GUIDANCE
program
development
and
management

GUIDANCE

program
development
and
management

3rd Edition

Herman J. Peters
The Ohio State University

Bruce Shertzer
Purdue University

CHARLES E. MERRILL PUBLISHING CO.
A Bell & Howell Company
Columbus, Ohio

Published by

Charles E. Merrill Publishing Co.

A Bell & Howell Company

Columbus, Ohio 43216

Standard Book Number: 0-675-08825-9

Library of Congress Catalog Card Number:
73-92004

1 2 3 4 5 6 7 8 9 10—78 77 76 75 74

PRINTED IN THE UNITED STATES OF AMERICA

To Annabelle and Carol

Table of Contents

0384936

7 THE COUNSELING SERVICE, 171

8 DEVELOPING AND MANAGING THE EDUCATIONAL GUIDANCE SERVICE, 207

9 THE VOCATIONAL GUIDANCE SERVICE, 257

Preface

Guidance: Program Development and Management, Third Edition, points the way to new guidance programs and staff involvements for the 1970s. The third edition is a blend of principles and practices. Guidance functions are the central focus of the instructional and pupil personnel program for the vast majority of boys and girls in elementary schools, secondary schools, vocational schools, and technical institutes. The primary objective of this book is to provide a frame of reference that will make for more effective guidance functions for children and youth. The material is articulated so as to be detailed and yet flexible for the variety of guidance programs needed in different settings. An effort is made to cast the guidance program in terms of the larger behavioral system concept which supplements and complements guidance, integrally interwoven with the instructional system for the pupil's learning about the outer world.

In the third edition:

Leadership principles are emphasized in Chapter one.

Principles of action are incorporated closely with practice. (Of course, the assumption is made that the user will have studied principles of guidance and counseling.)

Each chapter has been reexamined in terms of contemporary ongoing practices.

The case studies are new and represent a variety of points of view and settings for guidance program development and management.

With purpose, we have attempted to encompass the complex dimensions of initiating, developing, and sustaining effective guidance programs.

School counselors, guidance-oriented teachers, guidance-supportive administrators, and guidance-minded parents want specific assistance for their children in educational development, career exploration, course planning and selection, and personal fulfillment. School counselors are called upon to assist with educational planning, interpreting aptitudes, providing information about occupational trends and vocational opportunities, and resolving personal difficulties and aspirations. These functions are expected for all children and youth in all settings. Thus, guidance program development is truly a major thrust in seeking a better America.

The authors gratefully acknowledge appreciation to publishers for quotations, to our students for provocative questions, to our counselor colleagues for stimulating challenges to place theory into practice, and to our counselor educator colleagues for mutuality of support in this endeavor. Much appreciation is due Patty Mack of Charles E. Merrill Publishing Company for her cheerful and valuable editorial help—a word, too, for the other Merrill staff for their unseen but very effective assistance in getting this book through varied channels from us to you.

HERMAN J. PETERS

BRUCE SHERTZER

January, 1974

Introduction

PROGRAM DEVELOPMENT AND MANAGEMENT: AN OPERATING BASE

The mid 1970s educational trend emphasizes more than individualized development. Personalized learning about one's self and educational strategies is essential. As personnel services and guidance functions involving large numbers of boys and girls develop in effectiveness, as they become interrelated with instruction, and as they become more and more complex, their development and management become essential if the benefits of the services are to be extended to all who need them. Educational services and instructional functions relating to behavioral studies must be carefully organized and planned to meet the needs of the twentieth-century students; informal and accidental administration of these services is no longer adequate. Orderly functions—instruction and counseling on self-understanding—must be incorporated into the school system. These functions become more and more possible as school systems form educational parks, houses, and alternative schools with a wide variety of available resources. The courage to change is the challenge. Will the change be procedural and deceiving in its thrust? Will the change be procedural and reflective of basic attempts in new directions which truly allow for the exciting development of each person's individuality?

In other fields, too, as the complexity of administration has increased, there has been a growing need for formal organization. Business and industry have been organized to make possible the manufacture and distribution of goods to meet the demands of an expanding society. They have developed personnel services which are necessary for the accomplishment of their business and industrial objectives. Individually administered social services have proved inadequate. Welfare services now have been extended beyond individual and often accidental relief of need. Formal education, likewise, has supplanted tutoring in the home and the teaching of the favored few in the small private schools. The elementary and secondary schools have been organized to make available to all children that knowledge which is regarded as essential to cope with the frontiers of twentieth-century living.

During the twentieth century there has been increasing recognition of the need to assist young people in making educational and vocational choices. These choices are not discrete guidance concerns. They are inextricably interwoven with each person's life-style. They must include a look at each person's appropriation of time for learning, working, leisure, and "just free time." Action must happen in these areas.[1] The informal advice of interested adults had some value when youth also had many personal, direct contacts with the areas in which decisions had to be made. But today, with industry, education, and social relations so varied and complex, a child or adolescent has little direct, realistic experience or even indirect contact with the environment in which he will endeavor to adjust as a student and worker. Therefore, personal growth and self-development have been added as a third dimension to the guidance functions of educational and vocational decision-making.

In education, three trends have evolved which assist youth in developing the ability to make necessary decisions with increasing independence and adequacy. First, a number of counselors with specific and professionally useful techniques, and the ability to apply them with understanding, have been given school-supported time to provide professional guidance service for pupils. The number of such professionally prepared staff members is still inadequate, but the situation is improving.

The second trend is toward the increasing utilization of research findings about learning, individual differences, and variations in normal child and adolescent growth patterns.

The third trend is toward the development and management of sociological findings and material resources of the school and community in order to make them available to all youth. The conscious direction of human and material resources toward assisting each youth to understand himself, his environment, and his coping within it has been called the personnel or

---

[1]Jerry L. Davis and Marshall P. Sanborn, "Getting Student Action on Guidance Goals," *Journal of Counseling Psychology* Vol. 20 (May, 1973), pp. 209–13.

guidance point of view. When emphasized for the pupil who profits from regular classroom instruction, it is known as the developmental guidance approach. The guidance point of view must be implemented through cognitive and affective avenues. Behavioral science and the art of human relations must be organized for study throughout grades K–12 just as other subject matter is. This cognitive emphasis must be complemented by the affective-focused functions of guidance, especially counseling.[2]

The emphasis in this book is placed on the third trend. The purpose is to show ways in which the resources of the school and the larger community may be organized. This book will have special appeal to counselors, teacher-counselors, teachers, school administrators, and all who are interested in or responsible for guidance programs in secondary schools. It is intended especially for those students (counselor-candidates, teachers, and prospective administrators) who are actively engaged in studying the development and management of guidance programs. The organization emphasizes adequate guidance staff and services to provide all young people with opportunity for self-examination and with more adequate preparation for making decisions that are essential to their educational progress, career development, and personal fulfillment.

Although the writers assume that the reader has had a basic course in the principles of guidance, it seems appropriate to review briefly some basic principles underlying the guidance process. These principles will serve as a sort of multidimensional framework for the more detailed analyses of the development and management aspects of an effective guidance program.

The first attempts at an organized plan of guidance occurred in the early 1900s. The early emphasis was on vocational guidance. The guidance process has since encompassed educational, vocational, and personality development based on a point of view that the individual functions as a bio-social organismic whole. The term *guidance* is coming to mean *that assistance which enables the individual to move toward his fullest development.* It includes examining decisions made and to be made, determining courses of action, and resolving concerns and problems.

Some educators think of guidance and instruction as being the same. Naturally, there is a relationship between the two, but they are not the same thing, just as instruction and administration are not the same. Guidance is a part, hopefully an inherent part, of the total educational experience of the student. Guidance is considered to be a process by which the student achieves greater self-insight, self-understanding, and stability to enable him

---

[2]Leroy D. Klas and Herman J. Peters, "Counseling Interview Techniques: A Comparison of Theory and Practice," *Counselor Education and Supervision* Vol. 13 (December, 1973), pp. 137–143.

to become an intelligent consumer and producer in our society. Guidance is focused on the *inner* person, in contrast with instruction, which is focused on material, *outside* of the person. Guidance is based on thoughtful assistance to the individual so that he may understand himself—his abilities, interests, and goals. Instruction is based on thoughtful assistance to the individual so that he may understand the world in which he lives. Of course, both guidance and instruction have as their primary goals the enhancement and development of the individual. Organized guidance in the schools has come to mean those functions, activities, and services which have as their common goal the assistance given the individual toward the objectives stated earlier in this introduction. Organized guidance is rapidly becoming an essential and integral part of the total educational program of each modern school system.

Several of the all-inclusive principles of guidance are:

1. *Appropriate guidance services are available to each boy and girl.* However, guidance, as a major aspect of the larger framework of pupil-personnel services and a learning-oriented resources program, emphasizes attention to those pupils who fall within the bounds of normalcy in their adjustment to school and life. Other pupil-personnel services deal in a concentrated way with those pupils who deviate to a considerable extent, especially in the downward direction of defeat, retardation, and misbehavior.

2. *Guidance is a continuing process throughout the school career of a pupil.* The development and management of an effective guidance program extends from kindergarten through the twelfth grade to college.

3. *Guidance emphasizes the right of each pupil to learn about himself in an accurate and professional way.* This right is coincident with his privilege to learn about the world in which he lives through the instructional program. It is also coincident with his right and need to study the behavior of man.

4. *Guidance necessitates an adequate complement of staff who are educated, specifically prepared, and certificated to engage in counseling and other guidance functions.* Ideally, the counseling and other guidance functions would be separated from counselor operational procedures.

5. *The counseling process, a one-to-one relationship, is the heart of the guidance program.* The school counselor should not have other guidance duties. A general practitioner guidance worker should be assigned these duties. Too, sub- or paraprofessionals should assist both the counselor and the general guidance worker.

By using specialized techniques and tools and referring at times to the principles and methods of related fields of knowledge, organized guidance functions endeavor to bring the individual to his highest level of growth and development as he moves forward in his educational career. Although guidance and instruction use similar tools, special preparation is required to draw inferences from, and make recommendations for, work in guidance.

Organized guidance functions have of necessity been a part of the total educational program by the increasingly complex environment in which pupils develop, make decisions, achieve, and interact with many different kinds of persons in varieties of situations. If purposeful actions are to be taken and effective life streams entered, and if unwise choices are to be held to a minimum and harmful behavior prevented, then all boys and girls must receive adequate guidance. Effective guidance includes consideration of the instructional program of the school, the climate of the home, and the community forces in terms of the needs of the pupil. It is the function of organized guidance programs to assist each pupil in looking at, trying out, and appraising his developmental progress. Within his school career there is a margin for the individual's experimentation and limited failure. However, the same cannot be said for adult living; in fact, the margin narrows as one progresses through one's school career.

As a point of departure, six guidelines, serving as a design for program development, management, and operation will form the boundaries for the discussion in the chapters to follow.

1. *Theoretical Structure.* Administrators and other staff members must be sensitive to the development of a guidance point of view based on what they consider to be the best research in the fields of psychology, education, and sociology. An interdisciplinary base is essential. Before staff members study the organizational designs for a guidance program, they should already have developed a theoretical structure as a base for the implementation of the program. As Kehas has said, "Theory concerning the organization of guidance services must flow from, or necessarily be compatible with, particular theories in guidance. The lack of theory in the one area is a reflection of the lack in the other."[3]

2. *Cultural Considerations.*[4] The nature of the culture in a pluralistic society is today more often the cause of an individual's behavior than if the individual were to act out of a self-contained vacuum.

---

[3]Chris D. Kehas, "Towards the Development of Theory in the Administration and Organization of Guidance Services," *Counselor Education and Supervision* Vol. 1 (Winter, 1961), p. 97.

[4]Ronald G. Corwin, *A Sociology of Education,* (New York: Appleton-Century-Crofts, 1965).

3. *Development Patterns.* More than cursory awareness of the developmental patterns of boys and girls is needed: these developmental patterns are the first concern in developing the theoretical framework for establishing the guidance program.[5,6] Of particular importance is the need for an understanding of the search for learning of the pupils in each school system concerned with developing an effective guidance program.

4. *Budget and Facilities.* A fourth major guideline relates to budget and facilities, for the guidance program will require money and space. Just how these will be managed will be discussed in Chapter 15.

5. *Staffing the Guidance Program.* A fifth guideline for program development focuses on the staff needed to implement and carry out the organizational designs discussed throughout this book. Appropriate staff becomes the *sine qua non* of a successful guidance program, once the first four guidelines are accepted. Therefore, staffing considerations have been included in each section of this book.

6. *Accountability, Evaluation, and Research.* There should be continuity in appraisal through measurement and evaluation as the guidance program develops throughout the years. Thus, as with the other guidelines, measurement and evaluation permeates the total organization of a guidance program. Although appraisal may not be emphasized in every chapter, the reader should keep it in mind throughout the book. The difficulties in discerning this guideline will be discussed in Chapter 17.

BIBLIOGRAPHY

Cook, David R. *Guidance for Education in Revolution.* Boston: Allyn and Bacon, 1971.

Peters, Herman J.; Dunlap, Richard S.; and Aubrey, Roger F. *The Practice of Guidance.* Denver: Love Publishing Company, 1972.

Shertzer, Bruce, and Stone, Shelley C. *Fundamentals of Guidance.* 2d ed. Boston: Houghton Mifflin Company, 1971.

---

[5]The reader is recommended to Jerome Kagan and Howard A. Moss, *Birth to Maturity— A study in Psychological Development,* (New York: John Wiley & Sons, 1962).

[6]The importance of the developmental approach is seen in another piece of evidence, the publication of the journal of *Developmental Psychology* in 1969 by the American Psychological Association.

Educational Administration, Organization, and Leadership

Lipham[1] made a distinction between administration and leadership. Whether or not one accepts his definition, it is clear that some administrators do little but maintain an organization, while others effect some changes in the goals, programs, and/or procedures of an organization. It is this latter activity that represents leadership whether seen as part of or separate from administration. While these changes of goals, programs, or procedures have their expression within the organization, their legitimation must reside in the world surrounding the organization. Thus, the administrator is required to stimulate his staff as well as to convince his public.[2]

Chapter 1

What are some major characteristics of the current scene in education?

What factors influence educational administration and organization?

What major theories of administration have been proposed?

What relevance do these theories have for guidance administrators?

THE CURRENT SCENE IN EDUCATION

Education is a continuous process. While repetition has made this statement commonplace, it has not decreased its significance. From birth to death the individual participates in continuous experiences that modify subsequent behavior. This, of course, represents learning or education. In early childhood, education centers largely around the informal home life. Through childhood and adolescence in modern American society, the school as a

---

[1]James M. Lipham, "Leadership and Administration," *Behavioral Science and Educational Administration,* National Society for the Study of Education, Sixty-third Yearbook, Part II. Chicago: University of Chicago Press, 1964. Chapter VI.

[2]Roald F. Campbell, Luvern L. Cunningham, Roderick F. McPhee, and Raphael O. Nystrand, *The Organization and Control of American Schools.* Columbus, Ohio: Charles E. Merrill Publishing Company, 1970, p. 568.

1

social institution seeks to provide organized sequential educational experiences. These learning experiences comprise the multitude of organized and unorganized, formal and informal, planned and unplanned experiences that constitute life.

Any particular period of time in education is, of necessity, based upon previous experiences in other periods. But any description of the status of American schools is quickly made obsolete. Important changes took place in education during the decade of the sixties and during the early 1970s. Further modification will no doubt continue during the later 1970s. Despite these changes and those that will inevitably come, it seems appropriate to start this book with a brief status picture of the contemporary scene in American education.

The Magnitude of the Educational Enterprise

Americans have long supported both public and nonpublic schools. Slightly less than 19,000 publicly supported local school districts are distributed among the fifty states and territories. The number of school districts per state varies widely. For example, there is only one district in Hawaii, while Nebraska has more than 2,000. Each year, school consolidation and reorganization cut back the number of public school districts.

In 1970, the public school districts of the nation contained 66,849 elementary schools and 26,282 secondary schools. In that same year there were approximately 14,400 nonpublic elementary schools and 4,200 nonpublic high schools.[3] Nonpublic schools are those organized under church auspices as well as those under other private agencies. Beginning in 1967, public school enrollments began declining and they continue to do so at the present time. The number of schools, particularly elementary schools, diminishes gradually each year with further school consolidation.

Enrollments during 1971 in public and nonpublic schools as reported by the Census Bureau are presented below:

Level	Public	Nonpublic
Kindergarten	2,377,000	400,000
Elementary	29,829,000	3,678,000
High School	14,057,000	1,126,000
College	6,271,000	1,816,000

The lowered birth rates of the early 1970s are expected to level off and/or reduce the heretofore annually expanding elementary and secondary school enrollments.

---

[3]Based on statistics in "Statistical Abstract of The United States, 1972," Bureau of Census p. 102.

Individuals employed in professional positions in public schools in 1970 numbered more than two million. This includes some 1.3 million elementary school teachers and more than 929,000 secondary school teachers. Approximately 120,000 administrators and supervisors and 50,000 school counselors were employed in public schools. The numbers of individuals employed in nonpublic and public schools are as follows:

	Public	Nonpublic
Elementary school teachers	1,132,000	146,000
Secondary school teachers	929,000	80,000
Elementary school counselors	10,000*	–
Secondary school counselors	45,0000**	–
Principals and supervisors	120,000	–

Bureau of Census data indicate that during 1970, the public elementary and secondary schools expended $43.3 billion for current operation and $5.5 billion for capital outlay and debt service, equalling a total of $48.8 billion. The financing of nonpublic schools varies greatly among churches and other agencies supporting those schools. The 1970 census reports that current expenditures in this educational sector were $5.2 billion and that $600 million were spent for capital outlay or plant expansion.[4]

Heterogeneity—Different Humans

Americans have long taken pride in providing a public education for every man's child. The schools have played an important role in attaining what has long been an American goal: the provision of equality of opportunity for all. Despite the goal, numerous cases can be cited where equality of opportunity does not exist because of race, sex or economic class. For many it seems that in an imperfect world, ideals are goals toward which progress is slow.

Americans have sent their children to schools in increasing numbers and they have been remaining there for longer periods of time than ever before. Some 98 percent of youth between the ages of six and sixteen are now in school. The diversity present in a school's heterogeneous student population —regarding aptitudes, interests, purposes, and values—is indeed great. It represents a great challenge to those who serve these students.

---

*Estimated by authors.
**Obtained from *Occupational Outlook Handbook, 1972–73*. Washington D.C.: U.S. Dept of Labor.
[4]*Ibid.*, p. 105.

The heterogeneity of the student body has forced both an expansion in and a differentiation of the educational program. This expansion and differentiation—more subjects, extra curricular activities, and several curricula—contributes to increasing the range of individual differences as potential abilities in different fields are developed. A school that accepts all students can not have a single uniform program for all, can not provide a defined and single body of content for all, and can not set forth a common body of skills in which all students will achieve uniform excellence. Rather, standards of achievement based upon individual student's capabilities must be established. The high school diploma is to be viewed realistically as simply a certificate awarded to the individual who has completed that program of studies judged to be most appropriate to his purposes and abilities.

PUBLIC UNEASINESS ABOUT SCHOOLS

Many school observers believe that the magnitude of public uneasiness about the schools has increased during the early 1970s. Increasingly, lay citizens have become concerned about their local schools, and have begun questioning the school's goals, policies and practices. The late 1960s and early 1970s comprised a period of time when some became sufficiently disenchanted to try out alternative schools. Most so-called "free schools" were unable to continue beyond a year or two, due to a number of reasons, including internal dissension.

One may well wonder why, after years of unprecedented expansion, affluence, and apparent success, our schools should be faced with so much criticism. However, while it is true that Americans have long had faith in their educational systems, it is equally true that they have long been highly critical of them.

The discontent over busing, desegregation, disadvantaged students, alienation and a host of other crises spread widely among members of the public and led many to believe that somehow the schools failed to accomplish their purpose. Even affluent surburban schools were criticized for shortchanging students. Many parents became deeply worried that their children were being taught conformity, order, and acceptance rather than creativity, independent thinking, and self-sufficiency. They called for reforms to make school less constraining and more humane. Changes were made as experimentation and innovation became fashionable. The public attitude about schools now seems to be changing. More and more citizens are becoming aware that complex social problems can not be solved by the schools alone. More than ever they are demanding that the role of schools be clarified.

Uncertainty About School Priorities

As the American people become clearer in their understanding of democratic principles, and more determined to achieve them, their demands on the schools become more imperative. These ever increasing demands reflect both the social problems of today and the anticipated needs of tomorrow. Currently much uncertainty exists among educators as to what the priorities of the school should be. Thoughtful educators and lay citizens alike are concerned as to whether schools can accomplish the many responsibilities expected of them. Contrary to the assumption of many critics, most of the additions to the schools—headstart programs, racial integration, psychological education, career education, humanistic education, etc.—have not been occasioned by teachers or school administrators. These programs have found their way into the school because other social devices and vehicles for providing youth with the necessary skills, understandings, and attitudes have not proved adequate.

A society will not support nor long tolerate an educational system out of touch with the controlling social philosophy. Indeed, schools are expected to guide society's movement toward its goals and purposes. These premises are known and accepted. The current problem is to discern the expectations members of the public have for the schools and to develop programs that will be effective in preparing young citizens for living in an increasingly complex social system.

Today, some educators and lay citizens are urging that schools place first priority upon intellectual development, others just as strongly urge vocational development, and still others stress that top priority should be given to emphasizing personal and social development. These differential perceptions of what schools should accomplish make it difficult to obtain any operational agreement on the priorities to be established by the school. Resolution of priorities will inevitably involve educators, lay groups, and local, state, and federal governmental officials.

Fundamentally, priorities emerge from the basic socioeconomic forces in American society. These forces generate movement that stimulates political action which, in turn, leads gradually to policy formulation by local, state and national educational levels. Campbell and his associates graphically depict how this takes place (Figure 1–1).

Student Activism, Rights and Involvement

During the middle and late 1960s, student unrest and protest swept across American college campuses. Student demonstrations over the Vietnam War, the draft, student participation in educational discussions, pollution, and the impersonality of college environments became commonplace.

I Basic Forces	II Antecedent Movements	III Political Action	IV Formal Enactment
Social, economic, political, technological (usually national or worldwide in scope)	The Conant Studies, the Compact of the States, the National Assessment Movement	By organizations usually interrelated at local, state, and national levels, such as U. S. Chamber of Commerce, AFL-CIO, and NEA	May be at local, state, and national levels, through legislative, judicial, and executive agencies

Figure 1-1.   *A Flow Chart on Policy Formation in Education.* [*From Roald F. Campbell, Luvern L. Cunningham, Roderick F. McPhee, and Raphael O. Nystrand,* **The Organization and Control of American Schools.** *Columbus, Ohio: Charles E. Merrill Publishing Company, 1970, p. 39.*]

Student activism was not confined to college campuses. It soon became prominent in junior and senior high schools. For example, in a national survey of 1,026 principals, conducted by J. Lloyd Trump and Jane Hunt, it was reported that 56 percent of those in junior high schools and 59 percent of the high school principals had experienced some kind of student protest.[5] These protests often escalated into violence and many schools had to resort to the placement of policemen in school buildings.

While many student demonstrations were over political issues and conditions, others were directed toward establishing student rights in respect to dress codes, hair regulations, disciplinary procedures, smoking rules, assembly programs, student newspapers, examination and grading policies, and participation in decision-making about school policies and regulations. Student demands for individual rights and involvement in decisions about their education met varied responses. Some educators were caught in a dilemma of trying to respond in a way that respected the student's right of self-expression while simultaneously maintaining order. Most educators recognized the legitimacy of some of the student grievances and responded positively with changes in school policies and practices. While some educators believe that student unrest was merely a reflection of the times, and therefore a current fad, it seems more likely that the newly found power by the students will continue to exert itself during the future. Student demands generally represent sincere pleas for improvement in the educational program.

---

[5]J. Lloyd Trump and Jane Hunt, "The Nature and Extent of Student Activism," *The Bulletin of the National Association of Secondary School Principals*, Vol. 53 (May, 1969), pp. 150–158.

CURRICULAR CHANGES

Modifications are currently taking place in almost all subjects and curricular activities. Emphasis in subject matter and in teaching is shifting from the rote learning of facts and dates to understanding the fundamental intellectual structure of a subject. An essential ingredient of this approach is that students acquire an understanding of the means by which knowledge is discovered, and that they become active rather than passive learners. At the heart of the approach lies Bruner's hypothesis that "any subject can be taught effectively in some intellectually honest form to any child at any stage of development."[6]

Many organizations, professional societies, and individuals have been involved in modifying the contemporary curriculum. These changes include those fostered by the Illinois Committee on School Mathematics, the Physical Sciences Study Committee (physics), the Biological Sciences Curriculum Study (biology), and the United States Office of Education supported curriculum projects in English and social sciences such as *Man: A Course of Study.*

The impetus for many of the changes in subject matter areas has been instigated by the developmental work being done by those in the discipline in colleges and universities. Teachers in elementary and secondary schools are, of course, involved in both the development and testing out of new subject matter and teaching methods. An ever increasing thrust is to compress into shorter periods of time that which is to be taught, and to introduce concepts and content at an earlier grade level than that at which they were previously taught.

The body of contemporary literature dealing with curriculum modification and change is immense. Fundamentally, curriculum changes now require the study of everything that affects human life and organization. The task of planning, conducting, and testing curriculum content and methods is continuous, and requires the resources and talents of the entire school faculty. The search is neverending for relevant experiences conducive to learning, reflective of that which is needed to cope in contemporary society, and directed toward goals that are real and important to the student.

Emphasis Upon Career Education

Currently, dominant voices in education increasingly speak of career education as the necessary way of the future—the path the schools must follow if they wish to make themselves relevant. It is a point of view

---

[6]Jerome Bruner, *Toward a Theory of Instruction.* New York: W. W. Norton and Company, Inc., 1966, pp. 1–21.

articulated, for example, by Joseph P. Cosand, the United States Assistant Commissioner of Education, and Sidney P. Marland, Jr., Commissioner of Education, who speak of the need for education to be oriented toward some kind of useful work. Marland declared in December, 1971, that career education was the first priority of the United States Office of Education. These spokesmen and others have argued for an educational system which, from kindergarten to graduate school, concerns itself with career choices and vocational training, so that students can leave school at any point and find themselves with some marketable skill.

Many school counselors have long been troubled by the phenomenon of large numbers of students who are apathetic about educational-vocational planning and future careers. While career education has been defined as ". . . the total effort of public education and the community to help all individuals become familiar with the values of a work-oriented society; to integrate those values into their personal value structure; and to implement those values in their lives in such a way that work becomes possible, meaningful and satisfying,"[7] the evidence remains unclear as to whether the definition can be made operational, and whether educational practices can be designed to accomplish its purposes.

The United States Office of Education has encouraged and funded career education programs all over the United States. One outcome expected of the career education programs is to gradually eliminate the "general" high school curriculum now being taken nationwide by about half of the students, and replace it with vocational skill training. Moreover, classroom teachers are expected to emphasize the career implications of their subject matter to students. Also, vocational skill training is being presented in junior high schools rather than at high school levels. Finally, more use is to be made of involving the business-labor-industrial community in career education programs by providing observational work experience and work study opportunities for students. There is little doubt but that career education, with its emphasis upon learning useful skills and the perspective and motivation to use them, will continue to find expression in schools.

THE PRESS FOR ACCOUNTABILITY

Accountability has come to be a major challenge in education. No longer is it possible for educators at any level to suggest that the benefits and outcomes of education are to be found in the individual's life after he leaves school. That which education seeks to accomplish is to be assessed in the

---

[7]Kenneth B. Hoyt, "The Counselor and Career Education," *Guidance Newsletter,* Science Research Associates, (November-December, 1972), p. 1.

present, not in the future life of the student. Accountability (as we have all heard a good many times by now) is believed to be the key to improving productivity and managing the rising costs which plague schools today. No one knows much about productivity in education, let alone how to improve it. We learned, some seventy years ago, how to define, how to measure, and how to raise the productivity of manual work. But we have yet to learn what productivity really means in any other kind of work. The "cost-squeeze" on schools and colleges, which struck in the early 1970s, triggered rising demands that education account for its outcomes. Many questioned whether schools, despite having added layer upon layer of management and all kinds of specialized staff members, were any more productive (in achieving their outcomes) than they were forty years ago.

A major component in school accountability is to define objectives, develop practices, and assess how well these objectives are being met. Evaluation, based upon performance objectives, has become not only highly fashionable but, in many communities, almost mandatory. Previous globally stated school objectives, such as intellectual development, good citizenship, competence, and personal self-actualization, are now being reworked into performance objectives that can be assessed and judged as to how well school programs accomplished that which they promised and pursued.

Accountability involves not only the systematic planning of procedures, and an assessment of their effectiveness, but also includes careful reporting to keep both school personnel and the public informed of the school's program accomplishments, needs and problems. Sound reporting practices do much to gain the public's support and assistance. Their help must be obtained to promote educational improvements and to solve specific educational problems.

THE TEACHERS

Teaching as an occupation has become more and more attractive to young people choosing careers. No doubt, teaching became more popular because of better, more competitive salaries and work conditions. Contributing also to more young people choosing careers in teaching, has been the shift of their values toward careers which involve working with people as people, and not as objects to be manipulated. During the 1950s and 60s, the number of children increased at an unprecedented rate. New schools had to be built to accommodate them. The reason, obviously, was that the babies born during the post-war boom were then reaching school age. The teachers in the schools during this time were mostly elderly; the last period of massive hiring had been in the 1920s, an era when high schools grew as fast as colleges have recently. Between 1955 and 1970, therefore, an unusually large number of teachers reached retirement age, became disabled, or died. As a result, some five million college-educated young people found teaching jobs available during this period.

However, in the early 1970s, the traditional shortages in the supply of teachers, so characteristic during previous years, disappeared. During the 1970s, no more than two million teaching jobs will open up; some forecasts put the figure as low as one million. One reason is that the school-age population will be smaller, as a result of the decline in birthrates that began a decade ago. Another reason is that teachers today are the youngest group of workers in the country, therefore fewer vacancies will occur because of death and retirement.

Several outcomes, related to the oversupply of teachers, are becoming more and more evident. No longer do schools need to employ marginally prepared and/or noncertified teachers. More and more teachers have attained a higher level of preparation than ever before and this trend, no doubt, will continue. Currently, some 85 percent of teachers now have at least their bachelor's degree; about 30 percent have master's degrees, and 12 percent have completed a year or more of work beyond the master's degree. Another outcome is that teachers have become more militant about their professional needs. They have championed, at local, state and national levels, better educational opportunities for children and youth, and have been more aggressive during the last few years about the need for higher teacher salaries, bargaining rights, retirement benefits, improved job conditions, sick leave, tenure, and other benefits. The remaining years of the 1970s are expected to be a time when teachers make rapid strides in improving their professional services. More and more attention will be given to determining who enters the profession and to increasing the productivity of those who remain in it.

EDUCATIONAL FINANCES

Financing schools has become a thorny issue. Rising property taxes have called into question this means of supporting the costs of education. Not only have school costs risen faster than the available revenues, but the inequities and inequalities in educational programs associated with local property tax funding practices have been questioned legally. On August 30, 1971, the Supreme Court of the State of California decided, by a majority of six to one, that the system of financing schools in California through local property taxes violated the equal protection clause of the 14th Amendment to the United States Constitution. The court held that funding schools by local property taxes made the quality of a child's education a function of the wealth of his parents and neighbors. The idea that money determines the quality of education a child receives was also one of the major arguments in the *Rodriguez versus San Antonio School Board* (1972) case. However, the majority opinion of the United States Supreme Court (1973) did not agree with this idea.

Disparities in the financial support of schools within a state and among states—ranging from less than five-hundred to over two-thousand dollars per child—have been cited by many authorities. A wealthy school district with a high assessed property valuation per child spends more for each child's education than a poor district with a low assessed valuation per child. Hawaii is a notable exception because schools there are supported 100 percent by the state. This inequality of expenditure is believed to produce an inequality of educational opportunity.

An underlying assumption that has long been held is that increasing expenditures in low-cost schools will inevitably improve educational opportunity. This assumption was called into question by the large-scale study by Coleman and Campbell,[8] who reported that the differences among American public schools in class size, buildings, equipment, teacher preparation levels, library services, and other variables seemed to have less effect on success in schools than did social class (as indicated by family income). However, the conclusions from this study were not universally accepted. Many educators believed that the averaging of school data minimized the contributions that better school financing had made to the development of students.

The obvious inequalities (both nationally and state-wide) of financial resources among local schools has resulted in a search for a means to equalize local, state, and federal financial aid to schools. The proportion of school funds at selected years, provided by each sector, is presented in Table 1–1. As can be seen by examining the data presented in Table 1–1, the proportion of educational funds derived from the federal government almost doubled during the 1960s. Presumably, school financing in the future will increasingly come from state and federal sources.

EDUCATIONAL TECHNOLOGY

Technology has come to today's schools. In recent years, an ever-increasing array of technological equipment—computers, television, video reproductions, programmed learning materials, etc.—have been used to facilitate

---

[8]James Coleman and Ernest Campbell, *Equality of Educational Opportunity.* Washington, D.C., U.S. Office of Education, 1967.

Table 1–1.   *Proportion of School Funds by Source. [Source: Bureau of Census, "Statistical Abstract of the United States, 1972," p. 105.]*

Level	1960	1966	1970	1972
Federal	6.9	11.2	10.6	11.3
State	29.1	28.9	29.8	29.6
Local	39.3	33.0	33.1	32.0
All other	24.7	26.9	26.5	27.1

instruction. These technological developments have been called "convivial tools" by Ivan Illich[9] because they give each person who uses them the greatest opportunity to enrich the environment with the fruits of his or her vision.

Rising school costs and the demand for individualizing instruction led to a vanguard of experimental technological educational projects. However, the predictions made in the 1960s, that the instructional process would be revolutionized by educational technology, have not come true. Koerner[10] cites many reasons why the educational revolution failed to follow the technological applications. He points out that the equipment itself fell short of the claims for it. The most advanced hardware systems (e.g., electronic systems, computer-assisted instruction) have low reliability, high maintenace costs and are incompatible with other systems. Moreover, the development of the software (e.g., test banks, testbooks) lagged far behind the hardware. Finally, the attitudes of teachers toward applying technology in education have been largely negative. Koerner's analysis is that educational technology cannot, at the present time, do much to increase access to education, improve individualization of education, or reduce the unit costs of education.

EDUCATIONAL ADMINISTRATION AND ORGANIZATION

Educational administration—along with the administration of all other nonprofit-making enterprises—is usually classified as public administration, as opposed to private administration, which is concerned with the organization and administration of enterprises conducted primarily for profit. While it is true that some "private" schools are conducted for profit, these are so much in the minority that the general statement classifying educational administration as public administration holds true.

[9]Ivan Illich, "Convival Tools," *Saturday Review of Literature,* (May, 1973) pp. 63–67.
[10]James Koerner, "Educational Technology," *Saturday Review of Education* (May, 1973), pp. 43–47.

Schools—or any other social organization—do not operate automatically. They function through a definite organization of plans, personnel, procedures, plant, and finances. The central purpose of administration is to coordinate the efforts of people to achieve the goals of the organization. In education this means that administrative functions are those that center on enhancing learning. The terms "organization" and "administration," which are difficult to define precisely, are often used interchangeably in the educational administration literature.

Definition of Terms

Organization is basically concerned with making arrangements so that individuals can communicate with each other to realize their purpose. Organization may be thought of as the overall framework joining the functions of an enterprise. It is a process of so combining the work which individuals have to perform with the facilities or equipment necessary for its execution, that the duties, so formed, provide the best channels for the efficient, systematic, positive, and coordinated application of available effort. The underlying basis of an organization is built upon the relationship of the *functions* of an enterprise, rather than on individuals who perform those functions. Organization and/or reorganization is necessary because imperfections appear in existing patterns of functions, original purposes become modified or extended, conditions change, and/or new functions are discovered.

Whenever people engage in purposeful activity, whether work or play, they organize it—either to lighten the effort required or to make more systematic that which is done to improve or increase whatever is produced. Organization is the instrument for putting into systematic relationships the elements and activities which are essential to the purpose of the social system. Organization includes the dissimilar elements of operation and growth.

For most students, organization means that their attention is given to line drawings or charts which indicate relationships between and among individuals who are associated together for some purpose. Organization should be seen as the overall structure of the functions to be performed by the organization. In short, formal organization is a plan for the division of work and the allocation of authority.

Administration is concerned with the conduct, control, and management of an enterprise. Knezevich defines school administration as ". . . a social process concerned with creating, maintaining, stimulating, controlling, and unifying formally and informally organized human and material energies within a unified system designed to accomplish predetermined objectives."[11] It seeks to make sure that things are done. Because administration must "decide" and "do," it implies control, authority, and responsibility. As a process, administration seeks to manage situations by which people of differing skills, interests, and abilities focus their efforts to achieve the goals of an enterprise. Administration is a source for the decisions taken by a group to achieve their goal. Simon makes this quite clear when he states

> It should be noted that the administrative processes are decisional processes: they consist in segregating certain elements in the decision of members of the organization, and establishing regular organizational procedures to select and determine these elements and communicate them to the members concerned.[12]

Vested authority gives school administrators the right to act in the best interest of the community. Responsibility is attached to authority, which means that an accounting may be requested regarding the success or failure of the organization.

Campbell, Corbally, and Ramseyer[13] cite three primary types of activities which school administrators are required to perform to advance teaching and learning: (1) to discern and influence the development of goals and policies basic to teaching and learning; (2) to stimulate and to facilitate the planning and operation of appropriate programs for teaching and learning, and (3) to procure and to manage personnel and material to implement the programs of teaching and learning. The suggestion by Campbell and his associates that administrators not only discern but also *influence* goals and policies is a departure from typical formulations of administrator functions. Their point is that the division between policy making and administration is not a clear one, and that administrators necessarily influence policies as they discern and clarify it.

While the terms "organization" and "administration" are frequently used in education, the authors prefer to use the term "management." It is believed that this term connotes more clearly the focus of behavior exercised in the interaction of people, structure and purposes, particularly as applied to the guidance function. *Management* has been defined by Hersey and Blanchard as "working with and through individuals and groups to accomplish organizational goals."[14] They point out that the achievement of an organization's objectives through leadership is management, and thus everyone is a manager in at least certain portions of his life.

[11]Stephen J. Knezevich, *Administration of Public Education,* (2nd ed.). New York: Harper & Row, 1969, p. 11.

[12]Herbert A. Simon, *Administrative Behavior.* New York: The Free Press, 1957, p. 8.

[13]Roald F. Campbell, John E. Corbally, Jr., and John A. Ramseyer, *Introduction to Educational Administration.* Boston: Allyn & Bacon, Inc., 1962, p. 76.

[14]Paul Hersey and Kenneth Blachard, *Management of Organizational Behavior.* Englewood Cliffs, New Jersey: Prentice-Hall, Inc., 1972, p. 3.

Factors Influencing Organization and Administration

Many factors influence educational organization and administration. Three of the major factors will be identified and discussed here.

Size and Complexity. School operations are now on a larger scale and more complex than they were at an earlier time. As size increases, the management work increases in importance. Too, when work is of a very complex nature, as is teaching, good organization and administration are especially essential.

Size and complexity influence the management of an educational organization in that greater coordination of people and resources is necessary if the school is to realize its objectives. Coordination may be compared to a lens that brings everything about the school into focus for the community, faculty and students. If it is a poor lens (poor coordination), the image is fuzzy and obscure, and no one gets a clear picture of what the school is seeking to accomplish. It is a good lens (good coordination), the school projects more clearly the purposes that have been set for it.

School Goals or Purposes. The goals or purposes of the school influence its management. Two of the best known and accepted statements of educational purposes were formulated by educators in 1918 and 1938. The first statement, by the Commission on the Reorganization of Secondary Education, proposed for the school a set of seven cardinal objectives: health, command of fundamental processes, worthy home membership, vocational competence, effective citizenship, worthy use of leisure, and ethical character. The second statement, by the Educational Policies Commission, developed a number of objectives under four headings: self-realization, human relationship, economic efficiency, and civic responsibility.

More recently, the American Association of School Administrators set down, after two years of study, the "Imperatives in Education." The Commission did not envision these imperatives as goals, but believed that they represented certain activities within schools that should be revised and reshaped to meet current needs. According to them, it is imperative that schools strive:

1. To make urban life rewarding and satisfying
2. To prepare people for the world of work
3. To discover and nurture creative talent
4. To strengthen the moral fabric of society
5. To deal constructively with psychological tensions
6. To keep democracy working
7. To make intelligent use of natural resources
8. To make the best uses of leisure time
9. To work with other peoples of the world for human betterment.[15]

[15]American Association of School Administrators, Washington, D. C. *Imperatives in Education,* Report of the AASA Commission on Imperatives in Education, 1966.

Sergiovanni and Carver[16] point out that goals can be separated into those that are *explicit* (formally stated and pursued) and those that are *implicit* (not stated but informally pursued). The more compatible the two types of goals, the more successful the school. These two authors also classify school goals as *substantive* (those that represent society's hopes and aspirations for the schools) and *instrumental* (specific, more earthy and achievable). The former prescribe purpose while the latter (instrumental goals) guide action. The closer action is to purpose, the more likely it is that purposes will be carried out.

The importance of school goals is best understood as being the starting point for administration. Management is viewed as the source for activating school personnel to produce that which the school seeks to accomplish. Plans, procedures and policies are established so that the school's goals may be realized. Goals serve as the basis for organizing, allocating and coordinating available resources.

Administrative Skills. A third factor that influences administration lies in the values, skills, and personal characteristics of those who occupy administrative positions. Good ability and specialized preparation are essential to competent school management. Many have asserted that to organize and administer the work of others requires the professional skills and personal characteristics of a practicing social scientist.

Many administrators consider their work an artistic endeavor. They believe that management is largely an art practiced by those with intuition refined by preparation, common sense and experience. Important in this view is that those who manage school programs need to be keen students of society. They must be sensitive to others' behavior and knowledgeable about the community served by the school. They must have a grasp of learning processes and understand educational practices if they are to help the faculty, students and community to achieve the purposes of the school.

Management of a school program is a "thinking" and "doing" activity that involves working with people to develop healthy relationships. A large proportion of the time of most educational administrators is absorbed in establishing, supporting, modifying, and clarifying interpersonal relationships. More discussion will be found on this topic in a later section of this chapter.

In summary, the management of an educational enterprise is influenced by the values, beliefs, and skills of those who occupy administrative positions. Their behavior in the position can be attributed in large measure to the expectations they hold about themselves and others, their needs, skills and past experience.

---

[16]Thomas J. Sergiovanni and Fred D. Carver, *The New School Executive.* New York: Dodd, Mead and Company, 1973, pp. 35–36.

THEORIES OF ADMINISTRATION

Theory building in administration is of relatively recent origin. Initial efforts began at the turn of the twentieth century with the work of Frederick W. Taylor, who is often called the "father of scientific management." His work sparked the interest of others in studying ways of increasing production through good management procedures. Administration, prior to that time, was characterized by its dependence on and adherence to custom. Those in administrative positions followed the manner and methods handed down by their predecessors. Additionally, an astute administrator observed how other successful administrators achieved their goals and incorporated their best methods into his own behaviors. Even today, many administrative practitioners depend heavily upon custom and observation of other administrators, for several reasons—such activities require little effort, since it is not too difficult to find out from another how the latter approached certain problems, moreover, such practices offer a source of information for difficult or new administrative problems for which the individual has had no previous experience.

The past two decades have been a time during which serious, systematic efforts have gone into viewing administrative functions rationally and, to some extent, into constructing theories about administrative behavior. Here some of the major theories, models, or viewpoints about administration will be described briefly.

Scientific Management

The application of science and the scientific method were first applied to the field of management by Frederick W. Taylor, a man of great vision and ability. He started working for the Midvale Steel Company around 1880 and was interested in increasing the output of work. Taylor discovered that two major obstacles operated to the detriment of achieving this goal: fear by workers that increased output would bring wage reductions, and the use of suasion by management as the means of securing greater worker output. Taylor conducted exhaustive studies of men, materials, tools and machines to determine scientifically what constituted an honest day's work. He demonstrated that managerial problems can be solved by scientific principles and that it was unnecessary for management to engage in guessing.

Among the fundamentals of management that Taylor set forth are that (1) standards must be established to control production, (2) workers, materials, procedures and working conditions must be selected scientifically to meet standards, (3) workers must be given training to improve their skills, and (4) friendly cooperation between management and workers must be established to insure a stable and psychologically sound environment in the enterprise. These basic principles, initially stated by Taylor, have been amplified, clarified and reaffirmed so that even today, they serve as the main pillars of modern management.

Scientific management was furthered by the knowledge drawn from the now classical Hawthorne experiments which began during the 1930s, when efficiency experts assumed that increases in illumination would produce higher output by workers in the Western Electric plant located in Chicago. As lighting was increased for the experimental group the output increased, but output also increased for the control group which had not received any increase in illumination. This led Elton Mayo and his team of researchers to continue various experiments. They finally formulated the hypothesis that worker output was influenced by the attention being paid to the workers. At least two basic principles were derived from these studies: first, that organizational output is effected by the interpersonal relationships that are developed at work, not just pay and working conditions, and second, that involving workers in planning, organizing, and controlling their work is an important attribute of good management.

Mayo believed that many managers held negative assumptions about the nature of man and society in general. Managers, according to Mayo, were of the opinion that society consisted of a horde of unorganized individuals whose primary concern was self-preservation. Consequently, they organized work by the "Rabble Hypothesis." That is, workers, on the whole, were viewed as unreliable, unthinking, and untrustworthy, and as a result, an authoritarian task-oriented management was created and used. It may be recalled that Machiavelli in *The Prince* (1515) pictured men as rebellious, aggressive, selfish, and greedy, and therefore to be controlled by whatever means available to those who have responsibility to maintain order.

Theory X and Theory Y

The work of Elton Mayo and his associates led to the development of "Theory X-Theory Y" by Douglas McGregor.[17] His contrasting conceptions of human beings living and working in an organization, are as follows: Managers who subscribe to Theory X believe that people dislike work and seek to avoid it if they can; people are not creative by nature; people are innately lazy and unreliable and therefore must be coerced, controlled and directed; people treasure security and dislike responsibility; and people

---

[17]Douglas McGregor, *The Human Side of Enterprise.* New York: McGraw-Hill Book Company, 1960.

possess little ambition, and depend on external controls. In contrast, the basic assumptions of Theory Y are that people like to work as well as play; people strive to establish cooperative social relations and do not enjoy being loafers; people by nature are self-directed and exhibit self-control; people are naturally creative and can be motivated, and people strive for excellence in everything they do.

McGregor pointed out that administrators who accept Theory X assumptions employ procedures and practices that structure, control and closely supervise their employees. Those who operate under Theory Y do not usually structure, control or closely supervise the workers. He believed that management practiced under Theory X assumptions was no longer needed or relevant since the means used were questionable ways of motivating people whose physiological and safety needs were reasonably satisfied.

Administration as Decision-Making

Administration has been viewed as consisting mainly of decision-making by many individuals. Prominent among them is Daniel E. Griffiths.[18] Griffith's theory favors the process of arriving at decisions by procedures based on scientific principles. In formulating his theory, Griffiths sets forth four assumptions:

1. Administration is a generalized type of behavior to be found in all human organizations.
2. Administration is the process of directing and controlling life in a social organization.
3. The specific function of administration is to develop and regulate the decision-making process in the most effective manner possible.
4. The administrator works with groups or with individuals with a group referent, not with individuals as such.[19]

The major concepts of Griffiths' theory of administration are decision-making, organization, perception, communication, power, and authority. Each of these is described briefly here.

Decision Making. Griffiths considers making decisions the core of administrative practice. The process or continuum involves (1) recognizing, defining and limiting the problem, (2) analyzing and evaluating the problem, (3) establishing criteria or standards, (4) collecting data, (5) formulating and selecting preferred solutions (testing them in advance), and (6) putting into effect preferred solutions.

[18]Daniel E. Griffiths, *Administrative Theory.* New York: Appleton-Century-Crofts, Inc., 1959.
[19]*Ibid.,* pp. 71–74.

Organization. Administrative processes take place within the context of an organization. Therefore, the organization influences outcomes of decisions. Essentially, three types of organizations may be found. First, *formal organizations* are usually characterized ˙ by traditional hierarchal approaches whereby authority and power flow from the top downward. Major decisions that move the organization toward achieving its goals are generally made at the top of the organizational structure. Second, *informal organizations* are so structured that a network of interpersonal relationships exist among the members. Pressures produce flux and change in these interpersonal relationships. Different groups make decisions at different times and any group within the organization can alter the decision making process. Third, *neutral organizations* exist, such as social groups or coffee groups. Disinterest is the major characteristic of neutral organization.

Perception. Griffiths' concept of perception draws upon phenomenological psychology: an individual's interaction with his environment influences both his views and the environment. Each person within an organization behaves within his own framework of reference. His perceptions, in turn, influence decision making processes.

Communication. A person's perceptions influence his communications. Most communications within organizations are not very effective.

Power. Griffiths defines power as the control an organization holds over its members, and also as what is needed to attain the goals of an organization. According to Griffiths,

> ... power is a function of decisions made and can be operationally defined as $P = f(D)$. The person has power to the extent that he makes decisions which: (1) affect the course of action of an enterprise to a greater degree than do decisions made by others in the enterprise, and (2) influence other decisions.[20]

Authority. The individual who persuades others to accept his power possesses authority.

These six concepts interact in the administrative process. People and positions can be categorized in terms of formal and informal decision, or power points. The formal chart of an organization, iconic in design, represents key decision points. The process follows six steps:

1. Recognize, define, and limit the problem
2. Analyze and evaluate the problem
3. Establish criteria or standards by which solutions will be evaluated or judged as acceptable and adequate to the need
4. Collect data

---

[20] *Ibid.,* p. 87.

5. Formulate and select the preferred solution or solutions
6. Put into effect the preferred solution.[21]

Administrators, before starting the analysis of a problem, should be sure they understand its nature, and how it is related to the structure of the organization. If the problem is of a nature that a decision must be made, and if the decision is one that is to be made by the administrator, the decision can take one of three forms: intermediate, appellate and creative. *Intermediate decisions* flow from the top downward and include orders, commands, and policies that compel implementation. *Appellate decisions* originate from requests made by subordinates within the organization, but they are confirmed by established procedures. *Creative decisions* are those that break new ground, establish new policy, or change an existing policy or procedure.

In formulating and selecting the preferred solution, administrators engage in weighing the consequences of each alternative to select that solution with the biggest payoff or utility. Griffiths constructs a probability event chain, depicted here as Figure 1–2, by which the probable consequences of an action or alternative become known.

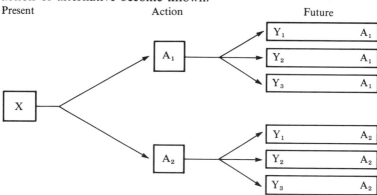

Figure 1–2.   *Griffiths' Probability Event Chain.* * [*Daniel E. Griffiths,* **Administrative Theory,** © *1959 by Appleton-Century-Crofts. Reprinted by permission of Prentice-Hall, Englewood Cliffs, N.J. pp. 104–105.*]

[*Read as follows: X is a decision to be made; A_1 and A_2 are possible courses of action. If one follows course of action A_1, the consequences are $Y_1 A_1$, $Y_2 A_1$, or $Y_3 A_1$. If one follows course of action A_2, the consequences are $Y_1 A_2$, $Y_2 A_2$ or $Y_3 A_2$. Probabilities of each consequence are approximated together with the desirability of each consequence, and from this, either A_1 or A_2 is selected as the course of action (decision).]

---

[21] *Ibid.,* p. 94.

When all alternatives are charted, a solution that best fits the problem can be selected rationally. Implementation, or putting into effect the preferred solution, follows. Implementation consists of three functions: (1) programming, (2) controlling and (3) evaluating. Programming consists of creating structures, or people and environment, to meet goals. *Control* means to set limits to be sure that performance corresponds with plans. For many administrators, this means establishing policy. *Evaluation* is to determine whether the decision has solved the problem and produced the desired outcomes.

Griffiths' formulation of administration as decision making has several implications for those who manage educational programs. First, administrators should strive for information and understanding of alternatives if their decisions are to be rational. Second, it is imperative that administrators be knowledgeable about the individuals and groups within the organization so that they can allocate wisely those functions and responsibilities necessary to achieve the school's objectives. Third, the administrator who understands that decisions are influenced by a person's psychological state is better able to judge the soundness of alternatives. Lastly, decision making can be shared. School personnel can be involved in deciding the utility of an alternative.

Administration as a Social Process

Jacob Getzels and Egon Guba[22] have theorized that administrative behavior is derived from the interaction of the positions, roles and role expectations within an organization and the individual's personality and need dispositions. They graphically portray this interaction, shown here as Figure 1–3.

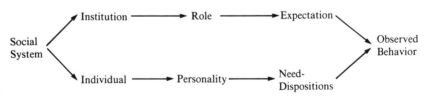

Figure 1–3.   *General Model of Social Behavior.* [*From Jacob W. Getzels and Egon G. Guba, "Social Behavior and the Administrative Process,"* **School Review,** *Vol. 65 (Winter, 1957) p. 426.* © *1957 by the University of Chicago Press. Used with permission.*]

---

[22]Jacob W. Getzels and Egon G. Guba, "Social Behavior and the Administrative Process," *School Review,* Vol. 65 (Winter, 1957) pp. 423–441.

Their model of administration is that it involves social behavior within a hierarchal social system. Any organization is composed of positions or statuses. Those who occupy these positions enact certain roles. Expectations are held by others for these roles. Individuals who occupy the roles possess personalities influenced by their need-dispositions.

Getzels and Guba point out that superior-subordinate relationships form a hierarchy in most organizations. This hierarchy of relationships is the locus for allocating and integrating roles and resources to achieve the organization's goals. These relationships carry certain expectations that influence behavior. Behavioral interaction between one individual and another results from their attempts to cope with an environment consisting of patterns of expectations for both which are consistent with their own independent value orientations. The upper level of Figure 1–3, the institutional or nomothetic dimension, defines acceptable institutional behavior. By it alone, one can visualize a dehumanized, over-simplified, and somewhat mechanical picture of the total situation. The psychological or ideographic dimension (lower level in Figure 1–3) introduces the flesh-and-blood aspect, for it is the individual who gives life and meaning to the activities associated with the organization. The observed behavior of individuals in an organization is based on interaction between the institutional and the personal dimensions.

Getzels and Guba point out that social systems evolve in organizations simply because people are involved. These individuals have different abilities, personalities, needs, and skills. Administration, according to Getzels and Guba, focuses on factors that influence behavior in organizations. It serves in an interpersonal way and as part of a larger social system.

The implications of administration as a social process lie in the premise that administrators respond to and deal with individuals who function as a result of the interaction between the nomethetic and ideographic dimensions. The work of Getzels and Guba provides the means to understand conflicts that occur between and among those who hold different roles, and between and among those who hold the same role. Their conception positions the administrator as a mediator between nomethetic and ideographic dimensions.

Guba has suggested that the power of an administrator is that of an actuating force. He diagrams this conception in Figure 1–4.
The administrator possesses power derived from delegated status and achieved prestige. Delegated status comes with his position or office, while achieved prestige reflects the individual's personality. Conflict is viewed as any alienating force. Conflict can be reduced by employing goals as integrating forces. To be an administrator means to be able to comprehend behavior by understanding how one organizational member relates to another, and

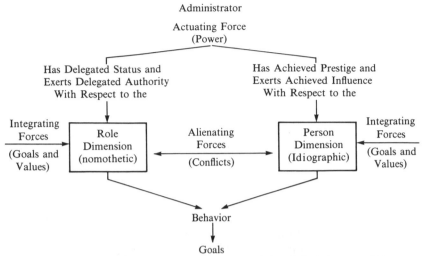

Figure 1–4.   *The Power Relationships of the Administrator.* [*From Egon G. Guba, "Research in Internal Administration—Is it Relevant?" in R. F. Campbell, and J. M. Lipham (eds.)* **Administrative Theory As a Guide to Action.** *Chicago: Midwest Administration Center, University of Chicago, 1960. Used with permission.*]

how each behaves, given certain constraints. According to Getzels and Guba, the unique tasks of administrators, at least with respect to staff relations, is to fuse the demands of the institution and the efforts and needs of staff members in a way that is at once organizationally productive and individually fulfilling.[23]

Administration as a Change Agent

Many hold conceptions of administrators as change agents. Administrators viewed in this way would be knowledgeable about the innovations and practices that hold promise for change, would be competent in transmitting this knowledge to others and would be skillful in creating strategies to bring the changes about. Naturally, any proposal for change that is not carefully planned, explained, and understood is likely to be rejected.

Schein has proposed that management be viewed as a process of influence. He states that behavior ". . . does not occur unless the individual is motivated and ready to change."[24] His description of the model follows Kurt Lewin's concepts about changing behaviors. The following statements by Schein explain the nature of his model:

---

[23]Getzels and Guba, *"Social Behavior and the Administrative Process,"* p. 441.

[24]Edgar H. Schein, "Management Development as a Process of Influence," in Harold J. Leavitt and Louis R. Pondy (eds.) *Readings in Managerial Psychology.* Chicago: The University of Chicago Press, 1964. p. 335.

Given these general assumptions about the integration of attitudes in the person, it is appropriate to consider influence as a process which occurs over time and which includes these phases:

1. *Unfreezing:* an alteration of the forces acting on the individual, such that his stable equilibrium is disturbed sufficiently to motivate him to make him ready to change; this can be accomplished either by increasing the pressure to change or by reducing some of the threats of resistance to change.

2. *Changing:* the presentation of a direction of change and the actual process of learning new attitudes. This process basically occurs by one of two mechanisms: (a) Identification: the person learns new attitudes by identifying with and emulating some other person who holds these attitudes or (b) Internalization: the person learns new attitudes by being placed in a situation in which new attitudes are demanded of him as a way of solving problems which confront him and which he cannot avoid, he discovers the new attitudes essentially for himself, though the situation may guide him or make it probable that he will discover only those attitudes which the influencing agent wishes him to discover.

3. *Refreezing:* the integration of the changed attitudes into the rest of the personality and/or into ongoing significant emotional relationships.[25]

Prominent among Schein's conception of administration as a change agent is communication between and among members of an organization. Communication and interaction are key ingredients by which change gains adoption.

Immaturity-Maturity Theory

Argyris[26] has proposed a theory to explain behavior within an organization. It is his thesis that neither the individual nor the organization alone is sufficient to account for life in an organization. Both factors—the individual and the organization—interact and influence behavior.

According to Argyris, seven changes occur in the personality of an individual as he develops, over time, into a mature person. The changes include (1) moving from a state of passivity to a state of increasing activity; (2) moving from being dependent upon others to being relatively independent; (3) moving from erratic, shallow, fleeting interests to crystallized deep and stable interests; (4) moving from a limited repertoire of behaviors to being capable of behaving in many different ways; (5) moving from a short time-perspective to a much longer time-perspective; (6) moving from a subordinate position in the family and society to an equal or superordinate

---

[25] *Ibid.,* p. 335.

[26] Chris Argyris, "The Individual and Organization: An Empirical Test," *Administrative Science Quarterly,* Vol. 4 (September, 1959) p. 146.

position and (7) moving from less control over oneself to self-awareness and control.[27]

Argyris questioned that worker apathy stemmed from forces within the individual. He suggested that the maturity of many people is thwarted by management practices that encourage passivity, dependency, and subordination. Consequently, employees behave immaturely. It is his contention that organizations fit the individual to the job, rather than the job to the individual, the reason being that the job is part of the design or conception of how the organization's goals can be met. The design, based upon four concepts of scientific management—task specialization, chain of command, unity of direction and span of control—comes first. When an employee is involved in a conflict, it is because he is put into situations in which he is dependent, submissive, and has no opportunity to use his creative abilities. The employee becomes frustrated and engages in such activities as absenteeism; aggressive and defensive behaviors (daydreaming, nurturing grievances). He becomes apathetic, disinterested and non-ego involved in the organization and its goals, deemphasizing in his own mind the importance of self-growth and creativity while stressing the importance of money and other material rewards.[28]

Argyris believes that the degree to which the individual is subordinated to organizational press variables—directive leadership and managerial controls—increases as one goes down the chain of command. Healthy people react to this subordination with frustration. Management often views informal activities that might counteract the frustration as detrimental to accomplishing organizational goals. This increases employees' subordination which, in turn, increases frustration, failure and similar reactions.

Systems Approach

In recent years, many have sought to conceptualize a *systems approach* to administration. Most simply defined, a systems approach is a planned method of procedure. Johnson and his associates have defined the systems concept more fully:

> *A system is defined as an array of components designed to accomplish a particular objective according to plan.* There are three significant points to this definition: (1) there is a design or an established arrangement of materials, energy and information; (2) there is a

[27]Chris D. Argyris, "Individual Actualization in Complex Organization," in Gerald Bell (ed.) *Organizations and Human Behavior, A Book of Readings.* Englewood Cliffs, N.J.: Prentice-Hall, Inc., 1967, pp. 209–210.

[28]Ibid., p. 210.

purpose or objective which the system is designed to accomplish; and (3) inputs of materials, energy, and information are allocated to plan.[29]

It is by means of systems that many common relationships among the various parts of the organization are established, and the system is the means through which these various organizational parts are commonly associated. System brings order and method to managing the enterprise.

The systems approach views the organization as a network of subsystems, each unit designed to accomplish a function that contributes to the overall objective by converting inputs into outputs, all of which connect and relate to each other to form a complex whole. Knezevich points out that the educational enterprise may be viewed as a

> ... kind of delivery or conversion system whose major components would be (1) a goal and priorities setting subsystem, (2) a resources subsystem, (3) a control subsystem, (4) a client service subsystem, (5) an educational manpower subsystem, (6) an environment relations subsystem and (7) a student manpower reentry and retraining subsystem.[30]

His statement illustrates a perspective of a total system in terms of its functions or outputs of special and interrelated parts.

Those who employ a systems approach to management emphasize the following points:

1. Goals or objectives are stated in behavioral terms so that meaningful procedures can be planned, and procedures implemented to meet them. Behavioral goals are capable of being assessed and evaluated.
2. Every subsystem should serve a useful purpose. Systems are static, and they tend to remain in an organization once established. Since an organization is dynamic, almost constantly undergoing change, it is essential that period checkups of all systems be held at definite intervals to determine if the subsystems are necessary and are serving a definite and useful purpose.
3. Quantitatively-oriented tools and procedures are used to analyze systems.
4. All systems within an organization should be coordinated so that through their use a unity of purpose is accomplished. Management gives priority to planning, programming, and assessing whether a

---

[29]R. A. Johnson, F. E. Kast and J. E. Rosenzweig, *The Theory and Management of Systems* (2nd ed.). New York: McGraw-Hill, 1967, pp. 403–404.
[30]Knezevich, *Administration of Public Education,* p. 542.

system should be installed, revised or eliminated. All systems in the
organization should reflect the basic plan of management.

5. A system should justify itself from the standpoint of costs. A
   system is a means to an end, not the end itself. The end should
   justify the system.

A systems approach relieves administrators of many details of management, making it possible for them to devote more time to planning, coordination, and evaluation. Many of the usual tasks are taken care of by the
system and only the unusual or exceptional matters are referred to the
administrator, who decides what is to be done in these cases. This procedure
is referred to as the "exceptional principle" in systems management. A
systems approach aids materially in achieving a good organization, but a
systems approach does not insure that a good organization exists.

THE RELEVANCE OF ADMINISTRATIVE THEORIES
FOR GUIDANCE ADMINISTRATORS

The purpose of outlining these theories of administration is not to suggest
that all will be equally useful to the guidance administrator. Nor is it
suggested that a particular formulation will necessarily correspond to the
style of a given administrator or his school system. Rather, the value of
outlining the above approaches to administration lies in suggesting that
there is a framework within which to operate as a guidance administrator.
There are few feelings more helpless than those of a young guidance administrator in his first management assignment without any particular strategy
or general plan to follow. There can, of course, be no "handbook" giving
specific instructions to follow, but it is hoped that presenting these broad
orientations to administration will give those who manage guidance programs a set of general principles to follow so that they have some sense of
security in their asssignment. As a person matures as a guidance administrator, he develops, clarifies and refines his own techniques and procedures of
management.

Especially relevant to the guidance administrator is the notion that these
and other theories of administration may be viewed as tentative maps of
unknown territory. As he becomes engaged in his work of managing a
guidance program, he can superimpose on the data that are assembled in
daily practice some of the theories—the maps—and reconcile some of the
areas of agreement and disagreement among them. This is not to propose
that a guidance administrator should necessarily take a little of this theory
and a little of that theory and put them together; in reality, however, that
seems to be what many practicing administrators actually do. Essentially,

though, these maps need to be integrated, and a "true map" constructed that best fits the individual. This, of course, takes time. The guidance administrator, however, is faced with the practical situation of dealing with the problems as they are presented to him. He can hardly wait until his ultimate map is drawn before he accepts responsibility and authority for managing a guidance program.

Successful management of a guidance program can no doubt be conducted within any one of several theoretical frameworks. Some would even argue that it is possible to manage a program without any theory of administration. Others would point out that those who claim to do so are managing a program according to some approach which is simply not articulated. According to them, the guidance administrator believes in something, therefore he operates within some kind of theoretical framework. However, it seems clear that knowledge of administrative approaches and the ability to use them can do much to make one an effective guidance administrator.

These various approaches to administration may be characterized as attempts to identify *why* and *what* administrators do. The elements of goal formulation, planning, decision making, executing, appraising, and leadership are present in each of them and will be discussed more fully in the next chapter. Each of these elements requires skills of those who manage educational programs. Katz has identified three areas of skill necessary for managing an enterprise: technical, human and conceptual. Each of these may be briefly described, as follows:

> *Technical skill.* This represents the ability to use knowledge, methods, techniques, and equipment necessary for the performance of specific tasks acquired from experience, education, and training.
>
> *Human skill.* This consists of ability and judgment in working with and through people, including an understanding of maturation and an application of effective leadership.
>
> *Conceptual skill.* This refers to the ability to understand the complexities of the overall organization and where one's own operation fits into the organization. This knowledge permits one to act according to the objectives of the total organization rather than only on the basis of the goals and needs of one's own immediate group.[31]

Katz points out that less technical skill tends to be needed as one advances into the higher levels of administration but conceptual skills are increasingly necessary. Presumably, human skill is crucial at all levels of management.

---

[31] Adapted from a classification developed by Robert L. Katz, "Skills of an Effective Administrator," *Harvard Business Review,* Vol. 33, (January-February, 1955), pp. 33–42.

ANNOTATED BIBLIOGRAPHY

Roald F. Campbell, Luvern L. Cunningham, Roderick F. McPhee, and Raphael O. Nystrand. *The Organization and Control of American Schools.* Columbus, Ohio: Charles E. Merrill Publishing Company, 1970, 592 pp.

   Chapter 9 presents a discussion of the kinds and types of school administrators, describes control and professional expertise, and examines the power of an administrator.

Richard A. Gorton, *Conflict, Controversy and Crisis in School Administration and Supervision: Issues, Cases and Concepts for the '70s.* Dubuque, Iowa: William C. Brown Company Publishers, 1972, 357 pp.

   Part II presents major concepts associated with educational administration. Gorton discusses decision making, communication, leadership, authority, power, influence, role expectations, and conflict. The informal organization of a school is also identified and analyzed.

Paul Hersey and Kenneth H. Blanchard. *Management of Organizational Behavior* (2nd ed.). Englewood cliffs, New Jersey: Prentice-Hall, Inc., 1972, 209 pp.

   Hersey and Blanchard focus on behavior within organizations, the interaction of people, and motivation and leadership. Elements of management common to many organizations are presented in a simple and scholarly manner.

Stephen J. Knezevich. *Administration of Public Education* (2nd ed.) New York: Harper and Row Publishers, 1969, 578 pp.

   This widely used textbook describes the fundamentals of educational administration and operation. His book is helpful to those who wish to understand more fully and clearly the practice of educational administration.

Robert L. Saunders, Ray C. Phillips, and Harold T. Johnson. *A Theory of Educational Leadership.* Columbus, Ohio: Charles E. Merrill Books, Inc., 1966, 174 pp.

   These authors present a comprehensive approach to administrative behaviors. They emphasize not only the operational components of theory but also the philosophical questions. The authors suggest principles to guide management practices.

Charles L. Wood, Everett W. Nicholson, and Dale Findley. *Concepts of Educational Leadership for the Secondary School.* Warren, Ohio: Charles A. Jones Publishing Company, 1974, 487 pp.

   These authors focus upon the principalship as an educational leadership position. Part II discusses administrative theory and educational leadership.

Guidance: Organizational Theories and Patterns

It will be a major misfortune if the broad goal of guidance as assistance to the individual in development comes to be replaced by any part-goal, however commendable or expedient in itself.[1]

Chapter 2

What is guidance and how does it differ from and relate to other pupil personnel services and helping professions?

What guidance services are provided directly to students?

Why is guidance extended within American Schools?

What organizational structures are in common use?

How is guidance organized within education?

GUIDANCE AND OTHER PERSONNEL SERVICES

The aim of guidance, simply stated, is to help every person develop the best that is in him as an individual and as a member of society. The need for and practice of guidance have been in evidence whenever and wherever man turned to his fellows for help with his existential problems and concerns.

Thoughtful men in every era have wrestled with the problems of their time. Every era has been, to some extent, a period of transition between a pleasingly plausible past and a frustrating free-wheeling future. Some men in every era have tried to modify or correct man's existential problems by advancing political solutions to man's plight. Other men turned to personal ministrations in individual instances to improve man's condition.

---

[1]Carrol H. Miller, *Foundations of Guidance* (2nd ed.). New York: Harper & Row, Publishers, 1971, p. 435.

No doubt, life has never run smoothly in any world constantly in a state of change. But today, economic, political, social, and psychological changes of a far-reaching nature seem to add to the complexity and hazards of man's condition. These changes bring to almost every individual a sense of personal uncertainty, insecurity, and frustration. The individual, driven back on his own resources to cope with feelings of personal inadequacy, often experiences dissonance, conflict, and disintegration. He turns to his fellow man to understand his and others' behavior, his relationships with others, his decisions, his choices, his situations, his goals, and his very being. Fundamentally, his essential and perennial problems remain: Who am I? Am I normal? What is good? Of what value is life?

The individual, therefore, seeks help to overcome unfavorable situations, to establish unity in his life and to achieve integration of self. He is led by these conditions to other people in the hope that they can provide knowledge, beliefs, or understanding that they have evolved or acquired about the nature of the world and the individual's place in it.

Those who engage in helping relationships endeavor through their intervention to contribute in a positive, facilitating way to the individual who seeks their help. Their focus is upon behavior and the individual who presents it. Their concern is with the individual's attitudes, motives, ideas, needs, and responses.

Definitions of a helping relationship are sufficiently broad in meaning and scope to include many nurturing and uplifting relationships established between and among individuals. The relationship that exists between teachers and pupils, husband and wife, mother and child, doctor and patient, counselor and client, is frequently viewed as a helping relationship, no matter how the term is defined. Consequently, at every stage of life, sources of help exist for the individual. It is true, however, that assistance is generally given more freely and systematically to children than to adults, presumably because adults are viewed as being more nearly in command of their lives. The home (parent-child relationship) is the principal institution which helps the young child. The church is also involved, not only through its instructions and advice to parents on the rearing of their children but also through its youth-serving activities.

Guidance Defined for School Structure

Most individuals seem to know almost intuitively where to turn for help with their concerns. Early in the child's school career, he comes to realize that the school staff is there as a principal source of assistance in addition to the home. Indeed, he inevitably turns to them to make his life more satisfactory. He seeks their help in coping with the exigencies that are

invariably produced by living within the social system for formal learning
—the school. "Guidance" is the term that has evolved to describe the
helping relationship extended by school staff members to students.

Definitions, particularly precise ones, of the term "guidance" are hard to
come by. It is a loose word, ambiguous and tricky. Various writers and
practitioners have defined it, but never to their or anyone's complete satisfaction.

Following are some of the more recent definitions of the term:

> Guidance is the systematic, professional process of helping the indi-
> vidual through educative and interpretive procedures to gain a better
> understanding of his own characteristics and potentialities and to relate
> himself more satisfactorily to social requirements and opportunities, in
> accord with social and moral values.[2]

> We intend to confine our discussion to the subject of student person-
> nel services oriented toward assisting an individual to develop a well
> delineated sense of identity. The term 'guidance' will be used to de-
> scribe these services.[3]

> In an educational context, guidance is seen as the sum total of
> helping services purposefully created and contrived to facilitate, or
> show the way for, realizing optimum human growth and development
> of all learners.[4]

> . . . guidance will be defined as a program implemented by profes-
> sional specialists within the school system whose primary task is the
> application of skills and theory derived from the behavioral sciences.
> These skills will be applied primarily toward the accomplishment of
> goals related to the affective domain . . . in contrast to the teacher
> whose goals are primarily related to the cognitive domain. . . .[5]

While we, as other authors, would wish to formulate a definition which
would win general acceptance and therefore contribute to such needed
standardization of terminology, the desire exceeds the grasp. Guidance, as
used here and throughout this book, is defined simply as *the process of
helping the individual to understand himself and his world so that he can
utilize his potentialities.* Immediately, several explanations and addenda are

---

[2]Robert Hendry Mathewson, *Guidance Policy and Practice* (3rd ed.). New York: Harper
& Row, Publishers, 1962, p. 141.

[3]Lawrence H. Stewart and Charles F. Warnath, *The Counselor and Society.* Boston:
Houghton Mifflin Company, 1965, pp. 19–20.

[4]T. Antoinette Ryan and Franklin R. Zeran, *Organization and Administration of Guidance
Services.* Danville, Illinois: The Interstate Printers and Publishers, Inc., 1972, p. 7.

[5]Merville C. Shaw, *School Guidance Systems.* Boston: Houghton, Mifflin Company, 1973,
p. 10.

needed to convey a fuller explanation of the term. First, by *process* is meant that guidance is not conceived as episodic or a single event but rather is conceptualized as assistance that is sequential and cumulative in nature, progressing toward a goal. Second, *helping* means that the individual who renders the assistance is obligated to benefit and not to injure the person who seeks his help. McCully has defined a helping profession as one which, "based upon its specialized knowledge, applies an intellectual technique to the existential affairs of others toward the end of enabling them to cope more effectively with the dilemma and paradoxes that characterize the human condition."[6] Further, McCully noted that the practitioner in applying his intellectual technique to the existential affairs of others could not do so completely as a scientist. Obviously, the point is that the extension of a helping relationship is in part an art since there is no sure external approach to the resolution of existential problems. Third, use of the term *individual* is routinely qualified by adding that guidance is extended to all pupils who are present in the school. Simultaneously it may be noted that individuals who exhibit severe forms of disordered behavior may well receive therapy and other types of specialized assistance. Further explanations of this aspect are given below. Fourth, use of the words *to understand himself and his world* needs amplification. The intent here is to convey that the individual gains a better "understanding of his own characteristics and potentialities" (see Mathewson's definition). He not only gains an understanding and acceptance of himself and his problems but he utilizes this understanding for his and society's development and improvement. In this case "acceptance" does not mean "conformity" in the popular sense of the term. Rather it means that he achieves an identity, knows who he is and what he can become, and is less vulnerable to anxiety about his existence in moving toward fulfillment of his potentiality. Finally, additions to the definition would include the notion that teachers and administrators have inherent guidance responsibilities in their roles as teachers and administrators. Guidance is not the exclusive province of one group or the other, but is necessarily engaged in by those who are able and interested. Those who specialize (by virtue of training and assignment) in the school's helping relationships are usually called "school counselors."

Problems of Defining Guidance

Many individuals have suggested that the term "guidance" is an outmoded term and conveys a variety of things to different people, possibly

---

[6]C. Harold McCully, "Conceptions of Man and the Helping Professions," *Personnel and Guidance Journal,* Vol. 44, No. 9 (May, 1966), p. 912.

never accurately describing that which is done under its name. As used in educational literature "guidance" has sometimes meant the directing of learning activities by teachers, sometimes it has meant a constellation of student personnel services, while at other times it is used in a more specialized way to describe the work of a counselor. While laymen narrowly define guidance as "steering," "channeling," or "directing" students, the practitioner views it broadly as helping individuals to become what they are capable of becoming. Perhaps if the divergent views of laymen and practitioners cannot be reconciled the label "guidance" will have to be abandoned.

Social psychologists, in an effort to highlight the interdependency of language and environment, point out that the Eskimo vocabulary contains numerous words for snow, in all its forms, and very few words for earth. In contrast, our vocabulary contains many highly descriptive words for earth, in all its forms, and relatively few for snow. Clearly, vocabularies, both in their diversity and specificity, incorporate that which is important to people. As it now stands, the term "guidance" is most commonly used to refer to a set of services, while its practitioners bear a title that derives from only one of its services. The word is devoid of the specificity required to incorporate what counselors mean when they use the term. If usage was restricted to the actual meaning of the word, those practicing guidance should be called "guides," not "counselors." They then could properly perform guidance, but no self-respecting counselor would agree to the title "guide."

Hoyt[7] has argued for retention of the word "guidance" for three reasons: (1) it permits the function to be viewed as a program of schoolwide assistance to youth (every staff member has a guidance role), (2) it provides a rationale for viewing the school counselor as a key, central figure but it does not make him solely responsible for its success or failure, and (3) retention of the word "guidance" means that the counselor is not forced to form his primary working relationships with specialists (psychologists, social workers) rather than with educators (he would not lose his commitment to education). In defending the continued use of the term, Hoyt defined guidance as ". . . that part of pupil personnel services—and therefore of elementary and secondary education—aimed at maximal development of individual potentialities through devoting schoolwide assistance to youth in the personal problems, choices, and decisions each must face as he moves toward maturity."[8]

---

[7]Kenneth B. Hoyt, "Guidance: A Constellation of Services," *Personnel and Guidance Journal,* Vol. 40, No. 8 (April 1962), pp. 690–697.
   [8]*Ibid,* p. 692.

While educators usually are aware of what they mean by guidance, they have never quite been able to explain the distinction to the public. The school's boiler fireman may refer to himself as an "engineer," but any parent who asks him to specify what he actually does knows immediately that he is not a professional engineer, but rather tends the furnace. The parent who is told by a member of the school staff that he is a "school counselor" and asks what this means receives an answer that only can confuse him. Frequently this answer includes little, if any, reference to actual counseling with students. Rather, the usual answer is a listing of many activities that better describe the several services that comprise the entire guidance program. Perhaps concern with this issue will dissipate when school counselors counsel and supporting guidance services are assigned to subprofessionals. But one thing is evident: we need to eliminate vague language and move to a term more clearly descriptive of what counselors do, and more understandable and acceptable to both laymen and professionals.

Some Communalities and Distinctions

The terms "guidance," "student personnel," and "counseling" have been used in the foregoing pages. Here, an attempt will be made to point up some distinctions and communalities between and among these terms as well as others, e.g., teaching, advising, and psychotherapy.

1. *Student Personnel.* Some authors have recommended that the term, student personnel, be used as a replacement for the term, guidance. Indeed, at the junior college, college, and/or university level, "student personnel" is invariably used to describe certain services (counseling, scholarship and financial aids, admissions and registrations, student health, housing) provided to students. To some degree, such services to college students parallel those provided to high school students under the name of guidance. However, at elementary and secondary school levels, *pupil* or *student personnel* has conveyed for many years a more extensive array of services than that provided under the name guidance. At these levels, such services as child accounting, health, guidance, psychological services are usually incorporated under the title, student personnel. "Guidance," therefore, is only one of many services provided in the complex of pupil personnel services.

2. *Guidance.* Since guidance has been defined above, it is sufficient here to note that it is a term that is less broad than "student personnel" but is broader than the terms "counseling" or "psychotherapy." The constellation of services usually incorporated under the term "guidance" includes counseling, informational, planning and placement, and student appraisal (see next section on guidance services).

3. *Counseling.* A major service incorporated in the guidance program is that of counseling. Chapter 8 discusses the development and management

of this service. In counseling, an individual(s) with a problem(s) is helped through a relationship with a professionally prepared counselor to voluntarily change his behavior or to clarify his ideas, attitudes, and goals. Counseling differs from guidance in that the latter conveys a wider complex of services and relies somewhat more upon cognitively oriented processes (information, planning) to help the individual.

4. *Psychotherapy.* Psychotherapy has been defined as the process of re-educating an individual at both the conscious and unconscious levels to help him achieve personality reorganization, to integrate insight into his personality structure, and to work out methods of handling feelings originating deep within his personality.[9]

Some individuals use the terms "counseling" and "psychotherapy" interchangeably. For example, Patterson[10] does not believe that counseling and psychotherapy differ essentially from one another. He suggests that they are similar in the nature of the relationships established, the processes used, their methods and techniques, their purposes, goals or results.

Other individuals believe that differences exist between the two terms. Generally, the differences are those of degree, rather than kind. Some of these differences will be summarized here. First, the goal of psychotherapy is often conceptualized as basic personality or intrapsychic change, while counseling goals are often more modest, incorporating goals such as decision making, self-assurance, understanding self and others, etc. Second, the psychotherapist is primarily concerned with the irrational and unconscious components of the individual's life, while counselors are primarily concerned with conscious, more rational components. Psychotherapists often work with the historical factors in the individual's behavior patterns while counselors usually concentrate upon present (ahistorical) factors. Third, psychotherapy is usually viewed as the help extended to individuals who are suffering from severe emotional distress while counseling is extended to the more "normal" individual with developmental problems or concerns. Finally, psychotherapy as a service is most often provided in hospital and clinical settings while counseling services are located in educational and other nonmedical settings.

Fundamentally, differences between counseling and psychotherapy appear to be differences of degree rather than kind. Tyler, for example, has defined counseling as "minimum change therapy."[11]

---

[9]Lawrence M. Brammer and Everett L. Shostrom, *Therapeutic Psychology* (2nd ed.). Englewood Cliffs, N.J.: Prentice-hall, Inc., 1968, pp. 6–9.

[10]C. H. Patterson, "Counseling and/or Psychotherapy?", *American Psychologist,* Vol. 18, No. 10 (October, 1963), Pp. 667–669.

[11]Leona E. Tyler, *The Work of the Counselor* (3rd ed.). New York: Appleton-Century-Crofts, 1969, p. 13.

5. *Teaching.* Teaching, often defined as the act of imparting knowledge, skills or attitudes, has sometimes been differentiated from guidance, counseling, or psychotherapy on such bases as (1) teachers are concerned primarily with groups, counselors with individuals, and (2) teachers teach subject matter while the student is the subject matter of counselors. Grant has argued that the teacher-student relationship is not counseling because (1) the internalization of the teacher-held value that learning is important is the major motivator of pupil learning; (2) teachers need to possess only information about pupils which reveals their ability, achievement, potential and interest, and need not possess other information of a highly personal nature; and (3) teacher understanding of intimate areas of the pupil's life (fears, anxieties, guilt, peer relationships) would interfere with or inhibit rather than facilitate teacher-pupil realtionships.[12] Patterson has stated

> The counselor does not teach, and whereas counseling may resemble teaching in some respects—such as being based on the same philosophy regarding the nature of man and the broad goals of education or human development—this resemblance is not identity, and is often overworked. It may be that the greatest resemblance between the teaching period and the counseling hour is that they both are fifty minutes in length.[13]

Tiedeman and Field[14] have reacted to the perception of a counselor which relegates him to a technician who assists the teacher rather than being a professional in his own right. These two authors have cited some distinctions between the functions of a counselor as contrasted to those of a teacher. They maintain that teaching involves a communication of the experiences of others, while guidance is centered upon the individual's perception of experiences. Teaching, by nature, creates discontinuity; guidance attempts to reduce discontinuity. Shoben,[15] too, differentiates between teaching and guidance in much the same way. He believes that the teacher's function is to draw students into the traditions of society while the counselor's function is to help particular children move in distinctive directions on the basis of their special characteristics and potentialities.

6. *Advising.* Primary among the characteristics of advising is that the individual being advised is related to a set of predetermined conditions and

---

[12]Claude W. Grant, "The Teacher-Student Relationship is not Counseling," *Journal of Counseling Psychology,* Vol. 7 (1960), pp. 148–149.

[13]C. H. Patterson (ed.), *The Counselor in the School: Selected Readings.* New York: McGraw-Hill Book Company, 1967, p. 76.

[14]David W. Tiedeman and Frank L. Field, "Guidance: The Science of Purposeful Action Applied through Education," *Harvard Educational Review,* Vol. 32 (Fall, 1962), pp. 483–501.

[15]Edward C. Shoben, "Guidance: Remedial Function or Social Reconstruction?" *Harvard Educational Review,* Vol. 32, No. 4 (Fall, 1962), pp. 430–442.

confronted with his capacity to meet these conditions. The advisor abstracts some facet or characteristic from the advisee, considers this representative of him, and relates it to his probability and possibility of being successful in the predetermined conditions.

7. *Conversation.* Conversation or talking (even purposeful conversation in an interview situation) is not synonymous with counseling. However, conversation is involved in the kinds of relationships described above as well as in other situations, but conversation differs from counseling. In social conversation, the individuals involved maintain any distortions and/or play any role that they either consciously or unconsciously desire. Usually no attempt is made to correct the distortions or challenge the role.

Finally, examination of the above terminology reveals that distinctions between and among the terms are not clear-cut, categorical, or precise. The boundaries of each are not clearly laid down, rather they are fuzzy, shading one into another. The terms and their definitions have been borrowed from other professions. Confusion inevitably results when a profession preempts certain terms to identify its functions that are engaged in by so many others. It may be noted, too, that the language adopted in the definitions is often reverential, sentimental, and hardly helpful. Hopefully, more systematic definitions and explanations will be formulated soon by the profession.

THE GUIDANCE SERVICES

Typically, those who write about guidance classify the help provided under its name into five or six services, such as pupil inventory, informational, counseling, follow-up, placement, evaluation, and the like. But this classification of services has not been adopted very widely by those who practice guidance to refer or to identify the services they provide. Rather, practitioners refer to the testing program, educational guidance, counseling, vocational guidance, the record system, etc. Consequently, in this book on guidance program organization and administration, the authors utilize the approach and terminology of those in the field. The reader will note that this has the fault of fragmenting the services. In reality, there are only four (perhaps only three, depending upon how each service is defined) guidance services provided *directly* to students. These include:

1. *The appraisal service.* The appraisal service, sometimes called pupil inventory, is designed to collect, analyze, and use a variety of objective and subjective psychological data about each pupil. Essentially, its purpose is to help the individual to understand himself. While the collection and analysis of these data do not constitute a direct service to the individual, interpreta-

tion of data leading to self-understanding is a direct service to students. In this book, Chapters 11 and 12, dealing respectively with testing and cumulative records, discuss pupil appraisal.

2. *The information service.* The informational service is designed to provide students with knowledge of and familiarity with the educational, vocational, and personal-social opportunities that exist for them in our society. The aim is that with such information students will make better choices and will engage in more mature, planful behavior. An often overlooked aspect of this service is that students must not only be provided with or exposed to such information but must have opportunities to react to it in a meaningful relationship with others. In this book, Chapters 8, 9 and 10 discuss this service.

3. *Planning, placement, and follow-up.* This service is designed to assist the student in selecting and utilizing opportunities within the school and the labor market that will enhance his development. The reader will note that this service and the informational service could be viewed as one. They are separated here because all too often the informational service is restricted to the collection and dissemination of information to students. Information exists and is available in many forms, and what is involved in this service are processes of helping the individual to interpret and to act upon information in ways that are meaningful to him. Again, the material contained in Chapters 8, 9 and 10 identifies and discusses these processes.

4. *The counseling service.* This service is designed to help individuals with psychological problems to voluntarily change their behavior by clarifying their ideas, perceptions, attitudes, and goals. Chapter 8 discusses how this service is developed and managed in schools.

Seemingly, analysis of services provided under the term "guidance" is often confused with procedures and processes. "Service" refers to the organization of work done in an activity while "procedures and/or processes" refer to the courses of action taken to provide services. Mathewson has pointed out that "guidance activity is something distinct in itself, requiring a *policy* to direct it, an *organized program* and *set of procedures* to fulfill its purposes and *professional competencies and attitudes* to conduct it effectively."[16]

GUIDANCE WITHIN AMERICAN SCHOOLS

Observers and critics of American schools as well as educators abroad have often inquired as to why guidance should be a function maintained

---

[16]Robert H. Mathewson, *Guidance Policy and Practice* (3rd ed.). New York: Harper & Row, Publishers, 1962, p. 4.

within the school. The question of why guidance should reside within the school and not some other institution of society is a challenging one which every practitioner needs to think through clearly and carefully.

Why Within the School?

Three practical, if not philosophical, reasons exist which demonstrate the efficacy of providing guidance within the schools. First to be mentioned is *accessibility.* If guidance is provided within the schools, its practitioners will be readily accessible to those who need their services. The student will not have to be transported to a community clinic or some other agency to receive help. He will not have to go after school, in the evenings, or at other times. If guidance were provided by another institution of society and its practitioners sought to render the service inside the school (or at least part of it), problems always seem to arise as to when they are to be given access to those who wish to utilize their services. The argument here is that it is not only more convenient to offer guidance within the school, but that the timing with which help is given is an important element in correcting or alleviating situations for which help is sought. Within the school, guidance practitioners can draw more easily upon the knowledge that they, teachers, and administrators have accumulated about the individual student. Above all, obstacles and barriers are not placed upon the individual who seeks help when the counselor is located within the school.

A second reason as to why guidance should be a function of the school rather than an external agency is that external agencies such as community clinics and bureaus are often understaffed and overcrowded. Waiting lists of weeks and months develop for individuals who seek help. As a consequence, community agencies, by necessity often restrict their services to those who are most in need—those who have severe emotional or physical impairments. By definition, guidance exists because the "normal" individual's learning is impaired or interfered with, but the individual is not disabled or unable to remain within the classroom. In short, the case for guidance within the schools is that situational, educational-vocational problems, and personal-social (identity) concerns (which often interfere with the individual's learning and utilization of his potentialities) would receive short shrift in another agency or institution of society. Community agencies are usually staffed and/or directed by individuals trained at the Ph.D or M.D. level. By virtue of their training and interests, their attention and skills are more directly focused upon the severely disturbed rather than the developmental concerns of youth.

A third reason which supports provision of guidance within the school is that those who staff it will be more responsive to the needs exhibited by students, teachers, and administrators. Because they are physically present in the school their intimate grasp of the character of the student body will enable them to provide the kind of services needed. Administratively, when they serve within the school they can be held accountable for their professional activities.

The student's need for an understanding of his personal characteristics if he is to engage himself meaningfully in life; his need to understand his relationships with others; and his need for formulating alternatives and engaging in planning behavior are conditions which must be dealt with within the school. The point here is that a great society cannot afford to lose the best that an individual can produce. It (the society) can do no less than provide services which facilitate his development. Finally, the school as a servant of society incorporates the services that the members of that society expect and demand of it. There is no preordained set of functions which it must provide. It provides within its systems those services that educators and the members of community believe will help individuals become independent responsible members of society.

Guidance—an American Phenomenon

No other country seems to have developed systematic guidance services within schools as are present in American education. Many reasons have been given to account for this phenomenon. A summary of these speculations is given below, but no doubt it is not because of any one of them but rather a combination of reasons that accounts for guidance being an American phenomenon.

1. Some have asserted that guidance developed in American schools because of their size. With compulsory education, American school enrollment increased and the high school became larger. The attempt to educate all the children of all the people brought many individuals into the schools who had no clear idea why they were there or what they wanted from the experience. School personnel, teachers and administrators, broadened the curriculum and extended other services in an attempt to meet pupil needs. Because of the numbers of students and because students had to make choices among curricular programs, teachers and administrators required assistance in providing individual help to the students. Hence, school counselors were employed to provide an individualizing influence to counteract the impersonality that comes to any institution which becomes large. This consolidation of small schools into large concentrations of population with varied curricular patterns has, no doubt, been a major factor in the development and spread of guidance programs in American schools.

2. The aims and principles of guidance fit snugly into American democratic ideals. Its aim of helping the individual to become all that he is

capable of becoming without regard to family, class, or social conditions represents a characteristic of an open society and is highly prized in America.

3. America has been able to afford the costs of guidance services. Guidance is expensive. It costs money which an affluent society can afford. However, many who practice guidance often point out that if their efforts are viewed as being preventive, the savings to the nation represented in providing guidance rather than custodial care offset much of the cost.

4. The expansion of professionalization and specialization has been instrumental in the development of guidance in American schools. When certain needs are in existence, individuals who specialize in meeting these needs develop. Other societies characteristically depend upon the amateur to cope with these needs in addition to performing other functions. Rather than relying upon teachers to provide guidance, counselors (specialists) were brought into being to provide a systematic service to youth.

Other countries such as Norway, Sweden, and England are beginning to implement guidance services within their schools. Many of these countries are extending compulsory education and revamping their system of education. Larger schools, offering more comprehensive programs, seem inevitably to be a result of this reorganization. In the years to come, observations of school guidance practices and programs within these countries will be fruitful for those who practice in America.

These observations about the nature of guidance and guidance services serve as a background for considering how it is organized within American education. Before doing so, it is necessary to have some understanding about organizational patterns in education.

ORGANIZATIONAL PATTERNS IN EDUCATION

Previously (see Chapter 1), *organization* was defined as "the structural relationship of the functions within an orgainzation." It was pointed out that organization may be thought of as the overall framework joining the functions of an enterprise. Theoretically, an ideal organization can be established for each enterprise. This ideal organization incorporates all the characteristics deemed desirable in an organization. It would be obtained by establishing what is desired by rational thinking and by using scientific experimentation to decide what the relationships of the various functions should be in order to approach perfection.

In actual practice, the ideal organization is seldom, if ever, obtained. There are several reasons for this. The personal influence of chief executives upon the structure of the organization is exceedingly important. Men differ in their beliefs, and not all top executives view organization with identical opinions and convictions. Also, the enterprise may lack the financial resources required to establish the ideal organization. Moreover, there is a tendency to stay with the old and established form of organization rather than to change to a new and untried form.

Several organizational patterns have been identified and discussed in the educational literature. Here consideration will be given to reviewing four general types of formed organizational patterns, followed by a discussion of how guidance may be organized in American schools.

Line and Staff

Enterprises organized according to this concept are such that at any given level of authority, individuals and/or departments may be classified by function into line or staff. Line structure involves the division of an organization according to authority from top to bottom and vice versa while staff organization is division according to functions performed. The military enterprise is often cited as the model of an institution organized by line and staff. Traditionally, only line personnel give commands while staff personnel are involved in training, quality control, etc.

The line and staff structure as it might be represented in school organization is presented graphically in Figure 2–1.

Two comments may be made about Figure 2–1. First, authority in the schools comes from the Board of Education who represent the community. The superintendent, as the school's executive officer, delegates authority to building principals and they in turn to teachers in classrooms. Accountability for this authority (responsibility) flows upward, i.e., teachers are accountable to building principals who are accountable to the Superintendent, who is accountable to the Board of Education, in turn accountable to the public. The second comment is that the curriculum director and the research director do not have authority but rather depend upon their professional skills and status to influence the enterprise.

Scalar Patterns

Organizations which employ scalar or hierarchical structure grade the duties to be performed according to degrees of authority and responsibility. All individuals and or positions are arranged in a hierarchy according to the degree of responsibility and authority they possess and use. Figure 2–1 also represents a hierarchical pattern in that the Board of Education possesses ultimate authority, followed by the superintendent who possesses executive authority, and the like.

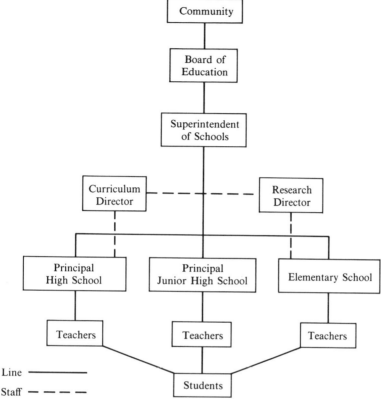

Figure 2-1.   *School Line and Staff Organizational Pattern.*

Spatial Patterns

This form of organization deals more with the "geography," the degree of centralization of functions in a main office, of an enterprise. For example, many argue about the merits of centralizing control in federal government agencies compared to decentralizing functions in the various state governmental agencies. Fundamentally, the question revolves around the efficiency with which functions can be carried out. Usually the central office retains general supervisory and administrative responsibility, while special services are decentralized into branch offices. Enterprises organized in this form have to cope with the problem of keeping lines of communication open to achieve articulation among decentralized coordinates.

Radial Pattern

This type of structure is often called "spherical" or "circular." Here the chief executive occupies the center position or hub, with all departments having equal authority and responsibility. Figure 2–2 is an attempt to portray graphically this organizational pattern in a school. Administrative fiat is to be avoided in radial structures with dependence placed upon recommendations and departmental concensus. If conflicting views emerge and concensus cannot be achieved, the central executive often makes the decision (reverting to vertical authority).

None of these four types of organizational structure may be found intact in a given educational enterprise; rather, elements of all may exist. It may be speculated that educational institutions, as public organizations, typically employ a scalar line and staff structure. Some administrators state that this kind of structure is followed because an accounting can be given for legal and fiscal authority.

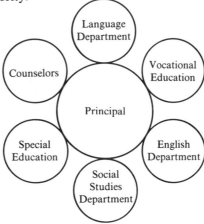

Figure 2–2.   *Radial Pattern of School Organization.*

Concepts of Authority and Responsibility

Administration, viewed as decision making, is most concerned with making correct decisions so that an enterprise accomplishes its work efficiently. Decision making involves value judgment as well as factual considerations. The concepts of authority and responsibility are of utmost importance in administrative structures. An individual who permits his behavior to be decided by a superior without independently reviewing the merits of that decision is said to have accepted authority. The authority exercised by a superior in an organization is usually asserted through obedience, suggestion, and persuasion rather than the threat of sanctions, such as discipline, or dismissal. Simon notes:

> Of all the modes of influence, authority is the one that chiefly distinguishes the behavior of individuals as participants of organizations

from their behavior outside such organizations. It is authority that gives an organization its formal structure, and the other modes of influence may best be discussed after this structure has been specified.[17]

Authority then is the power to make decisions which guide the actions of others. Authority reposes in the superior's position because he can formulate and transmit decisions with the expectation that they will be accepted by those in subordinate positions. Those in subordinate positions not only expect such decisions but their behavior is determined by these decisions. Authority is the "right to the last word." Simon has specified three functions for which authority is employed as a tool for coordination of a group: (1) enforcing responsibility to those who wield the authority, (2) securing expertise in decision making, and (3) permitting coordination of activity.[18]

Essentially, responsibility means accountability. An administrative structure not only has the right to decision but simultaneously is held to account for its actions and, in turn, enforces adherence by others to its decision.

Organization of Educational Institutions

The scalar line and staff administrative structure that characterizes American schools does not seem particularly appropriate to the educational enterprise. The fundamental purpose of the school is to advance teaching and learning; yet the structure most frequently employed seems to be based more upon administering a military enterprise or that of a company engaged in the production and distribution of goods. Line and staff administrative structures are built upon a model based upon superior-subordinate roles. Within the school building, the "superior" is the principal who not only has autonomous power to decide but the sanctions to enforce his decisions upon his subordinates—teachers, counselors and others. This casts teachers and others in the role of "employee." Associated with the role of employee is the condition to "obey" authority. However, school personnel (teachers, counselors, and administrators) are professionals and constitute a community of colleagues. Clearly, there is a lack of fit between the typical line and staff administrative structure and the kind of personnel associated with the school. What is needed is an administrative structure that will enable the professionals employed to utilize their competence and expertise to secure decisions based upon rationality and effectiveness, rather than authority.

Kehas has charged that the way authority has been defined and distributed in schools works against the development of a distinctive guidance

---

[17]Herbert A. Simon, *Administrative Behavior* (2nd ed.). New York: The Free Press, 1957, p. 124.
[18]Simon, *Administrative Behavior,* p. 135.

function. Pointing out that his argument is not to ask administrators to "understand counselors better" but rather a call for a functional allocation of authority based on competence and expertise instead of "ultimate authority," Kehas states

> Serious examination and study should be given to the question of authority in school systems, and primarily to the notion of the 'Autonomy of the principal in his school.' Such examination and study is necessary because of the central importance of this notion in the actual administration and organization of the schools. Further, I would argue that a redistribution of authority as regards the guidance function must come about—that authority for guidance in a system must reside with the chief guidance officer of that system, and that the involvement of others with the *basic* decisions regarding guidance must be circumscribed.[19]

Kehas envisions counselors as being primarily responsible to the director or supervisor of guidance for most of their activities and to the principal for others, based upon whether the activities center upon involvement with students or institutional obligations. Perhaps future school administrators will be able to subdivide the work of the school in such a way that the expertness residing in teachers and others can be utilized in the decision-making process. What is needed is some type of organization in which responsibility for decision is given to those who possess the expertise to make the decision. This would mean that the decisions in schools would be subdivided into component elements and each school member's activities would be restricted to those for which he evidences competence. The expert would be placed in a strategic position where his decisions would be accepted as premises by other members. Organization would thus be by process with "authority of ideas" placed in a superior position to "authority of sanctions."

ORGANIZATIONAL STRUCTURE FOR GUIDANCE

Many have commented upon the patchwork of organizing guidance services and its topsylike, chance-determined character in American schools. Lloyd-Jones[20] has described general educational programs as being divided into three patterns; classical, neo-classical, and instrumental. Guidance has

[19]Chris D. Kehas, "Administrative Structure and Guidance Theory," *Counselor Education and Supervision,* Vol. 4 (Spring, 1965), pp. 147–148.

[20]Esther Lloyd-Jones, "Personnel Work and General Education," in *General Education, Fifty-first Yearbook of the National Society for the Study of Education,* Part I. Chicago: The Society. Distributed by the University of Chicago Press, 1952, pp. 214–229.

been similarly characterized. Proponents of the classical point of view generally have refused to recognize guidance as a professional endeavor, assigning guidance duties to the academic and administrative faculty; administrators of neo-classical institutions have generally accepted guidance services; and those administering instrumental institutions have not only accepted guidance but have stressed the creation of an environment for experiment and testing of guidance patterns and functions.

Guidance Patterns, Approaches and Strategies

Glanz[21] cites four approaches to guidance programming in the schools. These four approaches are summarized here:

1. *Centralized-Specialism.* This approach utilizes professionally prepared counselors, psychometrists, social workers, and other highly qualified personnel in specified, defined, coordinated positions. Major responsibility for guidance and treatment of students' existential problems rests with these specialists. The specialists form a team with an administrative head and responsibility for their operations can be identified.

2. *Decentralized-Generalism.* This approach depends upon teachers and administrators to perform the guidance function within the roles historically assigned them. Specialists are usually avoided or are used only in a supporting role. "Every teacher a counselor" is a watchword and defense of those who employ this approach.

3. *Curricular Counseling and Guidance.* This approach seeks to integrate guidance within curricular activities. Group guidance approaches, orientation programs, guidancelike units taught in segments of the curriculum, classes in the study of occupations, and other activities are characteristic of this approach. Essentially, the hope is that these activities promote self-study and educational-vocational planning among students.

4. *Human Relations and Group Work.* This approach, as described by Glanz, seems to focus upon broad general outcomes of mental health. Various types of group work (principles of good mental health, adjustment, mature thinking, and effective interpersonal skills) are stressed.

Mathewson devotes a chapter in his book to the strategies employed for guidance. By strategy he means the decisions or choices by which the guidance process is selected and carried out. The series of decisions which

[21]Edward C. Glanz, "Emerging Concepts and Patterns of Guidance in American Education," *Personnel and Guidance Journal,* Vol. 40, (November, 1961), pp. 259–265.

determines behavior over a stretch of time is called a strategy. He pointed out that several strategies were represented in prevailing practice at that time (1962) and that no one strategy appeared to be dominant. In his work, seven strategies were conceptualized by dimensional lines, or continua, with the polar positions of each continuum identified. Here the seven continua are presented:

1. *Educative: directive.* The "educative" end of the continuum represents guidance conceived as a learning process in which the individual "learns" to make choices. At the other end (the directive) guidance is conceived as diagnosis of individual problems by an expert who then recommends problem-solving action for the counselee and/or his mentors.

2. *Cumulative: problem-point.* Guidance, at one end of this continuum, is viewed as a continuous and cumulative process for all students while at the other end it is seen as being required only at certain strategic decision-making points by a few students who need additional specialized assistance.

3. *Self-evaluative: mentor-evaluative.* At the self-evaluative axis, the assumption is made that self-constructs, self-definition, and identity can be achieved by the individual with little or no outside help while the "mentor-evaluative" pole assumes that the individual needs assistance and interpretation from others to achieve identity.

4. *Personal value: social value.* The "personal value" end of this dimension gives concern for the satisfaction of unique individual needs, purposes, and values while the polar position emphasizes social and institutional demands and needs.

5. *Subjective focus: objective focus.* The "subjective focus" is more oriented toward psychological states and events while the other focus is upon objective data (tests, ratings, etc.).

6. *Multiphasic: uniphasic.* The polar positions of this dimension include on the one hand that guidance is developed and treats the normal range of problems and concerns and, on the other hand, that guidance is restricted to a vocational orientation.

7. *Coordinative: specialized.* Guidance at one end of the axis is conceived as dependent upon cooperative procedures while at the other end it is conceived as being conducted by specialists.[22]

Finally, it should be noted that Mathewson has stated that these dimensions are interrelated and that gradations exist between the extremes.

---

[22] Paraphrased from pp. 97–99, *Guidance Policy and Practice,* (3rd ed.), Robert Hendry Mathewson. Copyright 1962, Harper and Row. Used with permission.

Scope, Timing, and Focus

Three questions fundamental to the organization of a guidance program —scope, timing and focus—have been raised by Shaw and Tuel.[23] A summary of their discussion of each of these questions is presented here.

> 1. *What is the scope of responsibility for guidance?* Basically, the question here is whether guidance services are intended for all students or for a segment of the school's population. Shaw and Tuel point out that if guidance is for a segment of the population, presumably it will be for those who deviate in some way from the generality. While a case can be made for dealing with almost any segment, theoreticians and practitioners are generally agreed that guidance should be aimed at all children. It is for all children because in their normal course of development they need assistance in learning how to deal effectively with learning problems, interpersonal and intrapersonal relationships, and skills.
>
> 2. *When is guidance to be given?* Here, Shaw and Tuel consider the question of timing or when intervention should take place. Historically, organized guidance services have been made available to secondary school age students. Earlier preventive intervention (guidance at the elementary school) might reduce problems experienced in later school years.
>
> 3. *What is to be the focus of guidance?* The issue is how guidance is to be accomplished and made most effective. Shaw and Tuel present the focus as either direct or indirect. The counselor who works with the individual student provides a *direct focus* while those counselors who concentrate upon improving the child's environment or helping significant others to understand the individual would be providing an *indirect focus.*

Shaw and Tuel have developed a schematic representation of the options available in respect to the scope, timing, and focus of guidance. It is presented here as Figure 2–3.

The developmental time phase (see Figure 2–3) is placed upon a continuum marked by "extensity" at one pole and "intensity" at the other. At the extensity pole, the program is aimed at the entire population and therefore, its scope is that of general prevention. At the other end of the continuum (intensity) the scope is diagnosis and remediation after pathology has developed, been recognized, and can no longer be tolerated. Between these polar positions lies selective prevention which implies early identifica-

[23]Merville C. Shaw and Jack K. Tuel, "A Focus for Public School Guidance Programs: A Model and Proposal," *Personnel and Guidance Journal,* Vol. 44 (April, 1966), pp. 824–830.

tion and special treatment of individuals predicted to have a high probability of developing pathology. Shaw and Tuel opt for a guidance model based upon general prevention. The reader is referred to their article for a discussion of the implications and advantages of their model.

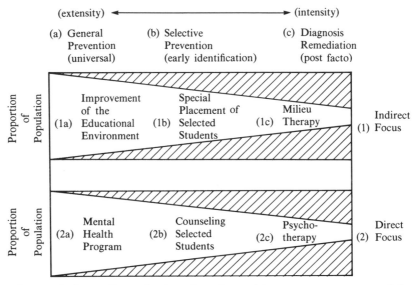

DEVELOPMENTAL TIME PHASE

Figure 2-3.   *Procedural options for guidance programs: a model comprising three dimensions (1) developmental time phase at which intervention is initiated, (2) proportion of population treated, and (3) level of focus at which treatment is aimed. Shaded areas represent proportions of population not reached by a given problem. [From Merville C. Shaw and John K. Tuel, "A Focus for Public School Guidance Programs: A Model and Proposal,"* **Personnel and Guidance Journal,** *Vol. 44 (April, 1966), pp. 824–830. © 1966 by National Vocational Guidance Association. Used with permission.]*

Typical Guidance Organizational Patterns

Patterns for organizing guidance in American schools vary somewhat, depending mainly upon the size of the school and the money made available for guidance.

Small Schools. Schools which have a limited enrollment (200 students or less) may not employ any full-time counselors. In these schools the principal, in addition to being an administrator, is expected to perform certain guidance functions such as testing, college advisement, program planning, and the like. Option 1 in Figure 2–4 represents this pattern. Other administrators have sometime delegated the major responsibility for counseling to a teacher who is given time from teaching for the assignment and have conceptualized their major responsibility as providing leadership in sensitizing teachers to the opportunities they have for extending guidance. Option 2 in Figure 2–4 represents in graphic form the organizational pattern for guidance in relation to other personnel in such schools.

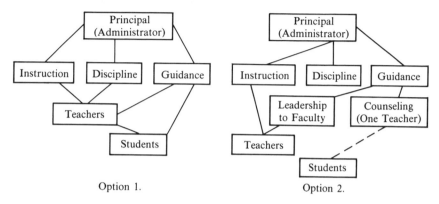

Option 1.   Option 2.

Figure 2–4.   *Typical Small School Organizational Pattern for Guidance.*

Large Schools. Schools with greater student enrollments (500 or more) or with a better financial base generally employ a more formal, centralized approach to guidance. Figure 2–5 attempts to depict graphically the position of counselors in relationship to other personnel in these schools.

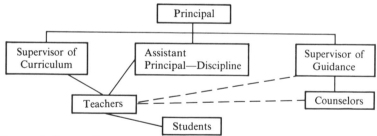

Figure 2–5.   *Organizational Pattern of Guidance in Large Schools.*

District-wide or system-wide guidance organization is sometimes elaborate and difficult to present clearly and accurately. Figure 2–6 presents guidance staff members and leaders in relation to school administration.

Counselors as Staff Positions

Some diversity exists in the way the position of counselor is viewed among secondary schools. However, the prevailing practice is for the counselor to be assigned a staff position. As such, he has no authority save his own personal prestige and status. Most counselors want it this way since the identity they strive to create among teachers, students, parents is that as counselors they are not administrators or teachers. The staff position is a favorable one for them inasmuch as students will be more inclined to view them as being obligated first to the individual and secondly to the institution.

Centralization and Specialization

Any comparison of guidance programs from school to school reveals considerable communality as well as diversity of organization. Diversity exists because of historical antecedents in institutions as well as because of differences in the leadership and personalities of those charged with the responsibility for the institution and for guidance.

Adaption is characteristic of most schools' guidance organization. Nevertheless, from our experiences in and continuing contact with schools it seems clear that more and more schools are moving to centralize their guidance services. The advantages and disadvantages of centralized versus decentralized guidance organization are summarized in Table 2–1.

In present-day practice, guidance services are usually headed by a director who is responsible for communicating to the staff, central administration, and the public regarding (1) guidance definition and goals, (2) personnel needs, (3) selection, assignment, and supervision of guidance personnel, (4) evaluation of the research in the guidance program, (5) needs for physical facilities and budget, and (6) the necessity and program for staff in-service education in guidance. Further elaboration of his responsibilities is given in Chapter 6. Within the typical school guidance organization, a full-time counselor is assigned 300–400 students for whom he is responsible for such activies as (1) counseling, (2) program planning, (3) test interpretation, and (4) educational and vocational planning. Counselors, in addition, serve as consultants to teachers, administrators, parents, curriculum specialists, and others in addition to performing their "counseling roles" with pupils. The reader is referred to Chapters 6 and 7 for a further discussion of counselor role and functions.

Administrative Deterrents to Guidance

Administration exists to move the school toward fulfillment of its goals; it is appropriately institution-centered and its objective is to facilitate the educational enterprise as a whole. On the other hand, guidance is responsible for protecting and preserving the interests of the individual; its objective is to help the individual attain his goals. Inevitably, conflicts emerge between counselors and administrators in situations wherein an individual

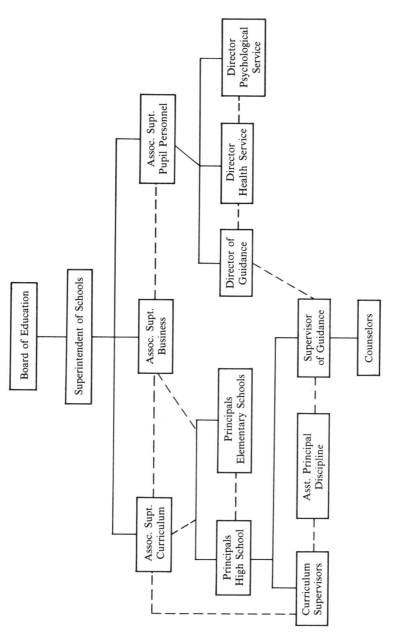

Figure 2-6.   Systemwide Pattern of Guidance Organization.

student's needs run counter to the needs of the institution. Filbeck's research results illustrate clearly the nature of this conflict. He states:

> The school principal studied in this investigation, in situations where the individual student is in conflict with the policies or practices of the school or with the larger social order, favors an approach by the counselor that: (1) is supportive of the school's policies, (2) is reinforcing for student conformity to social standards or norms of behavior, (3) is reinforcing of student acceptance of status quo, (4) promises to reduce the likelihood that students will overtly challenge or threaten the authority of the school.
>
> The counselors, on the other hand, tended to stress an approach that emphasized student decision-making based on individual values and factors.[24]

How this conflict is handled by administrators and counselors is most important. Hopefully, the conflict will be resolved not through use of authority but rather through a balanced consideration of the factors involved and the consequences to the individual and to the enterprise. Superiority of ideas should prevail rather than reversion to authority.

There is no desire here to make administrators scapegoats for ineffective guidance organization. Undoubtedly, guidance practitioners are equally at fault for their failure to identify and communicate clearly the kind of administrative structure that would facilitate guidance. It does seem important to note some of the chief administrative deterrents that often impair the operations of a guidance program. Though lack of counseling staff, leadership, facilities, and money are often cited as major deterrents, other equally serious impedediments may exist, with the factors mentioned being symptoms rather than causes.

Landy has cited a critical deterrent which highlights the previous discussion about authority. He states that "unfortunately, many administrators, who recognize their limitations in various areas of subject matter and methods of teaching, and who are quite willing to allow specialists in those fields to take on leadership roles, assume an expertness in the field of guidance that they do not possess."[25] Peters has identified and discussed nine factors which interfere with guidance program development.[26] Although these are not just administrative in nature, Peters' comments have relevant implications for the management of the guidance program. Of the

---

[24]Robert W. Filbeck, "Perceptions of the Appropriateness of Counselor Behavior: A Comparison of Counselors and Principals," *Personnel and Guidance Journal,* Vol. 43 (May, 1965), p. 895.

[25]Edward Landy, "Who Does What in the Guidance Program?", *The School Counselor,* Vol. 10 (March, 1963), p. 115.

[26]Herman J. Peters, "Interferences to Guidance Program Development," *Personnel and Guidance Journal,* Vol. 42 (October, 1963), pp. 119–124.

Table 2–1. *Advantages and Disadvantages of Centralization and Decentralization of Guidance*

Factor	Advantage	Disadvantage
Centralization	1. More economical and efficient coordination 2. Better opportunity to avoid duplication of efforts 3. Usually better qualified personnel are employed 4. Guidance personnel more likely to treat students from guidance point of view rather than from an institutional point of view 5. Referral resources are more likely to be identified and used	1. Specialists are more expensive to employ 2. May be a tendency to deemphasize teachers 3. Particular problems of students may be emphasized leading to compartmentalization of the student
Decentralization	1. Support is given to the guidance efforts and contributions of teachers 2. There is concern for the total learning situation	1. Too often, poorly trained personnel who lack adequate preparation are utilized 2. There is deemphasis of guidance because it is seen as "everyone's business" but no one's specific responsibility 3. Teachers see youth problems only within the context of the classroom or academic experiences 4. Only incidental or episodic guidance is given

nine factors cited by Peters, five are noted here: (1) guidance workers have tended to avoid the development of guidance theory, (2) guidance workers have assumed that their publics understand the nature and purpose of guidance when, in fact, they do not, (3) custom and self-interest are rationalizations for omission of needed guidance leadership, (4) counselors and staff members resist, either overtly or covertly, change and new ways of doing things, and (5) the counselor's broad role commitment to, and security in, his former teaching role induces a marginal professional identity with guidance.

Shertzer and Stone[27] viewed certain actions by school administrators as being detrimental to guidance. Among these were (1) inadequate programming of guidance because administrators have favored services extended to

---

[27]Bruce Shertzer and Shelley C. Stone, "Administrative Deterrents to Guidance Program Development," *Theory into Practice,* Vol. 2 (February, 1963), pp. 24–32.

large groups rather than to the individual; (2) administrators have appealed to the public and justified guidance services on nonlogical terms such as the superiority of "our school" over "their school"; (3) counselors are assigned administrative duties after administrators base their requests for counselor appointments upon the argument that counselors are needed to provide individual counseling relationships with students, and (4) administrators have fostered the notion that the existence of guidance services in the school is a cure-all for every educational difficulty.

Although it is true that vigorous professional administrative leadership alone can not overcome some of these impediments imposed by problems outside its sphere of influence, administrators can and should address themselves to important immediate and long-range problems which can be resolved. Though some changes may not suffice to produce the whole of needed reform, they will serve to effect many needed guidance improvements.

ANNOTATED BIBLIOGRAPHY

Duane Brown and David J. Srebalus, *Selected Readings in Contemporary Guidance*. Dubuque, Iowa: William C. Brown Company Publishers, 1973, 331 pp.
    The editors present in Part One, conceptions of the role of the counselor and in Part Two, ways of implementing the counselor's role. An article by W. Phillips on the range and scope of guidance services is particularly relevant to this chapter.

T. Antoinette Ryan and Franklin R. Zeran, *Organization and Administration of Guidance Services*. Danville, Illinois: The Interstate Printers and Publishers, Inc., 1972, 465 pp.
    Chapters one and two present, respectively, an overview of guidance and a systems approach to guidance management. The latter chapter deals with systems analysis and a model for producing a system.

Merville C. Shaw, *School Guidance Systems*. Boston: Houghton Mifflin Company, 1973, 407 pp.
    Chapters 1–4 present a case history of guidance in the public schools, current concepts of guidance, and a general model for guidance services. Shaw's treatment of these matters is comprehensive and insightful.

What to Expect from a Guidance Program

Increasingly, expectancies or expectations have come to be recognized as one of the most important shapers of behavior. Expectancies on the part of significant authority figures lead to individual behavior that is congruent with the expectancies. Thus, helpers whose expectations for a given helpee or group of helpees are high, elicit constructive gain or change, whereas helpers whose expectations for the helpees are low have retarding effects upon the behavior of the helpees.[1]

Chapter 3

What does a guidance program have to offer pupils?

How may a guidance program assist the teacher?

How do parents benefit from the guidance program?

What are community outcomes from a school guidance program?

How do the guidance functions facilitate the administration of the school?

This chapter attempts to point out how important it is to recognize just what it is that guidance does *for,* and *with,* and not just *to* the pupil, teacher, administrator, parents, and community. Guidance programs in the school are justified only because of the services which they offer to facilitate students' personal development—pupils' learning about the universe in which they live and about how to live in that universe. Personal development encompasses educational planning, experiencing, and evaluating for the next steps in lifelong learning. Personal development has for its key vehicle: work. Thus, career development becomes a central theme for expectancies for student and staff in the total guidance process of school and community.

---

[1]Robert R. Carkhuff, *The Development of Human Resources.* New York: Holt, Rinehart and Winston, Inc., 1971, p. 78.

Too often, guidance functions are perceived in terms of what a counselor or teacher does *to* a pupil rather than in terms of what guidance may do *for* and *with* him. Similarly, the guidance activities engaged in by the pupil are used by the teacher or counselor to help the pupil; however, the pupil is not aware of what guidance is doing for him. He equates guidance activities with other school tasks which he does for someone else. It is necessary for the school staff to assist the pupil in understanding what efforts are being made for him in a guidance way, as well as in the instructional subject-matter way. Etzioni has little expectancy that human beings can change. He states that mature people can be taught many things, e.g. speed reading and belly dancing; however, he emphasizes that when we turn to a change of persistent habits, basic values, and personality traits, the impact of educational efforts is much less noticeable. He further adds, "once we cease turning to ads, leaflets, counselors, or teachers for salvation, we may realize that more can be achieved by engineers, doctors, social movements, and public interest groups; and the educators will find new and much-needed allies."[2]

Perhaps this underscores the popularity of counseling which emphasizes specific behavioral changes and guidance approaches with direct interventionistic characteristics which focus on career development (which is much more manageable than personal development). Yet, despite its amorphous, developmental character, is not personal development the undergirding foundation for educational progress and career development?

Who has the right to intervene in the life of another? What direction should each intervention take? Kremer emphasizes that not only in professional literature but also in nonprofessional literature, it is underscored that "counselors must spend time examining their own values so as to find a firm basis for their pronouncements and the ways in which they use power to intervene in the life of another."[3]

Before the 1970s, it was not appropriate to focus on (or at times even mention) "intervention" or doing something *to* the client. In the 1970s there is strong emphasis on intervention. Whether it is in counseling or in teaching, there is definitely a strong movement for the professional persons, the ones in authority, to take action—granted that it has a cover of benevolent well-being. This is not to say that we necessarily argue with this change; we just think it is time to be more open about telling the public that we *do* have something to offer in guidance and counseling. However, if it is to work at all, the client will have to change his behavior accordingly.

---

[2]Amitai Etzioni. "Human Beings Are Not Very Easy to Change After All," *Saturday Review,* June 3, 1972, p. 47 (pp. 45–47).

[3]Bruce J. Kremer, "What the Hell are Counselors For?" *The Personnel and Guidance Journal,* Vol. 51, No. 10 (June 1973), pp. 707–709.

In one direction, Rosen states that counselors should be "positive participants in social change." It is not clear what he defines as "positive," although he focuses on "opening wide the gates of employment opportunity."[4] Guttliek and Riger[5] focus on intervention. They emphasize a more activist concern with social system change. Parenthetically it should be brought to the reader's attention that while there is much written on the interventionist approach and social system change, there is little clarity on the specifics of change needed. One will emphasize an entire reconceptualization, while another writer seems to be emphasizing procedural changes within the traditional value system. But now back to the Guttliek-Riger social intervention approaches (Figure 3–1). Besides examining this from a community psychology point of view, school administrators, school counselors, and teachers could examine these social intervention approaches as to feasibility in their settings, climate, organization. Community changes seem as urgent, or more so, as individual changes of behavior.

Besides intervention, there is another approach of far greater import. It is best described as participatory guidance or participatory counseling. There are hints of this in the literature, but it is most openly presented in the works of Ronald Laing.[6] Participation includes more than just the professional counselor and his client. One urgent priority, we believe, is to examine the nature of change in the modern world, including its speed and dimensions, so that we can better understand the distinctions that must be made between change in the past and that which is now ongoing. To do so, distinctions must be made among three kinds of cultures: postfigurative, in which children learn primarily from their forebears; cofigurative, in which both children and adults learn from their peers; and prefigurative, in which adults learn also from their children.

In participatory prefigurative learning, there is more than gaining information from children, adolescents, and youth. Rather it becomes a mutual experiencing of behaviors. How the counselor selects and differentiates his participation in mutual behaviors must surely affect his complacency, his value system, his ethical commitments, legal dimensions, and his authenticity. Whether this expectancy will or should achieve much headway, is in doubt in the middle 1970s. One might give the example of the not-too-long-ago demands by youth for participation in university student personnel work, administrative policies. Except for the vested interests of a few, and

---

[4]Howard Rosen. "Guidance Counselor—A New Activist Role," *Occupational Outlook Quarterly*, Vol. 14, No. 3, Fall, 1970, pp. 20–22.

[5]Benjamin H. Guttliek and Stephanie Riger. "Social Interventions in the Community: Three Professional Roles," *Professional Psychology*, Vol. 3, No. 3, Summer 1972, pp. 231–240.

[6]Ronald D. Laing. *See* the Annotated Bibliography at the end of this chapter.

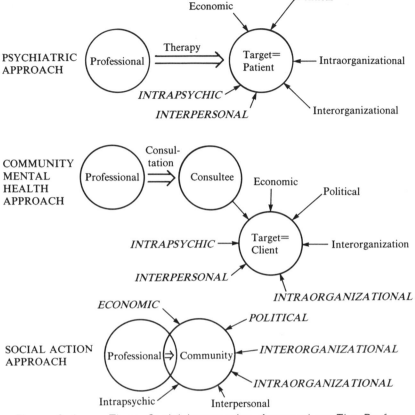

Figure 3–1.   *Three Social Intervention Approaches: The Professional-Client Dynamic.*[7] *(The significant social system vectors for each model are underlined.)*

the curiosity of still fewer, this kind of student participation seems to be fading almost as fast as it was initiated.[8,9]

CONTRIBUTIONS TO PUPILS

The guidance point of view stresses that guidance functions help a student adjust to himself and his environment more effectively by helping him

[7] Benjamin H. Guttliek and Stephanie Riger, "Social Interventions in the Community: Three Professional Roles," *Professional Psychology,* Vol. 3 (Summer, 1972), p. 236. © 1972 by the American Psychological Association. Reprinted by permission.

[8] Margaret Mead, "Youth Revolt: The Future is Now," *Saturday Review,* Vol. 53, No. 2 (January 10, 1970), pp. 23–25.

[9] Margaret Mead, *Culture and Commitment.* New York: Doubleday and Company, Inc., 1970, p. 113.

learn about both. Goals which bring out the basic purposes of school guidance (in terms of doing something for the pupil) are:

General Goals

1. To help the pupil understand and accept himself and make plans for developing educationally, vocationally, and personally.
2. To teach the pupil how to get along with other people, and to understand the world in which he lives, and to aid in its betterment.
3. To help each pupil get the most out of school by being an active learner.
4. To help the pupil explore his own interests and abilities, learn about various aspects of the world of work, and learn to make the most of his abilities.
5. To help him plan for more education and career development.

Process Goals[10]

1. To help the pupil plan the next steps in his education.
2. To help the pupil plan the next steps in his vocational development.
3. To help the pupil plan the next steps in his social-personal development.
4. To allow the pupil to experience and reflect on the process of experiencing sequential deterrent and interfering episodes.

Outcome Goals

1. To analyze general and specific, immediate, intermediate, and long-term outcomes of the contributions of the general goals and process goals.
2. To help the pupil determine where accountability for his development centers and what other influences have impact on it.
3. To allow the pupil to engage in a continuing process of reflecting on the direction of his life.

With this as our frame of reference, let us consider some specifics that guidance offers the pupil to help attain these goals. The appraisal, counseling, and information-giving functions of the guidance program aid each student by helping him see himself objectively; helping him control, as well as understand, trivial irritations and restore normal perspective; and helping him develop foresight based on "hindsight." Also, guidance functions are useful in promoting stability and self-direction; aiding the emergence of a "new" personality; aiding in emotional as well as educational adjustment. Further, guidance activities help the student recognize his special aptitudes, abilities, and limitations, and what they mean. This recognition will aid him

---

[10]Harold Hackney, "Goal Setting: Maximizing the Reinforcing Effects of Progress," *The School Counselor,* Vol. 20, No. 3 (January 1973), pp. 176–181.

in making wise subject choices for his educational progress and assist him in discovering the causes of any failures or setbacks in courses of study or human relations.

Another viewpoint emphasizes what guidance situations can do to help the child who seeks to find himself acceptable to other children. He will need to establish satisfying relationships with members of the opposite sex. Many children will need help in attaining a measure of responsible independence from parents.

Because of the individual attention given him in the guidance program, the student begins to see himself more clearly. He also begins to see himself in several new images; that is, as others see him. As the student becomes more self-aware, we expect some of the following things to happen. He will begin to see himself against a number of reference screens. His concept of self will be based upon such things as measures of his aptitudes and interests and upon other people's means of evaluating maximum self-development. Just as he uses a number of reference points in physical movement via visual perception, so he may now use a number of reference points in social-psychological movement via cognitive and conative perceptions. In the guidance function, the pupil is assisted to examine the meaning of these reference points *for himself.* The validity of their meaning requires the discernment resultant from the guidance process, especially the counseling function. "It is not irrefutable 'facts' that we find interesting, and that we act on, but the inference we make from them, often without recognizing the limits of their validity, without questioning how safe they are."[11]

Once the student has gained insight into his aptitudes, abilities, and limitations, he has a basis for making plans for the future. This planning for the future includes not only future experiences in human relations, but also choice of a course of study suited to his abilities, limitations, and interests, and career looking, exploring, deciding, and on-the-job working.

A pupil may expect from the guidance process important by-products for himself. The student will attain a better understanding of his social and physical environment. He gets a clearer idea of the surroundings in which he is to live, and he learns to live more successfully in them. Coupled with his knowledge learned in the instructional program, are his opportunities for more effective living.

As a result of the guidance program, the student may view his behavior in a more realistic way. As the student begins to recognize some of the reasons for his behavior, and is helped in seeing more acceptable forms of

---

[11]M. L. Johnson Abercrombie, *The Anatomy of Judgement.* New York: Basic Books, Inc., Publishers, 1960, p. 90.

behavior which will lead to more successful experiences both academically and socially, his directions for behavior become more real to him. Guidance will give him the psychological stamina for proper directional growth. More often than adults realize, boys and girls fail in their behavior (misbehave) because they do not know a sufficient number of alternative behaviors which are proper.

The complexity of the modern curricula necessitates careful choice. Small schools with limited curricula choices need to point this out to their students. If students do not realize what is involved in proper course planning, they will be deprived of knowing that future choices become more complex and grow out of choices made in high school.

The pupil learns for himself what is involved in finding and adequately preparing for a career for which he is suited. Encouraging self-reliance is another very important service that the guidance counselor provides *for*, as well as *to*, the pupil. As the student acquires a more adequate self-concept, he is better prepared to plan for a career that suits his ambitions, abilities, interests, and financial aspirations. The counselor helps the pupil in his vocational planning not only through helping the pupil acquire a more realistic self-picture, but also through disseminating and interpreting material describing vocational and educational opportunities. If guidance is effective, the pupil will have a growing awareness of what guidance is doing for his career development. If the pupil does not realize this, there is the danger that he will accept the guidance only as something done to him by ever-present and directing adults.

All the procedures a pupil must follow in furthering both his educational progress and career development are tedious but necessary. Incomplete procedures may deny the pupil learning opportunities for which he is otherwise eligible. As the student decides what he would like to do, he is given help by the counselor in filling in the many forms required for college entrance, industrial employment, and regional and national testing programs. He is also notified of, and helped in applying for, scholarships and business openings.

In addition to providing these aids in vocational planning, the counselor may introduce the student to employers who need full or part-time workers. In other words, the guidance office may serve as a school placement office. The manner in which the school placement program is organized will determine the effectiveness of the key factor of placement.

Another outcome of guidance is the encouraging and aiding of students to correct undesirable habits or improve present work and study methods. Such attention inspires the student to take a positive attitude toward available learning activities. This is implemented by an improved self-concept and increased awareness of the occupational opportunities awaiting him if he takes advantage of the opportunities for learning. These learning opportunities require effective study habits. The aid which guidance on study habits can bring to the pupil opens many gateways for mastering subject matter. Effective guidance programs will place major emphasis on helping the pupil understand what proper study habits and skills will do for him.

The process of schooling, in fact of all living, develops a self-concept of personal adequacy or inadequacy. The most dramatic kind of officially sanctioned failure occurs when one is told that one will not be promoted or allowed to move to the next sequential stage of one's development. The counselor can assist the student to focus on those things that he can do to enhance success and thus engage in more appropriate behaviors. In their study of 292 boys and 332 girls in the sixth grade in six different school systems in North Carolina, White and Howard found that a more positive self-concept was obtained by those students who had experienced no grade promotion failures.[12]

Interpreting the demands and the behavior of the adults with whom the pupil must work is another function of the guidance program, for many times the pupil is unable to understand the reasons for adult actions. He will function more effectively if, through the guidance programs, he acquires a better picture of reasons for the behavior and requirements of the school staff. This does not mean catering to the pupil, but rather that the guidance program must include outer-direction as well as inner-direction assistance for him. Knowing himself is necessary, but not sufficient. Knowing the key people in his life, the significant "others," is another force giving purpose, meaning, and direction in his life.

Guidance also provides a situation in which the student can receive in a friendly , permissive setting, assistance in understanding himself. In contrast to the classroom situation, in which the teacher must attempt to deal with all of the pupils as a group, the counseling situation provides a one-to-one relationship in which the student may discuss his concern with a competently trained school counselor. It is this philosophy of acceptance of the individual as he is that helps the pupil discuss himself frankly with the counselor and, thereby, receive help in academic and emotional self-improvement. The classroom teacher does guidance work for the pupil, but it is the school counselor who has specialized in graduate school in studying and practicing what counseling will do for the pupil's personality development as well as his educational progress and career development.

---

[12]Kinnard White and James Lee Howard, "Failure to be Promoted and Self-Concept Among Elementary School Children," *Elementary School Guidance and Counseling,* Vol. 7, No. 3 (March 1973), pp. 182–187.

Specific Areas Where Guidance Helps Career Development

So far we have discussed rather general activities which the guidance program may offer for each pupil's maximum development. Let us now look at some specific areas where various guidance activities may accomplish a major developmental task for the pupil. Pupils who find it difficult to discover a vocation for which they are suited are helped, at the appropriate time, by the school counselor who administers tests to help determine aptitudes and abilities. This not only helps the student know his directional strengths and interests, but it also helps the guidance person identify next life steps for the individual so that maximum use of his potential may be made.

Emotional Development

The student with emotional concerns will be benefited by counseling when he appreciates what can be done for him through the guidance process. Upon noting signs of emotional disturbance in a pupil, the teacher refers him to the counselor for assistance. Sometimes students' emotional problems are of such a nature that the guidance person thinks he cannot deal with them. In these instances, he is able to refer the students to agencies which are organized to help with particular kinds of children and youth concerns.

In addition to alerting the staff to recognize incipient problems, the counselor may help the student adjust to his home and school environment to obtain maximum successful pursuit of his academic work. If a student is upset or concerned about emotional conflicts at home or school, he cannot do an adequate job in his school work. It is the counselor's job, insofar as it is possible, to assist the student in resolving these problems so that he may perceive the many factors which influence his life.

Gifted Enhancement

The gifted student also profits from a guidance program because, through testing, his ability can be recognized. Once this outstanding ability has been discovered, it is necessary for the child to realize the many implications which accompany it. The student must be helped to develop the proper attitude, which is essential if he is to make maximum use of his potential ability. In addition to helping the student make the best use of his potential, the guidance person should inform the faculty of this discovery.

Student actions were found to be most effectively encouraged and produced through personal interviews. Contacts with teachers, parents, and written communication were effective, but less so. A key expectancy in a

Wisconsin Study of 108 high school students was that with appropriate encouragement on the part of counselors, other staff, and parents, students could be expected to seize available opportunities to exercise more control over their educational developments and assume more day to day responsibility.[13]

Slow Learner and the Child With Special Physical Needs

The slow learner and the handicapped are benefited by guidance through the recognition of their problem by testing, observation, and the case-study approach. Once the handicaps, physical, mental, or both, have been ascertained, the guidance person can assist the faculty by making suggestions on how to aid the student achieve maximum benefit from school. Finally, the guidance counselor can help the child think through the work necessary to success. The counselor can aid in helping the handicapped child to perceive various means of achieving his goals in life.

It is through an effective guidance program with competent counselors that a pupil has the best opportunity, not only to satisfy his own desires, but also to meet his responsibilities in society. The process may be generalized in the classroom, but it is individualized in guidance experiences.

The greatest satisfaction to both individual and society comes from the pupil's realization of his positive roles in life and his efforts to assume them with maximum effectiveness.

Pupil satisfaction comes from finding answers to such questions as: Who am I? What are my strengths? What can I do effectively? Where do I need improvement? What will I gain from self-understanding? There must be unity of thought in the developing pupil; anything else brings conflict, frustration, needless unhappiness, and minimal performance. Effective guidance coupled with expert instruction can aid in the pupil's fullest self-realization.

AID TO THE TEACHER

How will this increased pupil effectiveness in living with himself and his environment via the guidance process aid the classroom teacher? First, it will offer opportunities to increase the teacher's understanding of his students. Through in-service education programs carried on by the guidance person, the teacher will have a better understanding of the growth and development of children and adolescents. This knowledge will be supplemented by conferences between the teacher and counselor about individual students. If learning by the pupil is enhanced by teacher knowledge about

---

[13]Jerry L. Davis and Marshall P. Sanhorn, "Getting Student Action on Guidance Goals," *Journal of Counseling Psychology*, Vol 20, No. 3 (May 1973), pp. 209–213.

the pupil, then knowing the thoughts and feelings of the pupil should give the teacher many positive clues for making a better teaching-learning situation.

The school counselor assists in administering the testing program and in familiarizing teachers with the interpretation of the tests. These test results, accompanied by the proper interpretation, give information which assists the teacher to better understand his students' classroom behavior and performance. The tests, accompanied by information gathered by the counselor, may also give some idea as to the student's basic school functioning. If further tests, in addition to those administered in the course of the regular testing program, are needed to obtain more information, the school counselor will assist in administering these. This testing function of the guidance program is intended to give the teacher a better understanding of his students in order that he may do a more effective job of teaching.

GUIDANCE DATA

Data on the student's special interests, capabilities, and past experiences are provided on the cumulative record by the guidance faculty. This information is valuable to the teacher in the budgeting of effort toward each individual. Knowledge about the student's physical condition, medical history, family background, scholastic record, scores on standardized tests accompanied by interpretations of the test results, and personal characteristics helps the teacher provide better instruction for the student. Various schools of thought on the use of the cumulative record will be discussed in Chapter 12.

Prevention of Future Problems

In addition to providing information about the student's past, the guidance program also encourages each teacher to look for early manifestations of the children's strengths and limitations to prevent later problems in health, family, scholarship, personality, and general environment. By making the teacher alert to signs of these concerns before they become undirected or misdirected, the guidance program is taking preventive measures against extremely unpleasant situations which may occur later. A developmental approach in a favorable direction may be taken.

Behavioral Concerns

Cooperation in discovering and remedying the major difficulties which may upset the peaceful pursuit of each day of learning is an invaluable service provided by the guidance program. Student concerns that disrupt the classroom may be referred to the school counselor. The counselor will then consult with both pupil and teacher and work with them toward solution of the problem. This not only relieves the teacher of some of the responsibility for helping students with personal concerns, but also leaves him free to devote more time to the instructional program. In this way the teacher receives help in handling concerns for which he has had only minimal preparation, and is left more time for class preparation. This cooperation also provides individual help for the student when no other way is possible.

Guidance may also help the teacher by providing vocational and other pertinent information for his use. In addition, the counselor may aid the teacher in securing or preparing instructional material via visual aids, printed material from industry, business, unions, local fraternal organizations, service clubs, and the United States Employment Service Offices. The effective use of occupational information in various subject matter areas is one way of integrating guidance with instruction. This assists the student in becoming more aware and appreciative of the educational and vocational opportunities he will develop through effective learning in each teacher's classroom.

Parental Participation

The guidance program should also provide opportunities for meetings with parents under favorable conditions. This is in contrast to getting in touch with parents only when the student is in an unfavorable situation. The guidance approach in working with parents will aid the teacher in his teacher-parent conferences. This individualized help may have other benefits, such as encouraging parents to help in school projects.

The counselor also helps teachers by being ever ready to listen as each teacher is encouraged to discuss his educational concerns; this provides the teacher with both cognitive and conative experiences which are beneficial to sound mental health.

Acting as a general liaison service between the teachers and principal, children, parents, other teachers, and employers in guidance services is another way in which a guidance program assists the teacher.

BENEFITS TO PARENTS

The guidance program may help the parent in many phases of his duties relating to educational progress, career development, and personality fulfillment. By providing a clearer perception of the child's intelligence, abilities, interests, and potentialities, the program helps the parent know, understand, and accept the child as he is. Once the parent has a better picture of the child, the counselor may help the parent to find ways to help the child make greater use of his potential. The parent is then better able to see in which directions the child's energies may be directed in order for the child to achieve success and happiness.

The parent is provided with vocational information which helps him to understand the student's abilities and interests and to see the related job opportunities which are available. Not only will the parents be better informed as to the vocational areas for which their child is best suited, but they will feel more secure in offering advice to their children. This added confidence on the parents' part should result in an improved parent-child relationship.

The counselor's work with the parents will also provide a basis for projecting plans for their children's post-high school education or training. Guidance helps by giving the parents and children a sounder basis on which to make course choices for the next step in the child's educational progress.

Physical and emotional problems which prevent maximum performance in school may receive the attention of the guidance program. In such cases the counselor may work with the parents in obtaining the assistance of community-wide agencies and organizations which might be helpful to the health (mental and physical) of the child. The school counselor can recommend to the parent that professional help of a different nature, for example that of a state employment office counselor or psychiatrist, is needed in the particular concern.

In addition to the aid in referring parents to other community resources for help with their child, the counselor may encourage the parents to secure help with their home emotional problems when he thinks that such a situation is interfering with the student's performance at school. Along this same line, the counselor may provide information to the parent concerning good mental health.

The school counselor may also, in his counseling function, uncover the child's submerged concerns and other behavioral patterns. This outcome of the counseling process will lead to a better parent-child relationship as the parents learn to better understand each other. In fact, the counselor may assist the parents through counseling. Through counseling, the parents may gain a greater understanding of what problems are causing the child concern. The parents may be better able to perceive the problems in their own child-parent relationship and the effect of these problems on the behavioral patterns of the child. With this intellectual comprehension of their relationships with the child, the parents with the assistance of the counselor can work through better approaches for parent-child relationships.

The furtherance of the relationship between the parent, school, and community is an extremely important outcome of the guidance process. Helping to serve this function is the identification, collection, and processing of information essential to the parents' understanding of the child's health; scholarship; native ability; school necessities, such as books, special clothing, laboratory fees, etc.; time necessary for maximum achievement in class; personality problems; behavior problems; general maladjustments; and extraordinary accomplishments or potentialities.

The guidance program may also help parents assist in the improvement of the child's study habits at home; for example, the counselor may give the parents hints on how to improve study conditions. The climate for study at home, both physically and psychologically, may be improved through increased parent understanding of the study process resulting from guidance program.

The counselor may also serve as a coordinate between parents and teachers in the establishment of a time and place for problem discussion and analysis relating to boys and girls in their developmental processes. Counselors may act as consultants with teachers whom the parents cannot, at times, approach because of emotional involvement. Sometimes incidents occur which make it difficult for the parties involved to discuss the problem rationally. In this situation, the school counselor may serve as a go-between in attempting to discover the facts of the situation and resolve the differences between parent, teacher, and pupil. Parents and teachers can often work out concerns about a child's educational progress if each can reduce his tensions about working with the other.

Interpretation of modern schools to the parents and concern for the individuality of each pupil is another function of the guidance program. Through private conferences and public speaking engagements, the counselor is able to explain to the parents what the school should and is trying to do for their children. With this understanding of children and what the school is trying to do for them, the better informed parents feel more at ease about discussing school problems with their children.

Finally, research studies on the effectiveness of the school program of pupil placement, counseling, and pupil achievement demonstrate to the parents the vital effort of the school to understand their children. Objective data support the teacher and parent in that each may focus on the pupil rather than misconstrue the motives of the others.

COMMUNITY OUTCOMES

Guidance staff members providing information about the mental health, educational and vocational abilities, aptitudes, and interests of students at social and service organization meetings help to make the citizens of the community a better informed populace. The pupils live in a community, but too often the school staff forgets the action and reactions of the pupils in their school-community interrelationships. Clear understanding of pupil progress toward responsible citizenry is needed by the community patrons.

The guidance staff serves as representatives of the school and its policies as it works with the community to help the pupils who will be the future citizens of the town. In this way, the community is constantly improved through the efforts of the school. The guidance personnel in both private conferences with parents and students and also in speaking engagements in the community engage in activities that benefit the community.

The school counselors may also serve as helpers in projects designated to help the community. They may help service organizations choose projects which are most needed by the school, and they may also provide valuable assistance in organizing and carrying out the necessary work. Many service organizations have vocational guidance activities and are helped by the advice of the local school counselors. The school counselor may also work with the staff of the local employment office. Thus, the community benefits from the school guidance staff and program.

The guidance staff members are in positions, through follow-up studies of pupils after they leave school, to show the community the degree to which the school contributes to the community, as opposed to what the community continually gives to the school. The guidance staff may compile data showing the ways in which the pupils contribute to the community after leaving school. Information on former students who own local businesses, belong to civic organizations, and hold other significant positions helps to convince the community of the worthwhile job that the school is doing.

By making the citizens aware of the need for an active, progressive community, the guidance staff takes the first step in making the community more attractive to talented students. The school counselors and local citizens can work together to provide talented pupils with greater opportunities for learning. Through small group conferences, individual interviews, visits to business and industry, work experiences, and various communication media, the pupils may learn of the career opportunities in their community. The school counselor can arrange these activities through a continuing cooperative working relationship with community personnel. Service organizations often have programs for assisting boys and girls in many different ways; for example, vocational guidance committees of Kiwanis Club alert the pupils to local as well as national career opportunities. The good to the community is immediate and long term. The psychological climate is favorable to learning, and the pupil sees the community as a desirable place to live and work.

The community is also benefited by the guidance program because of the better adjustment of the students of the community. Juvenile delinquents and "problem children" arouse a feeling of unrest in the community. A more stable state of affairs prevails when the younger members of the community are well adjusted and are making developmental progress.

In addition to preventing delinquency, guidance may serve to prevent problems which may lead to mental illness. Through the efforts of the guidance staff, energy, money, and other resources of the community are more efficiently and intelligently used for preventive rather than curative purposes.

The members of the guidance staff can contribute to the community because they are experts in human relations and self-actualization processes. They are available to assist not only the students of the school but also the total community population toward better mental health.

FACILITATING ADMINISTRATION

The school guidance counselor helps the entire school in many ways. The counselor's work, in turn, reflects favorably upon the administration since it *is* the school in many citizens' minds. As previously stated, one of the ways in which the counselor helps the entire school is by aiding students in their choice of courses by counseling them individually on the basis of their aptitudes and interests. Working with students who are having behavior difficulties is another way in which counseling by trained personnel improves the school for all concerned. The guidance program, providing knowledge of the aptitudes, interests, and motivations of the student population, may help the administration determine the most effective teaching techniques.

The competent counselor is trained to conduct research to ascertain how many of the purposes of the school are being met and where improvement is needed in the areas assigned to guidance responsibility. By having research evidence of the achievement of the students, their interests, and their activities after leaving school, the school may study the ways in which it is accomplishing its goals. This gives the administration information on the phases of the school program which relate to the educational, career, and personality development of the pupils.

The guidance program increases the overall efficiency of the school program by providing more information and contacts between school and employer, thus providing more and better jobs for graduates. Employers will learn that the counselor has the time and the necessary information needed to make a good recommendation for vocational placement. Similarly, the school counselor works closely with college admissions officers concerning those pupils who are planning higher education. Using the placement information, the counselor, on the basis of research done in the area, may determine the effectiveness of the school program and may help to bring about improvements which will afford better course selection for students.

The guidance staff can aid in supplying information about school policies and goals to parents, thus aiding in the continued future support of levies and bond issues deemed necessary or desirable for the school. Also, the information may lead to further scholarship fund support from local organizations, for example, Parent-Teacher Scholarship Fund. Support may also be enhanced for research projects to determine the continuing effectiveness of guidance activities. New educational programs, such as in foreign languages, may gain support from a guidance analysis of the pupils' aptitudes for language learning.

The guidance program will assist the school administrative staff and others in leadership roles by providing counseling with pupils, scheduling, registration, college entrance papers, recommendations to, and interviews with, employers, career assemblies or programs, interviews with parents, committee meetings for planning school guidance activities, in-service training for the faculty, understanding of the teachers and their many problems, and interpretation of teacher-pupil relationship. Too often, members of the administrative staff engage in guidance activities. It is better to have competent school counselors do the guidance work and leave the administrator with full time for executive duties and educational leadership.

The guidance program also contributes to the development of a more "professional" teacher attitude. It provides concrete results about pupils' success (vocationally and academically); this feedback stimulates teachers to better their efforts since they are able to see that past efforts were worthwhile. Many times teachers wonder if they are really accomplishing anything and, if so, what. Through pupil follow-up provided by the guidance program, teachers may see that they they are actually contributing to students' success in life. This beneficial climate becomes the key for successful administrative leadership in developing an excellent plan for all pupils in their educational experiences.

EXPECTANCIES OF STRENGTHENED GUIDANCE PROGRAMS

The expectancies of a strengthened guidance program are found in the following salient points from the 1972 report of the National Advisory Council on Vocational Education.[14]

---

[14]"Counseling and Guidance: A Call for Change," *The Vocational Guidance Quarterly,* Vol. 21, No. 2 (December, 1972), pp. 97–101. Sixth Annual report of the National Advisory Council on Vocational Education, June 1972.

—State departments of education require work experience outside of education for all school counselors who work with students and prospective students of vocational education.

—Individuals with rich backgrounds of experience in business, industry, and labor, but with no teaching experience, be infused into the counseling system.

—Counselor education institutions require at least one introductory course in career education and least one practicum devoted to an on-site study of the business-industry-labor community.

—Responsible decision-makers embark on an immediate major campaign designed to upgrade the vocational knowledge and career guidance skills of currently employed counselors.

—Decision-makers in education make extensive provision for the training and employment of a wide variety of paraprofessional personnel to work in guidance under supervision of professionally qualified counselors.

—Concerted efforts, including computerized guidance systems, be made to get more accurate, timely data to counselors regarding vocational and technical training and job opportunities.

—Increased efforts be made to improve sound counseling and guidance services to members of minority populations and other disadvantaged persons.

—Special efforts be made to mount and maintain effective counseling and guidance programs for handicapped persons, for adults, for correctional institution inmates, and for veterans.

—Community service counseling programs be established and operated throughout the United States.

—Immediate efforts be made to lower the counselor-pupil ratio in elementary, secondary, and post-secondary educational institutions to a point where all who need counseling and guidance services will, in fact, receive them, while simultaneously encouraging more guidance in groups.

—Job placement and followup services be considered major parts of counseling and guidance programs.

—Career development programs be considered a major component in career education, both in legislation and in operating systems.

—The United States Office of Education create a bureau of pupil personnel services that includes a strong and viable counseling and guidance branch.

—The United States Congress create categorical funding for counseling and guidance in all legislation calling for these services.

—State departments of education and local school boards initiate actions confirming their commitment to the importance of providing sound counseling and guidance services to all individuals.

—All those who now criticize counselors be charged with responsibility for making positive suggestions for their improved performance.

The Ultimate Expectancy

The ultimate expectancy is self-responsibility in a social-technical world. External influences, dimensions, and values will only have social harmony and progress if they become internalized in a way that is befitting the pluralism of individuals. Personalized internal commitment is largely generated the same time that the conditions for generating valid information about opportunities, qualifications, free choice and associated changes are developed. What one infers and directly observes is essential for expecting outcomes. The pristine residency of responsibility for development must reside in the trust of one's being and becoming. The forging of this strong inner self must be built in the developmental process. It is too easily shattered, distorted, or disabled from early negative experiences.

SUMMARY

Guidance is focused on assisting not only pupils but also teachers, parents, the community, and the school administrative staff. Through many guidance activities, the various persons concerned benefit from objective data in better understanding the pupils. Understanding pupil behavior and pupil progress becomes the avenue for more effective pupil learning. This results in a better school and a better community for all concerned. Guidance emphasizes the substance of each pupil just as instruction emphasizes the substance of the subject matter of each area of learning.

ANNOTATED BIBLIOGRAPHY

Hollis, Joseph W. and Lucille U. Hollis, *Organizing for Effective Guidance.* Chicago: Science Research Associates, Inc., 1965.
 Chapter 3 discusses the identification of needs. This work emphasizes that the first echelon of guidance pertains to the role of a professional teacher.

Kowitz, Gerald T. and Norma G. Kowitz, *Operating Guidance Services for The Modern School.* New York: Holt, Rinehart and Winston, Inc., 1968.
 The entire text points out the usefulness of guidance activities.

Krumboltz, John D. and Helen Brandhurst Krumboltz, *Changing Children's Behavior.* Englewood Cliffs, New Jersey: Prentice-Hall Inc., 1972, 268 pp.

Specific ways to assist a student in the improvement of his behavior are given by Krumboltz and Krumboltz. Some of these concern reinforcement, gradually improving behavior, modeling, rewarding and other alternative behavioral approaches. The examples are specific and offer an initial thrust toward the desired goal.

Laing, Ronald D., *Divided Self.* New York: Pantheon, 1969.

_____. *Knots.* New York: Random House, 1972.

_____. *Politics of the Family.* New York: Pantheon, 1971.

_____. *The Politics of the Family & Other Essays.* New York: Random House, 1972.

_____. *Politics of Experience.* New York: Pantheon, 1967.

_____. *Self & Others.* Baltimore: Penguin Books Inc., 1972.

Laing, Ronald D. and David Cooper, *Reason and Violence.* New York: Random House, 1971.

Laing, Ronald D. and A. Esterson, *Sanity, Madness and the Family.* Baltimore: Penguin Books Inc., 1970. (1970/Penguin) (1971/Basic/Text Ed.)

Laing, Ronald D., et al., *Interpersonal Perception.* New York: Springer Publishing Co., Inc., 1966.

Rothney, John W. M., *Guidance Practices and Results.* New York: Harper & Row, Publishers, 1958.

This is a detailed analysis of what guidance services can do. It is a description and analysis of one of the few longitudinal studies in guidance, emphasizing particulary the benefits which students receive from a guidance program.

Differential Factors Influencing
Guidance in Different Kinds of Schools

I am not an educator. It does make sense to me, however, that experience must be at the heart of the educational process and that a system of vocational guidance and vocational education can become an integral part of such an experience-centered curriculum effort. Only the intellectually gifted can gain any significant understandings from reading about or hearing about the very fundamental thing that is going to occupy the majority of their life. Most of us, as John Dewey admonishes, "learn by doing."[1]

Chapter 4

What changes has the guidance movement undergone since its inception?

What factors contributed to the movement of guidance to the elementary school?

What are the current concepts of elementary school guidance?

What are the current concepts of secondary school guidance?

How does elementary school guidance compare to and contrast with secondary school guidance?

What implications for guidance at these levels are to be drawn from these differential factors?

The world of today has put new responsibilities on every level of its educational institutions. Human knowledge has grown so rapidly—geometrically in many specialized areas—that new and better ways are constantly being devised and tested to help us all learn better and faster. The rapidity of change in the patterns of life, the accelerating complexity of choices and alternatives confronting individuals, and the increasing impersonality brought about by urbanization have had their impact in the thrust of obligations placed upon the schools.

However, a refreshing willingness to experiment has permeated many of our schools. Programs that would have received scant attention before

---

[1]James A. Rhodes (former governor of the state of Ohio), *Vocational Education and Guidance: A System for the Seventies.* Columbus, Ohio: Charles E. Merrill Publishing Company, p. 43.

World War II have been tried out in hundreds of schools, and those that proved practical and beneficial have been retained. One such educational program that has been tried and retained and increased in scope, personnel, techniques, and resources has been the guidance function.

CHANGES IN GUIDANCE

The history of guidance has had many directions and many changes since its advent as an organized movement in 1908. Its founding father, Frank Parsons, opened the Vocation Bureau in Boston in that year with emphasis on job placement and occupation information. In the years since then, there have been significant changes in the concept, scope, and province of guidance. One such change in the *concept of guidance* has been that it has moved from a basically vocational orientation to a wider concern for all the *normal* problems of youth, such as school achievement, social and emotional adjustment, development of identity, and utilization of abilities and strengths. Many writers have urged that guidance move from its remedial orientation, in which children are helped after they have a problem, to a preventive function designed to keep children from being overwhelmed by problems. Increasingly, a developmental function is evolving in which guidance is designed to maximize growth of students in all areas of human development.

Another change has been in the *role of guidance* in the school. Guidance has changed from a specialized service added on to the regular school program to a service that is viewed as an integral part of the total school. Modern educators think of the school in terms of three basic services provided in an inclusive related program: instruction, administration, and pupil personnel (including guidance).

There also has been a change in the concept of *who is to perform* guidance services. In the early movement of guidance, almost total responsibility for the program was placed upon teachers. Teachers and administrators were relied upon almost exclusively to accomplish the guidance function. Within the last fifteen years or so has come the recognition that while every professional member on the school staff has an essential guidance function to perform, counseling specialists are needed if the program is to be effective.

A change in the *province of guidance* has evolved during the past decade. For many years, organized programs in elementary schools were rare. It was thought that elementary pupils had no career or college choices to make and that problem children could usually be cowed, coddled, or cajoled into submission by the teacher or principal. Guidance services are no longer restricted to the later years of secondary schools. It is becoming increasingly recognized by modern educators that guidance services are needed and must begin in the elementary school and be carried on throughout the individual's educational career.

WHY THE MOVEMENT TO ELEMENTARY SCHOOLS?

This recent emergence of guidance in elementary schools has come with striking emphasis. Several motivating forces contributed to its development: (1) The 1964 amendments to the National Defense Education Act of 1958 provided federal monies which supported the preparation of elementary school counselors and their employment at the local level. Most state departments of education initiated model or pilot elementary school guidance programs within their state. These pilot programs, many of which were placed in "leader schools," provided a dynamic thrust for elementary school guidance. It should be noted that the legislation enabling these programs to be generated came at a time when many educators and professional counselors were ready and willing to develop guidance in elementary schools. (2) More and more school officials and parents have accepted and are expecting that guidance will be available to *all* pupils, that it will not be confined solely to a crises-oriented program, and that it will not concentrate exclusively on pupils experiencing academic or other difficulties. (3) The increasing concern for America's talented manpower supply and its utilization has spurred interest in the early location and development of general and specialized talent. Guidance is looked to, rightly or wrongly, as a basic answer to this complex problem. (4) The shortage in the supply of professionally prepared elementary teachers gave rise in some schools to increases in the size of elementary classes; the result of this situation was that such teachers sought help in extending themselves to provide individual attention to the welfare of their pupils. (5) Psychological theory has steadily stressed the need for the early recognition of problems of troubled children. Remedial work with elementary pupils has revealed a close tie between emotional and adjustment problems and difficulties in acquiring scholastic skills. All of these forces have helped to turn the attention of educators to the guidance needs of elementary pupils.

CONCEPTS OF ELEMENTARY SCHOOL GUIDANCE

In examining some of the approaches to guidance at the elementary school level, it is evident that a number of views are currently being posited.

Here attention will be given to a brief description of some of these concepts of guidance at the elementary school level.

Elementary School Guidance as Good Teaching

One view is that guidance at this level is synonymous with good teaching. In this respect, Harper states that "Guidance at the elementary level is most significantly a point of view to be adopted and developed by the classroom teacher."[2] Ferris, too, argues that only teachers are needed for guidance because (1) schools cannot afford guidance specialists, (2) teachers are "closest" to children and consequently are in strategic positions to help them and (3) taking pupils out of classrooms for guidance is disruptive to both them and teachers.[3]

Hill[4] reported that many bulletins originating in and distributed by state departments of education stressed the central role of the teacher in elementary school guidance. His examination of these bulletins led to the conclusion that many personnel in state departments conceived the teacher as the only guidance functionary. However, Hill reported that there was no unanimity, some actual differences of opinion, and a good deal of uncertainty as to who was to do what in the name of guidance.

Essentially, conceptualizing guidance as good teaching means that elementary teachers are regarded as individuals who know their pupils well, recognize their problems, possess counseling skills, and can intervene appropriately and consistently when children need help.

Teachers Coupled with Outside School Specialists

A second view of guidance at the elementary school level is that the teacher, aided by specialists outside of the school, will carry on the function of guidance. Psychologists, social caseworkers, visiting teachers, health specialists, psychiatrists, and others working out of community agencies will be available to care for children with adjustment difficulties in the classroom. This is a modification of the view that guidance is synonymous with good teaching and invariably leads to a focus upon the problem-centered type of guidance. Building upon the basis of referral of troubled children, many elementary school educators have simply planned this approach as an extension of the teacher.

---

[2]Frances R. Harper, "The Guidance Oriented Elementary Teacher," *National Education Association Journal*, Vol. 49 (1960), p. 6.

[3]Robert R. Ferris, "Guidance in the Elementary School—A Teacher Does It Best," *National Education Association Journal*, Vol. 54 (1965), p. 48.

[4]George E. Hill, "Elementary School Guidance: Criteria for Approval by State Departments of Education," *Counselor Education and Supervision*, Vol. 2 (Spring, 1963), pp. 137–143.

The ASCA Elementary vice-presidents wrote a role statement in which the unique role of the elementary school counselor was set forth. This statement was divided into the following three parts.[5]

Rationale—Elementary school counseling concerns itself with the child in the developmental process of maximizing his potential, finding his identity, and learning to make choices and decisions.

Objectives—Elementary school counseling seeks to help the child identify his likes, dislikes, interests, etc.; define his role; feel positive about himself; recognize and accept his limitations; accept other people; feel good about learning and working; develop an interest in the future; and have an interrelatedness with people, things, and services. Elementary school counseling helps the teacher, the administrator, and the child's parents to understand and accept the child's self-concept, to relate to the child as a worthwhile human being, to provide teaching experiences and opportunities for learning decision-making, and to provide an effective learning environment. The elementary school counselor is a congruent person who accepts each person, provides the appropriate guidance and counseling, is able to identify changes and objectives; and who serves as an advocate for the children in an adult structure.

Implementation—Counseling services are planned and determined by the counseling staff in cooperation with the educational team whose focus is the learner as a person and as one who shares in the decision-making process.

A Services Approach

A third view of guidance at the elementary level is that it should be basically patterned after guidance in the secondary school. This view can be observed in many of the current textbooks written on elementary school guidance. Quite visible in these books is the services approach to guidance —counseling, pupil inventory, information, placement, and follow-up— which is consistently employed in guidance organization at the secondary level.

A Roles Approach

Most recently, responsibility for guidance at every school level (including that of the elementary) is being considered in relationship to the roles enacted by individuals engaged within the school. Within this view, the expectations attached to positions held by differing school personnel are

[5]"Elementary V-P's Define Counselor Role," *ASCA Newsletter,* Vol. 10, No. 3 (January, 1973), p. 2.

taken into consideration in delineating the possible kinds of help they extend to pupils. Due credit is given to the help inherent in the role of classroom teacher. Additionally, there is recognition that within the social system of the school, guidance specialists are needed to provide certain special skills, time, and privacy to youth that go beyond the classroom teacher's role. The presence of specialists is viewed as counterbalancing forces operating within the social system that limit the individual pupil in making the most of his abilities and opportunities.

These guidance specialists, elementary school counselors, are expected to establish and maintain helping relationships that free the individual and enable him to utilize the learning situation to his benefit. Building upon the work of teachers, counselors concentrate upon helping the individual achieve a personal identity and to reduce the emotional conflicts and concerns associated with normal development that often inhibit and impair him in the learning situation.

CONCEPTS OF SECONDARY SCHOOL GUIDANCE

The previous discussion of changes in guidance has already indicated some of the concepts of secondary school guidance. It was noted that the first concept of guidance was restricted to problems of vocational placement and occupational adjustment. In 1909, Frank Parsons viewed guidance as consisting of (1) self-understanding on the part of the student, (2) knowledge of the requirements for success, and (3) reasoning concerning the relationships between the two. During subsequent years, emphasis has been given to a broader function of guidance because "(1) 'guidance' though vague, has kept constantly before the personnel worker the truth that the whole child is affected by any problem and by its solution; (2) student problems ignore semantic distinctions; (3) at least logically, this stand tends to confine one's study of the individual to a few seemingly pertinent disciplines instead of seeking to understand him by a multidisciplinary approach."[6]

The extension of guidance to a broader concern for all the normal problems of youth has been conceptualized into a four-dimensional model by Mathewson: (1) *Classroom-Centered—Specialized.* Guidance is centered almost wholly in the classroom as opposed to being conducted by trained professional specialists; (2) *Self-Integrative—Prescriptive.* One pole of this dimension assumes that personal precepts and constructs about current and

---

[6]James J. Cribbin, "A Critque of the Philosophy of Modern Guidance," in Gail Farwell and Herman J. Peters, *Guidance Readings for Counselors.* Chicago: Rand McNally & Co., 1960, p. 86. Used with permission.

future prospects can be integrated by the individual as contrasted to the other pole where reliance is placed on rather directive forms of guidance; (3) *Personal—Social.* At the personal end, concern will be given to the satisfaction of needs and purposes through individual expression and experiences; whereas, at the social end, concern is based on social and institutional needs, demands, and consequences; and (4) *Subjective—Objective.* The subjective approach directs attention to psychological events having to do with self-defining and self-conceptualizing processes inside the pupil, while the objective approach directs attention to the evaluation and interpretation of objective data of all kinds.[7]

Other concepts of guidance have been outlined by Cribbin: (1) *guidance as identical with education,* in which it is thought that education is guidance and guidance is education; (2) *guidance as a mediating agency and a series of supplementary services,* in which guidance is viewed first as "inherent guidance" or the kind of help every conscientious teacher gives to his students and second, "organized guidance" which endeavors to facilitate the student along life's highway; (3) *guidance as distribution and adjustment* in which guidance is seen as the distribution of students to suitable educational and vocational opportunities and the providing of assistance in adjusting to these situations; (4) *guidance as assistance in making choices,* in which a guidance situation exists only when students need help in making choices, interpretations, or adjustments; and (5) *guidance as a clinical process,* in which techniques are stressed to provide comprehensive analysis of the individual.[8]

Some literature in the field of guidance has stressed the adaptive concept of guidance. McDaniel and Shaftel describe this function of guidance as the following:

> In order to fulfill their responsibility to the community, schools must continuously adapt courses and activities to the actual needs of the young people in their classrooms. Guidance counselors play a vital role in this adaptive function of contributing to the development of the curriculum. Counselors, working constantly with individual students, know their personal problems and aspirations, their abilities and aptitudes, as well as the opportunities and the social pressures awaiting them. Counselors can therefore provide the data which must serve as a basis for curriculum thinking, and they can help curriculum experts shape courses of study which will more accurately serve their intended purpose. A curriculum that is developed without an inner skeleton of guidance purposes fails in a basic responsibility to education.

[7]Robert H. Mathewson, "School Guidance: A Four Dimensional Model," *Personnel and Guidance Journal,* April, 1961, pp. 645–646.

[8]Cribbin, *Modern Guidance,* pp. 83–91.

The special techniques used by counselors in this adaptive function are the *individual inventory* and the *follow-up study,* which are primarily services to the school as a whole. The data that are gathered provide the factual basis upon which to initiate and implement changes in the school program.[9]

Peters and Farwell have urged a developmental concept of guidance. This concept of guidance may be seen in the following quotation from their book:

> It seems imperative that each pupil be provided with an opportunity to see and understand himself through the help of persons who have as a basic precept the guidance point of view, which is the third leg of our triangle. It is when each individual sees himself as a developing organism, influenced by the many forces of the world about him, that optimum growth and adjustment can be realized. Because of lack of experience, a boy or girl often needs assistance from others to realize his full potential. The classroom teacher, supported by guidance services, plays a key role.
>
> It is imperative that the emerging self be seen both by the individual and the people attempting to assist him toward maturity. Our complex society, the mobility of our population, and the extent of the world of work support the importance of skills and knowledge. However, these are of little significance if the individual cannot ascertain how they apply to himself as a living, maturing person. Those persons on the school staff who are skilled at placing the individual boy or girl at the center of the teaching-learning maturing process offer the greatest hope for the enhancement of the self of each child coming under their direction.[10]

ALTERNATIVE SCHOOL MODELS

There are initial thrusts with alternative school models in contrast to the 8-4, 6-3-3 plans. The middle school was one of the recent changes. Too, there has been a renaissance of the Montessori schools. In nearly all of the alternative school models, there is emphasis on individualized approaches to learning. Guidance adds another dimension—personalized learning. Guidance functions assist each singularly unique student to process the learning in terms of his own enhanced development.

---

[9]Henry B. McDaniel with G. A. Shaftel, *Guidance in the Modern School.* New York: Holt, Rinehart & Winston, Inc., 1956, p. 13.

[10]Herman J. Peters and Gail Farwell, *Guidance: A Developmental Approach.* Chicago: Rand McNally & Co., 1967, p. 33.

Two Year Colleges

According to Eli Ginzberg, teachers and counselors in two year colleges need to be alert to the high dropout rate. There is a need for careful guidance in matching curriculum and student aptitudes and interests. Contemporary and future labor market trends should be related to the students.[11]

Vocational and Technical Schools

The program of vocational guidance should not be counselor-centered but curriculum-centered, with experience as the basis of the curriculum. The school counselor and the vocational educator are important to the vocational guidance program.[12]

Gysbers and Moore[13] call for a needs-assessment, goal-setting approach to the development of guidance programs for school counselors. They indicate that school counselors "have tended to become process-oriented and reactive" in the usual guidance programs. They emphasize the need for team work and career development as the first steps in guidance practices and responsibilities.

A key aspect for guidance programming which—although emphasized as a differential phase in vocational education—should be in all school programs is the delivery of career development experiences to students as a part of the overall career education process. The basic challenge is a reordering of priorities of differential factors in guidance programs in all sorts of school situations.

In 1973, Fischer and Rankin[14] discussed a community counseling center which could offer total community service through the college staff. The community counseling center was originally charged with the task of providing educational and vocational testing to members of the community. There was also a demand for personal and family counseling. The scope of community guidance services is much broader than that of the secondary school. Emphasis on the need for counseling in junior and community colleges is given by DeBernardis: "The community college must provide realistic counseling and career guidance for all students."[15] Broudy, al-

---

[11]Eli Ginzberg, "Career Guidance—Is It Worth Saving?" *Impact*, Vol. 1, No. 1 (Fall 1971), pp. 4–15.

[12]James A. Rhodes, *Vocational Education and Guidance*, pp. 74–75.

[13]Norman C. Gysbers and Earl J. Moore, "Career Guidance: Program Content and Staff Responsibilities," *American Vocational Journal*, Vol. 47, No. 3 (March 1972), pp. 60–62.

[14]Guerin A. Fischer and Gary Rankin, "A Community Counseling Center for Total Community Service," *Community and Junior College Journal*, Vol. 43, No. 5 (Feb. 1973), pp. 48–50.

[15]Amo DeBernardis, "What Career Education Means For the Community College," *Community and Junior College Journal*, Vol. 43, No. 8 (May 1973), pp. 9–11; 42.

though he attempts to be impartial, does not really view "alternative schools" as meeting their key guidance component—providing for individual differences—any better than other more typical schools.[16]

DIFFERENTIAL FACTORS

Although the point has been made in Chapter 2 that the basic principles of guidance apply equally to guidance services at the elementary, secondary, and college levels, the guidance services most pertinent for each of the levels are determined, at least in part, by forces external to the movement. Guidance services at any school level are appropriate or inappropriate to the degree that they relate to the developmental age or needs of the population to be served; to the expectations held by administrators, teachers, pupils, parents, community leaders; and to the prevailing movements in the community and the broader social sphere.

A consideration of the differences in elementary and secondary schools reveals several major distinguishing factors.

Purposes of Guidance

One such difference is in the purpose of guidance at each school level. Farwell and Peters describe this difference:

> Guidance in the elementary school should assist the pupil to develop a harmonious and integrated personality core through carefully planned school experiences which reflect the integration of the forces impinging on the individual. This is in contrast to guidance services in the secondary school which assist adolescents to extend themselves to the optimum in all the various aspects of adolescent and adult living, such as educational planning, career choice, personal relationships, and living with one's self.[17]

Thus, the purpose of guidance at the elementary school level is focused on assisting pupils to integrate such primary group forces as the home, the school, the church, and peer relationships. These are the forces which form the base for the pupil's adolescent and later years. The aim of guidance, then, is to blend these forces into a harmonious whole.

---

[16]Harry S. Broudy, "Educational Alternatives—Why Not? Why Not," *Phi Delta Kappan,* Vol. 54, No. 7 (March 1973), pp. 438–440.

[17]Gail F. Farwell and Herman J. Peters, "Guidance: A Longitudinal and a Differential View," *Elementary School Journal,* Vol. 57, No. 8 (May 1957) p. 443.

The purpose of guidance at the secondary school level is more centrally focused upon the differentiating aspects of these forces as they affect the pupil's knowledge, acceptance, and direction of himself. Secondary guidance services have as their focus the assistance given to the pupils to extend themselves as their potentialities and opportunities will permit in areas of educational planning, career choice, interpersonal relationships, and intrapersonal acceptance.

Psychological Development

Another differentiating factor between elementary and secondary schools is in the psychological point of view of the pupils. One noticeable aspect is in the concept of time as held by pupils of these two school levels. The secondary pupil tends to be more "future-oriented," while the elementary pupil views time as "now." Elementary pupils as a group do not have a sense of immediacy in their decision-making processes; they are not autonomous in educational choices, career plans, and familial factors that affect their direction and movements to adulthood. They are concerned with learning the tool skills, such as reading, writing, and numerical concepts and manipulation; socialization processes; and adjustment to a real rather than a fantasy world. Secondary pupils view time with both a present and future reference. They learn that decisions have both immediate and long-term consequences.

Havighurst[18] has outlined the developmental tasks confronting elementary and secondary pupils. These tasks are grouped into three general areas: those resulting from physical maturation, those resulting from cultural pressures, and those resulting from the emerging personality. Some of the common major accomplishments required of the adolescent are: (1) achieving a satisfactory acceptance of his rapidly growing body; (2) becoming confident and happy in new social relationships with age mates of both sexes; (3) achieving self-directing independence from parents without losing mutual affection and respect; (4) making plans and preparation for adult economic and social status; (5) achieving confidence in respect to more sharply identified self-roles, and (6) building a system of values to which he can wholeheartedly commit himself. In contrast, the elementary pupil, age six to twelve, is engaged in developing a self-concept, weaning himself from close dependence on parents and adults, establishing a place for himself in a peer group, and achieving the motor, communication, and intellectual skills needed for greater personal and social effectiveness.

---

[18]Robert J. Havighurst, *Human Development and Education.* New York: David McKay Co., Inc., 1953.

In considering differences in psychological developments between pupils at the two levels, one notes the significantly greater dependent relationship of elementary children to their parents. The adolescent is characterized by his search for independence and meaning in his life; in this search his behavior quite often moves beyond the limitations established by adults.

More demands are made on the adolescent. More is expected of him— he is no longer regarded as a child, and his mistakes are not excused as a child's are. By adolescence, a person has learned that some behavior and attitudes are unacceptable to adults. Unless his socialization process has encouraged individuality as well as conformity, the adolescent is likely to be wary of asserting and expressing himself.

Farwell and Peters point out another difference in the psychological point of view between elementary and secondary pupils in that elementary children

> cannot verbalize their feelings to the extent that the maturing adolescent is capable of doing. Because the reasoning process in children is not developed to its fullest, it, too, is a differential factor in an elementary-school pupil's being insightful into the cause and effect of his behavior. Two cautions in interpretations of the last statement are in order here: (1) The mere fact that the elementary-school boy or girl may not have reached the highest level in his reasoning powers does not mean his feelings are not as sensitive or impressionable as are the adolescent's. (2) The mere fact that the pupil is in the adolescent stage does not necessarily mean that his reasoning powers insure insightful self-understanding.[19]

None of these developmental stages is easy for children or adolescents. Both groups need great areas of freedom in which to make their own decisions. Often both need parental support and the help of others to master the demands placed upon them.

Organization of the School

The organizational differences that exist between the elementary and secondary school lead to a major difference in the conduct of the guidance function. Typically, secondary teachers have each pupil for a limited time each day, normally in one class period of some forty to fifty-five minutes. Other pupil contacts are usually limited to the supervision of a club activity. As a consequence of this limited contact, the relationship between secondary pupils and teachers is, by its very nature, bound to be more superficial

---

[19]Farwell and Peters, "Guidance: A Longitudinal and a Differential View," p. 444.

and more impersonal than the relationship that exists between elementary pupils and their teachers. The extended relationship between elementary pupils and teachers makes it possible for elementary teachers to know their pupils much better than their secondary counterparts can hope to know their students. It places elementary teachers in an advantageous position in providing and drawing upon anecdotal records and other observations of behavioral patterns which will be useful in formulating a developmental, longitudinal picture of each pupil. Secondary teachers, because of their more limited contact with individual pupils, are able to provide such information for only a select number of students.

Another differential factor attributable to the organizational school pattern of the elementary as contrasted to the secondary school lies in the more flexible nature and structure of the day-long classroom for the elementary teacher. This comparatively unstructured time sequence may enable the teacher to perform his secondary role of a guidance person with an elementary pupil in assisting him to personally attain healthy emotional and social development. This is important for the sake of the child, and it is an essential condition for learning.

Curricular Differences

The nature of the curriculum offered in the two levels is another force outside the guidance movement itself which shapes guidance practices. The elementary school child has no curricular choices to make. He takes subjects common to all elementary pupils. As Riccio and Maguire state: "When the curriculum is differentiated, as in the case of reading groups, the elementary school student is *told* that he will read with the robins, or the bluebirds; he himself cannot decide to be a sparrow. But the secondary student does have a choice with respect to curriculum, and he is often at odds with his teachers who feel that he is college material and should not be wasting time in commercial or shop courses, or conversely, that because of his low mentality, he should be taking non-college preparatory courses."[20]

Another contrasting curricular factor is that subject matter in the elementary school is more impersonal in the sense that it does not require that its pupils examine their abilities, interests, and past performances. The secondary school curriculum with its points for decisions—termination of junior high school mandating a curriculum choice, confirmation of choice in grade ten or eleven, choice of extracurricular activities, choice of college and career plans—encourages its pupils to evaluate themselves in relation

---

[20]Anthony Riccio and Joseph H. Maguire, "Interdependence of Guidance Services at the Various Levels," *The Bulletin of the National Association of Secondary-School Principals,* Vol. 45, No. 265 (May, 1961), p. 138.

to a program of studies and related activities. Such a factor "sets" the stage for the guidance function by encouraging a greater state of readiness or receptivity among pupils involved in these decision points.

Materials and Methods

Another differentiating factor in the two levels is the guidance materials and methods used with the pupils. Although guidance at both school levels is concerned with normal pupils, psychologists and psychiatrists have found that their techniques for dealing with neurotic adults or adolescents do not necessarily apply to severely disturbed elementary school children. Bijou has stated that "historically, Anna Freud initially attempted to apply the techniques developed for the neurotic adult to the child. It soon became apparent to her that the child treatment situation differed from that of the adult in many significant details and that techniques applicable to adults would have to be modified. Many other therapists recently concurred with her impressions."[21] It seems clear that guidance workers at the elementary school level do not find all of the techniques successful at the high school level equally useful at their level. For example, elementary school counselors use such techniques as play therapy or children's art work to find out what is important and what has meaning to the child they are counseling.

The organization of elementary schools, particularly schools with limited enrollments, provides little opportunity for environmental manipulation as a guidance technique. The secondary school, with its large numbers of course offerings and extracurricular activities, permits its counselor, when necessary, to change somewhat the environment of his counselees.

Elementary counselors have to rely more heavily upon teacher-centered or counselor-centered instruments or reports as compared to secondary counselors who can and do utilize pupil self-reports. Such self-report instruments as the autobiography, questionnaires, checklists, and inventories have generally not been as effective with elementary pupils as with secondary pupils. On the other hand, "elementary counselors and teachers utilize such materials and methods as anecdotal records, children's works, such as art products, measures of social relations, reaction forms and dramatizations, and play therapy."[22]

Another illustration of the differential methods and materials used by guidance workers at the two levels is in the counseling service. While

---

[21]Sidney W. Bijou, "Therapeutic Techniques With Children," in L. A. Pennington and Irwin A. Berg, *An Introduction to Clinical Psychology.* New York: The Ronald Press Company, 1954, p. 611.

[22]Ruth Martinson and Harry Smallenburg, *Guidance in Elementary Schools.* Englewood Cliffs, N.J.: Prentice-Hall, Inc., 1958, pp. 114–124.

elementary pupils will refer themselves to the counselor, they rarely are ready for a sustained examination of their emotions and feelings associated with a problem. Leo Kanner observes

> Direct inquiry is usually not very productive. A sustained discussion of himself is not a part of the child's way of living. The necessity of answering pointed questions about his feelings tends to create an awkward situation for which there has been no precedence in his experience. He may find it difficult to relate even those things about which he knows . . .[23]

On the other hand, Slavson states

> The most outstanding characteristics of a child are his comparatively weak ego organization and his limited ability to deal with inner impulses and external demands. The second difference, which is a direct outgrowth of the first, is the basically narcissistic quality of the child's libido organization, his lack of ego control, hence impulsiveness, his still narcissistic character, hence self-indulgence and feelings of omnipotence. The third distinction is the surface nature of his unconscious. One is impressed with the readiness and almost complete unself-consciousness with which young children act out and speak about matters that are embarrassing to an older person. This can be attributed to the incomplete superego development, the lack of repressive forces (ego), and undeveloped sublimation channels. Finally, the child's identifications are in a fluid state.[24]

The above quotations seem to indicate that counseling elementary pupils would necessitate providing support, reassurance, and adroitly directed adult initiative in the sense of assisting the pupil to achieve a sense of direction and purpose in his behavior. Counseling would be concerned not only with *why* the child acts as he does, but also with *what* he intends to do or wanted to do. "Such interpretations of his true intentions evoke, if correct, an immediate and characteristic reaction. This automatic reaction consists of a roguish smile and peculiar twinkle of the eyes, a so-called recognition reflex. The child need not say one word, or he may even say 'no'; but his facial expression gives him away."[25]

---

[23]From Leo Kanner, *Child Psychiatry.* Springfield, Ill.: Courtesy of Charles C. Thomas Publisher, 1957, p. 220.

[24]Reprinted with permission from S. R. Slavson, *Child Psychotherapy.* New York: Columbia University Press, 1952, p. 143.

[25]Rudolph Dreikurs, *Psychology in the Classroom* (2nd ed.). New York: Harper & Row, Publishers, 1968, pp. 55–56.

Kowitz and Kowitz summarize the present development of guidance methods and materials with children by pointing out: "Although there have been a number of advances in therapy with children, few of these are within the area of counseling. The effectiveness of the counseling process with elementary school children is a field which deserves careful study and thorough research."[26]

Responsibility for Guidance

As we have already noted, many elementary schools place the teacher's role as a guidance worker secondary to his role as an instructor or teacher. Thus, a limit is placed on the extent of the teacher's guidance responsibilities. This situation contrasts with that in the secondary schools where counselors are employed with their primary role being in guidance. However, elementary teachers are increasingly demanding that specialized guidance personnel be assigned to their schools. Twenty years ago Smith reported that a survey of elementary teachers in St. Louis County, Missouri, revealed 93 percent favored such specialized persons in the elementary school.[27] This does not mean that teachers will not have guidance responsibilities, but rather that additional personnel workers are often needed to meet the guidance needs of elementary pupils. Effective guidance services at both levels will continue to depend upon the knowledge, skill, and professional attitudes of mentally healthy teachers, specialists, and administrators. It is imperative that the guidance function be coordinated at both school levels. Otherwise, incidentalism prevails with its attendant overlap, duplication, and omission.

Services Emphasized

The services approach to guidance (counseling, individual inventory, information, placement, and follow-up) has been seen by Hulslander as having implications for elementary school pupils. However, in the elementary school greater emphasis is usually placed on counseling and consultations with teachers and parents. As pupils move into junior and senior high school, the need for counseling services remains the same and an increasing emphasis is placed upon informational and planning services. Personal-social information on heterosexual adjustments and relations increases as does career information.

Elementary schools rely heavily upon group approaches[28] to collecting, providing, and interpreting information about "self" and impinging envi-

---

[26]Gerald T. Kowitz and Norma G. Kowitz, *Guidance in the Elementary Classroom.* New York: McGraw-Hill Book Company, 1959, p. 142.

[27]L. M. Smith, "An Observation on Elementary School Guidance," *Personnel and Guidance Journal,* November, 1956, p. 179.

[28]S. C. Hulslander, "The Content of Guidance Services for All Elementary Children," Report to the North Central Association of Guidance Supervisors and Counselor-Trainers, Purdue University, January 6, 1961, mimeographed.

ronmental influences. At the high school level these are increasingly supplemented by the individual counseling services.

Summary and Other Factors

A summary of these differentiating factors and other factors is provided in Table 4–1.[29]

IMPLICATIONS OF THESE DIFFERENTIAL FACTORS

If these factors—psychological development, school organization, curriculum, materials and methods—do, in fact, differentiate to some degree life in the elementary school from that of the secondary school, what implications are to be drawn from them in developing and managing guidance at these two levels? Examination of these differences does not suggest to the authors that the need for guidance is any less acute in the elementary school than in the secondary school. Even if elementary school teachers are

Table 4–1.   *Differential Factors of Elementary and Secondary Guidance*

Factor	Elementary	Secondary
Personnel	Considerable, sometimes complete, reliance placed on teacher to perform guidance	Greater use of counseling specialists with teachers
Services	More emphasis on individual inventory, orientation and information services	More emphasis upon individual counseling, step-up of career information, and personal-social information
Readiness for guidance	Fewer choice or decision points in the school for pupils, thereby less encouragement for self-study	A number of critical stages encourages self-study and readiness for guidance
Counselor's contacts	Conducted with pupils, teachers and parents	Fewer contacts between counselor and parents
Pupil appraisal	Greater stress on teacher or counselor-centered instruments	Use made of self reports or pupil-centered instruments
Problem areas	Problems more often centered in learning areas or home relationships	Problems involve not only learning areas but also heterosexual relationships, career and educational planning
Referral of pupils	Referrals mainly from teachers and parents	Increase of self-referrals
Concept of time	More "now oriented"	More "future oriented"
Counselor-pupil ratio	One full-time counselor for every 300 pupils	One full-time counselor for every 250 pupils
Cost of guidance programs	Estimated cost of $20.00 per pupil	Estimated cost of $30.00 per pupil pupil

---

[29]Martinson and Smallenburg, *Guidance in Elementary Schools,* pp. 28–126.

associated with 25–35 pupils throughout the day, it seems unlikely that the need for guidance is reduced. The need seems everpresent because the boundaries associated with the teacher's role simply do not permit the individual in that role to establish and maintain for a consistent period of time the conditions needed by the child to solve his personal problems.

The difference in developmental patterns would imply that the counselor and the teacher must be familiar with, understand, and know the psychological pattern characteristic of the age group with which he works. But knowledge of the psychological development of the individuals within the setting in which one is employed does not mean, for these authors, that guidance program development and management is any different. All counselors, at whatever level, are expected to know and to understand typical behavioral patterns of the individual for whom they provide a helping relationship.

The differences in curriculum, lack of pupil choice and impersonality associated with fundamental learnings at the elementary school level, do not seem to have much relevance for distinguishing between the organizations of guidance at the elementary school and the secondary school. Possibly, it may create in pupils a greater need for guidance, but the implications for distinguishing between guidance at these two levels are not readily apparent. Finally, if the informational service is conceived as a means for providing individuals with an opportunity to acquire and make use of environmental and psychological data they need for their development and growth, then presumably the age of an individual would not be a determining factor in his need for such information. The information itself may differ in nature, but all individuals, regardless of educational level, should have access to and be helped to incorporate these data if they are to function successfully.

The major implication to be drawn from these differentiating factors is that the counselor must know the situation in which he is employed. If he is to understand the behavior of those within the system, if he is to provide a helping relationship to them, then he must understand the forces associated with the system and which generate the behavior of those within it. Knowledge of these forces leads to formulation and implementation of the kind of role expected of counselors.

SUMMARY

Some of the changes that have evolved in the guidance function since its beginnings in 1908 are that the concept of guidance has broadened from that of vocational concern to a wider concern for all areas of normal youth; the role of guidance in the school has shifted from that of being an "added on" function to an integrated part of the school; the personnel to perform the service have changed to include teachers, specialists, and administrators; and the province of guidance has shifted from secondary only to include elementary and collegiate schools. Guidance has moved to elementary schools because it should be available to all pupils, because the national interest demands early identification and nurture of talent, and because early recognition and help given to pupils has a greater chance for success than that given later.

While no single clear concept of guidance characterizes the thinking of those who perform at the elementary school level, the developmental approach with its emphasis upon the strengths and the emerging self seems to be slowly catching hold both at the elementary and secondary level.

Those who develop and manage guidance programs in American public elementary and secondary schools need to understand the forces and factors that differentiate these two levels. Seven basic factors—purposes of guidance, psychological development, school organization, curricular differences, materials and methods, responsibility for guidance, and the services emphasized—need to be studied for an understanding of the differences existing between the two levels.

ANNOTATED BIBLIOGRAPHY

Grams, Armin, *Facilitating Learning and Individual Development Toward A Theory for Elementary Guidance.* Minneapolis, Minnesota: Department of Education, 1966.
    Provides much insight into the nature of elementary school guidance and implementation into a program. Chapter 6 discusses "The School Administrator and the Guidance of Learning."

Mathewson, Robert Hendry, *Guidance Policy and Practice* (3rd ed.). New York: Harper & Row, Publishers, 1962.
    Alternative possibilities of organizing and administering guidance programs are lucidly presented as well as a thorough development of procedures and practices required for the implementation of a strategy for guidance.

Shertzer, Bruce, and Shelley C. Stone, *Fundamentals of Guidance* (2nd ed.). Boston: Houghton Mifflin Company, 1971.
    Responsibilities for the guidance program and guidance relationships are examined.

Developing and Managing the Guidance Program

Structuring our schools for change, which is to say making them open systems, is necessary for the very survival of our schools as viable institutions ... the goal of education is to facilitate the development of full humanness in the context of the postmodern world. ... Responsible human beings who are willing to take risks on behalf of others is what is finally needed, which means that we have to remain aware of our freedom *not* to be professional.[1]

Chapter 5

What basic organization principles are relevant for guidance administrators?

What major administrative processes will be engaged in by guidance administrators?

What is the nature of leadership expected of guidance administrators?

What guidelines should be followed in initiating and implementing a guidance program?

What factors influence the development and management of a guidance program?

BASIC ORGANIZATIONAL PRINCIPLES

A good organization is of inestimable value in managing a guidance program; likewise a poor organization makes management extremely difficult. Too often guidance programs have grown without any real plan of organization. Counselors are added and the program takes on ever more functions, becoming larger and larger each year. From the viewpoint of efficient management, the absence of planned organization usually leads to undesirable conditions, including the following:

1. The functions (counseling, educational planning, etc.) become disproportionate in their relationship to each other as judged by the

[1]David R. Cook, *Guidance for Education in Revolution.* Boston: Allyn and Bacon, Inc., 1971, pp. 469, 540, 554.

relative importance of each function to the objectives of the enterprise.

2. Certain essential functions (research, placement, etc.) in the program are neglected or they are subordinated to other functions. Either condition makes it difficult to carry out an effective program.

3. Planning of new functions needed to strengthen the program is ignored.

4. Capable, competent professionals are confined to mediocre assignments.

5. The necessary coordination among the major functions is decreased, since those personnel engaged in each function tend to stress their individual operations and activities exclusively.

Some principles of organization have evolved over time, and experience shows that these principles are characteristic of most good organizations. These principles may be viewed as common guides to action, and their universality applies equally to organizing a guidance program or a manufacturing plant. These principles are identified and discussed briefly here.

Organization should be based upon the objectives of the enterprise. The very first principle in organizing any program is to consider the goals or objectives of the program. Answers to the question, "What is the aim of the program?" or "What is the program trying to accomplish?" are fundamental considerations in any organizing effort. The objectives permeate all activities within a program, and influence the number and extent to which all activities are established and conducted.

It is extremely difficult to judge the effectiveness of any program without an adequate knowledge of its objectives. What might be considered efficient to achieve one objective might well be very inefficient for another. Because objectives differ, the type and number of functions in an organization would differ from those of another.

The functions to be performed must be considered. The essential functions of the enterprise constitute the main elements of the organization. These functions are what must be related and coordinated in the organization. The nature of the enterprise determines the main functions, and these, in turn, determine the way the organization or program should be built.

Organizing a program based upon the functions to be performed provides continuity for it. Basic functions remain or they expand almost indefinitely; they are not limited in span of time or in ability, as are individuals. Building a program along functional lines makes for a powerful yet flexible organization. Functions may be modified, new ones added, and useless functions eliminated without disturbing the essential structure of the program.

Simplicity must be maintained. Simplicity has been defined as "that delightful perfection between too much and too little," and good organizations are those that employ simplicity in their structure. A complex organization is almost certain to create difficulties for those who manage it. A good organization includes only the necessary functions in the simplest possible manner. The true concept of a particular function—what is to be done, when, how, and why—is best understood by people when they are informed in a simple language and in a straightforward manner.

Efforts to make a program seem profound by adding unnecessary functions, giving old functions new names, and developing complex, unnecessary relationships among functions make for confusion. Efficient administrators work with ideas and relationships that are simple but fundamental, for they know that simplicity brings best results.

Channels of authority and responsibility must be established. A good organization must provide clearly defined channels through which authority (the right to act) and responsibility (accountability for an activity) can be exercised. Such channels are necessary in order that each member of an organization knows what his responsibilities are, and the boundaries of his authority. Definite channels eliminate the so-called "horizontal gaps" in organizations, i.e., areas at any given level in the organization which are not covered by a channel of personnel control. In those situations, the functions and activities of the personnel in such areas are not adequately synchronized with those of other parts of the organization. Establishment of definite channels tends to minimize overlapping of activities.

Delegation of authority and responsibility is either specially granted to or inherently implied in an organizational position. In the former case, it is given to an individual in order that he might act to gain the coordination that is essential to achieve an objective. In the latter case, the authority and responsibility are inherent to the position so that whoever holds the position, or performs the delegation function in the organization, automatically possesses the authority and responsibility that goes with the position.

The individual who delegates power always retains ultimate responsibility for duties delegated. Usually the individual delegates only that authority and responsibility necessary to successfully carry out the organizational functions. This leads to what is known as the "tapering concept" of responsibility and authority, i.e., responsibility and authority in most organizations become successively smaller (tapered) as successively lower horizontal levels of the organization are considered.

Span of control must be considered. Related to identifying clearly established channels of authority and responsibility is the span of control, or the number of persons reporting to a supervisor, director or executive. Opinions differ as to the appropriate number, but most managers agree that a number from four to eight is most satisfactory. It is believed that an executive can best utilize his time and ability if he has from four to eight persons to whom he can delegate authority and responsibility. On the other hand, the executive who has more than eight persons reporting directly to him dilutes his efforts over too wide a span, resulting in poor coordination. The principle is that the number of people reporting to any one person should decrease as that person moves higher in the organization. Top executives or managers or administrators should have fewer subordinates to supervise than the lower level managers. This traditional principle may not be too applicable to guidance programs whose personnel are highly educated. The amount of direct supervision should be determined by the maturity and self control of the individuals being supervised.

Definite responsibility should be established. Responsibility implies an individual trust or charge, that is, a dependence upon an individual to perform an assigned task promptly and efficiently. When a position in an organization is vested with certain responsibilities, it is up to the individual who occupies that position to see that the responsibilities are carried out satisfactorily. Responding to these fixed responsibilities is a means by which individuals develop and exercise initiative. The individual who knows the tasks and activities for which he is held accountable tends to overcome common obstacles in order to perform these tasks promptly and thoroughly. Fixed responsibility aids in getting the work of an organization accomplished.

The human element must be evident. The motivating power behind any organization is its personnel. For an objective to be realized, a function to be performed, a responsibility to be assumed, or an authority to be exercised, the presence of human beings is required. Therefore, full and continued consideration for the human beings in any organization is of paramount importance.

The individuals who comprise the personnel in any organization are not alike. They differ in their interests, in their capabilities, and in their energies. What one person seeks, another abhors. Similarly, the various functions to be performed differ so that in any program there are many functions to be performed by many different people. Arranging for some congruence between a person and a function or job is the mark of a sound organization. It provides overall harmony within the organization, and encourages efficiency among the members, for employees believe they are doing worthwhile activities and contributing to the objectives of the organization.

Periodic review of the organizational structure from the viewpoint of the human element is imperative in good organization work.

Operations should be systematized. In any enterprise there are operations that influence the relationship among the different parts of the organization. The handling of test data, for example, frequently concerns not only counselors, but teachers, parents, and principals. When operations occur at frequent intervals, it is necessary to establish some sort of a standardized procedure for handling them in the organization. The establishment of systematized operations is an important principle of organization. Systems bring order and method to work. A systematic approach reduces cost and simplifies the execution of that which is to be done.

Good leadership must be established. The element of leadership is always essential to the success of any organization. An organization could be very poor from the standpoint of its structural relationships, yet its accomplishments could be remarkable because of effective leadership. (A more detailed discussion of leadership is given later in this chapter.)

Clearly, these organizational principles establish that organization is an instrument through which management operates. Organization is the structure, while management is the executing and coordinating force that sees that the work is accomplished.

MAJOR ADMINISTRATIVE PROCESSES

The central purpose of guidance administration is to coordinate the efforts of people to accomplish the goals of the program in which they are involved. Those who serve as managers engage in goal setting, planning, organizing, decision making, motivating and similar processes.

Administrative processes were first identified in the writings of Henri Fayol. His work, published originally in French in 1916, was not widely read in the United States until much later. He viewed the major elements of administration as planning, organization, command, coordination, and control.[2] His five processes have been repeated, adapted, and extended by many others. For example, Gregg cited seven elements of the administrative process: decision-making, planning, organization, communication, influencing, coordinating, and evaluating.[3] Attention will be given here to those administrative processes engaged in by those who manage guidance programs.

---

[2]Henri Fayol, "Administration Industrelle et Generale," in Constance Starrs (ed.), *General and Industrial Management.* London: Sir Isaac Pitman & Sons, Ltd., 1949.

[3]Russell T. Gregg, "The Administrative Process," in R. F. Campbell and R. T. Gregg (eds.), *Administrative Behavior in Education.* New York: Harper and Row, 1957, p. 271.

Goal Determination

Goal determination is an important facet of management in the total educational process and the subsumed guidance process. Too often there is organization of procedures for implementing ill-defined and vaguely-stated goals.

Goal determination in guidance administration involves thinking through and deciding upon such things as: the purposes for which a guidance program is developed; the experiences that will result in the accomplishment of these purposes; the management of these experiences to provide continued, sequential, and integrative benefits; and the means for evaluating the direction of such experiences. In short, goal determination is the sorting out of the kind of behavior *expected* of students: what they are to do, to be, to believe, or to feel because they have been involved in some type of experience. It should be recognized that goal determination stakes out only intended or expected behavior, and that students' actual behavior may differ substantially.

It is important that the goals which are determined acceptable for a guidance program be clearly stated. These goals should be written in terms of behavioral outcomes as well as in terms of general principles. This is important because the staff will wish to evaluate the effectiveness of the program. If the output is to be measured, it will be far easier to gain an idea of the effect of the program if the input and the goals have been stated in terms of the behavioral outcomes rather than in terms of philosophical ideals. Illustrative of guidance program goals stated in terms of behavioral outcomes are:

1. Students develop a greater understanding of their abilities, aptitudes and interests.

2. Students, and their parents, are aware of opportunities and requirements for education and careers.

3. Students select courses and achieve in them in line with their abilities, aptitudes, interests, and opportunities.

4. Students who have the requisite ability finish secondary school.

5. Students who are capable of doing so continue their education beyond high school.

6. Students who continue their education beyond the high school are successful in their educational pursuits.[4]

---

[4]Based on Frank E. Wellman and Don D. Twiford, *Guidance, Counseling and Testing— Program Evaluation.* Washington, D.C.: United States Government Printing Office, 1961, p. 26.

A committee of college and university examiners has classified educational goals into six major classes: knowledge, comprehension, application, analysis, synthesis, and evaluation. In such a taxonomy, goals are arranged from the more simple behaviors, such as knowledge or remembering, to the more complex behaviors, such as evaluation or judgments of value. For those involved in goal determination, studying and carrying through the processes described in *Taxonomy of Educational Objectives* will be invaluable.[5]

Goal determination clarifies the actual intent of the guidance program. There are many different outlooks in initiating or extending guidance programs; therefore, it becomes important to consider—in the development and management of any guidance program—the part that goal determination plays in the guidance process.

Planning

Planning is an important ingredient in administering the guidance program. Planning involves all the preparation needed to reach a decision as to how the resources will be used. In essence, planning consists of developing work maps showing how the program's goals are to be accomplished.

Planning includes a look at the possibilities of the program's success. It means deciding in advance what is to be done. Planning should be realistic in nature, neither emphasizing only the assets nor excluding the liabilities of a particular situation. Planning is also the phase which so often involves active participation of the administrator with the staff. It is planning that enables the guidance administrator and his staff to anticipate the impact of various forces and to influence and control these forces.

Decision-Making

Decision-making means the arrival at a point where it is necessary to take a definite stand on the direction in which the program will be moved and built. Decision-making can be on a logical or psychological basis. Ideally, it would involve both. Decision-making should involve primarily two factors: (1) a rationale which is arrived at after determining the goals to be achieved and (2) the planning that has been done.

How does decision-making occur? Authorities have stressed two different kinds of answers. First, decisions are drawn from established premises which infer logical conclusions. Second, decisions are made on the basis of insight or immediate knowledge. In other words, intuition provides the

[5]Benjamin S. Bloom (ed.), *Taxonomy of Educational Objectives—Handbook I: Cognitive Domain.* New York: David McKay Company, Inc., 1956.

awareness of the complexities involved in the situation necessary to make the decision. Sarbin, Taft, and Bailey further point out:

> In practical decision-making contexts, a pervasive assumption, difficult to test and equally difficult to ignore, is this: the greater the amount of relevant knowledge about an event and the conditions under which it occurs, the more rational the decision process, i.e., the more it is derived from a complex, integrated set of postulates. This is common sense—the justification for specialization in human decisions. For the treatment of an eye injury, an ophthalmologist rather than a general practitioner is sought out, on the assumption that he has the tools and set of relevant postulates for acquiring relevant and complete knowledge for a diagnosis and for making a decision.[6]

Decision-making, then, is the conscious choice from among alternatives. It involves selecting a course of action to bring about a desired future state. The output of decision making lies in formulating policies to guide subsequent behavior in the program.

Often administrative decisions involve physical, social, and personal decisions. As one advances in leadership, he often spends time on decisions involving plant and equipment. Then he attempts to transfer this decision making to situations involving social and personal decisions:

> . . . it appears reasonable to assume that processes of judgment operate differently in the judgment of physical stimuli than in the case of social and clinical judgment. In this connection it is interesting to note that some tentative evidence is available to the effect that a judge's ability to discriminate behavioral stimuli *cannot* be predicted from his ability to discriminate physical stimuli.[7]

Coordination

Although the utilization of both human and material resources might have been placed under another rubric, it is included here as coordinating. Major consideration must be given to the coordinating of both the human and material resources. There has to be identification of who and what is available at the present time, what possibilities exist for obtaining additional resources, and what are the likely implications in regard to the total school

---

[6]Theodore R. Sarbin, Ronald Taft, and Daniel E. Bailey, *Clinical Inference and Cognitive Theory*. New York: Holt, Rinehart & Winston, Inc., 1960, p. 238.

[7]James Bieri, Alain L. Atkins, Scott Briar, Robin L. Leamac, Henry Miller, and Tony Tripodi, *Clinical and Social Judgment: The Discrimination of Behavioral Information*. New York: John Wiley & Sons, Inc., 1966, p. 107.

staff if the resources are obtained. Coordinating involves the unifying of people into a team to realize the organization's objectives.

The proper coordination of resources defines the possibilities for the direction of a guidance program. It makes possible the achievement of the goals of the guidance program. As soon as more than one person is employed in a guidance program, some means must be used to unify all efforts. Otherwise, one person may work at cross purposes with another. Coordination is achieved through establishing communications among people.

Directing

Directing is one of the key considerations in achieving organization and efficiency in the guidance process. Sometimes there is merely coordination with no one individual really directing the program. Eventually, whether by plan or default or under the subterfuge of committee action, some one person has to take final responsibility for directing the program. The person to take charge must be one who is knowledgeable about the determined goals. He must have the professional and personal competencies necessary to carry out his responsibilities, and he must have administrative support and freedom to exercise his professional judgment. The act of directing must be included in the framework of the goals to be achieved. Directing involves not only planning and the utilization of human and material resources, but also the *ethical* use and consideration of the resources as they are being involved. Directing or stimulating and influencing, when properly done, reflects the democratic process of concern for all personnel who are involved in a particular program, in this case, the guidance program in a school. Directing also serves in moving toward the goals previously determined rather than a mere coordination of activities being carried on in different directions.

Developing

Once the preliminary considerations have been made, and the program is in operation, it is necessary to look at the continuity of the program in action through a sequence of stages. It is not enough that the program is initiated. It is equally important to see that the program continues to develop, that it is dynamic in character, and that it moves forward. This involves careful examination of both the purposes of the program and the initial accomplishments.

Extremely important in the development phase of the guidance program is the stimulation that has been given for action. Stimulation of all the staff members involved in the guidance program is a very complex process because of the nature of the guidance program and the personalities involved. While there is no one definitive set of suggestions or recommendations for developing a program, there are several points to keep in mind. One is that mistakes are inevitable in the developing process and should not be construed as failure of the program. Emphasis should be placed on a realistic encouragement of the positive. There should be a realistic expectation by all persons concerned that improvements can be made. Stimulation should be directed toward meeting the goals previously determined, and should not be focused on personality interactions between and among the staff members. Feedback of results, and follow-up to compare accomplishments with plans are very important elements in motivating personnel.

Evaluating

The next step in the administration process is evaluating; sometimes authors use the term "appraising," sometimes, "assessing." In general, many of the terms have the meaning of taking a look at what has been done, for the purpose of modifying previous plans or adopting new ones. Because organization implements the goal-determining process in achieving objectives, it is extremely important in the educational process. The fundamental question is: "To what extent has the organizational plan been effective in reaching the goal previously determined?"

In effective guidance programs, as in other educational functions, it is necessary that the evaluation itself be conducted frequently—if not continuously. This is necessary because the dynamic nature of guidance requires it to adapt itself to the boys and girls in school at a particular time in a particular kind of developing culture. (Evaluating the guidance program will be fully discussed Chapter 17.)

Planning Future Steps

In describing the facets of the administrative process, authors often end with "evaluation." Frequently, it is only implicit rather than explicit that there is still another action. This is the phase of planning the next steps to be taken. Ending with evaluation means the loss of any pertinent follow-through action using the evaluation data. Equally important are the next steps, whether they involve modifying old ones, initiating new ones, or combining modified and new steps. The preparation of next steps gives continuity to the program. It is essential in guidance administration that continued efforts be directed toward improving what has already been accomplished.

Even though these administrative processes have been identified and discussed separately, it should be remembered that they are interrelated in practice. While interrelated, one or more may be of primary importance at any one time. The contribution of the guidance administrator lies in his ability to engage in such activities.

LEADERSHIP OF GUIDANCE ADMINISTRATORS

Most administrators are in accord that the ability to get along well with people is an important managerial skill. Counselors, teachers, and other school personnel—no matter how individually competent—do not constitute a good program by working by themselves. A guidance program is effective when leadership provides formulation of goals, encouragement, direction and unity of efforts.

Definition of Leadership

According to Knezevich, leadership has been viewed as

> (1) an attribute of personality (symbolic leadership); (2) a status, title, or position recognized in a formal organizational chart (formal leadership) and (3) a function or a role performed in an organized group (functional leadership). Leadership is, in essence, concerned with human energy in organized groups. It is a force which can initiate action among people, guide activities in a given direction, maintain such activities, and unify efforts toward common goals.[8]

Terry defined leadership as ". . . the activity of influencing people to strive willingly for group objectives."[9] Hersey and Blanchard, after reviewing several definitions of leadership, state that it is

> the process of influencing the activities of an individual or a group in efforts toward goal achievement in a given situation. From this definition of leadership, it follows that the leadership process is a function of the leader, the follower and the situational variables—$L = f(l,f,s)$.[10]

---

[8]Stephen J. Knezevich, *Administration of Public Education* (2nd ed.). New York: Harper and Row, Publishers, 1969, p. 95.

[9]George R. Terry, *Principles of Management* (3rd ed.). Homewood, Ill.: Richard D. Irwin, Inc., 1960, p. 5.

[10]Paul Hersey and Kenneth H. Blanchard, *Management of Organizational Behavior* (2nd ed.). Englewood Cliffs, New Jersey: Prentice-Hall, Inc., 1972, p. 68.

Leadership Styles

While leadership is often classified into three styles—autocratic, laissez-faire, and democratic—most leaders, given certain conditions, exhibit attributes of all three styles. In some situations, a particular style may actually be necessary for managing certain situations.

Autocratic leadership stems from the authority of the status leader. Communication flows from the top down and there is little feedback from subordinates. While the autocratic leader tends to be personal in his praise and criticism of members, he remains aloof from active group participation. *Laissez-faire* leadership extends freedom for a group or individual without any, or at most, a minimum of leader participation in a decision. Leaders who employ this style, supply needed materials, articles, equipment, and provide information when asked. However, they rarely participate in discussions of the work to be done or determine the tasks to be accomplished or assign responsibility. *Democratic* leadership depends upon group discussion to formulate policy and to arrive at decisions. Members participate in outlining the general steps to reach a goal. Members are free to work with whomever they choose and the division of tasks is decided by the group. The democratic leader tends to be "objective" in his praise and reproof of members' work. He seeks to be regarded as a regular group member.

Shortcomings of each leadership style have been identified by many authors. For example, autocratic leadership is generally criticised for neglecting personal relationships, creating dependence and stifling creativity, while democratic leadership is often criticized as being inefficient, overly concerned with relationships, and nonproductive.

The guidance administrator must function as a leader in situations that require specific skills, qualities, and characteristics. The mixture of his personal characteristics, his training, and his experiences will lead to the development of a leadership style. Hersey and Blanchard[11] point out that there are a wide variety of types of administrators. They depict a broad range of styles on a continuum moving from autocratic or authoritarian leader behavior on one end, to democratic leader behavior on the other. Their representation is presented here as Figure 5–1.

Trait or Situational?

Leadership has long been viewed as a personality trait that included such qualities as friendliness, alertness, sensitivity, presence, and so forth. Moreover, it was believed that individuals who possessed this trait would exercise it from one situation to another. According to such a view, leadership

---

[11]Hersey and Blanchard, *Organizational Behavior,* p. 71.

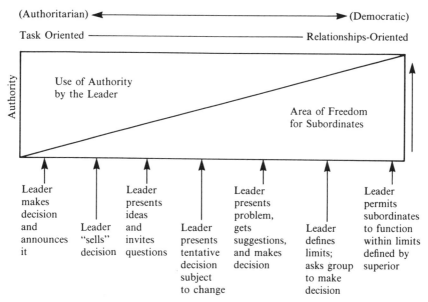

Figure 5-1.   *Continuum of Leader Behavior.* [*Source: Paul Hersey and Kenneth H. Blanchard,* **Management of Organizational Behavior** *(2nd ed.). Englewood Cliffs, N.J.: Prentice-Hall, Inc., 1972. Reprinted by permission.*]

training was unnecessary. However, researchers in the area of leadership have never been able to identify a personal trait or set of qualities that distinguish leaders from nonleaders. Rather, the studies suggest that leadership is a process varying from situation to situation, from leader to leader, and from task to task. In short, leadership is situational, depending upon many conditions and mixtures of personality.

Leadership in Guidance

An effective guidance program must have leadership. While leadership is never vested exclusively in any one person, guidance administrators are expected to provide leadership continuously and consistently. Those guidance administrators who have achieved prominence in their work are those who exhibit concern for both task accomplishment and the relationships among those with whom they work and interact. They have evolved a style of leadership that enables them to initiate structures that lead to goal accomplishment, while simultaneously exhibiting concern and interest in facilitating effective relationships among staff members.

Effective guidance administrators are those who help staff members clarify and understand program goals and objectives. They exercise leadership in conceptualizing guidance programs that serve students well, and they establish communications among staff members. They become involved directly with staff members, students, school administrators, teachers, and parents to secure their cooperation and assistance in solving mutual problems. Guidance administrators, then, are leaders who adapt their behavior to meet the needs of the group and the particular situation to facilitate the work of many people to accomplish the goals of the guidance program.

GUIDELINES FOR INITIATING AND EXTENDING GUIDANCE PROGRAMS

The administrative, supervisory, and teaching staff of each school district is responsible for organizing an effective guidance program for all pupils within the district. The organizational pattern in any given school district may well determine whether the guidance function operates optimally. In carrying out this responsibility, the staff will be helped by observation of certain key principles. As a set of general organizational guidelines for the development and management, the following points are useful. They will be detailed more completely in the remainder of the text.

Staff Receptivity to Guidance [12]

It is basic to the organization of the guidance program that staff members be receptive to the guidance point of view. To declare that the guidance point of view, emphasizing the uniqueness, dignity, and value of the individual pupil, should be held by the members of the staff is not to say that it will be so vague and diffuse as to be meaningless. Rather, it provides the backdrop for which guidance functions can be established. At all school levels, it is the school administrators and their supervisors who are responsible for facilitating receptivity toward the guidance point of view. Their beliefs and actions must express this point of view every day in their school activities and out-of-school life. One word of caution is in order. A guidance program cannot be arbitrarily introduced into a school. It must be carefully developed with consideration for the sensitivities of the staff and the needs of the students.

Articulation of All School Levels

Another guideline to the organization of a guidance program is articulation through discussion, eventual consensus, and continuing contacts by the staff at both the elementary and secondary levels. If guidance, as an integral

---

[12]Buford Stefflre and Fred Loafzer, "Value Differences between Counselors and Aministrators," *The Vocational Guidance Quarterly,* Vol. 10, No. 4 (Summer 1962), pp. 226–278.

function of education, is to contribute to the realization of the school's total objectives for its pupils, then it will be inherent in every level of the school district. Because the guidance function must be coordinated in all its various phases, this articulation will help bridge the gap between elementary and secondary levels and will avoid many unnecessary "starts" in collecting, interpreting, and using pupil data. Articulation of all school levels will enable guidance personnel to maintain an orderly accumulation and recording of a variety of information about each pupil. Most school districts have provided for this articulation by organizing an all-district guidance council and by employing a director of guidance who supervises the guidance program throughout the district. Cooperation and sincerity of purpose should pervade all participants in their guidance dealings with each level. Some time ago, Mathewson stated: "Guidance cannot be rendered exclusively in one spot; it must be pervasive. Therefore, a *systematic team* process is essential, compromising the efforts of teachers, parents, counselors, specialists, and the pupil himself."[13]

Developmental Needs of Children

The guidance function must be based upon and respond to the needs of pupils. This means that counselors must (1) understand students as individuals, (2) know students' personal and educational needs and (3) be skillful in formulating and arranging programs to facilitate student development. In organizing the guidance program, then, a determination of pupil needs at each school level must be ascertained. This can be accomplished through pupil checklists, questionnaires, tests, and inventories; through surveys and follow-up studies of graduates and dropouts; through staff surveys; and through parent and community opinionnaires. The guidance program is for the pupils to be served in a given school district. The given needs of the local setting are major determinants of the organizational pattern that is to be adopted. Not all programs should attempt to be like every other guidance program. In summary, a well-developed guidance program will provide needed services to all students, not just those with serious emotional problems or maladjustments. The function and organization of guidance emanates from the needs of pupils, the unique characteristics of the community, and the current conditions of the school.

Objectives Clearly Defined

In organizing the guidance program, it is necessary to have the objectives of the program defined for each school. Recommended practice is to have those objectives stated in written form. The procedure for defining guidance

---

[13]Robert Hendry Mathewson, *Guidance Policy and Practice* (3rd ed.). New York: Harper & Row, Publishers, 1962, p. 215.

objectives is long and arduous. The authors recommend that the Director of Guidance and the counseling staff (1) consult with school administrators, teachers and pupils as to what the school is seeking to accomplish, (2) start with several simply stated objectives and delete those that critical examination shows to be inappropriate, (3) modify and refine the objectives until they become meaningful, and (4) consult with teachers, parents, and students again and again. Guidance personnel in each school will want to examine the basic needs of its students and its underlying philosophy in deciding upon its objectives. Objectives must, of course, be stated in terms of observable behavior so that progress toward these objectives can be assessed. Once the members of the school staff have agreed on the objectives of the guidance program, they can determine the services needed to reach these objectives.

The definition and determination of objectives is one area in which real leadership must be exercised by the director of guidance. Members of the public, school administrators, and even counselors are all too often confused about the desired outcomes of guidance. The confusion often puts diverse pressures upon counselors to do something different from whatever they are doing, without consideration as to its desirability.

The problem of bringing the professional counselors of the school, the vocal members of the community, and teachers and school administrators to a common agreement on objectives is indeed a rigorous one. Perhaps this is the most difficult of all tasks which a director of guidance faces today. He cannot be neutral or insensitive in this matter; he must stand up to the challenge. Failure to do so is an abdication of leadership responsibility.

The only recourse is for the director of guidance to arm himself with professional knowledge of guidance, and knowledge of his staff, students, and community so that as a leader he is in a position to offer propositions that are well considered and based upon clarifying expectations which people hold for guidance. In this way, a basis would be established for arriving at a rational and operational definition of guidance objectives.

Coordination of Function

The major purpose of organizing guidance is to coordinate all the school personnel, resources, and materials that serve the needs of pupils in a learning situation. Without coordination of the guidance function, there will be much waste of personnel, materials, and resources with overlap and duplication of effort and anxiety over individual responsibilities. The student has enough problems in living and learning without the added bother of resolving the disjointed efforts of a poorly organized guidance department.

Coordination means that the many individual contributing parts of guidance must be synchronized into one complete productive unit. People and the services they perform must not be working against one another or out of relationship with each other. It is through coordination that counselors carry out their tasks in a manner which achieves the program objectives not only with optimum effectiveness but also with a high level of morale.

Clear assignment of responsibility and authority of the guidance staff is necessary for effective coordination of effort and services. Careful attention should be given to each person's assignment so that his duties are delineated and recognized and so that his efforts and responsibilities will not overlap others'. Coordination will evolve from cooperative planning of the program. Direct responsibility for the overall operation of the program should be delegated to a qualified staff member who has adequate time to carry out the assignment.

Professional Leadership and Personnel

Another guideline to organization of guidance is the acquisition of personnel who are competent personally and competent professionally. The Director of Guidance will furnish the technical leadership that, coupled with the executive leadership displayed by the top-level administrator and the cooperation of the rest of the staff, will facilitate the interpretation, promotion, and acceptance of the guidance program to accord with the educational needs, laws, and finances of the local community. There is no doubt that both technical and executive leadership will be needed to combat the problems that can well develop at any level of operation.

It may be said that the strength of a director of guidance can be measured by the competence of his counseling staff; however, this statement does not mean that a strong counseling staff has no need of a strong director of guidance. Clearly, staff strength is dependent upon leadership strength. The director of guidance and his counseling staff are dependent upon one another; the strength of one enhances the strength of the other.

Acceptance of this guideline would mean that much would be done to build up staff strength. Assessment and appraisal are common activities used to find and recruit the most competent counselors. Recruitment, selection and orientation of new counselors have taken on added importance as a function for guidance administrators in recent years. In-service education and individualized supervision of counselors have become increasingly important.

Not only are strong directors of guidance alert to the sources of competent personnel; they devise ways of improving the competence of the personnel already on the job. They find ways of deploying the services of the staff members to accomplish the task of the guidance program as effectively and efficiently as possible. If necessary, they separate the incompetents from the school system. This painful, unpleasant step is, of course, taken with due process observed.

Counselors and guidance administrators know that any program, whether new or old, needs the acceptance and endorsement of the school administrator. Without his continued support, any function will "wither on the vine." Teachers and pupils sense and frequently adopt the school administrator's attitude toward any program in the school.

Provision for Time, Facilities, and Budget

Schools have increasingly found that the effectiveness of competent counselors can be immeasurably increased through providing them the requisite time, facilities, and budget. Because of the relatively recent and rapid development of guidance services, provisions for the guidance function have often failed to keep pace in existing school programs. Few good standards have been developed in these areas that can universally serve educators.

To determine the physical facilities needed, the guidance director must have four kinds of data: (1) a mental picture of the way guidance will operate; (2) a projection of the school population to be served; (3) a plan for housing arrangements and (4) an indication of funds. A guidance budget will convey the proposed program and the anticipated expenditures necessary to support such a program. The budget should not provide simply for personnel but rather for particular personnel to carry out specific parts of the program. It should stipulate the equipment and materials needed to facilitate particular parts of the program.

Provision for In-Service Education

Few schools are without teachers who find it difficult to accept the guidance point of view; yet these teachers should be considered not as a threat but as a challenge. Guidance administrators who take pride in basing their services on accepting individual difference will seize every opportunity to assist these teachers and understand their views. Inasmuch as guidance has currently developed in many schools, in-service training is essential as a constant means of improving the guidance services of the school. Such a program will strengthen the teachers' understanding of guidance functions. As their understanding increases, they will acquire new interests, new competencies, and new motivations for performing the guidance function. Compelling staff members to participate in an in-service guidance program should be avoided. The effects of guidance services upon pupils should convince the more skeptical teachers of the need for guidance activities. Once these teachers have observed the benefits of guidance, they will realize the need for deepening their insights and skills through the in-service education program.

Use of Community Resources

Those persons involved in the organization of guidance services need to consider the agencies and resources that are available in the community. Service clubs often have standing committees that are vitally interested in the field of guidance. Community agencies, state mental health clinics, community youth guidance centers, university counseling and testing services, religious counseling services, psychological centers, and other similar organizations are but a few of the local services that can serve as a valuable adjunct to the school guidance program. The use of these referral sources should be contingent upon their professional status. Arbuckle notes that "The counselor, however, must be aware of all the services that are available, and he has some responsibility in trying to develop a closer relationship between the school and various community services, or even to develop and use community resources if they are not being utilized."[14]

The elementary and high school counselor's knowledge of community referral resources will be useful because most of his clients are still living at home with their families. Their problems quite often are family problems with which some agency might help. Developing respect, confidence, and cooperation with community resources takes time, but gradual growth can be expected with the constructive handling of each occasion that arises for working together. The long run benefits of such cooperation and common concern with community needs may be fully as important as the specific undertakings out of which they grow.

Evaluation Maintained

A final guideline for initiating and extending guidance programs is that a means for evaluation must be built into the school program. A more detailed discussion will be found in Chapter 17. It is through evaluation that insights are provided, enabling needed improvements to be most efficiently and intelligently planned. Continuous appraisal should be structured from the initiation of organized guidance services. It is true that school officials make value judgments about their various services without conducting the

[14]Dugald S. Arbuckle, *Pupil Personnel Services in American Schools.* Boston: Allyn & Bacon, Inc., 1962, p. 401.

evaluation program in a systematic manner, but if evaluation is to yield results for intelligent planning, an organized, on-going evaluation program will permit greater insight into real needs. The value of evaluation of the program from its beginning is that checks can be made upon procedures, methods, or materials that were installed on the basis of educated guesses of the staff. Further, evaluating at this stage facilitates stating the objectives of the program in terms of observable behavior.

CRITICAL FACTORS THAT INFLUENCE THE INITIATION OR DEVELOPMENT OF GUIDANCE PROGRAMS

Experience has demonstrated that several factors are critical in initiating or expanding a guidance program. Programs which survive and grow are those that are directed toward responding to student needs, those that build upon teacher awareness of guidance services, and those that utilize a team approach.

Determining Pupil Needs

Pupils often have educational and personal needs and problems which are not met in the school's instructional program. The guidance program can be developed effectively when as much information as can be collected regarding the individuals composing the student body is studied and known. It would be desirable to know everything about the individuals who represent the student body of a school including their present life styles, their past histories, and that of their family. This, of course, is impossible. However, careful study should be given to their needs. Some of the means for determining these will now be discussed.

Needs—Developmental Aspects

Guidance is to serve the pupils to facilitate their personal and emotional development. To determine needs, the staff may use any one or a combination of several approaches. Because guidance is basically a positive process, the staff should think of needs in terms of the developmental stages and functioning of normal boys and girls. Guidance functions should be provided in terms of the needs of the normal school population—the vast majority of the total enrollment. Guidance processes will facilitate the proper developmental growth processes. Illustrative of the developmental functions to be considered are those cited by Havighurst for middle childhood, adolescence, and early adulthood.

Developmental Tasks of Middle Childhood

1. Learning physical skills necessary for ordinary games.
2. Building wholesome attitudes toward oneself as a growing organism.
3. Learning to get along with age-mates.
4. Learning an appropriate masculine or feminine social role.
5. Developing fundamental skills in reading, writing, and calculating.
6. Developing concepts necessary for everyday living.
7. Developing conscience, morality, and a scale of values.
8. Achieving personal independence.

Developmental Tasks of Adolescence

1. Achieving new and more mature relations with age-mates of both sexes.
2. Achieving a masculine or feminine social role.
3. Accepting one's physique and using the body effectively.
4. Achieving emotional independence of parents and other adults.
5. Achieving assurance of economic independence.
6. Selecting and preparing for an occupation.
7. Preparing for marriage and family life.
8. Developing intellectual skills and concepts necessary for civic competence.
9. Desiring and achieving socially responsible behavior.
10. Acquiring a set of values and an ethical system as a guide to behavior.

Developmental Tasks of Early Adulthood

1. Selecting a mate.
2. Learning to live with a marriage partner.
3. Starting a family.
4. Rearing children.
5. Managing a home.
6. Getting started in an occupation.
7. Taking on civic responsibility.
8. Finding a congenial social group.[15]

The developmental task concept calls attention to the fact that growing pupils, during the many phases of their development, face a series of "learnings" to be mastered. These learning tasks result from the interaction between the pupil's maturing body and the pressures of his social and physical environment. For counselors the value inherent in this concept lies

---

[15]Robert J. Havighurst, *Developmental Tasks and Education.* New York: Longmans, Green and Company, 1952, summarized from Chapters 2, 3, 5, and 6. Reprinted by permission David McKay Company, Inc.

in its emphasis upon social expectancy and maturity. With some pupils social expectancy and maturity do not coincide. Unhappiness, low self esteem, and lack of confidence result. By knowing the developmental tasks confronting adolescents (and a thorough foundation in human growth and development is required to do so), those responsible for the guidance program can better plan appropriate courses of action. Counseling services can be extended to pupils to enrich their understanding of the situation in which they find themselves. Teachers can be consulted to attain their understanding and cooperation in a program tailored for such youth. Also important for the school counselor is that he will need to assess the behavior of adolescents by adolescent standards. Too often adolescents are judged by adult standards because they closely resemble adults in physical appearance. Consequently their behavior does not measure up favorably. Because it does not, it is often judged to be problem behavior. The guidance worker needs to know the norms or expected behavior typical of the group with whom he works.

Needs—Personal Resources

Too often guidance programs are built on a negative basis of problems, need in the sense of want, and handicaps. Guidance programs should also be built in terms of pupils' personal resources. The positive should be accentuated. The maximization of the positive will help to put weaknesses in proper perspective. Guidance programs will be far more likely to succeed if they are built on pupil strength rather than on pupil weakness.

A number of standardized inventories for surveying pupil concerns and problems is available: The Science Research Associates Junior Youth Inventory; the Psychological Corporation Mooney Problem Check List; the Minnesota Counseling Inventory.

The use of these survey instruments can focus on the immediate needs of pupils in a particular school. This may serve to initiate a guidance program in terms of pupil needs. However, pupil strengths, as previously mentioned, should also be considered.

1. *SRA Youth Inventory.* The SRA Youth Inventory is composed of 298 statements on matters which have bothered teen-agers all over the United States. The test has eight major areas: (1) My School, (2) Looking Ahead, (3) About Myself, (4) Getting Along with Others, (5) My Home and Family, (6) Boy Meets Girl, (7) Health, and (8) Things in General. The inventory is designed for use with all students in grades 7–12. Most students can take the inventory in thirty minutes and all should finish in forty minutes. Interpretation is on the basis of relative frequency of responses in a given area and is useful as a basis for getting an interview started. Norms are

provided from a stratified sample of 9–12 grade students and are presented in the form of mean responses in each of the eight areas.

2. *Mooney Problem Check Lists.* The Mooney Problem Check Lists have three forms, one for college students, one for high school students, and one for junior high school students, The college and high school forms have 330 items in eleven problem areas: (1) Health and Physical Development, HPD; (2) Finances, Living Conditions, and Employment, FLE; (3) Social and Recreational Areas, SRA; (4) Social-Psychological Relations, SPR; (5) Personal-Psychological Relations, PPR; (6) Courtship, Sex and Marriage, CSM; (7) Home and Family, HF; (8) Morals and Religion, MR; (9) Adjustment to College (School) Work, ACW, ASW; (10) The Future: Vocational and Educational, FVE; and (11) Curriculum and Teaching Procedure, CTP. The junior high school form has 210 items in seven problem areas: (1) Health and Physical Development, HPD; (2) School, S; (3) Home and Family, HF; (4) Money, Work, and the Future, MWF; (5) Boy and Girl Relations, BGR; (6) Relations to People in General, PG; and (7) Self-Centered Concerns, SC. The student underlines the problems of concern, circles those of most concern and summarizes in his own words. Most students finish in thirty-five minutes and practically all finish in fifty minutes. However, all should be given as much time as needed to complete the inventory. Scoring is in terms of frequency of response in each problem area. Norms are not presented, as the authors believe that local norms established by the test administrator will be more meaningful in test interpretation.

3. *Minnesota Counseling Inventory.* The Minnesota Counseling Inventory contains 355 true-false items. It provides a question score which indicates whether enough items have been answered to justify scoring and using the inventory. A validity score helps identify those students who are overanxious to display socially acceptable characteristics. Scores in Family Relations, FR; Social Relationships, SR; and Emotional Stability, ES, help in identifying areas of high and poor adjustment. Four other scales, Conformity, C; Adjustment to Reality, R; Mood, M; and Leadership, L, provide information on the methods students employ in making adjustment. The inventory is designed for use with ninth to twelfth grade students. Administration time is approximately fifty minutes. Norms are presented for boys in grades 9 and 10, girls in grades 9 and 10, boys in grades 11 and 12, and girls in grades 11 and 12. The norms are presented in standards scores converted from the raw score in each of the above areas. A table for this conversion is included in the manual.

Needs—Guidance Functions Approach

In inaugurating or revising a guidance program, Hollis and Hollis suggest a number of starting points. Those given below are illustrative.

Information Service may be the place to start if . . .

1. Systematic investigation has shown specific need.
2. Adequate guidance library facilities are available.
3. Faculty, administrators, and service personnel are willing to cooperate in the gathering and dissemination of information.
4. Individualized guidance records are nonexistent or inadequate.
5. Information on aspirations and plans of individual students is lacking.
6. Students' decisions are now based on inadequate information.
7. Students lack access to educational, occupational, and personal information that may help them in their development and enhancement of self-concepts.
8. Information is not being gathered to provide the necessary longitudinal or developmental approach.
9. Present information on existing records is thought to be of little value by teachers.

Testing, Measurement, and Individual Appraisal (TMIA) Service may be the place to start if . . .

1. No schoolwide standardized testing is now performed.
2. Faculty are willing to make use of results in working with students or planning classroom activities.
3. Remedial services are available for students, and assistance is needed in identification of individuals who may benefit.
4. Time is available for individual interpretation of results obtained.
5. Counselors will work with individuals to assist in building realistic self-images.
6. Individual work will be done in helping each student to recognize his potentials and establish realistic educational and vocational goals.

Counseling Service may be the place to start if . . .

1. Specific information has been obtained to prove the need.
2. Students are requesting assistance of the type offered by professional counselors.
3. Among the faculty and administration are well-trained individuals who are willing to cooperate with the service.
4. Counseling Service in the past has been basically an information service for students with vocational and educational needs.
5. Good community resources and referral personnel are available.

6. Individual guidance records or inventories, though inadequate, are available for most students.
7. Results of schoolwide testing are available for each student, and supplementary tests for an individual can be administered if warranted for counseling.
8. Adequate space is available where confidential counseling sessions can be held.

Placement Service may be the place to start if . . .

1. Placement has proved to be a definite need.
2. Curricular or job placement is not being offered by an existing service or is inadequate to serve identified needs.
3. Location of school is convenient for job placement.
4. Opportunity exists for educational placement of students in different (a) rooms in elementary school, (b) classes in junior or senior high school, (c) programs such as academic, general, or special education, or (d) cocurricular activities.
5. Students frequently change classes or vocational goals.
6. Few students participate in cocurricular activities.
7. Teachers often remark that a certain student should not be in a certain class.
8. Time is available for follow-through.
9. Adequate information service is available.

Follow-Through Service may be the place to start if . . .

1. Needs in this area are sufficiently demanding.
2. Present guidance personnel assist an individual at the time of request but provide little or no follow-through.
3. Information gathered is not sufficiently interpreted or applied with students who may benefit.
4. Continued assistance over an extended period is available to only a few persons, if any.
5. Responsibility for students is dismissed after referral has been made.
6. Individuals who have completed work with a guidance service receive no further information or assistance, even in the event of a change in circumstances that would affect their actions and decisions.
7. The guidance records pertaining to an individual are to be kept to date.
8. The staff has assumed the responsibility of offering to students continuing assistance in assessments of themselves and their environment and, when either or both change, assistance in reevaluation of the decisions previously made.

Research Service may be the place to start if . . .

1. Study has revealed a definite need for research.

2. The guidance staff is research oriented and willing to use the results obtained.
3. Information has been collected but analysis is lacking.
4. No present base line exists with which future progress can be compared.
5. The data for evaluation of guidance services are inadequate.
6. Specific information on the student body is lacking: number of students in academic programs, number planning to continue schooling beyond high school, and number with abilities beyond a certain point in each type of program; correlation of grades and academic ability; relation between the aspirations of a given group of students at one grade level and their aspirations at a different grade level.

Evaluation Service may be the place to start if . . .

1. Individuals involved in the program have indicated readiness for evaluation and willingness to implement necessary changes.
2. Objective information, such as furnished by Research Service, is available for making evaluation.
3. Criteria have been accepted so that an evaluation can be made.
4. A guidance program has been in existence for a period of time.
5. Guidance committee and personnel have displayed objective, unbiased viewpoints in the areas to be evaluated.
6. The specific effectiveness of the program is unknown.
7. The conditions and timing appear to be right for making modifications in the present program.[16]

Student Awareness of Guidance Services

Many schools have found it advantageous to determine the degree to which students are aware that guidance services are available to them. To do so, they develop some type of checklist or questionnaire. The one developed by H. Eugene Wysong is presented here as an illustration.

Student Inventory of Guidance Awareness (SIGA)[17]

We would like to discover the extent to which you are familiar with the guidance services offered in your school. By knowing how you feel about this phase of our school program, we shall be better able to initiate changes in areas which you indicate. Will you please respond as frankly and honestly as you are able? *DO NOT PLACE YOUR NAME ON THIS INVENTORY.*

---

[16]From *Organizing for Effective Guidance* by Joseph William Hollis and Lucile Ussury Hollis. © 1965, Science Research Associates, Inc. Reprinted by permission of the publisher.

[17]H. Eugene Wysong, "Evaluating Secondary School Guidance Programs: Development and Validation of Instruments." Unpublished doctoral dissertation, The Ohio State University, 1968. Material used with permission.

DIRECTIONS: Will you please check (X) *Yes* or *No* to indicate your feelings about each question. If you feel that you cannot give a definite *Yes* or *No* answer, will you please check (X) in the space marked (?).

Yes__No__?__   1. Does your school help you to consider information about yourself as it relates to your future educational and vocational plans?

Yes__No__?__   2. Have you been encouraged to investigate the personal and educational requirements for occupations you have considered?

Yes__No__?__   3. Have you had conferences with someone on your school staff concerning your educational and vocational plans?

Yes__No__?__   4. Does the school inform your parents of your standardized test results?

Yes__No__?__   5. If you had a personal problem, would you feel free to discuss it with someone on your school staff?

Yes__No__?__   6. Does your school help you to understand the meaning of your standardized test scores? (Examples: school ability, achievement, and aptitude.)

Yes__No__?__   7. Do you have access to the information you want and need to know about the various occupations you have considered?

Yes__No__?__   8. Do you know which member of your school staff is your school counselor?

Yes__No__?__   9. Is opportunity provided in your school for groups of students to discuss and understand their attitudes?

Yes__No__?__   10. Has your school counselor talked with you about your future educational and vocational plans?

Yes__No__?__   11. Has your school provided your parents an opportunity to discuss your educational plans?

Yes__No__?__   12. Do you have access to the information you want and need about colleges and other schools which offer post-high school education?

Yes__No__?__   13. When you entered high school, were you helped to learn about your new school and how to get along in it?

Yes__No__?__   14. Have you had an opportunity to discuss with your school counselor various approaches to solving problems with which you have been faced?

Yes__No__?__   15. Are you thinking about or planning what you are going to do when you finish high school?

Yes__No__?__   16. Has your school provided the opportunity for you to learn to present information about your abilities, training, characteristics, and experience to employers in a convincing manner?

Yes__No__?__   17. Have your parents ever talked with your school counselor?

Yes__No__?__	18. Have you been helped to plan the subjects and activities you need and want to take while you are in high school?
Yes__No__?__	19. Were you helped to become familiar with the employment possibilities in your community and the surrounding areas?
Yes__No__?__	20. Can you talk about your real feelings about things with your school counselor?
Yes__No__?__	21. Do your teachers discuss the various occupations which are related to the subjects taught by them?
Yes__No__?__	22. Do you know where your school counselor's office is located?
Yes__No__?__	23. Have you been helped to decide if you have the ability to succeed in college?
Yes__No__?__	24. Does your school use film-strips, films, pamphlets, books, etc., to help you understand problems of personal and social development?
Yes__No__?__	25. Have your ability and achievement test results been helpful to you in your educational and vocational planning?
Yes__No__?__	26. Have you received any help from your school in the improvement of your study skills and habits?
Yes__No__?__	27. Have you had an opportunity to participate in group discussions about the concerns of high school students?
Yes__No__?__	28. Has your school counselor discussed your ability and achievement test results with you individually?
Yes__No__?__	29. Were you helped before the ninth grade to plan your high school program of courses?
Yes__No__?__	30. Has your school provided opportunities for you to grow in your ability to make realistic plans for yourself?
Yes__No__?__	31. Has a counselor or a teacher helped you to examine your abilities, personality traits and interests as they may pertain to your future plans?
Yes__No__?__	32. Have you been satisfied with the course selections which you have made?
Yes__No__?__	33. Do you feel that your school experiences have provided you with opportunities to develop self-reliance?

SCHOOL _____ BOY _____ GIRL _____ GRADE _____

TEACHER AWARENESS OF GUIDANCE SERVICES

Classroom teachers are important in facilitating student personal development. Their responses to students do much to establish and promote a positive mental health. Their knowledge of student needs, based upon direct contact with them, is particularly useful in initiating or expanding guidance services. Again, some inventory can be utilized to obtain their judgments as to what services are present and what needs attention. An inventory, developed by H. Eugene Wysong, is presented here as an illustration of those that could be developed.

Teacher Inventory of Guidance Awareness[18]

We would like to obtain an indication of your awareness of the guidance services in your school and the extent to which you feel they are adequate. This information should be useful in improving guidance services to students. Please be frank in your appraisal. DO NOT PUT YOUR NAME ON THIS INVENTORY.

Part of Your School Program?	DIRECTIONS: To the left of each question, mark (X) to indicate whether or not the activity is carried out in your school. To the right of each question, mark (X) in the column which represents your opinion of the adequacy.	To What Extent?				
		None	Inadequate	Adequate	Too much	???
Yes __ No __ ? __	1. Is an organized program of guidance available to all students?					
Yes __ No __ ? __	2. Has the staff cooperatively planned the guidance program?					
Yes __ No __ ? __	3. Does the school have a standardized testing program which includes both ability and achievement tests?					
Yes __ No __ ? __	4. Have guidance services been provided to orient new students to the school?					
Yes __ No __ ? __	5. Do you discuss with your students the vocational applications of your subject matter fields?					
Yes __ No __ ? __	6. Have the seniors developed both immediate and long-range plans?					
Yes __ No __ ? __	7. Have you participated with the counselor and other teachers in case conferences concerning students?					
Yes __ No __ ? __	8. Are placement services provided to assist students to obtain additional education or training?					
Yes __ No __ ? __	9. Are organized activities provided to assist students in planning careers?					
Yes __ No __ ? __	10. Do the cumulative records contain information about the educational and vocational plans of students?					
Yes __ No __ ? __	11. Is individual counseling of students a part of the guidance program?					

[18]Wysong, "Evaluating Guidance Programs."

Part of Your School Program?	(continue with previous directions)	To What Extent?				
		None	Inadequate	Adequate	Too much	? ? ?
Yes __ No __ ? __	12. Are informational materials on education provided and effectively used by students?					
Yes __ No __ ? __	13. Do you know the educational and vocational plans of the students in your classes?					
Yes __ No __ ? __	14. Does the staff plan cooperatively the evaluation of the achievement of students in relation to their potential?					
Yes __ No __ ? __	15. Do the cumulative records contain information on the home and family background of students?					
Yes __ No __ ? __	16. Are teacher responsibilities in the guidance program clearly defined and understood?					
Yes __ No __ ? __	17. Are standardized test results interpreted for teacher use?					
Yes __ No __ ? __	18. Does the administrative staff support and assist in the development of the guidance program?					
Yes __ No __ ? __	19. Are informational materials available to students concerning personal and social development?					
Yes __ No __ ? __	20. Are group guidance procedures used in the guidance program?					
Yes __ No __ ? __	21. Do teachers accept and take advantage of the guidance services offered?					
Yes __ No __ ? __	22. Do you discuss with your students the educational implications of your subject matter field?					
Yes __ No __ ? __	23. Do the cumulative records contain information which indicate special abilities or talents of students?					

Part of Your School Program?	(continue with previous directions)	To What Extent?				
		None	Inadequate	Adequate	Too much	? ? ?
Yes __ No __? __	24. Do you seek the assistance of the counselor in helping students?					
Yes __ No __? __	25. Do you have an in-service education program for the staff on guidance services?					
Yes __ No __? __	26. Do you make referrals of students to the school counselor?					
Yes __ No __? __	27. Are the cumulative records of students accessible to teachers in your building?					
Yes __ No __? __	28. Is an opportunity provided for groups of students to discuss matters of concern to them?					
Yes __ No __? __	29. Are informational materials available to students concerning occupational opportunities and requirements?					
Yes __ No __? __	30. Are counselor-parent conferences held concerning students?					
Yes __ No __? __	31. Do students accept and take advantage of the guidance services offered?					
Yes __ No __? __	32. Is help given to students in planning an educational program to meet their individual needs?					
Yes __ No __? __	33. Do the cumulative records show an educational growth pattern of students?					
Yes __ No __? __	34. Do you hold conferences with parents concerning their children?					
Yes __ No __? __	35. Are organized activities provided to assist students in developing good study habits?					
Yes __ No __? __	36. Are teachers provided with summaries of important data from records and tests?					
Yes __ No __? __	37. Are parents informed of their children's standardized test results?					

Part of Your School Program?	(continue with previous directions)	To What Extent?				
		None	Inadequate	Adequate	Too much	???
Yes __ No __ ? __	38. Have students made realistic course selections in relation to their abilities and interests?					
Yes __ No __ ? __	39. Do the cumulative records contain anecdotal reports or summaries of student progress written by teachers?					
Yes __ No __ ? __	40. Does the guidance program include research and evaluation studies?					

BUILDING A TEAM APPROACH

Today's guidance program uses a team approach if for no other reason than the fact that few schools have sufficient counselors to serve the needs of all the students. The ratio of students to counselors in most schools is above the recommended 250 students to each full-time counselor. To counter the high student-counselor ratios, a team approach that involves counselors, teachers, paraprofessionals, psychologists and social workers has been used.

While team work in guidance has been long viewed as ideal, few schools have actually made it operational. McQueen states that

> Many professionals believe that during the seventies, the team concept will be adopted by counselors. Counselors will work more closely with teachers, administrators, social workers, school nurses, physicians, and psychologists. They will also work more closely with parents and other citizens and will make additional use of community resources, including persons who can contribute help in a variety of ways. Counseling and guidance services will be able to help more students because counselors will have more people to help *them*. The use of paraprofessionals and other kinds of aides, such as student assistants and volunteer mothers, will increase. Training for almost all helpers will be available. Many junior colleges have programs for paraprofessionals or guidance aides. Some forward-looking schools are already providing in-service training for community volunteers and student helpers. A counseling or guidance team might be made up of a counselor, a paraprofessional,

a volunteer mother, and some student helpers. There could be a variety of combinations, but all members would work together under the direction of the counselor to help students.[19]

Schools that employ a team approach must analyze carefully what each member is expected to do to make the guidance process effective and meaningful for students. It must be recognized that to do so requires several meetings and conferences to establish assignments and good working relationships. Cooperation and coordination of effort are even more urgent with a team effort.

Figure 5–2 depicts the operation of a team approach in a guidance program. Mathewson points out that study of what is presented reveals that

> (1) Some of the activities are intermittent, the functionary does not conduct them continuously; (2) other activities are interwoven with classroom or other functions so that they may be performed almost simultaneously with other duties; (3) there is reinforcement effect as a result of the team process which unites the lesser effects of several people into a combined process of substantial effectiveness; and (4) the process occurs over a span of years, and is centered around the work of the counselor, the data of the cumulative record and the growing self-situational understanding of the pupil himself.[20]

Effective team work does not just happen. It must be nurtured by the director of guidance through his coordination and leadership efforts. Otherwise, each team member goes his own way and the outcomes are often individual stagnation, isolation, and the lack of organizational achievement. The guidance administrator bears a heavy responsibility for encouraging participation among the members. Above all, he must develop a structure which increases members' productivity by pooling their knowledges and skills to solve crucial matters. The wise director of guidance knows that he must capitalize on the creativity of all staff members in building a team approach that places a premium upon the cooperative effort required to plan and carry through with guidance practices. Members want to be sure that their ideas about corrective or initiating actions are received and considered. All want some voice in determining what should be done, and all want an active role in following through with actions.

The employment of a team approach to guidance requires leadership. It is essential that the director of guidance be able to understand and work

---

[19]Mildred McQueen (ed.), "Trends in Guidance and Counseling," *Research Report.* Chicago: Science Research Associates, Inc., November 1972, p. 2.

[20]Mathewson, *Guidance Policy and Practice,* p. 208.

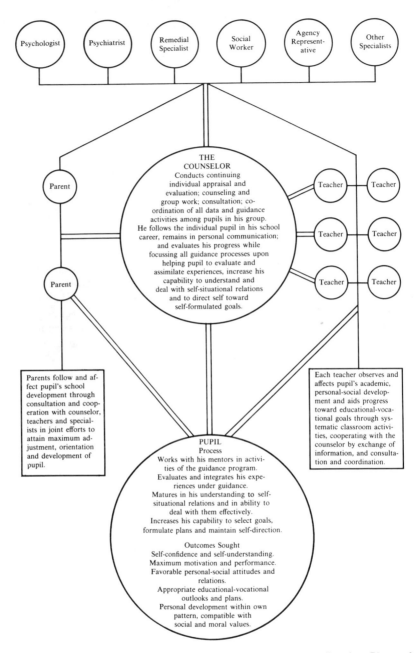

Figure 5–2.   "The Counselor as the Central Coordinating Pivot of the Guidance Process." [From Robert H. Mathewson, **Guidance Policy and Practice** (3rd ed.). New York: Harper and Row, 1962, p. 209.]

with team members. It is wise to remember that any team, regardless of size, is composed of individuals. Means must be found to involve all team members—counselors, teachers, parents, and psychologists—in crucial decision making areas. Both formal and informal communications are needed. Meaningful contributions can result from members pooling their expertise to solve problems and create practices that will benefit students. The guidance administrator must be able to recognize the "big ideas" that emerge from the team, and focus efforts upon making these operational. This is perhaps his greatest challenge when he works with a team.

ANNOTATED BIBLIOGRAPHY

Castetter, William B., *The Personnel Function in Educational Administration.* New York: The MacMillan Company, 1971, 385 pp.

Chapter 2 discusses how school systems deliver services, and how they create opportunities for members to derive satisfaction from their work. The basic theme is that a school consists of interrelated components designed to achieve certain purposes according to a plan. The author pays particular attention to the relationship between the individual and the system.

Miller, Frank. *Guidance Principles and Services* (2nd ed.). Columbus, Ohio: Charles E. Merrill Publishing Company, 1968, 536 pp.

Part II treats the development of guidance services. Miller identifies the necessary characteristics of a program, use of guidance committees, teachers' responsibilities and other organizational matters.

Munson, Harold L., "Guidance in Secondary Education Reconnaissance and Renewal," in *Guidance for Education in Revolution,* David R. Cook, ed. Boston: Allyn and Bacon, Inc., 1971, pp. 170–193.

Munson examines present day guidance strategies with regard to older conceptions. He identifies changes needed in the practice of school counseling programs, and sets forth some new directions.

Responsibilities of
Guidance Personnel

Further, he (the school counselor) cannot, by working alone, hope to achieve the overall objectives of the guidance programs. What is required is a smoothly functioning team effort where reciprocal roles are clearly established and where common objectives are being pursued.[1]

Chapter 6

What guidance duties and responsibilities are expected of the guidance staff?

What guidance duties and responsibilities are expected of other pupil personnel workers?

What guidance duties and responsibilities are expected of adminstrative officials?

What training should guidance personnel possess?

What professional organizations serve guidance personnel?

The development and management of an effective school guidance program will be facilitated through written job descriptions of each staff member's guidance responsibilities. The proper assignment of guidance duties insures that each staff member knows what he is to do. It helps to define his role not only for himself but also for his co-workers. Proper task assignment also aids in more effective articulation of the various guidance activities by the staff. Further, because guidance duties are interwoven with the total educational process, it is necessary that these duties become clearly delineated. Clear delineation will prevent or minimize overlap, confusion, and misemphases of staff members' primary and secondary educational roles.

[1]Duane Brown and David J. Srebalus, *Comtemporary Guidance Concepts and Practices.* Dubuque, Iowa: Wm. C. Brown Company, Publishers, 1972, p. 80.

The nature of the community, budget and facilities, historical factors, degree of guidance program development, and active leadership determine the precision and direction of guidance duties for the staff in a particular school system. It is clearly recognized that the duties to be given each staff member must be flexible within the local school system. However, flexibility must not be used as a basis for violating professional standards. Because the guidance program as an organized part of the total educational scene is relatively new, it is imperative that job descriptions reflect those duties which are professionally sound.

The following discussion of the duties and responsibilities of the personnel involved in guidance will be separated into three categories: the first dealing with the responsibilities of the immediate guidance staff; the second, with guidance responsibilities of related pupil personnel workers; and the third, with guidance responsibilities of the administrative personnel.

RESPONSIBILITIES OF THE GUIDANCE STAFF

These duties and responsiblities of the immediate guidance staff will be discussed here. Included in the personnel most directly charged with the responsibility of guidance are counselors, director of guidance, teachers, and the guidance advisory committee.

The School Counselor

The activities, tasks, duties, and responsibilities of counselors have been the subject of much attention. A large and ever-increasing literature has sought to determine and clarify what school counselors "ought" and "ought not" do. The next chapter, Chapter 7, presents a more complete analysis of this literature. Here, a summary will be given of the major activities of elementary and secondary school counselors.

For these two authors, the major activity of counselors, at either the elementary or secondary school level, is counseling. That is the reason why individuals are employed as counselors—to provide a helping relationship with students which enables them to examine and cope with their developmental concerns. The second major activity is that of consulting with teachers, parents, and administrators. All other assignments are secondary to the counselor's establishment and maintenance of individual and small group counseling relationships with students. While the proportion of time devoted to counseling may vary somewhat from school to school, it would seem that counseling contacts would occupy from two-thirds to three-fourths of a counselor's time. For each counselor and for each school, determination of time devoted to counseling will depend at any given period (week or month) upon certain characteristics of the social system of the school, e.g., need for counselor-teacher consultations and the like.

The recommendation that counselors spend from two-thirds to three-fourths of their time in counseling individuals and small groups is far from being met by them at the present time. This is clearly evident from a survey of guidance personnel in Indiana schools by Pruett and Brown.[2] The two investigators asked 85 secondary school counselors, 56 directors of guidance, and 24 deans of boys and girls to keep a log of their activities for a specified three-week period. Based upon an analysis of their logs, 42 percent of their time was spent with students and 11 percent with teachers and parents. Further, about one-quarter of their time was spent in nonguidance activities such as clerical work, attendance taking, disciplining students, and substitute teaching.

Undoubtedly, today's counselors in most schools have to engage in activities other than counseling. Hopefully, today's counselors will ward off those activities identified as nonguidance such as attendance taking, substitute teaching, and the like. But, the amount of time and effort that any one counselor devotes to "supporting guidance services" such as program planning, student appraisal, etc., will depend upon such factors as the size of the counseling staff available, the interests of the counselor and those with whom he works, and his conceptualization of the counselor role. Consequently, attention here will be given to identifying by educational level some of the supporting activities that a counselor, for any one of several reasons, may be expected to engage in for varying amounts of time.

Elementary School Counselors. Activities other than counseling engaged in by elementary school counselors include:

1. Consultation with teachers, administrators and other school personnel about individual children
2. Consultations with parents concerned about the behavior and development of their children
3. Observation and case study of certain children
4. Testing pupils and interpreting the data
5. Referral of children to special programs and personnel maintained within the school and the community
6. Consultation about development and use of a cumulative record system
7. Interpreting the character of the school to those responsible for curriculum change

---

[2]Rolla F. Pruett and Duane Brown, "Guidance Workers' Use of Assigned Guidance Time," *The School Counselor, Vol. 14* (November, 1966), pp. 90–93.

8. Conducting study groups of parents aimed at understanding children's needs and characteristics
9. Consultation about testing programs, reporting test results to teachers and parents and use of test data
10. Helping teachers design and implement career informational services for pupils

Nelson[3] reports that some fifty-nine elementary school teachers in an Indiana school district placed high priorities upon the following activities of seven elementary school counseling interns who had served in the schools for an academic year: counseling with teacher-referred children; providing feedback to teachers about pupils; consulting with teachers on pupils' problems; counseling with parent-referred children, and counseling with children who referred themselves. These teachers rated the elementary school counselors as being very effective in such activities as "being an understanding professional," "having readiness to talk with teachers about pupils," and "developing effective relationships with children, teachers, parents and others."

Secondary School Counselors. Activities (other than individual and small group counseling) in which secondary school counselors may engage include:

1. Educational and vocational program planning with a specified number of students

2. Interpreting test data to students and reporting test data to teachers

3. Consultation with teachers, administrators and other school personnel about individual students

4. Consultation with parents concerned about the behavior and development of their children

5. Referral of students to special programs and personnel maintained within the school and within the community

6. Organizing and administering college day and career day experiences

7. Administering external tests (college admission and scholarship examinations)

8. Organizing and administering career informational materials and experiences for students

---

[3]Richard C. Nelson, "Report on the Purdue-Tippecanoe Elementary School Counseling Internship for 1972–73." Mimeographed, Purdue University, Lafayette, Indiana, June, 1973.

9. Interpreting the character of the school to those responsible for curriculum modifications

10. Conducting study groups of parents aimed at understanding children's needs and characteristics

11. Consultation work about testing programs, reporting test data and their use

12. Consultations with administrators and teachers about development and use of cumulative record system

There is no anticipation here that any single counselor will be expected to do all these activities. Most counselors, especially in schools where more than one counselor is present, will counsel and engage in only two or three of the activities listed.

Director of Guidance

The title and function of a director of guidance seem to be generally found in the larger school systems. However, in many small schools in which only one person is employed as a guidance specialist, he is often given the title director of guidance. In such cases, titles do not convey functions, for such persons more appropriately serve as school counselors.

The contention here is that the title, director of guidance, should carry with it such functions as the supervision of counselors; communication with administrative officers of the school who have responsibility for financial accounts and control for providing physical facilities; and the responsibility for general program development and management. The title should be reserved for those who assume such responsibilities in order that it convey some indication of the individual's functions.

Biggers and Mangusse[4] sought to obtain a description of the work of guidance administrators employed in large city school systems. Some 104 directors of guidance responded to forty items that described their work. Approximately two-thirds of the respondents devoted full-time to administration of the guidance program. These 104 directors were in school systems that employed 7,200 secondary school counselors and 1,950 elementary school counselors. Over half of the directors were solely responsible for administering the guidance program. Each of the others had from one to twenty professional assistants who helped with the administration of guidance. Seventy-five of the 104 school systems had written job descriptions for the guidance administrator's position. The director reported directly to the

---

[4]Julian L. Biggers and David J. Mangusse, "The Work of the Guidance Administrator," *Counselor Education and Supervision,* Vol. 12 (December, 1972), pp. 130–136.

school superintendent in fifteen systems, to an associate or deputy superintendent in twelve instances, to an assistant superintendent in forty-four
systems and to another director in the remaining cases. Some 71 percent of
the directors reported a staff relationship with secondary school counselors,
50 percent had a similar relationship to elementary school counselors, and
almost all reported a staff relationship to principals. Some forty activities
were reported to be performed to some degree by the guidance directors.
Ten activities that were most often engaged in by the directors, and the
percentages that endorsed each item are as follows:

Activity	Percent (N=104)
Coordinate system-wide services	98
Improve the effectiveness of the guidance program	98
Read recent research reports	98
Develop and promote a philosophy of guidance services	97
Disseminate information to counselors	97
Plan guidance programs and activities	95
Prepare objectives for the guidance program	95
Conduct staff meetings and conferences	95
Disseminate information to principals	95
Conduct in-service training for counselors	94

Donigian and Wellington surveyed thirty-four New Jersey high school
guidance departments to determine the leadership behavior of guidance
directors most and least satisfying to school counselors. The *least* satisfying
director behaviors included that of neglecting to carry out "role implementation." That was reported as failing to assist counselors to fulfill their
professional roles, or to improve themselves. The *most* satisfying behaviors
were those in which directors demonstrated "professional competence,"
engaged in "program maintenance and facilitation," established "communications" and exhibited "professional regard and concern." These two investigators concluded that "The directors of the MS (most satisfied) group
were perceived to be less authoritarian and less autocratic in their relationships with staffs."[5]

---

[5]Jeremiah Donigian and Arthur M. Wellington, "Leadership Behavior of Guidance Directors Related to Counselors' Expectations," *Counselor Education and Supervision*, Vol. 10,
(Winter, 1971), pp. 146–152.

Today's director or supervisor of guidance (an individual who is responsible for guidance in a school system and who supervises three or more counselors) might order his major activities as follows:

1. Interpreting guidance to administrators, staff and members of the community

2. Supervising counselors through individual and small group conferences devoted to concerns about counseling

3. Coordinating the work and efforts of guidance personnel

4. Serving as a liaison with community referral agencies and personnel

5. Formulating budgets and planning physical facilities needed for guidance

6. Selecting and placing counselors

7. Coordinating and conducting research and evaluative studies of guidance

8. Devising innovative record systems, methods of imparting information, etc.

The effective director of guidance views himself as an educational leader who possesses expertise in guidance. He has a grasp of the total educational process as well as a theoretical rationale through which guidance is to be made operational within the educational process. Sensitive to educational change, the director (or supervisor) of guidance encourages staff members to examine why certain practices are used, to identify appropriate guidance purposes and goals and the means to attain them.

The Teacher

The role of the teacher is a complex one. The teacher must set priorities if the job at hand is to be done.

Instruction is the teacher's major function. However, for instruction to be of the greatest value, individual differences among students should be recognized. Adequate teaching techniques must be employed with the group, and the teacher must have time during the period the school is in session to assist students. The teacher, serving as a resource person, particularly in the area of vocational exploration, is able to provide information and help to a student. However, he should exercise care to permit a student to develop his own choice. Further, the teacher must be aware of personal biases and prejudices so that the entire picture is presented to the student. In his guidance role, the classroom teacher will become sensitized to some of the symptoms of various kinds of problems. Referral may then be a more logical course of action. The teacher can serve as one of the screens for ascertaining information and also as a screen against which the pupil may project his concerns.

Some ways in which teachers may create wholesome guidance activities for the students include independent work, pupil motivation, pupil planning, recognizing individual differences, helping children learn to evaluate, presenting challenging material, providing opportunities for social and emotional growth and security, and developing effective parent-teacher relations. Brown and Pruett, based upon their survey of 3,000 elementary school teachers, reported that these teachers viewed their guidance functions as (1) identifying student needs and problems, (2) making referrals, (3) working with parents and (4) working with students who have learning difficulties.[6] Further, Brown surveyed 1100 Indiana secondary school personnel to determine their attitudes toward teacher guidance functions. Consensus as to what these functions should be was not present among teachers, principals and counselors. Generally, vocational teachers were more willing to assume certain guidance responsibilities than teachers of academic subjects. However, there was no significant difference between or among the groups in their belief that the teachers "would occasionally perform counseling."[7]

Many debates have been held on whether teachers should counsel students. Those who engage in arguing the issue never seem to make clear what purpose is demonstrated whichever way the case is "proved." While it is believed by these authors that the teacher's *primary* responsibility lies in facilitating the intellectual development of students (by teaching), it is also believed that the teacher has a related or secondary responsibility for facilitating the emotional or personal development of students (by advising, counseling, or establishing close relationships with students). Because teachers are professionals, because they are mature human beings and because they are oriented toward and care about people, students expect them to be, and use them as, sources of help. Here are some of the ways it is believed that teachers engage in guidance functions:

1. By relating to, advising and counseling students who seek their help

2. By conducting their classes and other student contacts based upon established principles of good human relationships

---

[6]Duane Brown and Rolla F. Pruett, "The Elementary Teacher Views Guidance," *The School Counselor,* March, 1967, p. 198.

[7]Duane Brown, "Attitudes of School Personnel Toward the Teacher's Role in the Guidance Program," *Vocational Guidance Quarterly,* Summer, 1966, pp. 259–262.

3. By being attentive and responsive to pupil behaviors that indicate that help is needed

4. By studying and observing pupils; by learning their interests, aptitudes, behavioral patterns, goals, and values and encouraging them in appropriate ways to utilize their potentialities

5. By incorporating career information and resource materials in their subject matter areas and encouraging students to plan career activities

6. By referring pupils with educational, vocational, or personal problems beyond their (the teachers') competence to qualified counselors

7. By encouraging students to utilize counseling services

8. By consulting with counselors about individual students who need help or specialized attention

The Guidance Council and/or Committee

In large school systems, it has been suggested that a guidance council be established to provide continuity for the entire guidance program. The essential duties of the guidance council are (1) the establishment of system-wide guidance policies, (2) the coordination of the guidance services and (3) the evaluation of these services throughout all the grades and all the schools. The personnel composing the guidance council varies from system to system. In many cases, council membership is held by counselors, teachers, and the principal from each school, as well as representatives from the central system staff, that is, director of guidance, curriculum specialists, supervisors, and associate superintendents.

Many single-unit schools have established a guidance committee of either a policy-making or advisory nature with most being advisory in nature. In other words, the committee serves as a means of communicating to the guidance staff the needs and views of the staff and teachers and aids the school and guidance administrator and counselors in establishing policy. Typical of the responsibilities of guidance committees are studying the needs and purposes essential to the development of guidance services, evaluating existing services and procedures, and planning in-service activities in guidance for staff members. Most authorities believe the guidance committee's major service is its ability to be a vehicle for keeping all staff members informed of guidance policies, decisions, and plans. Membership on the committee is desirably held by teachers who are interested in guidance activities and by department heads.

RESPONSIBILITIES OF RELATED PERSONNEL WORKERS

As has been stated before, all professional staff members associated with the school have opportunites to engage in guidance activities. Some of the guidance responsibilities of the school attendance officer, social worker, school nurse, school doctor, school psychologist, school psychiatrist, school psychometrist, and the school librarian are presented in this section.

The School Attendance Officer

The actual function of the attendance officer is to enforce the attendance laws and to investigate and help children who are not attending school. In carrying out his official duties, the school attendance officer has an excellent opportunity to locate and refer to the school counselor or the proper agencies pupils who are chronically tardy or absent. Often, the attendance officer has unique opportunities to observe the environmental factors of the pupil's home.

The major activities of school attendance workers lie in interpreting to students and their parents regulations about school attendance. They consult with teachers and administrators about school attendance laws, admission of students, pupil tardiness and absences. In many school districts they are responsible for granting school leaving permits and student work permits. They often represent the school in juvenile court cases where school attendance or discipline is an issue.

Social Workers

School social workers have sometimes been given titles such as "visiting teachers" or "school home visitors." These titles convey that social workers are expected to be concerned with home and community factors that influence students' performance in school. Nebo sets forth this description of the functions of the school social worker:

> The main contribution of the school social worker is a specialized service which is based on his understanding of human behavior, skill in interviewing, and ability to use community resources. ... As a member of the school staff, the school social worker receives referrals from teachers and other school personnel, of the children who are exhibiting symptoms of social or emotional difficulty which are interfering with their learning, attendance or social adjustment.[8]

---

[8]J. C. Nebo, "Some Aspects of School Social Work Practice in Schools," *Social Work in Schools—Selected Papers.* New York: National Association of Social Workers, 1960, p. 8.

Today's social worker often devotes large amounts of his time to case study and counseling of handicapped children, consultation with parents of disturbed or handicapped children, arranging referrals to appropriate community youth-serving agencies and establishing programs for treating and preventing delinquency. The fundamental intent of school social work is to assist children whose problems in school stem from family and environmental causes. Such children who are emotionally immature, who are inattentive, who have made poor social adjustments, or who have poor attendance and discipline are prominent clients for social workers.

The Librarian

One essential function that can be performed by school librarians is orientation of new students, especially in the secondary school. The Illinois Library Association held a conference on the theme, "The School Library and the Guidance Program." The librarians concluded that their function was to help the individual find information and, in addition, assist him in reaching his highest level of self-realization.

Librarians may participate in the following activities:

> (1) providing authentic, pertinent, and adequate information about vocations, educational opportunities, social relationships and personal development; (2) assisting the individual in locating and interpreting information pertinent to problem solving; (3) aiding the individual in orienting and adjusting to educational opportunities, especially those available through the library; (4) assisting in obtaining information which will lead to utilizing available information about the individual in working more effectively with him; (5) providing opportunities through social contacts, assigned responsibilities, exploratory activities, and constructive environment which will lead to greater insights and satisfactory development of the individual; (6) providing such counseling services to the individual as are in keeping with the operation of the guidance program and the competency of the librarian.[9]

The School Nurse

The school nurse assists teachers and counselors by coordinating health status, behavior, home environment, and school progress as well as helping handicapped pupils adjust to their problems. She becomes a "watcher" of the development and growth of the pupil, especially the handicapped child.

Barr has suggested that, *with the school physician,* the school nurse may serve on the medical team, diagnose and prescribe treatment for physical

---

[9]C. A. Michelman, "Counselor and Librarian," *Library Journal,* February, 1953, p. 291.

handicaps and ailments which, when properly treated, may avoid or reduce mental problems. In this way, she can stimulate better adjustment and development of the child.[10] Also, through home visitations by the school nurse, solutions to problems of emotional adjustment may be accomplished indirectly through treatment of physical conditions.

In a study of 607 New Jersey school nurses employed during the 1956–57 school year, Klein found that health guidance was accepted as a major function by the school nurses and that 78 percent of the nurses in this study were provided time during school hours for follow-up of health problems. The nurses were not clinicians. However, some 88.6 percent of the nurses employed in schools which had a guidance director indicated that they were members of the guidance team.

Functions of the nurse in the area of health guidance were:

1. Instructing teachers on methods of handling specific health problems relating to an individual child's condition (e.g., diabetic, epileptic, or handicapped).

2. Counseling pupils on personal health problems and/or group conferences with faculty or staff personnel concerning current health problems, including prevention and control of disease.

3. Counseling faculty members on home situations of pupils which affect their adjustment.[11]

The nurse contributes to the guidance functions of the school by serving the staff as a consultant and resource person. Her work might better be labeled as teaching or informing rather than as counseling as performed by the counselor, although here, too, is a therapeutic element in the pupil's experience.

The Physician

The school physician like the school nurse can render an important service toward the guidance program. Physicians employed by schools are responsible for conducting routine physical examinations of pupils. Most school physicians are limited to periodic visits, diagnoses and referrals, and immunizations. When appropriate, they consult with school personnel and parents about a particular student's physical problem. Their recommenda-

---

[10]John A. Barr, *The Elementary Teacher and Guidance.* New York: Holt, Rinehart and Winston, Inc., 1958, p. 360.

[11]Ruth A. Klein, "The School Nurse as a Guidance Functionary," *Personnel and Guidance Journal,* December, 1959, pp. 320–321.

tions about an individual's health condition can facilitate enlightened school practices toward the individual.

The guidance program can be strengthened through cooperation between the teacher, the school physician, and the pediatrician, all of whom may furnish the school with information which would greatly help an individual in his adjustment to his environment. Teachers who carry out physicians' recommendations such as providing short rest periods, permitting a child to empty his bladder, and supervising exercises for minor orthopedic difficulties, avoid many problems.[12]

The School Psychometrist

A school psychometrist is a professional whose speciality is administering and interpreting individual ability and personality tests. His training has focuses upon intellectual assessment and the statistical treatment of psychological data. Psychometrists, often erroneously referred to as "school psychologists," usually have one year of graduate psychological preparation.

The major function of the school psychometrist is to administer, score, and interpret both individual and group standardized tests. Many spend much of their time screening children for placement in special education programs. The presence of a school psychometrist may be justified in a large school system, but since the functions of a psychometrist can be conducted by a school psychologist, the position seems necessary in smaller school systems. The school psychologist is able to perform more specialized functions than testing and test interpretation.

The School Psychologist

Individuals employed as school psychologists come from a variety of educational backgrounds. Some have had their training in clinical psychology, others in educational psychology, while still others have specialized in child psychology, counseling, learning, and so forth.

Holt and Kicklighter[13] point out that the first name associated with school psychology was that of the renowned Arnold Gesell. He was given that title when he was employed by the Connecticut State Board of Education in 1915 to examine children throughout the state who were performing poorly in school.

In 1925, Walter listed the following functions of the psychologist:

[12]Marlene G. Ions and Isa C. Grant, "Teacher and Pediatrician Work Together," *Education,* LXXVII (October, 1958), p. 99.

[13]Fred D. Holt and Richard H. Kicklighter (eds.), *Psychological Services In the Schools.* Dubuque, Iowa: Wm. C. Brown Company Publishers, 1971, p. 1.

1. Direction of group testing within the system

2. Diagnosis and therapeutics of problem cases—mentally retarded, superior child doing inferior work, child who has a special ability, child whose behavior does not meet the standards of the community

3. Analysis and disposal of problem cases

4. Bring a unique point of view to bear on educational problems

5. Conduct research problems

6. Render contributions to general theory and practice of education[14]

Because current teacher preparation provides more depth in the area of psychology, the psychological view toward educational problems is not as unique today as it was in 1925. The other functions, as listed by Walter, appear to be just as pertinent today. In 1955, the American Psychological Association reported that the school psychologist serves in an advisory capacity to school personnel, and performs the following functions:

1. Measuring and interpreting the intellectual, social, and emotional development of children

2. Identifying exceptional children and collaborating in the planning of appropriate educational and social placement and programs

3. Developing ways to facilitate the learning and adjustment of children

4. Encouraging and initiating research, and helping to utilize research findings for the solution of school problems

5. Diagnosing educational and personal disabilities, and collaborating in the planning of re-educational programs[15]

An APA committee from Division 16, chaired by Frances A. Mullen, proposed the following functions for school psychologists:

1. Service to the individual child: screening, diagnosis, placement, counseling, referral

---

[14]A. Walter, "The Functions of a School Psychologist," *American Education*, Vol. 29 (December, 1925), pp. 167–170.

[15]Norma E. Cutts (ed.), *School Psychologists at Mid-Century—A Report of the Thayer Conference on the Function, Qualifications, and Training of School Psychologists*. Washington, D.C.: American Psychological Association, 1955, pp. 30–31.

2. Services to the school as a whole: to school organization, to school policy, curriculum, teaching, group testing, personnel and inservice training

3. Service to the community

4. Research

5. Organization of psychological services[16]

White and Harris identified five categories of current school psychological programs: (1) The psychologist who is a permanent staff member of a single school system and travels from building to building because his services are extended from kindergarten through grade twelve; (2) the psychologist who is a member of a centralized staff, serving several school districts; (3) The psychologist who is employed by a large metropolitan bureau which reports to the city board of education; (4) the psychologist who is employed in a rural area, works alone, and travels from one distant school to another, and (5) the psychologist who is employed on a central staff or a county or state governmental agency and who serves as a consultant to school psychologists within his jurisdiction.[17] The major services of school psychologists, according to White and Harris, are four in number. These are identified here, and a brief summary is given of their discussion of each function.

1. *Educational diagnosis.* The school psychologist defines the educational status of a pupil—his assets and difficulties. The psychologist does this by means of tests, observations, interviews and history-taking.

2. *Educational remediation.* The school psychologist outlines a program, based upon the diagnosis, designed to secure improvement in the educational adjustment of pupils. Remediation processes may include selected teaching, tutoring, classroom modifications, alteration of family attitudes, and the like.

3. *Personality diagnosis.* The school psychologist employs (in addition to those cited for educational diagnosis) personality tests, diagnostic interviewing, compilation of personality and social history to assess the pupil's personality and the factors associated with adaptation and maladaptation.

---

[16]Report of the committee on Reconsideration of the Functions of the School Psychologist. *The Psychologist on the School Staff.* Washington, D.C.; American Psychological Association, Division 16, 1958, p. 3

[17]Mary Alice White and Myron W. Harris, *The School Psychologist.* New York: Harper and Row, Publishers, 1961, pp. 5–6.

4. *Personality remediation.* The school psychologist outlines a program designed to secure personality remediation. He may undertake some measures himself, collaborate on other measures with his colleagues, and/or secure the services of specialists, agencies, or other schools.[18]

Whether school psychologists provide therapy as part of their services is an unresolved issue. Most school psychologists have not been trained as psychotherapists. The issue was identified and discussed at the August, 1954, conference of school psychologists held at the Hotel Thayer, West Point, New York. Sponsored by the American Psychological Association and financed by U.S. Public Health Service, the report of the conference sought to establish ". . . a definite statement about the functions, qualifications, and training of school psychologists." The report was published under the title, *School Psychologists at Mid-Century*[19] and is usually referred to as the Thayer Report. Conferees could not reach agreement as to whether school psychologists extended therapy as part of their services, and concluded that ". . . the extent to which psychotherapy can be regarded as a proper function of the school psychologist has not been agreed upon . . ."[20] Herron argues that

Whatever functions the school psychologist carries out in schools, his greatest effectiveness lies in being trained as a psychotherapist. Whether primarily a tester, consultant, or therapist, he must know how to understand and relate to people, which is a major objective of psychotherapeutic training.[21]

Magary and Meacham estimated that between 1950 and 1960 the number of school psychologists in America increased five-fold, from 520 to 2,724.[22] However, Tindell judged that some eight to ten times as many school psychologists as there are now are needed if the recommended ratio of one full-time psychologist to 5,000 students is to be met.[23]

---

[18] *Ibid.,* p. 6.

[19] Norma E. Cutts (ed.), *School Psychologists at Mid-Century.* Washington: American Psychological Association, 1955.

[20] *Ibid.,* p. 48.

[21] William G. Herron, "Training School Psychologists to Do Psychotherapy," in Fred D. Holt and Richard H. Kicklighter (eds.) *Psychological Services in the Schools.* Dubuque, Iowa: Wm. C. Brown Company, Publishers, 1971, p. 48.

[22] J. F. Magary and M. L. Meacham, "The Growth of School Psychology in the Last Decade," *Journal of School Psychology,* Vol. 1 (No. 1), 1963, pp. 5–13.

[23] R. H. Tindell, "Trends in the Development of Psychological Services in the Schools," *Journal of School Psychology,* Vol. 3 (No. 1), 1964, pp. 1–12.

The School Psychiatrist

As limited as psychological services are in schools, psychiatric services are even more limited. The school psychiatrist's major responsibility is to consult with counselors and teachers who are helping pupils with serious maladjustment problems. He also has responsibilities for helping pupils with problems such as underachievement, reading difficulties of the gifted, poor attention, and pupil apathy. There should be greater emphasis placed on prevention than on treatment. To be most effective in preventing serious disorders, the entire staff must be made aware of how they can consistently promote better mental health. The school psychiatrist may also be used to coordinate the mental hygiene activities of the school. Through case conferences and staff meetings conducted in a seminarlike manner, he can help all members of the school staff develop a better understanding of how to improve mental health.

The services of a school psychiatrist are usually limited today to larger school systems, because psychiatrists usually practice in areas with a large concentration of population. However, referral to a psychiatrist may be arranged in many smaller communities. The major function of the psychiatrist is that of individual assistance to the individual with severe problems. Usually schools do not refer for psychiatric treatment without the consent of the parents.

RESPONSIBILITIES OF THE ADMINISTRATIVE STAFF

Basic to the development of an effective guidance program is administrative leadership provided by the board of education, the superintendent, and principals. In some schools, there is jockeying of leadership between the superintendent and the principal. Superintendents should be alert to the possibilities that principals do not hamper the development of the guidance program under the guise of building automony. It must be reiterated that careful job analyses will assist the principal to know his responsibilities in guidance. Because the rapid expansion of guidance services has come about in the last few years, many principals have not received adequate information about their guidance responsibilities. Often overlooked is the board of education's responsibilities for leadership in guidance program development.

Dean of Students

Deans in most schools serve in capacities similar to assistant principals or vice-principals. Because of that fact, the trend, for a long period of time, has been away from appointing deans of boys or deans of girls. However, some schools still adhere to the traditional titles, particularly that of dean of girls.

Most deans are charged with such responsibilities as attendance recording, reviewing students' reasons for being absent or tardy from school, administering discipline, administering the extracurricular activities, scheduling classes, etc. Their duties vary considerably from school to school, and are a function of the decisions that principals make as to the way they want assistance in supervising their schools.

Principals and Superintendents

Some guidance responsibilities principals and superintendents carry out vary with the size of the administrative unit. If the school is large enough to employ a director of guidance, such a person is expected to provide the technical leadership for the guidance program. However, in all schools, principals and superintendents are counted on to carry out the executive leadership inherent within their positions. This means that they believe in, and their actions exemplify, the guidance point of view. They will seek to activate such a philosophy among staff members. The support of the principal and superintendent will do much to strengthen the guidance program.

The principal and superintendent set the pace for guidance services. They can encourage effective and appropriate activities for the guidance staff. They must see that the counselor's time is not devoted to substitute teaching, taking attendance, punishing students, and the like.

Through their executive leadership, the principal and superintendent provide the means for informing the community of the guidance program. They are the ones with whom parents come in contact, and their communications about guidance establish impressions and attitudes that will remain with parents.

A superintendent, in order to exercise leadership in the area of guidance, must have some understanding of the basic philosophy underlying the guidance program, and some familiarity with the purposes of its basic services or components. Most guidance authorities would expect superintendents to

1. Employ a director of guidance for the system, and employ counselors who have been professionally prepared

2. Insist that the guidance staff formulate a clear statement of program objectives

3. Support systematic evaluations of the guidance program

4. Provide adequate guidance budgets and physical facilities

5. Establish continuing public relation activities that keep the board of education and the community informed concerning the guidance program

6. Develop inservice training programs that focus upon guidance practices, and activities that reach all levels of the school system

Most of all, school superintendents are expected to exercise leadership by being able to make soundly based decisions and by communicating effectively with all staff members. Occasionally, even guidance directors or counselors have been known to propose activities or programs that cannot be supported when balanced against certain needs or conditions of the school system.

In most school districts, the principal is the chief executive officer of the building. He influences considerably what occurs within the building. Many principals are viewed, by others and by themselves, as being responsible and accountable for all that takes place in their schools. Currently, many educators question whether or not principals should be autonomous—unconcerned with system-wide policies or with specialists whose expertise in certain areas would do much to improve educational practices. However, it is true that today's principalship can no longer be conducted as the headmastership of old. The principal should focus his leadership upon stimulating every professional in his school to optimum performance. He should marshall all available resources, both human and material, to accomplish the school's objectives. Dean conceptualized the principal's office as a service center for the school. He considered the ten most important services of this office to be:

1. A communication center for the school

2. A clearing house for the transaction of school business

3. A counseling center for teachers and students

4. A counseling center for school patrons

5. A research division of the school, to be used for the collection, analysis, and evaluation of information regarding activities and results of the school program.

6. A repository of school records

7. The planning center for solving school problems and initiating school improvements

8. A resource center for encouraging creative work

9. A coordinating agency cultivating wholesome school and community relations

10. The coordinating center of the school enterprise.[24]

The principal, in fulfilling his leadership role in guidance, is expected to:

1. Secure counselors who are professionally prepared for their positions and numerically adequate for the student body

2. Insist that written statements of counselor work activities be defined and be congruent with professional role statements

3. Delegate responsibility for actual supervision and administration of the program to well prepared specialists

4. Provide adequate facilities, materials and equipment

5. Encourage continuing and systematic evaluation of guidance

6. Provide for interpretation of guidance services and practices to the school staff and the public

7. Organize a school guidance council or committee, and encourage its development as an advisory or policy recommending body

8. Promote in-service education programs in guidance for the staff.

The Board of Education

The board of education, which represents the patrons of each school district, is responsible for broad policy development of the general planning, organizing, and leadership of the educational program in the community. Ryan and Zeran cite the following 10 responsibilities of school board members in the area of guidance:

1. Understand the meaning of these terms (as used in describing the guidance services): the analysis of the individual, information services, counseling, placement, and follow-up of school-leavers.

2. Recognize the need for developing a program offering these five guidance services to all boys and girls at all grade levels, and see that it is organized and operational.

3. Select the superintendent and other school administrators with regard to their attitude toward, and philosophy of, a program of guidance services.

---

[24]Stuart E. Dean, *Elementary School Administration and Organization.* Washington; D.C.: U.S. Office of Education, Bulletin No. 11, 1960, p. 376.

4. Study what is being done in the elementary and secondary schools in the area of guidance services.

5. Provide funds for facilities, supplies, materials, and for employing specialized staff and clerical assistance at all grade levels.

6. When employing replacements, appoint those teachers who are guidance-minded and who can supplement the skills and abilities of the present staff.

7. Ascertain that adequate time is provided for the specialized personnel and staff members to carry out guidance functions.

8. Inquire into the hierarchical and horizontal staff relationships of the organization which has been set up to carry out the guidance duties.

9. Encourage the in-service preparation of the staff at all grade levels in the development of their guidance skills.

10. Participate in these in-service programs in order to obtain basic understanding of testing, informational services, and counseling.[25]

In addition to these responsibilities, the school board member must become familiar with federal legislation which provides funds for school guidance, counseling, and testing and the training of school counselors. Another responsibility is that of studying the local situation. If written policies for guidance are not in existence, these should be established or if existing, they may be in need of revision.

PROFESSIONAL EDUCATION OF GUIDANCE PERSONNEL

The professional education recommended for guidance personnel involves a graduate program which provides didactic study and supervised experiences. The National Defense Education Act of 1958, as well as the Education Professions Development Act, and the Elementary and Secondary Education Act of 1965, and subsequent amendments support guidance and counseling in the secondary school. These federal acts constitute the greatest single impetus ever given to secondary school counseling and guidance. They served as the stimulus (1) to improve the development of elementary and secondary school guidance programs in the states and (2) to initiate, underwrite, and stimulate the development of university programs

---

[25]T. Antoinette Ryan and Franklin R. Zeran, *Organization and Administration of Guidance Services.* Danville, Illinois: The Interstate Printers and Publishers, Inc., 1972, pp. 280–282. Used with permission.

for the preparation of school counselors. The funds from these acts provided much needed monies for university personnel, clerical help, and training materials. Equally important, the program encouraged high caliber, professional leadership at all levels on the part of those who participated in bringing guidance into a functioning reality.

State Requirements

The minimum training requirements for guidance personnel are established by state departments of education. The state departments have enacted a variety of patterns, although a common core of content is reflected throughout. The status of certification requirements for school counselor and school psychologist is shown in Table 6–1.

Currently many state departments are in the process of changing their requirements for certificating school counselors and directors of guidance. In 1971, Thorsen[26] identified, state by state, some of the changes that were being initiated. Only five states were not engaged in modifying their requirements for certificating counselors. The nature of the changes in the other states included (1) increasing the required number of semester hours of graduate course work in guidance, (2) reducing the required number of years teaching experience, or providing substitutes for it, such as internship programs, (3) distinguishing the requirements for certification as an elementary school counselor from those needed by a secondary school counselor, and (4) formulating performance-based criteria. Thorsen also pointed out that twenty-three states and territories offer one level of counselor certification, nineteen offer two levels, and nine offer three levels. Advancement from level to level is most often based upon completion of successful experience and additional graduate course work. Moreover, once advanced level certification is reached, it is usually valid for as long as the individual is actively employed.

At the time Thorsen made his report, fourteen states required special certification for elementary school counselors. Although the trend is currently away from requiring teaching experience as a prerequisite for counselor certification, twenty-one states still required from one to three years of teaching experience in 1971. The trend is also away from requiring work experience other than teaching. In 1971, only thirteen states required such experience, and three of the thirteen offered alternatives.

Thorsen's report states that the degree and course requirements for counselors vary from state to state. Twenty-eight states require a master's degree

---

[26]Jack Thorsen, "Counselor Certification 1971," mimeographed (Washington, D.C.: American Personnel and Guidance Association, June, 1971).

*Hubert W. Houghton, *Certification Requirements for School Pupil Personnel Workers.* Washington, D.C.: Counselor Preparation Section, Office of Education, U.S. Department of Health, Education and Welfare; 1967.

Table 6-1. *Status of Certification Requirements for Guidance Workers, by State**

State	School Counselor		School Psychologist	
	Mandatory	None	Mandatory	None
1	2	3	4	5
Alabama	X			X
Alaska	X			X
Arizona	X		X	
Arkansas	X			X
California	X		X	
Colorado	X		X	
Connecticut	X		X	
Delaware	X		X	
Florida	X		X	
Georgia	X			X
Hawaii	X		X	
Idaho	X		X	
Illinois	X			X
Indiana	X		X	
Iowa	X		X	
Kansas	X		X	
Kentucky	X			X
Louisiana	X			X
Maine	X		X	
Maryland	X		X	
Massachusetts	X		X	
Michigan		X	X	
Minnesota	X		X	
Mississippi	X			X
Missouri	X		X	
Montana	X			X
Nebraska	X			X
Nevada	X			X
New Hampshire	X		X	X
New Jersey	X		X	
New Mexico	X			X
New York	X		X	
North Carolina	X		X	
North Dakota	X			X
Ohio	X		X	
Oklahoma	X		X	
Oregon	X		X	
Pennsylvania	X		X	
Rhode Island	X		X	
South Carolina	X		X	
South Dakota	X		X	
Tennessee	X			
Texas	X			X
Utah	X		X	
Vermont	X			X
Virginia	X			X
Washington		X	X	
West Virginia	X			X
Wisconsin	X		X	
Wyoming	X		X	
	48	2	32	18

163

or its equivalent for entry level certification as a school counselor. Moreover, the number of semester hours in required graduate guidance courses ranges from a low of twelve in Massachusetts to thirty-six in South Carolina (for those who did not hold a state teaching certificate). Among those courses which states listed as required for counselor certification, the following titles were most commonly specified: study and appraisal of the individual; counseling techniques; organization and administration of guidance services; educational and occupational information; principles and practices of guidance; tests and measurements; supervised practicum. Thorsen also pointed out that the psychology courses required by many states included personality theory, learning, and human growth and development. All but seven states required some type of supervised counseling practica or internship.

In 1971, five states were involved in developing performance criteria for certification. However, only the State of Washington had actually formulated and implemented a competency based model for counselor certification. Brammer and Springer,[27] describing the Washington plan, state that no course, credit or degree requirement is set forth in the plan. Both preparation and service agencies were encouraged to address themselves to the ultimate criterion of effectiveness, that is, what happens to children, parents, and teachers served by counselors. The Washington plan assumes that professional development is life-long, and that all counselors (no grandfather clause) must prove that they meet the observable criteria. A training consortium was established consisting of employing school districts, colleges and universities, and professional associations, in which all three of these groups participated in developing training programs and in recommending candidates for certification to the State Board of Education.

Four counselor levels of preparation are available in the Washington plan. The first is a *preparatory* or an intern level. The second is an *initial* level, (after basic skills are learned, but before nonsupervised practice begins). The third level is a *continuing* stage (after demonstrating counseling competence), and at the fourth level, the counselor serves as a *consultant,* that is, as a field-centered counselor-educator who serves as a training consultant in his school. Undoubtedly, performance-based counselor certification is the wave of the future.

Graduate Preparation of the School Counselor

The school counselor of the last quarter of the twentieth century must be a liberally educated person with competencies in his area of work; these

---

[27]Lawrence M. Brammer and Harry C. Springer, "A Radical Change in Counselor Education and Certification," *Personnel and Guidance Journal,* Vol. 49 (June, 1971), pp. 803–808.

competencies originate from a graduate program of preparation in counselor education. The counselor needs to have a basic understanding of the culture. This is obtained, in part, through interdisciplinary study.

The counselor must have a firm foundation in education both as a discipline of study and as society's formal means for inducting children and youth into society. Whether the counselor should have had teaching experience is a moot question, but almost all who debate this point want him to demonstrate a commitment to education. He must have an interest in working with pupils of the age level at which he counsels. He must be an active participant in the life of the school staff and student body.

The content of one-year graduate programs preparing school counselors usually includes the following areas:

1. Introduction to guidance

2. Testing and other forms of individual appraisal

3. Statistics

4. Adolescent development and/or child psychology

5. Educational-vocational theory and information

6. Organization and administration of guidance

7. Counseling theory and techniques

8. Group processes

9. Supervised counseling practica

10. Supervised internship.

Authority for training programs most frequently resides in university departments of education. Courses from other departments, for example, sociology and psychology, will be an inherent part of a counselor education program which strives to provide an interdisciplinary base in its preparation of elementary and secondary school counselors. These courses will, then, be taught by staff members from those departments.

Various professional groups have identified the characteristics of an adequate counselor education program. Standards for preparing *secondary school counselors* have been formulated, tried out, and adopted by the American Personnel and Guidance Association.[28] Committees of this Association have prepared statements which describe the role and preparation

[28]Committee on Professional Preparation and Standards, "Standards for the Preparation of Secondary School Counselors 1967," *Personnel and Guidance Journal,* Vol. 46 (September, 1967), pp. 97–160.

standards applicable to elementary school counselors and also for college and/or university counselors.[29]

The year 1964 marks the date when the Association for Counselor Education and Supervision (ACES) issued the first statement of standards for preparing secondary school counselors. Prior to that date, five years of study had been invested in preparing and drafting the initial statement of standards by hundreds of counselor educators, city and state directors of guidance and local school counselors. The three-year period, 1964–1967, was used to try out the Standards in some 100 counselor training institutions and to obtain reactions from more than 1,000 Association members. A mail poll was taken of the more than 2,000 ACES members and the 1967 edition of the Standards was endorsed almost unanimously.

The committee responsible for the Standards has indicated that the Standards are intended to be used in the following ways:

1. For institutional self-study by counselor education staffs and their school colleagues.

2. For the evaluation of counselor education programs by state departments of education which determine what programs will be recognized as adequate to prepare candidates for certification.

3. For the evaluation of professional counselor education by appropriate accrediting bodies.

4. For use by agencies and persons conducting research in the field of counselor education.[30]

Four major sections divide the content of the Standards. The first deals with philosophy and objectives, the second with curriculum, the third with selection, retention, endorsement, and placement and the fourth with administrative relations and institutional resources for supporting the counselor education program. Essentially, the Standards (1) identify counselor education as graduate education, (2) call for two years of study, and (3) recommend full-time study. The program of study encourages counselors to develop understanding and competencies in the foundations and dynamics of human behavior, the educational enterprise, and professional studies in school counseling and related guidance activities. Ten areas are identified in the "professional studies":

---

[29]Lee Isaacson (Chairman), "Guidelines for Graduate Programs in the Preparation of Student Personnel Workers in Higher Education," *Personnel and Guidance Journal,* Vol. 47 (January, 1969) pp. 493–498.

[30]George E. Hill (Chairman), "Standards for the Preparation of Secondary School Counselors—1967," *Personnel and Guidance Journal,* Vol. 46 (September, 1967), p. 96.

1. Philosophy and principles underlying guidance and other pupil personnel services.

2. The nature and range of human characteristics and methods of measuring them in individual appraisal.

3. Vocational development theory.

4. Educational and occupational information, its nature and uses.

5. Counseling theory and practice.

6. Statistics and research methodology, independent research and familiarization with data processing and programming techniques.

7. Group procedures in counseling and guidance.

8. Professional relationships and ethics in keeping with the APGA Ethical Standards.

9. Administration and coordination of guidance and pupil personnel services.

10. Supervised experiences.[31]

The supervised experiences set out by the Standards include laboratory experiences such as role playing, listening to tapes, testing, and examining case materials; counseling practica with individual and small groups of at least 60 hours' contact during the two years; and an internship or supervised experience in a school setting.

Clearly, adoption of the Standards was of major import for the profession. Stripling points out that ". . . we have assumed this responsibility for the protection of society against malpractices of inadequately prepared counselors, we have indeed taken upon our shoulders a worthy responsibility which calls for dedication on the part of each member of our association."[32]

PROFESSIONAL ORGANIZATIONS FOR SCHOOL COUNSELORS

Guidance personnel will desire to affiliate with other members of their profession. Through their membership they will contribute to their own professional growth and to that of their colleagues. One of the major na-

---

[31] *Ibid.,* pp. 99–100

[32] Robert O. Stripling, "The Role of Professional Associations in Counselor Education," *Counselor Education and Supervision,* Vol. 6 (Spring, 1967), p. 256.

tional organizations for guidance personnel is the American Personnel and Guidance Association. Its membership in 1973 numbered more than 31,000. The APGA publishes the *Personnel and Guidance Journal* ten times a year and maintains a headquarters office under the administration of an executive director at its "home," 1607 New Hampshire Avenue, N.W., Washington, D.C. Besides membership in the overall organization, eleven special interest divisions are available to those who meet the qualifications established by the divisions. The eleven divisions include the American College Personnel Association, Association for Counselor Education and Supervision, National Vocational Guidance Association, Student Personnel Association for Teacher Education, American School Counselor Association, American Rehabilitation Counseling Association, Association for Measurement and Evaluation of Guidance, the National Employment Counselors Association, and the Association of Non-White Concerns, the National Catholic Guidance Conference, and the Association of Group Work Specialists. Most of the divisions also publish journals and other materials of interest to its membership. The APGA also maintains branches at the state level, and chapters at the community level. In addition to the APGA, for those who qualify, membership in Division 17, Counseling Psychology, of the American Psychological Association, will aid in the professional growth of school counselors.

Many state teachers' associations have divisions or special interest areas for school counselors and other guidance personnel. Such divisions or groups often conduct conferences and carry on a publication program that enables the school counselor to communicate with others in his profession.

The professional school counselor will want to and will participate in the various professional associations and organizations available for him at the local, state, and national levels.

SUMMARY

Job descriptions of guidance personnel should be stated in written form. Appropriate assignment of personnel will facilitate the functioning of the guidance activities of the staff. The child welfare officer, the school attendance officer, the visiting teacher, the social worker, the school librarian, the school nurse, the school physician, the school psychometrist, the school psychologist, and the school psychiatrist, as well as the immediate guidance personnel and the administrative staff, all have guidance functions. Explicit duties in any one school or school system will necessarily be tailored to local needs. However, local needs should not be the rationale for distorting the professional dimensions of the guidance functions. Much needs to be done in the clarification of many roles which are changing in a dynamic twentieth-century educational system.

Training and professional preparation of guidance personnel are concerns for all workers in education. State departments of education establish the minimum course work and other professional experiences for guidance personnel. Professional organizations, such as the APGA, serve guidance personnel by providing an avenue for further professional growth and for communicating with persons who have similar interests, problems and commitments.

ANNOTATED BIBLIOGRAPHY

Calia, Vincent F., and Bartholomew D. Wall, *Pupil Personnel Administration.* Springfield, Illinois: Charles C. Thomas, Publisher, 1968.
  This book tends to deal with conceptual ideas in promoting guidance and other pupil personnel functions.

Holt, Fred D. and Richard H. Kicklighter (eds.), *Psychological Services in the Schools.* Dubuque, Iowa: William C. Brown Company Publishers, 1971, 312 pp.
  Section II presents the role and function of the school psychometrist and psychologist. The selected articles, by prominent writers, present different roles, professional relationships, problems, and issues.

Ryan, T. Antoinette and Franklin R. Zeran, *Organization and Administration of Guidance Services.* Danville, Illinois: The Interstate Printers and Publishers, Inc., 1972, 465 pp.
  Chapter 9 discusses the roles and responsibilities of guidance and related personnel.

The Counseling Service

Counseling is both a process and a relationship designed to explore the student's feelings, thoughts, and actions, and to learn to meet the challenge in his environment. In the elementary school, counseling is primarily preventive and developmental, secondarily remedial.[1]

"To us, therapy is a matter of assisting people to change the effects of developmental hurts or failures and to expand their awareness of choices and alternatives . . . our approach in working with people emphasizes potential rather than deficit . . ."[2]

Chapter 7

The opening quotations of this chapter refer to the return of developmental guidance as a key thrust in the guidance program. This interest in developmental guidance comes under the rubric "Psychological Education." Therefore, authority for implementing the counseling function in the school guidance program would be functionally located. This questions the notion of the absolute autonomy of the principal in his school—a notion which is of blurring validity in contemporary education. However, the key is not to separate or isolate any guidance functions; rather, the decisional processes should be based on competence of the guidance staff in cooperation with the principal. Maximum use should be made of the guidance staff scholar-

---

[1]Richard C. Nelson, *Guidance and Counseling in the Elementary School.* New York: Holt, Rinehart and Winston, Inc., 1972, p. 134.
[2]Bill L. Kell and Josephine Morse Burrow, *Developmental Counseling and Therapy.* Boston: Houghton Mifflin Company, 1970, p. 5.

ship, expertise in practice, and organizational knowledge relating to guidance functions. This chapter deals primarily with the counseling function.

GENERAL RATIONALE FOR COUNSELING

What then is the purpose of counseling? Perhaps it is to bring each youth to a level of realization and personal involvement that he has never before had—a level at which he can experience compassion without embarrassment, and love without the need for reciprocity; a level at which he lives with totality and completeness because he has learned to capture the essence of each moment and because he has learned to concern himself not with what he does not have, but rather to appreciate, within that fleeting moment of time in life which is truly his, all those experiences that touch his life. It is in this way that he grows, develops, and transcends those obstacles he finds in his path to maturity. It is in this way that he learns to reach out to touch others with kindness.[3]

Osipow and Walsh[4] emphasize a behavioral and developmental approach. They view counseling as a process to enhance the learning function by focusing on the relationship between the individual's overt responses and his environment. They feel that the goal of the counseling function is to help the individual develop his capacities for problem-solving and coping.

Other definitions of counseling may be found under specific headings of client-centered therapy, developmental counseling, existential counseling, behavioral counseling, traing-factor counseling, and rational-emotive counseling.[5]

QUESTIONS ABOUT COUNSELING

The counseling function focuses on individual and social aspects of behavior.[6] The goal of the counseling function is the changing of behavior, personality, or developmental functioning. Theories, approaches, or emphases of behavior, overlap of behaviors, force of influences on behavior, and prognosis for change of behavior vary. However, all seem to indicate

---

[3]Kenneth U. Gutsch and Herman J. Peters, *Counseling with Youth: In Search for Identity.* Columbus, Ohio: Charles E. Merrill Publishing Company, 1973, p. 122.

[4]Samuel H. Osipow and W. Bruce Walsh. *Strategies in Counseling For Behavior Change.* New York: Appleton-Century-Crofts, 1970, pp. 10–13.

[5]Louis M. Cunningham and Herman J. Peters, *Counseling Theories.* Columbus, Ohio: Charles E. Merrill Publishing Co., 1973, pp. 23–132.

[6]C. H. Patterson, *Theories of Counseling and Psychotherapy.* New York: Harper & Row, 1973, pp. xii–xxii.

organizational considerations of the counseling function which include attitudes, feelings, perceptions, values, and goals. Perhaps, stated simply, the
challenge is how one changes one or several facets of behavior.

One of the problems which counselors face is that they work under others
whose duties are neither technical nor of a particular professional bent but
who determine the limits of the program, the budget, and the interpretation
and defense of the program. Another problem is that the literature of
guidance does not reflect well enough the counselor's responsibility and
accountability to the institution or agency employing him. The counselor's
expectations for primacy range from relative independence of functioning
to firm ideas of supervision. Still another question concerns the confusion
surrounding the purpose of guidance, particularly in the area of counseling,
despite its public policy views of many years. The pressures and personality
needs of many guidance administrators may not be fully realized by counselors. The visible turbulence of administration may not be consistent with
the turbulence of counseling.[7]

Solutions to these problems reside first in intelligent cooperative compromise. This is difficult when the counselor views the administrator's
skepticism and impatience, and counters with similar attitudes. Inter-
communication between and among staff is needed for understanding how
each person perceives his job. Each must substitute his jargon with clear
explanation. Environment and personality have impact on everyone who is
involved with the system. Climate conditions of organizational development need to be analyzed for needed changes.

Central Purposes

The central purposes of counseling are to help the individual to:

1. Examine his personalized style of living commensurate with his
   developmental level

2. Analyze self-enhancing and self-defeating behavior

3. Study his integrity of living versus his compartmentalization of
   living

4. Face whether his values are "hand-me-downs" or whether they
   truly befit how he wishes to behave and become

5. Ascertain the courage he needs to change

---

[7]Joseph Samler, "The Counseling Service in the Administrative Setting: Problems and
Possible Solutions," in Vincent F. Calia and Bartholomew D. Wall (eds.) *Pupil Personnel
Administration.* Springfield, Illinois: Charles C. Thomas Publisher, 1968, pp. 133–138.

6. Increase his awareness and authenticity

7. Think of the impact of his awareness and authenticity on his educational and career development

8. Consider the forces involved in risk-taking for the fullness of development

9. Orient himself to a discipline of maximum development in terms of all the above purposes

The importance of the counseling function is emphasized by Kowitz and others in their article which analyzes recent changes in guidance and counseling.[8] These shifts suggest that in the future, guidance and counseling will be moving toward greater attention to the individual, with more concern for his dynamics than for his classification.

Standards

Professional and paraprofessional training standards and accreditation for counselor preparation have been formulated. However, they continue to be in the embryonic stages. Public policy of approach, as mentioned earlier, continues to look askance at true professional counselors in the schools, and public opinion is not much better toward agencies.

The preparation of counselors has largely been a bootstrap-lifting operation. Conflicts arise over the impact of the American Personnel and Guidance Association, American Psychological Association, and accreditation by the National Council for Accreditation of Teacher Education (NCATE) —largely on the basis that it is teacher-education-oriented rather than counselor-education-oriented. To inform himself about the continuing struggle for professionalism in counseling, the student should read:

American Personnel and Guidance Association, *ACES Manual for Self Study by a Counselor Education Staff.* Based on the 1967 edition of "Standards for the Preparation of Secondary School Counselors." Washington, D.C.

American Personnel and Guidance Association, *Standards for the Preparation of Elementary School Counselors.* Washington, D.C., 1967.

---

[8] Gerald T. Kowitz, Ronald R. Reeves, Gladys M. Dronberger, Neil E. Bishop, and Nelson T. Abbott, "Values in Guidance: Can ERIC Help?" *Measurement and Evaluation in Guidance,* Vol. 6, No. 1 (April, 1973), pp. 47–53.

American Psychological Association, "Accreditation: A Status Report," *American Psychologist,* Vol. 25, pp. 581–584, 1970.

American Psychological Association Committee on Counselor Training, Division of Counseling and Guidance, "The Practicum Training of Counseling Psychologists," *American Psychologist,* Vol. 7, pp. 182–188, 1952.

American Psychological Association Committee on Subdoctoral Education of the Education and Training Board: The Training of Technical Workers in Psychology at the Subdoctoral Level, *American Psychologist,* Vol. 10, pp. 541–545, 1955.

American Rehabilitation Counseling Association, "The Professional Preparation of Rehabilitation Counselors: A Statement of Policy," *Rehabilitation Counseling Bulletin,* Vol. 12, pp. 29–35, 1968.

Dickey, F. G., "What is Accrediting and Why Is It Important for Professional Organizations?" *Counselor Education and Supervision,* Vol. 7, pp. 194–199, 1968.

Goodstein, L. D., and Ross, S. "Accreditation of Graduate Programs in Psychology: An Analysis," *American Psychologist,* Vol. 21, pp. 218–223, 1966.

Guidelines for Graduate Programs in Preparation of Student Personnel Workers in Higher Education," *Personnel and Guidance Journal,* Vol. 47, pp. 493–498, 1969.

Hill, G. E., "Self-Study and Self-Evaluation of Counselor Education Programs," *Counselor Education and Supervision,* Vol. 5, pp. 68–72, 1966.

Hoch, E. L., Ross, A. O., and Winder, C. L., "Conference on the Professional Preparation of Clinical Psychologists: A Summary," *American Psychologist,* Vol. 21, pp. 42–51, 1966.

Kennedy, C. E., Danskin, D. G., Edelman, S. K., and Steffen, J. D., "The Practicum in Study of Student Development: Its Relation to Counselor Preparation," *Counselor Education and Supervision.* Vol. 9, pp. 272–276, 1970.

Miller, C. H., "Quality in Counselor Education," *Counselor Education and Supervision,* Vol. 1, pp. 124–130, 1962.

Van Hoose, W. H., "Conflicts in Counselor Preparation and Professional Practice: An Analysis," *Counselor Education and Supervision,* Vol. 9, pp. 241–247. 1970.

"Task Force on Paraprofessional in the Counseling Center." Proceeds of the Annual Conference of University and College Counseling Center Directors, University of Missouri, November 1971.

Essentials of Counseling

Webster states that the only essential requirement for counseling is humanness. By humanness is meant the capacity for an individual to be open to another human being without judging and without losing his own individuality.[9] The counseling function, then, is viewed as that part of the guidance program that provides an individual or a small group of pupils who seek better understanding of self and/or world and who try out experiences, with the assistance needed to implement this understanding, and with the professional counseling necessary to help achieve such understanding. The goal of developing and managing counseling functions is to make this service maximally accessible, since any person may be faced not only with problem-solving situations but also with developmental concerns which can best be resolved through the counseling service. Tyler states that an individual becomes a client because "he must deal with a situation, or situations, for which there is some doubt about the appropriateness of his responses."[10]

The counseling function has been described by many as "the heart of the guidance function." This is true because the counseling service is that part of the guidance function which gives true meaning to the phrase, "guidance is a personalized service." Underscored is the notion of personalized service, not merely individually focused service. It is the service through which all other guidance activities and services are brought together for the benefit of the individual student. Counseling brings into action concern for the individual and his singular uniqueness. Thus, the uniqueness of the guidance function is embodied in the counseling service. This lies in (1) the "content of experience" or the nature of the pupil's need for a counseling relationship, and (2) the "focus of attention" or point of primary purpose of the counselor.

The guidance administrator's work in the counseling function does not end after a school counselor has been employed. Problems arise in the operation of the counseling function just as they do in the instructional program. These problems require the attention and cooperation of the school counselor, staff, and administrators.

---

[9]Steven D. Webster, "Humanness: The One Essential," *The Personnel and Guidance Journal,* Vol. 51, No. 6 (February, 1973), pp. 378–379.

[10]Leona E. Tyler, *The Work of the Counselor,* (3rd ed.). New York: Appleton Century-Crofts, 1969, p. 16.

Goals for Counseling in Schools

The point of providing counseling services can be seen in the fact that most pupils at some time or another become concerned by uncertainties in their lives, and desire to be optimally functioning in daily living. Modern life has often been characterized as an age of turmoil, conflict, and uncertainty. Also, it is characterized as an age of freedom, excitement, and adventure. It is in the relatively calm, nonthreatening, and mutually participating counseling atmosphere that today's pupil is most likely to face his development courageously, to sort out the ideas and values that are valid for him, and to implement them with consistent responsible actions.

DEVELOPING AND MANAGING THE COUNSELING FUNCTION

The primary goals of the counseling function are:
1. To individualize for each pupil the cumulative effects of individual development, group forces, and mass techniques and media of the school.

2. To provide professionally prepared persons equipped to help individual pupils understand their personal characteristics, realize their potentialities, attain an appropriate concept of self, and experience behaviors resulting from the cognitive analysis in counseling.

3. To facilitate changes in individual pupils to enable them to make wise future decisions. To extricate themselves from immediate difficulties; their problems can be used to further self-knowledge and acceptance, as well as to acquire increased ability for self-direction.

4. To free the capacities of pupils to learn. Through counseling contact, the individual pupil will be able to strengthen his ego function and self-concept, and to plan activities to implement them.

5. To help the individual pupil find the opportunities that are right for him, and use his experiences to cope with current realities.

6. To realize that the residency of responsibility of behavior is in him.

7. To examine his options in terms of other people, and his possible contribution to them through his own self-fulfillment.

THE JOB OF THE SCHOOL COUNSELOR

The duties of the professional school counselor have already been briefly outlined in Chapter 6. There is considerable disagreement concerning the counselor's job, both in theory and in practice. The statements of the professional organization do not necessarily constitute unanimous endorsement. At best, they are so generalized to obtain approval, and they lack specification.

The following paragraphs delineate the job of the counselor, based on the role usually practiced by counselors employed in elementary, junior high, and secondary schools that also have directors of guidance and other pupil personnel workers.

The counselor's primary duty is to be responsible for counseling individual pupils assigned to him. He helps these pupils evaluate their experiences and their behavior in relation to these experiences. He will interpret standardized tests and inventories to pupils and utilize test results in counseling sessions. He will be familiar with tests of achievement, intelligence, aptitude, and interest, and with personality inventories to the extent that he can relate their results to others. He is concerned with the normal growth needs of pupils—more with personality development than with problem crises. Much of his work with pupils will be to provide educational and vocational guidance, but some of his contacts may involve "minimum change" therapy. The extent that he will provide therapy will be related to his preparation, experience, and skill. He should recognize the extent of his preparation, and should refer to other specialists those pupils whose problems go beyond his skills. He may use particular approaches for pupils emphasizing particular kinds of life style.

The school counselor's duties include more than counseling. The school counselor blends counseling with participation in interactive functions, such as:

1. *He aids teachers in understanding pupils.* He does this by knowing pupils and teachers and by being able to suggest means of meeting problems in classrooms. He provides data that will enable teachers to better understand their pupils. He understands the functions of classroom teachers. He is a behavioral specialist.

2. *He consults with parents.* His contacts with parents involve such work as interpreting test scores of their children, supplying them with information about college requirements and scholarships, interpreting behavior of their children, counseling them about their children, and interpreting the guidance function of the

school. He provides an important liaison between the school and the home. He interprets positive behavior as well as negative behavior exhibited by pupils.

3. *He selects and administers tests and inventories to pupils, and reports their results.* He is expected to be familiar with an extensive variety of standardized tests and inventories for the school's uniform testing program. He may either administer these himself, or he may supervise teachers or others in their administration. He is expected to report these test results intelligently and quickly to teachers, supervisors, and administrators. As testing becomes more computerized, his chief job should be the use of tests rather than the clerkship of testing.

4. *He collects and uses pupil records.* He knows the pupil records of his school and is instrumental in building and maintaining cumulative and other personnel records that are useful to teachers and administrators, as well as to counselors. Actual clerical work should be done by clerks.

5. *He conducts group guidance activities.* He may participate in orientation programs, occupation classes, or units within a class. Typically, he sponsors career days, college nights, and other guidance-related activities. He often works with a small group of students who have a common problem (for example, those who are underachieving in school). He should not be overwhelmed with group activities to the point that he neglects the counseling function.

6. *He has a working relationship with local business and industrial personnel.* He maintains personal contacts with many personnel officers and employers so that he will know employment possibilities for his students and will be in a better position to inform and counsel students in the area of local vocational offerings.

7. *He works with personnel in other school areas.* He will bring his knowledge, skills, and attitudes to bear on such matters as curriculum planning, extracurricular activities, school reporting to parents, and special provisions for handicapped pupils. He is concerned about all school activities that have a bearing on pupil guidance.

8. *He conducts research and evaluation studies.* He engages in research and evaluation studies to ascertain the effectiveness of his program. He uses the findings of such studies to revise his

procedures, to plan his activities and methods, and to establish policies. He conducts follow-up studies of graduates and dropouts. He may conduct community and school surveys.

9. *He participates in school activities.* He participates in a fair share of extracurricular activities. He views his participation in such activities as a means of learning more about pupils and teachers. Also, he does this as any other staff member participates in general school activities.

As pointed out in Chapter 6, the development and management of an effective guidance program will be facilitated through written job descriptions of each staff member's guidance responsibilities. Because there is frequently confusion regarding the counselor's job, it is recommended that a school develop a written statement of the counselor's role and duties. At this time especially, such a statement would be a useful document for the counselor, administrator, and other staff members. The process of attaining agreement concerning the counselor's role at the start of the counseling service would also encourage cooperation, and would facilitate understanding between the administrator or supervisor and the counselor. An agreement reached in the early stages of planning would have the additional advantage of minimizing difficulties that often arise later because the counselor does not perceive his role and actions as the school administrator does; of course, this statement should be reviewed periodically.

The Stanford program[11] emphasizes the experiences that are currently being used to prepare counselors at Stanford to clarify role expectancies. The key differences between the usual program and the Stanford program is the specificity of competencies based on the behavioral counseling approach. Trainees must demonstrate competence in eight facets of the program: (1) general counseling and behavioral change methodology, (2) practicum, (3) foundations, (4) group counseling, (5) decision-making, (6) research, (7) preventive systems, and (8) dealing with minority clients. Organizing training in counseling is illustrated in Figure 7–1.

Staffing the Counseling Functions

The staffing of the counseling function poses many questions for the school administrator and the director of guidance. What characteristics should we seek in counselors for our school? What preparation should

[11]C. G. Hendricks, Jeffrey G. Ferguson, and Carl E. Thoresen, "Toward Counseling Competence: The Stanford Program," *The Personnel and Guidance Journal,* Vol. 5, No. 6, (February, 1973), pp. 418–424.

Steps in Counseling

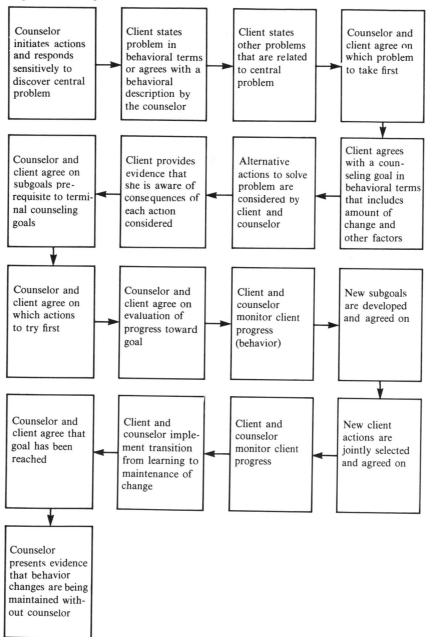

Figure 7–1.   *Stanford University Competency Model**

From C. G. Hendricks, Jeffrey G. Ferguson, and Carl E. Thoreson, "Toward Counseling Competence: The Stanford Program," *The Personnel and Guidance Journal* Vol. 5, (February 1973), p. 420. Copyright 1973 by the American Personnel and Guidance Association. Used with permission.

counselors possess before we employ them? What is a desirable counselor-pupil ratio? How should we assign pupils to counselors?

In resolving these matters, school officials will want to consider what others have found to be helpful, as well as what their own local conditions, finances, and attitudes warrant. Staffing the counseling function means defining the job of the counselor, assessing the capabilities of persons employed, and assigning them clear-cut responsibilities. Leadership must be provided to the counseling service. Adequate usage of the staff will be contingent on the preparation of the staff members and on the scope of the duties that they can professionally perform; what is basic is the school. Too often, it continues to be a model of the sick pupil rather than of the normal.

CHARACTERISTICS OF COUNSELORS

In selecting counselors, the administrator ordinarily relies on his judgment and on that of other staff members to decide whether or not candidates have the personal characteristics considered desirable for the school. What are some of the traits counselors should desirably possess? This is a question that is coming more and more to the attention of researchers. Those working in guidance agree that the personal characteristics of a counselor are important, but there is little agreement on just what these characteristics are; and as yet, there is no adequate means of assessing them.

Counselor Availability to Pupils

In counseling, one of the key components of a guidance program is the counselor's availability to pupils. In 1973, Matz and his colleagues reported on the current status of counselors.

In 1970, the equivalent of 50,700 full-time counselors were in the public schools. In spring 1970, with about 45,710,000 pupils (grades K–12) in these schools, the overall ratio was about 900 pupils per counselor.[12] The American School Counselor policy recommended one counselor for every 250 pupils. In secondary schools, over 90 percent of which had a counselor available, the aggregate pupil-counselor ratio was estimated at 420 to 1. Counselors on call were not included in the count of counselors in computing the ratios because FTE numbers of on-call counselors were not collected in the survey. If on-call counselors had been included, the ratios would have been somewhat lower. The ratios were calculated using all pupils—those in

[12]A. Stafford Metz, Leslie J. Silverman, Dyckman W. Vermilze, and P. J. McDounough, *Counselors in Public Schools, Spring, 1970.* Washington, D.C.: Department of Health, Education and Welfare publication, (OE)73-11106, National Center for Education Statistics, 1973, pp. 4–6.

schools both with and without counselors on regular assignment. A report on staffing characteristics in public schools is being prepared with pupil-counselor ratios based on pupils in schools with counselors on regular assignment. In the same report, it was stated that the number of pupils per counselor in elementary schools was proportionately much greater—3,500 elementary school pupils per counselor. Many elementary schools had no counselor available. The recommended ratio of 450 pupils per counselor in elementary schools was not met.[14] The situation in elementary schools outside the large cities and their suburbs was particularly deficient—about 6,300 pupils per counselor.

Table 7-1.   *Counselor Availability*[13]

Level and location of school	Pupils (pre-K-12)	Regularly assigned counselors (FTE's)	Pupils (pre-K-12) per regularly assigned counselor (FTE's)*
All schools**	45,710,000	50,700	900
Elementary schools	26,277,000	7,500	3,500
Large cities	5,742,000	2,800	3,020
Metropolitan areas outside large cities	8,928,000	2,800	3,150
All other areas	11,607,000	1,800	6,330
Secondary schools	17,375,000	41,200	420
Large cities	3,774,000	9,700	390
Metropolitan areas outside large cities	6,057,000	14,600	410
All other areas	7,543,000	16,900	450

*Pupil-counselor ratios were computed using unrounded numbers.

**Combined schools, with both elementary and secondary grades, are included in the totals but not in the detail by school level.

Note. Detail may not add to totals because of rounding.

Thorsen[15] reported on Counselor Certification in 1971 for the American Personnel and Guidance Association Board of Directors. Today most professional educators agree on some kind of certification. Certification requirements do, in effect, determine who will be school counselors. Rothney[16] emphasized this point. This contrasts, at least to some degree, with the thinking of Carl Rogers.[17] In 1973, Carl Rogers thought that

[13]A. Stafford Metz et al., Counselors in Schools, p. 5.

[14]The American School Counselor Association, "Report of the Committee on Guidance in the Elementary Schools," 1959, p. 9, (mimeographed).

[15]Jack Thorsen, *Counselor Certification 1971.* Washington, D.C.: American Personnel and Guidance Association, (mimeographed).

[16]John W. M. Rothney, "Who Gets Counseled and for What?" *The Education Digest,* November, 1971, pp. 41–44.

[17]Carl R. Rogers, "Some New Challenges," *American Psychologist,* Vol. 28, No. 5 (May, 1973), p. 382.

moves toward certification and licensure had failed. The greatest effect would be caused by freezing the profession, thus preventing standards from being outdated by the time they are implemented.

CHANGES IN COUNSELOR QUALIFICATION

In 1971, Thorsen[18] listed the significant certification changes which had taken place since 1967. These continue to change but do give a solid base line. His changes are classified by state.

Alabama. Increased Class A requirements from 12 to 18 semester hours in guidance, and changed certificate from nonrenewable to renewable. Class AA changed from life-term to 12 years, renewable.

Alaska. Complete change. Dropped 2 years teaching and one year other work experience. Now has Type A certificate for those who complete approved counseling program. Type C for those with counseling experience other than in school setting. Possible future revisions.

Arizona. Added "successfully completed an approved guidance program in an Arizona institution" as certification alternative.

Arkansas. Added elementary certification.

California. Currently requires (1) masters degree plus 30 semester hours, or (2) masters degree plus 3 years teaching. California recently placed responsibility for certification with the Commission for Teacher Preparation and Licensing, which will draw up new requirements, effective January 1973.

Colorado. Recognizes endorsements for "secondary emphasis" and "elementary emphasis." Dropped 1 year work experience.

Connecticut. New requirements effective September 1972: "Provisional"—one year full-time supervised school internship in place of STC or teaching experience, plus masters with 30 semester hours in guidance. "Standard"—added 15 semester hours in guidance beyond Provisional.

Delaware. Allows alternatives to teaching requirement, but still requires STC at appropriate level.

District of Columbia. Combined junior high, senior high, and vocational school requirements into one, requiring (1) masters in guidance, including practicum or 1 year teaching or counseling experience, or (2) masters degree with 30 specified hours, plus practicum or 1 year experience.

---

[18]Thorsen, *Counselor Certification.*

Florida. Added Rank IA certification, requiring 27 semester hours of graduate work above Rank II.

Georgia. No change.

Hawaii. Dropped STC and 3 years work experience. Added alternative of masters degree in guidance.

Idaho. Made mandatory the following courses: principles and practices, counseling techniques, and supervised practicum.

Illinois. Stiffened requirements to masters with 32 semester hours with practicum. Eligibility for STC now allowed.

Indiana. State guidance associations revising requirements. Exploring performance-based certification.

Iowa. Specific endorsement for elementary counselors and for secondary counselors. Elementary-secondary counselors (combined) requires masters degree with 45 semester hours in approved guidance program, with practicum at *both* elementary and secondary levels. New certification for "Director of Guidance Services."

Kansas. Certificate coded to recognize counselors for elementary and for secondary levels. New requirements similar to old Counselor I standard qualifications, but reflect appropriate level. Two years counseling an alternative to teaching.

Kentucky. New requirements effective September 1970. "Provisional" —experiences changed to 1 year teaching or 1 year supervised internship. Certification valid for five years, renewable with additional course work. "Standard"—thirty semester hours beyond Provisional, plus 1 year counseling required.

Louisiana. Now offers 2 years teaching plus one year accumulated work experience as alternative to 3 years teaching experience. Masters now with 21 semester hours guidance courses.

Maine. No change.

Maryland. Increased requirements to 30 semester hours with courses in personality, learning, and supervised practicum now required instead of optional. Added course in "counseling concerning minority groups." Added course in counseling young children (for elementary counselors). Added masters in guidance as alternative to specific content areas.

Massachusetts. No change.

Michigan. Certification requirements effective for the first time June, 1971. Require STC, recommendation from training institution, and not less than 18 specified semester hours in guidance (which can be waived for experimental programs).

Minnesota. Life certificate discontinued. Further revisions forthcoming.

Mississippi. Added "Class AA, Advanced Guidance Counselor" certificate which requires (1) Class AA, Guidance Counselor certificate qualifications, (2) two years counseling, and (3) 60 semester hours in specified areas. "Class AA, Guidance Counselor" changed teaching experience to 1 year teaching and 1 year counseling. Course requirements increased from 12 to 18 semester hours, and teaching reduced from 2 to 1 year for both "Permit" levels.

Missouri. Two year Temporary certificate changed to 3 year Provisional. Qualified masters degree as including minimum of 25 semester hours in specified areas. Stipulated extra courses needed for secondary teachers to become elementary counselors.

Montana. Added required recommendation of "appropriate college official."

Nebraska. Increased minimum preparation from 12 to 18 semester hours in guidance. Added separate endorsements for secondary and elementary counselors. Expanded sixth year program "to permit greater depth of study and skill development."

Nevada. Added specific endorsements for elementary and secondary counselors. Added alternative of completion of approved guidance program for both endorsements. Increased valid term of certificate from 3 to 5 years. For Professional endorsement (both elementary and secondary), changed two years teaching to two years counseling. Added masters degree plus specified advanced courses. Increased valid term of certificate from 5 to 6 years.

New Hampshire. Dropped 2 years teaching and teaching certificate.

New Jersey. Changes "imminent" with possible certification through college program.

New Mexico. Five-year School Counselor certificate changed to four-year School Counselor certificate. Revisions expected in near future.

New York. Dropped STC and teaching and work experience.

North Carolina. Dropped 3 year teaching requirement.

North Dakota. No change.

Ohio. Revisions effective January 1972. Renewal provision "upon expiration" added to the Provisional and Professional certificates. General but slight increase in required course hours. Added group methods course at Provisional level. Permanent certificate no longer requires 9 additional semester hours.

Oklahoma.   Dropped Temporary certificate. Committee working to establish Professional Counselor certificate expected to require an additional 30 semester hours beyond Standard certification.

Oregon.   Added 2 years teaching to Basic Norm and 2 years counseling to Standard Norm. Change expected toward competency-based preparation with certification based on "Washington plan."

Pennsylvania.   Bases certification upon recommendation from training institution, with preparation at the masters level. Apparently dropped teaching requirement.

Rhode Island.   Lowered teaching-work experience to 2 years teaching. Increased guidance course requirements from 15 semesters to 24.

South Carolina.   Established undergraduate "Associate Guidance Counselor certificate." "Secondary School Guidance Counselor" certificate has two options: (1) qualify for the Associate certificate and complete 21 semester hours of specified guidance at the graduate level; or (2) qualify for STC, receive a composite National Teacher Exam score of 975, and complete 21 semester hours of specified guidance courses at the graduate level. "Secondary School Guidance Counselor—Advanced Certificate" requires applicants to qualify for Secondary School Guidance certificate, with 9 semester hours beyond, and masters degree.

South Dakota.   Dropped Teacher-Counselor certificate.

Tennessee.   Endorses now for both elementary and secondary certification. Teaching reduced from 3 years to 2 years at appropriate level, or 1 year teaching plus 600 hours of supervised internship at appropriate level.

Texas.   Expects changes in direction of competency-based preparation and certification which "may alter certification requirements drastically."

Utah.   Added "Basic Professional" certificate which requires STC, two years educational experience, acceptance into counseling program, 16 semester hours in guidance, and recommendation of training institution. Valid for three years; renewable. Professional certificate now allows supervised internship as alternative to STC, and now requires three years counseling experience.

Vermont.   Now has three certification levels. "Probationary"—masters degree in guidance, or two years teaching plus ½ masters plus one year work experience. "Standard"—now requires masters plus two years counseling. "Continuing"—masters in guidance plus 5 years counseling plus plans for continuing growth.

Virginia.   No change.

Washington.   Certification is performance-based with no universal teaching or degree requirements.

West Virginia.   Teacher-Counselor certificate changed to a temporary license valid for one year, with no teaching requirement. Intended as emergency license. Counselor certificate allows 2 years counseling at appropriate level as alternative to teaching.

Wisconsin.   Grade B now called "Provisional" certificate with no changes. Grade A now called "Professional" certificate with 30 graduate semester hours in guidance allowed as alternative to masters. Added "Professional-Life" certificate with 18 semester hours above Professional. Added experimental Intern program which leads directly to certification with masters and one-year full-time supervised counseling internship.

Wyoming.   Added emergency "Limited Services" permit which is valid for one year, nonrenewable. Requires STC eligibility, one year teaching or internship, and 20 hours in guidance. Initial certificate now requires STC eligibility, 2 years teaching or 1 year teaching and 1 year counseling, plus internship, masters, 1 year accumulated work or counseling in vocational education, and technician's endorsement. Standard certificate increased counseling experience from two to three years.

Performance Criteria and the Washington Plan

Five states reported that work was currently being done within their state to develop performance criteria for certification. In Indiana, a committee with representatives from IPGA, ISCA, and ICES was exploring competency-based certification with demonstrated performance as a requirement for professional certification. Oregon anticipates a similar trend, as does Texas. Washington is the one state that has gone the furthest in developing a competency-based model for counselor certification and as such merits special mention.

The Washington plan calls for "behaviorally-stated performance standards related to client outcomes with no course, credit, or degree requirements specified."[19] Certification is based solely upon a training program developed by the training institution, the state professional association, and the employing district. Those who demonstrate their competencies by performances required by the training program are recommended to the State Board of Education for certification. The plan calls for three levels of certification: (1) a preparatory or intern level; (2) an initial level granted after basic skills are learned, but before nonsupervised practice; and (3) a continuing level granted after demonstrated counseling competence.

---

[19]Lawrence M. Brammer and Harry C. Springer, "A Radical Change in Counselor Education and Certification," *Personnel and Guidance Journal,* June 1971, pp. 803–808.

The plan, approved in 1968 with no provision for "grandfathering," called for the certification of all school counselors by 1973. Each school district is charged with developing a certification program for their counselors, which means, theoretically at least, that requirements for counselor certification could vary from district to district. This implies that if a counselor wished to move from one district to another, he could lose his certification in the process.

IMPROVING COUNSELING SKILLS IN THE PROGRAM

Aubrey emphasizes a number of ways for improving counseling skills. First, the counselor examines his own attitudes and practices. Then he has a commitment to change. Aubrey suggests:

1. Gaining new skills as an observer-participant with other counselors

2. Implementing a team approach to counseling, with each team member evaluating the other's counseling sessions

3. Analyzing taped counseling sessions

4. Using outside counseling experts and consultants

5. Assisting in training a counseling intern

6. Evaluating the feedback from counselees[20]

In summarizing the selection of school counselors for the counseling function, the following suggestions are made for employing officials:

1. The preparation needed for state certification should be considered as the minimal requirement and not as the optimal in preparation. Also, state certification needs drastic revision as do most, if not all, counselor education programs.

2. Contacts should be made with the candidate's institution staff for evaluation of the candidate.

3. An attempt should be made to match the candidate's personality characteristics with known qualities of the school and community.

---

[20]Roger F. Aubrey and Ray E. Hosford, "Improving Counseling Skills," *Focus on Guidance,* Vol. 3, No. 6 (February, 1971), pp. 1–7.

4. The school's emphases in counseling must be considered. Is it decision making? Is it therapeutic in nature? Is it some combination of the above?

Counselor Load

The question of an appropriate pupil-counselor load remains unanswered. In this chapter previous statements have been made as to desirable ratios. However, the problem lies in the fact that there has been no systematic research on the topic. Counseling personnel have relied on speculation to establish a pupil-counselor ratio that, on the surface, seems logical. As yet, no one has made any systematic attempt to establish criteria, investigate the facts, and draw valid conclusions to support a thesis as to pupil-counselor ratio. Therefore, we can only examine the case from the past and what is presently being recommended.

The historical approach to this topic is revealed in the writings of early authorities in the field. In 1939, Hamrin and Erickson made the following comment concerning pupil-counselor load: "It is proposed that every pupil have the advantage of the uninterrupted, sympathetic, and intelligent attention of his advisor or homeroom sponsor in an individual conference of at least one-half hour once a year. Since the average homeroom enrolls about thirty pupils, this would mean about fifteen hours of actual individual counseling for planning purposes by each homeroom teacher each year."[21] In 1941, Lefever, Turrell, and Weitzel approached the matter of pupil-counselor load by stating: Many schools might well adopt the plan of slightly increasing the pupil-per-teacher ratio for the purpose of releasing one or more faculty members for counseling and guidance activities.[22]

Moving to more recent literature, Roeber, Smith and Erickson state: "The rule of thumb followed in many localities is one period per day for each 75 to 100 pupils."[23] In 1958, Froehlich commented on pupil-counselor load to this extent: "It was planned to give the counselor approximately one period a day for each 100 pupils in the whole school."[24]

With the development of greater specialization in the guidance services, authorities have established a smaller pupil-counselor ratio. James B. Conant stated that each school counselor should be responsible for 250 to 300

---

[21]S. A. Hamrin and C. E. Erickson, *Guidance in the Secondary School.* Appleton-Century-Crofts, 1939, p. 296.

[22]D. W. Lefever, A. M. Turrell, and H. I. Weitzel, *Principles and Techniques of Guidance.* New York: Ronald Press Company, 1941, p. 225.

[23]Edward G. Roeber, Glenn E. Smith, and Clifford Erickson, *Organization and Administration of Guidance Services.* New York: McGraw-Hill, 1956, p. 104.

[24]Clifford P. Froehlich, *Guidance Services on School.* New York: McGraw-Hill, 1958, p. 72.

students.[25] Wrenn, reporting for the American Personnel and Guidance Association's Commission on Guidance in American Schools, has also recommended a counselor-pupil ratio of one full-time counselor for every 300 pupils in the school.[26] Martinson and Smallenburg, in making recommendations for elementary schools, speculate that one full-time counselor should be provided per 600 pupils.[27] One of the more extensive statements concerning counselor load has been made by Hatch and Stefflre. They cite the following recommendations:

One Counselor:

1 Hour per day	200 Hours per year	100 Counselees
2 Hours per day	400 Hours per year	200 Counselees
3 Hours per day	600 Hours per year	300 Counselees
Full-time	Full-time	500 Counselees

One Guidance Specialist:

1 Hour per day	200 Hours per year	50 Counselees
2 Hours per day	400 hours per year	100 Counselees
3 Hours per day	600 Hours per year	150 Counselees
Full-time	Full-time	250 Counselees[28]

Finley and Shertzer[29] found that the counselor needs approximately three and one-half hours of contact time per student each academic year, or that by spending 60 percent of his time in contact work he could serve 235 students. Quickly they caution that a counselor-pupil ratio is not enduring nor universal. The ratio must be built on student needs and counselor characteristics and the function which he performs. The counselor-pupil ratio is often given as 1 to 400 or 1 to 600. Just why this is done is not clear. Certainly preventive and developmental guidance would require as favorable a ratio in the elementary school as in the secondary school.

Behind all the speculation concerning pupil-counselor ratio, a vital aspect frequently overlooked is consideration of the duties the counselor must perform in addition to counseling. Though the average counselor should

---

[25]James B. Conant, *The American High School Today.* New York, McGraw-Hill, 1961, p. 44.

[26]C. Gilbert Wrenn, *The Counselor in a Changing World.* Washington: American Personnel and Guidance Association, 1962, p. 137.

[27]R. A. Martinson and Harry Smallenburg, *Guidance in Elementary Schools.* Englewood Cliffs, N.J.: Prentice Hall, 1958, p. 25.

[28]Raymond N. Hatch and Buford Stefflre, *Administration of Guidance Services* (2nd ed.). Englewood Cliffs, N.J.: Prentice-Hall, 1965, p. 185.

[29]Robert Finley and Bruce Shertzer, "What is An Adequate Counselor-Student Ratio?" *The School Counselor,* Vol. 15, No. 1 (September, 1967), pp. 32–38.

spend 60 to 70 percent of his time in counseling, the rest of his work is typically spread over a variety of time-consuming duties which need to be considered when establishing his work load. Until adequate research is completed in this area, there seems to be no clear-cut solution to the problem.

Full-Time or Part-Time Counselors?

Should counselors be assigned to the counseling function full-time, or should teacher-counselors be used? This question has been discussed, and positions emotionally taken by many practicing counselors. The advantages and disadvantages that have been given by many to support their positions are summarized in Table 7–2.

The school that is organizing its counseling function should base its decision on the question of whether it will obtain individuals qualified to perform the duties and role of the counselor. With the adoption of the National Defense Education Act of 1958, an increasing number of schools have begun to use full-time, rather than part-time, counselors. The Education Professions Act may reinforce this in the seventies.

Aubrey states that, "The present structure of public secondary schools contains a number of elements that preempt the time of counselors, and prevent innovation and inform." He emphasizes that the process of getting to students is hindered by quasiadministrative responsibilities and a time schedule which precludes easy avenues of communication. His suggestions for optimal change focus on regularly scheduled curriculum time for guidance purposes, based on the essential thrust of personal growth for each student, primarily through the opportunity of the group process.[30]

Specialized Counselors

Specialized counseling,[31] although on the scene for some time, is being recognized. A certificated counselor is one who devotes a major share of his professional time to a single area of guidance. Vocational counselors appear to be in heavy demand. Vocational counselors relate especially to vocational education programs which are expanding. However, the traditional areas of college and educational counseling take major precedence in counseling duties. Samler[32] raises a number of questions in regard to a new psychological specialty: vocational counseling. Despite changes, there is work to do.

---

[30]Roger F. Aubrey, "Organizational Victimization of School Counselors," *The School Counselor,* Vol. 20, No. 5 (May, 1973), p. 347.

[31]Robert W. Crary, "Specialized Counseling—A New Trend?" *Personnel and Guidance Journal,* Vol. 44, No. 1 (June, 1966), pp. 1056–1061.

[32]Joseph Samler, "A New Psychological Specialty: Vocational Counseling," *Vocational Guidance Quarterly,* Vol. 15, No. 2 (December, 1966), pp. 82–88.

Assigning Pupils to Counselors

In the organization of their counseling functions, many schools have pondered various ways of assigning pupils to counselors. Assignments by grade or class, by sex, by homeroom, by alphabetical listing, by curriculum areas, by free choice of the pupil, or some modification of these approaches have been tried. The assignment of counselees to the counselor is conditioned by many factors, such as counseling time, number of counselors available, supplemental duties of the counselors, and basic counseling point of view. Because these factors vary from school to school, no one approach can be recommended as applicable to all schools.

Table 7–3 presents some of the advantages and disadvantages of using various approaches.

Little research is available to ascertain the advantages of one method of assigning pupils to counselors over another. Roeber, Smith, and Erickson seem to favor a free-choice method; they believe that this method would recognize students' individual needs. They conclude that with any method used, with the exception of free choice of pupils, counselors should be alert to situations which may indicate a referral to another counselor who can work more effectively with the pupil.[33] Southard found that "student selection of adviser did not increase student rapport significantly at any dimension in the counseling relationship and that, regardless of selection or nonselection, students varied significantly from adviser to adviser in their degree of satisfaction with the counseling relationships. This suggests that the adviser was a more important factor in determining rapport than was the method of selection of an adviser.[34]

The most common method of assignment is by grade of class. Perhaps the reason for this may be found in the fact that this is an easy way to place responsibility. The second most common practice of assigning pupils to counselor is by sex. This practice seems to be a remnant from the days when deans of boys and deans of girls were responsible for guidance activities. Boy examines the proposition that girls prefer women counselors and boys prefer men counselors on the assumption that they would be reluctant to reveal their innermost feelings with a member of the opposite sex. He states:

> The validity of such a procedure is seriously doubted. Good counseling is good counseling regardless of whether it emanates from a man or woman. Training in the techniques, not the sex of the counselor, will be the determining factor.[35]

---

[33]Edward C. Roeber, Glenn E. Smith, and Clifford E. Erickson, *Organization and Administration of Guidance Services.* New York: McGraw-Hill Book Co., 1955, p. 123–125.

[34]Charles W. Southard, "Effect of Student-Selection of Adviser on Rapport," *Personnel and Guidance Journal,* Vol. 38, (April, 1960), p. 619.

[35]Angelo V. Boy, "The Sex of the Counselor—Does It Make Any Difference?" *The Bulletin of the National Association of Secondary-School Principals,* October, 1959, p. 67.

Table 7–2.	*Full-Time versus Part-Time Counselors*	
	Full-Time	Part-Time
Advantages	1. Can devote full-time to counseling activities with less chance of interruptions 2. Likely to develop more intense professional attitudes 3. Easier to obtain counselors 4. Person becomes identified as a counselor, not just another teacher 5. Available during all parts of day, not just certain hours of the day 6. Tends to be seen more as a specialist	1. Belief that teachers accept counselors more readily 2. See pupils in situations other than counseling relationship 3. Claim are in closer touch with pupils 4. Counseling is basically related to pupil educational needs
Disadvantages	1. Claims he may lose contact with pupils as they act in a classroom setting 2. Teachers may not accept counselor as well 3. May have more clerical and other noncounseling duties given to him	1. Has divided responsibilities and loyalties 2. Time factor limits activities he is able to do well 3. Too often his work becomes full-time in both areas 4. Often lacks the training for counseling work 5. Assumption of class contact is, at best, very limited

194

Table 7-3.	Assignment of Pupils to Counselors		
System	Advantages		Disadvantages
1. Assignment by sex	1.1. Belief that boys are more likely to discuss their problems with male counselors, and girls with female counselors		1.1. Belief that assignments in this manner add to the difficulty of establishing rapport with some pupils who have made poor adjustment to parents of like sex of counselor
	1.2. Belief that counselors of same sex as the client will better understand and know client's problems because of counselor's background		
2. By class or grade with the counselor moving with the students	2.1. Counselor has an opportunity to know his counselees well		2.1. Change of personnel or staff turn-over interrupts pattern
	2.2. Students identify and know to whom they can go for assistance		2.2. The diversity of problems requires counselor to be acquainted and skilled in many areas
	2.3. Pupil problem areas would provide diversity of experiences for the counselor		2.3. Personality conflicts could inhibit counseling success
	2.4. The greater span of time with pupils permits counselor opportunity to evaluate his effectiveness with them		
	2.5. Pupil cumulative records would not have to be transferred as often		
3. By class or grade with counselor remaining at that level	3.1. Counselor becomes experienced with problems at that level; becomes specialist in that area		3.1. Students required to adjust to a new counselor each year
	3.2. Counselor knows well curriculum areas of grade		3.2. Counselor required to learn new pupils each year
	3.3. Students learn to identify the person as the counselor for a particular grade		3.3. Cumulative records and data on pupils must be transferred each year

Table 7–3.	*(continued)*	
System	Advantages	Disadvantages
	3.4. During academic career students have advantage of working with different counselors	3.4. Curtailment of latitude of experiences for counselors
4. Homeroom teacher as counselor	4.1. Comes to know pupils in situations other than counseling relationship	4.1. Disciplinary role as teacher may interfere with counseling
	4.2. May have easier access to counseling time with pupils	4.2. Pupils may view counselor as just another teacher
5. Free choice of pupil	5.1. Easier to establish rapport	5.1. Could result in an unequal counselor-ratio for some members of staff; result in popularity contest of counselors
	5.2. Recognizes democratic rights of student to choice	5.2. May encourage pupils to shop from counselor to counselor
		5.3. Some pupils may never establish counseling contact
6. Alphabetical listing	6.1. Assignments easily made	6.1. Counselor required to know students, their problems at all grade levels
	6.2. If total school is included, gives counselor latitude of experience	
7. Curriculum or interest areas	7.1. Rapport may be established more easily	7.1. May foster division and cliques among pupils
	7.2. Counselor's function in curriculum planning is facilitated by knowledge of curriculum area	7.2. Problems arise when students change curriculum
	7.3. Counselor would become more familiar with career and occupational information related to curriculum area	7.3. May overemphasize educational problems

Organizing Referral Services

A more complete discussion of organizing the community resources for guidance is given in Chapter 13. We are concerned here with the development and management of referral sources and procedures for the counseling function. Referral, knowing when and how, is one of the basic competencies of the practicing school counselor. Referral should not be an escape; the counselor must not be a clearinghouse for referral agencies. No one expects the counselor to be effective with all of the pupils with whom he comes in contact. One of his most necessary skills is knowing when his counselee should be referred to another person or agency because his counselee's needs and problems are beyond his training, skill, and experience. The school counselor is not a psychiatrist and should not attempt to do a psychiatrist's specialized work. If he does, he is likely to find that the pupil's problems may be aggravated and intensified. The ability and willingness to make referrals is one of the basic responsibilities of all who engage in the counseling profession.

The counselor will want to work out some logical procedures for making referrals. The following suggestions may be helpful:

1. The counselor should avoid giving the pupil the impression that his concerns or problems are unusually serious, intense, dangerous, or alarming, but rather should strive to make him understand that his concerns or problems are of a different kind or sort from those handled by the school counseling service.
2. The counselor should contact the referral agency or person and arrange an appointment for the pupil. If possible, the counselor may find it advantageous to personally introduce the pupil to the referral person. The counselor should let the pupil know that he is interested to find out if the referral procedure worked out to the pupil's satisfaction.
3. The counselor should expect and be ready to provide the referral agent with the reason for the referral and other pertinent data that may be needed.
4. The counselor should make sure that the referral agent knows whether or not a report of the results of the referral is expected.

The counselor does not dismiss referral cases at the time of the referral. The counselor plans an approach to following up the progress of the pupil. It may be that the pupil would like to reopen counseling after the referral to discuss its helpfulness.

The counselor may find it convenient to prepare a referral form to send to the agency or person. Figure 7–6 illustrates how one school has organized such a form. The counseling service will also need to develop a list of the local and state psychological, psychiatric, welfare, special education, and other types of referral agencies and individuals that it can draw upon for assisting individual pupils. Many schools have found it helpful to organize a card file indexed under pertinent headings. Such a file of referral sources provides continuity to the counseling service and saves much needed time when there are changes of personnel. Figure 7–7 illustrates the type of card that might be used.

Another type of referral that the counseling function will want to work out is the method teachers and administrators will use to refer pupils to the counselor. Alert teachers and administrators will identify many pupils who conceivably could benefit from the counseling service, but who, unless referred by others, would not come to the counselor. The way this referral is handled by teachers and administrators is important to the outcome of the counseling process. If the administrator or teacher uses the referral as a threat, either implied or actual, or as a punitive measure, he will be building attitudes and apprehensions in the pupil that may inhibit the counseling process. Counseling will proceed much more smoothly and effectively if referrals are appropriately made in as personal a manner as possible. It is best if referrals are made so that the counselor is not tied to a particular course of action and so that the client can arrange the time when he wishes to use the counseling service. Again, the counseling service may find helpful, as having counseling services in other schools, the referral forms shown in Figures 7–5 through 7–7.

RECORD FORMS USED IN THE COUNSELING PROCESS

Chapter 12 discusses the development of a guidance record and data-processing system with its focus on individual pupil records. Attention is given here to an illustration of some of the record forms the counselor may use in its organization and development (Figures 7–2 through 7–7).

Record forms as used in the development and management of the counseling function have received scant attention. Variation in record forms exists from school to school, and properly so, because each school must adopt the record forms that best suit its own needs. The primary purpose of these liaison records is to expedite the clerical work of the counselor and to facilitate the use of the counseling service by teachers, administrators, and others.

In this section are presented several forms that illustrate what may be needed in the management of the counseling service. They have not been selected as the best records of their types, for no sure way is known to judge which are the best, except that which works for the school. These records do illustrate that schools are enough concerned about the organization of their counseling service that they have tried to reduce the time and effort needed to make such a service function.

Summary of Counseling Interview

Student's name: _____ Grade _____

Date: _____ Time: _____ Counselor _____

Interview initiated by: Student _____ Teacher _____

Administrator _____ Counselor _____ Other _____

Purpose of interview: _____

_____

_____

General attitudes or emotional state of student: _____

_____

_____

Summary of interview: _____

_____

_____

_____

_____

Decisions or plans: _____

_____

_____

Figure 7–2.

One form the counseling service may wish to prepare in its development is a summary of counseling interviews. Most counselors agree that fairly detailed notes of the interview should be maintained. These will be helpful in preparing for future interviews and also will provide a developmental view of the movement of the pupil during the length of the counseling contact. Summary notes of the interview need only to provide cues to the major topics that have been discussed and any plan or decision made. The key is to streamline the summarization so as to spend as little clerical time as possible and yet make the significant notations that will enable one to review the major substance of the interview. Typical forms may be made on 5 x 8 cards or mimeographed on 8½ x 11 paper. Figure 7–2 is an illustration of such a form.

Lou Utter suggests the form shown in Figure 7–3 for assisting the counselor with his record keeping of counseling notes. This form can also serve as an evaluative tool.[36]

Another form useful to counselors is one that summarizes some of their individual counseling activities and serves as a periodic progress report to the administration. Figure 7–4 is an illustration of such a form.

_____

[36]Lou Utter, "Counseling Situation—A Rating Scale," *Vocational Guidance Quarterly,* Vol. 8, No. 1 (Autumn, 1959), pp. 12–14. Used with permission.

Department of Guidance   Pupil's name _____

Counseling Situation—Rating Scale

                    First interview date _____   19 _____

Statement of problem: _____

_____

Counselee's recogni-
  tion of the real
  problem   Refusal _____ Semi-Refusal _____ Neutral _____
                             Semi-Accept _____ Acceptance _____

Counselee's charac-
  teristic of solving
  the problem   Negative _____ Semi-Negative _____ Neutral _____
                             Semi-Positive _____ Positive _____

Counselee-Counselor
  relationship (rap-
  port)   Negative _____ Semi-Negative _____ Neutral _____
                             Semi-Positive _____ Positive _____

Reinterview dates:
_____   Conclusions:

_____   Comments:

_____

_____

_____

Figure 7–3.

Figure 7–5 illustrates a form for referral of pupil by teachers and administrators to the counselor.

Another referral report is one to other pupil personnel workers either within or outside of the school. Such a form is illustrated in Figure 7–5.

An additional form that many counselors have found useful is one utilized in a card file that pulls together the referral agencies and person available in their community and state. The card file is indexed under such headings as: Health, Psychological, Psychiatric, Welfare, Special Education, Social Services, etc. Cards within the file might take the form shown in Figure 7–7.

Record forms are indispensable to the functioning of an organized counseling system. In developing them, efforts should be made both to achieve simplicity and to collect the essential facts that are needed. Such forms should be constantly evaluated as to their effectiveness. In this respect, consideration should be given to the views of all who use them.

```
┌────────────────────────────────────────────────────────────┐
│                  Report of Counseling Interviews            │
│                                                             │
│  This report summarizes the counseling interviews conducted from │
│  _____  To  _____  │
│           (date)                              (date)         │
│  Number of self referrals: _____ │
│  Number of teacher referrals: _____ │
│  Number of administrative referrals: _____ │
│  Other referrals: _____│
│                                                             │
│                      Nature of Interviews                   │
│                                                             │
│  Personal, emotional concerns:          _____  │
│  Understanding one's self               _____  │
│  Educational planning                   _____  │
│  Career planning                        _____  │
│  Appraisal of pupil                     _____  │
│  Subjects—progress                      _____  │
│  Financial problems                     _____  │
│  Employment needed                      _____  │
│  Referral to others                     _____  │
│  No problem                             _____  │
│  Accenting maximum achievement          _____  │
│  Developing identity                    _____  │
│                                                             │
│        Totals                           _____  │
└────────────────────────────────────────────────────────────┘
```

Figure 7-4.

```
┌────────────────────────────────────────────────────────────┐
│                      Referral Report                        │
│                  To the Guidance Department                 │
│                                                             │
│  Student's Name: _____ Grade _____  │
│  Reason for referral: _____│
│  _____│
│  _____│
│  _____│
│  _____│
│  Other comment or observation: _____│
│  _____│
│          Signature: _____│
└────────────────────────────────────────────────────────────┘
```

Figure 7-5.

Kirby High School
Department of Guidance
Referral Request

Student: _____ Grade _____
Reason for referral: _____
_____
_____
Progress reports expected: Yes _____ No _____
Telephone No. _____
Counselor: _____

Figure 7–6.

Boyville High School
Referral Index

Division: _____
Name of agency or person: _____
Address: _____
Telephone No.: _____
Director or contact: _____
Students Referred: _____
_____
Fee Schedule: _____

Figure 7–7.

INTERPRETING THE COUNSELING SERVICE

If the guidance function in schools is to attain its objectives of assisting individuals to attain maximum development of their potentialities, a counseling service must be organized and interpreted to pupils, parents, teachers, and administrators. Students, parents, teachers, and administrators often have widely varying perceptions of the counseling services. The effectiveness of the counseling service will depend not only upon the counselor's perceptions of his job, but also on how pupils, parents, teachers, and others interpret the service. That the image of counseling is not uniform and tends to be shrouded in the expectations that individuals have of the service can be seen in a number of studies on the subject.

Evraiff reports a study of the counselor's function as seen by administrators, teachers, junior and senior high students, and their parents. While all ranked counseling students concerning school problems as being the most important function of the school counselor, they differed in their perception of the counselor's role in such areas as conferring with parents, personal problems, future career plans, consulting with teachers, use of referral agencies, and pupil programming.[37] Bergstein and Grant found that parents, by their free responses and their rating scales, perceived counselors to be helpful to their children and to be more helpful than their family friends or school principals or people who were of average help. Parents perceived counselors to be helpful with educational-vocational problems rather than with personal-emotional social problems.[38]

King and Matteson reported that college students felt most free to take educational problems to the counseling service; next came vocational problems and then social problems. Students felt least free to take personal adjustment problems to the counseling service.[39] Heilfron submitted a set of types of problems to 107 high school juniors; the students rated these as needing the attention of a counselor. It was found students rated cases such as "Athlete," "Bright," and "Engineer," as needing a minimum amount of counseling. Heilfron concludes:

> Two major findings emerged from the study. Based on our sample: (1) high school students feel that students who are performing well academically and socially need much less counseling than students who are intellectually inferior, socially immature, or unrealistic in their aspirations; and (2) only students who display obvious character disorders should be referred to agencies outside the school for professional help.[40]

Teachers often view the counseling service as a threat to their relationships with pupils. Certainly few practicing counselors have not had the experience of criticism and hostile feelings from some members of the faculty. In discussing the interpersonal relationship between teachers and counselors, Peterson states: "Counselors are realistically a threat to teachers who realize that inevitably a part of the counselor's role is to listen to complaints, real or unfounded, made by students against their teachers."[41]

---

[37]William Evraiff, "Perceptions of the School Counselor," *The School Counselor,* Vol. 8, No. 3 (March 1961), pp. 78–82.

[38]Harry B. Bergstein and Claude Grant, "How Parents Perceive the Counselor's Role," *Personnel and Guidance Journal,* Vol. 39 (May, 1961), pp. 698–703.

[39]Paul T. King and Ross W. Matteson, "Student Perception of Counseling Center Services," *Personnel and Guidance Journal,* Vol. 39 (January, 1959), pp. 358–364.

[40]Marilyn Heilfron, "The Function of Counseling as Perceived by High School Students," *Personnel and Guidance Journal,* Vol. 39 (October, 1960), p. 136.

[41]Barbara Peterson, "Interpersonal Relationships Between Counselors and Teachers in a School Setting," *The School Counselor,* Vol. 7, No. 1 (October 1959), p. 12.

From these and many more studies, it can be seen that much more attention should be given by counselors to interpreting their services. Students, parents, teachers, and others often view the counselor as one who helps only with educational and vocational planning. This, of course, is an important aspect of the counseling service. But ways must be found of presenting the goals and objectives of counseling. A written statement of these can help bring about mutual understanding. A clear, objective presentation at meetings of parents, teachers, and administrators may facilitate a realization that counselors are concerned and equipped by virtue of their experience and training to yield a greater service to pupils, teachers, and others than that of conferring on educational-vocational planning. Chapter 15 will discuss some of the means that can be employed in interpreting the counseling service as it exists within the guidance function.

CRITICAL ISSUE

Some are raising the question whether counseling is really the heart of the guidance program. Counseling is the one unique guidance function of the school counselor's duties. If an opportunistic, expedient approach to counseling is taken, then, in the long run, guidance will be harmed in the school. If the counselor is assigned consultation, coordination, communication, then he becomes an administrator or translator or conveyor of pupil information. That these functions need to be done does not present a cogent argument for the usurpation of the counselor's time for this purpose. Counseling must maintain itself as the core of all of the guidance functions.

SUMMARY

All students have concerns and many need assistance at various times in their life experiences. Some would like intensive counseling. The school counseling service is established to provide an integrative developmental function that contributes not only to the troubled and the maladjusted but to the long-range choices and experiences of all pupils. Because of this, the job of the counselor is multiphased and variable in scope and role.

Professionally prepared counselors are essential in carrying on the counseling service. In selecting counselors for the counseling staff, attention must be given to their personal qualities as well as to their professional education. Meeting state counseling certification is seen as the minimum training required for the job of the counselor. Recommended counselor load is currently viewed as being one full-time counselor per 250 pupils. There are advantages and disadvantages in different ways of assigning students to counselors.

Basic to the organization of the counseling service is the preparation of record forms and the development of referral sources. The professional counselor was viewed as one who will affiliate with the professional organizations available to him at local, state, and national levels.

ANNOTATED BIBLIOGRAPHY

Peters, Herman J., and Michael J. Bathory, *School Counseling—Perspectives and Procedures.* Chicago: F. E. Peacock Publishers, 1968.

The focus of this book of readings is on articles which give meaning to counseling in schools. Wherever possible, articles dealing with school counseling are presented.

Shertzer, Bruce and Shelley Stone, *Fundamentals of Counseling* (2nd ed.). Boston: Houghton Mifflin Co., 1974.

This book is a comprehensive view of the basic principles and techniques for counseling.

Hansen, James C., Richard R. Stevic, and Richard W. Warner, Jr., *Counseling: Theory and Process.* Boston: Allyn and Bacon, Inc., 1972, 392 pp.

This book serves as a basis for one to develop one's "own personal theory of counseling—hopefully a theory that he will use to guide his own practice" (p. vii).

Developing and Managing the Educational Guidance Service

Decisions made by students and concerned adults should be based upon the most relevant available information. The information service provides for the collection, maintenance and dissemination of current educational, occupational and personal-social information for use by students, parents, teachers and administrators.[1]

Chapter 8

What differential levels of educational guidance and information are needed at the various school levels?

How may group activities be used to provide educational guidance?

How is pupil educational planning and placement organized?

How may programs for improving study skills be developed?

How may the college information program be facilitated?

Educational guidance is the assistance given to pupils individually and through group techniques enabling them to function more effectively in school by freeing their capacities to learn. Educational guidance helps students to recognize their present and future educational needs and opportunities. It includes assistance given to the pupil in adjusting to the school; selecting curricular and extracurricular offerings of the school; and planning, preparing, and carrying through an appropriate educational career.

Educational guidance is often the major part of the secondary school's total guidance function. The unity of the individual and his experience constitutes a major theme underlying the education approach to guidance.[2]

---

[1] *Guidance Services for Ohio Schools.* Ohio Department of Education, Division of Guidance and Testing, September 1971, p. 5.

[2] Joseph Zaccaria, *Approach to Guidance in Contemporary Education.* Scranton, Pa.: International Textbook Company, 1969, p. 18.

surrounding a pupil's scholastic success or failure and his adaptation to the conditions and policies that must be maintained if the school is to function as a social unit.

A major purpose of educational guidance is to present, by all of the resources available to counselors, teachers and administrators, pertinent information about the school's physical plant, different curricula programs, course offerings, state and local requirements for graduation, values of pursuing education, the opportunities and requirements for post-high school study, and the like. Through the educational guidance service, pupils receive assistance which enables them to understand themselves and how their particular potentialities may be developed. This complex undertaking can be discharged only by the cooperative effort of teachers, counselors, and administrators.

Educational guidance and vocational guidance are closely linked. The authors are aware that danger exists in devoting separate chapters to organizing the educational-vocational guidance services, for the reader may think of these processes as separate, distinct from each other, with separate objectives, goals, and procedures. Practicing school counselors know that a client's educational problems and plans are complicated by, and related to, vocational and personal choices and decisions. The separation of the discussion into two chapters has been done for greater ease of illustrating the organizational aspects of the educational-vocational guidance process.

Educational guidance is needed by almost every pupil at all levels from the time of entering school until leaving. It is carried on by all teachers and counselors to the extent that they recognize and understand the educational problems and developmental needs of their pupils. Thus the purpose of this chapter is to examine the development and management of the educational guidance service. Seven major aspects—differential levels of educational information, providing educational guidance through group activities, pupil educational planning, developing study skill improvement programs organizing college information, the kinds and sources of educational information materials, and the educational counselor's professional library— comprise the major elements of an organized educational guidance service.

DIFFERENTIAL EDUCATIONAL INFORMATION NEEDED

It has been stated that educational guidance begins on the first day the pupil enters school and continues until he terminates his academic career. This implies the need for differing kinds or levels of educational guidance as he progresses through school. It also implies that the educational guidance service will be continuous. However, at certain key points the pupil's need for information and guidance will be more critical than at other times. Such times occur as the pupil progresses to an organizational phase of the curriculum new to him—when he enters elementary, junior high or senior high. This new phase demands of him "new" ways of acting, planning, and responding.

The amount, content, or levels of educational guidance and information are not equally the same at these three levels, nor are they needed equally by all pupils within these levels. The point here is that even though we seek to organize and administer educational guidance as a service to all pupils, it cannot be done routinely. Guidance has always had as its focal point the consideration of each pupil as an individual.

The basic objective of educational guidance—to facilitate better adjustment and development of the pupil on the basis of actual individual needs and capacities—can be met, at least in part, by providing the pupil with information about his school—its curriculum, regulations, resources, and general policies. Knowledge of such information, coupled with knowledge of himself, should make it easier for the pupil to achieve directionality. In some areas the kinds of educational information needed by elementary, junior high, and senior high pupils will be different only in degree, while in other areas it will be different in kind.

Needed by all pupils and/or their parents at all school levels, varying only in degree, will be information regarding:

1. The school's physical and environmental plant
2. The school's schedule, including plan of the school day, holidays, vacations
3. The content of what is to be taught in any one year or subject area
4. Regulations concerning safety and traffic
5. Grade report policies and practices
6. Expected school behavior

In addition to this kind of information, those responsible for educational guidance will differentiate information needed at the following levels.

Elementary School

At the elementary school level, the information provided through the educational guidance service may be sought not solely by pupils but also by their parents. Some of it needs to be at their disposal prior to entrance;

other data may be presented later. The following information, in addition to that presented above, is needed by the elementary pupil and his parents.

1. Regulations concerning school visitors

2. How to understand peer attitudes and actions

3. How to achieve integration with groups

Junior High School

As pupils move into the departmentalized junior high school, they will need other types of information. Representative of the differentiated information to be presented at this level are the following:

1. Subjects to be taken

2. The school's extra-curricular activities

3. The improvement of study skills

4. Special services available to pupils such as remedial programs, health, counseling, and the like

5. The values of staying in school

Senior High School

The senior high school, with its numerous curricula, course offerings, and extracurricular activities, demands that the pupil examine his strengths, weaknesses, and plans for the future. Information of the following kind is needed by senior high school students:

1. Curricular offerings and subjects available within each curriculum area

2. Graduation requirements

3. Improvement of study skills

4. Opportunities for post-high school education

5. Requirements for post-high school education

6. Educational requirements for occupational choice

7. Scholarships and other financial aids

8. Methods of meeting military obligations

9. Occupational and career opportunities

How can such information be provided to pupils? Some of it will be provided through teacher contacts with pupils and their parents; other information will be provided through individual counseling. Some of the more basic information will be disseminated through group techniques, including orientation programs, homeroom discussions, guidance courses and study units within a course, college days or conferences, campus visits, and the like.

PROVIDING EDUCATIONAL GUIDANCE BY ORGANIZING GROUP PROCEDURES

The counselor often uses group guidance to provide information that enables pupils to better understand themselves and their problems. Ohlsen emphasizes that guidance groups assemble to obtain information, to exchange ideas, to learn more about working in groups, and to experience these activities.[3]

According to Driver, group guidance provides a learning situation. She says:

> Learning is focused on healthy growth in capacity for personal and social adjustments. The group gives an opportunity for improvement of attitudes and skills in human relationships. Individual counseling provides help in self-assessment of personal strengths and weaknesses, and in specific problem areas which the participant may not wish to present in group sessions. Prerequisite to the aim of skill in personal and social adjustment are the goals of self-understanding and acceptance, understanding and acceptance of others, practice in communication and interpersonal skills.
>
> Learning takes place in four ways: (1) through the discussion content and group activities, (2) through the personal relationships of group members, (3) through the interactions of group members with the leader during group sessions, and (4) through the counseling process in private interviews with the leaders.[4]

In group situations, the leader or central person strives to maintain a personal, permissive, and nonjudgmental atmosphere. Such an atmosphere encourages pupils to discuss their concerns, anxieties, and problems and to achieve insight into their attitudes and behaviors. Topics for group guidance

---

[3]Merle H. Ohlsen, *Guidance: An Introduction.* New York: Harcourt, Brace & World, Inc., 1964.

[4]Helen Irene Driver, *Counseling and Learning through Small Group Discussion.* Madison, Wisconsin: Monona Publications, 1958, p. 19. Used with permission.

are generally social issues of significance to the group. Group guidance is best conducted by counselors who have been trained to do so. However, teachers, and particularly homeroom teachers and teachers of special courses such as occupations, personal living, school orientation, and the like, have often had to conduct group guidance without the benefit of formal training in group techniques.

Are group guidance classes effective? Gribbons evaluated an eighth grade group guidance program carried on in nine classrooms in five urban communities. The nine groups were using the book, *You: Today and Tomorrow*,[5] which focuses the attention of the pupil on decisions concerning high school curriculum choice and occupational opportunities. By pre- and post-interviews with fifty-five boys and fifty-three girls randomly selected from the nine classes, Gribbons found that because of their participation in group guidance these pupils

> made significant increases in awareness and accuracy of appraisal of their abilities, values and interests. Considerable gains were made in the amount of information pupils possessed about educational and vocational requirements. Of more basic interest to vocational guidance practice is the evidence that pupils increased in their capacity to synthesize their understanding of the concepts of abilities, values and interests, and to apply this understanding to their own choices.[6]

Goldman has clarified the interaction of content and process represented in group guidance, group counseling, and group therapy through an extension of Kurt Lewin's writings on the group. He believes that many group guidance techniques are unsuccessful. The reason is that while the "content" of these activities—self-study, work world, college selection—is that of guidance, often the "process" is not. The "process" by which these activities are conducted reflects a teaching orientation rather than a guidance orientation. This, Goldman believes, is a fundamental explanation of why many group guidance activities in the past have not lived up to the hopes of those who engaged in them. Goldman has presented a two-dimensional chart (reproduced here as Figure 8–1) which demonstrates differentiation among three levels and three types of groups. The best indicator of differences among the three levels of process, according to Goldman, is the kind of evaluative questions likely to be asked. For example, a question illustrating Level I is "How much does he know?" At Level II, the question

---

[5] Benjamin Shimberg. *You: Today and Tomorrow*. Princeton, New Jersey: Cooperative Test Division, Educational Testing Service, 1958.

[6] Warren D. Gribbons, "Evaluation of an Eighth Grade Group Guidance Program" *Personnel and Guidance Journal,* Vol. 38 (May, 1960), p. 744.

would be "Does he have well-developed and well-substantiated opinions?" A question illustrating Level III might be "How does he behave in relation to peers and parents?" Goldman's analysis of the interaction of content and process in group situations seems particularly relevant to counselors and teachers engaged in helping youth with their educational planning and decisions.[7]

Educational information and planning is often the central topic of group guidance as conducted through such activities as orientation programs, homeroom programs, guidance courses and units within courses, and special activities.

Orientation Programs

The central purpose of school orientation programs is to help each person feel at ease, understand and adapt to his new surroundings, its traditions, rules, offerings, and activities. Orientation should begin before the pupil enters the new school program. As an example, the elementary pupil should be prepared for junior high school during his last year in the elementary school and then helped to feel comfortable when he enters the first year of junior high school. Responsibility for orientation programs is generally a function of the educational guidance service.

Specifically, counselors will be involved in ascertaining the problems of pupils that can be dealt with in group situations organized in the orientation programs. Also, counselors can use the orientation program to make sure that pupils know the counseling service is available for their use. McDaniel believes orientation programs can be used to develop readiness for counseling. He states the following elements as among those necessary to develop readiness for counseling when orientating a student to school: (1) the student's recognition of whatever problems he may have in his acceptance of, and adaptation to, the school situation; (2) the student's recognition of his own learning problems; and (3) the student's recognition of personal differences from other students in development, function, and interests.[8]

Often a committee composed of teachers, counselors, and administrators is appointed to define objectives, general procedure, and responsibilities for orientation programs. The committee will establish and maintain channels to transfer records of pupils to the new school and provide avenues for feedback of information from personnel in the new school to those in the former school.

---

[7]Leo Goldman, "Group Guidance: Content and Process," *Personnel and Guidance Journal,* Vol. 40 (February, 1962), pp. 518–522.

[8]H. B. McDaniel, *Guidance in the Modern School.* New York: Holt, Rinehart & Winston, Inc., 1956, p. 389.

Content	Level I Leader plans topics Lecture and recitation Facts and skills emphasized Units in regular classes	Level II Leader and group members collaborate in planning topics Discussions, projects, panels, visits Attitudes and opinions emphasized Separate guidance group meet on schedule	Level III Topics originate with group members Free discussion, role-playing Feelings and needs emphasized Groups organized as needed, meet as needed
Type A Usual school subject-matter: mathematics, English, etc.	1	4	7
Type B School-related topics: the world of work, choosing a college, how to study, etc.	2	5	8
Type C Non-school topics: dating behavior, parent-child relations, handling frustrations, etc.	3	6	9

Source: Leo Goldman, "Group Guidance: Content and Process," *Personnel and Guidance Journal*, Vol. 40 (February, 1962), p. 519. Reprinted by permission.

Figure 8–1. *Interaction of Content and Process in Group Guidance, Group Counseling, and Group Therapy*

Some of the activities carried on in orientation programs at the different school levels are outlined below.

Entering Elementary School

1. P.T.A. meeting to explain school objectives, policies, and regulations
2. Visiting day for children (and parents) to enroll and meet teacher
3. Tours of school to locate washrooms, offices, etc.
4. Letters and other forms of written communication to parents regarding school schedule and activities
5. Teacher, administrator, and parent meetings of each classroom to discuss the work for the year

Entering Junior High School

2. Prior to entering:
   a. Introduction assembly—all sixth grades visit junior high school they will attend.
   b. Tours of school to get "atmosphere"
   c. Visit classes—(1) either in small groups; (2) with a Big Brother or Sister assigned through student council to each entering student
2. Orientation days—first two days or so of school spent completely with homeroom teacher. Tours, programs, discussions on topics in the student handbook to present school policies and programs
3. Big Brother and Sister program during the year especially helpful in activity participation like Pep Clubs, etc.
4. P.T.A. meeting for all sixth grade parents with a panel discussion conducted by the junior high school principal, assistant principal, counselor, nurse, and teacher. Topics frequently presented are school objectives, policies, extra-curricular activities, special services available, typical school days, and the like.

Entering Senior High School

1. In the grade prior to entering:
   a. Study of high school handbook
   b. Talks by selected high school sophomores to individual homerooms or groups on such topics as "How To Prepare and Meet High School"
   c. Selection and discussion of curriculum areas in high school by counselor, teacher, etc.

    d. Activities assembly—officers of extra-curricular activities explain the clubs and organizations available upon entering high school.

    e. Films in homerooms or class groups on such topics as "What High School Can Do for You"

    f. Study and discussion of guidance literature such as the S.R.A. Junior or Senior Guidance Series covering the broad topic of "What Lies Ahead"

2. P.T.A. program for parents and entering high school students: introduction of high school administrators, counselors, etc.

3. Orientation day—newly entering high school students come to school one day early.

    a. Receive programs of study

    b. Meet teachers and pass through building to gain sense of location

    c. Informed about basic school policies and guidance services available

4. Big Brother and Sister program—upperclassmen assigned to each entering student for the purpose of aiding him or her during the year in program selection, school activities, and tradition.

Homerooms

The homeroom is the logical place for providing educational guidance: the sponsor can become well acquainted with each pupil, note his progress and development, be aware of his problems, and assist him through his school career. However, the homeroom as a vehicle for the educational guidance service has been abandoned by many schools. Many factors have contributed to this. One, the homeroom period has often been too short to permit accomplishment of any significant activities. Two, homeroom periods have often been used as administrative periods in which attendance was recorded, announcements were given, fund raising activities were conducted, and the like. Three, teachers have often been unable to do what they believe they should do or have not known what guidance personnel expected them to do in the homeroom situation. Many teachers have been assigned homerooms as sponsors with little interest in conducting such an assignment. Some have been assigned to homerooms with pupils they never had in class which makes more difficult their job of "knowing the individual pupil."

These adverse factors have been alleviated, at least to some extent, by school personnel who have envisioned the homeroom as an opportunity for teachers and counselors to help pupils in their educational planning and placement and have managed to locate personnel, time, and resources to make it work. Those who have found ways to make the homeroom a learning situation for guidance have indicated a few key principles upon which to build a program.

1. *Administrative attention and planning must be given to the organizational aspects of the homeroom.* Educational practice has indicated that there should be no more than thirty pupils in the homeroom and that pupils should be assigned to homerooms heterogeneously within each grade. A daily homeroom period of at least thirty minutes should be established. Dunsmoor and Miller recommend that the homeroom period be the first period of the day if it is to be true school home for the pupils.[9] Homeroom records should be brief. A folder in which is kept a student interest blank, schedule card, and form for recording student's plans and achievements, as well as notes of individual counseling interviews, should be adequate.

2. *Homeroom programs should not be imposed upon students and teachers.* School policy has often insisted that every teacher have a homeroom. Many teachers lack the interest or the training to accomplish the purposes of the homeroom. Consequently, programs may have to be started by using only those teachers who are interested and have the training or experience. This may mean a more limited beginning by making it impossible to have homerooms in every grade, but the probability is increased for the program to be successful. As for students, representation and participation on the program planning committee will help to alleviate their feeling that a program is being imposed on them.

3. *Leadership must be given by guidance personnel in developing guidance materials for the homeroom.* The lack of leadership in this area has probably been the chief cause for dissatisfaction with homerooms. The only semblance of leadership given to the development of materials for homerooms in many schools has often been some edict such as: "This week homerooms will discuss the curriculum offered in our school." Homeroom teachers need more information than this to conduct a good homeroom. They need suggestions as to resource materials and topics for discussion to stimulate such homeroom activities as committee work, discussion, debates, individual thinking, planning, working, and reporting. An outline of topics with suggestions for their introduction and discussion and a list of challenging questions to be mulled over by pupils will help many homeroom teachers conduct a more successful homeroom program. It goes without saying that resource materials suggested to teachers need to be readily available. The development and availability of materials is the most crucial factor in determining the success of a homeroom program. Alert counselors will provide leadership in this area.

[9]Clarence C. Dunsmoor and Leonard M. Miller, *Principles and Methods of Guidance for Teachers.* Scranton, Pa.: International Textbook Company, 1949, p. 274.

4. *Homeroom sponsors must provide variety in the approach to topics discussed.* Group discussions are not conducted every day. In some schools, three days of the week are given over to group guidance with two days reserved for individual counseling. Again, practice has indicated that it is necessary for counseling to be conducted in privacy. During the periods devoted to group work, the central person does not always have to be the homeroom teacher. Variety through student participation in individual reports, committees, and debates offers a change of pace. The use of resource persons from the community in their areas of competence and interest may heighten interest.

Curriculum choice and the courses available in each curriculum will be an important topic for discussion in homerooms beginning in the junior high schools and continuing through grade eleven. Genovese obtained the reactions, opinions and judgments of 3,471 pupils in Grades 10, 11, and 12 as to the value of topics or problem areas presented in homerooms. In the tenth grade, choice of vocation ranked first, and choice of high school courses ranked second; in the eleventh grade, curriculum choice ranked fifth, and in the twelfth it ranked eighth.[10] Pupil and teacher discussion of the relationship of curriculum choices to occupational choices, of the educational requirements for occupational choices, and of the relationship of high school courses to occupations conducted in a free, friendly manner will help to create an awareness of the elements involved in such choices and decisions.

Do homeroom teachers know the values to be found in the various high school subjects? Fry states:

> The homeroom teachers' knowledge of subject values is complicated by reason of the fact that they may possibly be clinging to prejudices regarding their own particular subject of specialization. Scattered information and hearsay tell us that the educational and vocational values to be found in school subjects outside the teachers' specialty are often unknown. They may be because of the blind spots resulting from the elective system which has characterized the education of teachers, or because teachers as a whole make little or no effort to understand what other subject teachers are attempting to achieve in their respective fields.[11]

Homeroom teachers will need opportunities to communicate with teachers in other subject matter areas to learn of the developments in these fast

---

[10]Clarence T. Genovese, " A Consensus of Senior High School Pupils Concerning Group Guidance Programs in the Homeroom." Doctoral Dissertation, University of Pittsburgh, 1941.

[11]Harry C. Fry, "The Homeroom Teachers' Responsibility for Curricular Guidance," *The Bulletin of the National Association of Secondary-School Principals,* October, 1959, p. 24–25.

changing fields. In some schools, administrators have found it useful to devote time in staff meetings to an explanation and discussion of the objectives and values of the courses in the different departments of the school. Thus, not only homeroom teachers but all teachers become more informed of the subject matter areas.

Counselors and homeroom teachers will need to work closely and cooperatively on problems and special cases arising or observable in the homeroom. Provisions must be made for referral to the counselor of those students whose problems go beyond the skills or time of the homeroom teacher. In a cooperative relationship, counselors can expect homeroom teachers to provide insightful information about their pupils that will aid the counselor in his contact with the pupil.

In summary, homeroom programs can be an effective approach for educational guidance. Guidance personnel can make it more effective if they assist homeroom teachers to develop materials, evaluate such materials, assist them in the preparation of forms for becoming better acquainted with pupils, and interpret the results of their work. If guidance personnel meet their responsibilities in these matters, homeroom teachers will achieve the purpose of the homeroom as stated by Willey and Andrew:

> To set up an ideal, intimate, democratic relationship between pupils
> and teachers in which the curriculum, extra-classroom activities, and
> the general guidance program might be better coordinated.[12]

Guidance Courses and Units

Many secondary schools have organized courses or units within a course to provide group guidance. Basic in such courses or units is the provision of educational guidance through such topics as orientation to school, curriculum offerings, extra-curricular activities, the meaning and value of education, understanding one's abilities, personal characteristics, and educational opportunities, and planning for college or other post-high school education. The emphasis in such courses or units is upon the individual to take cognizance of his own special situation.

Systematic cooperative planning is needed if such courses are to have value for students. Otherwise duplication will result in boredom for pupils. Warters states that the pupil personnel workers involved need to coordinate their efforts in order to (1) permit consistent emphasis throughout the program, (2) clarify their objectives, (3) plan for cumulative cultivation of fundamental comprehensive objectives, (4) determine the special objectives

---

[12]Roy DeVerl Willey and Dean C. Andrew, *Modern Methods and Techniques in Guidance.* New York: Harper & Row, Publishers, 1955, p. 513.

to be sought through particular courses at specific grade levels and the contents (facts, ideas, concepts) to be stressed in each course, (5) determine the learning experiences and materials most suitable for achieving particular objectives at particular grade levels, and (6) appraise the outcomes.[13]

School and College Day Conferences

Many remarks to be made about the school and college conference have application also for career conferences, career assemblies, or for any type of large group meeting convened for the purpose of giving information. Like other group guidance experiences, school and college conferences are of greatest value when students are prepared for participation. Conferences must be viewed as simply a part of the continuing guidance process, and in no instance should they constitute the entire program. Despite the universality of some principles, certain problems and their solutions are unique to the school and college conference, as the following discussion will demonstrate.

These conferences are known by various names, depending upon when they are held and who participates. The college conference—attended by college representatives only—may also be called "College Day" or "College Night" for obvious reasons. Some schools prefer to hold conferences during part of one or several school days, whereas others give over one entire day to meetings, and still others have conferences at night so that parents can attend. When representatives from institutions other than colleges—for example, technical and business schools, schools for training in beauty culture and nursing—are also invited to participate, the meetings are usually known as school and college conferences. Norris, Zeran, and Hatch[14] suggest the name "Further-Education Conference" for such conferences.

Purpose of College Day Conferences. The chief purpose of the school and college conference is, of course, to make available to high school students information concerning admissions requirements, housing facilities, educational programs, costs, scholarships, opportunities for student part-time work, occupational possibilities, and so forth. These conferences permit students—and their parents if the program is held at night—to meet representatives from the participating institutions for questioning and firsthand information. Conscientious representatives will present a realistic picture of their schools and will even direct some students to other schools better

---

[13]Jane Warters, *Group Guidance: Principles and Practices.* New York: McGraw-Hill Book Company, 1960, p. 231.

[14]See Willa Norris, Franklin R. Zeran, and Raymond N. Hatch, *The Information Service in Guidance* (3rd ed.). Chicago: Rand McNally & Co., 1972.

prepared to fill their needs. The unscrupulous, however, may use this opportunity for recruitment, and although instances of this are now rare, students should be taught to recognize the pitch.

The following conclusion was reached by a joint committee of high school and college educators after many months of studying the problem of providing high school students with the necessary college information:

> Secondary schools and colleges of Pennsylvania recognize their mutual responsibility in offering proper guidance to high school students who are interested in gaining admission to some institution of higher learning. It is the studied opinion of educators that guidance and not recruitment is the principal objective of high school-college relations. Guidance of the student normally begins in the earlier years of secondary education, and the college officers of admission are invited only to supplement the earlier guidance by supplying specific information about their particular schools.[15]

Suggestions for Organizing the School and College Conference. Before launching into actual plans for a school and college conference, some broad questions must be raised and answered. Basic policies and approaches must be decided. The questions that follow are suggestive only; local situations will dictate additions, deletions, and modifications.

1. What part, if any, should students play in planning for the conference? Students enjoy working on conference plans if they are permitted to make the real contributions they are capable of making. Frequently, organizations such as the Student Council or the Future Teachers Club sponsor school and college conferences. If students are to be brought into the planning, they should be in at the beginning, and they should have some voice in basic decisions. A steering committee from the sponsoring organization might be selected to serve on the planning committee.

2. Should other high schools be invited to share in the conference? If the high schools are small, certain advantages may be derived from combining with two or more schools for the conference. This decision should be made early in the planning stage, however, so that all may share in the planning.

3. What institutions should be invited to the conference? The committee must arrive at some means of determining the specific colleges

---

[15]"High School College Nights," *The Bulletin of the National Association of Secondary-School Principals,* September, 1957, p. 134.

and schools (e.g., technical institutes) to invite. One procedure calls for the committee itself to draw up the list; another way of handling the problem is by means of an unstructured survey of the students to discover their wishes; a third procedure, and probably the most successful, is one which combines the first two suggestions.

4. Does your state have a college-secondary school articulation committee? Educators in several states have become cognizant of the joint responsibility of high school and colleges in sharing the burden of guidance for those students going on to post-high school study, and they have developed a statewide program of cooperation to assist students in making their post-high school plans. If the state sponsors such a program, high schools will benefit by working through it.

5. What pattern should the conference take? Several patterns are possible. In some schools, part of one or more school days are set aside for conferences. Other patterns include one full day or one or several evenings devoted to conferences. One argument in favor of the evening program is that it permits parents to attend.

6. What grades should be permitted to attend? In the past it was believed only students in grades eleven and twelve could profit from these conferences. However, with increasing emphasis upon early college choice, the tendency now is to encourage students in grades nine–twelve to attend.

7. Should recent graduates who are attending schools or colleges be asked to participate? Distance from the institution plus conflicting schedules frequently preclude this question. When it can be arranged, however, participation by recent graduates can be valuable. If the returning students are provided with adequate speaking guides, their remarks may well illuminate some otherwise neglected areas. These students might appear with representatives from their school, or they might serve as keynoters in a brief general meeting at the beginning of the program.

8. What should be the format of the program? Here some broad, general outline can be drawn rather early, and the details can be put in later by the planning or program committee. Among decisions to be made here is whether or not a general meeting should be used to open the evening's program and if so, how long it should be and how it should be used. Preliminary meetings sometimes include a film or a keynote speaker. Usually instructions and final announcements are made at this time. The planning committee will want to consider the

number and length of the conference periods and the assignment of representatives to classrooms. Experience favors small group conferences in classrooms where parents, students, and representatives can meet on an informal basis. Time should be divided between presentation by the representatives and a question and answer period. Finally, the committee will need to consider how to end the conference— another general meeting, a social hour, lunch?

A word of caution should be inserted concerning the relatively unsuccessful exhibit-like conferences. These are sometimes held in the cafeteria or gymnasium where representatives set up their posters and display their wares for students and parents who wander aimlessly from one to another, picking up literature they will never read.

9. Should students be used in conducting conferences? Students have successfully served as hosts and guides, introducing representatives, initiating the question and answer period, recording attendance, and evaluating the conference.

10. What channels can be used for publicity? Local newspapers and radio stations are usually ready to cooperate to carry school news to the community. Within the school itself, the school paper, posters, bulletin boards, and the public address system can be used for publicity. However, a "whispering campaign" seems to bring the best results. The sponsoring organization can start it and keep it going.

11. How should the conference be evaluated? Students in the sponsoring organization will have specific reports to make about their jobs and experience with the conference. For parents and students who attend, an evaluation form can be attached to the program. Boxes can be strategically and conveniently placed for depositing completed evaluation sheets at the end of the program. The planning committee will want to review all evaluations carefully.

Warters feels that effective organization begins and ends with evaluation.

The systematic use of evaluation reports from previous conferences helps the planning groups to perceive the importance of protecting conference time and the need for exercising care in selecting speakers. The students may remove from their roster of potential speakers the names of some individuals who, according to the reports, apparently just did not take their jobs seriously, came to the conference more or less unprepared, although they had received letters of instructions, filled the time assigned them with wisecracks, jokes and personal anecdotes, and gave the students relatively little pertinent information. . . .

They (the reports) may show that a speaker who was good one year was not in other years because he failed to dust off his wares before presenting them to another group.[16]

Steps in Planning the School and College Conference. Planning is of prime importance. Long hours required for adequate planning pay off handsomely in a smooth conference that moves on time with seeming effortlessness. But, to realize this happy state at conference time, attention must have been given to even the smallest details, as well as to the larger ones: How should the representatives be conducted to conference rooms? What is to be done about hats and coats? What is the best day—or night—for the conference?

1.   Choosing the date. Adequate preparation demands that planning get under way a couple of months prior to the date set for the conference. Since many high schools hold their conferences in the fall, consideration should be given to putting the date on the school calendar before summer vacation starts. Not only will this procedure assure planners ample time for preparation, but it will also enable them to issue early invitations to those schools and colleges most heavily in demand by other high schools similarly planning fall conferences. The date chosen should not conflict with other school activities. If the high school is located in an area known for severe winters, some attempt should be made to avoid the months of the worst weather.

2.   Activating the planning committee. This committee may include student members of the sponsoring organization, its sponsor, and a member of the guidance department, or any workable combination of students and staff. The planning committee has the responsibility for reviewing broad organizational questions and arriving at some procedural decisions.

3.   Surveying students. Some simple form may be used to announce plans and purposes of the conference and to find out which schools and colleges students would like to have represented.

4.   Issuing initial invitations. Next, results of the survey are tabulated and a list of potential representatives drawn. Initial invitations indicating time, place, and purpose of the conference should be issued as soon as possible. Arrangements for keynoter, films, etc., are also made at this time.

---

[16]From *Group Guidance: Principles and Practices,* pp. 376–377, by Jane Warters. Copyright 1960. McGraw-Hill Book Company.

5. Drawing up a tentative program. As soon as replies are received from schools and colleges, names of representatives, student hosts, and room assignments can be put on the tentative program. Frequently, the tentative program becomes the final one with only slight changes.

6. Registering students. The tentative program and a registration form can now be distributed to students. At this time students sign up for conference periods. Many schools require that the registration form be signed by both parents and students, particularly if the conference is to be held at night when it is hoped that parents will attend.

7. Instructing representatives. A second letter can now be sent to school and college representatives and other speakers. Such items as time allotted for presentations and questions and answers, topics to be covered, specific questions students want answered, the approximate number of students and parents expected to attend various conference periods, the name of the student host, and the time and place to report on the date of the conference will be included in this second letter. A program should be enclosed.

8. Preparing students. All students serving as hosts or guides must know their precise responsibilities. Students planning to attend the conference must understand their purpose in participating. Sometimes preliminary meetings are called to arouse interest and guide thinking in preparation for the conference.

9. Holding and evaluating the conference. While the conference is in process, members of the planning committee often assume the role of trouble shooters, moving about constantly, averting difficulties, and looking for ways to improve the next conference. All participants are urged to evaluate the conference. A simple questionnaire or check-list attached to the program will facilitate evaluation.

10. Following up the conference. The writing of letters of appreciation, careful examination of evaluation sheets, and discussions and recommendations for future conferences by the planning committee constitute one form of follow-up. Another kind involves encouraging students to write to schools and colleges for additional information, to attend college-high school days, and to visit campuses.

Three general points need to be stressed in connection with conference planning:

1. Students have demonstrated their ability to perform many of the functions with a minimum of supervision.

2.   Conferences serve their purpose best when they are simply one part of the guidance process.

3.   Publicity—or lack of it—can make or break a conference. No service, regardless of its merit, can be counted successful if it is not used. The success of a conference depends upon attendance, which in turn is dependent upon good publicity.

Advantages and Disadvantages. Much time and effort are spent on planning and holding conferences, and sometimes counselors and others responsible for the program wonder whether the effort is well spent. This is the time to assess evaluation data and to weigh the advantages and disadvantages.

Some of the advantages frequently mentioned in connection with conferences follow:

1.   Students have a chance to get first-hand information to supplement or correct that provided by catalogs and literature.

2.   Students and parents are more likely to visit schools and colleges after they have met the representatives and feel they have some "contact" with the institution.

3.   The conference is an efficient way of providing many individuals with information in a relatively short time.

4.   The conference eliminates interuptions during the school year for meetings between students and visiting representatives, an administrative advantage chiefly.

5.   The conference offers opportunity for improvement of understanding and relationships between high schools and post-high school institutions.

6.   If it is held at night, the conference affords another chance for parents to participate in school affairs.

On the other side of the ledger, some disadvantages are cited:

1.   Representatives may not be good speakers or may give prejudiced presentations.

2.   Students are frequently unprepared for the conference.

3.   Often there is no follow-up.

4. Disinterested students may be forced to attend conferences or may do so to get out of class when conferences are being held during the day.

5. The conference is sometimes viewed as the total guidance program.

6. Students not planning to go to college are neglected when only colleges are represented at the conference.

Other Special Days

Other special days that are often the responsibility of the educational guidance counselor are such activities as scholarship recognition days, honor awards assembly program, subject career days, and the like. Elmer R. Ritzman reports a subject career day in which his school devoted the day to teacher-pupil discussions of the educational and vocational implications of each subject offered in the schools' curriculum. Teachers were assisted by the guidance department in obtaining materials and planning their day.[17] Also illustrative of these special days or events is the scholarship recognition banquet for superior students and their parents as conducted by the guidance department of Phoenix Union High School.[18] R. W. Chapman reports a scholarship recognition day for high school seniors in South Dakota:

> Since the first Scholarship Recognition Day in 1953, the event has brought numbers of brilliant young people to the campus annually. Here they receive recognition, certificates of achievement, and scholarship medals.[19]

EDUCATIONAL PLANNING AND PLACEMENT

Often the educational planning and placement of pupils has been a hurriedly done, once-a-year task, with little study or knowledge of the factors involved. Not only have pupils failed to exercise much thought or given attention and time to the planning of an educational program fitted to their needs, abilities and aspirations, but often the advice given to them by parents and teachers has been based on tradition and bias. The planning of

---

[17]Elmer R. Ritzman, "Subject Career Day," *Vocational Guidance Quarterly,* Vol. 8, No. 3 (Spring, 1960), pp. 155–156.

[18]Burce Shertzer (ed.), *Working With Superior Students.* Chicago: Science Research Associates, 1960, p. 315.

[19]R. W. Chapman, "Scholarship Made Attractive" *Vocational Guidance Quarterly,* Vol. 8, No. 1 (Autumn, 1959), p. 4.

a pupil's educational program is an important educational guidance activity. It should be undertaken in a serious and systematic manner, based upon pupil, parent, teacher, and counselor study of the individual and his opportunities.

As was stated in the introduction to this chapter, educational planning and placement are closely related to vocational choice and planning. There is little disagreement that the main task of the school counselor is in the educational-vocational guidance field. The major factors involved—pupil's intellectual level and aptitudes—are important determinants in both educational and vocational choices. Choices in this area can only be made wisely by the acquisition and understanding of data about the individual's aptitudes, interests, goals, and motivations.

Most students face initial educational choices during the seventh and eighth grades, when the junior high school curriculum provides for elective subjects. Some may face them earlier if the elementary school offers certain subjects, such as foreign language, music, art, on an optional basis. These early educational decisions, followed by the election of certain courses in the ninth grade, may determine to a considerable extent the curriculum sequence pursued in high school.

Selection of Curriculum

When the student enters senior high school, he will have to make a choice of a curriculum. The extent of different curricula offered varies from school to school. Even small schools generally offer a choice of college preparatory or general curriculum. In larger schools, eight, ten, or twelve different curricula may be available.

Segel, Wellman, and Hamilton have argued that the choice of curriculum at the eighth- and ninth-grade levels should be based on the following principles:

1. The voluntary selection of a curricular sequence is the privilege of each student.

2. Selection by the student of a curricular sequence and of vocational goals should be made only after all information pertinent to general *intellectual level* and specific aptitudes has been made available to him by his counselor.

3. *After the curricular sequence has been selected,* other factors, such as vocational interests, personality characteristics, emotional maturity, and socio-economic status should be identified and analyzed with respect to their positive and negative influences on the full development of the curricular plan.

4. Guidance in the selection of curricular sequences consists of more than counseling. A systematic program of measurement should be carried on to get the information referred to in principle 2. Counseling is but one aspect of the guidance program and is dependent upon other procedures.

5. After a student has enrolled in one curricular sequence, there should be provisions in school regulations and guidance procedures to permit periodic reassessment of (1) the original curricular choice or decision and (2) other personal environmental factors, to determine the validity of the chosen sequence and to determine whether a revision of plans is indicated, such as a transfer to another curricular sequence.

6. Effective guidance procedures at the junior and senior high school levels and appropriate articulation between high schools and colleges should reduce the need for college entrance examinations.[20]

This represents a somewhat different approach to curriculum selection than commonly taken. The usual approach is that the student and counselor give consideration to the students' aptitudes, achievements, personality traits, and interests. This approach would consist of two steps in which there is a separation of the original choice of curriculum from the analysis of information other than scholastic ability and specific aptitudes. In step one, tentative choice of curriculum would be based solely on ability and aptitudes. Step two would consist of considering other data, such as interests, personality characteristics, and the like, with respect to their influence in the development of the curricula plan. Segel, Wellman, and Hamilton predicate this approach because they believe the use of data such as interests, personality, and social status tends to influence counselors and students to make curricular decisions inconsistent with the students' educational potential.[21]

Basic to the selection of the curriculum is the decision as to whether a student will attend college. For many students, the decision to attend college, in turn, is dependent upon whether their occupational choices require a college education. These are matters that counselors will need to consider with the pupil. Involved in this consideration will be the student's ability to project himself, to develop long-range planning. Hahn and MacLean state that the individual must acquire as complete understandings as possible of the following:

---

[20]David Segel, Frank Wellman, and Allen T. Hamilton, *Individual Analysis.* Washington: U.S. Government Printing Office of Education, Department of Health, Education and Welfare, 1958, pp. 3–4.

[21]*Ibid.,* pp. 15–27.

1. Of himself in terms of his achievements, abilities, aptitudes, interests, motives, attitudes, and dreams

2. Of this personal dynamic structure in relation to the various occupational groups within which he may operate with greatest hope of success

3. Of the training necessary to develop knowledge, skills, and behavior patterns, and of institutions and curriculums in which they may be best obtained

4. Of the world of work and workers to which he must adapt himself, not only in his own field, but also in those that relate to, and interact with, his own[22]

Once a tentative decision of a curriculum has been made, the choice of subjects within the curriculum must be considered. Again, considerable variability exists from school to school in the latitude of choice of subjects within a curriculum. For example, it may be school policy that the student who undertakes the college preparatory course will be required to take the following subjects: four years of English; three years of social studies; four years of mathematics; four years of foreign languages; and four years of science. In other schools the college preparatory curriculum may be less rigidly defined with the consequent increase of the number of subjects to be elected.

The counselor and pupil will have to arrange a meaningful sequence of courses. For the majority of pupils, the goal will be to select a series of courses that lead to the development of marketable skills.

Three- or Four-Year Plan Sheets

Many school counselors have devised forms for use at the beginning of high school or just prior to entering which help the pupil to think through the subjects he will take in high school. For example, an eighth-grade student would tentatively plan the subjects he would take as a freshman, sophomore, junior, and senior. Figure 8–2 is an illustration of these four-year plan sheets. The advantages cited for these three or four year plan sheets include: (1) students have a better idea as to what lies ahead, (2) student planning will be less haphazard, (3) planning will be focused over a longer period of time, (4) the administration can estimate staff and facilities needed in future years, and (5) parents are better informed as to student and counselor planning. One disadvantage of such plan sheets is that

---

[22]Milton E. Hahn and Malcolm S. MacLean, *Counseling Psychology.* New York: McGraw-Hill Book Company, 1955, p. 49.

(Name of student)

(Address)

Choice of Curriculum:

Date Contacted:

Grade:

Homeroom:

___ Academic

9

___ Vocational

10

___ Voc. Agriculture

11

___ Voc. Homemaking

12

___ Business

___ Fine Arts

Stated Career Plan.

Date   Plan

Counselor:

Home Telephone:

231

Figure 8–2.   Everyready High School; Four-Year Plan Sheet

GRADE 9

Semester I

Subject	Grade	Units earned
English		
Phys. Ed.		

Semester II

Subject	Grade	Units earned
English		
Phys. Ed.		

GRADE 10

Semester I

Subject	Grade	Units earned
English		
Phys. Ed.		

Semester II

Subject	Grade	Units earned
English		
Phys. Ed.		

GRADE 11

Semester I

Subject	Grade	Units earned
English		
U.S. Hist.		

Semester II

Subject	Grade	Units earned
English		
U. S. Hist.		

GRADE 12

Semester I

Subject	Grade	Units earned

Semester II

Subject	Grade	Units earned

Figure 8–2. *(continued)*

counselors and pupils are reluctant to change plans even when the best evidence indicates changes should be initiated.

Test Data in Educational Planning

The counselor will draw upon test data to aid the student in educational planning and placement. Test data provide an objectivity to the measurement of human ability and achievement that never before existed. Even with their known limitations, tests have proven fairer and more reliable than any other method devised to screen ability and achievement. The collection of test data should be a continuing process. This is needed, not because major variations in ability are expected from year to year, but because in any given year tests may not precisely reflect the pupil's aptitudes and achievements. The test used may not have been a good one, or the score may have been recorded erroneously or inaccurately calculated. Repeated appraisals correct such inaccuracies and provide the counselor with a pattern of test data which, coupled with teachers', deans', and administrators' judgments of a pupil's aptitudes and achievements, serve as a base upon which predictions can be made for educational alternatives available to the pupil.

Other Data

Test data alone will not be the sole determinant of educational plans. The counselor will draw upon a considerable variety of other evidence. There are powerful ingredients in successful academic performance—attitudes, values, motives—that, at present, we have no reliable way of measuring. The counselor must avoid the temptation to discount the value of such attributes—staying power, zeal, judgment—because they are not easily measured. These attributes should carry due weight in any educational-vocational decisions to be made. No stone should be left unturned to insure that educational decisions are based on a wide range of evidence of student potential which is carefully gathered and sifted. The weighing and sifting of evidence demands judgment by a qualified and responsible counselor.

Individual Conferences for Pupil Planning

In order for the counselor to provide assistance to the student making educational plans, many schools establish a guidance policy that each pupil will confer individually with the counselor at least twice a year. Through consultation with a counselor, a program is developed which corresponds to the pupil's abilities, interests, and performances. Individual conferences are a means of working out an individualized educational program for the student.

As the counselor consults with the student about his educational plans, how can he help the student? Can the counselor look into the future to see what will be needed? Can the pupil plan now for a future in which careers and occupations will undergo radical change, and the pupil as a person will also? First, the counselor will have to search out all personal data about the pupil—his general ability, his specific aptitudes, his attitudes, values, and motives, his interests—and logically relate these for the pupil. The counselor's interpretation will give the pupil a cross section of his strengths and liabilities as they are now.

Second, some ferreting out of past data will reveal the direction, or tendencies, of the movements of pupil behavior. Developmental growth patterns should become apparent from the examination of the data by the counselor and by the pupil. Observation of his own developmental direction gives the pupil guidelines upon which to make at least tentative choices.

Third, the counselor can urge the pupil to be aware in the weeks and months ahead as to such things as what he likes to read, how well he does in courses in which he had indicated high interest, how he feels about working alone and working with others, and the like. Gradual shifting of the pupil's personality during the years beginning with junior high school and through senior high is to be expected. Eckerson has pointed up the changes that may take place during these years:

> During junior and senior high school, and to a lesser degree in college, a student is in the state of flux, living just one moment of life. If he has requested guidance, he may be balancing, teetering—undecided as to what direction his tendencies will carry him. His counselor will not deal with permanently molded material, but with a plastic, changing assortment of hopes, ideals, satisfactions, and determinations. It is the counselor's responsibility to help the student see himself now— poised between what he was in the past and what his propensities are leading him toward in the future.[23]

As the pupil's experiences and maturity develop, the counselor has the opportunity of assisting him to alter his course, widening his opportunities, and extending his thinking of himself and his future.

Fourth, the counselor can present a broad view of educational-vocational alternatives. Even though all data point to a specific occupation (which is rare) the counselor should introduce and acquaint the student with the general occupational field and the kinds of educational experiences needed for occupations in the different levels in that field.

---

[23]Louise O. Eckerson, "Guidance: A Letter to Counselors," *School Life,* Vol. 43, No. 1 (September, 1960), p. 11.

Parent Conferences

The counselor will want to be in close contact with the parent in formulating pupil educational plans. Parents differ greatly in their interests in the achievements and aspirations of their children. However, most parents want and need to know as much about their children as can be given to them. The acquisition of such information helps them to know the quality and quantity of school work their children are capable of performing and to formulate future education plans.

There are times when the counselor's judgment of the appropriateness of educational plans for the student runs contrary to parents' ambitions and dreams. Many parents are firmly convinced that a boy who plays the violin at age twelve will be a great musician at twenty-five or that a girl who plays "school" will surely develop into a teacher. The counselor's task with such parents is to help them realize that educational-vocational predictions can not be made on the basis of a single event, but rather on the basis of the child's longtime developmental pattern.

Many educational guidance programs conduct group meetings of parents at the eighth-grade level to acquaint them with the curricular and course offerings of the school. At such meetings, counselors can discuss the policies and processes of student educational planning. This general meeting usually sets the stage for individual conferences with parents. Because parents find it difficult to come to the school during working hours, many counselors have established evening hours for parent conferences.

Placement in Special Classes

Recent surveys[24] and school reports indicate a growing awareness of the need on the part of administrators to provide special classes for bright students and for the mentally slow. Conant has written:

> In the required subjects and those elected by students with a wide range of ability, the students should be grouped according to ability, subject by subject. For example, in English, American history, ninth-grade algebra, biology, and physical science, there should be at least three types of classes—one for the more able in the subject, another for the large group whose ability is about average, and another for the very slow readers who should be handled by special teachers. The middle group might be divided into two or three sections according to the student's abilities in the subject in question.[25]

---

[24]See Robert F. DeHaan and Robert J. Havighurst, *Educating Gifted Children.* Chicago: University of Chicago Press, 1957.

[25]See James B. Conant, *The American High School Today.* New York: McGraw-Hill Book Company, 1959, p. 49.

And again:

> In some schools, the main problem stems from the tendency of some academically talented pupils either to elect an easy program or to enroll in a vocational sequence to prepare for an immediate job. In other schools, the reverse situation is found: the main problem the counselor faces is persuading the overambitious parent of a child with little academic ability that eleventh and twelfth grade mathematics, physics, and foreign languages are too difficult.[26]

The school counselor will be a central person in identifying students for special classes. The counselor will do the initial screening for those students of less ability who may profit from placement in special education classes. From this pool of students, the final screening for special education classes is usually done by psychologists who have been certified by the state department of education.

A school testing program provides several kinds of information which can be helpful in identifying bright students for special or sectioned classes. Information from other sources must not be overlooked. To yield a more complete picture of a student, test data should be combined with information from other sources. The school counselor, in cooperation with other members of a screening committee for such classes, may establish a formula in which consideration is given to pupil ability, achievement test results, previous grades, teacher recommendations, and the like.[27]

DEVELOPING STUDY SKILL PROGRAMS

Among elementary and junior and senior high school students, a common educational problem is lack of effective study habits. Remmers and Hackett point out:

> ... most youngsters feel strongly about school failures. (Perhaps their outward "who cares about grades" attitudes is the best indication of that.) They want to know how to study better, how to perform better in class, and how to achieve better. Here are some of the statements connected with success in studies that one-fifth to one-half of the 15,000 students we surveyed checked as problems:

---

[26] *Ibid.,* p. 59.
[27] See Frank W. Endicott, *Guiding Superior and Talented High School Students.* Chicago: North Central Association of Colleges and Secondary Schools, 1961, pp. 12–16.

54% say I wish I knew how to study better.
53% say I have difficulty keeping my mind on my studies.
21% say I don't know how to prepare for tests.[28]

The educational counselor will receive many referrals of pupils who are having difficulty in studying or who seem to the teacher to be disinterested or resistant to studying. It is axiomatic that studying must be satisfying to the pupil if he is to engage in it. If he learns studying is not satisfying or is frustrating and defeating, he *learns* not to get involved in study activities if he can help it. In such cases, the counselor and teacher must carry on a remedial program of helping the pupil relearn satisfactions which can come to him through the methods and materials he is studying.

Good study habits are not acquired by chance but rather are the result of learning, training, and self discipline. To attain academic success in the different subject matter areas, the student has to develop those techniques of study pertinent to the individual subject area. Each teacher should devote time at the beginning of each school year to explain and to illustrate the kind of study skills needed for success in his course. Periodic reviews of these should be given during the year.

The educational guidance service can organize to improve study habits of youngsters by

1.   Enlisting the assistance of all teachers. Particularly, English teachers and librarians can help by teaching the use of encyclopedias, dictionaries, and reader's guides.

2.   Making available "how-to-study" materials. Many good materials are available in booklet, pamphlet, and book form. They contain discussions on how students can use their time and efforts to the best advantage in school. Hints on test preparations, taking notes, and planning homework are typically given.

3.   Introducing a short unit on study methods in the school curriculum. Study methods, or the lack of them, seemingly become a more visible problem at the ninth grade. A course or unit on study skills can be started in the junior high and continued through senior high school.

The Need for a How-to-Study Program

Because counselors and teachers have found so many students who lack the know-how of studying, of budgeting wisely their time, and of doing their

[28]H. H. Remmers and C. G. Hackett, *Let's Listen to Youth,* Better Living Booklet. Chicago: Science Research Associates, 1950, p. 18.

school assignments efficiently, many schools have organized how-to-study programs. Robinson, although referring to such programs at the college level, believes they can be of help to everyone. He indicates that "how-to-study programs have met with notable success. Measures of student progress have shown increased reading ability, greater skill in organizing work, better use of educational facilities, and more satisfying personal and social adjustment."[29]

Where should such programs be offered? DeForest and Brown reported that a "how-to-study" course or program offered in four of fifty "better schools" they surveyed was given in the following grades and in these ways: Two periods per week voluntary "How-to-Study" classes, Grades 10, 11 and 12; one homeroom period per week for six weeks in Grade 9; two weeks devoted to the study skills in English and Citizenship; and fifteen lessons course in "How-to-Study" offered by reading teachers, Grades 10, 11 and 12 (voluntary on part of students).[30]

Since study skills are so essential to the academic success of pupils, a program could be started in the junior high school, and continued through high school. From year to year and from school to school, many pupils with poor study skills have been overlooked and merely passed on from grade to grade. Even with how-to-study programs, teachers would retain their responsibilities to correct and improve study deficiencies. Counselors could develop a checklist that teachers may use to record their observations of pupil's study habits and skills. Such a checklist or questionnaire would ask for an indication of how a pupil meets his assignments, handles available time, concentrates on an activity, provides or cares for his equipment; attitudes toward work and class; and specific difficulties, such as following directions, comprehending materials, accuracy, use of reference books, poor vision, selection of main thought of paragraph, and the like.

There are a number of surveys or inventories available to assist in the identification of problems in the study skills area. The oldest and best known inventory is Wrenn's *Study Habits Inventory* which contains four different areas of concentration: (1) reading and note-taking techniques, (2) habits of concentration, (3) distribution of time and social relations in study, and (4) general habits and attitudes of work.[31] Reported correlations of inventory scores with grade point averages range from .24 to .58 which, of course, is positive but low.

---

[29]Francis P. Robinson, *Effective Study.* New York: Harper & Row, Publishers, 1961, p. 2. Used with permission.

[30]Richard F. DeForest and Marguerite A. Brown, "How the Good Schools Handle 'How to Study'," *Vocational Guidance Quarterly,* Vol. 9, No. 2 (Winter, 1960–61), pp. 131–32.

[31]C. Gilbert Wrenn and Robert P. Larsen, *Studying Effectively.* Stanford University, California: Stanford University Press, 1941.

After the most significant problems in the area of study skills are recognized and identified, a program can be activated. In order that the actual problems be brought forcefully and realistically to the students' attention, it is often necessary to use special techniques in instructing and assisting them. In working with this particular problem of study skills, inexpensive slides could be made illustrating students correctly and incorrectly performing study tasks. Equipment with which to perform this service will ordinarily be available in the audio-visual department.

More and more schools are providing reading laboratories conducted by specialists, but in many schools the responsibility of helping up-grade study competencies still rests with counselors and teachers. The following general suggestions can be given by counselors and teachers to pupils who need help in improving their study habits and skills:

1. Study in a place that is free from noise and distraction.

2. Study at regularly designated times which means budgeting time in and out of school.

3. Study material as soon after taking the class to minimize the amount of forgetting that normally occurs between class and actual studying.

4. Study the assigned material before class, taking notes or underlying the important points.

5. Take notes on the important points in class lectures or discussions.

6. Review daily both class and notebook notes.

7. Question yourself on an assignment and see if you can answer your own questions.

Many times students will ask specific questions: "How do I take good notes?" "I don't seem to understand my lesson when I read it—can I change this?" "How can I really study for a test?" These and other similar questions cannot be treated lightly nor answered vaguely. The teacher and the counselor must be prepared to give definite answers and to further illustrate them with selected examples.

Some pupils referred to the counselor will have certain attitudes that will need to be altered before more efficient study habits can be developed. In such cases, the counseling approach will be necessary for changing the attitudes before assistance and attention can be profitably given to remedying study habits.

One final point, the mere possession of knowledge of good study habits is not a guarantee that good methods will develop. It is essential that the counselor evaluate the effect of the information disseminated by checking periodically with teachers and pupils as to the habits being exhibited by the pupil. Without this continuous evaluation and communication, the effectiveness of the program will be dulled.

ORGANIZING COLLEGE INFORMATION

As the secondary schools and colleges move further into the period of greatly increased enrollments, the need for organizing college information for secondary students becomes more and more important. Each year a larger percentage of American youth are attending secondary schools and colleges. Nationwide, about 35 percent of secondary school graduates enter college, and this is increasing 1 percent each year.[32] This increase creates new and complex problems for counselors. Although secondary schools no longer exist solely to prepare students for college, the increasing proportion of graduates seeking further education means that ways must be found to adequately prepare those who do so. Obtaining adequate and accurate information about colleges and other educational institutions is part of the preparation needed. Two major questions face counselors as they search for effective ways to inform and prepare their students for the transition to higher education: What information is needed by students who wish to extend their education? How can such information be organized for its most efficient use?

College Information Needed

What kinds of information do students, parents, and school counselors want and need from educational institutions beyond the high school? Wright and Jung in their survey of the top 10 per cent (N = 3,479) of the 1955 Indiana graduating classes reported:

1. Information regarding further education had been introduced at only one grade level in the high schools of two out of three of the students.
2. The parents of four in five of the youths (79.3%) had not discussed the matter of further education of their children with any school official.

---

[32]See Ronald B. Thompson, *The Impending Tidal Wave of Students.* Columbus, Ohio: The American Association of Collegiate Registrars and Admission Officers, 1954, p. 48.

3. More than one-half (54.7%) of the youths knew of no scholarship that might have been available to them.
4. Six in 10 of the youth had not talked with a college representative about the possibilities of continuing their education.
5. Four in five of the youths had not discussed the cost of further education with their parents. As many as 38.1% of them thought that it cost too much for them to continue their education beyond the high school.[33]

Students planning further education will want to know the following information.

Should I go to college? Counselors have the problem of helping students determine whether they should go to college. Explorations of their abilities, interests, and occupational goals with the counselor will assist students to arrive at a decision. Counselors say this problem is sometimes complicated by the excessive recruitment practices of some colleges. A publication of the American Association of Collegiate Registrars and Admissions Officers states

> Probably the answer to this problem will be the result of many factors. As the numbers of our young people increase, society will have to decide how much college education it will provide and for whom. Colleges will have to decide the particular roles they wish to play in higher education and the kind and number of students they wish to serve. They will then face the problem of admitting only those who have reasonable probability of success in their chosen programs of study.[34]

The student's grades and rank in class will be important criteria in decisions as to whether to go on to college. Joseph P. Cosand, in 1953, reviewed twenty-one research studies in which college success had been correlated with average grade (seventeen studies) and rank in class (four studies).

> He reported a positive correlation ranging from 0.41 to 0.68 between average grade and college success. The correlation with rank in class ranged from 0.36 to 0.62. This seems to indicate that average grade in

[33]Wendell W. Wright and Christian W. Jung, *Why Capable High School Students Do Not Continue Their Schooling.* Bloomington, Indiana: Indiana University, Bulletin of the School of Education, Vol. 35, No. 1 (January, 1959), pp. 56–58.

[34]Committee on Special Projects. *Secondary School-College Co-Operation, An Obligation to Youth.* University of Kansas: The American Association of Collegiate Registrars and Admissions Officers, April, 1955, p. 5.

high school is a predicator of college success that is fully as reliable as rank in class. In fact, it may be a little more reliable than rank.

Cosand also reviewed twenty-six studies in which multiple correlations had been established between college success and combinations of two or three differing measures. In nearly every case the multiple correlations were higher than correlations obtained between college success and single measures. The range extended from 0.48 to 0.83. All of the highest eight correlations, ranging from 0.72 to 0.83, were obtained by using three measures. The highest correlations, 0.81 and 0.83, were obtained by using high school grades, an I.Q., and an English test.[35]

How to select the college or institution. Lovejoy's College Guide[36] lists 2,266 institutions of higher education. There are obvious differences in size, location, and tradition among these institutions. Some have impressive faculties and beautiful campuses. There are variations in tuition fees and in affiliation—church, state, community, and private. There are men's colleges, two year colleges, teachers colleges, technical schools, and specialized graduate and professional schools. How can students select from this field a manageable group of three or four in which they may be seriously interested? Jane Griffin and Thomas Morgan present seven questions which aid the student and his parents to do so:

> Do I want to go to a small college? A medium sized one? A large university?
>
> Do I want a coeducational college? One for men (or women) only?
>
> Do I want my college located in a medium-to-small town? A big city?
>
> Do I want a college in my home town? A short distance away? Far from home?
>
> Do I want to attend a religious denominational college? A federally supported college? A state- or city-supported college? A nondenominational private college?
>
> Do I want special courses not available at some colleges?
>
> Am I interested in junior colleges?[37]

Requirements for entrance. Colleges vary considerably in their requirements for entrance. However, the majority of colleges require the basic units found in the academic curriculum of the high school: four years of English,

---

[35]*Ibid.,* p. 19.

[36]Clarence E. Lovejoy, *Lovejoy's College Guide.* See latest issue.

[37]Reprinted from *LOOK* magazine, Dec. 6, 1960, issue "How to Get Into College in the Sixties," by Jane Griffin and Thomas Morgan.

two or more units each in mathematics, foreign languages, sciences, and social studies. Entrance examinations are fast becoming a common requirement for admission. Over 1,000 colleges and universities now require satisfactory completion of College Entrance Examination Board Tests. Some also require achievement tests in the "solid subjects" taken in high school. Every college sets its own formula for using these tests. Although these examinations are important, students are not always excluded just on the basis of low scores. Admission applications call for letters of recommendations from the high school counselor or principal. Also, many ask for statements on character, cooperation, dependability, and leadership traits. Some admission requirements ask that the student write an autobiography or an essay.

Accreditation of colleges. There are some 1,050 colleges that are accredited, degree-granting, four-year institutions in the United States. In general, those colleges and universities officially recognized by a national, regional, or state accrediting agency enjoy a higher educational standing than do those which have not been accredited. In addition, it is possible to transfer college course credit more readily if the school is an accredited institution. Accredited colleges and universities are those schools which have met certain standards in admission practices, curricular offerings, faculty and staff competencies, their system of records, guidance services, financial conditions, and physical facilities.

College and universities obtain regional accrediting from one of the following six agencies: the North Central Association of Colleges and Secondary Schools, Middle States Association of Colleges and Secondary Schools, New England Association of Colleges and Secondary Schools, Northwest Association of Secondary and Higher Schools, Western College Association, and the Southern Association of Colleges and Secondary Schools. Some professional organizations such as law, medicine, journalism, dentistry, and architecture have lists of approved schools.

Cost of colleges. An often vital bit of information needed by students is the cost of attending college. There is no sure way to estimate what college will cost, for costs change rapidly and vary widely from student to student. Costs for the average student to attend public tax-supported colleges today are about $2,025 per year, while it costs about $3,950 per year in private institutions. Four year costs range from about $8,600 to more than $13,000. If students attend college away from home, it typically will cost about $2,500 per year. Studies show college girls spend about $200 less per year than do boys. Students majoring in music, law, medicine, dentistry or engineering may have to pay additional costs. Often over-looked are incidentals and travel costs and various fees for health, laboratory, and library privileges and activities.

Financial aid. Many forms of financial aid are available for students. Financial assistance is given in the form of scholarships, student loans, part-time employment, remission of tuition, and so on. Many colleges now participate in the student loan provisions of the National Defense Education Act of 1958. Under the provisions of Title II, students may borrow up to $1,000 a year from the college for four years with no interest or principal payments until after they have graduated.

Organizing the Information

A deliberate program to inform students of the possibilities of further education is part of the educational guidance service. Some general considerations for organizing such a program include

1.   Such a program would be undertaken beginning with the first year of high school. It would be continuous throughout the remaining high school years. A weakness of too many programs for informing youth about further education is that they are not started until the senior year of high school. For many youths this is too late. A well-planned program to inform students about further education will be one that begins early in their school career to encourage them to consider themselves, their abilities, and their special aptitudes in light of their future and renders assistance in clarifying their objectives and decisions as they progress through high school.

2.   Such a program would need to extend informational and counseling services to parents. Individual and group conferences with parents of capable youth will be conducted to give them basic information about further education. In this way parents will be encouraged to consider the educational opportunities for their children. Parents are key people in the encouragement of youth to extend their schooling. Students and their parents need information of the financial assistance available for further education. Counselors can be of help to parents and students in devising an intelligent plan for meeting the costs of further education. Beginning in the tenth grade, students should be given information about scholarships, loans, and part-time employment.

3.   Greater use should be made of college representatives as consultants for those planning further education. Better communication

and closer working relationships between secondary school counselors and college personnel are needed. For many who enter college, there is inadequate communication between those who knew them in high school and those who serve them in college.[38] High school counselors will have to become adequately acquainted with college admission officials and college counselors. Familiarity of both persons with their overlapping objectives, problems, and resources will result in better communications and understanding. Articulation will be facilitated.

4. The organization of published descriptions and listings of colleges and their courses of study will often determine their usefulness to students. All catalogs and publications meant for the student should be easily accessible in the library or in a separate room near the counselor's office. Such an information center should contain college directories and catalogs as well as books and pamphlets giving information on scholarships, loans, work-study opportunities, and financial aid in general. Calvin Daane states

> The catalogs can be organized in several ways, each with advantages for efficient use. One good plan is to arrange the catalogs (alphabetically) in groups according to geographical location, with subgroups for junior colleges, technical schools, four-year degree-granting institutions, and graduate and professional schools. This will help many kinds of students including the student who is most interested in location, the student who can afford only two years of advanced education, and the student who has planned a long-range graduate program.
>
> A loose-leaf folder providing a key to efficient use of the catalogs should be established. Whenever composite listings are available, such as *Lovejoy's College Guide,* which lists the schools granting degrees in various majors, the folder should refer to both this listing and the alphabetical list for each subgroup. Schools with ROTC Units, seminaries, and other special facilities, listed in publications such as Brownstein's *College Bound,* can be similarly keyed. The loose-leaf folder, then, will afford maximum student use by anticipating questions and organizing information for ease in finding answers.[39]

Encouraging student use of these materials will need to be stressed during grade nine and beyond, in the homeroom programs, group guidance courses and units, and individual conferences.

5. Revolutionary changes have taken place and are continuing to occur with increasing frequency in processing educational and

---

[38]Committee on Special Projects, School-College Co-Operation, p. 1.

[39] *Working With Superior Students: Theories and Practices,* edited by Bruce Shertzer. Copyright © 1960, Science Research Associates, Inc., p. 194.

vocational information. While these changes are beneficial to the counselor in many ways, the tremendous increases in the quality and quantity of information about students and their educational opportunities make the work of the counselor more difficult in several ways.

Goldman has identified some of the serious problems which counselors have to cope with and which have been influenced by the improvements in data processing, storage, and retrieval. These problems are summarized here and include the following:

1. Counselors will be hard pressed to keep up, not only with the sheer volume of new information but with the hardware in which it will appear—film cartridges, closed-circuit television, computers, and other media.

2. Counselors bear some responsibility for maintaining flexibility of the new information.

3. Because the new information is printed, is in tabular form, or appears on a screen or computer-operated typewriter, pupils and their parents may attribute to it a greater degree of validity and reliability than is warranted.[40]

Goldman concentrated upon discussing a key issue for the counselor who works with educational information. That issue is how counselors can maintain a counseling relationship while simultaneously bringing into it relevant and necessary information about the individual and his environment. Counselors frequently report that in their view counseling is interrupted to supply educational guidance or vocational guidance needed by the counselee, and which could or should be obtained through some other guidance function. Two reasons for the seeming interruptions were offered by Goldman: factual information takes the client's (and counselor's) attention from his feelings, values, and inner life and counselors tend to be less accepting of the client's perceptions and values when external data are used. According to Goldman, two solutions to this state are possible. The first is to separate the two processes. This would mean that the counselor does only "counseling" without bringing assessment or environmental information into the counseling process. He would refer to an appraiser or an informational specialist when such information was necessary. The second solution is that of unifying the roles of counseling and utilization of external data. Pointing out that unification of the two roles is possible, Goldman identifies

---

[40]Leo Goldman, "Information and Counseling: A Dilemma," *Personnel and Guidance Journal,* Vol. 46 (September, 1967), pp. 42–47.

two necessary conditions. The first is that counselors have to maintain the same attitudes toward appraisal and environmental data as they do toward other information derived from the counselee. The second is that counselors must keep informed and up-to-date regarding assessment and informational resources, their reliabilities and validities. Preferably, counselors will choose the second alternative and combine the two roles. External data, for the counselee, need to be meaningfully explored if he is to engage in planful behavior and make choices that are appropriate to him. For the counselor, this means that he is an "interpreter of probabilities" in the best sense of the words.[41]

COMPUTER-BASED PROGRAMS

Many diverse reactions have been stimulated by the introduction of computer-based programs into education and guidance. While some view the new programs as a direct threat to job security, others view the developments as a way of both broadening their capabilities as professional guidance workers and reducing the many time-consuming technical tasks associated with the acquisition and delivery of critical data and information. In addition to aiding the counselor with a summary of individual student data, computer-based programs can: (1) aid in broadening vocational and educational awareness; and (2) assist in establishing educational-vocational planning and problem solving skills.

Educational and Career Exploration System (ECES)

ECES is a computer-based system supported by the International Business Machines Corporation. ECES reflects Donald Super's vocational development theory, that is, that vocational development is a continuing process which may be divided into life stages including growth, exploration, establishment, maintenance and decline. Students aged twelve to nineteen who, according to Super's classification, fall into late growth and exploration stages, form the experimental group.

The basic purpose of ECES is to help students investigate occupational alternatives and educational programs as they plan their futures. Oriented to the high school level, ECES is composed of three on-line directly available components: occupations (400 occupations categorized in various fields and levels reflecting Roe's[42] classification system), majors (400 post-secondary

[41]Ibid., p. 46.
[42]S. H. Osipow, *Theories of Career Development*. New York: Appleton-Century-Crofts, 1968.

programs of study), and charts (personalized information about the student and his computer interactions). A fourth ECES component, a batch-processed college finding program, is available off-line (by supplementary request system).

Information System for Vocational Decisions (ISVD)

The ISVD started in 1966, based on a grant from the United States Office of Education to David Tiedeman and Robert O'Hara of Harvard College. ISVD attempts to link together the student, the computer, and the counselor in such a manner that the student could first interact with the computer and then interact with the counselor for meaningful decisions based on the student's dialogue with the component. ISVD aims toward exploration, clarification and consideration of the information and decision.

Occupational Information Access System (OIAS)

This computer-based information's retrieval system is a component of the Career Information System (CIS), a statewide interagency consortium designed to provide current labor market information in usable forms to individuals, schools, and social agencies in Oregon. After he has completed a twenty-five item inventory specifying his geographical, economic, and occupational preferences, as well as noting physical limitations, the student is informed of the occupations (up to 230) that meet his specifications. If the student desires, job descriptions, training opportunities, cassette interviews, and visitation possibilities are made available to him. Occupations are organized by function into job families which emphasize similarities of job duties and career fields.

Cost estimates for this system indicate a range of between two and three dollars per student. Typical usage is estimated at thirty minutes per student. The OIAS is fully implemented in the schools of the Eugene, Oregon metropolitan area, with the system active in 40 of the 42 junior and senior high schools within that region.

ICSS/CTIS

A promising educational-occupational guidance data system which is currently in operation is the Interactive College Suggesting System and Career Training Information System, of Concord-Carlisle, High School, Massachusetts. This system provides individuals with current information on over three-thousand colleges and universities through a teletypewriter terminal. With the assistance of a counselor, the student must decide which of three-hundred characteristics on the worksheet provided by the system are important to him.

Other computer-assisted informational systems include the Computerized Vocational Information System (CVIS) at Willowbrook High School in Illinois; the System of Interactive Guidance and Information (SIGI) currently being developed by Martin Katz at Educational Testing Service, Princeton, New Jersey; and the Computer-Assisted Career Exploration System (CACE) being developed by Joseph T. Impellitteri at Pennsylvania State University. These and other models are described more fully by Joyce Chick in her work *Innovations in the Use of Career Information.*[43] Chick also details the principal advantages and disadvantages of computer-based informational systems. In addition, several comprehensive programs for computer-based training systems for vocational decision-making have been developed and are being tried experimentally in various school systems (Cogswell, 1967[44]; Super, 1969[45] and Tiedeman, 1967[46]). These systems range from those which deal with retrieval of educational and vocational information to those that are designed to be combined with a model course in vocational decision-making and individualized counselor guidance. Simulation and gaming techniques are one step removed from information and decision-making in reality.

The Life Career Game

Developed at Johns Hopkins University by Sarane S. Boocock, the "Life Career Game" involves both simulation and gaming. It simulates features of the education, labor, and marriage "markets" as these presently operate in the United States and are projected to operate in the future. The major objective of the game is to assist youth to acquire a better understanding of these "markets" and to provide them with preplanning experiences believed beneficial to their future development. Teams of two to four players participate in game rounds (discussion periods) during which they make decisions about the alternatives available to a fictitious person whom the teams represent. Each game requires players to complete job applications and college admission forms. Each of four areas—education, occupation,

[43]Joyce Chick, *Innovations in the Use of Career Information.* Guidance Monographs. Boston: Houghton Mifflin, 1970.

[44]Cogswell, J. F., "Exploratory Study of Information Processing Procedures and Computer Based Technology in Vocational Counseling," Systems Development Corporation, Santa Monica, 1967.

[45]D. E. Super, F. Minor, and R. A. Myers, "An Experimental Computer-Based Educational and Career Exploration System," *Personnel and Guidance Journal,* Vol. 47 (February, 1969), pp. 564–569.

[46]D. V. Tiedemann, et al., *Information System for Vocational Decisions,* Annual Report, Harvard Graduate School of Education, Cambridge, Mass., 1967.

family life, and leisure—is scored. Varenhorst reports that she has used the Life Career Game in California school settings, and has adapted it for use with both junior and senior high school students.[47]

Occupational Simulation Kits

Krumboltz and Bergland[48] have constructed lifelike problem-solving job experiences for seven occupations, such as accounting, appliance service and repair, electronics technician, and the like. Each simulated experience is contained in a self-administering kit. The format employed includes an introduction to the occupation, a statement of the problem and the information needed to solve it. Results from evaluative studies of the effectiveness of the simulated occupational experience were that (1) students from lower socioeconomic schools reacted more positively than their middle-class school counterparts, (2) the problem-solving booklet generated interest in the occupation it presents, and (3) students who personally choose their own kits sought further occupational information and tended to predict more favorable estimates of job satisfaction than equivalent students who had not personally selected their kits.

MULTIMEDIA TECHNIQUES

An example of the simultaneous application of several types of media to the information services is the Vocational Information for Education and Work project (VIEW) developed by the San Diego County Department of Education. Project VIEW is a regional center for the collection, synthesis and dissemination of career information. Phase I of the center, according to Gerstein and Hoover,[49] was designed to assess the types of career information needed by students, counselors, and teachers and to devise a useful and appropriate method for disseminating such information to local schools. Phase II was designed to develop an operational model-system for the 100,000 students in the 70 school districts.

The occupational information is gathered by combining national, regional, and state publications with educational-occupational community surveys. Special microfilm machines enable the student to view material by himself, select the parts he wants, and obtain a reproduction of the desired

---

[47]Barbara B. Varenhorst, "Innovative Tool for Group Counseling: The Life Career Game," *The School Counselor,* Vol. 15 (May 1968) pp. 357–362.

[48]John D. Krumboltz and Bruce Bergland. "Experiencing Work Almost Like It Is," *Educational Technology* Vol. 9 (March 1969), pp. 47–49.

[49]Martin Gerstein and Richard Hoover. "VIEW—Vocational Information for Education and Work," *Personnel and Guidance Journal* Vol. 45 (February 1967), pp. 593–596.

information through a simple and inexpensive mechanical device. The material can be easily updated by the counseling office through simple typing operations.

Life Style Films on Work

Ann Martin developed several life style films on workers that utilize the functional model of the *Dictionary of Occupational Titles.* The films stimulate the generic concept of work by communicating to the individual the following:

1. Identifies the three basic components of work: people, data, things.

2. Demonstrates the skill requirements that exist in work.

3. Demonstrates the training requirements that exist in work.

4. Identifies the interpersonal and supervisory relations that exist in work.

5. Demonstrates that work allows a person to fulfill a life style.

6. Demonstrates the satisfactions that result from work.

7. Establishes respect for the social as well as the economic value of work.[50,51,52]

Through group discussion that should follow the use of the material, the concepts introduced are broadened for the individual student, and thus greatly reinforced. The materials are available commercially through Mar-Media, Inc., Pittsburgh, Pennsylvania.

Educational Counselor's Professional Library

The educational counselor will need to maintain a professional library if he is to keep up with the constantly changing educational scene in America. He must be alert to collect materials providing information on such things as the ever increasing requirements for admission to colleges, technical institutes, and training programs; advanced placement and early admission practices; accreditation; scholarships and other forms of student aid; and

---

[50] Ann M. Martin, "A Multimedia Approach to Communicating Occupational Information to Non College Youth," Technical Report, U.S.G.E. Contract No. OE 6-85-952, Dept. H.E.W., Office of Education, 1967.

[51] _____, "An Interactive Media for Student and Teacher Growth," *Audiovisual Instruction,* Vol. 15, 1970, pp. 53–56.

[52] _____, "Guidance: The Learning Process and Communications Media," *Educational Technology,* Vol. 9, 1969a, pp. 46–53.

the like. In this respect, his professional library can become quite voluminous; it will of necessity consist of materials that are ever changing.

What books, pamphlets, and catalogs represent his minimum needs? What will such a library cost? Many experienced counselors view the following materials as essential in conducting educational guidance:

1.   One copy of a catalog from each post-high school educational institution (college, business school, nurses' training, junior college, technical school, etc.) within the state in which the school is located. Also, catalogs should be obtained from out-of-state educational institutions frequently attended by graduates from the high school. (Provided free to high school counselors)

2.   A general directory of colleges which gives brief descriptions of the institution and specific information on tuition costs, entrance requirements, degrees conferred, facilities, and where to write for further information.

3.   A general directory of scholarships and financial aid. Such material usually lists the scholarships available, amount, qualifications, and how and where to apply.

4.   Guides to planning and preparing for college.

5.   A general directory of approved home-study and correspondence course.

6.   Materials dealing with how-to-study, scheduling time, saving money and the like.

There are many good materials available which are invaluable to the practicing school counselor. As an example, the following might well be the professional library of the educational counselor.

General Directories

American Junior Colleges. E. Gleazer (ed.) Washington, D.C., American Council on Education, 1967.

American Universities and Colleges O. A. Singletary (ed.) Washington, D.C.: A.C.E.

Association of College Admissions Counselors Directory.

Mary E. Barre, *College Information and Guidance: Guidance Monograph Series,* Boston: Houghton Mifflin, 1970.

The College Blue Book, Yonkers-on-Hudson, New York: Christian E. Burckel and Assoc.

Guide to Correspondence Study, Minneapolis, Minnesota: National University Extension Association.

Home Study Blue Book, Washington, D.C.: National Home Study Council.

Clarence E. Lovejoy, *Lovejoy's College Guide,* New York: Simon and Schuster.

Clarence E. Lovejoy, *Lovejoy's Vocational School Guide,* New York: Simon and Schuster.

Ann Martin, *The Theory/Practice of Communicating Educational and Vocational Information, Guidance Monograph Series,* Boston: Houghton Mifflin.

Porter E. Sargent, *Handbook of Private Schools,* Boston: Porter Sargent.

Porter E. Sargent, *Junior Colleges and Specialized Schools and Colleges,* Boston: Porter Sargent Publications.

Financing College

American School Counselor Association, *How About College Financing,* Washington, D.C.: American Personnel and Guidance Association.

Norman Feingold, *Scholarships, Fellowships and Loans,* Vol. V, Cambridge: Bellman Publishing Company.

E. D. Hicks, *Financing a College Education: The College Selection Program.* Boston: Houghton Mifflin, 1969.

Need a Lift? Educational Opportunities for Children of Veterans, Ninth Edition, Indianapolis, Indiana: Scholarship Information Service, National Child Welfare Division, The American Legion.

Thersa Welking, *Financial Aid for College Students: Undergraduate,* U.S. Office of Education, obtain latest report. Government Printing Office, Washington, D.C.

Planning and Preparing for College

American School Counselor Association, *How About College?* Washington, D.C.: American Personnel and Guidance Association, 1960.

Samuel C. Brownstein and Mitchel Weiner, *How to Prepare for College Entrance Examinations,* Great Neck, New York: Barron's Educational Series.

Benjamin Fine, *Fine's American College Counselor and Guide,* Englewood Cliffs, N.J.: Prentice Hall, Inc.

Benjamin Fine, *How to be Accepted by the College of Your Choice,* Great Neck, New York: Channel Press, rev.

J. W. Brierly, *College Selection Handbook: The College Selection Program,* Boston: Houghton Mifflin, 1969.

Guide to College Majors, New York: Chronicle Guidance Publications.

National Vocational Guidance Association, *How to Visit Colleges,* Washington, D.C.: American Personnel and Guidance Association, 1960. (30c)

Francis Robinson, *Studying Effectively,* New York: Harper & Row Publishers, 1970.

Marian Tobriner, *Preliminary Planning Guide: The College Selection Program.* Boston: Houghton Mifflin, 1969.

SUMMARY

Educational guidance is the assistance given to pupils in planning, preparing, and carrying through an appropriate educational career. Related to vocational planning and development, education guidance begins with the pupil's admission to school and continues as he progresses through school. Educational guidance is provided through individual conferences and group procedures. Counselor conferences with pupils are essential to planning an individualized educational program. Group activities, such as orientation programs, homerooms, guidance courses and units, college conferences, and the like can contribute materially to the student's knowledge and planning of the educational process.

The lack of good study habits handicaps many pupils. The educational guidance counselor will organize how-to-study programs with emphasis upon early identification of pupils with inadequate study skills and a program of counselor-teacher cooperation to correct study skill deficiencies.

The educational guidance service will devise appropriate procedures for providing information about further education. College catalogs, printed supplementary materials, and visitations from college representatives will be organized for efficient use by students.

The educational counselor will need to maintain a professional library with a core of five or six essential types of materials.

ANNOTATED BIBLIOGRAPHY

Byrne, Richard Hill, *The School Counselor.* Boston: Houghton Mifflin Company, 1963, 295 pp.
   Chapter 5 (pp. 67–83) and Chapter 6 (pp. 84–106) discuss, respectively, the curriculum, counseling, group activities, and developmental concerns. In

Chapter 5, Byrne describes the principles related to programs of study and the principles relevant to "services" provided to an individual. He then inquires into how these two sets of principles relate and merge to form certain conditions in the school. In Chapter 6, Byrne seeks to establish a role for school personnel in helping youth with developmental problems. He illustrates how informational group activities may be useful to youth in certain decision-making situations.

Norris, Willa, Franklin R. Zeran, and Raymond N. Hatch. *The Information Service in Guidance,* 3rd ed. Chicago: Rand McNally & Company, 1972.

The chapter on educational information, Chapter 6, presents levels of educational information, and identifies the kinds and sources of information. An evaluation form for aid in selecting a college is given.

The Vocational Guidance Service

The schools have one final opportunity to prove their worth to the nation, in perhaps the most challenging undertaking of their history, by dedicating themselves to preparation of students for the world of work.[1]

Chapter 9

Vocational guidance has always occupied a prominent position in the guidance movement. Educators first became aware of the need for guidance through the difficulties they encountered in placing students in jobs. Moreover, they became aware that students needed help in making occupational choices. Since its origin in the early 1900s, when the guidance movement was almost exclusively concerned with the dissemination of vocational information, it has progressed to include the study of the attitudes and emotional factors involved in vocational decisions. Today, with hundreds of new careers available because of fast moving developments in science, technology, and international relations, the need for vocational guidance is just as insistent, if not more so. Students not only have the task of selecting

---

[1]Roman C. Pacinski and Sharlene Pearlman Hirsch, *The Courage to Change—New Directions for Career Education.* Englewood Cliffs, N.J.: Prentice-Hall, Inc., 1971, p. 8.

257

careers but also of becoming flexible enough to cope with the ever-present changes in the future of their career development.

VOCATIONAL GUIDANCE DEFINED

Many counselors prefer not to separate "vocational" from "educational" or "personal" guidance. Separating guidance into categories, according to their view, makes their efforts with youth appear much more fragmented than it really is in practice. The authors are aware that it is difficult to know when "vocational" guidance begins and "personal" guidance ends, but believe that it is important to separate them in this volume in order to deal adequately with the topics.

Some have viewed vocational guidance as a preventive or prophylactic aid for in-school youth. Others see vocational guidance as a service to help people make a satisfactory economic adjustment. Still others extend the scope of vocational guidance to include problems in social and personal adjustment.

Long ago, the National Vocational Guidance Association defined vocational guidance as "the process of assisting the individual to choose an occupation, prepare for it, enter upon and progress in it."[2] Super, in 1951, recommended that vocational guidance be redefined as ". . . a process of helping a person to develop and accept an integrated and adequate picture of himself and of his role in the world of work, to test this concept against reality, and to convert it into a reality, with satisfaction to himself and benefit to society.[3] His redefinition called attention to the fact that information about the self as well as about occupations is needed if vocational adjustment and understanding are to be secured.

Crites defined vocational guidance as "the process or program of assistance designed to aid the individual in choosing and adjusting to a vocation."[4] More recently Herr and Cramer have defined it as

> . . . a fusion of educational and vocational concerns for assisting students to locate themselves vocationally in the future and at the same time to make effective use of present educational experiences connected to such further choices. However it does not preclude the personal. Locating oneself vocationally in the future, however defined, must be predicated upon coming to terms with one's values and life purposes,

[2]"The Principles and Practices of Educational and Vocational Guidance." *Occupations*, Vol. 15 (May, 1937), p. 772.

[3]Donald E. Super, "Vocational Adjustment: Implementing a Self-Concept," *Occupations*, Vol. 30 (November, 1951), pp. 88–92.

[4]John O. Crites, *Vocational Psychology*, New York: McGraw-Hill, 1969, p. 23.

with one's personal characteristics and orientation toward or away from others—in short, those things about the self that can serve as reference points for sorting and evaluating alternatives made available by society.[5]

All of these definitions, while given at different times, indicate that vocational guidance is fundamentally concerned with vocational behavior. Vocational behavior is, of necessity, multifaceted. It is personal and cannot be separated easily or wisely from its antecedents. Its development is a function of many correlates and responses made by a person to personal and occupational stimuli.

Super has long insisted that vocational development is a process.

> It need hardly be said that vocational development is a process. It would be unnecessary to say it at all, were it not that the concept of development has not, until recent years, been applied to the study of vocational choice and adjustment. Despite statements in the earlier literature of vocational guidance to the effect that vocational choice is a process, and that this process is continuous, the continued use of the term choice connoted an event. The impression left was that at some moment in his life an individual chooses an occupation, after which he prepares for, enters, and then adjusts to it. Thus Ginzberg and Associates thought it necessary to report, as one of their major findings, the fact that occupation choice is a developmental process which typically takes place over a period of some ten years.[6]

Vocational guidance is concerned with the student and his planning, preparation for, and adjustment to the world of work. It seeks to engage the student in projecting ahead and in examining his attitudes, feelings, anxieties and aspirations that revolve around work. It encourages him to think about occupational status, job satisfaction and other facets of earning a living and living a full life.

If vocational guidance is to be effective, it must consider the student's goals, needs, drives, and opportunities. Vocational guidance may be examined from the standpoint of its *content* (the "what" of guidance) and its process (the "how" of guidance). Content, therefore, includes the manner in which students are to earn a living, while process refers to the appropriate changes which the individual makes within himself and his environment as a result of the focus of the guidance relationship.

---

[5]Edwin Herr and Stanley L. Cramer, *Vocational Guidance and Career Development in the Schools: Toward A Systems Approach.* Boston: Houghton Mifflin Co., 1973, p. 3.

[6]Donald E. Super, "Vocational Development: The Process of Compromise or Synthesis," *Journal of Counseling Psychology,* Vol. 3, (Winter, 1956), p. 249.

NEED FOR VOCATIONAL GUIDANCE

From the time a child is first asked the question, "What do you want to be when you grow up?" until he is started on a career that is right for him, there is no more important question he has to answer. In today's specialized occupational society, there are few questions more difficult. The importance of having a vocational objective is seen when one considers the societal backdrop in which earning a living is important, vocational roles are significant, and education is vocationally directed.

Several years ago Williamson characterized the stumbling blocks resulting in students' faulty thinking with respect to their vocational choices.

> ... the *attractiveness of the remote* ... the grass on the other side of the street always seems greener—until we have crossed that street ...
>
> ... the tendency *to glorify the unusual* ... students see doctors in the light of their most brilliant operations and fail to realize the long hours of routine treatment they are called upon to make.
>
> ... the *white collar illusion* ... only the professions are respectable.
>
> Students often imagine that there exists somewhere a *perfect niche* ...
>
> ... *misreading the signs* ... is a mistake made by those who jump to the wrong conclusions. A supposed liking for a particular subject is a sign pointing to success in that particular field.
>
> ... the *fear of the closed mind* ... once an occupation is chosen students are stuck with it forever ... Many students hesitate to make a choice for fear they will get into a blind alley job.
>
> Indolent students resemble *sparkless motors* ... only the stupid study. They are willing to be educated if it takes no work on their part.
>
> *The fallacy of the occupational labels* ... students state they are interested in manufacturing which could mean any of a dozen or so jobs.
>
> ... the *fallacy of the added cubit* ... "which of you by taking thought can add one cubit to his stature?" Wishing for ability and success is not enough; one must have ability.
>
> *The fallacy of perfectability* ... all of us like to believe we are potentially capable of greatness and that we have tremendous talent abilities. Students must face reality. Nature has set pretty definite limits to what any of us can do.
>
> ... the *fallacy of equal ability* ... all men are created equally. We should understand there is merit in true differences in ability.
>
> ... the *phrenological fallacy* ... there is no known relationship between aptitude for jobs and bumps on the head.
>
> ... the *fallacy of sequential training* is the pitfall of those who think that they should spend no time on studies which are not in the direct

sequence leading to the job they have chosen. Such students miss the rich experiences to be gained from wandering in the bypaths of education.[7]

Career Education

While these "stumbling blocks" were put forth many years ago, many educators claim they are still characteristic of the vocational behavior of many youth. These and other considerations led Sidney M. Marland, in his first major address as Commissioner of Education, to recommend that the "general education curriculum" be abolished and that a new "career education" be established. It was his opinion that those students in the general education curriculum were drifting in an educational wasteland and urgently needed exposure to the work world. Marland's proposal emphasized education as preparation for work. That, of course, is neither a new nor novel view of education; however, many students fail to develop any understanding—based upon what they do in school—as to what they will do later at work. Hoyt and his associates have defined career education as

> . . . the total efforts of public education and the community aimed at helping all individuals to become familiar with the values of a work oriented society, to integrate these values into their personal value systems, and to implement these values into their lives in such a way that work becomes possible, meaningful, and satisfying to each individual.[8]

The dominant purpose of career education is to provide students with the skills, attitudes, and information which they need to successfully enter the labor market at whatever point they leave school. Career education seeks to have schools provide a transitional bridge from school to work, for it is difficult for students to prepare themselves for jobs and to enter the labor market. Too many students have not been able to do so during the past ten years. While the high school dropout rate was the focus of attention during the 1950s and 60s, the unemployment rate among teenagers has climbed higher each year. The ratio of youth unemployment to adult unemployment rose from two and one-half times as high in 1950 to five times as high as the adult rate in 1970. Moreover, unemployment among minority group teenagers is twice as high as that for white teenagers.

---

[7] *Students and Occupations,* by E. G. Williamson, Copyright © 1937, Henry Holt and Company, Inc. Reprinted by permission of Holt, Rinehart & Winston, Inc.

[8] Kenneth B. Hoyt, R. N. Evans, E. F. Mackin and G. I. Mangum, *Career Education.* Salt Lake City, Utah: Olympus Publishing Company, 1972, p. 1.

Approximately 2.5 million American students leave the formal educational system each year without adequate career preparation.[9] The National Advisory Council on Vocational Education estimates that in 1970–71, there were 850,000 elementary and secondary school dropouts, 750,000 general education curriculum high school graduates who did not attend college, and 850,000 high school students who entered college in 1967 but did not complete the baccalaureate or an occupational program.[10] Many articles have been written about student dissatisfaction with what they study in school and the "irrelevance" of much of their educational experience.

Coupled with the urgent vocational needs of students are the changing needs in the American work force. It is estimated that by 1980, 101 million Americans will be in the labor force. This is one-sixth more than the 86 million in the labor force in 1970. Currently only about 20 per cent of American youth graduate from college. This leaves about 80 per cent with a need for other kinds of career skills. Moreover, it is estimated that by the end of the 1970s, eight out of ten jobs in America will not require a baccalaureate degree.

Changes Needed

The changes in education needed to accommodate career education have been discussed by Hoyt. Here the five changes that he suggests will be identified and discussed.

> One such change is the need for year-round school in which both students and teachers attend classes on a staggered basis throughout the full twelve months of the year. Hoyt states this is important to career education because it represents a way to avoid "dumping" large numbers of graduates on the labor market once a year.

> A second basic change lies in the need for the eighteen-hour school day and the six-day school week. Hoyt believes this would benefit career education by giving flexibility in establishing work experience and work-study programs and by allowing schools to contribute to adult education.

> A third change is the need for performance objectives. Hoyt believes this would help career education by giving opportunities to college students to explore occupational information without being locked in by Carnegie unit requirements, and by extending educational credit for student learning activities beyond the four walls of the school.

[9]U.S. Office of Education, *Career Education,* Washington, D.C.: Department of Health, Education and Welfare, Publication No. 72–39, p. 1.

[10]National Advisory Council on Vocational Education, "Counseling and Guidance, a Call for Change," *Vocational Guidance Quarterly,* Vol. 21 (December 1972), pp. 97–101.

A fourth basic change is the necessity to make it possible for some persons without standard teaching certificates to teach in our elementary and secondary schools. Hoyt's point is that some skills in career education come from those learned in the school of "hard knocks."

Fifth, we need to see the "open-entry, open-exit" system of education adopted as an integral part of American education. (No one ever finishes their education.)[11]

Uncertainty about the Work Ethic

Some educators believe that the old American work ethic is no longer a motivating force among the young. They believe that a large and growing number of today's school-age population have values that differ radically from those of past generations. One suggested difference in values concerns a change in the importance of "success"; in particular, a shift in the meaning associated with one's job.

Attitudes toward jobs and income are strikingly varied among different generations. Perhaps this is because older generations have known real poverty and insecurity, having lived through an economic collapse, while the younger generation has often experienced uninterrupted affluence and security. Rejection of traditional economic definitions of life's purposes is most frequent among those youth whose families have been the most comfortable and secure. However, this does not assert that it is common among young people to reject material well-being. Rather, the point is that when material well-being is increasingly taken for granted, the quest for economic security ceases to be a central task of life. In such situations, one's job is no longer the centerpiece of one's life.

Hodgson[12] reports that Department of Labor surveys found young people strongly work-oriented and concluded that even those unemployed were "not choosing not to work." Hodgson believes that some young people want different kinds of work and different things from work but that their will to work had not suffered any deterioration. Perhaps what is needed is what Bruner suggested—that "vocation" and "intention" should be put back into schools. He comments that

> ... I would like to explore, in the interest of relevance, whether we might not recapture something of the old notion of vocation, of ways of life, or to use the expression of so many undergraduates today, of "life styles". . . . I really believe that our young have become so isolated

---

[11]Kenneth B. Hoyt, "The Future of Career Education," *Guidance Newsletter.* Chicago: Science Research Associates, March–April, 1973, pp. 2–3.

[12]J. D. Hodgson, "Youth Motivation," *Chronicle Guidance Professional Service.* Moravia, N.Y.: Chronical Guidance Publications, 1972–1973, p. 3.

that they do not know the roles available in the society and the variety of styles in which they are played. I would urge that we find some way of connecting the diversity of the society to the phenomenon of school, to keep the latter from becoming so isolated and the former (from becoming) so suspicious.[13]

Need for Vocational Information and Help

The need for vocational guidance is clearly understood by students. Data collected from a national sample of students indicate that only 21 percent of them believe that they have sufficient information and help to plan their futures. Those students who believe they have sufficient help are those who make good grades, plan to go to college, and come from higher income families.[14]

Need for Career Identity Awareness

Moore[15] points out that many students need improved and expanded opportunities in order to become aware of their career opportunities. Such students form their occupational values and attitudes on the basis of fragmentary, incidental information and therefore their views of the work world are restricted. Vocational guidance gives students the opportunity to explore and conceptualize their notions of the work world. Finally, vocational guidance gives students the opportunity to generalize their emerging career identities through effective placement and follow-through activities.

General Research Findings

Results of several studies of youth's vocational development indicate

1. Many pupils choose from a narrow range of occupations.

2. A larger proportion of students aspire to enter the professions than actually enter. In some studies as many as 40 per cent of the students choose a professional occupation, while the number of people engaged nationwide in the professions is approximately 10 per cent.

---

[13]Jerome Bruner, "The Process of Education Revisited," *Phi Delta Kappan,* September 1971, pp. 18–21.
[14]Purdue Opinion Poll 85, *Counseling Needs of High School Students.* Lafayette, Indiana: Purdue University.
[15]Earl Moore, "Career Development: The Key to Relevancy," *Chronicle Guidance Professional Service.* Moravia, N.Y.: Chronicle Guidance Publications, 1972, p. 3.

3.   Boys evidence a striking lack of interest in clerical, sales, and related occupations though that field offers a relatively greater number of occupational opportunities.

4.   Many students select occupations either above or below their ability as measured by psychological tests. Pupils of high mental ability sometimes select vocations offering limited intellectual opportunities, and pupils of low mental ability sometimes select occupations for which they are not intellectually fitted.

5.   As many as a third of the students in high school are unable to indicate a choice of an occupation.

6.   There is a dearth of student information about earnings, requirements, and opportunities in various occupations. Many students believe they are going to earn much more than the average practitioner actually earns.

7.   Nine out of ten girls will work twenty-five years during their life time. Yet most girls' future planning seems to terminate with marriage.

Students who need assistance in vocational planning have a variety of concerns. To paraphrase Hahn and MacLean, some of the more common vocational problems of high school include

1.   *Uncertainty about vocational choice.* Many students will be uncertain as to vocational planning; some will be indifferent and express a "don't care" attitude; others in this category will be students of high ability who can succeed in many fields. The average adolescent experiences discomfort about his future, shows some anxiety regarding his vocational goals, and reveals a considerable number of mixed feelings about the outcome.

2.   *No choice of an occupation.* Among the high school population, many are so confused by the thousands of jobs available to them that they are unable to choose any in which they may find satisfaction. Some students find the societal pressure for an early decision of occupational area adds to their problems and complicates their choices. Experienced counselors know that students vary greatly in readiness to choose a life work.

3.   *Inappropriate vocational choice.* Students make inappropriate choices of vocations in a variety of ways; disparities between measured interests and abilities, between abilities and level of occupations chosen

(which may be too high or too low), or between abilities and interests that may be aptly geared together but out of line with personality structure, emotional patterns, social skills, etc. The average student believes that somehow, somewhere, his dreams will come true. He often fails to examine the probability of his wishes becoming reality.[16]

Buchheimer[17] believes that today's work world is a source of anxiety, resulting in part from fear of skill obsolescence. Principally, however, because work is dichotomized into productive and nonproductive, manual and intellectual, and training for work is dichotomized into vocational and academic, these dualistic conceptions have created anxiety. The anxiety is present because work is conceived of as either physical or nonphysical. Man becomes anxious not only through fear, loneliness, and lack of intrinsic motivation, but because he is unable to compensate and sublimate his need for physical and sensual experiences in pride of work. Modern man in the work world, according to Buchheimer, has moved from drudgery to anxiety. To ameliorate that condition, Buchheimer calls for schools to create tension rather than anxiety, to work toward the "individuated" related person who is creative rather than productive, to place a premium on "being" rather than "becoming" and to advance "educative work" to cope with anxiety. As examples of educative work, he cites such ventures as the Peace Corps, Job Corps, the CCC of former days and other community projects. Above all, schools must prepare for work, not merely for jobs, and the task of training in an automated society is "to train to *search* and to train to identify with many communities, to create tension and stress instead of anxiety and atrophy, to create selfhood through relatedness and individuation rather than individualism and competitiveness."[18]

Many social and economic factors have increased the need for vocational guidance. These include: (1) *industrial changes,* such as the increase in specialization and technological and scientific developments; (2) *vocational changes,* such as the increasing number of total jobs and sharp shifts in employment in certain occupational groups—such as the rise of clerical and kindred work and the decline of private household; (3) *population shifts,* such as the general increasing mobility of the population, the rural to urban movements, and the geographic movement southward and westward; (4) *changes in standards of living,* such as emphasis on increasingly higher living standards and keeping up with the Joneses; (5) *decreasing employ-*

---

[16]Milton E. Hahn and Malcolm MacLean, *Counseling Psychology.* New York: McGraw-Hill Book Co., Inc., 1955, pp. 47–49.

[17]Arnold Buchheimer, "From Drudgery to Anxiety," *Vocational Guidance Quarterly,* Vol. 14 (Winter, 1965–1966), pp. 77–82.

[18]Ibid., p. 80.

ment opportunities of youth, a situation which points to the need to identify potential dropouts and assist them to resolve their problems so that they may complete high school. These social and economic forces have increased the difficulty of vocational development for youth, and have increased their need for vocational guidance. As Drucker asserted:

> The problem today is not the lack of choice, but the abundance thereof. There are so many choices, so many opportunities, so many directions that they bewilder and distract the young people. No sooner have they shown a passing interest in this or that area than they are encouraged to make it their life's career.[19]

Above all, the need for vocational guidance can be seen in the opening remarks made to a counselor by over half of any high school's graduating students: "Mr. Counselor, I have to find a job in June." This need is ever present and insistent.

PURPOSES OF VOCATIONAL GUIDANCE

The major purpose of vocational guidance is to assist students, in systematic ways, to engage in vocational development. Counselors can help youth plan ways by which they can achieve satisfaction in work and life. Of necessity, such planning should take into consideration those processes and factors that aid or impede the individual's acquisition of values, knowledge, and skills that influence vocational behavior and development.

There is increasing recognition of the concept of vocational development. Tennyson and his associates[20] emphasize the fact that vocational choice is not a single choice made at one particular point in time, but rather is a long, on-going process. Their intent in emphasizing vocational development as a process is to create a philosophical undergirding for school vocational guidance procedures and practices. "Develop" means unfolding, evolving, and maturing by degrees and stages. Super and his colleagues state that ". . . the essence of development is progressive increase and modification of the individual's behavioral repertoire through growth and learning."[21] Development occurs over time and is marked by sequential stages. Each developmental step has bearing upon each succeeding stage. Each stage is

---

[19]Peter Drucker, *The Age of Discontinuity,* New York: Harper and Row, 1969, p. 274.

[20]W. Wesley Tennyson, Thomas A. Soldahl, and Charlotte Mueller, *The Teacher's Role in Career Development,* rev. ed. Washington, D.C.: National Vocational Guidance Association, 1965.

[21]Donald Super, et al., *Vocational Development: A Framework for Research.* New York: Teachers College Bureau of Publications, 1957, p. 36.

determined by prior ones and by the environmental factors with which the individual interacts while he progresses through a step.

Surveys have shown that interest in vocational development begins as early as the third grade. Starting from this point in elementary school, then, the process of vocational development might be considered—normatively, at least—to extend over something like a ten-year period. During this period, the maturity of the student's interest is steadily changing as is the level of information that he can deal with comfortably. For this reason, it seems desirable to maintain certain purposes or objectives at various points along the span of years during which vocational guidance should be present. The intent here is to present, somewhat in outline form, what appear to be reasonable purposes with regard to vocational guidance during the elementary, junior high, and senior high school years.

Elementary School Years

Almy believes that the six year old has lost some of his emotionally dominated behavior:

> He lives more in a world of reality and less in a world of phantasy.
> He can understand a number of relationships in the physical world.[22]

Further, in regard to self-awareness, "He knows his actions have consequences for other people and is more alert to their responses and feelings." Jersild has indicated that children, at an early age, ". . . have greater capacities for learning to meet, understand, and deal effectively with realities than has been assumed in psychological theories or in educational practice."[23]

Wellington and Olechowski sought to determine whether or not primary grade children could realistically "gain awareness" essential to formation of vocational attitudes and value formation. They used a class of 30 third-grade children in a suburban Chicago elementary school who studied a unit entitled "Shelter." The children's discussion of the material indicated that they had little understanding of the worker's role and functions. They had the children interview people they knew and, after completing the interviews, present their findings for discussion in class. Wellington and Olechowski concluded that the children in this project, among other things, (1) developed a more realistic understanding of the work world, (2) developed appreciations for different kinds of work, and (3) developed respect for

---

[22]Millie Almy, *Child Development*. New York: Holt, Rinehart and Winston, Inc., 1955, p. 200.

[23]Arthur T. Jersild, "Self Understanding in Childhood and Adolescence," *American Psychologist*. Vol. 6 (1951), pp. 122–126.

other people, the kinds of work they do, and the contributions made by providing products and services for everyone.[24]

Nelson demonstrated that as early as the third grade children have well-developed attitudes regarding occupations and levels of education. Moreover, as early as ages eight and nine, children tend to reject some occupations as of no interest to them. He concluded that elementary school children have already begun to assimilate perceptions and preferences which may be wholesome and meaningful, or distorted and ultimately harmful to aspirations and achievements.[25] Creason and Schilson asked a sample of 121 sixth-graders about their vocational plans. These two investigators reported that none failed to indicate some vocational preference, and only eight indicated that they did not know why they chose their particular reference.[26]

In his plans for vocational development, Kaback indicates that for pupils in grades one and two, vocational activities would be directed to providing information and understanding about the various kinds of businesses children can observe, and the interdependence of workers. At third and fourth grades, detailed examination of the kind of work children perform in their classrooms would stimulate extended discussion about occupations and their merits and opportunities, the nature of work, and so forth. Fifth and sixth grade projects would be concentrated upon observation about occupations they had learned about through visiting a working parent on the job.[27]

During the elementary school years, the general purposes of vocational development might well be to aid children in understanding that all legitimate occupations are necessary to our way of life, and hence deserve respect. The present emphasis given to the professions and white-collar jobs does not seem to be in the best interests of either children or society at large. It might be noted that the primary aim at the elementary level is to arouse an interest in occupations—generically—and this purpose might be well served by arousing interest in the occupations of parents or family members, or jobs done by the children themselves, or even occupations suggested by everyday phenomena. With care taken not to limit children's vocational interest, the elementary school counselor can develop an awareness of the kinds of activities pupils enjoy, the kinds of activities they do well, and the personal values they are in the process of forming.

[24]John A. Wellington and Nan Olechowski, "Attitudes Toward the World of Work in Elementary School" Vocational Guidance Quarterly, Vol. 14 (Spring, 1966), pp. 160–162.

[25]Richard C. Nelson, "Knowledge and Interest Concerning Sixteen Occupations Among Elementary and Secondary Students," Educational and Psychological Measurement, Vol. 23, (Winter 1963) pp. 741–754.

[26]F. Creason and D. L. Schilson, "Occupational Concerns of Sixth Grade Children," Vocational Guidance Quarterly, Vol. 18 (March 1970), pp. 219–224.

[27]Goldie Ruth Kaback, "Occupational Information for Groups of Elementary School Children," Vocational Guidance Journal, Vol. 14 (Spring, 1966), pp. 163–168.

Halverson has proposed several principles upon which vocational development in the elementary school could be based. His principles, paraphrased here, are:

1. Goals and objectives, defined in terms of the educational needs and interests of students at this stage of development, are needed.

2. Vocational development should be considered within the larger concept of the elementary school goals. Vocational development activities should not be fragmented or separated from the curriculum, but rather should be considered as an integral part of goals validated for elementary education.

3. Curriculum planning as it is influenced by vocational development should not be dominated by college preparatory emphasis.

4. Readiness for learning vocational behaviors must be determined by what has already been learned by the student, the projected goals that relate to the students' expressed or identified needs, and the general level of his intellectual, social and emotional maturity.

5. Concrete experiences and learning must precede learning of the abstract. Younger children function more successfully in the concrete realm than in the abstract. Readiness for abstractions increases with age.

6. If goals or objectives for vocational development are set forth, experiences and activities must be sequenced in a way that maximizes the likelihood that students will achieve these goals.

7. There are many subject areas and activities in the elementary schools that lend themselves to vocational development.[28]

Gysbers has labeled the vocational development phases that span the elementary and early junior high school years as perceptualization, conceptualization, and generalization. The perceptualization phase focuses on the processes necessary for the child to become aware of himself and his environment and to differentiate between them. Concept formation, in the *conceptualization* phase (grades four to six), is mediated by past experiences and given direction by the individual's values. The person's values are shaped by stereotypes, community and family input, and the breadth or narrowness of his knowledge about his work. The generalization phase is

---

[28]P. M. Halverson, "A Rationale for a Career Development Program in the Elementary School." Paper presented to the Program Development Committee of the Cobb County, Ga., Schools, January, 1970. Mimeographed.

a period during which the student uses the already formed concepts about differences among people and occupations to generalize to wider radii in these domains.[29]

Norris, Zeran, and Hatch have suggested that vocational information provided at the elementary levels should (1) develop wholesome attitudes toward all fields of work; (2) develop an awareness of the wide variety of workers; (3) help the child answer the myriad questions he may have about occupations; and (4) bring out varying rewards of work since influences of home or community may indicate remuneration in the form of wages or salary is the only reason for working.[30]

Dinkmeyer cites the following objectives of vocational development activities at the elementary school level:

1. To increase the child's understanding of his abilities.

2. To provide opportunity for the child's exploration of the aptitude, interest and personality factors necessary on certain jobs.

3. To make the child aware that his self-image will determine his choice of work and way of life.

4. To help children develop realistic attitudes and methods in dealing with school achievement as an aspect of vocation.

5. To help pupils understand that rapid changes taking place in the world of work will necessitate advanced training.

6. To help the child understand that all legitimate occupations are worthwhile.[31]

JUNIOR HIGH SCHOOL YEARS

In grades seven, eight, and nine, it is desirable that the vocational guidance service provide students with an opportunity to become informed of their abilities and personal qualities. The informational aspect of the vocational guidance service will help students review the world of work in general and acquaint them with the overall occupational local patterns. Consideration will be given to the educational opportunities in high school

---

[29]Norman Gysbers, "Elements of a Model for Promoting Career Development in Elementary and Junior High Schools." Paper presented at National Conference on Exemplary Programs and Projects Section of the Vocational Education Act, Amendments of 1968, Atlanta, Ga., March 1969.

[30]Willa Norris, Franklin R. Zeran, and Raymond H. Hatch, *The Information Service in Guidance for Career Development and Planning* (3rd ed.). Chicago: Rand McNally & Co., 1972, pp. 158–159.

[31]Don C. Dinkmeyer (ed.) *Guidance and Counseling in the Elementary School: Readings in Theory and Practice.* New York: Holt, Rinehart and Winston, 1968, p. 309.

and beyond, that relate to occupational choices. Tentative formulations of education and vocational plans will be initiated. The emphasis on activities at this level is on exploratory activities. Vocational guidance in the junior high school must be integrated with instructional content, yet must not lose its own identity and become wholly instructional in nature, in the sense that characterizes other material to be learned.

Norris, Zeran, and Hatch have proposed that at the junior high school level, the aims of occupational information are: (1) to learn about broad fields of work; (2) to see the relationship of these fields to curriculum choices; (3) to secure information about specific job employment; (4) to understand the means for obtaining accurate, up-to-date information about the occupational world; (5) to understand the significance and scope of vocational planning; and (6) to understand that the work world is never static, but always changing.[32]

Gysbers and Pritchard have suggested vocational guidance objectives for junior high school students:

1. The student further differentiates his self-characteristics (interests, values, abilities, and personality characteristics) from those of others, and can identify broad occupational areas and levels which may be more appropriate for him.

2. The student differentiates between the several broad occupational areas in terms of (a) a potential satisfaction each might offer him, (b) the nature of work tasks performed, (c) the future impact technology might have on particular occupational areas, (d) the contribution and importance of particular occupational areas to our society, and (e) the future demand for workers in broad occupational areas.

3. The student identifies different educational areas that are available both in the immediate and more distant future, the nature and purpose of each, and the avenues toward which each can lead. He tentatively assesses what each offers him in terms of his possible vocational choices. He demonstrates how knowledge and skills acquired in different subject matter areas relate to performing different work roles. He recognizes the personal and social significance that work has in the lives of individuals at varying levels within the occupational structure.

4. The student identifies future decisions he must make in order to reach different goals. He identifies those personal and environmental efforts that impinge upon his future decisions. He assesses possible steps he might take in minimizing negative

---

[32]Norris, Zeran, and Hatch, *The Information Service, op. cit.,* p. 160.

factors and maximizing positive ones, and considers the possible consequences each has for him.

5. The student makes a choice of a broad occupational area to study in greater depth.

6. The student can differentiate between the major occupations that make up a broad occupational area, and can make some differentiation of these occupations in terms of (a) the amount and type of education needed for entrance; (b) the content, tools, setting, products or services of these occupations; (c) their value to society; (d) their ability to provide him with the type of life style he desires; (e) to what extent they can satisfy his interests and values; (f) in what ways they do and do not seem appropriate for him.

7. The student selects education or training in the light of his tentative broad career purposes.[33]

HIGH SCHOOL YEARS

In high school, two general purposes of vocational guidance emerge. The first purpose is to provide the student with an opportunity to work out vocational plans for himself. This means helping the student define his problems and to resolve them in as realistic a manner as possible. The counselor assists the student to discuss and think through his occupational dilemma. Through individual and group procedures, the student is helped to reduce his indecisions and conflicting feelings about vocational development. He learns to utilize his strengths in the development of a course of action or a career plan. Although such a course of action may be only tentative, the student should work out present and possible vocational opportunities if he intends to secure employment in the local community. The second general purpose of vocational guidance is to provide students with factual, specific vocational information. Such information would include psychological test evidence about the student himself, and knowledge about various occupations and opportunities in specific fields. Consideration should be given to particular occupations and to high school and post-high school educational opportunities in the student's area of interests and abilities.

The National Conference on Guidance, Counseling and Placement in Career Development and Educational-Occupational Decision-making (Gysbers

[33]Norman C. Gysbers and David H. Pritchard (eds.) *Proceedings, National Conference on Guidance, Counseling and Placement in Career Development and Educational-Occupational Decision-Making.* Columbia, Mo.: University of Missouri, October, 1969, p. 73–74. Material used with permission.

and Pritchard) recommended these vocational guidance objectives for the secondary school:

1. The student develops awareness of his need for more specific implementation of his career purposes.

2. The student develops more specific plans for implementing his career purposes.

3. The student executes plans to qualify for entry-level jobs by taking appropriate courses at the high school level, by on-the-job training, or by pursuing further training in college or post-secondary vocational education geared toward acquiring qualifications for some specific occupation.[34]

It should be noted that these suggested objectives of vocational guidance involve an overall progression from general to specific. In addition, it should be emphasized that vocational development involves a long process, during which objectives should be determined in the light of the kind of level of interest maturity and the imminence of the time of actual occupational choice. The senior high school years are the time when students test their aspirations by developing plans for converting them into reality.

THE CONTRIBUTIONS OF VOCATIONAL COUNSELING

Counseling will be advantageous to the student as he strives to develop a self-acceptable vocational plan. In organizing the vocational guidance service, opportunities for counseling should be provided at crucial stages in the sequential development of the student's experiences in career planning. Counseling is needed to help the individual determine, understand, accept, and use the known information about himself so that he can relate it to the relevant facts about the vocational world. Those students who are referred to the school counselor or who are self-referred seek vocational counseling because there is some doubt about their particular course of action or career plans. Some students will desire an objective verification of their potentialities; others seek additional information about occupations.

Vocational counseling is thought of as the assistance given to students in decision making. Appropriate decisions are made when an individual is cognizant of his strengths and limitations. Herman and Molen present the following components of a formula to assist the counselor in gathering the necessary facts and making positive conclusions: (1) The equation of awareness. The student must have knowledge of his abilities, his real interests, and his performances; (2) The equation of self-knowledge. The knowledge of

---

[34]Gysbers and Pritchard, *Proceedings,* p. 74.

one's potential is combined with self-knowledge and work experience which results in a measure of possible job opportunities open to the student; (3) The equation of vocational understanding. The knowledge of the two previously discussed equations makes known the possibility of numerous vocational opportunities that are applicable to a person's abilities and interests.[35]

Nature of Vocational Counseling

As a service, the intent of vocational guidance is to help students make vocational plans and decisions that are appropriate to them. Vocational counseling may be seen as a cornerstone for the vocational guidance service. It is viewed as a cornerstone since the individual, to come to an appropriate decision, must know as much as possible about himself and the work world. It is through individual and small-group counseling that the student will be able to deal with the complexity of the work world and the affective components related to his future involvement in it. At present, many issues cloud the nature of vocational counseling. Some believe that the introduction of external data into counseling means that counseling, per se, stops or is interrupted. The reader is referred to Chapter 7 in which this was discussed. It may be remembered that Goldman held that counseling need not be interrupted to consider external data if two conditions are present: counselors maintain the same attitude toward appraisal and environmental data as they do toward other information and counselors keep informed and up-to-date regarding assessment and informational resources, their reliabilities and validities.[36]

Boy and Pine[37] urge counselors to examine periodically the rationale which undergirds their use of information and advice as part of counseling procedure. They pose

> An important series of questions every school counselor should ask himself is—do I change the behavior of my counselees by giving them advice and information? To what degree do my counselees change and make decisions on the basis of advice and information I give them? How enduring and lasting are changes in the behavior of my counselees as the result of information and advice I give them? Do I give information and advice because the counselee needs information and advice, or do I give information and advice because I need to?[38]

---

[35] Jerry J. Herman and Robert Vander Molen, "An Equation for Use in Vocational Counseling," *Vocational Guidance Quarterly,* Vol. 8, No. 1 (Autumn, 1959), p. 41.

[36] Leo Goldman, "Information and Counseling: A Dilemma," *Personnel and Guidance Journal,* Vol. 46 (September, 1967), pp. 42–47.

[37] Angelo V. Boy and Gerald J. Pine, "The Counseling Process: A Perspective on Information and Advice," *Vocational Guidance Quarterly,* Vol. 14 (Spring, 1966), pp. 201–204.

[38] *Ibid.,* p. 202.

While Boy and Pine acknowledge that school counselors, in carrying out their educational and vocational guidance responsibilities, will become involved in informational relationships, they warn counselors to be aware that dispensing information can be a means of insulating themselves from counselees, that it can be a means by which counselors feel more secure and omniscient.

The following extract from Borow would seem to point up the need for vocational counseling:

> ... the individual's encounter with vocational development tasks may be viewed as instances of reality testing in which he takes a variety of social roles, tests them for consonance with self, often unconsciously, and develops a progressively differentiated and stable self-image. Thus, in motivational terms, his striving to arrive at an appropriate vocational goal may be interpreted as a search for a work role that is harmonious with the need structure resulting from the gratifications and frustrations of early life (Roe), as a search for the new ego identity that marks the adolescent stage (Erikson), or as an attempt to implement an already emerging self-concept (Super).[39]

Samler thought that the reservations about the nature and use of information in counseling were four in number. These were (1) vocational counseling and its use of occupational information is based upon a theory (trait and factor) that is unsatisfactory and incomplete; (2) informational resources used in counseling are incomplete; (3) occupational investigation is not psychologically based; and (4) even with proliferation of occupational material, there is reason for concern that the realities of work, the work force, and the labor structure are not really considered.[40] Because of these reservations, Samler identified seven proposals for occupational exploration in counseling. These proposals, in his words, are stated here:

1. Occupational exploration is not a separable part of the counseling process.

2. The client's needs should be identified and their strength assessed.

3. The client's potential for commitment to task is assessed.

---

[39]Henry Borow, "Conjunction of Career Development and Curriculum: Problems and Potentials," *Conference on Implementing Career Development Theory and Research Through the Curriculum.* Washington: National Vocational Guidance Association, August, 1966.

[40]Joseph Samler, "Occupational Exploration in Counseling: A Proposed Reorientation," Henry Borow (ed.), *Man in a World at Work.* Boston: Houghton Mifflin Company, 1965, pp. 413–414.

4. The client is helped to become aware of the nature of career development and progression. His potential for orderly career is assessed.

5. The working world should be seen as a totality. Within it the individual should be seen as a psychosocial as well as an economic entity.

6. The process of occupational exploration is psychological in the sense that the client's perceptions are taken into account.

7. Occupational exploration should provide a model for decision making, not necessarily, the decision itself.[41]

Patterson[42] believes that vocational counseling includes the following elements: (1) an atmosphere of acceptance and understanding is created so that the client can engage in self-analysis; (2) the client is encouraged to express his self-concept in terms of his needs, conflicts, anxieties, hopes, desires, and expectations, particularly as they relate to his aptitudes, abilities, interests, and concepts of work; (3) the individual is provided with information about himself through tests and inventories for self-exploration; (4) the individual is assisted to explore vocational opportunities through use of occupational information; and (5) the client is helped to relate information about himself and about occupations in terms of self-concept, to develop plans, set goals, and increase his understanding of himself in relation to the work world.

Samler[43] views vocational counseling as a psychological enterprise which must go beyond cognitive formulations and into feeling because work can be a road to self-acceptance and mental health. However, he questions that commitment to therapy (personality restructuring) is an encompassing substitute for vocational counseling. He points to other aspects of personality change that do not depend as much upon restructuring the personality. This statement of his view about the nature of vocational counseling parallels an earlier statement in which Samler, while recognizing the importance of the psychological aspects of vocational counseling seemed to differentiate between vocational and psychological counseling. In this work, he discussed the processes of vocational exploration as related to the individual's psychological needs and explains "Since such problems are by definition in the area of personality adjustment, it is proper so to label them. It is not, however, necessary to change sports jackets for white coats, to abandon vocational

---

[41] *Ibid.*, pp. 414–429.

[42] C. H. Patterson, "Counseling: Self-Clarification and the Helping Relationship," Borow, *Man in a World at Work, ibid.,* p. 446.

[43] Joseph Samler, "A New Psychological Specialty: Vocational Counseling," *Vocational Guidance Quarterly,* Vol. 15 (December, 1966), pp. 80–82.

counseling with the client for personal adjustment counseling."[44] And again he states "It cannot be denied that he (the vocational counselor) must be a clinical worker and should be as competent in understanding behavior as is any clinical practitioner. But he is not a therapist, at least not in the usual sense."

Patterson[45] has reacted to the position taken by some extremists who insist that vocational counseling *is not* counseling but rather is vocational guidance, or teaching, or advising, or decision making. The need for and the reason why vocational counseling developed, according to Patterson, is because

> It is the recognition of and dealing with affective factors in vocational development and choice, including the self-concept as related to occupational perceptions and preferences, and affective reactions to information which involves the self-concept—such as scores on tests of aptitudes and abilities—which makes consideration of vocational problems counseling rather than "guidance."[46]

Patterson does not view vocational counseling as being a lower level activity than therapeutic counseling nor does he believe that the preparation of vocational counselors requires less time than the preparation of therapeutic counselors. Rather, his judgement is that therapeutic counselors can be prepared in one year but two years of preparation are required for vocational counselors. The reason is that vocational counselors must be taught "tests and measurements and occupational information *and* their use in counseling."

Patterson prepared a statement which was accepted and became part of a policy statement issued by the APGA's Professional Preparation and Standards Committee:

> Counselor education programs do not prepare vocational counselors, educational counselors, or personal counselors, as such, but prepare counselors who are qualified to deal with all these areas. All counseling deals with the total counselee. It is not possible to categorize his needs into educational, vocational, social or emotional. Thus, in order to deal adequately with the vocational aspects (or any single aspect) of a counselee's development the counselor must also be prepared to recognize and deal with other aspects of his development.[47]

---

[44]Joseph Samler, Occupational Exploration in Counseling: A Proposed Reorientation," in Henry Borow (ed.), *Man in a World at Work.* Boston: Houghton-Mifflin Company, 1964, pp. 411–433.

[45]C. H. Patterson, "Counseling: Vocational or Therapeutic?" *Vocational Guidance Quarterly,* Vol. 15 (September, 1966), pp. 61–65.

[46]*Ibid.,* p. 63.

[47]American Personnel and Guidance Association Professional Preparation and Standards Committee, "The Relationship of Short-term and Specialized Programs to the APGA Policy Statement, The Counselor: Professional Preparation and Role," *Personnel and Guidance Journal,* Vol. 43 (January, 1965), pp. 538–539.

While theoreticians may debate the nature of vocational counseling, the work of the school counselor as he assists students in their vocational development goes on. Noting that career development studies of adolescent girls are uncommon despite projections of the expansion of women in the labor market, Anderson and Heimann sought to test the supposition that short-term vocational counseling would contribute to the career development and vocational maturation of junior high school girls. "Vocational maturity" measures used in the study included (1) verbal expressions concerning approaches to planning for vocational choice, degree of awareness of training, need for making a choice, assumption of responsibility for making a choice (collected by structured interview schedules) and (2) knowledge of self and occupations (collected by a revised test of knowledge of the work world and a self-discrepancy scale based on differences between scores on 36 measures and self-estimates of these scores). Some 60 eighth grade girls drawn randomly from two Phoenix, Arizona, schools were divided into two equal groups designated experimental and control. The 30 experimental subjects were involved in six individual counseling sessions during the six weeks prior to completion of the eighth grade. Counseling, by two male, third-year graduate students in guidance, was highly structured and utilized leads designed to encourage the counselees to think about career choice, occupations, and self-concepts. Counseling sessions averaged 35 minutes in length. Based upon their findings, Anderson and Heimann report

> Analysis of results indicated the experimental subjects had more favorable scores in the predicted direction than did the controls in every case. However, when subjected to a series of analysis of variance tests, only differences on the VMS (vocational maturity scale) reached the 0.05 level of significance.[48]

The reader will note that differences between the two groups were not statistically significant in the case of knowledge of occupational information and self-estimating capability. These two authors believe that counseling was effective in increasing subjects' measured vocational maturity and drew the implication that girls at the eighth grade level were developmentally ready for preliminary planning activities. In other words

> Given the opportunity to sit down with a counselor at regular intervals and think about and discuss themselves, the world of work, and their perceptions of their vocational future, they will benefit significantly by becoming more vocationally mature as reflected by their increased scores on the VMS. To the extent that increased vocational

---

[48]Dale G. Anderson and Robert A. Heimann, "Vocational Maturity of Junior High School Girls," *Vocational Guidance Quarterly,* Vol. 15 (March, 1967), p. 194.

maturity is regarded as a suitable objective of our educational system, the present findings provide one justification of short-term, vocational counseling at the eighth grade level with girls as a regular school activity.[49]

Clients' Knowledge of Occupations

Clients will differ considerably in their knowledge of occupations. Some students who have made a definite choice of an occupation that seems appropriate for them may have little need for occupational information. Other students will seek aid from the counselor and, according to Hoppock, will need to know: (1) the range of vocational opportunities open to them; (2) the sources of vocational information available and how to appraise their accuracy; (3) how to choose an occupation; (4) how to find a job; and (5) the significant specific things about an occupation.[50]

Counselor's Knowledge of Occupations

The school counselor is not expected to know everything about the some 22,000 occupations available to youth. He will have to separate a core of essential knowledge from that not quite so essential and master it. Hoppock believes vocational knowledge essential for a counselor includes: (1) the first jobs of the school's dropouts and graduates; (2) the principal employment opportunities for the school's dropouts and graduates; (3) those occupations that are being seriously considered by his students; (4) sources of information about occupations and how to appraise its accuracy; and (5) labor legislation.[51]

Having learned this core of information about his students and community, the counselor can then extend further his knowledge of occupations.

Some General Principles for Vocational Counseling

The counselor will need skill in the incorporation of vocational information in the counseling process. Such skill will include judgment as to when and how facts about occupations should be brought in. Tyler discusses three principles useful as guides in this respect:

> The first of these has to do with economy of the client's time. He should not have to acquire detailed information about occupations that

---

[49] *Ibid.*
[50] Robert Hoppock, *Occupational Information* (3rd ed.). New York: McGraw-Hill Book Company, 1967, pp. 18–19.
[51] *Ibid.*, pp. 6–15.

are completely out of the question for him. This means that often the facts about jobs are brought in after he has taken some tests designed to get at individual strengths and weaknesses.

The second principle governing the use of occupational information is that it should be brought in such a way as not to break down or confuse the essential structure of the counseling relationship. If the counselor explains the facts in an authoritative way, the client may lose the sense that his is a situation in which he is to make his own decision and see it instead as one in which he is called upon to accept or reject a decision made for him by someone else.

A third principle in the use of occupational information . . . There should be plenty of opportunity for the expression of feeling and attitudes. The girl who has been seriously considering social work needs a chance to express the disappointment she feels when she discovers what very low salaries many social workers receive.[52]

Shostrom and Brammer believe there is danger in giving vocational guidance information too early or when not solicited by the client. They cite some general principles to guide the counselor in his use of occupational information in the counseling situation.

1. *Objectivity.* Information should be given without personal reference.

2. *Occupational facts.* Occupational facts should be presented directly from printed matter rather than from memory.

3. *Suggesting occupations.* When occupations are indicated to the counselor but not the client, the counselor may suggest them as possibilities to consider.

4. *Timing.* Occupational information and suggestions are held in abeyance until (1) the individual appraisal phases are completed, (2) the client feels a need for such information, or (3) the counselor feels that occupational information would serve an instrumental or therapeutic function.

5. *Synthesis.* The counselor has a responsibility to help the client relate occupational facts to the predetermined data from tests and the personal history of the client.

6. *Verification.* The counselor helps the client to verify and clarify the occupational information gained in his library research.

[52]Leona E. Tyler, *The Work of the Counselor,* third edition. New York: Appleton-Century-Crofts, Educational Division, Meredith Corporation, 1969, pp. 129–131.

7. *General education.* Counselors should avoid de-emphasizing the general educational values of certain courses of study.[53]

Counselor's Use of Occupational Information

Baer and Roeber list seven uses of occupational information in the counseling interview:

1. *Exploratory use.* Occupational information is used to help the counselee to make an extensive study of the work world.

2. *Information use.* Counselees are assisted to make a detailed study of a few occupations.

3. *Assurance use.* The counselor uses occupational information to assure the counselee that he has made an appropriate or inappropriate choice of vocations.

4. *Motivational use.* Occupational information will be used to arouse the counselee's interest in school work or in vocational planning.

5. *Holding use.* Occupational information will be used to retain the counselee in counseling situations until he gains some insight into his real needs and into his behavior.

6. *Evaluative use.* The counselor will check the accuracy and adequacy of the counselee's knowledge and understanding of an occupation.

7. *Startle use.* The counselor will ascertain if the counselee is uncertain or anxious after he chooses a particular vocation.[54]

Test Interpretation

One of the major responsibilities of the vocational counselor is to interpret the results of psychological tests and inventories to students. Test interpretation in vocational counseling has two main problems. One, how may the counselor present the test results and their predictive possibilities so that the counselee understands them? and two, what methods can be used with the counselee to facilitate his use of such information? The Bixlers urge counselors to:

---

[53]Lawrence Brammer and Everett L. Shostrom, *Therapeutic Psychology* (2nd ed.). Englewood Cliffs, N.J.: Prentice-Hall, Inc., 1968, pp. 407–417.

[54]Reprinted by permission from *Occupational Information* by Max F. Baer and Edward C. Roeber, Copyright © 1951, pp. 424–72; also see 1964 ed., pp. 425–451, Science Research Associates, Inc., p. 468.

1. Give the client simple statistical predictions based upon test data.

2. Allow the client to evaluate the prediction as it applies to himself.

3. Remain neutral toward test data and the client's reaction.

4. Facilitate the client's self-evaluation and subsequent decisions by the use of therapeutic procedures.

5. Avoid persuasive methods: test data, not the counselor, should provide motivation.[55]

The Counselor's Approach

Bramner and Shostrom point out that vocational counseling can be viewed in several ways. First, it can simply be a process of confirming a choice already made by a counselee; second, vocational counseling can be viewed largely as a process which helps to clarify vocational objectives. Finally, vocational counseling can be viewed as permitting clients to discover facts about themselves and the working world.[56]

Presumably, whatever view is held must be implemented by certain techniques. Selecting practices which help the client examine what he is like and wants to become requires artful judgment, based upon counselor experience, insight, and skill. Some time ago, Super addressed himself to this matter:

> Since vocational development consists of implementing a self concept, and since self-concepts often need modification before they can be implemented, it is important that the student, client, or patient put his self-concept into words early in the counseling process. He needs to do this for himself, to clarify his actual role and his role aspirations; he needs to do it for the counselor, so that the counselor may understand the nature of the vocational counseling problem confronting him. This calls for the cyclical use of nondirective and directive methods. Schematically, vocational counseling can be described as involving the following cycle:
>
> 1. Nondirective problem exploration and self-concept portrayal
>
> 2. Directive topic setting, for further exploration
>
> 3. Nondirective reflection and clarification of feeling for self-acceptance and insight.

---

[55]Ray H. Bixler and Virginia H. Bixler, "Test Interpretation in Vocational Counseling," *Educational and Psychological Measurement.* 1946, 6, p. 155.

[56]Brammer and Shostrom, *Therapeutic Psychology,* pp. 401–402.

4. Directive exploration of factual data from tests, occupational pamphlets, extracurricular experiences, grades, etc., for reality testing.

5. Nondirective consideration of possible lines of action, for help in decision-making.[57]

CONSULTING WITH PARENTS

Many students are influenced by, and dependent on, their parents when they plan their vocational careers. Few students decide on vocations that are at extreme variance with their parent's aspirations and wishes. In a vocational guidance situation, the counselor may find the help of the parent very desirable. Some students may ask that their parents be included in the guidance process while others may resist this. Some students may use the counselor as a force against their parents by misrepresenting the counselor's statements. Parents differ in their attitudes toward participation. Some will call the school counselor and ask to accompany the student. Generally, parents want to be apprised of the results of psychological tests and inventories.

In working with parents about a vocational problem, the counselor is bound by the professional confidentiality of his relationship with the student. Extreme care, skill, and tact will be required if the student is not to lose confidence in the counselor. The school counselor is not free to divulge any information received in the counseling relationship without the student's consent. In vocational counseling, the school should maintain a policy of encouraging parents to talk with the counselor, although it should not be necessary for the counselor to see the parents of every student.

ORGANIZING GROUP PROCEDURES FOR VOCATIONAL GUIDANCE

Group procedures which present vocational guidance information are ordinarily organized in three ways: (1) through a course organized specifically for the purpose; (2) through a special unit in one of the school subjects such as social studies; and (3) through special events, such as plant visits and career conferences. In some schools, the vocational guidance service has utilized all three ways, or some combination of them. Care must be taken when all three are used to avoid duplication of material and purposes. Group vocational guidance is concerned primarily with disseminating voca-

---

[57]Donald E. Super, *The Psychology of Careers,* New York: Harper and Brothers, 1957, p. 308.

tional information, broadening the vocational horizons of students, and stimulating interest in vocational counseling among the individual members of a particular group.

Hoppock has written that the teaching of occupations to groups has the following advantages: (1) it saves time in counseling because many general questions are answered in the group procedure; (2) it provides a background of information that improves counseling in that clients have information against which to discuss the individual aspects of their problems; (3) it gives the counselor an opportunity to know his clients better; (4) it focuses collective judgment on common problems; (5) it provides some assurance that complex problem cases will not monopolize the counselor's time; (6) it keeps the counselor up-to-date; (7) counselors recognize the need for it; and (8) it may permit a part-time counselor to spend full time on guidance and thus become more competent.[58]

Norris, Zeran, and Hatch have summarized the disadvantages of group activities as being: (1) many problems of students require the face-to-face relationships of counseling and cannot be considered in a group situation; (2) group activities are not equally effective with all students; (3) the organization of a group with sufficient homogeneity of interest, maturity level, and problems poses administrative problems; (4) there is a shortage of teachers competent in group techniques; and (5) the school curriculum is already overcrowded.[59]

In organizing any or all of the three group procedures, the emphasis should be evenly divided between projects involving study of self and study of vocational informational materials. The group procedure used should provide the student with an opportunity to engage in self-study prior to studying occupational fields. From this self-study of aptitudes and interest patterns, specific occupational information materials could be explored and analyzed. The instructional content related to group study of the occupational fields would then be centered around the expressed interests of the members of the group. The occupations likely to be followed by the majority of the members would serve as a guideline for group study.

Courses in Occupations

Objectives of the occupations course as taught in secondary schools and colleges in Illinois have been identified by Wright. He established some twenty-five objectives. Ranked in order, the first four of these are:

> To help students appraise their own interests, abilities, aptitudes, and personality characteristics with respect to the needs of occupations. To acquaint students with sources of occupational information, and to

---

[58]Hoppock, *Occupational Information,* pp. 167–169.
[59]Norris, Zeran, and Hatch, *Information Service,* pp. 406–407.

educate them in the skills required to find, use, and organize such materials. To help students develop wholesome attitudes toward work and other workers. To create a desire in each student to be of service to society by filling a useful place in the world of work.[60]

Two different approaches characterize the courses being taught in occupations. The first approach (and the earliest) is based on the belief that the acquisition of data about the work world is the starting point for vocational guidance. Brayfield states the assumptions of this approach to be

1. The individual who has been formally exposed to occupational information will make more appropriate vocational choices than the individual who has not been so exposed.

2. The individual will make specific application of the content of the course to his own situation with a minimum of individual assistance.

3. The individual completing such a course will develop attitudes and skills which will carry over as new problems of vocational adjustment arise.[61]

The second approach is based on the belief that the acquisition of information about the self is the proper starting place for vocational planning. Super has written that the assumptions underlying this approach are "developed to a point at which it is reasonable or desirable to expect them to commit themselves to a vocation."[62]

As the student moves into these tracks, he progresses nearer to one type of vocational goal and further away from other possible goals. Eli Ginzberg has aptly characterized this as the irreversibility of vocational choice.[63]

Finding personnel qualified to teach courses in occupations is one of the difficult problems confronting the administrators of the guidance program. Without question, counselors would be persons best qualified to teach a course in occupations, since their preparation includes courses in occupational information, vocational development and group procedures.

Sinick, Gorman, and Hoppock[64] reviewed forty-four studies—thirty-four of which were experimental—on the teaching of occupations at the elemen-

---

[60]Ralph E. Wright, "Teaching Occupational Information in Illinois Secondary Schools," *Personnel and Guidance Journal,* September, 1956, pp. 30–33.

[61]Arthur H. Brayfield, "Putting Occupational Information Across," *Educational and Psychological Measurement,* 1948, 8, pp. 485–495.

[62]Donald E. Super, "The Critical Ninth Grade: Vocational Choice or Vocational Exploration," *Personnel and Guidance Journal,* Vol. 39, (October, 1960), pp. 108–109.

[63]E. Ginzberg, S. W. Ginsberg, S. Axelrad, and J. L. Herma, *Occupational Choice.* New York: Columbia University Press, 1951.

[64]Daniel Sinick, William E. Gorman and Robert Hoppock, "Research on the Teaching of Occupations: 1965–1970." *Vocational Guidance Quarterly,* Vol. 20 (December, 1971), pp. 129–137.

tary, secondary, and post-secondary school levels. One implication they drew from their review was that occupations courses accomplished more than dissemination of information. They found that such courses may have salutary effects on noncognitive variables such as attitudes toward work, realism of interests, vocational maturity, motivation, independence, and decision-making. In another study, Sinick and Hoppock[65] presented practices that were associated with the teaching of occupations that had been rated as "exceptional" or "good" by some 97 percent of the personnel in 696 Illinois high schools. These practices are cited in Table 9–1.

Table 9–1.   *Practice Related to the Teaching of Occupations in Illinois. [From Daniel Sinick and Robert Hoppock, "Research Across the Nation on the Teaching of Occupations,"©Vocational Guidance Quarterly, Vol. 14 (Autumn, 1965), p. 23. Used with permission.]*

Practice	Percent
File of occupational information	89
Information on training opportunities	88
Career Days and related activities	45
Short units on occupations (about 1 week)	42
Community occupational and other surveys	42
Community occupational and other surveys	38
Units on occupations (about 6 weeks)	34
Exploratory courses	32
Occupations courses (semester or longer)	16
Supervised work experience	14

Units Within School Subjects

When vocational information is presented as a special unit within one of the school subjects, systematic organization of the material is most necessary. Otherwise, teachers will tend to present it only if and when they think of it. The contents of the unit will vary with the type of students and the length of the course, as well as the grade level at which it is taught. The teacher's background and experiences will likewise be factors in determining its content.

Such units are often of an exploratory general nature. A frequently cited objective is to assist students to gain the perspective to view an occupation within the framework of the entire occupational structure. Another goal is student participation in the unit. Participation will help students become more knowledgeable at grouping occupations and studying and describing the changes taking place in them.

---

[65]Daniel Sinick and Robert Hoppock, "Research Across the Nation on the Teaching of Occupations" *Vocational Guidance Quarterly,* Vol. 14 (Autumn, 1965), pp. 21–25.

The contents and methods of such units are often similar to that of a standard guidance course. However, the time allotted for such units is usually only two to nine weeks. Consequently, only cursory treatment is given to most essential topics: (1) self-understanding and appraisal; (2) career planning; and (3) educational planning.

Baer and Roeber describe three occupational units that can be offered in an occupations course or as separate units within a school subject: Unit I, Exploratory; Unit II, Making Career Plans; and Unit III, Securing a Job and Progressing in it.[66] Important in organizing such units is that teachers and counselors do not attempt to cover everything known or all the things needed by students at various stages in their vocational planning. It is better to cover a few topics adequately than to cover many topics superficially or inadequately. The whole job of vocational guidance does not have to be accomplished in one unit within the classroom. The use of students in the planning of such a unit will be invaluable. The content of the unit should be determined by the vocational needs, interests, and maturity level of the students. If a unit is planned to help students with their problems, it is important that they be permitted and have the opportunity to make their needs known to instructors and counselors. If a unit is organized within a school subject matter area, it will need to be related to the other guidance services to avoid becoming a substitute for them.

Plant Visits

Many vocational guidance programs provide field trips or visits to plants, businesses, and industries in the local and surrounding communities. Such visits can have value to students if they are well planned and well timed. Visitations can provide first-hand experiences in the use of tools, skills, materials, and processes. The following are some suggestions for the organization and conduct of plant visits.

1. *Give attention to preliminary arrangements.* Go over arrangements carefully with the host. Make sure of the arrival and leaving times. Know in advance where the group is to report and to whom it is to report. Arrange transportation. Clear the visit with the school administrator. If necessary, secure parent's permission.

2. *Time the visit.* If the trip is to have maximum value, it will come after some study of vocational information and will be made with a purpose in mind.

3. *Brief students before making the visit.* Point out what to observe on the visit and how to behave. Explain to them the purpose of the visit.

---

[66]Baer and Roeber, *Occupational Information,* pp. 361–462.

4. *Discuss the visit at the next class meeting.* Discussion will provide an opportunity to correct any misunderstandings resulting from the visit and to point up significant features. Discussion will stimulate a need to seek additional information about the abilities needed to perform certain jobs, worker characteristics, preparation, responsibilities, and the like.

5. *Prepare news releases and letters of appreciation.* Students in the group can prepare and send letters of appreciation to the host. A news release can be prepared by the group or by a committee either before or after the visit and sent to the local newspaper.

Career Conferences

The career conference is a group activity organized for the purpose of providing vocational guidance information of a supplementary or preliminary nature. The career day has often been described in the guidance literature, and such descriptions show it to be as varied as the students and staff involved. A wide variety of plans and programs have been employed: those organized for a school class or by a regional association of high schools; those organized for a single day or spread over several days or weeks.

Criticisms. Career days or conferences have been criticized as being ineffective if their major purpose is to assist the student in his career planning. Some of the criticisms that have been leveled include the following:

1. Students are often not prepared for participation in the career conference. They frequently have little knowledge of the information which may be supplied through such a conference. Quite often they are simply told they may attend if they desire.

2. Career conferences are often viewed as the entire vocational guidance service or as a substitute for it. Career conferences are often thought to be substantial in themselves needing no preliminary preparation of students nor follow-up activities.

3. The career representatives are predominantly from professional occupations. Workers in skilled and semi-skilled occupations—occupations into which most students will enter—fail to be adequately represented. The careers discussed usually are those that require a college preparation, yet only 25–50 percent or so of the students plan to attend college.

4. Speakers and career representatives may not give a valid picture of their occupation. The speaker's attitude toward his job—either

enthusiasm or apathy—may give students a false or misleading impression of the job. Students may receive inaccurate or colored information which they accept as authoritative.

5.   Students may strengthen vocational goals which are inappropriate. Career conferences may restrict rather than broaden the perspective of students toward the world of work. The emphasis upon the professions encourages many students to make unrealistic choices.

6.   Career conferences require too much staff time and energy to organize and execute. Students view them as a "day off." Days and weeks are required for career conferences planning, which takes away time and energy for individual counseling.

Values and Purposes. Despite these limitations, the career conference continues to be popular as a much used auxiliary activity in the vocational guidance program. The values and purposes of career days are seen by many to include the following:

1.   The career conference is a means of presenting vocational guidance information to large numbers of students. Through special speakers, films, discussions, and exhibits, large numbers of students are reached and receive some occupational information.

2.   It introduces students to occupations found in the local community. Local employment opportunities and trends in various occupations are stressed. Students have an opportunity to meet the business and industrial leaders of the community who may be their future employers.

3.   It supplies firsthand information. Career representatives provide information about the qualifications, preparation, and requirements for entrance and progress within their various occupations. Students have an opportunity to see, hear, and question people actually working in the occupation.

4.   It helps students think about their vocational choices. It can present accurate information on careers of interest to the majority of the student body. It may serve as a motivational activity for the further study of their choices. If some students decide not to pursue an occupational choice or if some reasonable doubt is generated as to the appropriateness of their choice through accurate information acquired during a career conference, then the conference has been as worthwhile to those students as to those whose appropriate choices are strengthened.

5. It may serve as a means for an expanded guidance program. Following career conferences, a number of students will seek counseling. This influx of students may point the way for an expansion of the guidance staff to perform such services more uniformly.

6. It has high public relations value. Through visiting the school and through participation in the conference, parents and community leaders become more informed as to the school's needs. Teachers and administrators become better acquainted with the occupations in the community. This information can be used advantageously in the classroom and in counseling with students. The publicity given to a conference will be a means of interpreting the needs of the pupils and the school to the community.

Organizing the Career Conference. Norris, Zeran, and Hatch set forth the ideas that career days should be preceded by self-analysis study in order for students to have some idea of their interests, aptitudes, and abilities in relation to various occupations or fields of work. Also, information should be made available beforehand to give students a general understanding of local and national trends and to stress the importance of careful planning for a career. The conference should be followed up with classroom discussions, and the counselor or teacher should suggest additional sources of information for interested students.[67]

The key to a successful career conference lies in its planning and organization. Preparation for the conference will begin several months before the conference is conducted. Several key questions must be examined and answered prior to the organization of the conference. These questions were posed in the discussion of the school and college conference in Chapter 8, and a review of them by the reader may be helpful.

The following points are suggestions for organizing the career conference:

1. A carefully selected planning committee should be set up to begin work at least three months before the expected career day. The committee should be composed of student leaders, faculty members, and counselors. In some schools civic leaders and businessmen are also represented. The committee should be chaired by a counselor who has the ability to get things accomplished as well as previous experience in conducting or organizing a career conference.

2. Schedule the conference. Some schools schedule the conference in the fall of the year to permit follow-up activities of the conference throughout the remainder of the year and use it to serve as motivation

<hr>

[67]Norris, Hatch, and Zeran, *Information Service,* pp. 459–460.

for vocational planning of pupils. Other schools prefer spring conferences as a kind of culminating activity for the vocational guidance
service. Usually a large assembly hall and a number of small meeting
rooms will be necessary for the conference.

3.   Obtain staff cooperation. The success of the conference will
depend upon the cooperation of the faculty and administrators. They
should be actively involved in the conduct of the conference. For
example, the business education department teachers and students can
type the letters and notes to speakers and mimeograph programs. The
home economics department teachers and students can plan the luncheon or dinner for the participants.

4.   Decide upon the pupils who are to attend the conference. Practice among schools varies widely in this respect. Some have limited the
conference to juniors and seniors, while other schools have included
all students in the school. If all students in high school are included
every year, they will be able to attend four such conferences and
thereby increase the breadth of their contacts with different occupations.

5.   Survey students' vocational interests. Student interests in occupations should be the central basis for selecting the occupations to be
represented in a career conference. A checklist, similar to the one
illustrated in Figure 9–1, can be given to students to ascertain the
occupations in which they are interested. If a checklist is not used, a
questionnaire could be presented on which students write two, three,
or four of their preferred occupations in order of greatest interest to
them. The checklist or questionnaires are then returned, tabulated and
analyzed.

6.   Determine the occupations to be represented at the conference.
A decision will have to be made about occupational groups which
attract only a few pupils. Factors which guide such decisions are the
consultants available, the number of class periods to be given to small
group meetings, and the physical facilities.

7.   Set up a schedule for the conference. The size of the anticipated
group meetings should be considered in assigning special or individual
rooms. Arrange for any luncheon or dinner provisions. Schedule pupils
to the conference meetings. A 3 X 5 card on which pupils indicate the
meetings they plan to attend can be utilized for this. Mimeograph or
print a schedule of all activities, participants, room numbers, student
chairmen, and faculty sponsors.

Wilson High School is planning its Eleventh Annual High School Career Conference. A number of well qualified men and women will explain and discuss the occupations in which they are employed. They will be available to answer questions you have about their vocations. It will be possible for you to attend three different meetings. In order to make the selections of these career representatives, it is necessary to have an expression of your occupational interests.

From the list below, check three choices. Indicate this by numbering your choices (1, 2, 3) in the spaces provided.

____	1. Accountant	____ 21.	Railroad engineer
____	2. Airline Hostess	____ 22.	Secondary school teacher
____	3. Armed Forces	____ 23.	
____	4. Artist	.	
____	5. Airline pilot	.	
____	6. Baker	.	
____	7. Beautician	.	
	.	.	
	.	.	
	.	.	
	.	.	
	.	.	

Name   Grade

Figure 9–1.   *Wilson High School Career Conference*

8. Select and orient the career representatives or speakers. The choice of representatives and speakers is an important determinant of the success of the conference. (A speaker file should be established and screened from year to year.) Efforts should be made to secure speakers who present information that is objective and informative. The invitation to the career representative should indicate the time schedule and the person to be contacted at the school. An outline of suggestions should be sent to the representatives concerning the kinds of information the students will want: description of the occupations, requirements, rewards, entrance, and advancements. The schedule of the events should also be sent to these participants.

9. Brief all pupils, teachers, and administrators on the conference activities. Pupils should be prepared to utilize the consultants available to them. Each pupil should know the time period, subject, room number, career representative, and student and faculty leaders of his choice.

10. Publicize the conference. The career conference should be publicized to the student body through the school paper and bulletin board

displays, as well as in the local newspaper and radio and television outlets.

11. Evaluate the conference. At the close of the conference, some means of evaluation should be conducted. A simple questionnaire procedure in which pupils indicate the amount and/or quality of information received, the value of such information in increasing knowledge of the occupational field, and the general worthwhileness of the day is helpful in planning and conducting future career conferences.

12. Acknowledge the services of career representatives and others. Personal letters of appreciation should be sent to all speakers and participants as well as notes of thanks to faculty and student participants.

MATERIALS FOR VOCATIONAL GUIDANCE

Essential to the vocational guidance service is the collection, housing, and use of an abundant supply of economic-social-occupational materials. Not only will counselors obtain much data and information from these materials, but also they are essential for student use in vocational planning. It is recommended that in those schools employing two or more counselors, one of the counselors be assigned the responsibility for the acquisition, housing, filing, and methods of using vocational guidance materials. Three major problems of an administrative nature are involved with such literature.

1. Problems related to securing vocational guidance materials

2. Problems related to filing and housing the literature

3. Problems related to the use of the information

Securing Materials

Generally, arrangements are made with the librarian for the acquisition of materials. If little or no vocational guidance literature is available, a first year budget of approximately $250 would not be unduly large in a medium sized high school.

Hopke[68] has identified major developments in the field of occupational literature from 1950 to 1964. The developments are summarized here:

---

[68]William E. Hopke, "A New Look at Occupational Literature," *Vocational Guidance Quarterly,* Vol. 15 (September, 1966), pp. 18–25.

1. The National Vocational Guidance Association's review, rating, and publishing of reports on occupational literature in each issue of the *Vocational Guidance Quarterly.*

2. Progress has been made in lowering the reading level of occupational informational materials (see below).

3. More information about service, skilled and semiskilled occupations.

4. Publication of the Labor Department's *Occupational Outlook Handbook.*

5. Introduction of materials suitable to the elementary school level.

6. More attention is being given to psycho-social concepts and relationships in occupational materials.

7. Introduction of literature which is based upon job or career family approaches.

As current developments in the use of occupational information materials, Hopke cited that (1) some schools provide private study cubicles in a high school's learning center equipped with closed circuit TV; (2) the publications by Doubleday and Company of a two-volume encyclopedia of careers for student and parent use, and (3) the revision of the *Dictionary of Occupational Titles.*

In discussing the general goals to be considered in securing informational materials, Baer and Roeber state that such materials ought to provide (1) realistic and accurate information, (2) up-to-date information, (3) many types of information, (4) appeal to various levels of ability and experience, and (5) coverage of characteristics of any given kind of work or training opportunity.[69] Hoppock advises the counselor to appraise materials by asking five questions: When was it published? Where (geographic area) does it apply? By whom was it written? Why was it written? How were the facts collected and presented?[70]

The advanced reading level of occupational informational materials is a major concern and a serious weakness of many materials. Several reading level studies have reported that the large majority of materials are well above the level of the intended audience. For example, Ruth analyzed the readability of approximately nine per cent of the items in a career information kit and reported that the mean reading level of the materials was 14.7. Many items were found to be in the category of the 16th and 16th plus, and only one item was found to be on the 9th grade level. Ruth concluded that

---

[69]Baer and Roeber, *Occupational Information,* pp. 310–312.
[70]Hoppock, *Occupational Information,* pp. 45–50.

most items are closer in their readability to that of professional journals, and that the reading ease scores of these materials appeared too high to have usefulness as reading matter to be pursued by most high school students.[71]

The National Vocational Guidance Association has formed certain standards to be followed in the publication of vocational guidance materials. Their standards are given below.[72]

Standards for Use
in Preparing and Evaluating
Occupational Literature

As the title suggests, this statement on *"Standards"* has been prepared to assist those who are writing, publishing or evaluating material descriptive of a single occupation or of a group of related occupations. The present guide, undertaken at the suggestions of the Trustees of the National Vocational Guidance Association is a revision of the "Standards" written by the Publications Committee of the Occupational Research Division of NVGA in 1950 and widely used since that time.

However, the concern of NVGA for the quality of occupational material goes back at least to 1924 and has been expressed in a series of publications written by individual members or committees of the Association. The writers of this report have sought to revise the 1950 statement in terms of present concepts and conditions.

Basic Concepts

In undertaking this revision, it was clear that the task was not so much the correction of the 1950 "Standards" as it was the addition of some basic concepts which would orient writers and publishers of occupational literature to the ends such publications can serve. The guidance profession particularly needs occupational information which can be used effectively with youth. While the maturity necessary for sound occupational choice is an outcome of many factors, a broad knowledge of occupations is essential as background information. This knowledge can be acquired in part by the use of written materials if these are prepared and used appropriately. Appropriate occupational literature will also be useful to adults and to professional persons in counseling and personnel services.

1. *A basic standard for any occupational publication should be the inclusion of a clear statement as to its purpose and the group to whom it is directed.*

For example, a publication designed to inform the counselor or teacher is unlikely to meet the needs of a junior high school student. Similarly an occupational pamphlet intended to recruit for a particular

---

[71]Roger A. Ruth, "Readability of Occupational Materials," *Vocational Guidance Quarterly,* Vol. 11 (Autumn, 1962), pp. 7–10.
[72]Publications Committee of the Occupational Division of the National Vocational Guidance Association, Vol. 12 (Spring 1964), pp. 217–227. Used with permission.

profession will be an acceptable aid in guidance only if it takes into account the needs of youth.

2. *Occupational information should be related to developmental levels which will vary with age, educational attainment, social, and economic backgrounds.*

For example, elementary school children need information that will expand their knowledge of the world of work, of the contributions and inter-relationships of many kinds of workers, of the varieties of settings in which skills may be used, and of the satisfactions to be found through work. Junior high school students need more information about the relationship of abilities and interests to educational choices and occupational requirements. At the senior high school level more comprehensive information is needed by both the job-bound and the college-bound student.

Materials should be slanted to give youth help in planning next steps or in recognizing occupational implications of current studies or activities. They need to be related to the present or immediate future particularly for younger groups to whom five or ten years is meaningless. These generalizations are intended merely to suggest how important it is that occupational materials be based on an adequate understanding of the needs of the intended audience.

3. *Consideration should be given to the implications of the material for all groups in our society.*

For example no statements about the advantages of a particular occupation should be made which involve or imply unfavorable comparisons with other occupations. When photographs are used, they ought to be as nearly as possible representative of all groups and areas in our society. To be truly representative, photographs should be identified as to locality and show ethnic groups proportionate to the local population.

Occupational information, particularly when prepared for youth, ought to be useful in stimulating aspiration and in encouraging individuals of all backgrounds to develop to their greatest potential. However, care should be taken to avoid the false stimulation which may result from too great stress on material values, status symbols, and the like.

4. *The description of an occupation should be an accurate and balanced appraisal of opportunities and working conditions which should not be influenced by recruiting, advertising, or other special interests.*

5. *Occupational information should include the nature of personal satisfactions provided, the kinds of demands made and the possible effects on an individual's way of life.*

Guidelines for Content

The quality and specificity of detail in occupational materials will vary with the intended use of the publication. For example, a publication intended for adults considering retraining or additional training should include more specific information about earnings and fringe benefits than one designed to help students explore the job world. The following is intended not as a schedule for analyzing occupations but as a check list to insure that a particular publication contains the necessary information.

• Definition of the occupation as given in the *Dictionary of Occupational Titles* or as determined by the U. S. Employment Service. (The D.O.T. title should be included if definitions are provided by state employment services, professional and trade associations, unions, licensing bodies, or job analysis.)

• History and development of the occupation including its social and economic relationships.

• Nature of the work such as duties performed, tools or equipment used, relationships to other occupations, possible work settings and fields of specialization.

• Requirements such as education and training, aptitudes, temperaments, interests, physical capacities, and working conditions.

• Special requirements such as licensure or certification imposed by law or official organizations.

• Methods of entering the occupation such as direct application, personal reference, examination, apprenticeship. (Explanation should be made of the assistance which may be offered by unions, employers, professional and other organizations, public or private employment agencies, school and college placement offices.)

• Opportunities for experience and exploration through summer and part-time employment, work study programs, programs of the Armed Forces or voluntary agencies such as the Peace Corps, youth organizations and community services.

• Description of usual lines for advancement or of possibilities for transfer to related occupations either through seniority, experience, on-the-job or in-service training, additional education, and examinations.

• Employment outlook as suggested by trends likely to affect employment the next five, ten, or twenty years. (Factors affecting particular groups such as geographic area, age, sex, race, physical disabilities, and the like should be considered, as well as factors affecting outlook such as supply and demand, retaining programs, replacement needs, automation, and other technological developments.)

• Earnings, both beginning and average wage or salary according to setting, locality and other significant factors as well as supplementary income and fringe benefits such as commissions, tips, overtime, bonuses, meals, housing, hospitalization, vacations, insurance and retirement plans. (Related to earnings are costs or deductions for tools, equipment, uniforms, supplies, and the like.)

• Conditions of work and their implications for the individual's way of life, including where significant, daily and weekly time schedules, overtime, seasonality, physical conditions such as travel required, setting—indoor or outdoor, noise, confusion, temperature, health hazards and strength demands.

• Social and psychological factors such as work satisfactions, patterns of relationships with supervisors and other workers, and with unions, associations, or other organizations in which membership may be required or desirable.

• Sources of additional information such as books, pamphlets, trade and professional journals, motion pictures, slides and other visual aids, pertinent literature provided by government agencies, unions, associations, industry, schools, colleges and universities.

Criteria for Style and Format

The intended use of the occupational material will be a critical factor in the consideration of style and format.

• Style should be clear, concise, interesting, and adapted to the readers for whom the material is intended.

• Publishers are encouraged to be creative and imaginative in presenting factual information in a stimulating fashion. The typography should be inviting, the total format pleasing, and the illustrations should be of a quality to enhance the effectiveness of the material and to make it appropriate for the age level for which it is planned.

• Charts, graphs, or statistical tables should be properly titled and interpreted. Sources and dates of basic data should be given.

• The occupational book or pamphlet should state specifically, the publisher, date of publication, the sponsoring organization, group or individual and the author. Information about the author's training and experience should be provided. Pages should be numbered in sequence and the price, when applicable, should be included.

• In view of the changing nature of occupations, it is important that information be kept up-to-date. Provision should be made for review and revision when the original publication is issued and new editions should state whether or not contents have been revised. Dates of original publications and of the data used should be given on both first and revised editions. When information about wages or other data subject to relatively rapid change is used, date and source should be indicated.

Guide for Preparing
Industrial Careers Brochures

This guide has been prepared by the National Vocational Guidance Association as an aid in writing brochures about career opportunities in a single industry. While the purpose of such brochures, generally, is to provide information about a business or industry, recruit employees, and promote good public relations, the emphasis in this guide is on the vocational needs of the readers. The aim should also be to provide information that can be useful to counselors and teachers of "careers" courses.

Fundamental to the satisfaction of vocational needs is the recognition that individuals differ due to various combinations of aptitudes, temperaments, interests, capacities, training and experiences, and that these factors determine suitability for different types of work. Research and experience indicate that suitability for work is a condition for easier training and may be associated with greater job satisfaction, productivity, and suitability of employment. At the same time, it is necessary to recognize that suitability for work is dynamic, conditioned by opportunities and training available, and by early work experiences.

Therefore, in describing work activities within an industry, opportunities for an individual's occupational growth and advancement should be included.

In order to provide up-to-date, usable information, career brochures need to be revised regularly.

Industrial careers brochures should be adapted to the needs of certain groups of potential workers and job seekers; some of these groups are:

1.   Those who are interested in an industry, such as aircraft or electronics manufacturing, rather than in a specific occupation, because of glamor, financial rewards, or familiarity. They need an industrial careers brochure to introduce them to the world of work as well as specific job information.

2.   Those who have chosen a specific occupation, such as stenographer or machinist, that exists in many industries. They need information on the industry's locations, growth, wage levels, working conditions, and its products or services.

3.   Those who are considering an occupational change because of technological or economic developments, age, handicap, or other personal reasons. They need information about related occupations and retaining programs in industries where their skills can be utilized.

In presenting information, the writer should consider ways in which individuals think about jobs. For example, some job seekers tend to think of job opportunities in terms of occupational classifications, such as sales, transportation, repair and maintenance, or the professions. Others think in terms of school subjects, such as mathematics, bookkeeping, languages, or woodworking. Some individuals think about jobs available to technical school or college graduates. Others think in terms of working with people, ideas or things, or in situations involving outdoors work or physical activity.

The writing style and vocabulary should be understandable at the junior high school level. Technical terms and concepts, where used, should be defined. To avoid high turnover to industry and disillusionment to the career seeker, writers are urged to present opportunities as accurately as possible.

The cover and format should be eye-catching. Pictures and illustrations showing individuals on the job should be included to provide greater understanding of the work setting.

A Suggested Brochure Outline

I. Introduction
    A. Purpose and uses of brochure
        1. Sponsoring organization
        2. Audience for brochure
    B. Scope of information
        1. National or local data
        2. Geographic distribution of jobs
    C. Sources of information
    D. Date of data collection
    E. Publication date

II. Industry characteristics and trends
    A. Description of products or services
    B. Role of the industry in the economy
    C. Size of the industry
        1. Number of employees
        2. Volume of products or services
        3. Physical plant
    D. Employment outlook
        1. Past trends and current situation
        2. Seasonal or cyclical factors
        3. Forecast

III. Occupations in the industry
    A. General occupational groups
    B. Individual occupations
        1. Entry Jobs
            a. Opportunities: scholarships, summer jobs, apprenticeships

        b. Requirements: education, experience, licensing, equipment, personal traits

  2. Promotional opportunities

        a. Channels

        b. Steps

  3. Earnings

        a. Entry salaries

        b. Median after 5, 10 years

        c. Tops ranges

  4. Fringe benefits

        a. Sick leave

        b. Vacation

        c. Insurance

        d. Retirement

  5. Working conditions

        a. Plant environment

        b. Locations

        c. Hours

        d. Employee facilities

IV. Unions and professional organizations

Writers of industrial brochures who wish information on assistance with vocational guidance aspects may call upon the National Vocational Guidance Association, 1605 New Hampshire Avenue, N.W., Washington 9, D.C.

Types of Vocational Information Materials

Vocational guidance materials are voluminous and ever changing. The vocational guidance information service must include features that allow full coverage and must have a built-in mechanism for keeping materials up-to-date. In organizing the service, a wide variety of materials will be needed by students. Baer and Roeber point out that vocational materials can be written only when research findings are available, and that only a small proportion of such materials are based on original research—firsthand investigations to determine the facts of occupational life.[73]

Kuntz and Jetton[74] were interested in learning of the extent and use of various types of occupational materials and how counselors evaluated these materials. They surveyed 706 certified counselors in Texas, Missouri, Arkansas, and Oklahoma and received 412 responses. Using only the 268 completed returns from secondary school counselors, they reported the

---

[73]Baer and Roeber, *Occupational Information,* p. 35

[74]James E. Kuntz and Clyde T. Jetton, "Use and Appraisal of Occupational Literature by Secondary School Counselors," *Personnel and Guidance Journal,* Vol. 39 (February, 1959), pp. 441–443.

"usefulness" and the "use" ranks of fifty-two sources of occupational information. Table 9–2 presents this information.

Samler has pointed out that much of the vocational guidance literature is oriented to the economic aspects of vocations and that counselors need to secure materials that present the psychological picture of occupations:

> The point to be made here is that the type of occupational information literature available to the counselor does not reflect the ideas and insights suggested as essential for man at work. Further, that, as is evident, there *is* such a literature, but it does not happen to be in the sources generally used by the counselor. It does not *happen* to be there because the basic orientation of present occupational literature is toward job analysis and the Economic Man. We must look, therefore, to the psychological and sociological sources.[75]

Some of the various types of materials included in a school's vocational guidance library are given below.

1. Published materials:
    (a) Occupational monograph—general study of an occupation which presents the nature of the occupation, size, and distribution of labor force, outlook, personal requirements, preparation, working conditions, and other detailed information of an occupational field
    (b) Occupational abstract—composite and concise summary in approximately 3,000 words of the available literature in the occupational area
    (c) Occupational briefs—written descriptions of about 1,500 words of the various types of specialities in an occupation
    (d) Job description—statements of the duties, qualifications, and other factors involved in a job in an industry
    (e) Occupational titles and definitions—material which gives names, titles, definitions, code numbers, and a brief description or definition of the occupation
    (f) Career fiction—portrayal of an occupation through the experiences of fictional characters
    (g) School publications—locally prepared publications of occupational pamphlets
    (h) Biographies
    (i) Textbooks

---

[75]Joseph Samler, "Psycho-Social Aspects of Works: A Critique of Occupational Information," *Personnel and Guidance Journal,* February, 1961, p. 462.

       (j)   Bulletins
       (k)   Recruitment literature

2.   Audio-visual materials:
       (a)   Tape recordings
       (b)   Slides
       (c)   Films
       (d)   Posters and charts
       (e)   Bulletin board materials
       (f)   Pictures of former students at work

3.   Dramatization materials

4.   Role-playing materials

Sources for Materials

Part of the job of the counselor who has responsibility for the acquisition of vocational guidance materials is to know where to obtain them. National, state, and local sources are available to the counselor. Baer and Roeber have extensive listings of these sources giving addresses where applicable.[76]

1.   National sources:
    (a)   Governmental agencies such as the Government Printing Office, Women's Bureau, Department of Labor, Bureau of Labor Statistics, Bureau of Census, Department of Commerce, Department of Defense, and the like publish materials of a vocational information nature, some free.
    (b)   Private publishers such as Science Research Associates, Bellman Publishing Company, Chronicle Guidance Publications, B'nai B'rith, Charm Magazine, New York Life Insurance Company.
    (c)   Professional Societies, unions, and trade associations such as American Institute of Accountants, American Society of Auctioneers, American Federation of Labor, and the Home Economics Association.

2.   State sources such as the state employment service, state department of education, and veterans commission should not be overlooked.

3.   Local sources such as local governmental agencies, organizations and industries, school surveys of school leavers and of occupational opportunities.

Filing and Housing Materials

A meaningful organization of materials is necessary if they are to be used by many students. Some orderly method of cataloging, filing, and housing

---

[76]Baer and Roeber, *Occupational Information,* pp. 163–309.

Table 9–2.   *Relative Use and Usefulness of Various Sources of Occupational Information*

Sources	Usefulness Ranks	Use Ranks
1. Occupational Pamphlets	1.0	7.5
2. Life Adjustment Booklets (SRA)	2.0	5.0
3. Career Monographs	3.0	7.5
4. Occupational Outlook Handbook	4.0	3.0
5. American Job Series (SRA)	5.0	16.0
6. Personnel and Guidance Journal	6.0	19.0
7. Materials from Professional Associations	7.0	12.0
8. B'nai B'rith Vocational Materials	8.0	24.0
9. School and College Placement	9.0	29.0
10. Chronicle Guidance Reprints	10.0	31.0
11. Guidance Bulletins (Simmons College)	11.0	33.0
12. Vocational Guidance Series	12.5	18.0
13. Career Index	12.5	27.0
14. Occupational Guides	14.0	14.0
15. Vocational Guidance Pamphlets (N.A.M.)	15.0	10.0
16. Occupational Abstracts (Personnel Services)	16.0	30.0
17. American Occupations Monographs	17.0	43.0
18. U. S. Navy Occupational Handbook	18.0	2.0
19. Seventeen Magazine	20.0	45.0
20. Monograph Series (Bellman)	20.0	45.0
21. Labor Information Bulletin	21.0	36.0
22. Occupational Trends	22.0	13.0
23. Occupational Outlook Bulletins	23.0	9.0
24. Guidance Index	24.0	38.0
25. The Guidance Leaflets	25.0	23.0
26. Jobs in Action (SRA)	26.0	25.0
27. Career Opportunity	27.0	40.0
28. Occupational Outlook Summary	28.0	11.0
29. Way of Life Series	29.0	16.0
30. Industrial Arts Index	30.0	48.0
31. Institute for Research Publications	31.0	35.0
32. The Labor Market	32.0	26.0
33. Occupations in the Federal Civil Service	33.0	22.0
34. Air Force Publications	34.0	4.0
35. Career Opportunity	27.0	40.0
36. Army Publications	36.0	7.5
37. High School Career Booklets (Ladies Home Journal)	37.0	28.0
38. America at Work Series	38.0	46.0
39. Charm Magazine	39.0	21.0
40. Mademoiselle	40.0	17.0
41. Glamour	41.0	15.0
42. Industrial (Small Business Series)	42.0	34.0
43. Journal of Living	43.0	51.0
44. Commonwealth Vocational Guidance Monograph Library	44.0	47.0
45. Farmer's Bulletin	45.0	42.0
46. The Labor Force	46.0	37.0
47. Dictionary of Occupational Titles	47.0	1.0
48. Monthly Labor Review	48.0	39.0
49. Dodd, Mead Career Books	49.0	49.0
50. Candid Career Books	50.0	44.0
51. Independent Woman	51.0	50.0
52. Labour Gazette	52.0	52.0

the bound and unbound materials must be worked out at the beginning of the collection. A filing plan or system may be purchased from commercial companies: SRA Career Information Kit from Science Research Associates, Bennett Occupations Filing Plan from the Sterling Powers Publishing Company, and the Chronicle Plan for Filing Unbound Occupational Information from Chronicle Guidance Publications. The SRA and the Chronicle Guidance plans are based on the *Dictionary of Occupational Titles* code, while the Bennett filing plan is an alphabetical subject index by fields of work.

Some counselors have constructed their own filing systems. Many are based on the *Dictionary of Occupational Titles* codes; others have used codes from the United States census classification or the Standard Industrial Classification System. Alphabetical filing arrangements have been found to be advantageous in some schools. Filing systems based on occupational interest inventory areas, such as the *Kuder Preference Record* furnish group headings under which brochures or pamphlets may be collected and have the advantage of simplicity in following up occupations for students who have taken such inventories. School subject matter areas may be used to file and collect materials. Under such an arrangement, the literature is grouped in accordance to the subject matter areas to which it is most closely related. If the material cuts across one or more fields, it is filed in the subject matter folder to which it is most closely related, and cross references are made on other pertinent folders.

Goals for any filing and housing system used would be that the plan be simple, provide for expansion, be attractive, and be psychologically appropriate.[77]

Typical equipment to house the vocational guidance library includes bookcases or shelves for bound materials, file cabinets for unbound materials, index card files, and file folders. A bulletin board for display of materials is most important. Vertical racks are used in some schools to encourage student use of the material.

Encouraging Use of Materials

Vocational guidance materials may be part of the general school library or they may be housed in the general guidance office. The guidance staff should give consideration to both possibilities. Some school officials have an operating principle that the library should be the central location for all printed learning materials. The best location depends upon where the materials will have the greatest use. Hatch and Stefflre believe that the general guidance office should include

---

[77]Baer and Roeber, *Occupational Information,* pp. 316–317.

a. One or more occupational files mounted on casters for classroom as well as counseling use.

b. File of charts and films.

c. Up-to-date references of educational institutions.[78]

Teachers may be encouraged to use the vocational guidance materials by making available a movable file which can be transported to various classrooms. In respect to encouraging students to use the materials, Norris, Zeran, and Hatch state:

> Students may or may not be permitted to borrow materials for examination at home. Some schools, fearing that materials will be lost or damaged if students are allowed to remove them from the library, insist that they be referred to on the school premises. It is the authors' belief, however, that students should be invited and encouraged to make free use of the available information by being allowed to check out most booklets and folders for home use.[79]

Student and staff use of vocational guidance materials will be increased through observing the following guidelines:

1. The materials to be used are emphasized by guidance personnel and teachers.

2. Students have easy access to the materials.

3. A simple, convenient filing system is used and explained.

4. Attractive displays of materials are prepared often.

VOCATIONAL PLACEMENT

Opinion differs as to whether the high school has the responsibility of placing students in jobs. Some high school officials say their institution and personnel have little or no responsibility to place students as other private and governmental agencies exist to do this. Other school officials are of the opinion that the high school has a responsibility for job placement for its students. It is the belief of these administrators that their institution knows the student best and therefore can place him in a job that is best for him.

---

[78]Raymond N. Hatch and Buford Stefflre, *Administration of Guidance Services. Organization, Supervision, Education.* Englewood Cliffs, N.J.: Prentice-Hall, Inc., 1958, p. 202.
[79]Norris, Zeran, and Hatch, *Information Service,* p. 374.

They believe job placement is the last practical step in the educative process to make the student's education effective. Personnel in the high school who believe the school should provide placement designate a staff member who has the ability, time, and facilities to conduct an active program of securing jobs for students and give them information on ways to apply for positions.

In organizing the vocational guidance function, working relationships should be established with the coordinator of the work experience program and the placement director. Both of these staff members have contributions to make to the vocational guidance program, such as giving occupational information in homerooms, in classrooms, and in guidance rooms. Careful records should be kept showing the type of jobs entered by students. The coordinator of the work experience program and the placement director will be useful in guiding students about occupations in the local community. They should conduct follow-up studies of students while they are in school and after they graduate.

Those schools which do not maintain a vocational placement office within the school will find helpful the local branch of the Employment Security Division. One of the functions of the Division is to provide, without cost to the school or individual student, the administration, scoring, and interpretation of the *General Aptitude Test Battery.* Another function is the placement of those students who are ready to enter the labor market. The Employment Security Division can furnish a wealth of vocational information of help to schools and to vocational guidance counselors.

BUILDING THE VOCATIONAL GUIDANCE SERVICE

The process of building the vocational guidance service involves a number of steps.

1. Plan basic policies for the vocational guidance service. Policies should cover personnel, budget, facilities, and publicity.

2. Survey the vocational needs of the students. For example, students in rural areas may need further information regarding opportunities in agriculture and related occupations.

3. Inventory the existing vocational guidance materials of the school. All the materials should be brought together in one place, and a file which lists all the titles of materials should be maintained.

4. Establish budgetary procedures, such as those needed for clerical assistance and the purchasing of materials.

5. Give one counselor responsibility for supervision of the vocational guidance materials. Decide upon a system for storing and filing the materials.

6. Publicize the vocational guidance service. Use all media available to teachers and pupils.

7. Evaluate the vocational guidance services and materials.

THE COUNSELOR'S PROFESSIONAL LIBRARY

Counselors doing vocational guidance work will need certain basic materials which will aid in their performance. A minimum professional library could be obtained for approximately $200. Some of the professional materials that counselors would use quite often are given below.

1. *Dictionary of Occupational Titles,* Vol. I, II, III.

2. *Occupational Outlook Handbook.*

3. *Occupational Outlook Quarterly.*

4. *Employment Service Review.*

5. A copy of a comprehensive annotated bibliography such as Forrester's, *Occupational Literature: An Annotated Bibliography.*

6. A subscription to the *Vocational Guidance Quarterly.* The *N.V.G.A. Quarterly* contains a section of current occupational literature.

7. A subscription to a monthly guidance service such as that given by Chronicle Guidance Service or Science Research Associates.

8. Borow, Henry (ed.), *Career Guidance in a New Age.* Boston: Houghton Mifflin Co., 1973.

9. *Manpower,* official monthly journal of the Manpower Administration, U.S. Dept. of Labor.

SUMMARY

Vocational guidance was defined as that assistance given to the student to plan, prepare, and adjust to the world of work. It involves the counselor's establishment of a helping relationship by which the student can make appropriate changes within himself and his environment. Vocational guidance has differential purposes for elementary, junior high, and senior high school vocational guidance. The counselor's use of vocational information with students and parents was treated. Organized group procedures such as courses in occupations, units within a subject matter area, plant visits, and career conferences are a means of providing vocational guidance. Some of the types and sources of vocational guidance materials from national, state, and local areas for the students' and counselors' use were cited.

ANNOTATED BIBLIOGRAPHY

Borrow, Henry, (ed.), *Career Guidance for a New Age.* Boston: Houghton Mifflin Company, 1973, 348 pp.
 A companion volume to NVGA's 1964 volume, *Man In A World At Work,* this book explores the relationship between a person's career, and environmental changes and influences. The distinguished contributors to the volume include Carroll H. Miller, Donald H. Blocher, Donald Super, C. Gilbert Wrenn and others who have achieved prominence for their work in different aspects of vocational guidance.

Herr, Edwin L., and Stanley H. Cramer, *Vocational Guidance and Career Development in the Schools: Toward a Systems Approach.* Boston: Houghton Mifflin Company, 1972, 356 pp.
 Herr and Cramer present vocational guidance as a subsystem within the social system represented by the school. Their volume is exceptionally well written, carefully documented, and very practical.

Hoppock, Robert, *Occupational Information* (3rd ed.). New York: McGraw-Hill Book Company, 1967, 598 pp.
 This book deals with the kinds of occupational information that counselors and clients need, theories of occupational choice, use of occupational information in counseling, methods of teaching occupations, and the like. The chapters dealing with group methods of imparting vocational guidance will be worthwhile reading for school counselors.

Peters, Herman J., and James C. Hansen (eds.), *Vocational Guidance and Career Development. Selected Readings* (2nd ed.). New York: The Macmillan Company, 1971, 466 pp.
 This book of readings contains articles by many nationally recognized authorities in the field and conveys some of the problems and achievements of those who practice vocational guidance. The concept of work is treated in Section I; societal and cultural factors affecting work are dealt with in Section

II; vocational development theory is covered in Section III; the informational process and resources are the subjects in Section IV; vocational counseling is treated in Section V; Section VI deals with vocational guidance; Section VII covers career development of the disadvantaged; career development of women is the subject of Section VIII; and Section IX is devoted to adult career development.

Social - Personal Guidance

Our attention is directed to three characteristics of the simplest form of social system: (1) it consists of individuals; (2) there is interaction between and among individuals; and, (3) interaction is not randomly directed—it aims at achievement of goals.[1]

Chapter 10

Why is personality guidance needed?

What are the purposes of personality guidance at the elementary, junior high, and senior high school levels?

How may personality guidance be provided through counseling?

How may personality guidance be provided through group procedures?

What guidelines for development of social-personal guidance will be helpful?

Personality guidance has only recently reached the perspective point of looking at the total boy or girl. It is relatively new on the horizons of the guidance program. Personality guidance is an outgrowth of the mental hygiene movement at the beginning of the twentieth century, of clinical psychology's rapid growth, and of a general concern for the individual. Educators are becoming increasingly aware of the need for personality guidance as they study the difficulties confronting their students, particularly as these students make an effort to learn the subject matter in the classroom. As obvious as the need may seem, it has only been in recent years that educators have been truly concerned about the total person in the learning situation. Perhaps the recent emphasis on the total person has been

---

[1]Thomas J. Sergiovanni and Fred D. Carver., *The New School Executive: A Theory of Administration.* New York: Dodd, Mead & Company, 1973, p. 177.

314 SOCIAL-PERSONAL GUIDANCE

due in large measure to the heterogeneous school population now in attendance throughout the country. The qualitative and quantitative phases of child personality as such include a wide variety of constructs, involving such terms as coping, adjustment, maturity, development, individual differences, behavioral patterns, organization, dimensions, and, theories of behavioral processes.

It has been argued that it is impractical to establish a personality phase of guidance in the schools. Yet, not recognizing the influence of the personality of the students has been a failure on the part of our school systems and of education in general. This is not to say that teachers have to become psychiatrists to deal with human behavior but rather that consideration should be given to such items as the following:

1. Schools will have to be held responsible by the community for developing social awareness and social feeling in children.

2. The present problems of curriculum should be subordinated to the problem of living together.

3. Teachers must be reoriented in their thinking as to what is relatively important and what is relatively useless.

4. The present curriculum should be studied and evaluated to see whether our present selections are the best choices possible for teaching the basic principles of mutual survival.[2]

We can prepare students for the life they are living and will live in no better way than by helping them assess their personalities.

It is recognized that the development of wholesome personalities is the most important purpose of education. If this is true, why is it so neglected in the schools?

The impelling force behind the need for personality guidance in the schools is mental hygiene and study of human behavior. We teach social studies, language studies, science studies, and others. In these times of man against man we should be teaching human behavioral studies in grades K–12. This will give a cognitive base for affective action in counseling.

We cannot afford to ignore the personality growth of the student in our school offerings. To do so would be to deprive our children of the opportunity and right to become well-rounded, healthy individuals. By providing for personality development, we can help them become self-sufficient members of our society, individuals who can make their contributions to the orderly functioning of our democratic world.

---

[2] Willard Beecher, "Psychoneurotics; Why Our Schools Haven't Helped Them," *The Clearing House,* Vol. 20 (May, 1946), p. 520.

Today, with the emphasis on a sound mental health for success in one's career and in further learning, personality guidance becomes an important part of the school guidance program. An immediate caution is in order here. As stated, it is not the purpose of the school counselor to act as an amateur psychiatrist. The effective counselor has certain beliefs which should generally apply to most students and which should be kept in mind when dealing with the various students. The counselor's basic premises are that to believe in each and every student is important, that social adjustments are continuous (and in some cases difficult), and that each student makes choices and must accept the responsibilities that accompany those choices.[3]

Personality guidance is not carried on by the schools alone. It is accomplished by all the organized institutions in the community and most frequently by such social units as the family, employment resources, community child guidance agencies, private medical staff trained in this area, the church, the recreational agencies, and the special corrective and protective services. All these groups have as their common objective the promotion of the welfare of the individual. They, too, are interested in promoting a sense of security, self-esteem, and productive satisfaction for each person. Looked at in this way, carrying through personality guidance is not by any means the exclusive responsibility of the school nor of any single agency or institution. Because the pupil is in school during most of his daily living, his personality development can be observed, assisted, and reported by the school staff, especially the school counselor.

Although in recent years there has been some attention on the personality development of the pupil, it has often been more in the nature of lip service than any real effort on the part of the schools to have a total concern for the individual and his personality development. With the main focus of the school on the learning of subject matter, there must be a concern for the personality guidance of the pupil if learning for each boy and girl is to reach its maximum of development within his or her limits.

Dalton in his book defines personality guidance as "a construct of the dynamic organization within the individual which specifies his potentialities for action."[4] Implementation of this definition seems to necessitate a carefully considered plan of action in the guidance program which deals with social-personal guidance.

Opinions differ regarding what this plan would embrace. Some educators contend that it would encompass the total involvement of the person in the counseling practice. Others see personality guidance at different levels of

---

[3]Dean C. Andrews and Roy DeVer L. Willey. *Administration and Organization of Guidance Programs.* Harper & Brothers Publishers: New York, Copyright 1958, p. 197.

[4]Robert H. Dalton, *Personality and Social Interaction.* Boston: D. C. Heath and Company, 1961, p. 127.

assistance. These different levels of help are best expressed by Buhler and others in their stages of assistance to boys and girls. Buhler gives five approaches in working through adjustment concerns of children:

1. A first approach is supportive in nature. It emphasizes encouragement and confidence stimulation.
2. A second approach assists the child to understand himself at the level of insight.
3. With some children's concerns, it is necessary to effect a new structure of parent-child relationships.
4. A deeper level of assistance which requires a counselor of doctoral level competency in counseling is that of a transference relationship. The counselor becomes the key figure of importance in the child's life.
5. At the psychiatric level, there is the approach which calls for a complete personality restructuralization.[5]

Not everyone has the ability to reveal his real inner self. Before the counselor can make any suggestions for help or give direction, the counselee must disclose his inner feelings. Many times repressed feelings lead to depression and loneliness. Myrick and Moni suggest two procedures used to elicit self-disclosure—"the friendship flag" and "the card game."[6]

Personality guidance is a multiple process which helps an individual understand and accept himself and the reality of his environment and how he may best plan and make progress. The objectives of both the school and of personality guidance should be in agreement with what Horace Mann wrote: "Self-government, self-control, a voluntary compliance with the laws of reason and duty, have been justly considered as the highest point of excellence attainable by a human being."[7]

Personal views seem to dictate the meaning of personality guidance in a particular school situation. Some staffs advocate personality guidance as merely the knowledge of how to behave in a social situation. Others view personality guidance as a basic understanding of the self. These persons would extend the scope of personality guidance to include a clearer look at the self through a study of the individual's strengths and limitations.

This study of one's self is best done in the counseling process. The importance of personality guidance is indicated in an analysis of psychologi-

[5]Charlotte Buhler, *et. al., Childhood Problems and the Teacher.* New York: Holt, Rinehart and Winston, Inc., pp. 284–313.

[6]Robert D. Myrick and Linda S. Moni, "The Counselor's Workshop: Helping Children Disclose Themselves," *Elementary School Guidance & Counseling,* Vol. 7, No. 1 (October 1972), p. 55.

[7]Lawrence A. Cremin (ed.), *The Republic and the School: Horace Mann on the Education of Free Men.* Teachers College, Columbia University, 1957, p. 57.

cal factors pertinent to one's development. The self-concept is the residence for responsible living. A healthy self-concept provides the individual with a safe base from which to explore reality, to take risks as he attempts new and more difficult tasks, to surmount repeated and inevitable failures, to try again.

Personality guidance is concerned with an individual's aspirations, motivation, drive, and with the implementation of these factors in his educational process and career development. It is intimately interwoven with educational and vocational guidance. The impact of personality is noted by Bayley. She emphasized the life-giving push of emotions in daily living, when she stated "It is important, then, to learn what we can about emotions —how they develop and how they can be directed to help produce the most desirable personality characteristics."[8]

Sidney M. Jourard states "The behavior undertaken by a person when he is aroused to emotional tension is healthy (a) when it is effective in reducing or changing the present tension-level and quality to one which is more desired and (b) when the emotional behavior does not jeopardize health, self-esteem, or any other things which are valued by the person."[9]

NEED FOR PERSONALITY GUIDANCE

Each growing boy and girl needs the assistance of a guidance program based on the developmental approach. When one thinks through the developmental approach as a basis for the guidance function, it is necessary to examine the need for personality guidance. The first situation which reveals the need for such guidance is the concern of youth for direction. The burdens of uncertainty are reflected by youth today. In a study of issues considered as problems by high school students in 1935, mental hygiene ranked eleventh. By 1957, it ranked fifth (see Table 10–1).

The complex of contemporary concern for mental health in our society plus the insecurity of world conditions have cast shadows on the adolescent. The estrangement of man from man has further deepened these shadows. As was emphasized in the beginning of this chapter, adolescents are truly in search of identity. This identity can be best achieved through the developmental approach to personality guidance. A continuing personality guidance experience will assist each pupil to develop a foundation of

---

[8]The Association for Childhood Education International, 3615 Wisconsin Avenue, N.W., Washington 16, D.C. "The Emotions of Children: Their Development and Modifications," by Nancy Bayley. From *Childhood Education,* Vol. 21, No. 4, (December, 1944), p. 156.

[9]Sidney M. Jourard, *Personal Adjustment—An Approach Through the Study of Healthy Personality.* New York: The MacMillan Co., 1963, p. 114.

self-understanding which will serve him well during the rigors of adulthood as well as during the turbulence of adolescence.[10]

Table 10-1.   *Mean Ranks Given Fifteen Issues Considered as Problems by High School Students in 1935 and in 1957*[11]

	1935			1957		
Issue	Mean Rank	Standard Error	Rank of Mean	Mean Rank	Standard Error	Rank of Mean
Money	6.5	.11	1	6.4	.13	2
Health	6.61	.13	2	8.9*	.13	12.5
Personal attractiveness	7.0	.10	3	7.3	.11	4
Study habits	7.1	.11	4	5.7*	.12	1
Personal and moral qualities	7.2	.10	5	6.9	.10	3
Philosophy of life	7.5	.11	6	7.6	.12	5.5
Manners and courtesy	7.9	.10	7	8.1	.11	8
Home and family relationships	8.2	.12	8.5	8.0	.13	7
Getting along with other people	8.2	.11	8.5	8.3	.13	10
Recreation	8.3	.11	10	10.1*	.11	15
Mental hygiene	8.5	.12	11	7.6*	.13	5.5
Safety	8.6	.11	12	9.6*	.11	14
Civic interests, attitudes, and responsibilities	8.7	.10	13	8.2*	.11	9
Daily schedule	9.2	.12	14	8.5*	.14	11
Sex adjustments	10.0	.13	15	8.9*	.14	12.5

*Change from 1935 significant at 1 per cent level.

The student is influenced by the personality of the people with whom he deals in the school situation as well as by the professional help that they supply. Although the counselor must base his work on a rational interpretation of substantive knowledge about human behavior, he is and must be alert to the image which he gives as a person. The school counselor lives the integrity of his person and his profession. By his demeanor as well as by his rationality, he gives meaning to his love for truth, to his passion for excellence, to his dignity, to his character, and to his understanding of human frailty. As the individual pupil looks to himself and looks to others for a source of strength in developing, he often looks to the teacher and to the school counselor as models for his own personality.

[10]Jerome Count, "The Conflict Factor in Adolescent Growth," *Adolescence,* Vol. 2, No. 6 (Summer, 1967), pp. 167–181.

[11]Dale B. Harris, "Life Problems and Interests of Adolescents in 1935 and 1957," *The School Review,* Vol. 67, No. 3 (Autumn, 1959) p. 337. Copyright 1959 by the University of Chicago Press. Used by permission.

Walters states: "Since the learning of subject matter is related to the child's personality, a teacher can profit by mastering the principles of personality development. In particular, the principles underlying the acquisition of self-concept and the level of aspiration can be effectively applied in motivating children to learn in the classroom."[12]

Topp discusses behavior difficulties in childhood as important for the future. Topp states

> Provision should be made by school systems for personal guidance of children throughout the grades, either by freeing teachers from part of their group-teaching activities and training them in the correct approach to individual pupil problems, by providing enough mental hygienists to handle the personality problems which arise, or by making both provisions.[13]

This emphasizes the need for personality guidance in the school guidance program. The developmental aspects of the identity of the self as described in the sequential steps of child and adolescent progress also give emphasis to the need for personality guidance (see Table 10–2).

Many other factors have increased the need for personality guidance. Studies of children's personality adjustment in the socio-economic status of their families have found that the higher status children showed fewer indications of maladjustment. This finding might be of particular concern to those teachers and counselors who work in schools of depressed or deprived areas. This suggests that the need for remedial personality guidance is perhaps more dominant here. In the higher socio-economic levels, the need for personality guidance to reinforce positive development and maximum use of ability is dominant.

Another indication of the need for guidance is in the current efforts in working with each "kind" of student.

The need for personality guidance is emphasized by Shertzer and Dreyfus:

> A continuous screening of superior and talented students should be in operation in the school. This enables the school to detect and challenge the late bloomer. Factors of either an emotional or environmental nature that might impede identification at any given time could thus be offset.[14]

---

[12]Sister Annette Walters, "Role of the School in Personality Development," *Education* 77 (December, 1956), p. 219.

[13]Robert F. Topp, "Behavior Difficulties in Childhood as a Portent of the Future," *Elementary School Journal,* Vol. 51 (December, 1950), p. 199.

[14]Bruce Shertzer (ed.), *Working With Superior Students,* Chicago: Science Research Associates, 1960, p. 114.

There is a real need for an intimacy with one's self and with a few others. Intimacy or a satisfaction with living within one's self and with others is a challenge at any time but especially when there is so much leisure time.[15]

PURPOSES OF PERSONALITY GUIDANCE

The entire existence of personality guidance is predicated upon the fact that it assists the individual to achieve more effective learning. Personality guidance in the school has this justification for existence. Surveys have shown that a need for such assistance begins when the child enters kindergarten or the first grade. Starting from this point in the elementary school, the process of personality guidance is gradual and at times imperceptible. It is, however, the key process in the total development of the pupil during the period from kindergarten to the sixth or seventh grade. It is during this period that the student is forming a foundation for personality that will tide him over the rigors of adolescence and through his adult years. Because it is developmental, it seems desirable to maintain certain purposes or objectives at various points along the span of years during which personality guidance should be present in a school guidance program.

Elementary School Years

Lambert states

> The forgotten years of childhood are the school years between nursery and adolescence. Reams have been written about school management, IQ's, failures or success in learning the three R's, and problems within the classroom, but very little about what makes the six to twelve year old tick. Possibly this is because Johnny and Mary have lost the charm of babyhood and have not yet acquired the bloom of the teenager. Children of this age are not so lovable as they were at three nor so exciting as they are in adolescence.[17]

During the elementary school years, it is very important to consider personality guidance in the total guidance program. The emphasis on a foundation for later life makes it imperative that the school counselor understand the nature of the growing boy or girl. Several items, as empha-

---

[15]Edward A. Dreyfus, "The Search for Intimacy," *Adolescence,* Vol. 2, No. 5 (Spring, 1967), pp. 25–40.

[16]Erik H. Erikson, "Identity and the Life Cycle," *Psychological Issues,* Vol. 1, No. 1. New York, 1959, Monograph 1, p. 120. Reprinted by permission.

[17]Clara Lambert, *Understand Your Child From 6 to 12.* New York: Public Affairs Committee, Incorporated, 1957, p. 1.

Table 10-2.   Stages of Development Preceding and Following the Identity Crisis[16]

	1.	2.	3.	4.	5.	6.	7.	8.
I. INFANCY	Trust vs. Mistrust				Unipolarity vs. Premature Self-Differentiation			
II. EARLY CHILDHOOD		Autonomy vs. Shame, Doubt			Bipolarity vs. Autism			
III. PLAY-AGE			Initiative vs. Guilt		Play Identification vs. (Oedipal) Fantasy Identities			
IV. SCHOOL-AGE				Industry vs. Inferiority	Work Identification vs. Identity Foreclosure			

Table 10-2. (continued)

	Time Perspective vs. Time Diffusion	Self-Certainity vs. Identity Consciousness	Role Experimentation vs. Negative Identity	Anticipation of Achievement vs. Work Paralysis	Identity vs. Identity Confusion	Sexual Identity vs. Bisexual Confusion	Leadership Polarization vs. Authority Confusion	Ideological Polarization vs. Confusion of Ideals
V. ADOLESCENCE								
VI. YOUNG ADULT					Solidarity vs. Social Isolation	Intimacy vs. Isolation		
VII. ADULTHOOD							Generativity vs. Self-Absorption	
VIII. MATURE AGE								Integrity vs. Disgust, Despair

322

sized by Lambert, should be taken into consideration as one begins to look at the six-year old growing through the childhood years. First, you cannot make the child fit into one pattern. Second, the child has worries of his own and needs help in getting over his fears and concerns. Third, the child needs the opportunity to find friends of his own selection when he gets to school. Fourth, the growing child will try out some of his ideas in tell-tale tall tales, and this expression must be interpreted in terms of his whole development. As he moves into the later childhood, he is concerned with broadening his horizon and is beginning to sense ideas about people. He is beginning to be a little more self-conscious. He is undergoing continual change and rapid development. In order to have a sound program in personality guidance in the elementary school, it is important that the school counselor recognize these developmental patterns. Goals and purposes are clarified in terms of and based on a healthy self-concept.

The child firms or alters emotional patterns set in the early childhood years. The school can be a place to allow the child to unfold in terms of a healthy self-concept. It is a spiraling process growing in depth and extent over the years. It is difficult to perceive the increments of development of self-concept in these formative years. However, like flowers growing through the soil, development is there and it is being nurtured. If a child learns coping with, rather than mere adjusting to daily living, he will enjoy a healthy self-concept and be more able to handle his tensions.

Junior High School Years

In grades seven, eight, and nine, it is desirable that the personality service provide the student with an opportunity to begin to appraise himself. The junior high school student is becoming increasingly aware of his movement into adolescence and is concerned about the self. The self-concept needs to be considered as a second facet of development integrally intermeshed with the foundation which was built in a personality guidance development in the early years. It is at this time that the individual can think through his concerns and the possible meanings for them. Just as he engages in exploratory activities in the instructional program, the pupil may wish to have exploratory experiences in taking a look at his personality formation. This helps him gain a true sense of self-identity which will provide strength as he makes decisions for further education and a career in the senior high school. Johnson, Busaker, and Bowman have stated that:

> A question asked at some time or other by most junior high school pupils is "Am I normal?" . . . The need for accurate and timely

information on what is "normal," both in terms of changes and of differences among individuals is apparent.[18]

High School Years

In adolescence there is a need for a carefully thought-through program of personality guidance. In a sense, this is the last chance for the adolescent to take a look at himself and his goals and objectives in terms of environmental reality. The problem of control and freedom is one that needs to be considered by each adolescent. The decision-making concerns of the adolescent are mediated and altered by his self-concept. The adolescent is rapidly solidifying his identity of self and can profit from personality guidance. Jersild states, "To understand the adolescent we need to study all that we can see and measure in his make-up, but we need also to take account of his inner life—his experience as a separate self"[19] The adolescent is attempting to make congruent his idealized self and his self as viewed by himself and others. This is the crucial concern of adolescence and youth.[20]

PROVIDING PERSONALITY GUIDANCE THROUGH COUNSELING

Counseling sessions will be advantageous to the student as he strives to develop a better understanding of himself, especially as this understanding facilitates more effective learning. From brief individual sessions in the lower grades to longer time period interviews in the senior high school years, the individual pupil can use the counseling interview as a catalytic experience for taking a look at his total person. Counseling is needed to help the individual understand how the nature of the inner person relates to the demands of the outer world and, further, how he reacts to this relationship. It is important that personality guidance be viewed as a positive aspect of a total developmental guidance program. It should not be viewed merely as an aid only for those who are disturbed or in need of remediation. Counseling should provide a climate that will assist students to understand themselves so that they will use their abilities to greater advantage. Some students will desire simply to take a look at themselves. Others will desire to take a look at themselves in terms of greater improvement. However, in

---

[18]Mauritz Johnson, William E. Busaker, and Fred Q. Bowman, Jr., *Junior High School Guidance*. New York: Harper & Row, Publishers, 1961, p. 33.

[19]Arthur T. Jersild, *The Psychology of Adolescence*. New York: The Macmillan Company, 1963, p. 17.

[20]Herman Peters, "Processes of Personal Developing in Adolescence," *Adolescence*, Vol. 2, No. 8 (Winter, 1967–68), pp. 435–444.

each case, counseling should be viewed as a means for helping normal students make the fullest use of their abilities, rather than as a process for those who are mentally ill or disturbed.

There are two methods by which we may approach personality appraisal in the senior high school. The first of these is the clinical approach. This involves the use of selective personnel for counseling and guidance interviews. The other is by means of the present state of knowledge concerning the student. This includes day to day observation of students by their teachers. The key is the use of the counseling or individual process of guidance.

One of the difficulties of providing personality guidance through counseling is the lack of feeling of security and competency by the school counselor. Many school counselors have had extensive training in the guidance activities of testing, orientation, and program planning, but do not feel secure in a counseling interview when it focuses on personality development. This is an area in which the school counselor needs considerable practical experience so that he will feel at ease in dealing with the typical concerns of the growing boys and girls.

The counselor may also have difficulty in distinguishing between symptom and cause. Too often, the counselor and other school staff members are bent upon treating or working with the symptom rather than the cause of the behavior. To be sure, it is far more difficult to reach the true causes of an individual's personality functioning than it is to seek out the symptoms for that behavior. Nevertheless, it is important that the counselor has training in looking for the basic reasons for behavior. It is only then that he can determine whether he has the competency to continue counseling for this particular purpose, or whether he should, through the parents, suggest a number of proper referral sources. A developmental approach to social-personal guidance through counseling requires the use of positive techniques and tools as well as those which are concerned with difficulties. For a personal resources checklist, see Chapter 5, Figure 5-1. The checklist provides a base for counseling through strength, used with SRA inventories, Moony Problem Check List, or Minnesota Counseling Inventory, it is found to be helpful.

Counselor's Knowledge of Personality Development of Boys and Girls

It is important that the counselor be as competent in understanding childrens' and adolescents' personality development as in understanding their intellectual development.

Some General Principles of Social-Personal Counseling

The counselor should keep in mind a number of general principles of social-personal counseling. All these principles need to be considered in the organizational structure of the guidance program to insure that they receive adequate attention.

1. The individual's personality is learned primarily in relations with other people and his self-reflections.

2. The experiential background of the individual is expressed in his present social-personal actions which have evolved over a period of time.

3. The resulting individual's self-concept may shift from realism to unrealism depending on the respect or lack of it as perceived by him.

4. When the individual cannot meet needs or reduce tension, he resorts to a variety of behavior mechanisms.

5. Each individual has types of behaviors that are more likely to occur than others. These have reduced the tensions in the past.

6. The individual needs time in an organized guidance service to integrate his many ideas of self. This is a process.

7. Personality counseling for developmental purposes must be incorporated in a guidance program which permits voluntarily scheduled interviews for this purpose. This is the real base for educational and vocational counseling.

Use of Tests in Personality Guidance

There are a number of excellent instruments which with careful usage may facilitate the counseling process on personality guidance. Inventories, rating scales, checklists, and similar instruments may serve to focus the pupil's and counselor's attention on the particular phases of the individual's personality development. As noted elsewhere in this book, it is important to use great care in interpreting the results of any test or inventory. This caution is particularly important in personality guidance. The use of instruments for personality guidance should be carefully delineated in a written statement of procedures. The procedures should be written in consultation with the school board and administrative staff and the parents so that everyone is alerted to the nature of the instruments being used in the school. In programming for personality guidance, it is wise to inform all concerned of the purposes and nature of the instruments to be used before initiating their use; this procedure avoids the misunderstandings that sometimes arise after a program is in operation.

The school counselor will make use of such inventories as the SRA Junior Inventory, Youth Inventory, the Mooney Problem Checklist, the Bell Adjustment Inventory, and the Minnesota Counseling Inventory. These are excellent instruments when used as a part of the counseling practice. Care should be taken however so that the total focus of the personality guidance program is not pinpointed upon any one or several of the instruments. The use of checklists or rating scales by students and teachers may be effective in providing a base for personality guidance through counseling. Other personality tests are suggested in *Design for a Study of American Youth,* by John C. Flanagan, John T. Dailey, Marion F. Shaycoft, William A. Gortiam, David B. Orr and Isadore Goldberg. Some of these are the Binet, Rorschach, Inkblots, Woodworth Personal Data Sheet, and Minnesota Multiphasic Personality Inventory.

In the use of testing instruments for clinical interpretations, Goldman states

1. The counselor must *know his tests.*

2. Since he uses test and other data to build a model of the person, it is necessary that the counsleor *know a great deal about people,* their personalities, their functioning, and how they differ from one another.

3. The clinical process involves creative skill in producing likely hypotheses combined with scientific rigor and cautiousness.

4. ... the counselor must know quite a bit about the situations about which he makes inferences.

5. The counselor needs to study himself as an interpreter. The school counselor needs to use these guidelines in establishing the total guidance program. Particular emphasis is needed in applying these principles in social-personal guidance.[21]

The Counselor's Approach

A primary task of the counselor is to help each child discover, appreciate, and accept his uniqueness. This is the area in which the counselor adds his most distinctive and unique contribution. It is also

---

[21]Leo Goldman, *Using Tests in Counseling* (2nd ed). New York: Appleton-Century-Crofts, 1968, pp. 204–206.

an area in which many individuals face frustrations when they cannot accept or do not understand this part of self.[22]

The counselor's approach to personality guidance in the elementary, junior high school, or senior high school must be in terms of the developmental characteristics of the boys and girls at the particular grade level of concern and in terms of sound counseling theory. There is yet to be developed a sound counseling theory for personality guidance of boys and girls with normal concerns. Effort is being directed to this point. However, the best that can be done at this stage of the development of the counseling process is to make applicable what is known about the counseling process as derived from theory applicable to clinical and counseling situations.[23] However, it should be reemphasized here that the counselor's approach to personality guidance must be considered with the usual care in that it is here that the counselor is dealing with the highly sensitive inner core of the human personality. Because it is a highly sensitive core does not mean that the counselor should avoid or neglect it, but rather that he must use extreme caution and proceed slowly. Research is needed in this area to determine the best approaches of personality guidance through counseling when dealing with school boys and girls.

Personality Guidance Counseling and Parents

As in many aspects of the school guidance program, parents should be kept informed of the purposes and procedures for personality guidance. Since personality guidance is an integral part of the total guidance program and is merely identified as personality guidance for focus or emphasis, the parents should be given help through conferences, meetings, and individual approaches in understanding the processes used in this aspect of the program. Myers emphasizes that the developing independence of the boy or girl is a feature of the entire span of childhood. But it accelerates in adolescence and is usually identified as the major factor in the second decade of life.

Myers goes on to point out some factors in child emancipation from parents, which should be considered by the school counselor:

[22]Lillian V. Cady, "Developmental Guidance: One Definition and Rationale," *The School Counselor,* Vol. 16 (January, 1969), p. 219.

[23]Bruce Shertzer and Shelley C. Stone, *Fundamentals of Counseling.* Boston: Houghton-Mifflin Company, 1968.

Angelo V. Boy and Gerald J. Pine, *Client-Centered Counseling in the Secondary School.* Boston: Houghton-Mifflin Company, 1963, p. 289.

Herman J. Peters and Miahael J. Bathory, *School Counseling: Perspectives and Procedures.* Chicago: F. E. Peacock Publishers, Inc., 1968.

1. Emancipation requires much sacrifice by the parents. They must relinquish authority.

2. Emancipation is more than a mere letting go by parents; it is ideally a product of positive steps to cultivate responsibility.

3. The effect of small family size must be considered.

4. Emancipation should be achieved with good feelings all round.

5. The necessary prolongation of economic dependence must be considered.

6. The discrepancy between parental intellectual understanding of relaxation of controls and attitudes toward them must be considered.

7. The contemporary changes in values and loyalties must be considered.

8. The maturing adolescent is reaching a height of capacity for insight into his development of self.[24]

One-to-one counseling is important but manipulating, changing, or controlling the child's environment are also possibilities for counseling [25] Environmental change can be enhanced by consulting with parents. The counselor can serve as school interpreter for the parents—he can interpret school programs, philosophies, services, attitudes toward each child, and so forth.

Parents have the greatest effect on their child's environment. Armin Grams suggests that parents can ready their child for learning, by providing a sound emotional base, adequate social skills, encouraging special talents and developing values.[26]

ORGANIZING GROUP PROCEDURES FOR PERSONALITY GUIDANCE

Group procedures in personality guidance are often organized in ways similar to those for vocational guidance: (1) as a particular class unit for this purpose; (2) as a special unit within another subject area, for example, English or social studies; (3) through special events or special group conferences. In some schools, personality guidance is considered an integral

[24]Charles E. Myers, "Emancipation of the Adolescent From Parental Control," *The Nervous Child,* Vol. 5 (1946), pp. 251–62.

[25]James C. Hansen and Richard R. Stevic. *Elementary School Guidance.* The Macmillan Co., Copyright, 1969.

[26]Armin Grams. *Facilitating Learning and Individual Development.* St. Paul, Minnesota, Department of Education, 1966, pp. 49–78.

part of the health education program. Group procedures for personality guidance are concerned primarily with getting at dissemination of information about psycho-social matters, a discussion of how an individual's development contributes to learning effectiveness, and how a better self-understanding will lead to a happier life. The use of group procedures for guidance functions is illustrated in this report from a school system.

> On November 1st, an open house was held for all parents. An attempt was made to talk with as many as possible to familiarize them with the guidance program as well as the total school program.
>
> Group sessions were held with the freshman class. These sessions took place early in the school year and were devoted to question and answer sessions concerning the problems of high school.
>
> During the first few weeks of school, small groups of seniors received information and discussed various possibilities after graduation. They were advised of important dates for tests and certain deadlines that were to be met.
>
> During the month of May, the eighth graders from Adena Junior High School in Clarksburg were invited to spend an afternoon at Adena High School for an orientation program. The program followed the same format as the one sponsored each year by the guidance department in cooperation with the Student Council. The council members planned an assembly program explaining the various activities, policies, etc., to familiarize them with their new school environment. The guidance counselor discussed registration procedures.
>
> The following week, registration for the eighth graders was held in their building. The guidance counselor, junior high principal, and teachers (8th teachers) were available to answer questions and to advise individuals with problems. Parents were invited to arrange an appointment for a conference if they desired.
>
> In cooperation with Mr. Pack, the juniors checked questionnaires concerning Career Day which was held at Chillicothe High School. These juniors had received group instruction on what to expect and what to look for during Career Day.
>
> Group sessions were sponsored by the guidance counselor for the 9th, 10th, and 11th grade students prior to scheduling, so they would have an opportunity to ask questions concerning the curriculum and complete registration forms.[27]

Group procedures often have units on helping the child adjust socially, get along with his classmates, get along with his parents, understand people who are different from him, face problems in daily living, develop responsi-

---

[27]Guidance and Counseling Activities," *A Summary of Guidance Activities in the Ross County Schools—1966–67.* Chillicothe, Ohio; p. 6.

bility, and often define a code for effective living. There are a number of cautions in group procedures for personality guidance. First, care must be taken that there is a readiness on the part of the student to discuss some of the intimate concerns of how he feels and acts. Second, the counselor in charge of the group procedures must be sure that the students understand the purposes in a positive way. There is often the danger that the students see this as preaching, sermonizing, or "bawling out." Third, there must be provision for follow-up with the counseling process because an effective group-procedures class may stimulate student questions which are best considered in the privacy of the counseling office. Fourth, the counselor in charge of the group-procedures class must be skillful in the group discussion and must be alert to group dynamics when the topic is on some phase of group guidance.

In determining the effectiveness of group procedures based on a criterion of greater perception in understanding the self, Froehlich found that there is no difference in the effectiveness of the individual and group processes.[28] Caplan did work on group processes with particular emphasis on group counseling with adolescents with social problems. He was concerned about the changing self-concept of school achievement and behavior of boys with problems in a large high school in San Francisco. Group procedures were used in creating a permissive situation in which the boys involved were given opportunities to better understand themselves and why they were in the group. The purpose was therapeutic in nature. As the meetings increased in number, there seemed to be evidence that the boys had come to a better understanding of some of the difficulties in their development. Caplan found significant differences in favor of the group-counseled boys as against the controlled groups.[29]

> The purpose of the study was to evaluate the effectiveness of a program of developmental counseling in helping a selected group of high school students to cope more effectively with their roles as students.
>
> All 10th-grade teachers responded by identifying one or more students. The 28 most frequently nominated students (all boys) were contacted and invited to participate in a voluntary project designed 'to help sophomores with problems of school and grades.'
>
> Behavior changes in the population were studied under four basic criteria: (1) changes in achievement-oriented coping behaviors as

[28]Clifford P. Froehlich, "Must Counseling Be Individual?" *Educational and Psychological Measurement,* Vol. 4 (1958) pp. 681–689.

[29]Stanley W. Caplan, "The Effect of Group Counseling on Junior High School Boys' Concepts of Themselves," *Journal of Counseling Psychology,* Vol. 4 (Summer, 1957), pp. 124–128.

measured by academic grades; (2) changes in social coping behavior as measured by disciplinary referrals (disciplinary referral was viewed as a situation in which the students' coping behaviors are grossly inadequate to meet role expectations); (3) changes in personal feelings of adequacy of coping in social roles as measured by the S.R.A. Youth Inventory; and (4) persistence in the role of student as measured by rate of drop-out between 9th and 10th grades.

The counselor led discussions on massed versus distributed practice, the SQ3R study method, study scheduling, concentration, homework, work meanings, test preparation, and effects of recitation on reading retention. Four short 'how to study' films were shown. The district remedial reading specialist was invited in for one full session with each group.

Results were evaluated under the four types of criteria mentioned earlier.

1. *Changes in academic grades.* The mean changes in grade-point averages between first semester (pre-counseling) and second semester (post-counseling) were computed for both experimental and control groups. These means were compared using a t test. The mean differences for the two groups are shown in Table 10-3. The differences were in favor of the counseled group and were statistically significant at the .02 level of confidence.

2. *Changes in disciplinary referrals.* The number of disciplinary referrals to the principal during the second semester was obtained for each group. These differences are shown in Table 10-4. Eight control group students were referred for a total of 17 times, while five experimentals were referred for a total of 10 times. These differences, while in favor of the experimental group, were not statistically significant. They are obviously of *practical* significance, however.

3. *Changes in feelings of adequacy of coping.* Changes in the subjects' feelings of adequacy in coping were assessed using the S.R.A. Youth Inventory. This problem checklist that inventories common adolescent problems was considered a rough indicator of the subject's feeling of adequacy of coping within each of the eight areas measured. Table 10-5 shows the changes for experimental and control groups in terms of change in numbers of individuals who scored above the 75th percentile on each area. Scores above this point are usually considered 'high.' A 2×2 chi square statistic was computed comparing the number of control and experimental scores above the 75th percentile pre-counseling and post-counseling. The chi square indicated a difference in favor of the experimental (counseled) group significant beyond the .01 level.

4. *Persistence in school.* Perhaps the most crucial indicator of success of the developmental counseling program lay in the degree to

Table 10-3.[30]   *Mean Grade-Points of Experimental and Control Groups During 1st and 2nd Semesters.*

Group	Semester I	Semester II	Difference
Experimental	1.57	2.08	+.51*
Control	1.33	.86	−.47*

*significant at the .02 level (or p > .02)

Table 10-4.[31]   *Referrals to Principal Due to Acting-Out Behavior.*

Group	Number of Referrals			Total No. of Pupils Referred	Total No. of Referrals
	Once	Twice	Three Times		
Experimental	2	1	2	5	10
Control	2	3	3	8	17

Table 10-5.[32]   *SRA Youth Inventory Pre- and Post-Test Comparison of Number of Control and Experimental Group Members Who Marked More Items as Problems in Each of Eight Areas than 75 Percent of High School Pupils in the Nation.*

Area	Pre-Test		Post-Test		Change	
	Exp. Gp.	Cont. Gp.	Exp. Gp.	Cont. Gp.	Exp. Gp.	Cont. Gp.
School	11	10	8	11	−3	+1
Looking Ahead	7	4	3	5	−4	+1
About Myself	6	5	5	8	−1	+3
Getting Along With Others	9	3	3	4	−6	+1
Home and Family	7	9	5	10	−2	+1
Boy Meets Girl	4	4	2	3	−2	−1
Health	9	7	4	9	−5	+2
Things in General	8	5	2	5	−6	0
Total	61	47	32	55	−29	+8

[30]Ronald L. Benson and Don H. Blocher, "Evaluation of Development Counseling with Groups of Low Achievers in a High School Setting," *The School Counselor,* March, 1967, p. 219. Material used with permission.

[31]*Ibid.*

[32]*Ibid.*

which affected the school-staying behavior of the subjects. The counseling treatment terminated at the end of the subjects' 10th-grade year. All 12 of the experimental (counseled) students returned the following fall to enter 11th grade. Three, or 25 percent, of the control (non-counseled) group dropped out of school during the summer. This difference was not tested statistically but has obvious practical significance in terms of the drastic social consequences associated with dropping out of school.[33]

In a review of the number of research studies on the use of group procedures, it seems that the evidence points toward a trend in concern about self and concern in understanding self but that there is no outstanding gain in the change of behavior. However, group procedures which initiate deeper thinking on the part of the student as how he might become a better person may prove of value in the counseling interview if the pupil is encouraged to engage in this process. A checklist for determining the completeness of the personality guidance phase of the total school guidance program may be developed through the use of a part of the guidance services evaluative criteria in the 1960 edition of the *National Study of Secondary School Evaluation.* (Also see Chapter 17.)

EVALUATIVE CRITERIA[34]

Personal and Social Development

Checklist

Accurate information is available about the following items for all students:

( ) 1. Special talents and interests—musical, artistic, athletic, inventive, literary, dramatic, scientific.
( ) 2. Special achievements (other than academic) in school and out of school.
( ) 3. Participation in student activity program.
( ) 4. Educational intentions.
( ) 5. Vocational preferences at successive stages of development.
( ) 6. Evidences of vocational aptitudes—interests and skill in performance.
( ) 7. Membership in out-of-school clubs or organizations.
( ) 8. Employment during out-of-school hours and during vacations.

[33]*Ibid.,* pp. 215–220.
[34]Evaluative Criteria, Section G, Guidance Services, in *National Study of Secondary School Evaluation.* Washington, D. C.: Cooperative Study of Secondary School Standards, 1960, p. 282.

( )   9. Use of leisure—reading, hobbies, movies, radio, television.
( ) 10. Conduct of citizenship record.
( ) 11. Nature of social activities.
( ) 12. Periodic ratings by teachers on personality traits.
( ) 13. Attitudes toward school and school activities.
( ) 14. Religious interests and activities.
( ) 15. Results from interest inventories.
( ) 16. Interpretations of aptitude tests.
( ) 17. Interpreataions of personality and attitude inventories or scales.
( ) 18.
( ) 19.

Supplementary Data
1. Describe method for securing this information and indicate who is responsible for securing it.

Evaluations
( ) a. How extensive is the information concerning personal and social development?
( ) b. How up to date are records of personal and social development?

Comments

Courses in Group Guidance

The staff needs to exercise caution in the use of a course structure for classes in group guidance. Actually, group guidance is a misnomer. There are group procedures for individual assistance, that is, guidance. Further, care must be taken that group guidance classes do not become instructional lessons devoid of personal application.

The enrollment in a group guidance class should be no more than twenty-five. Ideally, the group guidance classes should be a function of both the junior and senior high school program. They should be staffed by certificated school counselors. The homeroom plan of yesteryear is not effective. The classes for this group experience should be scheduled as any other part of the instructional program. The staff should acquaint itself with materials on group guidance as a basis for determining the substance of the group procedures classes.

Units Within School Subjects

Often social-personal guidance may be promoted through a discussion of units within school subjects. One danger in approaching personality guidance through units within school subjects is that the student will see this merely as another intellectual attainment and will not relate it specifically to himself. The teacher must not assume that because a topic is discussed the student will see that it may have some relation to himself. It, of course, becomes imperative that the methodology of presentation provide opportunities for the student to think in terms of how this may reflect on his development.

Units of a guidance nature within a social studies, English, problems of democracy, or other course will vary in length according to the time available and nature of the subject. Generally, four to six weeks is needed to complete units on educational and vocational development and planning. The teacher and school counselor can work this out through in-service conferences. Care should be taken to appraise the unit's worthwhileness in the guidance of the pupils. The timing should fit into the total guidance plans as well as the instructional program.

The Use of Community Resources for Providing Personality Guidance

In every major metropolitan area, there are many resources which, if coordinated with the total school guidance program, may be excellent complementary and supplementary agencies for the development of the personality guidance phase of the guidance program. Children's mental health centers, service organization projects, family agencies, United Fund agencies, and often central school staff agencies in the larger cities have excellent resources for assistance in providing personality guidance for boys and girls. In developing a personality guidance program, the director of guidance or the school counselor must take care to organize definite procedures for use of the referral agencies. Inadequate preparation in the use of community resources may cause frustration, disappointment, and disapproval by parents who are hurriedly led into accepting the services of the agencies without proper orientation as to their purpose and function.

Essential to the proper development of the entire guidance program and to each phase, including the social-personal guidance part, is the collection, housing, and use of related materials. This is a very similar process to that described in Chapter 12.

Counselors and other staff members will obtain much data and information from these materials. These materials also serve to bring into more tangible form some of the abstract notions about human behavior. It is recommended that procedures similar to those used for handling materials for vocational guidance be used for materials for personality guidance.

FOLLOW-THROUGH AND GENERAL GUIDELINES FOR SOCIAL-PERSONAL GUIDANCE PROGRAMMING

It is important to the development of the personality guidance program that provision be made for a follow-through of personality development. Many behaviors of the pupil are transitory in nature and of little concern in his longitudinal development. However, it is necessary for the teacher and the counselor to be alert to those incidents of behavior which seem to form a sequence and later, over a few months, a pattern affecting the development of the boy and girl. These may be positive or negative in nature. A records procedure needs to be used which will be of benefit to the boy or girl in recording positive as well as negative data which are of longitudinal interest. Unless positive data are recorded, negative incidents that have been recorded may be used to draw invalid conclusions about a personality. It becomes important to decide what will be carried through in observing the personality development of boys and girls.

A number of guidelines are worthwhile. First, incidents or records of incidents which seem to be of momentary duration should be discarded no later than the end of the school year in which the behavior took place. Second, if possible, it is wise to summarize the nature of the incidents if they are viewed to be a pattern of development. Third, the materials should be available only for professional staff use and should be so secure that students or others who are in or near the office may not have access to them and misinterpret their purpose.

The staff members who participate in the group procedures class should realize that the atmosphere and the tensions and the permissiveness and other climatic facts may be quite different from those in the usual classroom. Although the atmosphere should be one of acceptance, permissiveness, and warmth, support must be given, perhaps far more frequently than in the usual instructional classroom. Counselors or the staff members in charge need to know their roles of group procedures and need to have practice in this important experience in dealing with the human dynamics of human behavior.

The process of building a social-personal guidance program involves a number of steps.

1. The guidance committee, including counselors, teachers, and administrative staff, should determine the emphasis to be given to developmental, remedial, and therapeutic guidance for social-personal concerns.

2. *Study* the social-personal needs of the students for focus and limitations of the program. Be sure that parents, staff, and students are aware before the study begins of the purposes of the instruments used.

3. *Relate* the social-personal phase of the guidance program to the learning effectiveness of the pupils as well as to their total development.

4. With an adequate number of certified school counselors, *allow* ample counseling time for social-personal development concerns of a positive as well as remedial nature.

5. *Include* the social-personal phase of the program in the guidance budget.

6. If there is more than one counselor, one should be *designated* as chiefly responsible for social-personal guidance.

7. *Decide* on procedures for handling confidential data (see Chapters 6 and 14).

8. *Evaluate* the program.

THE COUNSELOR'S PROFESSIONAL LIBRARY

Counselors will find few professional books relating specifically to social-personal guidance. There are many books on personality and the make-up of the individual. Keeping in mind the basic approach of this book—developmental guidance—the counselor will find the following books helpful in expanding the details of social-personal guidance.

1. James F. Adams, *Understanding Adolescence: Current Developments in Adolescent Psychology* (2nd ed.). Boston: Allyn and Bacon, 1973, 511 pp.

2. L. Joseph Stone and Joseph Church, *Childhood and Adolescence.* New York: Random House, 1972. 576 pp.

3. Lawrence B. Schiamberg, *Adolescent Alienation.* Columbus, Ohio: Charles E. Merrill Publishing Company, 1973. 148 pp.

4. John E. Horrocks, *Assessment of Behavior.* Columbus, Ohio: Charles E. Merrill Publishing Company, 1964. 736 pp.

5. Walter M. Lifton, *Working with Groups* (2nd ed.). New York: John Wiley & Sons, Inc., 1966.

6. Sidney M. Jourard, *Healthy Personality: An Approach From the Viewpoint of Humanistic Psychology.* New York: Macmillan Publishing Co., Inc., 1974. 480 pp.

SUMMARY

Social-personal guidance is an organized phase of the total program. It is concerned with the individual's attitudes and feelings of innerself as well as his relations with others. Differential factors in social-personal guidance in the elementary, junior high, and senior high schools were given. In the elementary school, social-personal guidance focuses on the child's growing understanding of the widening horizons of ideas about people. In junior high school, there is need for opportunity to begin appraising self-understanding in relation to other persons. In the senior high school, social-personal guidance becomes a part of the adolescent's look at his goals for the fullness of adulthood.

Counseling and group procedural approaches to social-personal guidance were considered. The proper interpretation of tests was emphasized. Group procedures were analyzed in terms of (1) class units for social-personal guidance, (2) as a special unit within a subject area, and (3) through special events or special group conferences. Some research evidence was presented. Further representative helpful materials were given in the list of five books in the counselor's professional library.

ANNOTATED BIBLIOGRAPHY

Combs, Arthur W., Donald L. Avila, and William W. Purkey, *Helping Relationships.* Boston: Allyn and Bacon, Inc., 1971, 360 pp.
In all aspects of helping another, these authors give sound ideas and approaches. Learning as *change* will be particularly helpful to school counselors.

Curran, Charles, A., *Counseling—Learning.* New York: Grune & Stratton, 1972, 258 pp.
The author emphasizes the learning relationship in the "I-Myself" congruency.

Gutsch, Kenneth A. and Herman J. Peters., *Counseling with Youth: In Search for Identity.* Columbus, Ohio: Charles E. Merrill Publishing Company, 1973, 128 pp.
Exploring how one relates in the social-personal world is the theme of this book. The counselor as an agent of change is discussed in relation to social-personal development.

Managing the Testing Program

An individual's concept of himself, his motivations, and the way he is perceived by others may be colored by test results. In recent years, educational and employment opportunities, at least in part, have been and are defined by test scores of one sort or another. ... If tests and their use are to escape eventual oblivion, test consumers must be informed thoroughly about the strengths and limitations of the techniques and instruments they employ. Their behavior must be congruent with this information.[1]

Chapter 11

What criticisms are made of tests and testing?

Why should a school have a testing program?

What sources may be consulted to obtain information about tests and testing?

What are the major components of a testing program?

What guidelines are useful in managing a testing program?

CRITICISMS OF TESTS AND TESTING

Lewis Carroll, speaking through his most famous character, Alice, once said that the best place to start is at the beginning. As appropriate and as intuitively satisfying as that advice is, it is of little help in deciding where to start in setting forth the major components of a testing program and its management. There is little doubt but that the educational historian who writes the story of American schools from 1945 to the 1970s can fail to note the extensive and pervasive use of standardized tests, at every level and for a wide variety of purposes. James D. Linden, a psychology professor at Purdue University who specializes in tests and measurements, estimates

---

[1]James D. Linden and Kathryn W. Linden, *Tests on Trial*. Boston: Houghton Mifflin Company, 1968, p. 1, p. v.

that some 250 to 300 million standardized tests were administered during 1972–73 in the schools of this country. The trend, which has been steadily in the direction of greater use of such tests, shows little sign of abating. The overwhelming proportion of these tests was used to assess student achievement and ability.

It is equally dubious that the educational historian can fail to note, as one of the distinctive features of this period, the ever-increasing crescendo of criticism of and controversy over standardized testing in schools and other settings. This criticism ranges over the construction, the publication, the sale, and, above all, the use of tests. The tensions created by the upsurge of testing and its criticisms have been felt by counselors, teachers, students, parents, and even test experts and publishers. Here some of the major criticisms will be described briefly, since it is believed that all school counselors, and particularly guidance administrators, should be familiar with the nature of the criticisms and the controversy that surround standardized testing. While the focus here is on standardized tests, it should be noted that teacher-constructed tests are subject to even more conflicts.

Criticisms of Test Validity and Reliability

The validity and reliability of standardized tests have been subjected to much criticism. Simply defined, *validity* refers to the degree of accuracy or truth with which the test measures what it purports to measure; *reliability* refers to the consistency and scope of a test. Criticisms of the validity and reliability of standardized tests strike at the very heart of testing, for if tests fail to measure what they are designed to assess, or fail to measure consistently, then little confidence can be placed in their results. There would be little use in administering them.

Standardized personality inventories have been criticized repeatedly as being invalid measures. Questioning the validity of group intelligence tests led New York City public school system, the largest in America, to discontinue their use in 1964, and to substitute an extensive achievement test program. Other large city school systems, including those of Washington, D.C., and Los Angeles also discontinued group intelligence testing. Test validity and reliability are highly technical components of tests, and when criticisms of this nature are made by those who are expert in tests and measurements, they are particularly serious. It should be pointed out that there are different forms of validity and reliability for different tests, based on the purposes for which the tests are designed. No test measure is exact. Some tests are more valid and reliable than others, but none is perfect in either respect. The criticism of imprecision applies equally well to other measurements that are important in our daily lives. Yet no one argues that these measures—temperature, mileage, and so forth,—should be abandoned because they are inexact. While the consequences of imprecision in testing are doubtless more serious than measures of this kind, nevertheless, test scores—properly obtained, interpreted and used—are highly useful estimates of behavior.

Cultural Bias

Another criticism of tests is that they reflect middle class experiences, achievements, and school successes. This is particularly true for those used to assess intelligence and achievement. Consequently, children born and reared in impoverished environments, or those who are culturally different, are penalized because their experiences limit their effectiveness in test situations. The items, activities and objects used in intelligence and achievement tests tend to be drawn from middle class culture. Consequently, a student who is a member of a middle class group has a better chance of scoring well than a student from a lower class home has because he is generally encouraged to develop verbal abilities and to reason critically. Thus, scholastic aptitude tests used in selecting students for college have been a target of much criticism.

Bloom has estimated that insecurity and an impoverished environment can cut ten I.Q. points from a child's test performance by age four, and another ten points by age seventeen.[2] Conversely, many studies have shown that the intelligence scores of underprivileged students have climbed—sometimes as much as eighteen points in eighteen months—when they receive special help, tutoring, or improved schooling. Some childrens' ability-test scores have varied as much as forty points from one period of their lives to another. Herrnstein observed that:

> The correlation between I.Q. and social class (usually defined in terms of occupation, income, and patterns of personal association) is undeniable, substantial and worth noting. A cautious conclusion, based on a survey of the scientific literature, is that the upper class scores about thirty I.Q. points above the lower class. A typical member of the upper class gets a score that certifies him as intellectually "superior," while a typical member of the lower class is a shade below average (that is, below I.Q. 100).[3]

Most test experts admit that those with impoverished backgrounds do poorly on tests. However, they do not advocate that testing be abandoned

---

[2]Benjamin S. Bloom, *Stability and Change in Human Characteristics.* New York: John Wiley and Sons, 1964, p. 77.

[3]Richard Herrnstein, "I.Q.," *The Atlantic,* Vol. 228 (September 1971) p. 50.

but rather that conditions be improved for such children, both at home and at school. They argue that standardized tests are an objective, fair and democratic means by which able students receive due recognition, no matter what their class or race. Finally, they urge that greater research effort be given to developing more culturally "fair" tests.

Restricted Conceptions of Ability

Another criticism of testing is that it fosters limited conceptions of ability. Most tests used in schools are based heavily upon verbal and quantitative skills. Many educators have observed that such skills do not exhaust all types of achievement needed in American society. The prominence given to these skills by testing throughout the schooling period tends to discourage the development of other kinds of qualities—such as persistence, social abilities, creativity, and honesty—and serves to reduce the diversity of skills available to society.

Lifelong Branding

A charge often made is that test results are used to label or brand people for life as "average," "superior," or "inferior." The charge stems from the belief that students who are given intelligence tests in elementary schools are classified by teachers into groupings based upon their tests results. Moreover, these test results (and labels) are transferred from teacher to teacher, and from school to school, and follow a person throughout his life. Further, many assert that the individual so labelled comes to believe the label and reacts to the expectations held by others for him that are implicit in the classification. He becomes the part associated with the label or classification. Because the individual acts to meet the expectations associated with the classification, it is asserted that test data determine his life chances. The classification remains with the individual and influences what he does regardless of how he changes or how his environment changes.

Invasion of Privacy

Another criticism is that testing is an invasion of an individual's privacy. The right to privacy—to have one's personal thoughts, records, behavior, and reports free from inspection or examination by another—is a very fundamental right that is increasingly being given protection by state laws. Many individuals are concerned not only that administering a test violates a person's right to privacy, but that test results are posted in a cumulative record that follows an individual through school and on into his work position. They are concerned about the individuals who have access to the test data in this record.

The criticism of invasion of privacy is more often leveled against standardized inventories of personality, values, beliefs, and attitude scales than other assessment devices. Cronbach has pointed out that

> Any test is an invasion of privacy for the subject who does not wish to reveal himself. . . . Virtually all measures of personality seek information on areas that the subject has every reason to regard as private, in normal social intercourse. He is willing to admit the psychologist into those private areas only if he sees the relevance of the questions to the attainment of his goals in working with the psychologist. The psychologist is not "invading privacy" when he is freely admitted and when he has a genuine need for the information obtained.[4]

Cronbach's criteria for justifying testing are that (1) the individual consents to the administration of the personality inventory, and (2) the psychologist needs the information. Many school personnel justify the administration of ability and achievement tests on the grounds that they have a "genuine need" to know the information obtained in order to provide appropriate instruction and other forms of assistance to an individual.

Inaccessible Test Data

Another charge against testing is that feedback about test results is not given to the person tested. This charge stems from the practice of testing an individual and withholding from him the outcomes of the test. The practice was initiated and continued because it was believed that those who did poorly would find the results disturbing and inimical to their functioning. Also it was believed that too many naive students and their parents would misunderstand test interpretations and use such data in harmful ways. Brim states

> It is natural for a person to have an interest in any facts about himself. If someone else knows something about him that he, himself, does not know, then of course, he will try to find it out, especially if it is something of such importance as his intelligence test score.[5]

Brim's point seems well taken. Individuals believe that if they take tests, they have a legitimate interest in and a right to all the information yielded by the tests.

---

[4]Lee J. Cronbach, *Essentials of Psychological Testing* (3rd ed.). New York: Harper and Row, Publishers, 1970, pp. 509–510.

[5]Orville G. Brim, Jr., "American Attitudes Toward Intelligent Tests." In Bruce Shertzer and Shelley C. Stone (eds.), *Introduction to Guidance: Selected Readings*. Boston: Houghton Mifflin Company, 1970, p. 235.

Control by Test Publishers

Another criticism is that test publishers not only influence educational practices by the tests they publish and distribute, but that in doing so they exercise control over what is taught and valued in the classroom. This criticism stems from the practice of using achievement tests at the end of the year to evaluate student gains and losses. The argument is that it is the test publisher—not the professional classroom teacher—who selects test items and who, therefore, determines the content that is treated in the classroom. In response, test publishers argue that they do not design standardized achievement tests for a local school and that a particular teacher exercises judgment as to what material is selected and presented to a class.

Ebel has pointed out

> Those who know well how tests are made and used in American education know that the tests more often lag than lead curricular change, and that while tests may affect particular episodes in a student's experience, they can hardly ever be said to determine a student's destiny. American education is, after all, a manifold, decentralized, loosely organized enterprise. Whether it restricts student freedom too much or too little is a subject for lively debate. But it does not even come close to determining any student's destiny, not nearly as close as the examination systems in some other countries, ancient and modern.[6]

Mechanistic Decision-Making

Traditionally, educational testing has been designed to measure the progress and attainments of students. However, it is charged that these data are too often mechanistically used, without regard to other factors, to make decisions about the individual. Without question, test scores are often used by the individual to make decisions, and by others to make decisions about the individual. Included in this charge is that the individual "disappears" steadily when test data about him are accumulated to make an institutional decision. He becomes more and more a manipulated being, caught in the grip of computer processed data that mechanistically indicate whether he is to be accepted or denied.

Illustrative of this charge is that school administrators have used end-of-year achievement test data to evaluate teachers and to determine whether to continue their employment. Those teachers whose classes do not exhibit sufficient gains have been released from their contracts without any consid-

---

[6]Robert L. Ebel, "The Social Consequences of Educational Testing." In Bruce Shertzer and Shelley C. Stone (eds.), *Introduction to Guidance: Selected Readings.* Boston: Houghton Mifflin Company, p. 231.

eration given to the experiences and previous background of students in their classes. Such ill-advised, mechanistic decision-making practices are, of course, condemned by all knowledgeable educators.

Increasingly, test authors and publishers are designing tests to be of more direct help, not only in institutional, but in individual decision-making as well. In respect to the charge that test data lead to mechanistic decision-making, Ebel has written that:

> A large proportion of the decisions affecting the welfare and destiny of a person must be made in the midst of overwhelming uncertainties concerning the outcomes to be desired and the best means of achieving such outcomes. That many mistakes will be made seems inevitable. One of the cornerstones of a free society is the belief that in most cases it is better for the person most concerned to make the decision, right or wrong, and to take the responsibility for its consequences, good or bad.
>
> The implications of this for educational testing are clear. Tests should be used as little as possible to *impose* decisions and courses of actions on others. They should be used as much as possible to provide a sounder basis of *choice* in individual decision making.[7]

Encourage Test-Taking Skills

A final criticism of testing to be reported here is that testing provides an incentive to students to develop specious test-taking skills rather than encourages them to develop skills that facilitate "true" learning. Moreover, according to this charge, students learn for the sake of passing tests rather than for mastery of the content. This criticism is based on the notion that learning how to survive tests becomes overly important to students, and that they process material with the view of how it will appear and how it must be dealt with on a test.

In summary, examination of these criticisms reveals that most are based upon the abuse of test data. While the technical shortcomings of some standardized tests and inventories cannot be overlooked, the most serious limitation, at present, is the way test data are viewed, interpreted and used. Fincher has written that

> There remains a great need for better education and understanding concerning the uses and applications of all psychological tests. Because tests have been identified with abusive practice in the employment area, they are often rejected for the wrong reasons in other areas. They are regarded too frequently as intrinsically discriminatory and ipso facto,

---

[7] *Ibid.,* p. 233.

morally reprehensible. That tests have served other social needs in a
most valuable way at other times is not fully appreciated.[8]

Without question, teachers and counselors need both pre- and in-service
training in the appropriate use of test data. Since counselors are often the
most qualified personnel in the schools in respect to test data, they must
exercise leadership in initiating and developing sound practices of test
interpretation, use and reporting.

TESTING: VALUES AND PURPOSES

Criticisms of tests reflect the dissatisfaction held by many adults and
students. For example, Brim reported that of a representative group of
Americans over eighteen years old, many were opposed to using tests to
help decide on admission of students to college (41 percent); using tests in
job selection (37 percent); using tests to help decide on job promotions (50
percent), and using intelligence tests to help establish special classes in
school (25 percent). High school students were even more opposed to the
use of intelligence tests: 50 percent were against their use in job hiring; 62
percent were against their use in promotion decisions; 54 percent were
against using them to help select students for college; and 50 percent were
against their use to help establish special classes in schools.[9]

Despite intense criticisms and the dissatisfaction, test usage has not been
abandoned in schools. Several reasons could be advanced for their continued use. Ebel states

> If the use of educational tests were abandoned, the encouragement
> and reward of individual efforts to learn would be made more difficult.
> Excellence in programs of education would become less tangible as a
> goal and less demonstrable as an attainment. Educational opportunities
> would be extended less on the basis of aptitude and merit and more on
> the basis of ancestry and influence; social class barriers would become
> less permeable. Decisions on important issues of curriculum and
> method would be made less on the basis of solid evidence and more on
> the basis of prejudice or caprice.[10]

In short, the consequences of abandoning testing are more adverse in their
social implications than the harmful consequences of continuing testing.

---

[8]Cameron Fincher, "Personnel Testing and Public Policy," *The American Psychologist*,
Vol. 28 (July, 1973) p. 488.

[9]Orville G. Brim, Jr., "American Attitudes Toward Intelligence Testing," In Bruce Shertzer
and Shelley C. Stone (eds.) *Introduction to Guidance: Selected Readings.* Boston: Houghton
Mifflin Company, 1970, pp. 234–235.

[10]Ebel, "Consequences of Testing," p. 234.

Tests—used with skill, wisdom, and concern—can benefit the individual. Here, consideration is given to their values and purposes.

Fundamental Purposes

The fundamental purpose of standardized tests is to provide an objective view of some aspects of an individual's behavior. A test has been defined as a "systematic procedure for observing a person's behavior and describing it with the aid of a numerical scale or a category system."[11] If used properly, test results can help counselors provide counselees with an objective viewing of their assets and liabilities.

Four purposes for which tests are given have been identified and described by Cronbach.[12] These purposes are paraphrased here, as follows.

> *Prediction.* Tests are given to obtain a measure of ability, achievement, and/or other characteristics that will offer a solid basis upon which individuals can make decisions. Decisions involve predictions as to how well individuals will do at a later time. Prediction based upon quantitative data is likely to be more reliable and accurate, and is likely to provide a balance against wishful thinking.
>
> *Selection.* Tests are used by institutions such as colleges, businesses, and industries to accept some individuals and to reject others. The decision to hire an individual or to admit a student to college is a selection decision.
>
> *Classification.* Classification is an arrangement according to some systematic division into classes or groups. Classification involves deciding which of the many treatments, groups, or assignments a person should receive. Examples of classifications include diagnosis of mental patients, choice of school or curriculum, assignment to a military occupational specialty, and the like. *Placement* should not be confused with classification although it is a kind of classification. Placement tests (assignment of individuals to different *levels* of work within a type of work) differ from classification tests (assignment to different *types* of work) in terms of the kind of validity data available and in terms of providing more individualized descriptions.
>
> *Evaluation.* Tests are used to assess and to evaluate programs, methods, treatments, and scientific experiments.

While these four fundamental purposes describe accurately and fully the use of tests, their use in educational practice may be understood more

---

[11]Lee J. Cronbach, *Essentials of Psychological Testing* (3rd ed.). New York: Harper and Row, Publishers, 1970, p. 26.

[12]*Ibid.,* p. 22–25.

completely by considering separately how teachers, counselors and administrators use tests.

TEACHERS' USE OF TESTS

Tests may be viewed as an extension of the teacher's ability to observe
pupil behavior. Naturally, the more complex the behavior, the more difficult
it is to observe or to measure. Standardized ability and achievement test
data are frequently used by teachers. Some of the specific ways that teachers
use test data include:

1. To serve as a basis for grouping pupils

2. To measure growth or progress in subject matter fields

3. To analyze or diagnose learning difficulties

4. To predict individual pupil achievement

5. To discover special achievements and abilities of pupils

6. To discover inadequacies in curriculum

7. To provide information for grading students, for promoting students, and for making meaningful reports to parents

In short, teachers use test data so as to discharge more effectively their
instructional responsibilities. Tests are the means, not the ends, for understanding pupils and for keying instruction to their needs.

COUNSELORS' USE OF TESTS

The counselor's uses of test data are not fundamentally different from
those cited for the teacher. Specifically, counselors use standardized test
data

1. To provide information to each student about his abilities, aptitudes, interests, and personal characteristics so as to enrich his
   self-understanding.

2. To help students predict future performance such as in college
   success, and work potential.

3. To help students arrive at decisions basic to planning their educational and vocational futures.

4. To diagnose student problems, such as reading, studying, relating to others, etc.

5. To evaluate the outcomes of guidance or counseling.

ADMINISTRATORS' USE OF TESTS

School administrators have long realized that an effective way of insuring that a given educational objective will be emphasized in the classroom is to measure periodically the extent of its realization. They have sought to develop testing programs that systematically furnish up-to-date information on the educational development and status of pupils. Such information is considered basic data about the educational process.

Some of the ways that administrators use test data are:

1. To obtain an overall measure of the effectiveness of the school program

2. To identify content areas in which corrective action or supervisory aid should be given

3. To inform the public about the school's success or failure

4. To clarify educational objectives to teachers, pupils, and parents

5. To discover inadequacies in curriculum content and instruction

6. To help make decisions regarding the grouping of students for instructional purposes

In summary, school administrators use test data to help analyze and refine educational objectives and programs. As the content and learning experiences are appraised by the use of tests, a clearer view can be obtained as to how well the school is meeting its objectives. Moreover, test results help to indicate particular points of emphasis needed in developing school policy and planning.

SOURCES OF INFORMATION ABOUT TESTS

An effective testing program consists of the best possible tests and their results are used in accordance with sound psychological principles. This means that tests must be studied carefully and systematically, and that an understanding of the psychological principles of testing must be developed. There are several sources of information that can be used in gaining information about these two matters. These will be identified and discussed here.

Test Publishers' Materials

About 90 percent of the tests used in American schools are published by only a few companies. These companies—Educational Testing Service, Science Research Associates, Harcourt, Brace and Jovanovich, California Test Bureau, The Psychological Corporation, Consulting Psychologists Press, Houghton Mifflin Company, and Personnel Press—publish catalogs that cite and describe their products. The descriptions usually provide information about the age or grade level for which the test is intended, the price, the level of training required for administering the test, who may order it and how. In addition to the catalogs, a *technical manual* and/or an *examiner's manual* or handbook for administering, scoring, and interpreting the test are available from the publisher. In some instances, the technical information about the test is incorporated in the examiner's handbook or manual. A specimen set of the test may be purchased from the test publisher. It includes the test or inventory, the manuals, scoring key, profile forms, and so forth. Needless to say, all these materials are sources that must be examined in collecting information about tests.

Yearbooks and Standard References

Another major source of information about tests is the series entitled *The Mental Measurements Yearbook,* edited by Oscar K. Buros.[13] At present, it consists of seven volumes which cover almost all commercially available educational, psychological, and vocational tests published in the English-speaking countries. The third to seventh yearbooks include critical reviews, by one or more test experts, of most of the tests. In addition each yearbook lists the publisher, date of publication, price, forms, age levels, and other data.

Another publication edited by Buros is *Tests in Print,*[14] which presents a comprehensive bibliography of tests, and which serves as a classified index and supplement to *The Mental Measurements Yearbook.* It contains a comprehensive listing of tests available and also a listing of out-of-print tests. It does not, however, contain reviews of the tests.

---

[13]See Oscar K. Buros (Ed.), *The Seventh Mental Measurements Yearbook.* Highland Park, N.J.: Gryphon Press, 1972.

[14]Oscar K. Buros (Ed.) *Tests in Print.* Highland Park, N.J.: Gryphon Press, 1961.

Journal Reviews

Other sources of information for those who use tests include the reviews of newly published tests, or their revisions, in educational and psychological journals. Among the journals which either contain a special section or which give some attention to tests are *Psychological Abstracts, Educational and Psychological Measurement, Measurement and Evaluation in Guidance, Journal of Consulting Psychology, Journal of Educational Measurement, and the Journal of Counseling Psychology.* A comprehensive critical survey of all types of tests is published every three years in the February issue of the *Review of Educational Research.*

Textbooks

Other sources of information about tests are the various textbooks designed for courses in test and measurements. Examples include: Anne Anastasi, *Psychological Testing* (3rd ed.). New York: Macmillan, 1968; Lee J. Cronbach, *Essentials of Psychological Testing* (3rd ed.). New York: Harper and Row, 1970; and N. M. Downie. *Fundamentals of Measurement* (2nd ed.). New York: Oxford University Press, 1967.

Other Resources

Counselors and test administrators in other school districts are another source of information about tests. Based upon their experiences with a particular test, they can provide helpful information about the administration, scoring, interpretation, reporting, and use of test data.

ETHICAL STANDARDS

Test publishers are obligated to restrict sales to individuals qualified to administer and interpret those tests they purchase. Purchasers of tests that are most difficult to interpret are especially screened to determine whether they are qualified to use the tests, since their misuse would be very serious.

Test publishers are obliged to meet the standards and ethical practices set down for test development and use. These can be found in *Technical Recommendations for Achievement Tests*[15] and the *Technical Recommen-*

---

[15]American Educational Research Association, Committee on Test Standards, *Technical Recommendations for Achievement Tests.* Washington, D.C.: National Education Association, 1955.

dations for Psychological Tests and Diagnostic Techniques.[16] Both sets of recommendations suggest practices in developing, publishing, selling, and scoring tests.

Equally important is test security, control, and proper use by the practitioner. He is equally responsible for safeguarding tests and for using them properly. Both the American Personnel and Guidance Association,[17] and the American Psychological Association[18] have ethical codes that address themselves to the professional's use of tests. Frequent review of these ethical standards is advisable for all counselors and test users.

MAJOR COMPONENTS OF A TESTING PROGRAM

Thoughtful attention must be given by all educational personnel to the tests being administered and used in their school districts. The guidance administrator should feel a sense of responsibility to make sure the tests being given are needed, that they have been selected wisely, and that resulting test data are being used in beneficial ways. Here some of the major components of a testing program will be discussed.

Types of Tests

There are several ways of classifying tests used in the school, based upon purpose, content, form, procedures, and functions.

Standardized vs. teacher-made tests. Standardized tests are those administered and scored according to specific instructions. Norms based on large samples of students are available to compare a subject's performance with that of others in a similar population category or group. Teacher-made tests are constructed for informal pupil evaluation within the classroom and usually do not have extensive norms available.

Individual- versus group-tests. Individual tests are those administered by a trained examiner to one subject at a time. The examiner observes the subject's responses to oral questions and assigned tasks, and he records the subject's responses. Examples of individual tests include the Stanford-Binet Intelligence Test, Wechsler Intelligence Scales, Rorschach Ink Blot Test,

---

[16]American Psychological Association, *Technical Recommendations for Psychological Tests and Diagnostic Techniques.* Washington, D.C.: American Psychological Association, 1954.

[17]American Personnel and Guidance Association, "Ethical Standards," *Personnel and Guidance Journal,* Vol. 18 (January, 1963) pp. 59–60.

[18]American Psychological Association, *Casebook on Ethical Standards of Psychologists.* Washington, D.C.: American Psychological Association, 1967.

and the Thematic Apperception Test. Group tests, on the other hand, are those that can be administered to more than one individual at a time.

Speed versus power tests. A speed test is one in which the examinee completes as many items as possible within specified time limits. A power test is one in which the examinee demonstrates the extent of his knowledge, or scope and depth of his understanding, with the time limit either eliminated or made very generous. Items on a power test usually range from easy to extremely difficult.

Performance versus paper-and-pencil tests. Performance tests require the subject to manipulate objects or to assemble parts, or to actually perform tasks, while paper and pencil tests require the examinee to mark an answer sheet or to provide written responses.

Objective versus subjective tests. Objective tests require little or no judgment on the part of the scorer, while subjective tests require the scorer to exercise judgment in evaluating the examinee's answers.

Maximum versus typical performance. Maximum performance tests are those that require the individual to perform at his best, to do the best he can to demonstrate his ability. Typical performance tests are those that seek to determine what the individual usually does or is most likely to do in given situations.

Another way of classifying tests is according to the purpose for which they are designed or the aspects of behavior they sample; for example, according to mental ability, aptitude, achievement, interest, and personality. These five types of tests will now be discussed briefly.

Ability Tests. Mental ability tests were the first psychological tests to be developed. Various terms (intelligence, academic ability, scholastic aptitude) have been and are still used to designate their purpose, which is essentially to estimate intellectual functioning.

Intelligence, while difficult to define, functions in educational achievement. Study after study has pointed out that different curricula require or attract different degrees of ability, at both the high school and college levels. In general, students in scientific and liberal arts courses have the highest ability test scores; those in business or commercial subjects come in next highest, and those in vocational education or trade courses come in last. Differences in the ability scores of students in different institutions have been found, which, like curricular differences, are in line with popular expectations. Some of these can be expressed in generalizations: liberal arts college students tend to be intellectually superior to teachers college students; those in small rural colleges tend to be inferior to those in large urban universities; and those in highly-endowed private institutions tend to be more able than those in state universities (at least when freshmen classes are compared). Documentation for these statements can be found by examining nation-wide testing programs, such as the Scholastic Aptitude Test of the College Entrance Examination Board.

Individual ability tests such as the Stanford-Binet Intelligence Scale and the Wechsler-Bellevue Intelligence Scales (now in three forms: *WPPSI* for children aged four to six and one-half; *WISC* for ages seven to 16; and *WAIS* for older individuals) provide both a qualitative and quantitative evaluation of a person's intellectual functioning. They are used primarily to evaluate students for special education classes, and as a means for determining the accuracy of group ability test scores of those who are in the top or bottom ranges. Of more concern to a testing program are standardized group ability tests.

Most group ability tests yield an estimate of the individual's ability to learn, by requiring him to perform activities regarded as showing evidence of intelligence. Prominent among test items are those that emphasize knowledge of vocabulary, numbers, and ability to reason. Some tests yield a single score, while others yield separate scores for verbal and quantitative aspects, and a total score. Some of the most common standardized group tests of ability include: California Test of Mental Maturity (California Test Bureau); Henmon-Nelson Tests of Mental Ability, Revised Editions (Houghton-Mifflin Company); Lorge-Thorndike Intelligence Tests (Houghton-Mifflin Company); Otis Self-Administering Tests of Mental Ability (Harcourt, Brace and World); School and College Ability Tests (Educational Testing Service) and SRA Primary Mental Abilities Test (Science Research Associates).

Achievement Tests. A test that assesses the attainments or accomplishments of a person after a period of training or education is called an achievement test. This is the type of test that accounts for, by far, the greatest number of tests given in schools, industries, colleges, and the military services. Schools use achievement tests to classify students; industry uses them in selecting employees; colleges use them in selecting students; and the military services uses them in classifying and assigning personnel.

There are several types of achievement tests. One type consists of achievement test *batteries.* This type is used to assess a person's growth in broad subject matter areas, such as reading, science, mathematics, social studies, etc. These test batteries provide individual profiles of subtest scores, in addition to a total score on the entire battery. Such tests permit horizontal or vertical comparisons, or both, so that a pupil's relative standing in different subject matter areas can be compared to a uniform normative sample. *Readiness* or prognostic tests are used to predict how well an individual may be expected to profit from subsequent training. Foremost among the areas sampled are reading and number skills. Readiness tests are frequently employed for making decisions about entrance into first grade. Some authors classify readiness tests as ability rather than achievement tests. *Diagnostic* achievement tests are designed to enable teachers and counselors to determine the pupil's performance and to yield information on the causes of difficulty in reading, arithmetic and language.

Some of the more commonly used standardized achievement tests in the elementary school grades include: The Metropolitan Achievement Tests (Harcourt, Brace and World); *Stanford Achievement Tests* (Harcourt, Brace, and World); *The Iowa Tests of Basic Skills* (Houghton Mifflin Company); *California Achievement Tests* (California Test Bureau); and *The Sequential Tests of Educational Progress* (Educational Testing Service).

Frequently used achievement tests in secondary schools include: The Cooperative Achievement Tests (Educational Testing Service); The Essential High School-Content Battery (Harcourt, Brace and World); and The Iowa Tests of Educational Development (Science Research Associates).

Aptitude Tests. An aptitude test is used to estimate the probable future success of a person in certain post-secondary school educational or training programs, or in certain occupations. Such tests are designed to identify those with promise or with prospects of success in a field where the individual has as yet had no substantial training or experience. However, the differences between an aptitude test, an achievement test, and an ability test lie more in use than in content. As stated previously, achievement tests are used to ascertain what and how much has been learned or how well a task can be performed, and its focus is on evaluation of the past without reference to the future. An ability test is a measure of an individual's current status, while an aptitude test is used to predict an individual's future performance or status on the basis of what at present he can do.

Some aptitude tests, such as those for mechanical, clerical, or musical aptitudes, attempt to identify and measure the combination of traits or specific aptitudes believed to be associated with them. For example, mechanical aptitude is believed to include, among other things, spatial perception, speed, and mechanical reasoning. The term *multifactor tests,* is used to describe an aptitude test battery or group of tests designed to measure several relatively independent abilities, such as verbal reasoning, numerical ability, memory, and muscular coordination. The principle underlying such test batteries is that since each measurable aptitude is usable in several occupations, a standard test battery can be constructed and normed in such a way that it will yield scores for a number of specific occupations. Such batteries are valuable in that they permit those who take them to explore a great variety of occupational possibilities.

Some commonly used aptitude tests include: Bennett Test of Mechanical Comprehension (The Psychological Corporation); Minnesota Paper Form Board (The Psychological Corporation); Minnesota Rate of Manipulation Test (The Psychological Corporation); The Purdue Pegboard (Science Research Associates); The SRA Mechanical Aptitude Test (Science Research Associates); Minnesota Clerical Aptitude Test (Psychological Corporation); General Clerical Test (The Psychological Corporation); Measures of Musical Talent (Psychological Corporation); Gordon Musical Aptitude Profile (Houghton Mifflin); Drake Musical Aptitude (Science Research Associates); Meier-Seashore Art Judgment Test (The Psychological Corporation); Differential Aptitude Tests (The Psychological Corporation); The Guilford Zimmerman Aptitude Survey (Sheridan Supply); General Aptitude Test Battery (United States Employment Service); Flanigan Aptitude Classification Tests (Science Research Associates); and Multiple Aptitude Test (California Test Bureau)

Vocational Interest Inventories. The interests of an individual are believed to be motivating forces, and as such, play an important part in his endeavors. An *interest* is usually defined as the "likes" and "dislikes" of an individual, or the feeling of intentness, concern, or curiosity about some object. Knowledge of a person's likes, dislikes, and indifferences is important both to the individual and to those who help him.

Interests are learned, and in that respect they are similar to attitudes. Some consider interests a special type of attitude. *Occupational differences* in patterns of interests were the basic discovery that led to the development of standardized vocational interest inventories. Vocational interest inventories assess, by means of lists of activities and occupations, the extent of the similarity of an individual's interests to those in different occupations.

Some interest inventories used in secondary schools include: Kuder Preference Record, Form C and Form D (Science Research Associates); Strong Vocational Interest Blank (Stanford University Press); Minnesota Vocational Interest Inventory (The Psychological Corporation); Lee-Thorpe Occupational Interest Inventory (California Test Bureau).

Standardized Personality Inventories. Assessment of personality is much more complex and much less objective than assessment in the areas previously identified. Most standardized group personality inventories are not very good for assessing individual behavior. They are best used with groups as a screening device to identify individuals who *may* be in need of psychological help.

The use of standardized group personality inventories, over the past forty years, has been cyclical. Periods of doubt about their usefulness have followed periods of acceptance. Their use in schools requires careful examination of the purpose for giving them. As is true with all tests, the training and experience of the individual who administers the instruments, and interprets the results is crucial. Their misuse by an inadequately trained person can lead to many problems. Even more importantly, students or counselees can be harmed by careless, inaccurate or ill-founded comments based, presumably, on "objective data."

Most schools administer standardized personality inventories on an individual need-to-know basis. In the past, some schools have administered them to an entire grade (such as the freshmen class) to screen out those most in need of help. This seems to be a highly dubious practice in terms of outcome and expense. It is best to use them in individual cases when the need to do so can be clearly established.

Some representative personality inventories include: Bell Adjustment Inventory, Revised Edition, 1962 (Consulting Psychologists Press); California Personality Inventory (California Test Bureau); California Test of Personality (California Test Bureau); Personal Inventory (Harcourt, Brace and World); Personal Profile (Harcourt, Brace and World); A Survey of Interpersonal Values (Science Research Associates); Guilford-Zimmerman Temperament Survey (Sheridan Supply Company); Minnesota Counseling Inventory (The Psychological Corporation); Mooney Problem Check Lists (The Psychological Corporation); and SRA Youth Inventory (Science Research Associates).

INITIATING A TESTING PROGRAM

The procedural matters of the test program require considerable staff time. Each year, changes may need to be made in the testing program because certain information is needed or new data are revealed about previous tests used.

Where to Start? The basic need for more information about individuals, in order to assist them, is a sound basis for a testing program. It is essential that all members of the school staff have a part in the total testing program. This staff involvement, in turn, encourages teachers to think more systematically about individual appraisal.

Organization of a testing committee that will carry out the wishes of the staff and follow the school philosophy will be of immeasurable value in the development of the testing program. An initial function of the committee is to determine what information is known about pupils. What is needed? How will the findings be used? The place to start is with the needs of individuals and the goals of the school. The end result that is desired is information upon which services may be built to help students. Information should include facts about the pupils, the local community, regional area, and national concerns.

How to Proceed? The determination of a need is a call to action. Planning for the testing program should include time to develop data that will indicate and support what is being done. The development of a minimum testing program is a starting point. It is safe to state that no one program would be satisfactory in all schools; however, a general program can be suggested.

Table 11–1.   *A Minimal Testing Program*

Elementary	
Grade 1	Reading readiness test (compatible with reading program)
Grade 3, 5, or 7	A mental abilities test
Grade 4, 6, or 8	An achievement battery
Secondary	
Junior High School	
Grade 7, 8, or 9	A mental ability test
	An achievement battery
Senior High School	
Grade 10, 11, or 12	A mental ability test
	An achievement battery

The minimal testing program illustrated in Table 11–1 may take several years to evolve. It could start in one or more grades one year, and have other tests added over the next few years. "Minimum" possesses different meanings to different people. For these two authors, a "minimum testing program" would include two measures of ability and two measures of achievement obtained during the twelve years the student is in school. Their advice to most schools is to reduce the multiplicity of tests given, and to concentrate upon how those given are to be utilized in meaningful ways. The procedure for managing even a minimum testing program should include: test selection; administering the tests; scoring the tests; recording test results; interpreting the results; and distributing the findings to pupils, parents, and staff members. It is essential to note how the various phases of a testing program relate to each other.

Test Selection Considerations. After the test committee has decided upon the information that is needed about the pupils, the committee or a test coordinator should start the process of finding instruments that will give the information pertinent to the program objectives. The identification of concerns demands answers to questions which can be answered, in part, by specific tests. These tests must not be mistaken as the total guidance process, but the use of the test results constitutes a useful part of the guidance process. Testing is an aid to student self-understanding and educational and vocational planning. Specific tests should be selected with these factors in mind. As previously stated, the test manuals provide information that will give test users insight into the value of the instrument for use in specific instances. However, test manuals must be examined carefully for overestimations of the value of the test. In the past, some claims have been presented about certain tests which little or no research data substantiates. Clear, concise statements about research findings are essential; interpretations of these findings will add immensely to the value of a test. Buros' *Mental Measurement Yearbooks* are excellent sources of information. In addition to these factors in test selection, it is essential that the validity and reliability of tests be considered.

Practicality is a criterion to be considered in test selection. This includes cost and amount of time that is necessary to administer, score, and interpret the test. Another criterion in test selection is ease of administration and use; that is, the student and test user must be able to understand all of the test administration's phases completely. In addition, the method of scoring should be examined in light of machine scoring, hand scoring, cutout stencils, strip keys, and specific test scoring techniques. Reading level is also an important factor in the selection of a test. It may be noted that the reading range of a typical sixth-grade class is approximately eight years compared to a range of approximately six years in mathematics.

The time limits for administering tests are important considerations both in the elementary school and the secondary school. Long periods of testing (over thirty minutes) in elementary schools will cause children to become inattentive and restless. In high school, achievement tests generally have no undue time limit. Recent research indicates that time is not an important factor in the consistency of scores unless the time is limited. Test length and difficulty should be appropriate to the range of capabilities of the subjects being tested. The "norm group" sample should be examined for size, representativeness, and normality so that the local test-taking population may be compared with the test "norm group."

Test selection considerations may be summarized as the gathering of all information about an instrument so that it is known whether it is valid, reliable, honest in its claims, practical, and functional in the local program. A good test should enable the student to demonstrate his knowledge, basic skills, or behaviors believed important to him and the institution. The real value of the test lies in its ability to be meaningfully interpreted to individuals after it has been administered.

Test selection may be facilitated by gathering information about various tests. A "Test Evaluation Form" may be useful in doing so (see Figure 11–1). Care needs to be given to obtain a comprehensive picture of each instrument. Any one item may be misleading.

DEVELOPING TESTING PROGRAMS

Judicious development of the school's testing program, based upon need, is a responsibility of most guidance administrators. Test data can be obtained that will be helpful for curriculum revision decisions. Experimental situations can be encouraged by use of test findings, especially in the determination of special programs such as remedial and advanced. The needs of the total group of students can be partially analyzed by the testing program. These measurements can contribute to the improvement of the educational process. The findings, or test results, may be used to determine the effectiveness of the instructional program. The teacher will see how fast instruction should proceed and at what grade level instruction will be planned. Expected achievement levels, based on ability levels, can be identified and examined by testing data.

The development of a testing program is an on-going process. A plan should be made to initiate some testing each year until an adequate program is in operation. The reasons for giving tests should be examined and appraised. Decisions should be made as to which objectives shall have priority in the development of the program. Selection, administration, and use of tests will then follow.

The development of a testing program will include

1. Defining the uses to which test data will be put, or specifying the reasons for administering each test.

2. Identifying those tests to be given system-wide; most schools initiate some testing at each educational level, usually starting with elementary school grades, then senior high, followed by junior high school grades.

3. Sequence-developed ability tests are usually initiated first, followed by achievement tests, then prognostic and diagnostic instruments, followed by interest inventories, and pupil aptitude testing, and then personality inventories.

4. Coordinating the use of test data with guidance and instructional practices.

5. Implementing ways to report test data to those who need to have them and to interpret tests to students and their parents. Imple-

	Does not apply for this type of test	Sufficiently covered	Included, but poorly covered	Excessive data hides essential data	Not included
Name of appraiser _____ Date of appraisal _____ School _____ Name of test _____ Type of test _____ Age and grade levels _____ Date of publication _____ Name and address of publisher _____ _____					
A. Dissemination of Information.	1	2	3	4	5
1. A detailed test manual is provided.					
2. The manual is up to date.					
3. Manual copyright data and revision dates are clearly indicated.					
Comments: _____ _____					
B. Interpretation.					
1. Test manual, record forms & other accompanying material assists correct interpretation of test results.					
2. Manual explicitly states the purposes & applications for which test is recommended.					
3. Professional qualifications required for administration and interpretation are given.					
4. In revised editions, nature & extent of the revision & the comparability of data for the revised & the old test are explicitly stated.					
5. Manual presents quantitative data to support implied relationships.					

Figure 11-1. *Test Evaluation Form*

Figure 11-1. *(continued)*

	1	2	3	4	5

6. When the term "significant" is employed, manual makes clear whether statistical or practical significance is meant.

7. Manual clearly differentiates between an interpretation for a group as a whole and the application of such an interpretation for individuals.

Comments: _____

_____

C. Validity.

1. Type of validity is clearly stated.

2. Validity indices stated indicate that the test measures what is purports to measure.

3. Criterion for validity are clearly defined.

4. Date validation data were gathered is reported.

5. Test scores used in validation are determined independent of criterion scores.

6. Manual gives specific warning in regard to margins of error in interpretation.

7. The validation sample is sufficiently described for the user to know whether the persons he tests may be properly regarded as represented in the sample.

8. Manual gives clear description of diagnostic categories.

9. Manual reports number of cases in validation sample.

10. Appropriate measures of central tendency, variability, & standard errors of estimate for all computations are reported for the validation sample.

Figure 11-1. *(continued)*

	1	2	3	4	5
11. Differentiation is made in validity between subgroups & the total validation sample.					
12. Validity of predictions are estimated separately at different age & mental ability levels.					
13. Reports of validation studies describe all conditions likely to effect motivation of subjects taking the test.					
14. Manual reports all available information which will assist the user in determining what psychological attributes account for variance in test scores.					
15. Manual reports correlations of the test with other previously published & generally accepted measures of the same attributes.					
Comments: _____					
_____					
_____					
D. Reliability.					
1. Manual reports such evidence of reliability as would permit the reader to judge whether scores are sufficiently dependable for the recommended uses of the test.					
2. Manual notes the absence of necessary evidence of reliability.					
3. Manual cautions user against interpreting profiles or score differences if the reliability of these differences between an individual's scores is low.					
4. Results of reliability studies are quantitatively expressed.					
5. Manual reports reliability for various age and mental ability levels at which the test is given.					

Figure 11–1. *(continued)*

	1	2	3	4	5

6. Manual avoids any implication that reliability measures demonstrate the predictive or concurrent validity of the test.

7. Reports of reliability, procedures, and samples are described sufficiently for reader to judge whether the evidence applies to the persons and problems with which he is concerned.

d_1) Equivalence of Forms.
1. If two forms of a test are made available, with both forms intended for possible use with the same subjects, the correlation between forms and information as to the equivalence of scores on the two forms are reported.

2. Manual warns user against assuming comparability when necessary evidence is not provided.

3. When two trials of a test are correlated to determine equivalence, the time between testings is stated.

d_2) Internal Consistency.
1. If the manual suggests that a score is a measure of a generalized, homogeneous trait, evidence of internal consistency is reported.

2. When a test consists of separately scored points or sections, the correlations between the parts or sections are reported.

3. Coefficients of internal consistency are determined by the split-half methods or methods of the Kuder-Richardson type, if these methods can be applied.

d_3) Stability.
1. Manual indicates the degree of stability expected when scores are repeated after time has elapsed.

2. Manual warns against assuming stability when such evidence is not presented.

Figure 11-1. *(continued)*

	1	2	3	4	5

Comments: _____

_____

_____

E. Administration and Scoring.

1. Directions for test administration are clearly presented.

2. Where subjective processes enter into the scoring of a test, evidence on degree of agreement between independent scoring is presented.

Comments: _____

_____

F. Scales and Norms.

1. Scales used for reporting scores are presented so as to increase the likelihood of accurate interpretation and emphasis.

2. Standard scores are used rather than other derived scores.

3. Local norms are available along with comparative data on the national level.

4. Manual indicates amount of emphasis on local norms for accurate interpretation.

5. Norms refer to clearly defined population.

6. Manual reports the method of population sampling.

7. Number of cases on which norms are based is reported.

8. Manual reports whether scores differ for groups differing in age, sex, amount of training, and other equally important variables.

9. Profile sheets or other appropriate means of recording and interpreting test scores are provided.

367

Figure 11–1.   *(continued)*

	1	2	3	4	5
10. The curve of the normalizing sample is sufficiently complete and normal so that test scores may be interpreted on the basis of normal distribution.*					
Comments: _____					

*For additional information on technical requirements regarding test construction and evaluation, we refer you to "Technical Recommendations for Psychological Tests and Diagnostic Techniques" prepared by a joint committee of the American Psychological Association, American Educational Research Association, and the National Council on Measurements Used in Education.

menting ways to report test data to teachers, students, and parents.

6.   Evaluating the testing program in terms of its objectives.

Scoring

The acquisition of the raw test score may be obtained either by hand or machine scoring.

Hand scoring. This is advised only when a small number of answer sheets is to be scored. Accuracy is a major consideration in this method of scoring. IBM answer sheets that have hole-punched scoring stencils are fairly easy to use. Carbon-backed answer sheets such as the *Otis scoreeze* is another method of hand scoring. The *strip key* scoring device is among the most difficult to use. It is important to have dependable clerical help to do the scoring. This is not considered the job of the school counselor.

Machine scoring. Large numbers of answer sheets can be scored in a short period of time by test-scoring machines. This is not an infallible method, and answer sheets should be periodically checked for errors. Commercial test companies have established machine scoring services, and some colleges and universities also provide this service. In the past few years, commercial test companies have developed "a packaged" test program. This includes the use of test materials (booklets and answer sheets), scoring, profiling, and posting data.

Communicating, Reporting, and Disseminating Test Data

A basic assumption that underlies the test program from its very beginning must be that interpretation and usage are the reasons for the existence of a testing program.

From the guidance point of view, pupils (and their parents) have the right to know their test results—in terms they understand. If tests have been given for administrative or research purposes, there may be no need to report test results to individuals. However, unless their knowledge would endanger the results, pupils, parents, and staff should know the purposes of the tests before the testing.

Test data serve as a base for reporting each pupil's progress to his parents. It is necessary for public relations to report to the community and interested parties what students are being taught and what academic results are being achieved. However, this does not mean public release of test scores with individual identities. This would violate ethical testing practices.

Test information communications is an area that needs continuing research and experimentation. Goldman states

> Schools sometimes tend to neglect the counselor's responsibilities for test interpretation. It is not unheard of for students in high schools to take tests and inventories in home-rooms, to score them and prepare their own profiles, and then to be given only the most general interpretations in a group and frequently under the supervision of a teacher with little or no training in measurement. This sort of thing may sometimes be encouraged by using the package programs, in which answer sheets are shipped to the test publisher or distributor, who scores them and sends multiple copies of each pupil's profile back to the school. In some instances, copies go to classroom teachers, presumably with the assumption that all teachers are qualified to interpret the results. Even more appalling, some schools turn over a copy of the profile to the student, asking that he take it to his parents for *their* interpretation.[19]

There are many ways for communicating and reporting test results through checklists, profile sheets, and test forms. Ways must be developed to communicate the meaning of the test results to various groups. The test coordinator and others of the counselor staff are responsible for determining ways information is reported.

In Sidney, Ohio, High School, one of the counselors, William Heath, had an illustrative profile of the Iowa Tests of Educational Development made in a chart as large as the backdrop of the auditorium stage. This permitted staff and parents to view this one profile with equal advantage from any seat in the auditorium. Heath could then interpret the guidance information derived from such a test profile.

---

[19]Leo Goldman, *Using Tests in Counseling* (2nd ed.) New York: Appleton-Century-Crofts, 1970, p. 344.

Durost suggests that the best method of reporting and developing test information for parents is in terms of *stanines* because

1. They are more dependable than any of the other common methods of reporting scores because they are broader units, although precise enough for our purposes.

2. Stanines make the test results comparable for the individual from test to test as long as the group on which they are based is the same.

3. They are relatively easy to explain to parents.[20]

The stanine scale is a simple nine-point scale of standard scores. (The word *Stanine* was originally derived from 'STAndard NINE-point scale.') In this scale, raw scores are converted to scores (levels) that range from 1 (low) to 9 (high). The percentages of the cases of a total distribution of scores that fall into each of the nine stanine classifications for a normal population are shown in Figure 11–2.

Meaning of Stanines
STA=Standard Score
NINE=Nine-Step Scale

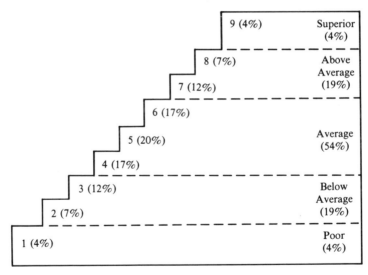

Figure 11–2.   *Percentage of Cases at Each Stanine Level*

The Columbus, Ohio, School staff has devised a testing profile program which is given here.

AN INTRODUCTION TO THE COLUMBUS TESTING PROFILE[21]

The Columbus Testing Profile is designed to provide, for the individual student, a meaningful graphic presentation of standardized test results. This Profile will be initiated for each pupil as he enters the first grade, and will become an integral part of the student's cumulative record as long as he is enrolled in the Columbus Public Schools.

The Profile should prove an invaluable aid to teachers, counselors, administrators, and parents in interpreting the results of aptitude and achievement tests as they relate one to the other, and in noting consistency, improvement, or regression in the student's level of achievement from point to point throughout his school career.

Space is provided on the inside part of the Profile, as will be detailed later, for posting results on all tests administered as part of the required testing program. An additional profile area is provided on the reverse side to accommodate posting of other tests, supplementary to the required tests.

As may be noted from instructions on the front of the Profile, two changes are made in the reporting of test results.

First, all tests are reported in terms of T Scores. These are standard scores wherein the mean is 50, and each standard deviation is represented by 10 points above or below the mean. The range of 20 (low) to 80 (high) encompasses the practical range of achievement. Thus, Academic Aptitude is reported in terms of T scores rather than as I.Q. However, when profiled, the student's score is graphically shown as below average, average, or above average ability or expectation of success.

Achievement tests also are reported in T scores rather than in grade-level equivalents. When profiled, these scores are revealed as below average, average, or above average achievement as compared to the achievement of students in the grade at which the test was given.

The second change in the reporting of test results involves the use of Standard Score Bands. It is well recognized that many circumstances may cause the true score achieved by the student to vary from the derived score. To plot a specific point for the test would be to denote greater accuracy of measurement than is inherent in the test. Each test designer has determined the Standard Error of Measurement for his instrument. This latitude for error has been used to determine the Standard Score Band which indicates the probability range within which the true score will be found.

It will be noted that the chart heading on the Profile also classifies the Standard Score Bands according to Stanines. The Stanine score is a simple nine-point scale ranging from 1 (low) to 9 (high) with a mean of 5 and a standard deviation of 2. Scores or bands falling primarily within Stanines

---

[21] Division of Special Services, Department of Child Study and Student Counseling, Columbus (Ohio) Public Schools, 1967. Reproduced by special permission.

1, 2, and 3 are generally considered as representing below average performance. Stanines 4, 5, and 6 encompass what is considered average performance, while Stanines 7, 8, and 9 represent above average performance. A difference of 2 Stanines is considered as a significant variation.

This method of profiling test results has two distinct advantages, as follows:

> First, comparatively small variations in scores, which might at first seem significant, lose this significance when the Standard Error is taken into account. The Standard Score Bands will in many cases overlap, indicating that performance on the two tests was relatively consistent. The graphic portryal also makes atypical performance easy to note. When the plotted score on one test in a given area is grossly at variance with others in the same area, then there could be cause to question the validity of that score or to explore the reason behind the major shift in performance.
>
> Second, the profiling of academic aptitude and achievement tests in the same manner permits an immediate evaluation of performance in comparison with expectation. The child with above average academic aptitude would normally be expected to be above average in achievement. The same relationship would hold true for those with average or below average aptitude. There are many factors such as motivation or lack of motivation which would affect this consistency. However, significant differences between expectation, as indicated by the academic aptitude tests, and performance on achievement tests become readily apparent and subject for further study.

In the future, the Profile will be initiated at the first grade and will follow the student through school. The only Profiles which will need to be initiated at higher grade levels will be those for students who transfer into the Columbus Public Schools. However, for the 1967–68 school year it will be necessary to prepare a Profile for each student in every school. Detailed information on this procedure will be provided after consultations have been held between Department of Child Study personnel and school personnel.

The name of the student and the date of birth should be completed in ink, using the legal, or reproducing, pen. The "School" blank should be completed in pencil as this will change due to normal progression and transfers.

In Grades 5 through 10, tests administered at the scheduled testing time, and submitted by the prescribed deadline, will be machine scored, and the conversion from raw score to the appropriate Standard Score Band will be done by computer. Furthermore, rather than the scored tests being returned for hand posting, the tests will be accompanied by computer-prepared pressurized labels giving the name of the student, the code of the administering school, the test and grade level code, the subsections of the test where applicable, and the T Score bands. This label need only be affixed in the appropriate space, and the bands plotted on the chart. This service should result in a considerable saving of time for teachers, clerks, or counselors.

Tests administered in Grades 1 through 4 will be scored, converted, and posted by hand, at least for the present time. Consideration is being given to the practicability of machine scoring and/or computer labeling at lower grade levels in the future.

Tests differ in the number of scores derived. For example, one academic aptitude test may yield only a total score, while another will give verbal and non-verbal subscores as well as a total score. Therefore, the size of the printed labels will differ according to the test administered. Labels will be one-half inch wide when one score is given for plotting, three-fourths of an inch wide when two scores are provided, and one inch wide when three scores are provided. Since each space on the Profile is one-fourth of an inch wide, a one-score label will take up two spaces a two-score label, three spaces; and a three-score label, four spaces. Enough space has been allowed in each section of the Profile to permit posting of the tests required by the Columbus testing program.

There will be no problem in the first grade in determining where to record the first score. This will be the Readiness Test, which will be posted under Reading Achievement on Line 1. However, for pupils beyond the first grade, this could not be the case. Ideally schools may wish to convert the present I.Q. and achievement scores on the current records to Standard Score Bands, and bring the Profile completely up to date. Conversion tables for all commonly used achievement tests will be prepared and made available to schools should they wish to update the Profile. This, of course, would make the Profile more meaningful for both the educator's understanding of the child, and for use in parent conferences. If this is to be done, now or in the future, it is essential that space be left for recording the earlier tests in chronological order. A guide outlining which lines on the profile will be used or reserved for tests at each grade level is attached. Careful observance of this guide will assure that room is left for updating the profile with tests being in the proper sequence.

Figure 11–3 shows the projected format for the pressurized labels. The first line contains the student's name, last name first. Due to space limitations on the answer sheet, the first name may be imprinted in full, or as shown in Figure 11–3 only in part. The governing factor is the length of the name. Also printed on the first line is the code number of the school at which the test was given.

STEVENSON, ELIZAB   102
HN6   10/66   41-46

Figure 11-3.   *Format of data on a one-score pressurized label.*

The second line carries the identification of the test. This is coded, and the key to coding is printed on the reverse side of the Profile. Figure 11–4 shows this coding. It will be noted that the letter code of the test is followed by a figure. This figure denotes the grade level at which the test was administered.

CODING

MRR	Metropolitan Readiness	SR	Stanford Reading
LCR	Lee-Clark Readiness	CRT	California Reading Test
ASR	American School Readiness	HN	Henmon-Nelson Intelligence
KA	Kuhlman-Anderson Intelligence	CAT	California Arithmetic Test
CTMM	California Mental Maturity	MA	Metropolitan Arithmetic
O	Otis Intelligence	OST	Ohio Survey Test
MR	Metropolitan Reading	CLT	California Language Test

Code to be followed by number to indicate grade at which test is given.

(i.e., HN4=Henmon—Nelson given in the 4th grade)

Figure 11-4.*Key to profile coding.*

Following the test code is the date of administration in month and year. If the test yields only a single score, as in Figure 11–3, the Standard Score Band would not include the second line. This results in a label that is one-half inch in width. In referring to the Space Allocation Guide which follows, we note that Lines 9, 10, 11, and 12 are reserved for sixth grade Academic Aptitude tests. This particular label requires only two lines, though the California Test of Mental Maturity for the same grade level requires the full four lines allocated to Academic Aptitude tests administered in Grade 6.

Figure 11–5 shows how this label would be placed on the Profile to utilize Lines 9 and 10.

After affixing the label, the next step is to plot the Band Score within the spaces on the Profile chart falling within its limits. This is done on the line immediately to the right of the Band Score—in this case on Line 10 as shown in Figure 11–5.

Figure 11–6 depicts the label for another sixth grader in a school which utilized the California Test of Mental Maturity. Two subscores are given in addition to the total score. The Band Score on Line 2 is preceded by the notation that it represents the non-verbal score. Line 3 carries the verbal data, and Line 4 shows the total score. Here a one-inch label is required, and all four lines on the Profile will be needed.

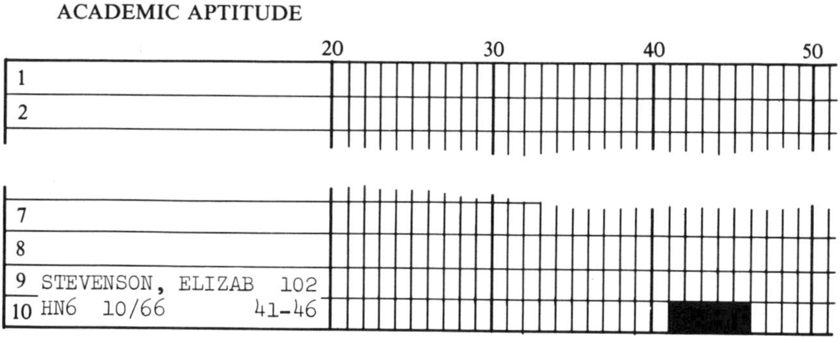

ACADEMIC APTITUDE

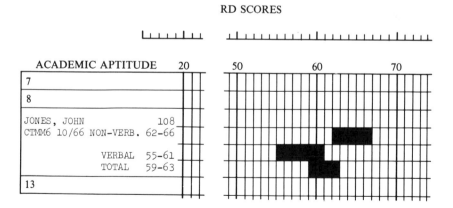

Figure 11–5.   *How an attached label and plotted band score for a one-score test should look.*

```
JONES, JOHN                      108
CTMM6 10/66 NON-VERB.    62-66
              VERBAL       55-61
              TOTAL        59-63
```

Figure 11–6.   *Format of data on a three-score pressurized label.*

Figure 11–7 shows how this label would be attached and profiled.

RD SCORES

Figure 11–7.   *How an attached label and plotted band scores for a three-score test should look.*

HENMON-NELSON (3-6)   Form A

Raw Score	T-Score Band	Raw Score	T-Score Band	Raw Score	T-Score Band
1	20–25	31	41–46	61	56–61
2	22–27	32	42–46	62	57–61
3	24–29	33	42–47	63	57–62
4	26–31	34	43–47	64	58–62

Figure 11–8.   *Conversion table, shown in part.*

In the first four grades, the data will have to be posted by hand at the present time. Once the test is hand scored and the raw score determined, the Standard Score Band will be found by referring to the table supplied for the particular test at that grade level. Figure 11–8 shows a portion of such a table for the Henmon-Nelson at the fourth-grade level. A raw score of 63 converts to a Band Score of 57–62. This band figure is the only score that will be posted and plotted on the Profile.

Figure 11–9 indicates how the data for such a test would be posted on the profile.

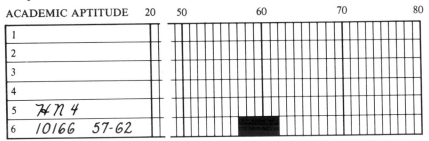

Figure 11–9.   *How test data on a one-score test should look when posted by hand.*

Figure 11–10 illustrates the band posting procedure for a test which yields more than a single score. In this example a California Reading test given in Grade 4 is depicted.

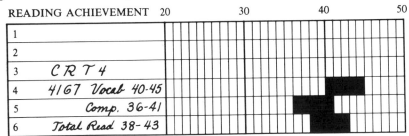

Figure 11–10.   *How test data on a three-score test should look when posted by hand.*

As mentioned earlier, tests administered in grade 5 and above as part of the city-wide testing program will be scored and converted to Band Scores by computer, and pressurized labels will be prepared. This can be done only when the tests are administered at the prescribed time and submitted to the Department of Child Study and Student Counseling by the deadline indicated. Make-up tests or tests not submitted in time must be hand scored and posted. This practice must be observed because it simply is not feasible to program the computer for small numbers of tests. However, conversion tables from raw scores to Band Scores will be provided for all authorized tests at all grade levels. Posting of individual make-up tests will be performed in the same manner as for those in Grades 1 through 4.

SPACE ALLOCATION ON TESTING PROFILE

ACADEMIC APTITUDE

Second Grade	Lines 1, 2, 3, and 4
Fourth Grade	Lines 5, 6, 7, and 8
Sixth Grade	Lines 9, 10, 11, and 12
Eighth Grade	Lines 13 and 14
Tenth Grade	Lines 15 and 16

READING ACHIEVEMENT

First Grade	Lines 1 and 2
Fourth Grade	Lines 3, 4, 5, and 6
Fifth Grade	Lines 7, 8, 9, and 10
Sixth Grade	Lines 11, 12, 13, and 14
Ninth Grade	Lines 15, 16, 17, and 18

ARITHMETIC ACHIEVEMENT

Fifth Grade	Lines 1, 2, 3, and 4
Sixth Grade	Lines 5, 6, 7, and 8
Eighth Grade	Lines 9, 10, 11, and 12

LANGUAGE ACHIEVEMENT

Eighth Grade	Lines 1, 2, 3, and 4
Tenth Grade	Lines, 5, 6, 7, and 8

COUNSELING WITH PUPILS, PARENTS, AND TEACHERS

From the guidance vantage point, test results are to aid in facilitating the pupil's educational progress, career development, and personal fulfillment.

The test results feed into the other parts of the guidance program, discussed in other chapters.

Counseling about test data needs to be arranged for each individual. Time is important in conducting test interpretations. Test information that is meaningful to the individual is not gained through hasty interpretations or simply by disseminating results to groups. Since test information reflects upon the pupil's self-concept, a counselor cannot merely "give" test results. The pupil must be ready to examine the results. The imparting of test information by "telling" defeats the purpose of it. Counseling about test information is not focused alone on objective data, for the counselor must consider the client's feelings, desires, aspirations, previous experiences, and self-image. The counseling process must allow time for the pupil to rationally and emotionally accept his test results.

In counseling, the development of self-understanding is often a goal. For many students who come for counseling, lack of self-understanding can be remedied, at least in part, by using tests. But if counselees are to make use of tests they must understand tests, and be able to accept the results for what they are; and tests must be selected to provide information needed and wanted by the counselee. Patterson states

> Tests, then, are introduced in counseling when the client, either overtly or covertly, indicates a desire or need for the kind of information they can help to provide. The counselor tells him what sorts of data the test can supply, describing the appropriate tests in nontechnical terms. The client then decides whether or not he would like to be tested, after which, if the decision is affirmative, the counselor arranges for the administration of the appropriate tests. This is all done in a simple, matter-of-fact way without disturbing the attitude of respect for the client, or infringing upon his responsibility for making decisions. There is no implication that the tests, or the counselor's use of tests, will solve the client's problems. Tests are presented as one source of information, and the decision as to whether to act upon the information is left up to the client.[22]

Interpretation of test data means that communication takes place between counselor and counselee. Basically, the counselee wants to understand the inferences about him that these test data give, and the counselor wants to make sure that the counselee does indeed understand. The methods by which communication of test data is fostered have been discussed

---

[22]C. H. Patterson, "Counseling: Self-Clarification and the Helping Relationship," in Henry Borow (ed.), *Man in a World at Work*. Boston: Houghton Mifflin Company, 1964, pp. 449–450.

in relation to educational planning (see Chapter 8) and vocational planning (see Chapter 9). It is fundamental to any method of communicating test results that test data are interpreted objectively, without counselor evaluation. The counselor must always remember that the counselee is emotionally involved in test results obtained from him. The counselee will not always be "rational" or logical in his thinking, understanding, and use of test data. He may react because he feels threatened by test results and seek to rationalize or to reject data. One or more emotional states—doubt about accuracy, fear, anger, or satisfaction—may be exhibited by the counselee in examining his test data, and these emotional reactions and attitudes are what the counselor has to be prepared to cope with in test communication sessions. Patterson provides three guidelines which are useful to counselors in communicating test results with counselees. These are

1. The client should not be abruptly faced with the test findings, nor should they be presented all at once or too rapidly. He should have time to absorb their meanings and implications.

2. The client should be given opportunity to express and discuss his reactions and feelings. It might be well to begin by obtaining his reaction to the testing experience in general before presenting any results. Some such question as "Well, what did you think of the tests?" might elicit some feelings and attitudes and serve to prepare the counselor for specific emotional reactions.

3. When feelings are expressed, the counselor should recognize them and respond to them in a therapeutic manner. They should not be ignored or passed over. Nor should resistance to acceptance of test scores be handled by defense of the tests, or of their reliability and validity, by arguments, reasoning or persuasion.[23]

Parents and teachers are entitled to test results. The counselor should explain the test results in terms that parents and teachers understand. Because parents are deeply emotionally involved in their children's school progress, the counselor will often be giving parents test results through a counseling process rather than through a short reporting procedure. Teachers may be given the test information on a staff or consultant basis. However, the counselor should be alert to teacher involvement in test results. A teacher may feel that achievement test results reflect on his teaching. The counseling approach would then be necessary. It becomes important to consider these factors in organizing and administering the testing program.

---

[23] *Ibid,* p. 451.

EXTERNAL TESTING PROGRAMS

"External" testing programs are increasingly being brought into schools. The term "external tests" refers to those state and national tests usually administered for college admissions purposes. These are established by outside agencies, and their control resides only minimally within the local school district. Generally their results are used, not by the local school, but by other institutions. Examples of external tests include: National Merit Scholarship Qualifying Tests (NMSQT); Scholastic Aptitude Test (SAT) of the College Entrance Examination Board (CEEB); Preliminary Scholastic Aptitude Test (PSAT); National Secondary School Admissions Test (SSAT); Junior Scholastic Aptitude Test (JSAT); Tests of Professional Aptitude; Federal Government Tests, such as the General Aptitude Test Battery (GATB), and the Federal Service Entrance Examination (FSEE); and American College Test (ACT).

Many educators are highly critical that external tests are time-consuming for the student and staff. It is believed that too many students take them, and take too many of them. Since certain batteries are used by colleges for selection and admissions, students often feel pressure to do well on them.

STATE-WIDE TESTING PROGRAMS

State-wide programs were first initiated in Iowa in 1929, when the State University of Iowa initiated an Every Pupil Achievement Testing Program. By 1939, similar testing programs concerned with areas of scholastic achievement could be found in twenty-six states. Growth in these programs from this time on appears to be stable but increasing slightly. In 1954, Berdie[24] was critical of the scant attention being given the extensive activities of the statewide testing programs; he reported that these programs "are found in many of the forty-eight states, most states having at least one such program and some states, having more than one." Impetus to these programs followed passage of the National Defense Education Act in 1958; additional emphasis was given through encouragement and financial support for the establishment of testing programs across the country.

The programs run the full range of variety, employing many different measurement devices. Some states require that specific tests be given by all schools to all pupils at certain grade levels; other states recommend that a testing service utilizing those instruments appropriate to the local situation be provided in the schools. In some states, a system of achievement testing

---

[24]Ralph F. Berdie, "The State-Wide Testing Programs," *Personnel and Guidance Journal,* Vol. 31, (April, 1954), p. 454.

in certain high school subject areas is required, as in New York, with the Regents Examinations; in other states a system of achievement testing is made available to schools but is not required, as in Ohio with the Ohio Test of Scholastic Achievement. These are examples of tests developed by the state departments of education. In other states, the testing programs utilize commercially built tests, as in Hawaii, where administration of the Differential Aptitude Test Battery to all eighth grade students is required. Other states provide a list of recommended tests from which schools may choose those they prefer. Virginia has required that certain testing programs be carried on by schools; this state now emphasizes the importance of results in the study of individuals instead of group survey. These examples represent the diversity of means taken in state-wide testing programs.

State testing programs are guided by purposes based on the value of the objective information available through the means of standardized tests. The testing program in each school is influenced by the state testing program, but it must also reflect the needs of the local community. This requires wise management.

GUIDELINES FOR MANAGING A TESTING PROGRAM

In most schools, it is the responsibility of the director of guidance to administer the testing program. This requires that he keep in constant touch with test developments and testing practices. Some guidelines are suggested here that have implications for his management of this area.

1. A test advisory committee for the system should be formed to formulate and review testing policies and practices. Such a committee should contain a mixture of teachers, counselors, administrators, students, and parents.

2. Subcommittees should be established to constantly review and evaluate new tests, as well as tests currently in use. This requires members with training and experience in testing. Such subcommittees should be prepared to recommend changes in test selections and testing practices.

3. Written policies and procedures should be clearly established for selecting, ordering, and distributing test materials; for issuing reports on test data; for scheduling testing dates; for administering, scoring, storing, and reporting test data; and for safeguarding and determining who has access to test data.

4. The director of guidance and the testing committee should conduct annual reviews of the testing program to determine whether tests

can be deleted rather than added. Few tests should be given, but those tests that are administered should be usable by students, counselors, teachers, parents, and administrators. The annual review should include an examination of (a) how the testing program is interpreted to the community; (b) how the inservice education of staff increases faculty members' knowledge of tests and their uses, (c) how well the procedures interpret test results to pupils and their parents; and (d) the objectives, costs and outcomes of the testing program.

5.   Administrative attention must be given so that counselors do not use the major portion of their time in administering tests. If they do so, little time exists during the school year for counseling. Almost all standardized group tests of ability and achievement can be administered by teachers, or even better, by subprofessionals. Training programs can be established and conducted for those who are to administer and score the tests.

6.   Administrative attention must be given to the statistical summaries of test results that are needed by teachers, administrators, other school personnel, and the public. Reports should be clear, concise and accurate. They should facilitate understanding of test data and encourage sound practices of test use and interpretation.

7.   While school- or grade-wide testing programs have a variety of legitimate uses—for instruction, guidance and administration—the chief value of test data is to help the individual understand himself and engage in planning endeavors. This means that communication about his test results is an obligation that must be met. Sound practices must be developed for interpreting tests to those who have taken them.

ANNOTATED BIBLIOGRAPHY

Cronbach, Lee J. *Essentials of Psychological Testing* (3rd ed.). New York: Harper and Row, 1970, 752 pp.
    Cronbach's book is a handbook for those engaged in testing operations and practices. It is written clearly and concisely, and is a comprehensive treatment of the field.

Goldman, Leo. *Using Tests in Counseling* (2nd ed.). New York: Appleton-Century-Crofts, Inc., 1971, 483 pp.
    Goldman's revised text is directed primarily to selecting and interpreting tests. He presents current thinking about practices which are useful to counsel-

ors, and he illustrates his practices in ways that are helpful to counseling professionals.

Stone, Shelley C., and Bruce Shertzer (eds). *Testing.* Guidance Monograph Series, Set III. Boston: Houghton Mifflin Company, 1968.

This set of nine monographs is devoted to examining such topics as controversial issues in testing, historical development of measurement, basic concepts in testing, types of test scores, interest and personality inventories, automated data processing in testing, and so forth. Each monograph has been written by well-known professionals in testing and measurement. Among the authors are Frank Womer, N. M. Downie, Robert Bauerfeind, William C. Cottle, and James Barclay.

Student Records

Little imagination has been applied by administrators, teachers, or guidance specialists to the effective use of records, and the cumulative record is usually resorted to only when a specific child has already manifested some learning or behavior problem.[1]

Chapter 12

What kinds of school records are being used?

What is the cumulative record?

What principles are involved in developing a guidance record system?

What records are used for reporting pupil progress?

What questions arise on the use of the cumulative and other guidance records?

RECORDS

Appropriate records are essential to a guidance program. Guidance records are a part of the total school records and a part of the total school record system and may be used for research and other functions. The school staff should always bear in mind the primary purposes of guidance records: (1) to appraise the present in terms of the past, (2) more importantly, to provide the staff with a basis for guiding the pupil's future development because the individual must not be shackled to his past.

Heayn and Jacobs speak of the fact that the school has become the repository for student records for all students, years of schooling—kindergarten through the twelfth grade: "Of interest and importance here is the increasing amount of intimate information beginning to appear in the folder

---

[1]Merville C. Shaw, *School Guidance Systems.* Boston: Houghton Mifflin Company, 1973, p. 120.

side-by-side with such familiar items as subject-matter grades and standard-ized testing results."[2]

Information that will be of particular interest to guidance specialists includes the outcomes of standardized ability tests, achievement tests, grades, and the meaningful interrelationships of these. Shaw states that "Records should be analyzed on a district-wide basis, schoolwide basis, and on a teacher-by-teacher basis."[3]

Classification

Essential school records have been categorized by a number of authors. Classification should reflect the purposes and functions of the records to aid in assigning proper staff responsibility. Bristow and Proctor presented a complete classification of records:

1. Registration and classification forms
2. Attendance records
3. Routine permits and passes
4. Reports to parents
5. Health and physical training records
6. Cumulative records
7. Reports to college[4]

In addition to these more formal types of records, there are the guidance records used in the counseling process and in case studies. These are impor-tant records because they form the basis for guidance action. Further, they become the primary source of much data that will be included on the more formal, permanent guidance records. As Rothney has pointed out, the gathering, coordinating, and reporting of information on pupil progress is a complicated task. It deserves much more attention than has been directed to it. It is more than a bookkeeping and housing process.[5]

Ayer has diagrammed the interrelations of basic and supplementary child accounting records (Figure 12–1). Central to the accounting system is the pupil's cumulative record. The cumulative record card is the picture of the pupil's total educational development. The census registration card is a composite of basic home and census data. The permanent office record is

---

[2]Maurice H. Heayn and Howard L. Jacobs, "Safeguarding Students' Records," *Personnel and Guidance Journal,* Vol. 46, No. 1 (September 1967), p. 63.

[3]Shaw, *Guidance Systems,* p. 120.

[4]A. B. Bristow and W. M. Proctor, "Senior High School Records and Reports," *The Clearing House,* Vol. 4 (March 1930), pp. 413–431.

[5]John W. M. Rothney, *Evaluating and Reporting Pupil Progress.* Washington, D.C.: Na-tional Education Association, 1955, p. 27.

the school executive's card on the pupil's development. It serves as a ready reference for administrative work. The pupil's report card is used to forward information to both pupil and parent about the child's educational progress. The teacher's classbook or register is a form or set of forms used by the teacher as the foundation for observation and for completion of other reports mentioned above. If this approach is used in developing a record system, there is need to establish a firm system of sound articulation for the flow of records and information.

The Georgia State Department of Education reported on records used in four typical Georgia high schools. The basic records used were (1) the student cumulative record card, (2) the student report card, (3) the homeroom compilation of grades, and (4) the course grades report. In addition, some schools kept other records, such as autobiographical forms, in the guidance counselor's office.[6]

Key Dimensions

In the use of any records, and particularly for guidance purposes, key dimensions of records need to be considered. These are

1. Is the information needed in terms of guidance program objectives? Too often, information is gathered because it is part of a record form developed for some other school. This information becomes a deterrent to use, because the staff cannot relate it to the guidance objectives for their school.

2. If the information is needed, where does it fit into the guidance program? The mere accretion of pupil data, even in terms of guidance objectives, is useless if it does not reflect itself in a particular guidance function. The guidance function means some kind of feedback to the pupil.

3. Is the information usable in terms meaningful to the staff?

4. Have adequate procedures been designed for gathering the data, safeguarding it, and yet making it available for use whether by traditional or computerized methods?

5. Has there been follow-through to determine the use of the data especially with the volume of material that can be turned out via electronic means?[7]

---

[6]Georgia State Department of Education, Report on *Internal Student Record Keeping and School-to-College Communications* (mimeographed), in cooperation with Educational Testing Service.

[7]Henry R. Kaczkowski, "The Current Status of Cumulative Records," *The Vocational Guidance Quarterly,* Vol. 7, No. 4 (Summer, 1959), pp. 211–213.

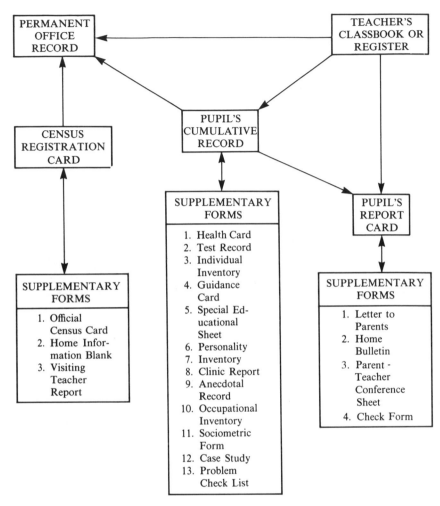

Figure 12–1.   *Interrelations of Basic and Supplementary Child Accounting Records.* [8] *(Connecting straight lines indicate the chief directions for the transfer or interchange of data.)*

THE CUMULATIVE RECORD

The guidance-centered instrument commonly employed for housing developmental information about a pupil is known as the cumulative record.
This instrument holds the key to the longitudinal developmental pattern of

---

[8]Fred C. Ayer, *Practical Child Accounting* (rev. ed.). Austin, Texas: Steck-Vaughn Co.,
1953. Used with permission.

the pupil. Often, the cumulative record folder contains other record instruments, e.g., test profile sheets for the pupil. These are inserted in the cumulative record folder or the information from the other records is transferred to the cumulative record form.

The cumulative record plan will vary for each school system. Any standard cumulative record must be modified to satisfy the unique requirements of each school and school system. To use a standard cumulative record and omit inapplicable items thereon often proves frustrating to teachers and counselors—somehow they feel compelled to fill in the blanks, regardless of the accuracy of the information. This is the danger of imposing a record card or system from one school on another.

Purposes of the Cumulative Record and Other Guidance Records

There are many uses for guidance records. The central—although not exclusive—purpose is for the school counselor to assist the pupil to maximum developmental progress. These records may be used by others to assist the boy or girl. The records may be used by, or with, school administrators, state education officials, teachers, counselors, parents, and, of course, pupils. Ayer does an excellent job of delineating the purposes for which guidance record systems are organized and developed. The following uses of records are based on Ayer's analysis.

Guidance records help school principals and superintendents to:
1. Identify pupils quickly
2. Have information available for parent and pupil conferences
3. Study pupil progress
4. Study changing characteristics of pupils
5. Provide a basis for pertinent school policies, e.g., instructional development
6. Provide data for research
7. Obtain data for the school's classification and grouping programs

Carefully used, the records may help state officials to:
1. Publish reports on pupil characteristics
2. Determine school holding power of pupils or conversely, the drop-out situation
3. Design budgets
4. Check pupil mobility
5. Determine needs of exceptional children

Professionally used, the records help teachers to:
1. Determine pupil developmental patterns
2. Know specific data about the child

3. Become acquainted with a pupil's educational progress
4. Review for parent or pupil conferences
5. Use as a base for instructional programming
6. Make periodic reports
7. Assist in teamwork with the counselor
8. Individualize instruction

If properly developed and organized, guidance records help the school counselor to

1. Know pupils as individuals
2. Counsel a pupil on his progress
3. Become aware of pupils in need of developmental guidance, that is alerting them to their potentialities and opportunities
4. Assist pupils to better understand their own record of progress
5. Form a basis for follow-up studies
6. Gather data for guidance research studies
7. Assist pupils in educational and vocational planning

Guidance records help parents to:

1. Understand their children
2. Know specifics about the educational development of their children
3. Realize that the school is vitally interested in the progress of their sons and daughters
4. Focus attention on their children rather than on a school staff member
5. Make decisions pertinent to selected policies of parent-teacher organizations
6. Continue or modify relevant conditions at home

The pupil in counseling will find that the guidance records, particularly the cumulative record, are useful to him to:

1. Understand his developmental pattern
2. Make better choice of courses
3. Determine any discrepancy between potential and performance
4. Plan his career objectives
5. Note the areas of improvement needed
6. Know the record that will be used in relevant conferences with parents
7. Raise questions in the counseling interview which will make it more meaningful to him[9]

The many uses of guidance records immediately suggest the importance of responsibility and confidentiality in professional use as well as proper format and housing.

---

[9]Based on Ayer, *Child Accounting*, pp. 17–25.

Items of the Cumulative Record

Each school staff responsible for the development of guidance records should determine (1) what data are needed, (2) what data can be obtained, and (3) what data are used. It is better to gather a small amount of specific information, and use it, than to gather a great deal of general data, only to leave it resting in files unused, or at best minimally used.

Ideally, schools would gather data on each pupil in the following priority sequence:

1. Identifying data
2. Physical health information
3. Home and family information
4. Educational development data
5. Academic test data
6. Vocational interests
7. Vocational development data
8. Key experiential data
9. Pupil self-concept data

The identifying data include: legal name, sex, birthdate and evidence of birth, current address, and telephone number. Other data commonly included in this area seem to these authors to have overtones which are more likely to be prejudicial than helpful to the pupil. As with any item, the question should be asked, "Do we really need it to better help this pupil." Similarly for home and family information, there is too often a gathering of data not needed for every pupil. Special information needed for a particular pupil can be ascertained at the time the identifying data are gathered. The other items are self-explanatory except, perhaps, items 8 and 9. The school staff has a responsibility to include positive key experiential data in the pupil's record. Too often, one finds only negative data there. Too, there should be some evidence which reveals the pupil's open appraisal of himself. This would counterbalance possible misleading inferences which might be drawn from the use of only standardized response instruments.

Another way of considering the items to be included on guidance records may be studied from the plan below, which is based on research by Heayn and Jacobs.[10]

Classification of Cumulative Record Data

An analysis of the contents of a cumulative folder suggests that information be classified according to two general categories: matters of record, and matters of judgment.

---

[10]Abridged from Maurice H. Heayn and Howard L. Jacobs, "Safeguarding Student Records," *Personnel and Guidance Journal,* Vol. 46, No. 1 (September 1967), pp. 64–67. Material used with permission.

Matters of record. Information in this category belongs in two categories: unrestricted and restricted. The former would include matters judged to be in the public domain; the latter would include information of a private nature. Information pertaining to the individual through no effort of his own is ascribed status. Information about what the student has accomplished in the course of satisfying the requirements of the school is achieved status.

An example of information classified according to this scheme is as follows:

Matters of Record—Unrestricted

Ascribed	*Achieved*
Name	Date of leaving school
Sex	Absences
Birth date	Tardies
Place of birth	Activities
Nationality	Honors
Names of parents	Change of educational status
Address of parents	Previous schools attended
Home telephone number	
Names of siblings	

Matters of Record—Restricted

Ascribed	*Achieved*
Health record	Disciplinary record

Matters of Judgment. Judgment items should be explanatory. They should aid the student in the learning process, and should not be used in a punitive or negative manner. Examples of information classified as matters of judgment would be: standardized test results; rank in class; psychological reports; psychiatric evaluations; social service reports; medical information; legal information; agency reports; student descriptions; and staff recommendations.

As records become more judgmental, and move from public domain to private, the need for interpretive ability, trustworthiness, and professional sophistication on the part of the recipient of the information increases proportionately.

Release of Information

The decision to release information, regardless of classification, is based on the prerequisite that the request is presented formally by an identified representative of a recognized and established agency, institution, or employer expressing a legitimate interest in, and need for, the information contained in the student's folder. It must be in accord with student rights as described by school directives, or state laws and regulations.

There are several levels of openness.

Level I. This information includes all matters of record—unrestricted to any appropriate user of the folder. Release of Level I information should be left to the discretion of the administrator or pupil personnel worker upon verification of the legitimacy of the request.

Level II. This information should include all matters of record—restricted to appropriate personnel. The inquirer after Level II information must satisfy, to the best judgment of the administrator or pupil personnel worker, the need to possess such information for the student's benefit.

Level III. This information should include the following matters of judgment: student descriptions; staff recommendations; rank in class; and standardized test results. The student or parent must give consent to release this information.

Level IV. This information should include the following matters of judgment: psychological reports; psychiatric evaluations; social service reports; medical information; legal information; and agency reports. The cumulative record folder should not contain this information. Some other manner should indicate the existence and location of the material. Responsible use for the pupil's interests is the basic criteria. The inquirer must demonstrate, to the satisfaction of the student, the personnel worker directly responsible for this information, and his essential need to know, possess, interpret and properly use this material. The information, if granted, shall be confidential. Under no circumstances should this information be shown to the student, nor shared verbatim with the parents of the student.

The release of confidential information requires the express authorization of the appropriate school staff, and written and witnessed consent to release the information is required from the student or parent.

An outline of general regulations seems necessary to supplement the foregoing, in order to reduce the perplexities confronting the keeper of the records.

General Regulations:

I. Types of requests for information
   A. Telephone requests. Requests for information via the telephone shall not be honored.
   B. Written Requests. Requests for information by letter may be honored under the following conditions:
      1. If the request is made under an official letterhead;

2. If the inquirer is properly identified in the correspondence;
3. If the purpose of the request is clearly stated; and
4. If the type of information required is exactly stated;

C. In-person requests for information. Upon presentation of proper identification, a request for information via personal visit shall be honored under the following conditions:
1. If the purpose of the request and the exact nature of the information requested is be stated and found satisfactory by the administrator or student personnel worker;
2. If the material is interpreted to the visitor by a qualified staff member. Under no circumstances should the record be open to visual inspection;
3. If the staff member is present during the entire in-person visit; and
4. If a record of the visit is made.

II. Sources of requests for information.

A. Parents or Legal Guardians.
1. Parents or legal guardians shall have the right to know the entire record of the student until the student's 21st birthday.
2. In the event of a legal separation or divorce, the contents of the record shall be released only to the parent with whom the student is in legal residence.
3. If the request is made by the parent not having legal custody, information shall not be released unless approval is given by the parent having legal custody.

B. Family Members Other Than Parents. Requests for information contained in the student's record shall not be honored when made by a student's relatives or immediate family members other than parents, whether the request is made by letter or in person. The release of information to those persons can be made only with the consent of the parents or legal guardians.

C. Staff. Staff members shall respect and observe the importance of the student record. The utmost personal and professional responsibility is required in the uses to which they put their special knowledge about a student. Staff requests for information should be directed to the student personnel worker directly responsible for the record.

    D. Board of Education Members. Requests for information from members of the Board of Education may be honored under the safeguards established for staff requests.

    E. Peers. Requests for information contained in the student's record from a student's peers shall not be honored.

    F. Agency or Institution. All information released to an agency or institution should be directed to a specifically named representative therefrom. Requests for information originating from any federal, state, county or local agency having any legitimate interest in the student's record may be processed according to these regulations.

    G. Other Sources. Requests for information from sources not specifically identified in these regulations may be processed in accordance with safeguards established by the school administrator after consultation with the chief student personnel officer.

Consent, the right to withhold information and location of student's records must be cognizant of the basic guidance principle: the individual's right to positive development.

Items for the School

Items for the school's cumulative record should be derived from its educational objectives, purposes of the guidance program, and planned research. Too often, much-publicized cumulative record cards are adopted by schools with the result that much unused information is gathered. Worse yet is the plethora of cumulative record checklists which, too often, implicitly indicate a need for all items in every school system. General topical areas should be considered and specific items should be developed by representatives of the school staff. Eliminating the problems created by simple adoption of another school's record form may demand more effort than developing a form appropriate to the particular school.

Responsibilities for Cumulative Records

Every school staff member has a professional responsibility to apply his ethical principles in the use of records. Records are instruments which must be used with discriminating care. In decisions on what to include in a record, in interpretation of records, in housing records, the staff must keep in mind that these records reflect a human being—a person of dignity. Great care must be exercised that records do not preclude a pupil's becoming his best possible self. To label may be to force a pupil into a life-long role far below that which he might properly have assumed.

Confidentiality of Records

The details of confidentiality of records are discussed in Chapter 14. However, it can not be overemphasized that records require the same discretion in use as do the results of the counseling process itself. The following statement is directly appropriate.

Recent actions regarding the disposition of student records and the subsequent concerns expressed by individuals and groups in education, guidance, and psychology clearly call for a statement of position by this Association.

1. The American Personnel and Guidance Association asserts itself in the rights and responsibilities of parents to learn and know of their children's status in educational institutions. This statement recognizes that parents, as legal guardians of their children, have quite a different role from that of a third party with regard to the understanding of the institution's impressions and actions pertaining to their children. In fact, only through continuing cooperation and mutual understanding between the home and the school can the best interests of the nation's school children be served.

2. These rights and responsibilities should be expressed in a manner which will be of the greatest value for the individual student being considered. Interpretation of a student's school record to his parents is a function that requires qualified professional personnel. Such records often contain some information which is confidential or technical in nature.

3. The best interests of the student are served when school records bearing upon parental questions concerning a student are interpreted by appropriate professional personnel, who are qualified: (a) to judge the validity of the information; (b) to determine how it may best be interpreted; and (c) to distinguish between that which should be regarded as confidential and that which may be disclosed to parents or other authorized school personnel.

4. Such interpretation may or may not include the actual display of record information. This decision is and must be part of the professional responsibility of appropriate school personnel and *not*, ultimately, the responsibility of the parent. The reasons for this are several: (a) the three statements in the preceding paragraph; and (b) the removal of any doubt among school personnel

regarding the person with whom rests the ultimate decision as to any visual inspection of records. Failure to do so will almost certainly result in the reduction of information entered in school records. Any such reduction will work a very real disservice to the student.

5. It is, therefore, the position of the American Personnel and Guidance Association that the best interest of the student is served when school record information is interpreted by appropriate professional personnel. Any decision as to the display of such information for visual inspection by the parent or guardian must rest with the professional judgement of the appropriate school personnel.

6. School record information may contain material prepared by other sources such as clinics, physicians, psychiatrist, psychologists, etc. These records should be prepared in a form for use by appropriate school personnel. It should be made clear whether such records are the property of the school or of the agency or clinic which was the source of the records. In the event of any doubt by school personnel as to their competence to interpret such material to parents, or in the event that the originators of such material do not expect it to be interpreted by school personnel to parents, then the parents should be referred to the originator of the materials for consultation.

7. Educational institutions are responsible for insuring through selection, training and review of practices of their personnel, that appropriate personnel are competent to use and interpret information.

8. Educational institutions are responsible for insuring that the content and manner of records gathered are limited to those materials which in the institution's judgement contribute to its efforts to educate the student. Records should differentiate between those entries which are observations and those which are inferential in nature.[11]

The statement above reflects two key points: (1) the importance of working with records as a professional tool and (2) the difficulty of devising specific guidelines for every possible use of the records. As in any profession, the counselor's judgement becomes the ultimate determinant as to what to do.

Boyd, Tennyson and Erickson surveyed school counselors about the methods they employed in releasing pupil personnel information to requesting

---

[11] *The Use of Student Records,* Washington, D.C.: American Personnel and Guidance Association, June 1, 1961.

Table 12-1.   F Values for Variables Influencing Counselor Disclosure of Pupil Information by Type of Information Requested

Counselor Variables		Scholastic Aptitude Tests	Multiple Aptitude Tests	Achievement Tests	Personality Inventories	Interest Inventories	Teacher Anecdotal Comments	Vocational Interview Information	Personal Interview Information	Community Agency Reports	Teacher Personality Ratings	Social and Descriptive Data
(1) Rural	N=563	31.86^*_2	14.31^*_2	18.66^*_2	0.08	0.64	4.51	0.86	6.38	0.00	0.01	0.11
(2) Urban	N=346											
Student ratio												
(1) 0–400	N=506	0.13	0.16	0.46	0.12	0.24	0.54	0.05	0.17	0.05	4.09	1.65
(2) 401+	N=404											
(1) Junior High	N=257	2.15	0.56	4.36	2.27	28.34^*_2	28.01^*_2	16.12^*_2	13.93^*_2	27.24^*_2	0.77	2.20
(2) Senior High	N=253											
Years since graduate level courses												
(1) 0–3	N=621	0.01	3.09	6.42	1.12	0.16	0.22	0.48	0.54	7.56^*_2	3.44	0.92
(2) 4+	N=290											
Years experience in counseling												
(1) 0–3	N=396	0.03	0.91	7.02^*_1	15.36^*_2	0.90	5.11	0.28	1.44	9.29^*_2	6.76^*_1	0.35
(2) 4+	N=515											
Written school policies												
(1) yes	N=402	12.31^*_1	11.39^*_1	13.60^*_1	2.84	1.70	0.52	2.69	0.16	0.14	0.75	0.69
(2) no	N=447											

Note: Numerical subscript on significant F values indicates the sample in that variable more likely to treat the request for information conservatively.

*Significant at .01 level.

Source: Robert E. Boyd, W. Wesley Tennyson, and Reynold Erickson, "Counselors and Client Confidentiality," Counselor Education and Supervision, Vol. 12 (June 1973), p. 283. Used with permission.

Table 12-2. *F Values for Variables Influencing Counselor Disclo-sure of Pupil Information by Requesting Source*

Counselor Variables		Student	Parent	School Administrator	Teacher	Employer	College Admission	Social Service Agencies	Government Protection Agencies
(1) Rural	N=576	1.93	9.44^*_1	29.01^*_1	25.79^*_1	38.69^*_2	16.72^*_2	22.70^*_2	27.33^*_2
(2) Urban	N=352								
Student ratio									
(1) 0-400	N=505	4.59	0.68	0.31	0.36	1.65	3.34	0.06	0.23
(2) 401+	N=398								
(1) Junior high	N=266	2.39	0.03	11.37^*_2	8.50^*_2	0.18	51.15^*_1	13.93^*_2	1.10
(2) Senior high	N=254								
Years since graduate level courses									
(1) 0-3	N=638	0.16	0.52	1.60	0.41	0.15	3.86	3.00	0.21
(2) 4+	N=293								
Years experience in counseling									
(1) 0-3	N=408	0.46	1.06	1.08	0.60	6.52	0.01	3.13	6.43
(2) 4+	N=523								
Written school policies									
(1) yes	N=411	0.03	2.01	2.38	3.08	22.21^*_1	8.69^*_1	7.61^*_1	18.85^*_1
(2) no	N=457								

Note: Numerical subscripts on significant F value indicates the sample in that variable more likely to treat the request for information conservatively.
*Significant at .01 level.

Source: Boyd, Tennyson, and Erickson. "Client Confidentiality," p. 283. Used with permission.

sources. Complete confidentiality was rarely, if ever, extended to school-age clients. The information most readily shared concerned pupils' educational-vocational development. Requested information was released in some form. Tables 12–1 and 12–2 illustrate the patterns of disclosure by type of information requested and by requesting source.[12]

It is well to review counselor privileged communication in regard to records.[13]

Privileged Communications. Fifteen states have statutes granting full privileged communications to school counselors, including Indiana (the first in the nation), Michigan, North Dakota, Idaho, and Montana. In an APGA Legislative Flier (May 23, 1971) McDonough reported that Iowa and Nebraska school counselors also had privileged communications statutes, but neither state supplied that information for this study.

Several states have specialized or limited privileged communications: Colorado and Delaware have statutes protecting student records; Maryland has a statute granting privileged communication to counselors approved by the State Drug Abuse Authority for counseling students with drug abuse problems; Washington has a similar statute, but at the time of this writing, it was not clear whether the law applied to school counselors or not.

Six states have bills pending. New Jersey has a bill similar to the Maryland drug abuse law. Oregon has a bill concerned with the privacy of student records. Illinois, North Carolina, and Utah have general privileged communications bills pending. Wisconsin has "a much debated bill in our current legislature."

Another four states have expressed strong interest in the issue. Alaska reported the possibility that privileged communication might be considered by petitioning the State Supreme Court, a route not used by any state so far. Arkansas, Massachusetts, and South Dakota have committees either developing bills or investigating that possibility.

In total, fifteen states have addressed themselves to the privileged communications issue. But privileged communications warrant a fairly close inspection so that states know what they are asking for when they seek such legislation.

Forms

The type or form of records which may be used is determined by the school district, county, or state. Most states have laws directly relating to

---

[12]Robert E. Boyd, W. Wesley Tennyson and Reynold Erickson. "Counselors and Client Confidentiality," *Counselor Education and Supervision,* Vol. 12 No. 4, June 1973, pp. 278–288.

[13]Jack Thorsen. *Counselor Certification 1971.* Washington, D.C.: American Personnel and Guidance Association, 1971, p. 9 (mimeographed).

record systems. In 1955, Segel published a U.S. Office of Education pamphlet on this matter. He stated

> Heretofore, little information has been compiled about the role of
> state departments of education in the development of cumulative
> school records. The present publication, therefore, should interest persons of the State Department of Education level who deal with this type
> of record.[14]

General requirements for each state were indicated. To comply with most state laws on this matter requires adoption of a cumulative record.

If the reader wishes to examine representative cumulative record forms he may write to one of the following:

American Council on Education, 1785 Massachusetts Avenue, N. W., Washington, D.C.

Chronicle Press, Moravia, New York

Educational Records Bureau, 437 W. 59th St., New York, N.Y.

Georgia State Department of Education, State Office Bldg., Atlanta, Georgia

California State Department of Education, Sacramento, California

The main advantage of a standardized form is that it is easily obtained. Its major disadvantage is that it probably is not entirely applicable to any one school system. The locally developed form has the advantage of staff involvement, with greater probability of subsequent use. One disadvantage is the time-consuming process of development. Another results from increased pupil mobility from school system to school system; transfer of different kinds of records then becomes a difficult task.

Housing of the Records

Records are for use. Therefore, records must be readily accessible. It is necessary to use modern methods of record reproduction if they are to be fully used. The expense of duplication may far offset the expense of using staff for clerical functions. Further, such use of the staff may engender reluctance to use the material. Guidance records should be readily available

---

[14]David Segel, "Cumulative Records: State Laws and State Department of Education Regulations and Services," Guide Lines No. 5. Washington, D.C.: U.S. Office of Education, May, 1955, mimeograph, p. 1.

to counselors. Counselors must develop a plan for record accessibility for teachers. This can be best achieved by having a separate record office in close proximity to the counselor's office. Care must be given, too, to the proper safeguarding of the records.

Machine-Electronic Innovations

As more comprehensive schools are developed and small schools are consolidated, staff members will have to catch up in their use of modern methods for data processing. Schools have barely scratched the surface in this area.

Holt states

> The over-all objective in using mechanical aids is to increase school efficiency. This is done by:
>
> 1. Improving the accuracy of records. The use of machine punch cards can assure the attainment of absolute accuracy since all cards are prepared from the original.
> 2. Relieving teachers of the routine clerical function of attendance. Attendance lists are prepared and automatically recapped.
> 3. Relieving teachers of the time-consuming task of correlating test data with work in the classroom. Cards with test data may be sorted automatically and classified to achieve many desired results.
> 4. Providing rapid and more widely disseminated information. The facts one teacher has can be made readily available to everyone in the school or system.
> 5. Helping counselors reduce time spent in compiling records, thus allowing them more time for guiding and counseling students.
> 6. Streamlining registration so that conflicts are greatly reduced, if not eliminated.
> 7. Aiding planning by having more kinds of data readily available as needed.[15]

There is need for a study of machine use of records for guidance purposes. On the horizon is the possible reorganization of guidance programs based on the changes in record processing through electronic innovation. This may well be a topic for study by the American Personnel and Guidance Association or the United States Office of Education.

---

[15]C. C. Holt, "Mechanical Aids for Teaching," *California Journal of Secondary Education,* Vol. 35 (April 1960), pp. 255–256.

Grossman and Howe give a number of advantages of the use of data processing in schools: accuracy, speed, reproduction, easy access to information, collation of information, compactness, automated process, and efficiency.[16] These lend themselves to the efficient use of time, energy, and skill. The emphasis on time is well described by Martin.[17] Overlap may be minimized with data processing.[18]

DEVELOPING USE OF CUMULATIVE RECORDS: SOME PRINCIPLES

In organizing and developing the cumulative guidance record system, the staff should state their priorities of record use. Guidance for (1) positive pupil development, (2) pupil educational planning, (3) career thinking, (4) areas of limitations, (5) recommendations, and (6) in-service education are suggested priorities.

Positive Pupil Development

A basic principle is to record those data which reflect the positive direction of a pupil's development. This does not mean that note should not be made of negative or deviant behavior. It does mean that care should be taken to make sure that, if a negative note is included in the record, it is a part of a pattern and not an incident.

Several years ago, pupil-kept cumulative records were being used advantageously to assist pupils in understanding themselves. This may be worthwhile if the pupil-kept record is unofficial and if all items on it (for example, test score) are expressed in terms understandable to the pupil.

Pupil Educational Planning

The principle of assisting pupils in educational planning has a high priority for guidance action. Focus on the educational progress of the pupil permits other data to be related to this important purpose of guidance. Educational achievement of the pupil is the basic *raison d'etre* for the boy or girl in the classroom. Concern for his total development is justified only because it forms the undergirding for educational achievement.

---

[16]Alvin Grossman and Robert Howe, "Human Economy and Data Processing," *Personnel and Guidance Journal,* Vol. 43, No. 4 (December 1964), pp. 343–347.

[17]Wainright E. Martin, Jr., *Electronic Data Processing—An Introduction.* Homewood, Illinois: Richard D. Irwin, Inc., 1965.

[18]Paul R. Lohnes and Thomas O. Marshall, "Redundancy in Student Records," *American Educational Research Journal,* Vol. II, No. 1 (January, 1965), pp. 19–24.

Career Thinking

Consistent with educational planning on the part of counselor and pupil is his career thinking. Records should facilitate the use of data in thinking through one's career objectives. Career thinking gives added incentive to educational performance. Career thinking needs to evolve from the fantasy stage to the reality state. To leave this to chance is to risk our greatest resource—the youth of our country.

Areas of Limitations

Guidance records are also useful if they assist the pupil in defining areas of limited performance. A principle of the record system is that it should confirm positive direction. It may be useful in doing this by disclosing areas of limitations. Put into proper perspective, this knowledge can facilitate growth. Emphasized as a separate discontinuity in one's life, without any relation to total development, an area of limitation may become the seed for discouragement.

Recommendations for Placement

Care must be taken when using record information as a basis for post-high school recommendations. Records should be carefully distilled and abstracted for information that reflects the pupil as he is now, not as he was several years ago. If the two are congruent, there is little reason for concern. However, the very essence of education is to produce changed behavior. Therefore, the immediate record is probably far more useful in most cases than the data of several years ago.

In-Service Education

Guidance records contain material for in-service education of the staff. Analysis of data on local school pupils provides an opportunity to bring theory to a practical level of application with the pupils. The staff—often to their surprise—will get an enlarged and more accurate picture of the total student population by studying the records. Too often, in their preoccupation with one segment of the pupil parameter, the staff loses sight of the total student body.

Cost

In the Georgia study previously mentioned, clerical work load and cost per student (annually) surveys were made. It should be noted that counselors did this kind of clerical work in one of the four schools. The cost is minimal when one thinks of the many benefits derived from a well developed, organized, functional record system.

REPORTING PUPIL PROGRESS

Both pupil and parent have a need and right to know of the boy's or girl's school progress. Rather than being just another task, pupil progress reports offer a real guidance aid both to pupil and parent. School staff must always realize that pupils and parents are sensitive to the progress reports. Therefore, the staff must expend the necessary time to be sure that the method and instrument used for pupil reporting is accurately reflecting the objectives for the particular report.

Report cards should reflect accuracy, honesty of reporting, cooperation in development, simplicity, positive stimulation for guidance, articulation with other records, total development of the child, and practicability.

Usually elementary school progress reports are better guidance instruments than high school report forms. The elementary school reports are more analytical and comprehensive, and thus facilitate encouragement of the pupil's strong achievement area and remediation for his weak performance area.

It should be noted that this progress report incorporates marks on subject matter, learning process, and attitudinal development. All of these are important for optimal pupil progress.

QUESTIONS ON THE USES OF CUMULATIVE AND OTHER GUIDANCE RECORDS

Some questions which all school staffs have to resolve in their use of records are outlined here for discussion purposes.

How permanent should be the keeping of guidance records? Seemingly, everyone writes that more and more information about a pupil should be recorded. Further, many guidance authorities emphasize that this information should be passed on from grade to grade. Does not the emphasis on the past deny the pupil's right of becoming—becoming a significantly different person than he is and was?

How can the positive and negative be properly balanced in the use of cumulative records? Because the negative is often more discrete and dramatic than the positive, it is recorded. Soon it looks as if the general character of the pupil is negative, and teachers act negatively toward him. The chain reaction is in motion. To avoid this reaction, it is necessary to achieve proper balance in the data recorded on guidance records, especially the cumulative record.

How may guidance records be used with objectivity? A staff member must understand his own biases in the flow of his career. He may, unwittingly, look for specific facts to justify his thinking. Any fact on a record must be interpreted in terms of the total array of pertinent data.

How may guidance records facilitate research? Records form a tangible basis for guidance research. With available data, staff can derive many facts about the characteristics of pupil ability and performance. From these results, the staff may proceed to specific, useful guidance approaches, e.g., the use of expectancy tables, and regression equations in course decision making. Additional research ideas are stimulated from the efforts put into the functional guidance record system.

How may the record system be refined and further developed? Through administrative leadership, staff team effort, and school counselor expertness in guidance records, the record system can be analyzed for further development. The school records study group can assess use, interpretation, cost, design, and staff-pupil-parent reaction to the record system. A handbook to accompany the guidance records may facilitate their more effective use. The study group also can investigate the use of electronic equipment. Pilot use may be made of new forms of records to determine the efficacy of a change.

SUMMARY

Records are essential to a guidance program. Records include census data forms, attendance records, routine office-facilitating forms, reports to parents, health records, cumulative records and reports to colleges. Key dimensions of the record system are (1) objectives for records, (2) place of records in the guidance program, (3) usability of records, (4) processing record data procedures, and (5) evaluation of the records.

The cumulative record is the primary guidance instrument for recording purposes. The cumulative record has administrative, instructional, and guidance uses. The cumulative record needs to be designed in terms of personal, educational, vocational, and social data. Every school staff member has a professional responsibility to apply his ethical principles in the use of records. The counselor needs to know his responsibilities in keeping the confidentiality of selected record data. The use of new electronic devices for data-keeping should be explored and developed according to each school's needs. The central focus of recordkeeping should be to assist in developmental guidance of each pupil.

ANNOTATED BIBLIOGRAPHY

Ayer, Fred C., *Practical Child Accounting.* Austin, Texas: The Steck Company, 1953.

    This is an excellent treatment of guidance records. Trends, purposes, uses, and examples of guidance records are presented.

Hatch, Raymond N., and Buford Stefflre, *Administration of Guidance Services* (2nd ed.). Englewood Cliffs, N.J.: Prentice-Hall, Inc., 1965.

    Excellent treatment is given in Chapter 5 to the record-keeping program, selection of the record form, and maintenance of the cumulative record. The authors discuss practices that may be used to screen, enter, and summarize data on pupil records.

Organizing and Using Community Resources

Counselors are constantly faced with the impacts upon the student of both family life and community life. Rarely is there an adequate awareness of the student's world outside the school, the world that is almost always more vivid to him than the world of the school. . . .[1]

Chapter 13

Why is there a need for organizing community guidance personnel?

What are the types of community resources typically available to school guidance resources?

How may school guidance personnel identify the community guidance resources?

How may school guidance personnel organize information about community guidance resources for their use?

How are coordinative and cooperative relationships established between school guidance and community guidance resource personnel?

The school's acceptance of greater responsibility for all aspects of a pupil's development and growth has made it imperative for the school counselor to understand and utilize the varied community resources at his disposal. The interdependence of home, community, and school cannot be overlooked if the guidance needs of individual boys and girls are to be taken into consideration. Guidance personnel must look about themselves to discover every possible source of aid in their efforts to provide the best possible program for the students in their school. Not only must guidance department personnel make maximum use of other school services that are avail-

---

[1]C. Gilbert Wrenn, *The World of the Contemporary Counselor.* Boston: Houghton Mifflin Company, 1973, p. 182.

organizations, and associations that may contribute to the school's guidance program.

Community guidance resources are those efforts on the part of persons, agencies, and organizations which seek through study and analysis of each individual to provide formal and informal experiences to stimulate him to grow toward his highest potential developmental level. In some communities there is a dearth of such provisions, which may be due to inadequate resources or lack of planning. In others, especially larger cities, the problem is one of integrating the varied services offered by many specialized agencies.

WHY UTILIZE COMMUNITY RESOURCES?

Underlying all modern programs of education is one fundamental principle: the child is a whole being who is educated by a total environment. Psychologists have disclosed the essential unity of personality as it develops through interaction of mind and body, beliefs and emotions, thinking and doing. Thus, a student's mind cannot be abstracted and educated apart from these other vital aspects of his total existence. Sociologists have revealed the essential unity of one's life experience, showing that all influences which impinge upon the individual educate him in some manner and to some degree, for better or for worse. Therefore, the guidance process cannot be confined solely to the school. The psychosociological findings of our time compel recognition that, when the school seeks to promote the constructive guidance of the whole child in relation to his total environment, it thereby commits itself to a conception of guidance as a community-wide function and enterprise. From this conception of guidance, the trend is toward centralizing guidance activities of the school—through coordination—bridging the gap between the school guidance resources and the resources available in the community.

Supporting the school and supplementing its contribution to the development of youth are the various community services for improving the mental and physical health and well being of the child. Both the school guidance personnel and the personnel in these agencies are striving to carry on preventive work with youth. The major obstacle to effective preventive work is that it is complex and demands that matters often considered trivial be regarded as important. Preventive work, to be effective, requires consideration of innumerable and diverse factors which operate in various combinations to produce early symptoms, but which previously seemed to have no special bearing on the problems they produce. Preventive guidance personnel too often perform in isolation from one another, emphasizing the enormous importance of the specific problems they see, but failing to realize the problems and contributions that similar workers in other institutions and agencies are meeting and making. Ryan and Zeran view the community as a very important factor in a functioning guidance program.[2]

Preventive guidance work in the school will most likely fail to attain effectiveness as long as it is done separately, without regard to the other influences shaping the lives of youth; hence, working with other agencies concerned with youth is a necessity. The very nature of preventive guidance work in the school demands a coordinated attack from experts in all related fields on problems that are seen as interdependent.

Additional reasons for utilizing community resources are summarized as follows:

1. The complexity of the problems of juvenile delinquency and maladjustment requires in response a broad program consisting of health services, guidance and counseling, case work, and recreational facilities to meet the tensions and conflicts of youth. Such a program must be broader in scope than one touching the child only during school hours. It must stimulate, organize, and coordinate all character-building agencies, of which the school is only one.

2. Some problems of youth are better cared for by community agencies that have been established to perform that service. Referral to them of such cases, e.g., pupils with family financial problems, is appropriate. The school guidance program has definite limits of responsibility which it should not exceed.

3. It is estimated that some form of exceptional anxiety exists in one out of eight children in our schools. It is rightfully expected that the school counselor, although concerned with every student, will devote the major portion of his time to normal students with normal anxieties. Therefore, referral resources in the community are greatly needed to assist in care and treatment of many types of exceptional problems.

4. The individual child needs protection from the confusion that surely results from the guidance activities of a multiplicity of agencies. It is the school guidance department's responsibility to obtain good working relationships and to coordinate the work of the school and community so that the child may have unified assistance.

---

[2]T. Antoinette Ryan and Franklin R. Zeran. *Organization and Administration of Guidance Services.* Danville, Illinois: The Interstate Printers and Publishers Inc., 1972, p. 383.

TYPES OF COMMUNITY RESOURCES

Caring for the physical, mental, social, and recreational needs of children in the schools requires the assistance of child guidance clinics, speech and hearing clinics, service clubs, parent organizations, medical services, religious associations, youth organizations, and the like. Responsibility for the guidance of youth is shared by the school and other community agencies. The director of guidance will find many resources and agencies available in his immediate and larger communities. Some of these resources may be designed to serve a limited clientele, but the director of guidance must know all the community agencies and organizations that provide assistance in any form to youth. The specialized resources of communities have not been utilized to the fullest in most school guidance programs.

The following material reports on some of the resources found in most communities. It is not a complete analysis of community agencies, organizations, and associations available in every community, but suggests the extent and availability of this source of help in providing youth with those understandings and insights which are becoming increasingly necessary as our lives become more complicated and complex.

Medical Services

Some of the larger school districts have the services of a physician. Most schools have at least the services of a school nurse who aids the physician in periodic physical and dental examinations. The handling of medical referrals usually is the responsibility of the school nurse. Parental cooperation is needed in arranging for special medical referrals and any remedial program conducted as a result. If parents are unable to pay for such services, financial assistance is often obtainable from welfare agencies or social and fraternal clubs. The school nurse or director of guidance should know community medical and dental specialists in such fields as (1) ear, nose, and throat; (2) heart and circulatory system; (3) orthopedics; (4) dermatology; (5) chest and respiratory system; and (6) oral hygiene, dental surgery, orthodontia, and prosthetics.

National, state, and local health offices provide information about health services. These include:

1. Local or county health departments
2. American Cancer Society
3. American Dental Association
4. American Diabetes Association
5. American Foundation for the Blind

6. American Heart Association
7. American Medical Association
8. American Public Health Association
9. Arthritis and Rheumatism Foundation
10. Association for the Blind
11. Cerebral Palsy Foundation
12. National Foundation (March of Dimes)
13. Multiple Sclerosis Society
14. State heart associations
15. State tuberculosis and health associations
16. Drug rehabilitation centers

Mental Health Agencies

School counselors are basically concerned with helping the wide range of normal children and youth with their problems, while the staff in community mental health clinics give help to the more seriously disturbed children and adults. They may serve as an ancillary service to mental hospitals—preparing patients needing hospital care, and their families, for the new situation, offering follow-up treatment to discharged patients on furlough, supervising patients in foster homes, and offering outpatient treatment for nonhospitalized persons. Particularly helpful to school counselors has been the widespread establishment of child guidance clinics. The increase in child guidance clinics has been due to a growing awareness of what may be accomplished through the coordinated services of psychiatrists, psychologists, vocational counselors, and social workers. Children who are referred to child guidance clinics usually display troublesome personality traits or unacceptable behavior—symptoms of serious underlying disturbances. Maladjustment, especially in young children, may be indicated by *chronic* thumb-sucking, nail-biting, masturbation, enuresis, night terrors, and the like. Or it may be indicated by personality traits, such as extreme sensitiveness, seclusiveness, apathy, fantasy, moodiness, obstinacy, etc. In general, children between the ages of three and sixteen are treated. Feeble-mindedness and pathological states of long standing, such as epilepsy, childhood schizophrenia, and the like, are not treated routinely by a child guidance clinic.

In some communities, the child guidance clinic emphasizes treatment of parents. The psychiatric social worker often counsels the parent, while the clinical psychologist works with the child. Some communities have set up traveling clinics with branch offices to serve sparsely settled and rural areas. In the traveling clinics, teams from the central office make regular visits to rural and small communities. Usually a local staff from the health or welfare agency assists in the work. It should be kept in mind that these agencies complement the work of private medical and psychological staff engaged by parents.

Some of the local, state, and national associations that provide information about mental health work include:

1. State and local mental health centers
2. County and state mental health associations
3. American Association on Mental Deficiency
4. American Association of Psychiatric Social Workers
5. American Red Cross
6. Big Brothers (Optimists Club)
7. Boy and Girl Scouts
8. Family and children's agencies
9. National Mental Health Association
10. State Psychological Association

Social Agencies

There are many children who present problems for the school counselor that will require aid outside of school agencies. Three types of social agencies exist: public private, and commercial. Public agencies are supported through taxation, private agencies exist through voluntary contributions, and commercial agencies are financed by fees. Commercial agencies are not included in the following discussion as they are operated for profit to the owner, with no community-wide responsibilities.

The public and private social agencies are usually operated for some special aspect of the community welfare and, as a result, function in cooperation with each other. Social agencies have their budget, clientele, and nature of service defined through legislation, whereas private agencies can determine their own clientele. Community agencies may serve certain groups, such as the blind, deaf, or adolescent. They exist to serve a social need—a service wanted either by the community as a whole or some particular segment of it. In some cases fees may be charged on a sliding scale to help defray expenses.

Often the problem with which a student is struggling is a family problem, one which some social agency might help. Dependent children, because of some disaster in the home, often require such aid and care. The breaking up of a home and the necessary assumption of parental responsibility by some extra-home agency require adequate planning of no small proportions. Financial assistance through county and welfare departments may be obtained for the children. Other students who chronically do not conform to socially acceptable behavior in the home or the school need the attention of trained and experienced professional social workers provided through the social agencies of the communities. Such workers become acquainted with the home background of children—the complete study and evaluation of a situation, its interpretation in terms of stresses and strains involved in causation, and the carrying out of treatment measures designed to remedy the fundamental difficulties. The methods used in social work are principally threefold: case work, group work, and "community" or social welfare organization. Case work, or individualized services to persons and families with various problems is the most highly developed and represents the core of professional practice. Group work is usually associated with leisure time activities for young people. Social welfare organization includes various processes of cooperation between agencies and groups interested in similar objectives.

Most large communities have established a council of social agencies. From this council, the director of guidance and staff members may obtain help in locating professional assistance and the information needed in making a referral to such agencies. Social agencies may be supported by Community Chest organizations, churches, and city, county, and state governmental organizations dealing with problems involving child support, family counseling, and vocational employment of minors. Some of the organizations from which information may be obtained are:

1. Aid to the blind, county department of welfare
2. Aid to dependent children
3. American Public Welfare
4. American Red Cross
5. American Social Hygiene Association
6. Association of the Junior Leagues of America, Inc.
7. Child Welfare League of America
8. Children's Aid Society
9. Council of Social Agencies
10. County child welfare services
11. General relief
12. Family Service Association of America

Service Clubs and Fraternal Organizations

A knowledge of the service and fraternal organizations is very useful to the director of guidance and the counseling staff. Such organizations are interested in vocational guidance, and many have standing committees to provide personnel and financial aid for special guidance projects such as career conferences, the occupational information library, and field trips to business and industry. They will also provide food, clothing, and medical care for families who need help. Many provide college scholarships, student loan funds, and part-time jobs for students in the community. Some of the service clubs that may be of assistance are:

1. American Legion, Child Welfare Division
2. Amvets
3. Benevolent and Protective Order of Elks
4. Daughters of the American Revolution
5. Fraternal Order of Eagles
6. Independent Order of Odd Fellows
7. International Association of Lions Club
8. Kiwanis International
9. Knights of Pythias
10. Loyal Order of Moose
11. Optimists International
12. The Shriners of North America

Religious Groups

Many churches provide pastoral counseling, youth group activities, and other programs of social service, such as counseling on juvenile delinquency. Young people often have questions about moral issues, doubts about religious teachings, and conflicts over church membership. In some cases, such as religious doubts, they prefer to discuss the matter with the school counselor rather than their pastor. In other situations, referral to workers in the church is in order. The counselor will be guided in such referrals by the preference of the client in that, before a referral can be made, the client must accept and agree to it.

Information about services may be obtained by contacting the following organizations:

1. Local council of churches
2. American Friends Service Committee
3. Catholic Welfare Bureau
4. Jewish Family Service
5. Lutheran Welfare League
6. National Council, Protestant Episcopal Church, Department Christian Social Relations
7. National Jewish Welfare Board
8. Salvation Army

9. Young Men's and Young Women's Christian Association
10. Young Men's and Young Women's Hebrew Association

Governmental Agencies

Youth services are also provided by governmental agencies which are created by law, regulated by law or official pronouncement, and supported by taxation. Such agencies may be erected to perform one simple and clear-cut service, or they may offer many and varied services. Governmental agencies serve the political areas for which they were created; such areas may be local, countywide, statewide or nationwide in scope.

One governmental agency which has a service that should be utilized in many secondary schools is the United States Employment Service. Through the state and local branches of this agency, the director of guidance or the counseling staff members may arrange for high school senior students to take the *General Aptitude Test Battery.* The results are interpreted to the students by counselors from the agency and used in the vocational placement of students, without cost to the school or student.

Another referral source for the counselor is the local branches of the Division of Vocational Rehabilitation. This agency exists to provide for rehabilitation services of physically and mentally handicapped and to bridge the gaps between rehabilitation and gainful employment. Through intensive counseling, physical and psychological rehabilitation techniques, selective placement, and workshop procedures, apparent unemployables acquire the skills to become occupationally established. The agency provides guidance in the selection of new work or job placement, training in school or industry for a job better fitted to client's disability, and removal or correction of the disability to fit the client for a new job. Eligible for the services are men and women of working age (sixteen years of age or older) who have substantial job handicaps resulting from physical and mental impairments. Such impairments may be visible or hidden disabilities such as amputation, spastic paralysis, partial blindness, tuberculosis, arthritis, deafness, and heart disease. This service is available at no cost to employers and employees.

The following governmental agencies provide varied services and information useful to the school's guidance program.[3]

A. State Departments of Health

1. Divisions of child hygiene
2. Divisions of dental hygiene

---

[3]Based on Herman J. Peters and Gail F. Farwell, *Guidance: A Developmental Approach.* Chicago: Rand McNally & Co., 1959, pp. 478–479.

   3. Divisions of communicable diseases
   4. Divisions of public education

B. State Departments of Public Welfare
   1. Divisions of social administration
     (a) Services for crippled children
     (b) Services for the blind
     (c) Child welfare services
     (d) Public assistance services
   2. Divisions of Mental Hygiene
     (a) Community child guidance services
     (b) Community welfare classes for retarded children
     (c) Special state schools

C. Divisions of Vocational Rehabilitation

D. State Departments of Education, Divisions of Guidance, and Divisions of Special Education

E. State Schools for the Deaf and for the Blind

F. United States Department of Health, Education, and Welfare
   1. Children's Bureau
   2. Bureau of Public Assistance
   3. Office of Education
   4. Public Health Service

Children and Youth Organizations

Almost every community has organized children and youth agencies which extend worthwhile recreational and socializing experiences. Some communities have coordinated their children and youth organizations to more effectively combat juvenile delinquency. These organizations have two major aims in their programs: (1) to meet the needs of normal young people, varying as they do in race, nationality, religion, and economic and cultural backgrounds; and (2) to meet the special needs of the so-called "vulnerables" or predelinquents.

The staff members in these organizations quite often are knowledgeable about children's home backgrounds and can provide the counselor with many observations as to the way the child functions in such organizations.

Organizations which may be contacted for services in this respect are

   1. American Junior Red Cross
   2. American Youth Hostels
   3. Boys' Club Federation

4. Boys' Clubs of America
5. Boy Scouts of America
6. Catholic Youth Organizations
7. Camp Fire Girls of America
8. Child Study Association of America
9. Distributive Education Clubs of America
10. Future Business Leaders of America
11. Future Farmers of America
12. Future Homemakers of America
13. Girl Scouts of America
14. Girls' Service League of America
15. Vocational Industrial Clubs of America.

Universities and Colleges

More and more colleges and universities are conducting field service functions for schools in their area or state. The Departments of Education and Psychology and the Divisions of Guidance and Counseling will help school counselors initiate or extend a guidance program, select and train personnel, conduct child study projects, improve counseling procedures, evaluate the guidance program, plan physical facilities for guidance, and carry on teacher in-service training conferences. The colleges and universities often provide test scoring services and consultant services on use and interpretation of tests. For more information on these services, contacts should be initiated with the state supported colleges and universities.

IDENTIFYING COMMUNITY GUIDANCE RESOURCES

One of the basic steps in the improvement of a guidance program is to take stock of what is currently available in terms of community resources. Even in schools in which a guidance program of some consequence has been in operation for a number of years, it is not uncommon to discover community resources not previously recognized.

School counselors have yet to be particularly effective in understanding their communities and in knowing how to discover and make available the countless resources that exist wherever people live in association. Even in communities that seem barren of resources, there is an infinite wealth that counselors have often failed to tap. A study by Hoyt and Loughary bears this out. They surveyed the school counselors in non-metropolitan secondary schools in Iowa as to their acquaintance with and use of referral sources. Among their findings was that the mean acquaintanceship of Iowa counselors with referral sources was 58 percent while the mean usage was only 12 percent. Their conclusions were

1. School counselors in the non-metropolitan high schools of Iowa are not well acquainted with referral sources available to them.

2. In view of the expected need and opportunity to refer students in non-metropolitan Iowa high schools, it does not seem that school counselors are making very good use of referral sources available to them.

3. The better trained counselors in non-metropolitan Iowa high schools are making better use of referral sources than counselors with little or no training.[4]

Guidance personnel need to identify the community resources available to them. They must know the services provided by these diverse organizations, the type of clientele that can be referred, the procedures for referral, and the like. Several sources may be used to gain a knowledge of the community resources available to the school. General information is available from the public library card catalog. Directories of social agencies are often published in the larger cities. The city directory may also be an important source of information about agencies which may extend services to youth. State colleges and universities, through their departments of education, are another source of information about referral agencies for aid for many kinds of problems. Scanning the telephone directory for agencies, organizations, and associations may be helpful in identifying local community resources useful to the guidance program.

Another way of identifying and locating the community resources is by a survey questionnaire. This technique permits the school to obtain information from large numbers of persons. It enables the school to make a complete survey of the community and its environs as a basis for an analysis of guidance resources which could be used and therefore improve the school's program materially. By obtaining the facts concerning local resources, facilities, and their scope, a determination can be made of the relative opportunities and avenues of possible referrals. Questions on such a survey questionnaire should be simple, clear-cut, and so phrased that they will have the same meaning to all who answer them. In some schools a committee has been formed to help steer the course of a proposed survey questionnaire. This committee is often composed of the director of guid-

---

[4]Kenneth B. Hoyt and John Loughary, "Acquaintance With and Use of Referral Sources by Iowa Secondary School Counselors," *Personnel and Guidance Journal,* February, 1958, pp. 388–391.

ance, administrators, teachers, and counselors. Tracing the work of such a committee may show the following steps.

1. A specific statement of the purpose of the questionnaire is developed and later incorporated in the questionnaire or in the covering letter accompanying the questionnaire.

2. A preliminary draft of the information wanted is prepared and an investigation conducted to find out if any of the desired information has already been assembled by other agencies.

3. The final draft of the questions to be asked to obtain the desired information is completed.

4. Members of the committee secure the names of persons, agencies, and associations to be contacted. Such a list may be obtained by the methods given above. The questionnaire is then sent to these sources.

5. The principal facts uncovered in the survey that relate significantly to its purpose are then summarized and assembled into a pamphlet or booklet for school and community use (see the following).

ORGANIZING INFORMATION ABOUT COMMUNITY GUIDANCE RESOURCES

Once community resources have been identified and information received as to the type of services they provide, the persons served, the procedures for referral, their charges or fees, and so on, a card file should be established to facilitate the use of such information. The director of guidance should have responsibility for maintaining such an up-to-date file of community resources.

A comprehensive and itemized card file of community resources is essential to the guidance department. In this file there should be many standardized cards which provide summarized data concerning each particular resource agency—data which can reveal at a glance the suitability of that resource to the specific guidance purpose. Such data should therefore be organized and classified to indicate which among the many possible factors are significant in each instance. Provision should thus be made for recording upon the file card these factors: the nature of the agency, name and telephone of person to be contacted in using the service, its address, business hours, fees, persons eligible for its services, facilities, professional staff, and the procedures for utilizing its services.

No guidance program can function with full efficiency unless all appropriate data about such resources are systematically recorded on a standard card form. Cards of this type can easily be filed in any one of numerous useful ways: by type of community setting, by kind of problem, by basic approach, or even alphabetically by item name. Efficiency in the card file can be increased by using different colored cards for each separate file.

However comprehensive the resource file, it may sometimes not include the type of item needed or desired by the counselor or teacher. For example, since the materials of a particular vocational guidance agency often become outdated, the source becomes obsolete. It is therefore necessary that the resource file be constantly extended and revised through systematic routine procedures. Alert perusal of current newspapers, brochures, and similar sources, along with regular canvassing of teachers, students, and interested laymen, will provide up-to-date information at relatively slight cost and trouble.

Every community resource of whatever type must be thoroughly investigated as a basis for making a preliminary rating of that agency's potential guidance value. Before any pupils are referred to any agency, the director of guidance should make sure the professional staff of the agency are qualified to perform the needed service. Evidence of their qualifications can be obtained through their training and professional membership. For example, information on psychologists can be secured through the state psychological association, information on physicians through the American Medical Association.

Guidance personnel will find that, as they become familiar with the resources available to them and learn how to use them, they will identify more and more students who can profit from the services provided by community resources.

INITIATING THE REFERRAL PROCESS

Roberts, Hallick, and Loeb state that "The term 'intervention system' may be used generally to describe a segment of the social welfare structure (excluding the family or private enterprise) that plays a role in improving or maintaining people's incomes, health, or social functioning."[5]

When the referral decision is made, the counselor or guidance team needs to make judgments concerning the services needed and student-parental involvement. It is in meeting the needs of the special students for remedial, preventive and rehabilitative psychological and social care and attention that school counselors most often experience concern about the adequacy of their professional skills and the legal-ethical processes to follow.

---

[5]Leigh M. Roberts, Seymour L. Hallick and Martin B. Loeb, *Community Psychiatry,* Doubleday & Company, Inc. (Anchor Books) 1969, p. 176.

The counselor's or guidance team's primary considerations are: (1) What judgment do I have of the needs of this student? (2) How is this related to the information I have? (3) Based on the student's life processing, what referrals will be helpful? What will be disruptive? (4) What sources of assistance are available? (5) How soon should referral be initiated?

Experience provides the most useful discerning criteria for counselor preparation and action.

DEVELOPING WORKING RELATIONSHIPS

Intelligent use of community resources comes to realization if guidance personnel establish close working relationships with the personnel from such resources. The true basis for such a relationship is a thorough understanding of the community agency, association, or organization by school personnel, and in turn, community resource personnel understanding of the school guidance function. Stoops states

> The school must take the initiative in making personal contacts, if possible. This soon becomes a *two-way matter,* in that the agencies are founded to serve the community, and their services can sometimes best serve the people by serving with the schools. No administrator should ever assume that the responsibility of the school could be transferred to an agency; when the referral is made through the school, the agency would, in joining with the school, serve in the capacity of assisting. As long as the pupil remains in school he remains a responsibility of the school, but the school is not responsible for meeting all his needs. He may, for example, need extensive medical treatment. This is not the responsibility of the school, but making an educational experience available to him in spite of his illness is.[6]

In developing cooperative relationships, it must be remembered that such relationships take time. Developing respect, confidence, and easy cooperation is not the work of one month or even a year. Gradual growth over a longer period of time, based on the constructive handling of each occasion that arises for working together, is to be expected.

Certain general principles are suggested as possessing the key to the development and maintenance of the school's working relationships with its community resources.

1.   The school and community resource agency share a concern for the welfare of youth. Productive cooperation presents problems which

[6]From *Guidance Services,* p. 156, by Emery Stoops (ed.). Copyright 1959, McGraw-Hill Book Company. Used by permission.

must be dealt with openly and with good will. Both must recognize that the essence of a team approach resides in the development of cooperative and integrative efforts for the benefit of students served.

The 1972 issue of *Impact* emphasizes the use of the Community Resource Survey for assisting students to learn about occupations in their community. The Resource Survey provides for involvement, exploration, and contact with persons in a variety of occupations.[7]

2. Some one person in the guidance program, usually the director of guidance, must be informed of and thoroughly understand community resource agencies and their functions. He will need to know their function, purpose, *modus operandi,* chief services rendered, readiness to cooperate with the schools, channels of referral, and the like. He must convey this information to the counselors, teachers, and administrators of the school. They must have a clear understanding of the entire program—what it is for, whom it is for, and who is to do what. Faculty members must know the part they are to have in it and must understand the relationship of the school and community agencies. In turn, the director of guidance is responsible for developing an understanding of the school's function among the staff of the community agencies.

3. A comprehensive referral system must be worked out. Policies governing referral must be well formulated and clearly understood by professional persons in both the school and the community agency. It would seem to be good administrative procedure for the director of guidance or one of the counselors to have the central responsibility for making referrals. Nothing can be more detrimental to the relationship between the school and the community agencies than haphazard referral. Properly completed referrals necessitate a recognition of the time element. Most referral agencies have long waiting lists which must be taken into consideration.

4. There must be provisions for adequate communication between the school and its community resources. Both need to exchange and share pertinent case histories and other types of information that will lead toward changes in treating behavior problems. However, personnel in both the school and the community agency must maintain the confidentiality of material received in a counseling interview unless the client's permission to release such information has been secured. But both groups need to keep informed concerning the disposition and outcome of cases. Inquiries, data, case study material, and miscellaneous information must move smoothly.

[7]"The Career Kaleidoscope," *Impact,* Vol. 2, No. 2, 1972, pp. 4–11.

5. The school and the community resource recognize that each has something to contribute to youth. Each needs to respect the other. Personnel in both the school and the community agency must be certain of their objectives and operate within their limits of competence.

SUMMARY

Fostering good working relationships among school guidance and community resources personnel is an important area of the guidance director's responsibility. The complexity of modern living and intensity of problems require, at times, specialized attention of community resources, private and public. Community resources that relate to guidance must be utilized because the school has accepted responsibility for a great many aspects of the pupil's development and growth. If his needs are not being met within the school itself, then the school, as a social agency of the community, must call upon these available resources. Examples were given of the types of community resources that exist in most communities. Communities will have some of each of the following agencies either under private or public auspices: medical services, mental health agencies, social agencies, service clubs and fraternal organizations, religious groups, governmental agencies, and children and youth organizations. Ways were suggested for identifying the resources that relate to guidance in any local community.

Resources that are identified must be screened before any referral of pupils is made. A card file should be maintained of the local resources. The intelligent selection and utilization of community resources can be realized through the establishment of closer working relationships with them. The goal of coordinate, cooperative relationships is to guide each child as needs arise by utilizing every available service. Such a procedure will insure that pupils become more self-directing and will attain places as participating and worthwhile citizens. Thus, coordination between the school and the community resources becomes the key to successful working relationships.

ANNOTATED BIBLIOGRAPHY

Hill, George E., *Identifying the School's Guidance Resources.* Athens, Ohio: College of Education, Ohio University, Pupil Services Series, No. 3, 1959.
    This booklet focuses upon identifying the resources available in the school for guidance. It contains an inventory or checklist for systematically identifying the personnel, facilities, materials, and money available for guidance in any school.

Norris, Willa, Franklin Zeran, and Raymond Hatch, *The Information Service In Guidance.* Chicago: Rand McNally & Co., 1966. (Also see 1972 edition.)

Part IV presents local sources of information. Chapter 10 describes local community surveys and job analysis and follow-up results. Chapter 11 presents local sources of work experience and placement programs. These two chapters provide ways and methods of obtaining information about the community that are useful to those in guidance programs.

Stoops, Emery (ed.), *Guidance Services.* New York: McGraw-Hill Book Company, 1959.

Chapter 8 discusses the use of community resources as part of the guidance program. The chapter contains a good discussion of ways guidance personnel can work cooperatively with community agencies.

Legal and Ethical Considerations in a Guidance Program

Authority is another name for the willingness and capacity of individuals to submit to the necessities of cooperative systems. Authority arises from the technological and social limitations of cooperative systems on the one hand, and of individuals on the other. Hence the status of authority in a society is the measure both of the development of individuals and of the technological and social conditions of the society.[1]

Chapter 14

What are the legal determinants for guidance services?

What are professional determinants for guidance services?

What legal factors are involved in counseling?

What are ethical bases for guidance work?

What are sources for legal and ethical consultation in the guidance program?

In the development of a guidance program, legal and ethical matters and standards involving the procurement and use of information, counseling records, and other guidance data must be professionally arranged. Assessment and evaluation of guidance programs are now being carefully studied by school counselors, counselor educators, supervisors, and school administrators. Consequently, attention is being given to the matters of legal and ethical standards of the guidance program. Normally, a lag is discernible between the professional development of sound guidance principles and practices and the legal standards which affect these services. Implicit in the development of guidance programs are questions revolving around the legal standards and ethical relationships in the guidance function.

---

[1]Chester I. Barnard, "The Theory of Authority," pp. 632–641 in Talcott Parsons, Edward Shils, Kaspar D. Naegele, and Jesse R. Pitts (eds.), *Theories of Society.* New York: The Free Press of Glencoe, Inc., Vol. 1, 1961, 682 pp.

The school counselor is subject to the legal and ethical responsibilities appropriate to all school personnel. This chapter pays particular attention to those legal and ethical responsibilities which are within the domain of the guidance function.

LEGAL DETERMINANTS FOR GUIDANCE SERVICES

The foundations of the legal determinants for guidance services are to be found in the laws of the land. Article X of the Bill of Rights reserves to the individual states the powers not delegated to the United States by the Constitution. Each state, thus, has the inherent constitutional obligation to establish and maintain public education in the state. The Kalamazoo Case in 1874 confirmed the right to tax for the purpose of maintaining high schools. Each state has implemented its right and responsibility by organizing its own educational system. A structure of legislative and administrative documents to meet the educational needs of boys and girls has evolved in each state.

The administrative organization at the state level is represented by state departments and boards of education. Through these bodies, according to legal requirements, standards for the operation of school have been formulated and adopted. The state departments of education carry out the policies of the state boards of education. These policies are within the legislation enacted by the state legislators.

Included among these educational standards is the requirement of providing for the program of guidance services for boys and girls. In most states, standards of certification of school counselors and other guidance personnel are noted.[2] Testing programs are frequently the focus of laws in many states. The following discussion expands upon these three legal determinants for guidance services: (1) state requirements for guidance services in the schools, (2) school counselor certification, and (3) state testing programs. The recognition of the need for inclusion of a program of guidance services in the operation of public schools, while it has lately developed, has been generally recognized. Counselors are being prepared in graduate programs across the country to move into positions in both elementary and secondary schools to give individual assistance to boys and girls. Interestingly, there are no state standards for counselors in college and university settings.

---

[2]Hubert W. Houghton, *Certification Requirements for School Pupil Personnel Workers,* Washington, D.C.: Office of Education, 1967, 147 pp.

The patterns of requirements for guidance services show variety and differences of agreement among the states. The patterns also show differences in emphasizing various aspects of guidance function.

The State of Washington has developed the most comprehensive competency-based model for counselor certification. According to this plan, the State Board of Education grants certification to those who have successfully completed a training program developed by the training institution, the professional association, and the employing district. The objectives of the training program are stated in behavioral and performance standards related to client outcomes, and have no course, credit, or degree requirements specified.

The Washington plan, approved in 1968, calls for three levels of certification: (1) an intern level, (2) a supervised practice level, and, (3) a continuing level after competence has been demonstrated. One of the unique results of this approach to certification is the fact that each school district ends up with a program tailor-made to what is perceived to be the needs of that district.[3]

Most states are participating in federal reimbursement assistance under the National Defense Education Act, Title V-A, for programs of guidance and counseling. Standards vary from state to state on minimums of qualification.

Counselor Certification

Change in the certification requirements of school counselors and guidance personnel has followed the establishment of minimum standards for guidance services. Recognized as mandatory and obligatory is the professional preparation required to insure ethical and effective operation of counseling and guidance services. The professional school counselor has qualified himself via his commitment to education and through his educational background and supervised experience, as well as his personal growth, to become a technically qualified, humanely developed adult, effective in his working relationships with boys and girls, their teachers, parents, and others. Consideration of the programs of counselor education which work with the needs and requirements of the practical situations of boys and girls in school, has impressed upon the certification agencies in most states that minimal preparation standards should be mandatory. Such standards should then be enforced, employing the help of professionally qualified experts from the schools, universities, and state departments of education.

[3]Thorsen, Jack, *Counselor Certification 1971,* a paper at APGA Board of Directors Meeting, June 23–26, 1971, pp. 8–9.

The continual upgrading of counselors is a joint responsibility of the local school system, the state department of education, and appropriate university staff. Too, the impact of the counselors' professional organization is noteworthy. The state plan for the formulation and adoption of certification standards for school counselors ought to reflect the wishes, desires, background, experience, and careful thought of counselor educators, school counselors, state department of guidance supervisors, administrators, teachers, and the public.

Surveys of the scope of counselor certification requirements have been popular in recent years. However, the trend is that the point of study is more quantitively than qualitatively oriented. Surveys, whether by graduate students in counselor education or by various agencies of the state or national level, indicate that the broad coverage of requirements in certification has been, for the most part, accomplished.

Lloyd's dissertation,[4] in May, 1960, is representative of an early interest in qualitative aspects of counselor certification requirements. He reported that 59 per cent of the states had two levels of certification requirements, one for entry and one for professional level. It should be kept in mind that, often, professional level means a second certification step. The first level is also professional. Further, he learned that 64 per cent of the states had a two-year or less requirement of teaching experience. Included, also, was the requirement of adult work experience by 57 percent of the states. He concluded that certification regulation should apply to all counselors, regardless of the amount of time spent in counseling activities, and that all existing plans should have upgraded academic requirements. Derived from the results of his studies, his recommendations for counselor certification requirements included the following:

1. Teaching certificate
2. Adult work experience
3. Broad general areas of academic background
4. Personal attributes of particular importance in the counseling relationship
5. Minimum of master's degree
6. Renewal of certificate after successful experience
7. No additional teaching or work experience required for renewal of certificate.

He concluded his study by reporting that "the feasibility of establishing uniform counselor certification in all states should be investigated. The

[4]David O. Lloyd, "An Evaluative Study of Guidance Counselor Certification in the United States," unpublished dissertation, Tempe, Arizona: Arizona State University, (May 1960), p. 149.

results of this study indicate a marked agreement in all areas except that of level."[5] Again, this represents the widespread acceptance of consistent standards and requirements for guidance services programs and school counselors. It should be noted that counselor certification requirements are still awaiting that frontier breakthrough in standards pertinent to the appraisal of the personality of the effective counselor and the teaching requirement.

Statewide Testing Programs

A further determinant of the legal foundations for guidance services is found in a number of statewide testing programs (also, see Chapter 11). State departments of education, in performing their leadership and regulatory functions, incorporate these data in evaluative research. Such procedures provide an objective means for measuring outcomes of instructional programs. Further, these data can be valuable to counselors in helping boys and girls to assess their strengths and weaknesses. However, testing programs are not necessarily guidance oriented.

The base of legal responsibility is clearly shown to be that of the state, and the evolution of those practices which are most highly valued is determined by the progression of practices contributed by professional leaders in the school, the university, and community. The legal commitments which entail compliance among the many schools are regularly found to be minimal, and to represent the consensus of the best and basic features which must be included for all boys and girls in all locations. The school counselor, in organizing and developing a guidance program, must ever be alert to the need for educating his colleagues and patrons toward the optimal guidance program.

PROFESSIONAL DETERMINANTS FOR GUIDANCE SERVICES

Professional competence and leadership among guidance personnel is important and necessary for both legal and professional arrangement of guidance services. Guidance personnel have the responsibility for defining roles, encouraging growth, demanding competent practice, and instituting measures of improvement in the guidance program.

The contributions of research, experience, and conceptualization in the evaluation of the guidance process enable wiser consideration for advancement and comprehensive coverage of the need of boys and girls in the school's program. This professional activity is basically the discussion of the

---

[5] *Ibid.*, p. 165.

issues and questions involved in the life situations of counselors and gives rise to careful thinking on the larger and more encompassing issues and ethical considerations.

Professional guidance groups and associations have been responsible for consolidating the best practices and developing the consensus of approaches through scholarly study and objective analysis of diverse measures. Such groups have, through their study efforts, created their own standards of professional competence and excellence, and have joined forces with other educational groups to study the possibilities of accrediting counselor education programs at the universities and including guidance services in the schools. Professional standards and accreditation are discussed in the following sections.

Counselor Education Standards[6-10]

With the increased demand for school counselors and the growing strength of counselor education programs at the universities, professional interest has been developing for the establishment of standards for counselor education in institutions.

Historical Perspective

The selection of prospective school counselors is a significant activity in the general concern for standards for counselor education. A broad survey of significant research on this question, and derived conclusions, has been made available in an article by Hill. His report delineates the variabilities of (1) variety of roles and relationships; (2) diversity of skills, understandings, interests, and attitudes expected in the counselor's position; (3) variety of personalities; and (4) hierarchy of guidance positions. All of these variables greatly complicate the work of the school counselor.[11]

---

[6]American School Counselor Association, "A Standard of Policy for Secondary School Counselors," Washington, D.C.: American Personnel and Guidance Association, 1964.

[7]Association for Counselor Education and Supervision, "Standards for Counselors Education in the Preparation of Secondary School Counselors, *Personnel and Guidance Journal* Vol. 42 (June, 1964), pp. 1061–73.

[8]Gilbert C. Wrenn, *The Counselor in a Changing World.* Washington, D.C.: American Personnel and Guidance Association, 1962.

[9]James B. Conant, *The Education of American Teachers.* New York: McGraw-Hill Book Company, 1963.

[10]Subcommittee Report, *Preparation of Elementary School Counselors* (memorandum), Association for Counselor Education and Supervision, 1967.

[11]George E. Hill, "The Selection of School Counselors," *The Personnel and Guidance Journal* Vol. 39, No. 5 (January, 1961), pp. 355–60.

He then indicated a basis for considering the selection of counselors, as follows:

1. Selection and training programs must be geared to some clear conception of the nature of the educational personnel work for which the trainee is headed.
2. Selection and training programs will become more realistic as the guidance profession evolves greater clarification of its own goals and responsibilities.
3. Selection and training programs that assume counseling to be the sole, or even major, activity of all school counselors are currently not realistically geared to the demands of the school situation.
4. Selection and training programs must prepare workers of tremendous breadth. Currently, the school counselor must fit a professional demand of almost impossible complexity.
5. Significant research assessing the effectiveness of selection procedures must cope with the evaluation of the counselor's effectiveness. This poses problems of considerable complexity.[12]

In April 1960, at the division business meeting of NAGSCT (National Association of Guidance Supervisors and Counselor Trainers) in Philadelphia, a cooperative national study of counselor education was launched.[13] Local study committees were organized to examine the ten essential elements of counselor education programs, as follows:

1. Philosophy and objectives of counselor education
2. Counselor educator curriculum content
3. Staff qualifications and staff ratio
4. Facilities, including guidance laboratories and libraries
5. Selection standards and procedures
6. Practicum methods, facilities, and supervision
7. Placement, endorsement of candidates, and followup
8. Field services, in-service training, and relationships with state agencies and schools
9. Research
10. Administrative organization, support, and coordination of counselor education.[14]

---

[12]Hill, *ibid.*

[13]Robert O. Stripling and Willis E. Dugan, "The Cooperative Study of Counselor Education Standards," *Counselor Education and Supervision,* Spring, 1961, p. 34.

[14]Willis E. Dugan, "Critical Concerns of Counselor Education," *Counselor Education and Supervision,* Spring, 1961, p. 6.

Initially the phases of this study were planned to encourage discussion, gather data, stimulate research, and produce preliminary statements leading to the preparation of position papers on the above-named ten major aspects. Position papers were given in evaluative criteria.

A publication of import was the APGA (American Personnel and Guidance Association), Commission's report of The Commission on Guidance in American Schools.[15] *The Counselor in a Changing World*, which represented the future thinking which this committee attempted. This blueprint for school counselors stressed the importance of increasing awareness of "social forces and their influence" and of young people themselves. Because of the stress of societal forces, the program of guidance services has been a "direct outgrowth" of the values of society, which emphasize the importance of each person and his opportunity to realize his fullest development. The school counselor aids boys and girls in their development by counseling, parent and teacher conferences, continuing study of the characteristics of young people, and liaison with other personnel resources. The report emphasized the importance of the eventual development of a coordinated pupil personnel service from the present guidance program. This goes along with the work of IRCOPPS (Interprofessional Research Commission on Pupil Personnel Services). A broader undergraduate program is encouraged to develop cultural awareness. The report concludes by discussing the education of a school counselor. Here is raised the controversy of teaching experience as a necessary prerequisite to school counseling; the report emphasizes that such experience is not the only avenue to knowledge of schools and people. Besides, many prospective counselors do not wish to teach prior to becoming a school counselor.

The nature of the graduate program is outlined as a two-year study and experience plan with the following designated areas:

1. Major core in psychology
2. Major core in the study of societal forces and culture changes
3. Supervised experience in both individual and group situations
4. Applied or technique courses, not more than one-fourth of the graduate program
5. Elementary research methods
6. Understanding of basic educational philosophies and curriculum patterns
7. Introduction to ethical and legal determinants in counseling[16]

State Departments of Education were enjoined to consider in their certification requirements the suggestions of the report, such as the following:

---

[15]Wrenn, *Changing World.*
[16]*Ibid.,* pp. 167–168.

1. Require a core of social sciences and humanities
2. Require supervised experience, subject to the approval of the graduate institution
3. Free the requirement of teaching experience if supervised internship in a school situation is available

This report has been important in directing the thinking of school counselors and counselor educators to the issues in guidance today. The survey and debate over the various propositions has excited discussion and study as never before. This report has influenced the following statement on standards for counselor education.

An early professional report concerning standards for counselor education was the announcement of a statement of policy, "Standards for the Preparation of School Counselors," by the American Personnel and Guidance Association in the December 1961 *Personnel and Guidance Journal.* [17] The statement was announced to be a "point of view stressing high quality in the preparation of counselors" for excellence of counseling in the nation's schools. The introductory remarks reported that "it is not a final statement, but represents a point of progress toward a final statement of standards."

Following the description of the roles and responsibilities of the school counselor was the delineation of the course work preparation of school counselors, marking these areas for concentration during the "minimum of two years of graduate education."[18] These were:

1. Behavioral and social sciences, biological sciences, humanities
2. Processes of education
3. Professional studies in counseling
4. Supervised practice in counseling

To promise the best results by those who complete the counselor education programs, three aspects of selection were cited:

1. Selective admission
2. Selective retention or continuous evaluation throughout the program of preparation
3. Endorsement for certification for counseling

Reflecting the importance of supervised practice in counselor education was the section delimiting the three separate experiences: (1) laboratory experience, (2) counseling practicum, and (3) internship.

These were controversial aspects of the policy statement, and questions were raised as resolution of these issues was sought. For example, some

---

[17]"Standards for the Preparation of School Counselors," *The Personnel and Guidance Journal,* Vol. 40 (December 1961), pp. 401–07.
[18]*Ibid.,* p. 403.

questioned the emphasis on the social and behavioral sciences, saying it masked the infiltration of greater numbers of psychology courses. Perhaps, an even larger issue appeared in the probability that a background of preparation and experience in education will not remain as minimal entry qualifications; "such knowledge and familiarity with these processes of education may come through teaching, but other experiences also are suitable and acceptable."[19] Additional items, which seem to be lesser issues, seemed to some to be critical issues in cases of individual decision. These are "full-time, continuous study" and the "minimum of two years of graduate education."

The standards are offered as guidelines for legal qualifications of counselor education programs, for certification policies by state departments of education, and as aids to school administrators in the employment of school counselors. Additionally, this policy statement could be used by counselor education institutions as a means of upgrading the quality of the program through self-evaluation and/or evaluation by consultants and professional associations.

Further discussion of this policy statement occurred, as evidenced at the North Central ACES (Association of Counselor Educators and Supervisors) meeting in January 1962, at Lincoln, Nebraska. Action was taken by counselor educators, and state supervisors on resolutions which questioned basic proposals of the policy statement. These resolutions are worthy of support and study. The unpopularity of the term "guidance" was noted, implying that it has serious negative implications for the school guidance movement. Although the policy statement was announced as representing the contributions of many counselor educators, state supervisors, and school counselors, the issue was raised that this statement reflected unjustifiably an air of finality, and that it should be revised and made subject to wide review. An additional issue was raised when declaration was made that the place of the school counselor was in the school setting, with a "commitment to education" as shown by his qualification for teacher and counselor certification.[20] The raising of these issues and rational consideration of them is the logical avenue for the development of professionally qualified and responsible school counselors. School counselors need to participate more fully in the design of university programs designed to prepare their new co-workers. Counselor educators and supervisors need to participate more fully in the school counselor's ever-changing work setting.

The polemic nature of the APGA Policy Statement on "Standards for the Preparation of School Counselors" was illustrated in the resolution passed

---

[19] *Ibid.*, p. 404.

[20] Statement of Resolutions, North Central ACES Meeting, January 4–6, 1962, Lincoln, Nebraska.

in the APGA Senate at the Chicago 1962 National Convention. The resolution called for a new look at a policy statement on counselor education standards.

Further effort was undertaken as evidenced by

1. The publication of the Chicago position papers and reactions in *Counselor Education—A Progress Report on Standards.* Washington, D.C. American Personnel and Guidance Association, September 1962. 90 pp.

2. Action to revise the policy statement (published in December, 1961).

3. An early 1963 meeting of the standards committee under the leadership of Professor Robert Stripling, University of Florida to consider current progress in the formulation of counselor education standards.

In March, 1967, the Standards for the Preparation of Secondary School Counselors[21] were adopted. Most guidance personnel viewed the adoption as a forward-looking movement to attain quality in counselor education. And few doubted that more quality was needed. Presumably, the Standards can become guidelines for legal qualifications of counselor education departments, for certification policies by state departments of education and as aids to school administrators in the employment of school counselors.

The state is the authority for the existence of most institutions offering counselor education programs. The institution receives support and direction through a state board or agency, and yet maintains a degree of autonomy to apply professional judgments to educational decisions. Private institutions have similar relationships with boards and may have more widely varied degrees of autonomy. Further, the State Departments of Education influence the nature and quality of counselor education through their certification requirements.

The range of issues in counselor education was delineated by the differential premises in the article of Peters and Van Atta.[22] Ten areas were identified to show the range of extremes in the varying claims of counselor education programs. The differential premises were the following:

1. Generalist counselor versus specialist counselor
2. One year of graduate study versus two years
3. Clinical approach versus educational programming
4. Principles versus techniques

[21]"Standards for the Preparation of Secondary School Counselors—1967," *Personnel and Guidance Journal,* Vol. 46, No. 1 (September, 1967), pp. 96–106.

[22]Herman J. Peters and Ralph E. Van Atta, "Differential Premises in Counselor Education," *Counselor Education and Supervision,* Vol. 1, No. 1 (Fall, 1961), pp. 36–39.

5. Development of counselor as a person versus emphasis on resources, techniques, and testing materials
6. Psychological versus educational (or psychology versus education)
7. Secondary school guidance versus guidance function
8. Counseling function versus guidance function
9. Selection procedures for counselor education for a clinical person versus those for a flexible generalist
10. Training the ideal school counselor as envisaged by the coun-
    selor educator versus the one perceived to fit into a school
    administrator's plans

Peters reports the following differential premises in guidance programming suggested from a statewide study of guidance services.

1. Some schools emphasize a guidance information-centered program.
2. Some schools emphasize a developmental-focused guidance program.
3. Some schools point toward a crisis-oriented guidance program.

The information-centered program deals mostly with educational-occupational information gathering and dissemination to students. The developmentally focused programs attempt to excite every pupil to work toward
his appraised potential. The crisis-oriented program deals with special pupil
groups, e.g., troubled students. Ideally, adequate provision would include
all of these. Currently, schools espouse only one, and do little to ensure
practices consistent with their premise. Conversation among counselor
educators, supervisors, and counselors includes discussion of the central
purpose of guidance. Although not meant to be exclusive, the central objective often becomes so in reality.[23]

In 1973, Wrenn stated that after forty years of counselor education, the
priorities had been wrong. Emphasis should be placed on the process of
selection of counselor candidates rather than on didactic counselor education courses. "The person of the counselor applicant is more significant than
the amount of cognitive materials to which he is exposed."[24] In 1974, the
Association for Counselor Education and Supervision approved the report
of the ACES Commission on Standards and Accreditation.

Following the development of standards for programs of guidance services and counselor education, discussion has been directed toward imple-

---

[23]Herman J. Peters, "Differential Premises in Guidance Programming," paper at the American Educational Research Association Convention, Atlantic City, New Jersey, February 21,
1962 (mimeographed).

[24]C. Gilbert Wrenn, *The World of the Contemporary Counselor.* Boston: Houghton
Mifflin Company, 1973, p. 274.

mentation of these standards in policies of accreditation, whether by school and college associations, state organizations, or professional groups. Recognition and official authorization of the qualified status of programs thus accredited offers assurance of and confidence in program quality.

Present accreditation standards affect, to some extent, guidance programs in schools as well as counselor education programs in higher graduate institutions. Generally, the five regional accrediting associations for secondary schools and colleges have created standards for secondary school guidance programs. For example, the guidance service standard of the North Central Association of Colleges and Secondary Schools relates that this program is designed to help boys and girls make adjustments to several problem classifications—educational, vocational, social, civic, and personal. A sufficient number of trained counselors should be provided to permit individual conferences with pupils, utilizing test data and related information in counseling and pupil records.[25] Professionally trained counselors with a minimum of fifteen graduate semester hours in guidance and counseling should be employed, preferably full-time, to meet an approximate ratio of one counselor to 300 pupils.[26] The prodding of this accrediting group has provided many member schools and prospective members with the stimulus for establishing a program of guidance services.

Through the National Study of Secondary School Evaluation and its publication, *Evaluative Criteria,*[27] the program of guidance services has received continuing and growing emphasis on striving for excellence in the school program. Through self-evaluation, schools are encouraged to develop programs of finer quality than those resulting from maintenance only of minimum standards. In direct reference to guidance services, the criterion states that these are "an integral part of the educational program and are especially designed to assist in focusing the entire educational process on the individual." The specially prepared school counselor is responsible for the coordination and correlation of the guidance services and other pupil personnel services for the individual student. The expectation is clearly indicated that the guidance program will be highly related to the school's philosophy and objectives and the characteristics of the school and community. Individual items within the outline of checkpoints to be evaluated indicate acceptance of the most appropriate and excellent characteristics of the best program. The outline of the evaluation criteria on guidance services follows:

---

[25]The North Central Association of Colleges and Secondary Schools, *Policies, Regulations, and Criteria for the Approval of Secondary Schools,* p. 9.

[26]*Ibid.,* pp. 17–18.

[27]National Study of Secondary School Evaluation, *Evaluative Criteria: 1960 Edition.* Washington, D.C.: National Study of Secondary School Evaluation, 1960.

Within the scope of this outline are included various activities and techniques which afford an excellent program of guidance services. Within the section on preparation and qualifications of guidance staff, the personal, professional, educational, and experiential qualifications of the counselor are checked to determine the degree of adequacy of those personnel charged with immediate responsibility for the guidance services program.

An extension of the accreditation activity is found in the approval by state departments of education of colleges and universities engaged in teacher education and, more recently, counselor education. It has been the mutual purpose of offices of certification and colleges and universities to ensure the quality of teacher education; this interest has led to the establishment of the National Council for Accreditation of Teacher Education, in 1954.[29] Some states have been willing to recognize graduates of programs accredited by the NCATE as qualified for legal certification. The use of this accreditation procedure is credited with eliminating many administrative difficulties. The general practice previously had been that each state granted approval to those institutions in which the programs met the minimum demands for state certification. This similar practice has evolved in some states in the

---

[28] *Ibid.,* pp. 275–288.
[29] Edgar Fuller, "State School Systems," *Encyclopedia of Educational Research.* New York: The Macmillan Company (3rd ed.) 1960, p. 1392.

approval granted to institutions with acceptable programs of counselor education. For example, in Ohio the Division of Teacher Education and Certification has approved thirteen graduate programs of counselor education. Course titles identified with certification requirements are submitted by Ohio's counselor educators, and are then used by the state officer in assessing the candidate's application for certification. Along with this process, the counselor educator's recommendation is utilized in granting certification. Approval of counselor education institutions by the State Department of Education has helped to guarantee that minimum course requirements are offered in each institution.

Closely related to accreditation, although not so demanding in terms of meeting minimum standards as a guarantee of qualification, are processes of evaluation. Various evaluative propositions have recently been put forth (see Chapter 6). The question is one of distinctive counselor role. In the following case summary the school counselor is seen as a teacher.

The State, ex rel. Fox, v. Board of Education, City of Springfield, Ohio.[30]

[Cite as State, ex. rel. Fox, v. Bd. of Edn., 11 Ohio App. 2d 214.]

Schools—Guidance counselor a teacher—Certificate to counselor a teaching certificate—Performance exclusively as guidance counselor not vested.

1. Pursuant to Chapter 3319 of the Revised Code, *a guidance counselor is a teacher, and the certificates issued to guidance counselors are teaching certificates.*

2. A teacher performing under the terms of a written contract to teach cannot acquire and maintain a vested right to perform exclusively as a guidance counselor.

(No. 636—Decided December 19, 1966.)
In Mandamus: Court of Appeals for Clark County.

Mr. Richard P. Faulkner, for relator.
Messrs. Cole, Cole & Harmon, for respondent.

Kerns, J. The relator, Layne Reiger Fox, has invoked the original jurisdiction of this court to obtain a writ of mandamus to require the respondent, Board of Education of Springfield, to employ her as a guidance counselor.

Relator has been in the Springfield City School System for eleven years, where she has a continuing contract as a teacher.

---

[30]Taken from 11 Ohio Appeals 2d, 214–216.

During the school years 1960–61, 1961–62, and 1962–63, the relator received the regular notices appointing her to the position of teacher at a stipulated salary, and each of these notices contained a further stipulation that she would receive a supplemental salary in given amounts for additional duties as a part-time guidance counselor. See Section 3319.08, Revised Code.

During the school years 1963–64 and 1964–65, the relator received and approved similar notices, but during this period she devoted full time to her duties as a guidance counselor.

On May 26, 1965, relator was notified orally by the Superintendent of Schools, Paul G. Gunnett, that she was being returned to her classroom teaching duties.

Thereafter, she received the usual notice as to teachers' salaries for the 1965–66 school year. She signed and returned the notice to the respondent board, and during the 1965–66 school year performed her duties as a classroom teacher.

This case does not directly involve any question of salary. *The precise issue rather, as disclosed by the prayer of the petition, is whether the relator has a clear legal right to resume her employment as a guidance counselor.*

The relator contends that she acquired "limited contract" status as a guidance counselor while actually employed under her written "continuing contract" as a teacher.

In claiming this dual status while performing under the same contract, the relator, Mrs. Fox, apparently envisions some categorical distinction between "guidance counselors" and "teachers" which is not discernible from applicable statutes.

Relator admits that she performed no administrative duties, and, manifestly, she is not a "nonteaching employee." Chapter 3319 makes provision for only one other group—"teachers." By statutory definition, guidance counselors are "teachers" (Section 3319.09, Revised Code), and the *certificates issued to guidance counselors are "teaching certificates"* (Section 3319.22, Revised Code).

Hence, the rights of the relator stem exclusively from her position as a teacher rather than from her assignment as a counselor, and the facts fail to disclose that she was denied any benefits due her as a teacher. On the contrary, during each year of tenure, she has had a written contract in accordance with statutory requirements. Each year she accepted the written contract, signed it, entered upon and performed under the terms of the contract, and accepted the payment for her services as prescribed therein.

At no time did the respondent board employ the relator under a limited contract for counseling duties, and at no time did the relator request or claim that she was entitled to a limited contract. Indeed, the intent evidenced by all the acts of the parties to the written "limited contract" status presently claimed by the relator is but the imaginative product of a belated statutory search for relief from the classroom.

The position occupied by the relator in this case appears vulnerable for still another reason. *She obviously could not comply with her written contractual obligation "to teach" while at the same time performing under an independent, unwritten, and limited contract to counsel. Performance under one necessarily precludes any possibility of performance under the other.* And the relator, having accepted the benefits and protection afforded by the continuing written contract, must be presumed to have waived her asserted right to any independent and preferential status under the alleged unwritten contract.

In essence, the relator urges that she acquired a vested right to perform exclusively as a guidance counselor while under contract with the respondent as a teacher.

After reviewing applicable statutes in the light of the facts of this case, we perceive no clear legal right to the relief sought herein. Accordingly, the prayer for a writ of mandamus is denied.

Writ denied.

Sherer, P. J., and Crawford, J., concur.

LEGAL BASES

School counselors must know and understand the legal considerations which focus on their day-to-day relationships with boys and girls. Only by being aware of the laws and other legal documents pertaining to guidance services, especially, and to the school's total educational program, can the school counselor operate effectively and securely.

Discipline

School counselors and teachers are under the same legal regulations in regard to discipline problems. The school counselor should view discipline from a point of view consistent with guidance. Behavior is caused. Punishment, per se, is not the solution to many of the behavioral infractions occuring in schools. Because punishment is such an obvious and easily wielded technique, punishment soon becomes the only form of discipline. Punishment should be a last resort, not a first course of action. In analyzing legal action in regard to discipline of college students, Bakken brings out a principle which is applicable to elementary school, junior high school, and senior high school pupils. Bakken emphasizes that "No discipline in college should be administered to teach the individual and the study body that the rules and regulations of society must be obeyed. The minimum which will accomplish this educational purpose is advisable. Counseling an individual will many times secure the needed results without further action."[31]

---

[31]Clarence J. Bakken, *The Legal Basis for College Student Personnel Work.* Washington, D.C.: The American College Personnel Association, 1968.

The legal considerations involved in working with boys and girls in school are determined by state and federal laws, various administrative documents, and judicial decisions. The legal considerations of basic importance are those which regulate the attendance of children in schools.

Compulsory Attendance Laws

Practically all states have compulsory attendance laws which require all children between certain ages to attend school full-time. The exceptions to this fairly uniform pattern are South Carolina, which has made no legal provision for compulsory attendence, and Virginia, which allows the local district to exercise its option to adopt or suspend operation before the school laws are enforced.[32]

Presently, the laws of several states require an even higher basic age for dropping out of school than the age specified in child-labor laws for employment. The age ranges usually begin with six, seven, or eight, and extend to the upper age of sixteen, seventeen, or eighteen. Four states—Ohio, Oklahoma, Oregon, and Utah—require compulsory school attendance until age 18. However, about two-thirds of the states allow children to leave school when employment is necessary, after completion of the eighth grade. Other exceptions are noted for children who face economic hardships, who dwell unreasonable distances from transportation sources, or who are too handicapped physically or mentally to profit from school or study. Some states require employed minors to attend continuation school for a few hours a week. Some states provide for a cooperative program of working and schooling.

Responsibility for enforcement of compulsory attendance laws is assigned to attendance officers, formerly recognized as "truant officers." Adjustment of their point of view has recently changed the concept of their role from policemen to guidance workers who are interested in the individual and the special circumstances which bring him to a violation of compulsory attendance laws. The attendance officer is now becoming recognized professionally as a guidance worker familiar with the problems of delinquent children and their parents. More frequently, he is becoming known as a "visiting teacher" or school social worker. The symptomatic identification of attendance problems is now being attended to by workers trained in the field of child and adult welfare.

Involvement of the school counselor with compulsory attendance laws is, perhaps, less immediately demanding. But his familiarity with state legal

---

[32]Bureau of Labor Standards, U.S. Department of Labor, *State Child-Labor Standards: A State-by-State Summary of Laws Affecting the Employment of Minors under 18 years of Age.* Washington, D.C.: U.S. Government Printing Office, Bulletin 158, Revised 1960.

requirements and local administrative regulations is a necessary knowledge which he may be called upon to offer as information pertinent to the welfare of all boys and girls in school. The counselor often has an additional opportunity to discuss with students the necessity of being excused from school attendance on a temporary or even permanent basis. Indeed, it is our hearty recommendation that potential school dropouts be interviewed and/or counseled before they make the often wasteful and unrealistic decision to leave school. Often affecting the short-range planning to leave school is the financial lure of immediate employment. There are several sources of information on the advantages and disadvantages of leaving school which are available to students and counselors. There are, too, legal restrictions on the employment of youth which must be recognized, if pertinent to the situation. It should be pointed out that effective guidance measures should be taken to identify predisposed dropouts. It is a little late after the dropouts occur.

Laws Affecting Employment of Boys and Girls

Knowledge and understanding of work and labor laws for youth is necessary for school counselors. When involved in the placement of boys and girls in employment, counselors want to be sure that these placements have been made in accordance with the law, not only to protect the boys and girls but "to retain the confidence of employers and public." A bulletin of the U.S. Department of Labor cites the following reasons why this knowledge is important to youth placement workers:

1. More regulations govern the employment of young workers than of adults.
2. Public interest is especially concerned with the job adjustment of young people.
3. Discharge as a result of labor inspection is particularly distressing for young workers.
4. Youth placement involves cooperation with more community agencies and organizations.
5. Early work experiences are especially important.
6. More youth placements result when placement workers can advise employers with confidence.[33]

Although school counselors are not responsible for enforcement of labor laws, and are not expected to make interpretation of difficult points, they

---

[33] *Self-Training Unit on Child-Labor Laws for Youth Placement Workers.* Washington, D.C.: U.S. Government Printing Office, Bulletin 202, 1959, p. i.

must be expected to have a general knowledge of these laws and to work with them accordingly. Students may need to have the social, economic, and individual benefits of such regulations described for them, to learn to appreciate their protective and developmental features and not to regard them as needless restrictions.

Although each state has its own child-labor law, the variations among the laws are offset somewhat by the general standards of the Fair Labor Standards Act. Provisions of this law apply to any employer hiring boys and girls under minimum ages of sixteen and eighteen to be engaged in the production or delivery of goods in interstate or foreign commerce. In such activities, the minimum age of sixteen has been established in certain hazardous occupations, such as handling explosives, logging, or operating certain power driven machines. In addition, the Walsh-Healey Public Contracts Act requires that a minimum age of sixteen for boys and eighteen for girls be met if they are employees working on goods for government contracts in excess of $10,000.

Supplementary to federal law are the child-labor laws in every state. These have been found necessary to supplement federal standards and to make application to all employment possibilities. It is reported that there has been exchange of experience and information among the states which has effected a pattern among the derived laws. The provisions of state laws delineate minimum age standards, employment certificate or work permit procedures, hours of work, and hazardous occupation. These provisions are supplementary to and complete the coverage of all employment opportunities for boys and girls other than those specified under the Federal Act. The variations among the state laws do not warrant a point-by-point discussion in this material, but are of import to the school and its guidance program.

The initial opportunity for boys and girls to learn of the legal standards and requirements for their employment opportunities comes within the program of the school. Appropriately, within the activities of the occupational information service of the guidance program, the counselor can realize his responsibility for providing this information in an individual conference, upon a student's request. After-school and part-time employment are concerns for many school youths. The potential school-leaver may also fall within the age span regulated by the child-labor laws.

Regularly, in most states, the local public school officials are delegated the responsibility of issuing such work certificates or permits, which insure that the conditions for employment are satisfied, that the student is physically fit for the job, and that he has met the educational requirements. It is pointed out that these work permits also serve as a means for identifying where boys and girls are working and determining that they are protected as the law intends.

School personnel in the guidance program need to maintain familiarity with other legal requirements affecting the employment of boys and girls. The most useful source of information is likely to be the state department of labor. Examples of laws which might be useful to know are the Workmen's Compensation laws, Wage Payment and Wage Collection laws, Vocational Rehabilitation programs, Health and Safety regulations, and Social Security benefits.[34]

Enactment of Fair Employment Practices regulations by some of the states is also of interest and concern in the legal performance of guidance activities. Counselors must be aware of lawful employment practices and procedures, some of which vacillate. In Pennsylvania in 1961, according to the Fair Employment Practices Act and Fair Education Opportunities Act:

> It is illegal for elementary or secondary schools to supply either employers or institutions of higher education with transcripts or other documents containing information which will reveal the race, religion, color, ancestry, or national origin of the student.[35]

Such information must be obliterated or expunged from transcripts or documents before they can be sent on to employers or colleges and universities. In Ohio, under terms of the Fair Employment Practices Law, counselors are obliged not to cooperate with employers following illegal practices. The counselor must refer all qualified persons to an employer, who then makes the employment decision on the basis of qualifications and not on race, color, religion, national origin, or ancestry.[36] School counselors should become aware of the legal standards for employment practices with which they are to work.

Recent and Related Legislation

Current problems arising from the increasing proportion of the high school-age population and the greater numbers of unemployed youth should be of significant interest to counselors and other guidance personnel. Recent legislation[37] affecting the health, education, and welfare of youth,

---

[34] *Some Facts for Young Workers About Work and Labor Laws.* Washington, D.C.: U.S. Government Printing Office, Bulletin 208, 1959, pp. 15–18.

[35] Department Advised Concerning Illegal Information, *"Official Notices,"* The State Council of Education and Superintendent of Public Instruction, Harrisburg, Pennsylvania, Notice No. 28, September 1961.

[36] William A. Briggs, "The Counselor and Ohio's Fair Employment Practices Law," *Ohio Guidance News and Views,* XI, No. 4 (March/April, 1961), pp. 2–3.

[37] Department of Health, Education, and Welfare, *Report of Legislation Programs for Education of Youth,* 87th Congress, 1st Session, January–September 1961, (mimeographed), 7 pp.

in particular, should be recognized and implemented when possible. Of course, counselors have been aware of the extension of the National Defense Education Act, because of their interest in the Titles relating to Guidance, Counseling and Testing program, and to the Scholarship Loan Program for college students especially. Another enactment provides grants for prevention and control of juvenile delinquency by establishing authority for a coordinated and comprehensive effort to curb youth offenses. Demonstration projects, expanded programs for training additional personnel in the delinquency field, and technical assistance for communities designing an antidelinquency program are the phases of this legislative achievement. Another enactment of potential use is that which extends the training programs for practical nurses. Changing legislative measures affecting the educational and welfare opportunities for youth demand the counselor's ever alert attention.

The pressure and conflicts of adolescence and certain special difficulties of young people about to start their working life has been the interest of a group known as the National Child Labor Committee. A new division formed by this group in 1958 is known as The National Committee on Employment for Youth. For their purposes the list of problems for concentrated study was

> 1,000,000 teen-agers looking for their first full-time jobs each year
> 500,000 high school students wanting vacation or part-time jobs for the first time
> About 600,000 unemployed teenagers
> 900,000 high school dropouts
> Countless numbers of slow learners who are intellectually and educationally disadvantaged
> 450,000 children with court records whom many employers consider undesirable
> Hundreds of thousands of children of minority groups, handicapped by discrimination
> Over a quarter of a million children, ages ten to thirteen, legally working in commercial agriculture, and thousands more of all ages working illegally
> About 100,000 school-age migrant farm children.[38]

Working With Parents

Additional legal determinants in working with boys and girls must be given consideration by counselors. Working with parents is a relationship which school guidance personnel should be most expertly qualified to handle. Legal considerations involving the place of the parents begin primarily

---

[38]National Child Labor Committee, *Primer on Employment of Youth: 1958 Annual Report,* 419 Fourth Avenue, New York 16, N.Y., p. 9.

with the state laws which require that each child of compulsory school age must be sent to school. The laws of compulsory attendance have been upheld by the courts. All states have such laws.[39] However, there are certain limits upon the extent of participation by parents in the conduct of public schools. School boards are legally responsible for the conduct of the schools and may not properly delegate this responsibility. It is of interest to note that teachers can and do enjoy a reasonable degree of academic freedom. Parents who disagree with the subject matter taught or the methods employed may take action to demand change. The parents may discuss this disagreement with the teacher, or register a complaint with the board of education, or even seek redress in court "if he feels his child's constitutional rights have been impinged."[40] The wise use of this power by parents is necessary so that it is not detrimental to effective teaching.

Recently, there have been reactions between schools and parents which leave much to be desired in understanding and good feeling, to say the least. The legal bases for countermanding the parents' desires notwithstanding, the social relationships which govern the degree of effectiveness of cooperation, harmony, and mutual spirit require reasonable, cooperatively conceived methods of mutual assistance.

Typical problems involving the referral of children for psychological testing were considered by the Tri-State Pupil Personnel Conference held at Cincinnati in 1961.[41] When considering the problems of obtaining parental permission for such testing, it was pointed out that, although such a practice is highly desirable, it is sometimes impractical, especially in lower socio-economic communities. Delaying the contact of the pupil personnel program with the activities of—specifically—the visiting teacher, until the parent could or would give permission, was considered to be impractical. The conferees concluded that there should not have to be a hard and fast rule in this procedure. It was pointed out that the prescribed practice in Indiana can entail the use of legal notice, which has been found to motivate parents to accept their legal responsibilities. Another problem area concerns the availability of pupil records to parents. The most recent legal test of this topic occurred in New York in the *Thibabeau Case.* The situation involved the desire of a parent to inspect the permanent record of his child. The case was brought to the court seeking an order[42]

---

[39]Madeline Kinter Remmlein and Martha L. Ware, "School and College Law," *Encyclopedia of Educational Research.* New York: The Macmillan Company (3rd ed.), 1960, p. 1189.

[40]*Ibid.*

[41]Program notes from group meetings of the Tri-State Conference on Pupil Personnel, October 19–21, 1961, Cincinnati, Ohio. Printed in *Tri-Stater,* January 1962.

[42]Letter from Walter Crewson, Associate Commissioner, The State Education Department, Albany, New York, to City, Village and District Superintendents of Schools and Supervising Principals on "Availability of Pupil Records to Parents," November 21, 1960, p. 1. Used with permission.

to restrain the board of education from carrying out its directive that parents be permitted to inspect the records of their children which would include progress reports, subject grades, intelligence quotients, tests, achievement scores, medical records, psychological and psychiatric reports, selective guidance notes and the evaluation of students by educators.

In reviewing this case for New York school administrators, Walter Crewson, Associate Commissioner of the State Education Department, stated in the letter

The schools of the State recognize that in the manner of the education of children they act as the agent of the parents of these children and in that capacity, accordingly, they must depend upon parental cooperation and understanding.

He also related

The schools of New York State have long aimed at providing for each individual student the best possible educational opportunities. To this end, schools necessarily gather and use comprehensive information concerning students in order to establish programs of instruction to meet the students' needs. Further, such information contributes to the background against which decisions regarding courses of action are determined by individual students, their parents, and school personnel.

Within the judicial decision it was noted that

The educational interests of the pupil can best be served only by full cooperation between the school and the parents, based on a complete understanding of all available information by the parent as well as the school.

It is, of course, to be understood that, at the time of the inspection of such records by the parents, appropriate personnel should be present when necessary to prevent any misinterpretation by the parent of the meaning of the record, since some of the records here in question may not be properly evaluated and understood by some parents. The resolution under review here contains provisions for such safeguarding procedure.[43]

The decision concluded by dismissing the appeal to restrain the board of education from carrying out its directive. The interpretation for school administrators by the Associate Commissioner recommended that policies

---

[43] *Ibid.*

to determine the content and uses with reasonable safeguard of pupil records could well be adopted. He stated

> The decision asserts the right of parents and reflects the interest of the people in the work in the public schools. All school personnel will welcome the interest, they will appreciate the fundamental right . . . The decision, while pointing to the accessibility of certain school records to parents, should not be viewed as modifying time-honored methods of communication between the schools and the home.
>
> The decision does not mean that isolated bits of numerical data, such as, I.Q.'s and achievement scores, should be presented, bare of interpretation, to parents, since free availability of this type of information without experience in its application could be less than helpful . . . The vast majority of parents will doubtless continue to recognize that it is to their advantage to get information in consultation with school personnel, as in the past, and that a high value should continue to be placed on the receipt of information in an atmosphere of good faith and trust . . .
>
> The opinion of the Commissioner in the matter of permitting parents to inspect school records of children is only an official information of a practice which has long been carried out with school health records. Physicians and school nurse-teachers are thoroughly informed concerning the matter of privileged communication and physician-patient relationship. They have consistently recognized that, with respect to pupils, this privilege relates to a third person and that, in the case of a minor, parents have the legal right to be informed of the medical findings in relation to their children . . .
>
> The phrase, "Psychological and psychiatric reports, selected guidance notes and the evaluations of students by educators" in the judicial decision refers to types of information, the availability of which to parents may sometimes cause concern. In connection with these types of information, certain considerations should prevail. First, in regard to reports or anecdotal materials, it has been considered desirable practice to record observations separate from interpretations. If observations are carefully made and factually recorded, they should be helpful when used with parents.
>
> Also, a function of guidance is assistance to the student in self-understanding and in educational planning. "Guidance notes," to be most useful in this process, should be understandable as used by students, parents and counselors in discussions of their implications in relation to other available data concerning the student and his environment.
>
> Further, in order to prepare certain reports and summaries, school or referral agency staff members frequently make notes in terms of their reactions, speculations or observations. These notes often serve as personal memory-aids in expectation of later preparation of reports which

are to become a part of the student's record. Such notes ordinarily are not placed in the student's file, but represent ideas which, when combined with findings from test materials and from other sources, aid in the preparation of the student's records. These personal notes, unlike test materials and prepared reports, remain on the work sheets or jottings of the teacher or other professional personnel involved.

Whatever system of record keeping is followed, it is urged that all school personnel should share the responsibility of insuring that the student's records are appropriate and pertinent. A student's records should not include speculation, labeling, irrelevant information, or comments of questionable usefulness in educational planning. Great care and discretion must be exercised in the preparation of such records as well as in their interpretation and use.

In summary, there are two basic considerations in relation to the school's maintenance and communication of information about the student. First, the parents or guardian have the right to be informed about the abilities, school progress and problems, and the planned educational program of their children. Second, the school, in communicating such information, must assume the obligation of making sure, to the best of its ability, that the information is understandable and useful to the parent in the interests of the child's development through education.[44]

The framing of Crewson's interpretative statements was built upon the positive nature of the parent-school relationship and asked that reasonable procedures and safeguards be utilized by school personnel in the presentation of this information to parents. This appears to be in conformity with the opinion attached to the Commissioner's statement concerning the possibility of libel suits against school personnel. The opinion stated

> that a carefully worded professional opinion, rendered in line of duty by a physician, psychiatrist, psychologist, guidance counselor, principal or teacher, does not constitute a criminal libel, if it is reasonably related to the educative process and if it accurately reflects true facts.[45]

The attached legal opinion concluded: "that such a lawsuit *based on such a professional opinion* against such persons would not be successful.[46]

It was reported that clarification had been given in the New York situation, indicating confidentiality of a counselor's "working material, i.e., 'marks accumulated while the teacher is reaching a balanced judgment.' " That this is an area for clarification will be attested by all counselors.

---

[44]*Ibid.,* pp. 2–4.

[45]Letter from Charles A. Brind, The State Education Department, Albany, New York, to Dr. James E. Allen, Jr., Commissioner, The State Education Department, November 17, 1960, p. 3.

[46]*Ibid.,* p. 6.

The APGA Code of Ethics emphasizes under the counseling rubric that "The member's primary obligation is to respect the integrity and promote the welfare of the counselee or client with whom he is working." Most if not all counselors would agree with this. The question is whether or not society also supports this ethic. There is a lack of specific statutes and court cases upon which to base support for school counseling.

Also listed under "counseling" in the APGA statement is that "The counseling relationship and information resulting therefrom must be kept confidential, consistent with the obligations of the member as a professional person." Legislation is necessary if this obligation is to be sustained.

Thorsen reported in 1971 that seven states had granted full privileged communications to school counselors up to that time: Indiana, Michigan, North Dakota, Idaho, Montana, Iowa, and Nebraska. Also in his report to the APGA Board of Directors, Thorsen added that several states had granted limited privileged communications; Colorado and Delaware had statutes protecting student records; and, that Maryland had granted privileged communication to counselors involved in drug abuse problems. New Jersey, Oregon, Illinois, North Carolina, Utah, and Wisconsin were also considering various privileged communications legislation. Alaska, Arkansas, Massachusetts, and South Dakota were generating interest in 1971. In all, twenty-one states had addressed themselves to the privileged communications question by 1971.[47]

Wrenn states that the possession of information that a client gave in an interview to the effect he said he violated a law or social convention does not make the counselor legally liable to disclose this information to any officer of the law or an official of the law. He has an ethical problem on his hands but no legal one until he is under oath.[48]

The counselor must act with prudence and the full realization that he is dealing with minors. He stands in *loco parentis.* As he takes the place of the parent, so must he tell the parent if the parent requests the information. Parents have the right to know about their children.

The key to communicating with the parent revolves around (1) clarity of the information and (2) adequate conference time to explain the meaning of the guidance information relevant to the parent's child.

Although the topic has been growing in conversation among counselors, one may look at the disadvantages of privileged communication for the school counselor. The school counselor works with school and community officials. Each is interested in promoting the welfare of the boy or girl. None

---

[47]Jack Thorsen, Counselor Certification 1971, paper at APGA Board of Directors at its meeting June 23–26, 1971, pp. 9–10.

[48]C. Gilbert Wrenn, "The Ethics of Counseling," *Educational and Psychological Measurement,* Vol. 12 (1952), pp. 161–177.

can evade the law. The judicious use of information, privileged in nature, is the real challenge for anyone who believes in the resiliency of a human to become something better than he now is. All of guidance is predicated upon the proposition that, with reasoned understanding and controlled emotion, each human can reach his potential of benefit to himself and society. The hard core of ethical considerations for the school counselor revolve around (1) the developmental stage of the pupil, (2) the question of loyalty, and (3) the use of information about the pupil. Because the pupil is in a developmental stage of intellectual growth, little experience, and legal minority, considerable adult direction is needed. The question is always "How much?" Whether the counselor has a primary loyalty to the school or the pupil is another question. It is to be hoped that the fundamental loyalty is in the pupil. The use of information requires that the school counselor know his school, his community, and his staff as well as his professional responsibilities in counseling and guidance.

Currently, it seems that, if a counselor seeks and receives confidential information as a normal part of his guidance function, there is no clearcut analysis as to how he should proceed, if it becomes necessary to consider the revelation of the material. As Stevic stated, "There has been little written on the legal status of the school counselor. As a consequence it is necessary to generalize from the legal position of those who work in a similar setting."[49]

Perhaps the basis for legal action by the school counselor will arise out of his code of ethics. The moral commitment to a set of professional behavioral standards really is the bulwark against the misuse of one's responsibilities. The rapidly developing profession of school counseling has been thrust into its adulthood. This has necessitated a consideration of a definitively stated code of ethics. The next section will analyze this contemporary action.

ETHICAL BASES FOR GUIDANCE WORK

The ethical bases for school guidance work are centered in the *Code of Ethics* of the American Personnel and Guidance Association (see Appendix). Every school counselor should study this code. Every school counselor should conduct his professional responsibilities within the intent and purpose of this code.

Perhaps one of the more encompassing ethical decisions in guidance work revolves around the right to intrude into another's personal life. Williamson states

---

[49]Richard R. Stevic, "The Legal Status of the Secondary School Counselor," *Guidance Journal,* Vol. 1, No. 1 (Summer, 1961), pp. 8–15.

Most individuals reared in our western culture resist intrusion upon their 'private life.' By private life I refer to their psychological pattern of self-concepts, motivations, and perceptual framework. Since the days of the Renaissance, western culture has been perfecting in home, school, and community, the *practice and concept of* the *dignity* and *worth* of each *individual.* One index of dignity and worth is the right of each individual to become his potentiality, to perfect his individuality as he wishes—within the outer limits required by the rights of other individuals to become themselves.[50]

The ethical concerns of school counselors arise out of their concern for human relationships with pupils, co-workers, parents and patrons. As a profession develops, there arises a need for a code of ethics. Because counseling is so intimately involved with the person-to-person relationship, the school counselor must know what he should do. The "should," the "ethical," is as important as the "must," the "legal."

Arising out of the code of ethics and its refinements are solutions to the following questions:

1. What is the school counselor's basic responsibility?

2. To whom does the school counselor owe his allegiance?

3. What is the school counselor's relationship to and with parents?

4. What is the school counselor's responsibility to the teaching profession? to the guidance profession?

5. How does the school counselor assess his competency limits?

6. What is the school counselor's responsibility to himself?

7. What are the ethical dimensions in working with his teaching and administrative colleagues?

The precise answers do not seem readily available.

Ethical Responsibilities in the Use of Guidance Data

There are ethical responsibilities related to activities of the guidance program which involves the reliability of the educational and occupational information sources. In the effort to feel confident and assured, the counselor must be alert to biased, even untruthful, sources of information. Propaganda about educational or vocational opportunities may be quite useful, but should be so labeled and qualified.

---

[50]E. G. Williamson, "Uses of the Counseling Interview," *Current Status and Future Trends in Student Personnel.* Pittsburg, Kansas: State College of Pittsburg, July 1961, pp. 31–43.

In making educational plans, students are well advised to consider pros and cons of enrolling in nonaccredited schools or colleges. It does not seem appropriate that students should become dupes of false advertising or victims of false claims. High tuition charges and promises of certain, lucrative placement are often come-on's to be guarded against.

Counselors have become concerned about the difficulties of determining the reliability of each and every opportunity for post-high school education or training. Minnesota counselors have framed a list of check points to help determine the degree of confidence warranted.[51] A discussion of this problem by Hummel[52] indicates that, often, the request by a student for information is the first step towards the acceptance of that information as advice. When the counselor does not intend to imply consent of this information, he must be alert to the potential danger of "advice without consent." It would be appropriate for the counselor to base his information on consideration of the following points: (1) status of the college, school, or institute by accreditation, licensing or regulatory bodies; (2) quality of the educational opportunities provided; (3) successful placement of graduates in the occupational fields for which training is offered; (4) survey of offerings of similar institutions; (5) investment of funds, time, and energy in an institute's program as to whether it will give satisfactory returns, such as appropriate job placement; and (6) thorough understanding by the students of the educational information provided and the length of time for curriculum has been offered.

In New York, a list of registered private business schools has been provided to be used in working with students and parents weighing the merits of private business schools.[53] In other states, such as Ohio, no state approval or accreditation agencies are functioning to give this assurance to counselors. Students are urged to visit or write to training and educational institutions beforehand to obtain full information concerning accreditation.

An example of professional activities in the structuring of standards for occupational information appears in the National Vocational Guidance Association's *Guidance Information Review Service.*[54] This service has classified publications according to type and recommendation. The recommendation is phrased as "highly recommended," "recommended," or "use-

---

[51]Guideline—Private Trade or Technical Schools," *Minnesota Guidance Cues and Views,* Code: XXXIII-B-3, (Winter, 1960–61), pp. 8–9.

[52]Dean L. Hummel, "Advice Without Consent," *Ohio Guidance News and Views,* XI, No. 4 (March/April, 1961), p. 1.

[53]Bureau of Business and Distributive Education, The State Education Department, The University of the State of New York, Albany, New York, Bulletin No. 143, May 1, 1961.

[54]See copies of National Vocational Guidance Association publications, *The Vocational Guidance Quarterly.*

ful," according to the degree of adherence to NVGA Standards for Occupational Literature.

Sources for Legal and Ethical Support

Depending on local conditions, the school counselor receives legal and ethical support through (1) the school attorney, (2) his state educational association, (3) the American Personnel and Guidance Association. As time goes on, there will be more legal precedents for having a counselor's guidance action.

In regard to insurance, Gauerke emphasizes that a teacher should carefully check the protection afforded him by the school's insurance coverage. Teachers sometimes are not included for certain contingencies. "A teacher should carry adequate insurance to offset his liability in the event of accident to a pupil. A personal liability policy is one means of safeguarding life earnings and protecting against the disaster of a large verdict." This is also sound advice for a school counselor.[55]

SUMMARY

This chapter discusses legal and ethical considerations in a functioning guidance program. The head counselor or director of guidance needs to be alert to state standards for guidance, counselor certification requirements, and state recommended programs, e.g., testing. Further, the director must be alert to some of the thinking and policies related to the professional training of the school counselor. Although nebulous in many areas, the legal requirements must be appraised by the school counselor. His status in regard to counseling with privileged communication, confidentiality of information, and *loco parentis* laws are key points for consideration. The ethical bases of his profession are centered in the Code of Ethics of the American Personnel and Guidance Association. The school counselor has sources for legal and ethical understanding and support.

ANNOTATED BIBLIOGRAPHY

Drury, Robert L., and Kenneth C. Ray, *Principles of School Law*. New York: Appleton-Century-Crofts, 1965, 356 pp.

---

[55]Warren E. Gauerke, *Legal and Ethical Responsibilities of School Personnel*. Englewood Cliffs, N.J.: Prentice-Hall, Inc., 1959, pp. 264–265.

A general guide to legal bases for behavior in schools, whether by staff, parents or pupils.

Huckins, Wesley, *Ethical and Legal Considerations in Guidance.* Boston: Houghton Mifflin Company. 1968. 70 pp.
  A general discussion on the topic is given.

Ware, Martha L. (ed.), *Law of Guidance and Counseling.* Cincinnati: The W. H. Anderson Company, 1964, 178 pp.
  This book takes a look at a number of specific areas of concern for the law as it relates to the practice of counseling and guidance.

Budget, Facilities, and Public Support for Guidance

However, the relationships are particularly critical since both by law and in practice, the executive-administrative function controls and regulates all activities of the school. One of their major tools for control is the budget. Thus, to some extent, the development of the guidance services will be dependent upon the willingness of the executive-administrative activities to allow it to develop.[1]

Chapter 15

How much do guidance programs cost?

What should be included in a budget for guidance?

What physical facilities are essential for the guidance function?

What is the importance of building public support for the guidance program?

What procedures may be used to strengthen public support for guidance?

Organization of the guidance program is the means for putting the various elements and activities into systematic relationships to achieve the purposes of the program. An organization is characterized by structure, form, personnel, and activities. Organization of the guidance program includes the dissimilar elements of (1) operation and (2) growth. Operation is concerned with the means needed to achieve the purpose or objectives of the guidance program. Operation as applied to guidance includes (1) establishing policies; (2) selecting, organizing, and coordinating personnel; (3) developing the services and activities as a means of attaining the objectives of the program; (4) securing the finance essential for the program; (5) obtaining the physical facilities needed to carry on the program. The formation of

---

[1]Gerald T. Kowitz and Norma Gress Kowitz, *Operating Guidance Services for the Modern School.* New York: Holt, Rinehart and Winston, Inc., 1968, p. 259.

policies, the selection, assignment, and coordination of personnel, and the development of services and activities of guidance have been discussed elsewhere in this volume. This chapter will discuss the development of a financial budget to provide for the guidance needs of the students and the obtainment of the physical facilities to provide an appropriate setting for the conduct of the guidance function. The second element of organization —growth—is the improvement of the entire guidance process through constant interpretation and evaluation. It involves the interpretation of the guidance program to the community so that its people are continuously informed of the purpose, value, conditions, and needs of the guidance program. Evaluation—the attempt, through careful examination and study of facts and conditions, to determine the efficiency and worth of the general and specific activities—will be discussed in Chapter 17. The interpretation of the program to gain public support will be discussed in this chapter.

THE COST FACTOR OF GUIDANCE

Each of the fifty states has provided for a state education authority responsible for seeing that the education plan as a whole is continuously executed. The character and extent of this state authority—the state department of education—varies greatly, although the long-time trend has been to delegate considerable responsibility to local communities. The local board of education is the popular authority, at the community level, for planning, executive organization, and appraisal. It is the agency legally responsible for providing a considered proportion of the financial means to carry out the educational program. Control over securing and authorizing expenditures of moneys rests with the board, while the administration of finance normally rests with the superintendent of schools. School finance is highly detailed and technical. In terms of internal organization of the school district, it usually becomes the first or second subdivision of the executive authority, as districts grow.

For accounting purposes, the United States Office of Education divides educational expenditures into three major categories: current expense, capital improvement and debt service. The first category, *current expense,* includes all moneys used for the daily operation of the school. This involves six classifications: (1) general control, or the expenses of the board of education and general administration; (2) instruction, including the costs of the principal's office, teachers, clerks, instruction aids, and instructional supplies; (3) plant operation, including salaries, fuel, light, heat, water supplies, and incidental expenses; (4) plant maintenance, or upkeep expense —repairs and replacements; (5) auxiliary agencies, or services to children and community, including health, transportation, other child services, public libraries under boards of education, and other community services; and (6) fixed charges, including state and local contributions to retirement funds, insurance and judgments, rent, and other unclassified items. *Capital improvement* is the financial outlay for items with a life expectancy of more than one year, such as additions to buildings or equipment. *Debt service* includes the payment of short and long-term loans and the interest payments on these loans.

As one seeks to ascertain the cost of the guidance function in schools and to study guidance costs, he encounters several difficulties:

1. The guidance program is a newly organized service in many school districts and, as a result, few financial records covering any extended period of time are available for study.

2. The method of reporting costs (as described above) makes it extremely difficult to ascertain exact costs of guidance expenditures. For example, counselors' salaries and the costs of test materials and educational-occupational informational materials are often placed in the classroom instructional budget.

3. The use of teachers as part-time counselors adds another difficulty in computing the exact amount of time they spend in guidance work.

4. The range of guidance services and activities has made it difficult to obtain accurate cost figures. For instance, should the class time that junior high teachers spend in an orientation program to prepare their students for senior high school be included?

5. Another complicating factor in obtaining true cost figures is the problem of breaking down costs relating to heat, light, maintenance of rooms, etc. In the very few cases where guidance costs have been studied, this cost has not been determined.

The "how" and the "why" of the guidance process are described in many articles in the professional guidance journals, but there is a paucity of information as to the cost factor. "How much does it cost?" is one of the questions most frequently asked by administrators, school board members, and parents. The director of the guidance program has responsibility for the budget; and the budget is the foundation of the entire program.

Because many public pressures to economize are brought against school administrators and board members, the guidance director is in real need of guidelines that enable him to establish orderly budget practices. Such practices are needed if the costs of the guidance program are subjected to attack. The public recognizes that education is not directly concerned with the profit motive, but that it is fundamentally a service whose purpose is to develop students into responsible and responsive citizens. Nevertheless, general financial guidelines for the efficient and economical management of a guidance budget will facilitate public acceptance of the program. A realistic view of the costs of personnel services must be taken; otherwise, financial obstacles to implementation of the guidance program will not be surmounted. In some communities, acuteness of need is not enough to overcome pressures for economy that are present; therefore, financial guidelines are essential.

For several years, a "rule of thumb" was that guidance costs amounted to approximately 5 percent of the total costs of operating a school. Programs of "acceptable" quality were offered at less than that level of expenditure.

Some twenty-five years ago, Crosby[2] undertook an extensive study of guidance costs in California schools. He reported that costs in ten schools ranged from 1.4 percent to 5.9 percent of annual current expenditures, or from $5.24 to $13.03 per student per average daily attendance. The ratio of costs of personnel to costs of materials ranged from 10 to 1, to 38 to 1. Palm[3] obtained guidance costs from directors of guidance in six Minneapolis-St. Paul area high schools in 1960, and reported that the total high school expenditures ranged from $118,827 to $692,806, with a mean expenditure of $465,334 for the six schools. Total costs of the guidance services ranged from $6,400 to $33,578 with a mean expenditure of $24,532; this mean expenditure represented approximately 5.3 percent of the total high school expenditure.

The great variance in expenditures for guidance services from one section of the country to another, and the lack of uniformity of budgeting and accounting procedures make accurate estimates of guidance costs difficult. Table 15–1 presents some data on guidance costs from eleven different sources during the decade of the 1960s.

As can be seen from examining Table 15–1, the range of costs per pupil (from $60 to $11.30) is great indeed.

Data in Table 15–2 present costs of guidance drawn from a sample of 404 Ohio public schools that participated in the National Defense Education Act (NDEA), 1965–1966.

---

[2]Joseph W. Crosby, *The Cost of Guidance Services in Selected High Schools.* Los Angeles: California Test Bureau, Report E, January, 1956.

[3]Harold J. Palm, "High School Guidance: What Does It Cost Today?" *Vocational Guidance Quarterly,* Vol. 9, No. 3 (Spring, 1961), p. 171.

Table 15-1. Comparable Data From Identified Studies 1960-67
on Cost of Guidance Services in Secondary Schools

State Source of Data	Bibliographic Reference	Academic Year	Sample	Mean Pupils Per Counselor	Mean Total Guidance Cost/Pupil	Mean Counselor's Salary/Pupil	Mean Clerical Salary/Pupil	Mean Testing Cost/Pupil	Mean Materials Salary/Pupil
Arkansas	2	1966-67	240 counselors*		$11.30				
California	10	1963-64	151 districts* 514,958 students	358	32.90	$27.43	$3.93	$.77	$.24
Connecticut	1	1965-66	240 districts* 214,546 students			24.41	1.36	.53	
Eastern Suburb	7	1966-67	1 township	250	60.00				
Hawaii	3	1966-67	State*	475	18.02				
Maine	6	1966-67	68 schools*	358	26.21				
Massachusetts	5	1966-67	470 schools* 344,240 students		27.70				
Ohio	8	1962-63	379 districts* 380,732 students		20.74	19.72	1.48	.60	.27
Ohio	4	1965-66	404 districts* 690,844 students	422	25.40	22.81	1.73	.60	.23
Pennsylvania	9	1963-64	23 schools* Montgomery Cty.		25.20	21.85	2.00	.74	.32
United States	11	1960-61	5,718 districts* 8,860,000 students	482	17.80	17.26		.57	

*NDEA participating schools and/or school districts.

Table 15-1   (Continued)

BIBLIOGRAPHIC REFERENCES

1. Conecticut Department of Education; Hartford: letter dated September 27, 1967.

2. Franks, Jim Paul. "Evaluation of Guidance Services in Arkansas for 1966-67." Little Rock: Arkansas Department of Education; 1967.

3. Hawaii Department of Education, Special Services Branch; Honolulu: letter dated October 13, 1967.

4. Hopfengardner, Jerrold D., Russell F. Getson and Glenn A. Saltzman. "The Cost of Guidance Services in Ohio Secondary Schools: A Study of NDEA—Participating Schools, 1965-1966." Columbus: Division of Guidance and Testing, Ohio Department of Education; 1968.

5. Massachusetts Department of Education; Boston: letter dated September 25, 1967.

6. Maine Department of Education; Augusta: letter dated September 27, 1967.

7. Mathewson, Robert H. *Guidance Policy and Practice*. New York: Harper and Row, Publishers; 1962.

8. Saltzman, Glenn A. "Cost of Guidance in NDEA Participating School." Columbus: Division of Guidance and Testing, Ohio Department of Education; 1963.

9. Schreiner, Frank J. *A Cost Analysis of Public Senior High School Guidance Programs*. Unpublished doctoral dissertation. Philadelphia: Temple University; 1965.

10. *Staff Ratios and Costs of Guidance Services*. Research Brief No. 11. Sacramento: Bureau of Pupil Personnel Services, California State Department of Education; November 1964.

11. Warner, O. Ray. *Cost of Secondary School Guidance Services*. Washington: Office of Education; U. S. Department of Health, Education and Welfare; 1965; #OE 25046.

468

Table 15–2.   *Cost of Guidance Services in Ohio.* *

SAMPLE: 404 public school districts that participated in NDEA, 1965–1966. (This represented 54% of Ohio's school districts and 72% of Ohio's secondary school enrollment.)

COUNSELORS: 1,611 (1,344 certificated)
1,335.54 counselor equivalents

RATIO: 421.89

SALARIES: Certificated $9,787   (Salaries include the 11% contri-
Non-Certificated   7,649   bution by employing school dis-
All Counselors   9,623   tricts to the State Teachers' Retire-
ment System.)

TOTAL COST FOR GUIDANCE SERVICES PER PUPIL:

	$/PUPIL	%/COST
Counselors' Salaries	$22.81	90%
Clerical Salaries	1.73	7
Testing	.60	2
Guidance Materials	.22	1
Miscellaneous	.04	0+
TOTAL	$25.40	100%

PERCENTAGE COST/PUPIL FOR GUIDANCE SERVICES WAS OF TOTAL COST/PUPIL IN AVERAGE DAILY MEMBERSHIP: 5.8%

COST PER PUPIL ACCORDING TO SCHOOL DISTRICT ENROLLMENT (7–12):

ENROLLMENT	COST/PUPIL
300 or less	$17.62
301–700	22.49
701–1,100	22.96
1,101–1,500	23.02
1,501 or more	26.72
STATE MEAN	$25.40

---

*Data from: Jerrold D. Hopfengardner, Russell F. Getson, and Glenn A. Saltzman, "The Cost of Guidance Services in Ohio Secondary Schools: A Study of NDEA-Participating Schools, 1965–1966." Columbus: Division of Guidance and Testing, Ohio Department of Education; 1968.

Governmental Support

McDaniels, describing the impact of federal government financial support on counselor education, notes that of the estimated total dollars spent on school guidance programs, federal funds have accounted for less than 10 percent of the total. He states

> The local school systems are carrying the bulk of the financial burden for school guidance programs. In the first year of NDEA, Federal funds accounted for forty-five percent of the total spent on guidance programs in the nation. The figure has been reduced percentage-wise each year since. The principal function of Federal funds has been that of priming the pump for local effort.[4]

Governmental support for public school guidance services has come through a variety of acts: The National Defense Education Act of 1958 and its later amendments, the Elementary and Secondary Education Act of 1965 and its later amendments, and many Vocational Education Acts and amendments. However, it is true that the categorical financial support provided by the federal government for guidance has decreased since 1968.

This reduction of federal funds earmarked for guidance occurred at a time when local funds were drying up and inflation costs during the early 1970s were spiraling. The costs of guidance programs have advanced rapidly. McCreary[5] points out that among the 136 California school districts that received NDEA funds, the average cost of guidance services per secondary school student rose to $46.78 in 1968–1969, an increase of $13.88 per student over that reported in 1963–1964. Salaries of counselors and clerks accounted for 97 percent of the costs in 1968–1969, compared to 95 percent in 1963–1964.

Perhaps the only point to be made from these studies is that there exists wide variation in guidance costs in different schools. Such studies usually fail to convey exactly what is being done through the services and personnel representing the costs. In addition, the cost figures are from programs of a few years ago; personnel costs have risen considerably since many of the studies were reported. The director of guidance must be aware, and must point out, that what was considered an adequate program a few years ago is probably insufficient today. He must attempt to know what is being done elsewhere, what it costs per pupil, and what is included in this cost. He should know the percentage of the total school costs represented by the guidance program and should make a cost analysis of his program. Such costs may vary from 5 to 10 percent of the total school budget, particularly if fairly extensive guidance services are provided.

---

[4]Carl McDaniels, "The Impact of Federal Aid on Counselor Education," *Counselor Education and Supervision,* Vol. 6 (Spring 1967), Special Issue, pp. 266.

[5]William H. McCreary, "Inflation Hits Guidance Costs," *The School Counselor,* Vol. 18 (November 1970) pp. 94–95

BUDGETING FOR GUIDANCE

The rapid expansion of guidance personnel and services in the modern school makes it imperative that attention be given not only to planning, but also to financing such a program. It is no longer sufficient in most schools for the costs of guidance to be imbedded in other funds. Budgeting guidance costs provides the school with a financial forecast of the services to be performed, the policies to be followed, and the points to be emphasized. Budgeting forms the basis on which to justify requests for expenditures to meet the various requirements of the program. The guidance budget can be a constructive instrument for representing a program for developing children. It can reveal the principles and ideals of its makers. It can also have serious limitations.

Limitations of the Budget

Every administrator acknowledges that budgets may have serious limitations, some of which were enumerated years ago by Engelhardt and Engelhardt:

1. The budget is not a watchdog of the treasury.
2. The budget cannot be substituted for good administration.
3. The budget will be as good as the executive who makes it.
4. The budget improves as administration improves.
5. The budget should not be discarded because of failure to use it advantageously.
6. Responsibility should not be placed in the budget.
7. The budget should not be followed blindly.
8. Judgment should be used. Remember the budget is based on estimate.
9. The budget should not be allowed to run the school and kill initiative.[6]

Functions of the Budget

Despite its limitations, the guidance budget can serve many practical purposes. De Young has discussed the purposes of educational budgets. Included among the functions he describes are the following: (1) the budget is a servant of education in that it is a means to an end, not the end itself; (2) the budget gives an overview of each program and of the complete school program; (3) the budget develops cooperation within the school, in that

---

[6]N. L. Engelhardt and Fred Engelhardt. *Public School Business Administration.* New York: Bureau of Publications, Teachers College, Columbia University, 1927, p. 553.

those in charge of business activities and operations and those in charge of educational activities become better acquainted in cooperatively developing educational standards and finances; (4) the budget stimulates confidence among the taxpayers, in that a detailed expenditures forecast aids in presenting the needs of the school; (5) the budget authorizes expenditures, in that it serves as a basis for accounting control; (6) the budget projects the school into the future, in that budget-making means planning ahead. Planning ahead involves forecasting building programs and facilities.[7]

The Budgetary Process

Responsibility for the total school budget preparation rests with the superintendent, or in large school districts, with the assistant superintendent, who has responsibility for business affairs. The director of guidance prepares a budget detailing expenditures for guidance operations over a given period of time. His budget is then merged into a final document for the school district.

Knezevich[8] has identified three major phases of budget preparation. These include (1) determining the educational program for the period in question, (2) estimating expenditures necessary to realize the program; and (3) estimating revenues or receipts anticipated from local, state, and federal sources. He refers to these three phases as the *educational plan,* the *expenditure plan* and the *revenue plan.* He points out that while few executives in the past have included the educational plan in the budget document, more will do so in the future, for it is difficult to justify a budget request without a statement of goals envisioned.

Budget Items

The preceding chapters have discussed ways and suggested plans for the organization of the guidance program. The director of guidance should carefully plan for these provisions to be included in the guidance budget. Attention must be given to separating the guidance items from those included in the instructional budget. His guidelines for determining this will be the services and activities provided in the guidance program, including: (1) counseling; (2) educational guidance—group activities, individual activities, and materials; (3) vocational guidance—group activities, individual activities, and materials; (4) personality guidance—group activities, individual activities, and materials; (5) records and supplies; (6) testing materials; and (7) appraisal, evaluation, and interpretation.

---

[7]Chris De Young, "The School Budget" in *School Business Administration,* pp. 140–143, Henry H. Linn (ed.). New York: The Ronald Press Co., 1956.

[8]Stephen J. Knezevich, *Administration of Public Education* (2nd ed.). New York: Harper and Row, Publishers, 1969, pp. 434–435.

From these services and activities, budget items can usually be classified as salaries, materials, equipment, facilities, repairs, travel expenses, and miscellaneous expenses.

1. *Salaries of personnel.* The salaries of all full-time and part-time counselors and specialists must be included in the guidance budget. These include the director of guidance, counselors, psychologists, psychometrists, social workers, and other personnel whose duties are primarily and directly involved in guidance. Teacher-counselors who work only part-time in the guidance area should have their salaries apportioned accordingly. Too often the part-time guidance salaries of such people are charged to the classroom instructional costs. If the varied class load in a school system is five periods a day, with one period for preparation, the teacher-counselor should have only that portion of his salary actually devoted to guidance work credited to the guidance budget; that is, the preparation period should not be included in the guidance costs.

Salaries of secretarial and clerical personnel should be included on a basis proportional to the time devoted to guidance activities.

2. *Materials for guidance.* All printed materials, tests, inventories, and record supplies used in testing and guidance surveys should be accounted for in the guidance budget. Examples of guidance materials charged to the guidance budget are testing materials and their scoring costs, school handbooks, occupational briefs, monographs, abstracts, books and pamphlets on educational and career planning, cumulative record cards, record forms, and the like.

3. *Equipment.* The initial outlay for equipping the guidance offices greatly exceeds the cost of additions that come later, but all costs of new equipment and improvements must be included in the guidance budget. Equipment includes such items as tape recorders, one-way-vision mirrors, file cabinets, desks, chairs, book cases.

4. *Facilities.* Again, there are ordinarily few expenditures beyond the initial outlay for partitions, doors, paint, lights, etc. But any renovations should be included in the guidance budget.

5. *Repairs.* Any repairs to facilities and equipment should be included in the guidance costs.

6. *Travel expenses.* All travel expenses of guidance personnel in attending professional meetings, visiting other schools, traveling to career days, etc., should be charged to the guidance budget.

7. *Miscellaneous expenses.* Expenditures involving general office supplies, mimeographing, postage, keynote speakers for career days, and the like would be charged here.

Note that the above listing does not include costs of heat, light, and custodial care as such items are difficult to apportion to different departments.

Problems in arriving at an appropriate guidance budget are numerous. Frequently, sufficient school records have not been kept, and, therefore, it is difficult, if not impossible, to determine how much money has been spent in the past for guidance services. The following guidelines are important in establishing a systematic procedure for making up a budget:

1. *Initiate accurate records.* To provide information for future budget analysis, all counselors and other guidance personnel must keep accurate records of cost, time, and guidance activities. Such records are essential not only in evaluating the guidance service, but also in the establishment of future budgets.

2. *Report to the board of education data concerning the guidance budget.* In order that the school board may more fully understand and appreciate the guidance services and the necessary costs, the director of guidance should make regular and detailed reports of the guidance activities and budget to the school board.

3. *Obtain public support.* If the school board is to have the backing of the community, parents and other persons must have an understanding of the service of the guidance program.

Publicity in the local newspaper, radio and TV programs, school orientation programs, and similar activities are essential for good public relations. An enlightened public assures an efficient and expanding guidance program.

SALARY DIFFERENTIAL FOR COUNSELORS

Many school districts pay salary differentials to counselors ranging from $100 to $1000 or more per year. In some cases the differential is given only to the director of guidance, and is awarded because of his administrative responsibility. In most cases, additional salary is given to counselors who are employed on a longer basis during the school year, usually a week or so before school starts, and a week or so after it terminates. Justification for paying counselors more than teachers of comparable education and experience has been based upon the operation of the law of supply and demand.

Since the shortage of school counselors no longer exists, doubtless the salary differential will no longer be given except for longer time contracts.

ACCOUNTABILITY

There is little doubt but that the public has become increasingly concerned about educational costs. This concern, as well as others, has led educational administrators to search for ways by which they can *account* for the outcomes achieved by programs and personnel which cost money. While many educators have limited accountability procedures to cognitive outcomes, others have sought to apply systematic planning, programming, and outcome assessment to affective concerns or the personal development of students. Even more educators have moved to a planning, programming and budget system for guidance.

The planning, programming and budget system (PPBS) is a means by which expenditures are related to the accomplishment of planned goals and programs in relationship to other programs. Knezevich[9] points out that PPBS is one way to relate resources to objectives, and it is a means by which decisions are facilitated when various educational purposes and activities compete for funds. According to Knezevich, *planning,* in the PPBS, is mission-oriented or concerned with the attainment of objectives within certain time constraints. *Programming* means that plans are translated into output-oriented activities or operations, and *budgeting* is the description of programs in terms of output, or missions-to-be-accomplished, categories. Budgeting forces recognition of the fiscal implications of implementing a program. Under the PPBS, it is no longer sufficient simply to cite the input categories such as numbers of personnel employed or the expenditures needed for operations and maintenance. Moreover, an important characteristic of the PPBS is that fiscal planning goes beyond one year at a time. The first year's budget is but a part of a three or five year time span that is needed to accomplish program objectives. Systematic analysis of alternative ways of meeting objectives is fundamental to the PPBS, for without analysis PPBS simply becomes program accounting.

PPBS Applied to Guidance

Humes[10] has described the application of PPBS to guidance in the Greenwich, Connecticut, schools. The program analysis developed for junior high

[9]Stephen J. Knezevich, *Administration of Public Education* (2nd ed.). New York: Harper and Row, Publishers, 1969, pp. 435–436.
[10]Charles W. Humes, Jr., "Program Budgeting in Guidance," *The School Counselor,* Vol. 19 (May, 1972) pp. 313–317.

school services was set forth by Humes. The *goals* included (1) helping all students attain their maximum personal and educational development by offering a variety of services; (2) providing all students the opportunity for couseling services; (3) providing educational and/or occupational informational services, (4) providing staff and parent consulting services; and (5) providing information and statistics which study changes in the character of the student body. Ten objectives were cited. Two are given here as illustrations:

1.   To demonstrate individual growth increase in personal and educational development for 90 percent of the students, based on a rating sheet that will be completed by the counselor at the beginning of the seventh grade and end of the ninth grade.

2.   To provide counseling for all students who desire, or who are referred to, the counselor for counseling within three days after request, with verification of this to occur by examination of guidance office records.[11]

Four *constraints* or limiting factors that might prevent realization of goals were noted. These included counselor role expectations that were outmoded, negative attitude of building principals, limited clerical assistance, and lack of teacher and parent understanding of guidance. It was Humes' opinion that the PPBS, by its very nature, would facilitate clarification of counselor role and functions.

Esterday[12] has also described how the guidance staff in a hypothetical school district became involved in planning programs, based upon objectives, by converting the activities into budgets. To achieve the stated objectives, three alternative programs were fashioned for a three-year period. Alternative *A* called for continued emphasis upon individual counseling contacts with students, Alternative *B* was a modified procedure of individual and group contacts, and Alternative *C* was mainly group activities. The comparative inputs and procedures are reported in tabular form by Esterday and are presented here as Table 15–3.

While the objectives are not reported in Table 15–3, ten of them were stated in Esterday's article. Most counselors would probably disagree that no secretary is needed for the first year with 1,000 students; a part-time secretary is needed during the second year, with 1050 students, and a full-time secretary during the third year, with 1100 students. However,

---

[11]*Ibid.,* p. 315.
[12]Glen A. Esterday, "Budgeting for Planned Guidance Program Development," *The School Counselor,* Vol. 17 (September 1969) pp. 17–22.

Esterday's point is to illustrate how budgets may be planned for longer periods of time, to build toward certain goals. Progress toward these goals is understood better than in traditional budgets which provide only an isolated year. Data in Table 15–3 also establish a cost-for-services/services-for-cost relationship that all may see and understand better.

Table 15–3.   *Comparative Inputs and Procedures. [Source: Glen A. Esterday, "Budgeting for Planned Guidance Program Development,"* **The School Counselor,** *Vol. 17 (September 1969), p. 20.]*

| | Alternative A | | | Alternative B | | | Alternative C | | |
	69-70	70-71	71-72	69-70	70-71	71-72	69-70	70-71	71-72
Pupil enrollment	1000	1050	1100	1000	1050	1100	1000	1050	1100
Counselors employed	4	4	4	3	4	4	3	3	3
Counselor-pupil ratio	1:250	1:262	1:275	1:333	1:262	1:275	1.333	1:350	1:360
Secretary employed	0	½	1	1	1	1	0	1	1
Emphasis of counselors' work	indiv	indiv	indiv	group	tran-sition	indiv	group	group	group
Anticipated number of different students in *individual* counseling	1000	1050	1100	800	950	1100	800	840	880
Total program costs	$42,372	$44,615	$48,193	$38,167	$46,645	$47,793	$33,615	$37,418	$38,933
Cost per pupil enrolled	42.37	42.49	43.81	38.17	44.42	43.45	33.62	35.64	35.39
Cost per pupil *individually* counseled	42.37	42.49	43.81	47.71	49.10	43.45	42.02	44.55	44.24

Truly, budgeting lies at the heart of management, for it represents the fiscal interpretation of the guidance program. The reduction or approval of proposed expenditures has more than financial significance; such acts directly affect the quality and quantity of guidance services.

PHYSICAL FACILITIES FOR GUIDANCE

Although many counselors and guidance personnel have successfully carried on their work in the absence of suitable facilities, the physical setting of the guidance suite can have a positive or negative effect on work with students. It is important to conduct counseling in as favorable a physical setting as possible. Many schools, built some time ago, were planned without space for the guidance function. In such schools, officials have the problem of finding appropriate space that can be utilized for guidance. If the school has sufficient space available, then identifying suitable quarters for the guidance program is not a difficult problem; but if the school is already overcrowded, considerable ingenuity may be required. However, even schools with limited space and over-taxed budgets have managed to provide some guidance facilities. Probably no counselor ever has an ideal situation in such arrangements. Some schools have converted an unused classroom into counseling offices; others have made use of cloak closets, storerooms, hallways, or corridors; and still others have partitioned a reception room or an office in the administrative quarters. Admittedly, these are less than ideal arrangements; nevertheless, these facilities may be made adequate for carrying on guidance services.

There has been little research in the area of physical facilities used in the guidance function. Stripling, writing in 1954, made a plea for more research to provide guidelines for those who are engaged in designing and building physical facilities in guidance. He listed thirteen questions that guidance workers should be able to answer when planning guidance facilities:

1. Why do we need physical facilities for student personnel work?

2. What facilities are needed?

3. How many square feet do we need in our guidance office?

4. How many conference rooms will we need? How large should they be?

5. How many square feet should there be in the reception room to the guidance office?

6. How many square feet do we need for storing records? For other storage facilities?

7. What space do we need for clinical services?

8. What kind of room do we need for play therapy? Should it be soundproof? What other use, if any, can be made of such a room?

9. What would be the advantage of having rooms equipped with one-way vision glass?

10. What facilities do we need for individual testing?

11. How should we arrange space for student health services?

12. Where should we locate the office of the visiting teacher?

13.   Where should student personnel services be located?[13]

Cocking, Editor of *American School and University* has written:

> All new secondary schools have an area labeled guidance. Here again
> we have recognition of an emphasis on program. There seems, however,
> to be a lack of imagination and information regarding the amount and
> character of space needed for specialized guidance services. . . . It is felt
> that the lack of definitive information concerning the purpose and
> character of guidance areas will continue to hamper their design. Con-
> tinued and detailed study of these areas will provide much needed
> information for school planners.[14]

Planning Guidance Facilities

Early planning is important, in that time and costly mistakes can be
avoided. Certain basic physical facilities are essential if the guidance program is to be performed efficiently. The planning for guidance physical
facilities should be a cooperative effort of counselors, teachers, and administrators. Architects should be included so that they may better understand
the guidance function and needs.

Committees established for planning guidance facilities will be most helpful to the architect when they describe the philosophy and functions of
guidance, and set forth the educational specifications needed to develop the
building plans. Educational specifications translate educational needs into
space requirements. They are prepared prior to the working drawings and
physical specifications of the building. Such committees are not responsible
for formulating actual building plans. The architect will take the educational specifications for guidance and fit them into a cohesive pattern with
the plans developed for other areas by other committees.

Those who are responsible for planning physical facilities to house the
guidance program must strive for flexibility. Buildings are long-lasting
structures, and the guidance program will no doubt change several times
during the life of the building. Flexibility can be shown in space designed
for private interviewing rooms, rooms for group work, reception areas,
clerical personnel, testing areas, and storage of files and papers.

Some time ago, Twiford suggested that diagrammatic schemes reflecting
each school's plan for guidance facilities may be advantageous to the architect

---

[13]Robert O. Stripling, "How About Our Physical Facilities—Are We Selling Student Personnel Services Short on Space?" *Personnel and Guidance Journal,* Vol. 33 (November, 1954),
pp. 170–171.

[14]Walter D. Cocking, "Secondary School Design Since World War II," *American School
and University,* 1955–1956, Vol. 27, pp. 185–191.

and to school officials. From such schemes, the architect can use his imagination and skill in developing the layout. Figure 15–1 presents two such schemes suggested by Twiford. Scheme 1 shows the preliminary planning stage which indicates the relationship of the guidance area to other areas in the building. Scheme 2 presents a more detailed pattern of the guidance area and its location with reference to related educational services.[15]

CRITERIA FOR PHYSICAL FACILITIES

Some criteria that may be helpful to those who plan physical facilities for guidance may be set forth:

1. The facility should provide privacy for counseling.

2. The facility should be located so that it is accessible to students.

3. The facility should be planned so that it can be enlarged or extended at reasonable cost.

4. The facility should be tailored to facilitate guidance activities.

5. The facility should reflect concern for esthetics. (That does not mean useless ornamental fabrication but certainly the appearance of many guidance facilities can be enhanced with some thought and effort.)

Some of these criteria will be discussed more fully.

Privacy

The most important criteria in planning guidance facilities is the matter of privacy. The counseling relationship, by definition, implies the presence of two people—the counselor and the client. Auditory and visual privacy in counseling is a fundamental requirement. The experienced counselor knows the difficulty that is often encountered in helping a boy or girl state the real problem which prompted him or her to seek help. Certainly the counselor must have the client's confidence before attempting to proceed with the counseling interview. One important element in facilitating such confidence is the client's feeling of security which comes from privacy. Nothing can limit the relationship of a counseling interview more quickly

---

[15]Don D. Twiford (ed.), *Physical Facilities for School Guidance Services.* Washington: U. S. Department of Health, Education and Welfare, 1960, p. 5.

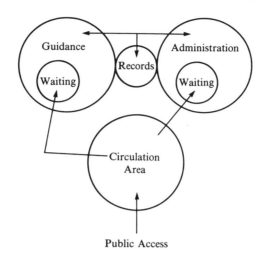

SCHEME 1

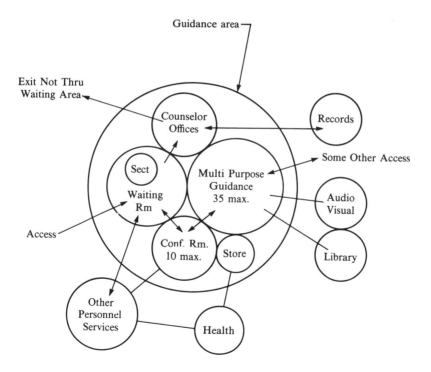

SCHEME 2

Figure 15-1.   *Diagrammatic Schemes Reflecting Plan for Guidance Facilities.*

than knowing that others are able to listen to what is being said or to watch what is going on. Consequently, counselors need offices that ensure privacy when they are interviewing students. If schools use partitions to divide a room to provide counseling offices, it is important that floor-to-ceiling partitions be used so that interviews may not be overheard by others who may be waiting to see the counselor.

Location

The question often arises as to which location is best when planning guidance physical facilities in new schools. Should the counseling offices be located near the administrative offices and school records? Or should they be placed away from the principal's office so that students and teachers do not consider the counselor as another administrative officer? Parker surveyed 177 high school principals, 182 secondary school counselors, and 113 university counselor-trainers and state guidance supervisors on attitudes toward the location of counseling offices. He submitted six different floor plans to them to obtain their opinions of the best location of the counselor's offices and related rooms. He found that, while principals preferred the counselor's office to be near the administrative offices, counselors, and counselor-educators avoided choosing these plans. Counselors seemed to prefer to separate themselves, insofar as possible, from administrative duties and from administrative quarters. Three-fourths of the respondents were dissatisfied with their present plans.[16]

If the school has more than one floor, on which floor should counseling offices be located? Should they be located on the first floor and near the school entrance, so that parents may come and go easily? These questions will have to be answered in the light of the conditions of a specific school, although there are some general conditions that it will be helpful to keep in mind. No matter what location is chosen, there will probably be advantages and disadvantages. Some suggestions that may be of assistance in making the decision as to location of counseling offices are

1. They should be near or adjacent to record files because, when these records are not readily available for the counseling interview, inadequate counseling may result.

2. They should be located as centrally as possible so that they are easily accessible to students, teachers, and parents.

3. They should be located near other special services, such as the health clinic.

[16]Kenneth H. Parker, "Location of Guidance Facilities Within the School Plant," *Personnel and Guidance Journal,* Vol. 36 (December, 1957), pp. 251–54.

Space

If only a small space can be provided for guidance quarters, the entire space may need to be used for counseling offices. Space should be chosen that is large enough for carrying on guidance services other than counseling —e.g., a reception room for students and parents and a room for small groups. Counseling rooms should neither be too large nor too small. Using too large a room for counseling seems to have an adverse effect on the intimate relationship that must be established. It is difficult, in the absence of any research on the subject, to specify the size of the counseling office. Perhaps the minimum practical size is around 6 by 8 or 9 by 10 feet. Many offices are larger than this. Sufficient space should be alloted for some filing equipment, shelves, and cupboards. Other factors—light, ventilation, and heat—need to be considered.

Reception rooms should be large enough to accommodate five or six chairs and a table. If a testing room is used for individual testing, it should be large enough for one or two tables and chairs. If it is used for small group testing and guidance, additional space is required.

Hatch and Stefflre[17] suggest the following allocations of space would be typical:

Purpose	Square Feet Needed
Counselor's office	100–125
Conference room	400–500
Reception area	200–250
Additional space for receptionist	100
Space for guidance records	3 per 200 students
Space for information service files	25
Placement coordinator's office	125
Individual testing room	100–125

Furnishings

The counselor's office should look as pleasant and inviting as possible; its appearance should be such that it provides a comfortable and relaxed atmosphere in which conversation can proceed easily. The general appearance depends on a combination of factors, such as color, cheerful decor, neatness, lighting, arrangement of equipment and furnishings, pictures, or displays. Certainly the office should be attractive, but too elaborate furnishings may have an adverse effect on other school personnel. Most schools

---

[17]Raymond N. Hatch and Buford Stefflre, *Administration of Guidance Services* (2nd ed.). New York: Prentice-Hall, Inc., 1965, p. 236.

have found it advantageous to follow a pattern similar to that set by other offices in the school. Expensive furnishings, such as a rug of exceptional quality, may be in proper taste in a school where expensive equipment and furnishings are used throughout; but, in other schools, such furnishings may be completely out of taste. The most important things, neatness and cleanliness, can be attained in every school.

The counselor's office should contain a nominal amount of furniture and equipment. The essential pieces are a desk, a chair for the counselor, and one or two chairs for visitors. There should also be some filing equipment where records can be kept within easy reach, and a bookcase. Other items, such as table lamps, pictures, and draperies, will add to the appearance of the office. It is also important that the counselor have a telephone in his office, since he often needs privacy in conversing with parents about their children, or in talking with referral agency personnel about specific students who need assistance. Here are some suggestions that may be of assistance:

1.   Chairs and desk should be arranged informally, to avoid a cold, formal atmosphere.

2.   When the counselor is interviewing a student, the student's chair should be placed near the counselor's desk, preferably at the side rather than in front of it. When the counselor talks across the desk, or to a student who is several paces away from the desk, there is too much suggestion of separation and authority.

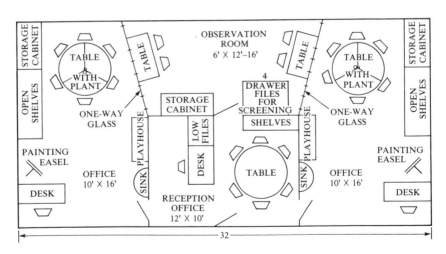

Figure 15-2.   *Elementary Counseling Center—Option 1.* [*Source: Richard C. Nelson, "Physical Facilities for Elementary School Counseling." **Personnel and Guidance Journal**, Vol. 45 (February, 1967), p. 554. Used with permission.*]

3. If there is a window in the office, the student who is being counseled should not be seated facing it. The glaring light may make him feel uncomfortable and ill at ease.

4. If possible, the student being interviewed should not be asked to sit facing the door, since this may interfere with the student's feeling of privacy.

5. Professional books and any filing equipment should be within easy reach of the counselor's desk. Then, if he needs to refer to a book or record during the interview, the interruption to obtain it will be brief.

6. During the interview, the counselor should watch for reactions to the physical surroundings, so that adjustments may be made to improve any condition that seems disturbing to a student.

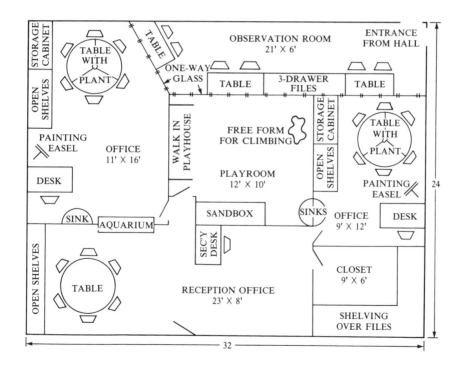

Figure 15–3.   *Elementary Counseling Center—Option 2.* [*Source: Richard C. Nelson, "Physical Facilities for Elementary School Counseling,"* **Personnel and Guidance Journal,** *Vol. 45 (February, 1967), p. 554. Used with permission.*]

Nelson[18] has proposed three possible physical arrangements within which elementary school counselors work based upon the assumptions that these facilities would (1) be attractive, (2) be designed to accommodate both group and individual counseling, (3) permit and encourage the use of play media, and (4) permit observation of counseling for the benefit of counselors-in-training and in-service education for practicing counselors. Nelson's three options are reproduced here as Figures 15–2, 15–3, and 15–4. Nelson's options assume a school population up to 700–800 pupils and one or two counselors who may work from time to time with counselor-trainees or counseling interns.

The major difference between options 2 (see Figure 15–3) and 3 (see Figure 15–4) is in providing more floor space for the reception office. Access to the observation room is gained from outside the counseling center except in option 1 (see Figure 15–2) and is a distinct advantage because it permits observers to enter without notice by the children.

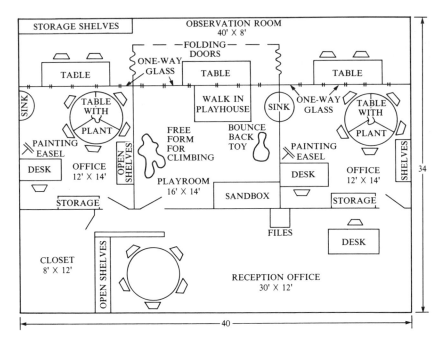

Figure 15–4. *Elementary Counseling Center—Option 3.* [*Source: Richard C. Nelson, "Physical Facilities for Elementary School Counseling,"* **Personnel and Guidance Journal,** *Vol. 45 (February, 1967), p. 555. Used with permission.*]

---

[18]Richard C. Nelson, "Physical Facilities for Elementary School Counseling," *Personnel and Guidance Journal,* Vol. 45, No. 6 (February, 1957), pp. 555–556.

Nelson suggests that the elementary school counseling office contain storage space for paper supplies and clay, open shelves for storing hand puppets, picture books, and a small play house. The observation room would contain: (1) one-way glass placed for viewing counseling rooms, (2) storage areas for files and equipment, (3) tape recorders with earphones for hearing and recording interviews, (4) chairs for observers, (5) work tables, and (6) draperies so that lights may be on in the observation room when counselors are in the counseling rooms.

THE NEED FOR PUBLIC SUPPORT

The director of guidance has interpersonal relations with many people—individuals and groups, laymen and professional workers. As a counselor, he has a professional responsibility to help people in the community become better informed about its schools and to enlist their cooperation to improve the total educational enterprise. Interpretation of the guidance program involves organized efforts to get public understanding, participation, and support for its services and activities. This has sometimes been called *public relations.* The term, public relations, does not mean a high-pressure campaign to sell the community on the guidance program as it is. Instead, public relations should mean informing and educating the community concerning ways in which children grow and learn, the objectives of the guidance program, and the means used in attaining the objectives. Public relations means building understanding among parents so they can intelligently evaluate the program and aid in its improvement. Public relations should be an inherent part, or a by-product, of the work of the school, rather than an external effort tacked onto a program. Its goal should be education by sharing and learning, rather than salesmanship and exhortation.

The basic reason for developing a good public relations program is to speed up the rate at which the guidance program can advance from its present state toward being a better program. It is assumed that the best rate of progress is reached when it results in the joint efforts of interested parents and professional guidance personnel. To do otherwise—to try to improve the guidance program without public support—proves halting and sporadic. The public does not support programs or services it fails to understand. The best way to make certain that a community supports a guidance program is to make sure it understands the program. It will understand the program better if it is involved in helping to develop the program.

School guidance programs are relatively new in terms of organization and services. Consequently, people in the community need to know the purposes, values, and services of such programs. A school that supports a guidance program best operates in a community that supports guidance.

The need for interpreting the guidance function to the public becomes apparent when one realizes that schools belong to the public; the public supports and maintains them. Thus, it is important that people in the community understand the work of the school and be in general agreement with its programs.

Cooperation between guidance personnel and the public should be a two-way affair. In addition to providing financial support, a community can be helpful to the guidance program and, therefore, to the school in many ways: its many community resources can be made available and organized for maximum utility in facilitating referral of students; the intelligence, training, and experience of citizens in various avenues of life, such as leaders in the professions, business, industry, labor, and government, can be drawn upon in a cooperative attack on some of the stubborn problems facing the guidance service; the interest and encouragement of citizens can be used to stimulate innovations in guidance practices and procedures.

Another reason which underscores the need to interpret the guidance function is that many parents do not understand the role or function of the counselor. Chapter 7 cited a few studies which showed that parents misinterpreted and misunderstood the counselor's job. A good public relations program continually emphasizes the kind of activities, the responsibilities, and the duties given to school counselors, as well as the objectives inherent in the kind of helping relationship they establish in the counseling process.

People are interested in, and want to know, what happens in their schools. They differ in their understanding of guidance, their aspirations for their children and their confidence in the school's programs. Therefore it is essential for the community to be kept fully informed of the purposes, programs, and needs of guidance.

A public can only be informed when it receives information. This means that some means to disseminate information must be established. However, the director of guidance and/or the school counselors cannot ethically use public relations programs to advance their personal interests. They should not use the dissemination of information as publicity to build a paper reputation for themselves. When interpretation of the guidance program degenerates into surface publicity for personal advancement, the spirit and morale of the many who must comprise any school program suffer. Good guidance programs are the efforts of many individuals.

Purposes of Public Relations

Some years ago, the American Association of School Administrators cited some purposes of school public relations programs. The Association has pointed out that, in a broad sense, school public relations involves all the contacts through which an impression or image about the school is established in the minds of people. Such an image may be created intentionally or unintentionally. The eight purposes of an intentional public relations program still seem relevant and are paraphrased here in respect to guidance. These purposes are:

1. To inform the public about the guidance program

2. To establish confidence in the guidance program

3. To rally support for proper maintenance of guidance programs

4. To develop an awareness of the importance of guidance

5. To improve the partnership concept by uniting parents and counselors in meeting the guidance needs of children

6. To integrate the home, school, and community in improving guidance for all children

7. To evaluate guidance programs and children's needs

8. To correct misunderstandings about the aims, objectives and activities of the guidance program.[19]

Human Relations and Public Relations

Public relations are designed to inform the public. The public is people; therefore the key to good public relations is effective human relationships. Human relations are the ways an individual relates to his social environment. They are the ways he behaves toward and responds to other human beings and include his communications to others and their communications to him.

A good public relations program includes more than periodic release of data. Founded upon human relationships, public relations communications will convey not only ideas, but feelings, aspirations, problems and goals. Such a program seeks to communicate the picture of how counselors are conducting their mission.

PROCEDURES FOR STRENGTHENING PUBLIC SUPPORT

The creative director of guidance will be inventive in determining opportunities to keep the public informed of the work of the guidance program,

---

[19]See American Association of School Administrators, *Public Relations for America's Schools,* Twenty-eighth Yearbook. Washington, D.C.: The Association, 1950, p. 12.

and in enlisting public support and assistance. The opportunities and avenues he uses will be based upon his intimate knowledge of the community, and will follow the principles inherent in any sound public relations program. As a result, interpretation, cooperation, and participation of the community can be anticipated.

Some Suggestions

Many have pointed out that public relations is an art which, when done well, presents not a sales campaign but accurate and well-reasoned information on guidance operations. To present a balanced view of guidance operations, it is imperative to prepare positive information on many aspects of the program. Various releases can be used to project the special skills, preparation, and insights of counselors, and how well certain operations are doing. Guidance personnel can become more competent in interpreting their programs to the community by following sound principles and practices of public relations. They will strengthen public support for guidance by observing the same basic professional relationships with the public as they maintain with their professional colleagues.

Public relations is, of course, more than just telling and selling. That which is done should reflect sensitivity to community interests and desires. Pumping out data about guidance to the community is not sufficient. An ever-widening range of topics about guidance is of interest to the people in a community. Some suggestions to be borne in mind in public relations work include: (1) In working with the public, the supervisor must remember that he is not dealing with an uninformed populace to whom even elementary matters must be clearly "spelled out"; therefore, patronizing or condescending attitudes are to be avoided. (2) In dealing with the public, there should be no favoritism given to influential members, but rather relationships should be characterized by sincerity, frankness, fair-dealing, and impartiality. (3) To achieve the most fruitful kind of cooperation, the director of guidance should lay honestly before the public the problems that concern him, and invite the assistance of the public in solving these problems.

Knezevich has formulated some statements that describe the development and execution of a public relations plan. His suggestions are reproduced here and include:

1. Define the missions (or image or posture) of the educational system to be projected.

2. Determine what kinds of communications will help or hinder the development of the posture desired, recognizing that distortion of the truth or news management must be avoided.

3. Identify the optimum avenues for projecting the missions of the school (based on an understanding of the appropriate media, frequency of communication, and the tone of the message).

4. Know the variety of the public to be reached (classified by religion, socioeconomic status, nationality, political belief, age level, educational orientation).

5. Develop an organization to operate the plan which involves many people but recognizes that a team of specialists is needed.

6. Allocate the resources to accomplish the public-relations program.

7. Execute the program.

8. Evaluate the effectiveness on a continuing basis.[20]

Currently all media—newspapers, television and radio—exhibit growing interest in what takes place in schools. Their interest exerts even greater pressure to inform and interpret guidance to the community.

Some additional suggestions for the conduct of a program to reach the public include

1. Establish many first-hand contacts among media personnel. Personal contacts stimulate interchange of ideas and understanding and support.

2. Present all the facts and present them in *detail.* Otherwise, suspicion will be aroused that information is being withheld, and public interest and confidence will be lost.

3. Use familiar terms. When new terms have to be used, definitions should be given and repeated. The language used should be unequivocal and forthright.

4. Use specific incidents and projects rather than abstract generalizations. By so doing, abstractions are reduced to more definite terms. To tell a group of parents that one of the goals of the guidance program is to improve the social adjustment of students, will not make as lasting an impression as illustrating the point with an example of a student who does not get along with schoolmates, and the procedures used by guidance personnel in helping him solve the problem.

5. Do not oversimplify any issue. To oversimplify issues builds narrow and inadequate public understanding.

---

[20]Knezevich, *Public Education,* p. 479.

6. In selecting news items, consider their news value and their promotional value to the school. Many studies of readers' interests indicate the following order of interest: news about people, news about things, news about ideas.

The Outreach of Guidance

The promotion of guidance services is based on understanding the people contacted directly and indirectly. The counselor in a school must achieve an understanding of the school, the professional staff, the pupils, and the parents. By achieving an understanding of the people involved, assistance can be better given to help meet the goals of educating children. Through such assistance, the teaching staff and community will more quickly realize the importance of guidance. In other words, the public relations of guidance should be "built in" in all areas of the guidance outreach.

1. Pupils. The very existence of guidance is due to young people's being in school. Students are not automations, but have a wide variety of needs and problems that are ever-changing. Group approaches of the school cannot meet the individual needs of the students entirely, so special programs of guidance must be employed to assist girls and boys in attaining their goals in life. The basic assumption of such programs is the worthiness of each individual and a respect for his individuality. Yet guidance must be known to the students. They must understand what to expect from counselors. They must feel free to consult with counselors, to use their services, and know that the guidance worker's intent is in their interest. The personal attitude of the counselor is important in inspiring understanding and confidence, but a warm smile and a friendly handshake is not enough. Pupils must feel that their contacts with counselors are helpful. If they believe counselors can help them with their planning and problems, they will develop a positive feeling toward guidance.

2. Teachers. The counselor serves students through assisting classroom teachers to understand pupils. He assists teachers by providing them with data about pupils, by interpreting behavior of pupils, and by carrying on intensive personal contacts with students referred to him by teachers. The counselor accomplishes more by skillfully and sincerely involving the teacher in a mutual problem, through a planning session or a case conference, than by acting as an expert in telling the teacher the answers.

3. Administrators. The fact that a counselor is on the staff demonstrates that someone had a vision of what this service could do. By

working with administrators and helping them develop and expand their ideas as to the objectives, procedures, and services of the program, the counselor constructs the bases for a smoother functioning program. Factual material about services rendered tells administrators a better story than idealized brochures which extoll the virtues of the program without supporting facts. Such material helps administrators interpret the program to the community.

4. Parents. Parents are a special group within the community. They often are the most valuable public relation resource available to the counselor. A testing program, counseling, the securing of a scholarship, a better adjustment in class, an improvement in grades, the blossoming of an extremely shy girl after being encouraged to enter a co-curricular activity, the feeling that someone is interested in their particular child—all of these will be noticed by parents. In turn, parents will discuss these things with their friends and neighbors. Thus, further understanding and support from the community will be achieved.

Avenues for Public Understanding

The community will judge the school not only by the reactions of the children to their school work and by the friendliness and sociability of the staff, but also by the tone and efficiency with which the school operates as an organization. The counselor's normal contacts with outside-of-school professional people such as those in the social agencies provide a good opportunity to demonstrate to the public how efficiently the guidance program can operate, and can serve to strengthen the public's confidence in the guidance program. For example, careful maintenance of records involving outside individuals and organizations, precautionary measures to safeguard confidential information, punctuality in making and keeping appointments, systematic follow-up of problems referred to outside agencies, prompt and courteous response to requests for information—all help to create a sense of respect for and satisfaction with the school's guidance program.

In the space available here, it is not possible to catalog all the ways of reaching the public that are available to the school's guidance program. Avenues for interpretation vary to a great extent according to the community. However, ten of the most typical channels that can be utilized toward this end are briefly described:

1. Television and radio. Several schools and agencies have used television and radio as vehicles for announcements about guidance programs. Talks, panel discussions, forums, "mock" interviews and case conferences are often presented on both television and radio. Some

schools have been able to establish elaborate programs for interpreting their programs to the public by using pupils and actual recordings of school activities.

2. Community newspapers. Community newspapers are used to announce and report guidance activities. They are used to report surveys, follow-up studies, workshops, special studies, special reports, and awards. Particularly, human interest material about pupils, their plans, and their achievements can be used by newspapers.

3. School newspapers and newsletters. Several school counselors say they arrange to be interviewed by student reporters once or twice during the time when the school newspaper is being prepared each month. They provide information about special programs dealing with guidance, about course changes, new courses, scholarship examinations, college and career information, scholarship recipients, and individual pupils' career choices, special awards, and honors.

Many schools use the school newsletter as a means of acquainting parents with guidance activities, testing programs, and other curricular and guidance information.

4. Open house. The open house program in most schools has been used as a vehicle for conveying information to the parents about their pupils and about the guidance services available. In some schools, the counselor has used the open house for short interviews with parents. This practice has its problems, created by too many people, too much noise, and too little privacy. Other counselors have prepared displays or have had pupils prepare projects, posters, and exhibits, or have given a talk as part of the evening program.

5. Bulletins and brochures. Bulletins and brochures are used to discuss the over-all guidance program or to describe specific programs and activities, such as the results of a follow-up survey. Brochures are designed for and distributed to pupils, teachers, parents, general citizenry, community club groups, community leaders, school boards, business, industry, government organizations, and other guidance agencies.

6. Faculty meetings. Faculty meetings are often used to plan or to discuss case conferences, to talk about guidance services available to teachers and pupils, and to show teachers how to assist in the guidance program and methods for assuming their responsibilities in guidance. New services, programs, and activities are introduced and interpreted in faculty meetings.

7.   Speakers' bureau. School counselors have gained recognition for guidance through providing speakers to community groups. Speakers' bureaus, upon request from various organizations, have been able to come up with the names of speakers in almost any area of guidance and occupational information desired. The more complete the list of people equipped to do this work, the more adequate is the information about guidance in the community. This first-hand contact is probably the most valuable and most effective.

8.   School assemblies. School assemblies are used for such things as making announcements about guidance services, presenting talks or lectures about guidance services and procedures, presenting information about colleges and careers, and presenting former students who describe conditions and problems they have faced since leaving school.

9.   Bulletin boards. Bulletin boards are used for making announcements of guidance services, examinations, scholarships, panels, talks, broadcasts, articles about guidance in newspapers or magazines, and visits of business, industrial, college and state employment personnel. Newly available brochures, bulletins, and college catalogs are often displayed.

10.   School yearbooks. Many school yearbooks exhibit pictures and provide information dealing with the guidance program. In schools where the guidance program is outstandingly popular, several pages are often given to this subject.

ANNOTATED BIBLIOGRAPHY

Shertzer, Bruce, Rolla F. Pruett, and Norbet J. Nelson, *The Guidance Physical Facility.* Indianapolis, Indiana: Indiana State Department of Public Instruction, Bulletin 213, 1965.

Twiford, Don D., *Physical Facilities for School Guidance Services.* Washington: U. S. Department of Health, Education, and Welfare, Office of Education, 1960.
    This booklet is a concise statement of suggestions for planning and improving physical facilities for guidance. The different areas of the physical arrangements are described and sample floor plan layouts are presented.

Warner, O. Ray, "Cost of Secondary School Guidance Services." Office of Education, U. S. Department of Health, Education, and Welfare; 1965; 25 pp.
    This booklet is helpful in analyzing various costs of secondary school guidance services.

Improving Guidance through In-Service Education and Communication

Professional energies can now focus on improvement efforts rather than programs associated with numerical growth. Quality programs may be possible if broad-scale quantity endeavors are not required. . . . Looking only to the immediate future and the problems arising out of our first five years with the league, it is apparent that staff development and school improvement of the kind described here (school-university staff development collaboration) must be legitimized by the school district as an approved and rewarded in-service activity.[1]

Chapter 16

Why is in-service education in guidance important?

Who is responsible for conducting guidance in-service education programs?

What basic principles should be observed in carrying out an in-service education program?

What approaches may be utilized in in-service education programs?

What methods may be used to keep the staff informed of guidance activities, developments, and personnel?

In-service education for guidance work is sometimes conceived as the formal activities organized for the purpose of extending and broadening the knowledge, understandings, and skills of the guidance worker. This definition is somewhat narrow in that it ignores many of the day-to-day contacts among teachers, administrators, and counselors which influence, favorably or adversely, the development and management of the guidance program. Thus it needs to be understood that the in-service education program consists of formal and informal aspects. It includes all the activities engaged in by professional personnel during their service designed to contribute to their improvement on the job. In this chapter, attention will be focused upon those activities that are promoted and directed by local school officials for this purpose in the area of guidance.

---

[1]Jack R. Frymier (first part of quote) and John I. Gallad (second part of quote), "Models of Staff Development," *Theory Into Practice,* Vol. 11, No. 4 (October 1972), p. 205, p. 213.

In-service education should be designed to advance the guidance competencies of teachers, counselors, and administrators. If there is a desire for improvement in the guidance program on the part of the staff—a desire arising from an interest in meeting needs—and, if given an opportunity through an organization to pursue needed changes, improvements, and cooperation, improvement will most likely occur. If there is no desire to improve, the finest in-service education program will be futile in practice. The degree to which in-service education becomes a cooperative program is dependent upon the degree to which a staff understands and accepts the principle that an effective guidance program can help them and that they can help the guidance program. Teachers and staff members sometimes resent an in-service education program. Some reasons why they may fail to cooperate in an in-service education program in guidance may be summarized here: (1) teachers object to a program which may add to their already overloaded schedules, especially in these days of specialization; (2) many schools have in-service programs just because they think it is "the thing to do"; (3) many teachers are not sure what is expected of them in projected in-service programs, or of what value they may be to them; (4) it is not always possible for schools to provide time during the school day for faculty members to participate in training programs, and as a result, the day of the teacher is extended; and (5) in-service education has often been considered a group procedure exclusively, and although each faculty group will have several common training needs, some faculty members will have training needs not common to the group. In spite of these blocks to in-service education, the fact remains that the growing complexity of the educational enterprise makes expertise necessary in all areas and at all levels. In view of the harm that can be done to an individual in the name of guidance, competence in this area is an essential condition among all personnel performing various guidance responsibilities.

The basis purpose of in-service education in guidance is to promote the improvement of guidance understanding, attitudes, and skills among the professional staff. With the rapid expansion of knowledge in the area, continuous in-service education is needed.

THE IMPORTANCE OF IN-SERVICE EDUCATION

The assumption that in-service education is important to a functioning guidance program is based on the belief that all staff members of the school are key persons in the guidance organization. The quality of each staff member's contribution depends upon his competence. If he is inadequately prepared, lacking in the knowledge and skills to perform the guidance functions expected of him, he can have a deleterious effect on the program. Several factors account for the need for in-service programs, including the rapid turnover of school personnel, new knowledge that accumulates about techniques and practices, and the changing character of many communities.

Relating Guidance to Contemporary Challenges of Education

A major outcome of systematic in-service education programs is that they relate guidance to contemporary challenges confronting counselors, teachers, and students. Three characteristics of such programs may be set forth.

1.   A good in-service education program in guidance uses relevant processes for selection of goals and activities. This involves what may be called purpose-establishing behavior. The intent is to help staff members choose with care the ends for which they strive. It is a function grossly neglected in most in-service education programs.

2.   A good in-service education program in guidance is based upon selecting and using means appropriate to learning and other goals. Here we are dealing with effectiveness of performance and with purpose-achieving behaviors. The aim is to help staff members find and employ, without wastefulness, the necessary and proper means to reach the chosen ends.

3.   A good in-service education program in guidance provides staff members with the opportunity to respond to an increasing range of phenomena and relationships with understanding, appreciation, and appropriate action. This characteristic has to do primarily with the emerging person and his performance.

Perhaps the chief outcomes sought are in the form of increasing openness—both to the world (i.e., to new experiences) and to the self, with a continuing dialogue between the patterns of thinking established by earlier experiences and the insights provided by new experiences, so that reformulation results in new behaviors with which to confront an ever-engaging world. The entire process involves self-other delineations leading to new integrations and mutual enhancement. It is a process through which the staff member comes to know who he is in relation to other professionals, and the ways he can use to improve his work.

Alleviating Background Deficiencies

Many members of the staff will have had no preservice preparation in guidance. Therefore, some attention must be given to alleviating deficiencies in their background preparation. The thought here is not to take the teacher out of the field for which he has developed some especial competency, but rather to assist him to develop additional skill with which to further enhance his competencies. Some writers have pointed out that many teachers without formal training (and even without being aware of it) are doing a competent job of performing the guidance role expected of them. However, there should be a much more systematic basis for the development of guidance services than dependance upon the chance that the teacher might do a creditable job in this field. The work of making teachers into better guidance personnel must be carried on continuously. The importance of doing so is revealed through a survey of staff members: often one sees unevenness in preparation, immaturity of beginning teachers, the complex nature of the guidance function, and the harm resulting from work poorly done.

The need for in-service education in the area of guidance varies considerably from teacher to teacher. It will vary as much as teachers vary in training and experience, and it will vary as does their capacity to profit from such an activity. The variance of skills and insights of individual teachers needs to be cut to a minimum if the school as a whole is to develop a guidance point of view. A carefully executed plan of in-service training should be established to assist teachers in reaching maximum proficiency in performing their role and in seeing guidance as a total program.

Clarifying Individual Differences

It is often pointed out that the future of our country lies in the undeveloped potentialities of the young people who attend our schools, no two of whom are alike. These young people differ in mental, emotional, and physical characteristics. Knowledge in the field of differential psychology is growing rapidly, and the major generalizations from this increased knowledge must be understood and put into use by teachers. To understand a pupil's potentialities, teachers need to be able to make use of factual, objective, and anecdotal records of his behavior as an individual and as a member participating in relation to various groups. These understandings and skills are often made more meaningful in service and they have a better chance of being adopted in classroom practice.

Learning New Developments

Extensive developments in ability, aptitude, achievement, interest and personality tests and inventories make it necessary for teachers to know about and keep abreast of continuing progress. In the field of guidance there is a constant procession of new practices. Many techniques for understanding and studying pupil personnel have recently been improved. For example, the use of behavior observation and sociometry[2] is a skill for studying children with which few teachers are familiar. Behavior observation and sociometry can be best learned in service.

The information most useful to teachers for developing competence in dealing with personality problems of pupils usually results from observations and ratings, daily diary records, autobiographical materials, tests, and interviews. The use of these methods requires training. Teachers must learn what to observe about students, they must know how to write and study significant behavior samples. The faculty should become informed of the new developments that seem important and give promise of contributing to the betterment of the school. What better place than in-service to extend skills and to become better informed?

Utilizing Community Resources

Many new understandings and approaches pertaining to the relations between school and communities have evolved during recent years. The best use of community resources involves ways of working that teachers, counselors, and administrators must learn. The human and material resources of most communities are rich and varied. Yet the yield of these resources will be insignificant compared to what is potentially possible if ways of identifying and classifying them, acquainting the staff, and using them are developed. For example, involving staff members in a survey of youth-serving agencies in the community—their purpose, location, hours, clientele, professional personnel, fees, etc.—has proved beneficial for many teachers and counselors. Such an undertaking has led to greater use of these agencies by school personnel, and has improved communications between the school and agency personnel.

Developing Common Goals

Another important reason for conducting in-service education is that it may serve as a means to develop common goals for the guidance program among the staff. Social psychologists have repeatedly emphasized that to change a group's norms and values it is necessary for the group to experience and communicate about a common set of influences. In-service education is an excellent way to achieve this experience and communication.

[2]James R. Barclay, "Sociometry: Rationale and Technique for Effecting Behavior Change in the Elementary School," *Personnel and Guidance Journal,* Vol. 44, No. 10 (June, 1966), pp. 1067–1076.

Integration and coordination of the work of every person in the guidance program can be achieved through in-service programs.

The goal of in-service education activities is learning, change, and improvement. Observation of education practice and the findings of research indicate increasingly that an attack upon an educational problem by all persons concerned is a superior means of clarifying the understanding of all, of obtaining a commitment to policies and practices developed to remedy problem situations, and of insuring intelligent participation in attempts to implement suggested solutions. There is a need to perceive the beauty in repetitive experiences, how they enhance one, and how new dimensions are seen where before they seemed to be absent.

Finally, the importance of in-service education is seen in that if teachers are to make significant contributions in this area, they should be familiar with the guidance services and possess the ability to use guidance techniques in accordance with their responsibilities to students. Their responsibility in this respect is twofold. First, the staff needs to be acquainted with the basic concepts of guidance and have the knowledge of how to administer and use such techniques of guidance as will be of service to their pupils. Careful study of guidance techniques will help the teacher to develop some skill in their use. It should give the teacher the confidence essential to positive action in helping pupils identify and solve their problems. In-service education could be expected to give systematic direction to their efforts. Second, teachers need information as to ways to make the best use of professional guidance workers on the staff. They need to know how guidance specialists and their skills are made available to them. They need to know what is expected of them in providing guidance services. They need to become aware of their own limitations. Some guidance techniques, essential and beneficial in the hands of the trained, experienced school counselor might prove disatrous in the hands of the teacher untrained in their use. Recognition of one's own limitations and the appropriate time for referral to professional service is in itself a skill which the teacher should develop.

THE RESPONSIBILITY FOR IN-SERVICE WORK

Appropriate preparation and organization are necessary if an in-service education program in guidance is to make the effective contribution that is intended. The most important single task in the preparation of an in-service education program is the formulation of its general purposes and planning the manner in which they are to be realized. The purposes of an in-service program should be clear and compelling in their importance; they should relate to a need or a problem that has arisen out of the guidance functions of staff members. Purposes should not be contrived nor academic: there are enough problems of immediate relevancy and deep concern that there need be no difficulty in finding one or more of sufficient importance.

Leadership is essential for an in-service education program. Tentative, flexible ways of accomplishing the purpose of the program must be worked out. Analysis of selected problems into appropriate smaller divisions and a tentative determination of possible ways each of the divisions may be related to the whole must be visualized by those responsible for the conduct of the program. Leadership must be given to the organization, preparation, and the functioning of the program. Leadership will be needed to estimate the demands of the program, as in-service programs should not strain the available resources of time, energy, and money.

Leadership for such programs is the responsibility of the director of guidance. Any in-service education program in a particular building is the direct responsibility of the principal. Principals are responsible for reviewing and approving programs and for providing the impetus to move from decision into action by encouraging staff members to try new ideas and plans. The principal's conviction of the importance of in-service education in guidance will encourage and support the staff to cooperate and to become involved. Among the leadership functions exercised by the principal are providing time, facilities, and resources to stimulate and strengthen the program. For in-service education in guidance, the principal will usually delegate to the director of guidance the specific responsibility for coordination of the program. The guidance director's interest, competencies, and responsibilities relate him very closely to such a program. He will assume the responsibility for expediting the program, clearing requests for outside consultants, and coordinating the scheduling of activities. The director of guidance will seek ways to provide communication and interaction necessary for in-service work. He will need to determine avenues for identifying the guidance concerns of teachers and counselors and of enlisting the aid of large numbers of them in the planning of activities. He will plan to capitalize on the strengths provided by members of the teaching and counseling staff.

Both principal and director of guidance should be involved in the planning and carrying out of the program if recommendations and conclusions of such programs are expected to result in action. The specific form of organization of an in-service education is not as important as are the attitudes of those in positions of leadership. If the principal and director of guidance believe in their teachers and their ability to see and solve problems, opportunities will be created for teachers to work on significant problems.

In a broader sense the program must come from the entire school staff. In order for an adequate program to take place the guidance director must work with the total staff in determining what form the program will take and how it will be implemented. If there is a guidance committee in the school they can do some basic work in surveying the needs of the staff and community and recommending a program which will be of interest in some way to to every member of the staff. It is doubtful that the director of guidance will obtain the desired cooperation and thus the desired benefits from his efforts if the staff is dictated to and not consulted on the program content and form.

PRINCIPLES OF IN-SERVICE EDUCATION

Guidelines or criteria to consistently direct action in planning, organizing, and conducting in-service education activities are necessary. The in-service education program in guidance, just as any academic course or any purposeful activity of the school, must be developed in the light of what is to be accomplished, the area to be served, and the facilities and means available for the implementation of the program. It is imperative that the program be organized around local conditions.

Some ten years ago, Twiford formulated the following basic principles for building in-service education programs in guidance:

1. The school administration, authorized by the board of education, is responsible for the initiation, development, and maintenance of a continuing program of guidance in-service education:

Giving emphasis to in-service education as an administrative responsibility of the local school tends to identify it as a school-centered function, and encourages more extensive provision for planned in-service opportunities.

In carrying out this responsibility, the school administration recognizes in-service education as an integral part of the school's total educational program. In-service education, therefore, is provided during the regular school day, with no additional expenditure of time or money required on the part of the counselor. If special seminars, workshops, conferences and the like, sponsored by outside agencies, are included in the school's program of group procedures or resources, any expense involved through such activities may be assumed by the school or school system.

2. The school administration delegates responsibility to a designated person, or persons, for program planning and coordination:

The integrative and coordinative function may be conducted through an in-service committee and its chairman, or it may be vested in a specific individual (i.e., the guidance director) who may seek assistance from an advisory committee.

3. The in-service program is planned in terms of definitive objectives, based upon the uniqueness of needs within a particular school setting.

The nature of the tasks and functions related to the guidance program is determined by underlying concepts held by the school administration about the guidance function itself, including goals and expectations, and the definition of staff roles.

Appropriate in-service education experiences are planned in accordance with the philosophy and needs of a given school situation, and the professional development status of individual staff members responsible for carrying out the guidance function in that particular school setting. Not only are there differences among staff personnel as to breadth of professional preparation and competency in applying counseling skills, but inevitably there are also differences among counselors as persons. The counselor as a person is a matter of concern which rightfully should begin in the counselor selection stage and continue throughout the preparation period, with special attention provided as the counselor begins to function professionally on the job. Neither at this point nor at any other will the counselor have professional and personal needs identical with those of other counselors. Thus, not only program needs but individual needs of counselors will vary with school settings.

4. The organizational structure and procedures are flexible and adaptable to changing needs:

A core of stability is provided through a clear statement of general program purposes and an organizational framework which provides a continuing and varied pattern of specific activities to meet the common as well as differing needs of counselors.

The school administration has a responsibility for making group experiences available which may meet individual counselor needs but which are not necessarily mandatory for all counselors. Group activities in the school's planned in-service program may include various conferences (such as case conferences and conferences with consultant-specialists), workshops, demonstrations, and study groups. In addition, certain group activities centered outside of the school may contribute to professional development. These may include State or regionally sponsored workshops, conferences, and meetings, as well as program activities of local, State, and national professional associations. Such activities, though not directely planned and sponsored by the administration, may nevertheless be regarded as within the broad context of professional development and recognized as in-service education resources.

5. The school administration provides for and encourages the participation of all eligible staff members:

The school administration encourages, and perhaps should require, the continuing professional development of each staff member. As motivation, the administration may set up a system of incentives, including eligibility for higher pay status upon the completion of certain professional development requirements. Participation in in-service activities may be a part of such a system.

School systems that require evidence of progress as a basis for salary increments or promotion may choose to grant credit for participation in certain professional development activities. A number of things may be recognized by school systems as contributing to professional development, such as service on committees, conference attendance, and travel.

6. The evaluation of guidance in-service education is continuous and geared to a broader evaluation of the total educational program, its accomplishments and needs:

The guidance in-service program takes its place among procedures designed to carry out better the goals of the total educational process. The extent to which these goals are achieved, and particularly as reflected in a higher quality of guidance program, is an indication of the effectiveness of the in-service program.

The increased effectiveness of the counselor as a professional practitioner is perhaps a more direct indicator of the success of the in-service education program. The cumulative personnel record of the counselor should record his continuing professional growth and development.[3]

Basic principles of guidance in-service education programs include recognition of key concepts relevant to any in-service education program and the growth needs of teachers, counselors, and administrators. The following basic principles contain suggestions that may be useful to a staff that is planning such a program. It should be recognized that these principles are not mutually exclusive nor is a sequential step significance implied. This is true because practically all of the actions indicated by the basic principles should be involved when a group plans its work and no two groups of school personnel would proceed in an identical sequential manner.

1. *Staff members will be interested in and will work on problems that are meaningful to them.* In-service education programs will need

---

[3]Don Twiford, *Inservice Education for School Counselors.* Washington, D.C.: U.S. Government Printing Office, Bulletin OE–25844, No. 33, 1965, pp. 8–10.

to be built on topics that involve staff members emotionally and intellectually. Action as a result of such programs will occur when whatever is done is important to the staff. Planning should start with the guidance problems faculty members think important. All should participate in identifying problems.

2. *The goals of the in-service education program in guidance and the methods for obtaining them should be determined by the staff.* After determining need or identifying problem areas, careful consideration should be given to the goals of the program, and ways of approaching them. Activities should lead to positive results and actions.

3. *Opportunities should be available for staff members to relate to each other.* The goals of a program will be more quickly realized when staff members can relate to each other. Small groups or subgroups can accomplish this. Individual work and general group meetings are other ways. Individuals must feel free to express themselves; some will take initiative, accept responsibility, and provide leadership for others. Initial steps taken by individual members must bring them a feeling of achievement.

They must be aware of their competence to contribute. Participation in larger meetings is often facilitated if teachers are given an opportunity for satisfying participation in smaller groups.

4. *Many and varied types of resources are made available and are used.* In-service education programs demand the identification and use of two types of resource assistance: materials dealing with current research findings and educational literature related to the content of the problem being considered and the human resources provided by consultants or authorities in the field under study. Special care should be given to making existing resources available to groups. Expansion of professional libraries is often needed. Certain individuals in each school may be given the responsibility for assembling appropriate materials and identifying personnel that will be helpful for the problem under study.

5. *Simple means are utilized to reach decisions and to move to action.* Decisions on problems and topics discussed by the school staff must be made and actions taken. Too many teachers have experienced the exercise of diligent work over a period of time which resulted in specific ideas for action and proposals that were then filed away. Administrators must be in constant contact with what goes on in inservice groups. They must be prepared to act quickly on the decisions reached by committees or the group. Encouragement must be given by

administrators to staff members to try ideas and plans. Realism can best be achieved when the proposed practices are made close to the problem. In-service education programs must be more than talking exercises with nothing happening in between. Pretesting of ideas and trying out recommendations will come through the creation of an attitude and climate supporting such action by school administrators.

GUIDANCE ACTIVITIES FOR IN-SERVICE EDUCATION

In-service education cannot begin until someone has decided that either the performance of personnel, a procedure, a practice, or an activity of some kind, needs to be done better. Diagnosing staff needs is crucial for the success of a program because if it is inadequately done the program will fail to be readily accepted. Diagnosis involves evaluation of a staff's readiness to change. Readiness develops as a result of staff dissatisfaction with present procedures, plans, or performances.

It has been stated that in selecting in-service education topics or problems, local needs must prevail. Those responsible for the conduct of such programs might well determine if a topic is worthy of the attention of staff members by using such criteria as

To what extent does the proposed topic aim at remedying deficiencies which members possess?

To what extent does the proposed topic encourage exploration and experimentation among staff members?

To what extent does the proposed topic appear promising with respect to helping members develop competencies in the area?

To what extent does the proposed topic contain means for its evaluation?

To what extent does the proposed topic possess qualities which make it an educational activity?

The following topics have been pursued by guidance personnel for in-service education work. They are given merely as illustrations of subjects, problems or activities around which an in-service education program may be built.

Career development
Psychological education

Identifying and using community resources
The use of specialists
The teacher's role in guidance
The study of pupil behavior
The behavioral objectives of guidance
The guidance point of view
The services of guidance
Techniques of referral
The use of guidance techniques
Understanding the counseling process
Improving school records
Improving pupil-teacher relationships
Improving parent-teacher conferences
Accountability in Guidance
Using tests for guidance purposes
The relationship between guidance and curriculum planning
The availability and use of educational-occupational information
Problems that confront graduates and dropouts
Occupational opportunities for graduates and dropouts
Improving descriptions of child behavior
Interpreting tests to parents and pupils

IN-SERVICE EDUCATION APPROACHES

A wide range of approaches have been used to conduct in-service education programs in schools. It is important to keep in mind that there is no one best in-service education acitivty, and there is no one best way to get a program started. The approach in each school must be one which fits that particular school situation and emerges from the problems of primary interest to teachers, counselors, and administrators. The attention here is focused upon some of the more formal approaches to in-service education in guidance in contrast to the various activities in which teachers might independently engage in order to improve themselves. The emphasis upon programmatic activity should not be construed to mean that wide reading, convention attending, or anything else conducive to facilitating guidance insight and competency is depreciated.

Teachers' Meetings

The majority of teachers' meetings should be devoted to improving the educational program of the school. The major problems of a school are the concern of all teachers. An in-service education purpose—to make teachers conscious of their needs and difficulties, which are often only vaguely realized—can be met in meetings of the total staff. Such meetings can be made to serve as a clearing house for the exchange of ideas on common guidance problems. Information can be exchanged leading to a better understanding of pupils.

Guidance personnel can furnish leadership to stimulate discussion of guidance problems of teachers. Some schools have devoted one or more of such annual meetings to the area of guidance.

Visits to Other Schools

Another approach to in-service education is that of visiting other schools to observe their guidance practices. The purposes of such visits are to discover the especially good and promising guidance practices that are being utilized, and to obtain information for use in planning and managing the guidance program. Like any other important in-service education approach, visits to other schools need careful planning preparation. The school to be visited must know the nature of the visit, the length of the stay, the number participating, and so forth.

Workshops

In recent years, guidance workshops have become popular and widely used. The number of schools conducting such approaches prior to the opening of school is increasing. The advantages of workshops over formal professional courses are that the former (1) are tailor-made to deal with specific problems which are of concern to the group, (2) are likely to be of greater immediate practical value, (3) are group directed, and (4) are of shorter duration, their length being specifically fitted to the tasks to be accomplished.

Depending upon its purposes, size, and membership composition, workshop activities may range from intensive work on a single problem or local concern (such as planning a testing program), to a consideration of a number of larger related problems of broader and more general interest (such as consideration of the complete personnel services). Workshops should culminate in the preparation of some planned program of action.

Crabbs[4] reported positive results from conducting a "listening" workshop for teachers. The focus was upon developing listening skills and the methods used included a brief lecture, experiential activities that were videotape recorded, and demonstration and critique of model listening.

---

[4]Michael A. Crabbs, "Listening Workshops for Teachers," *The School Counselor,* Vol. 20 (September 1972), pp. 61–63.

Use of Small Group Procedures

Recent emphasis upon "change" and innovation in education has led to the use of small groups (six to eight members) working in in-service education programs. In some programs the intent is not merely to have those staff members who are involved keep pace with changes; rather, the members are viewed as the primary objects of change. Fundamentally, small groups have been used to facilitate staff members' experiential or affective learning as to how their attitudes and interpersonal relationships influence their work.

While the idea of using small group methods to develop teacher effectiveness is not new, few studies in this area have been reported. Shaw and Wursten[5] surveyed the literature about working in the schools from 1953 to 1963, and reported only four studies of group counseling with teachers or student teachers. In addition to group counseling, other group methods have been advocated for in-service education programs. For example, Jacobson[6] and Roberts[7] have used study or discussion groups designed to increase understanding of specified educational topics. Newman[8] reports a psychological consultation service for schools which utilizes, in part, small group procedures. Case study groups involving writings, films, and recordings followed by critical "what to do" discussions have been reported by Pharis.[9] Horrocks[10] and Gordon and Spears[11] have used discussions combined with review of "actual hypothetical case studies" as a means of improving teacher observation techniques. Recently, sensitivity training groups in which teachers explore their relationships with students, parents, and colleagues, plus their professional goals, have been used or advocated by Mail[12] and Rogers.[13]

It is essential to point out that small group experience is not intended to be "therapeutic," because the participants are not emotionally disturbed,

---

[5]Merville C. Shaw and Rosemary Wursten, "Research on Group Procedures in Schools, A Review of the Literature," *Personnel and Guidance Journal,* Vol. 44 (September 1965), pp. 27–34.

[6]S. Jacobson, "When School People Get Together," *The National Elementary Principal,* Vol. 44, No. 6 (May 1960), pp. 25–29.

[7]J.D. Roberts, "A Hard Look at Quality in In-service Education," *National Elementary Principal,* September, 1964, pp. 15–21.

[8]Ruth G. Newman, *Psychological Consultation in the Schools.* New York: Basic Books, 1967.

[9]W. L. Pharis, *In-Service Education of Elementary School Principals.* Washington, D.C.: National Education Association, 1966.

[10]J. E. Horrocks, *Instructors Guide for Case Study Tests in Human Growth and Development.* Columbus, Ohio: Charles E. Merrill, 1960.

[11]I. J. Gordon and W. D. Spears, "Interpersonal Perception: The Effect of Training in Perceptual Theory, Observation and Analysis of Behavior Upon Accuracy of Production of Children Self-reports." Morovia, New York: Chronicle Guidance Professional Service, Chronicle Guidance Publications, Inc. 1965–66.

[12]Dorothy Mial, "The Principal—A Change Agent," *The National Elementary Principal,* Vol. 49, No. 1 (September 1964), pp. 27–31.

[13]C. R. Rogers, "To Facilitate Learning," in *Innovation for Time to Teach.* Washington, D.C.: National Education Association, 1966, pp. 4–19.

but rather are normal and healthy people. Quite the opposite, the experience recognizes teachers as professionally competent persons who can "learn" by intelligent and adult discussion of their ideas and attitudes about pupils, schools, and teaching. Such an experience is seldom afforded to teachers in the school. For example, counselor educators proclaim that teachers have a guidance function, yet teachers are only infrequently involved in describing their observations of "problem pupils" and even less frequently are they provided the opportunity to "work through their feelings about pupils."

Dinkmeyer and Arciniega[14] point out that participation in the small group experience gives counselors access to teachers' attitudes and beliefs regarding children. These two authors present several suggestions for "C" groups (labeled "C" because it collaborates, consults, clarifies, confronts, is concerned, and cares). Among their suggestions are that (1) only one group should be started initially to demonstrate its effectiveness and to stimulate other staff members' interests; (2) an experienced teacher who is socially powerful and well-accepted should be included; (3) organizational groundwork should be established early so that conflicts with other meetings are avoided; (4) administrative involvement and interest should be actively sought and obtained; and (5) an initial topic to be treated by the group should be a specific student situation or concern common to group members. Some functions performed by the leader of C Groups, according to Dinkmeyer and Arciniega, are

1. Structuring the group from the beginning so purposes and focus are apparent.
2. Being sensitive to verbal and nonverbal cues.
3. Linking related ideas of members in an attempt to underline similar problems, therefore bringing cohesiveness to the group.
4. Enabling quiet members to participate verbally as well as through spectator therapy.
5. Helping the group focus on what is happening here and now, as well as in their classrooms.
6. Focusing on assets and strengths to develop feelings of inadequacy.
7. Helping the group to clarify problems and find alternate solutions.
8. Enabling teachers to make a commitment to action.[15]

Using Consultants

Many formal and systematic in-service education activities have involved the use of consultants from universitites, state departments, central educa-

---

[14]Don Dinkmeyer and Mike Arciniega, "Affecting the Learning Climate Through 'C' Groups with Teachers," *The School Counselor,* Vol. 19 (March 1, 1972) pp. 249–253.
[15]*Ibid*, p. 251.

tion bureaus, and other school systems. It was stated in the discussion of principles of in-service education that it is important at the outset of the program to survey the availability of specialized consultants.

It is important that consultants be appropriately used. They should not dominate the thinking and activities of the faculty. Their skills, insight, and knowledge should be available as a resource to be used when needed by local staff members.

Study Groups

Small informal study groups of teachers who are interested in a particular concern in which they wish to pursue more intensively or extensively may be utilized profitably. Again, leadership, time, and resource materials, must be supplied by the guidance personnel.

University Courses

Many universities have extended their services to schools by providing extension courses conducted in the local school district. In the area of guidance this type of in-service education permits faculty members to develop competencies under the leadership of professionals in the field. In many cases, university credit is given for such courses.

COMMUNICATION

Keeping people informed is important. This is especially true in an area as important as guidance. Those who have responsibilities to perform can do so with a great deal more proficiency if they understand what is going on about them, especially concerning those things which relate either directly or indirectly to their own task.

The teacher needs to know what information is available for use. He should know how to obtain that information quickly. He needs to know how best to use that information. It is important, too, for the teacher to know how he can best contribute to the general stock of information. To the teacher who has had some training in the guidance field, the answers to these questions may be only a matter of routine information. To the teacher who has not had the benefit of such training, a program of orientation and in-service training should prove very helpful.

The planning of such a program for dissemination of information should be the task of the director of guidance and the principal. They must see the school organization as a whole. They need to plan for the development of good rapport among the various personnel that enter into the making of this whole. It is here that the development of adequate channels of communication are imperative. The answers to many such items as are raised in the preceding paragraph can probably be answered best by the director of guidance and the counselors. They have the training, the expert knowledge, and the skills which are needed in the field of guidance. How best can these skills and these services become available to the teacher? Administration must provide the channels of communication and assist in developing the proper climate for maximum use of such skills and services.

All concerned need to have a clear understanding of the school's philosophy and objectives. Only then can roles be clearly defined and understood. Teachers need to be advised regarding the ways and means through which they can make their maximum contribution to the guidance effort. They need to be advised as to the extent that they as teachers are to use directly the services and information provided by the professional guidance staff of the school.

The quality of communications between teachers and counselors needs continued attention in most schools. Many factors cause poor communications: Teachers and counselors become very busy; often, they have conflicting schedules; they are inconveniently located to talk to each other; or there is a lack of privacy. Sherman and Shapiro[16] reported the results of a communication survey of 418 teachers selected at random from 22 cooperating schools in five counties of the New York metropolitan area. Table 16–1 reports data obtained by these two researchers from the "Teacher-Counselor Communications Inventory."

Table 16–1   *Counselor Attitudes and Characteristics as Perceived by Teachers.* [*Source: Robert Sherman and Ida Shapiro, "Teacher-Counselor Communication,"* **The School Counselor,** *Vol. 17 (September 1969), p. 56. Used with permission.*]

Rank Order	Item	(N=422) Percent	Rank Order	Item	(N=422) Percent
1	Friendly	67	10	Highly professional person	17
2	Cooperative	56	11	Escaping from classroom	17
3	Likeable people	42	12	Too soft	15
4	Understanding	35	13	Discouraging of communication	7
5	Encouraging communication	33	14	Condescending	7
6	Professional toward teachers	32	15	Indifferent	7
7	Well trained	29	16	Too status conscious	6
8	Efficient and effective	28	17	Demanding	2
9	Removed from reality	19	18	Hostile	1

[16] Robert Sherman, Dominick Allaggin, Mary Cohen, Josephine Nadler, Burton Silverman, and Ida Shapiro, "Teacher-Counselor Communication," *The School Counselor,* Vol. 17 (September 1969) pp. 55–62.

It should be noted that most percentages reported in Table 16–1 tend to be less than a majority for given items because the inventory permitted free choices among many possible responses. While these 418 teachers indicated some dissatisfaction with their communications with counselors, a positive view is generally held. Although it is not reported in the tabular data, some 81 percent of the teachers considered counselors "essential" or "helpful" to the school. Teachers want to establish communications with counselors on a personal, informal basis. Particularly they want to discuss with counselors (1) the status of pupils they refer to counselors, (2) ways teachers can help particular pupils, (3) identifying characteristics of students who need spe cial help, and (4) test data interpretations.

No effort should be spared in planning a system of channels of communication. The use of special devices may save much time in explanation and meeting. They should be for the purpose of informing and advising personnel of the plans, procedures, and objectives which are being envisioned. Several devices for communication within the staff must be considered. Administrative bulletins from the central office are useful for general and specific administrative direction. Special service bulletins are helpful in providing information regarding some special program, as for instance, the career day. The newsletter is a useful device for giving information regarding progress of a program in action. The staff might profit too, by reading news releases regarding the program and its progress which have been published in local papers or in magazines for the information of the public. A well-informed staff is an essential factor in developing satisfactory public relations.

In considering the devices for communication, it cannot be expected that everything described above will be used in one system. The time of the individual staff members is valuable. They prize it highly and will resent having it taken up by unnecessary reading being thrust upon them. Some criteria therefore should be stated regarding these devices. They should be clear and concise. This means that they should be expertly written. The proper selection of those who prepare communications will help on this point. Communications within the staff should be clear, concise, and brief. They should be regular and on schedule. Knowing when to expect them is important. Lastly, they should be interesting. Special devices such as illustrations, cartoons, and catchy phrases appeal to the eye of professional people such as teachers, as well as to others.

Effective communications do not just happen; they must be nurtured. The assumption that there is a democratic working relationship when each staff member is permitted to go his own way not only leads to individual stagnation, but to lack of organizational achievement as well. All staff members desire to communicate with each other so that their efforts lead to positive outcomes for students. Communication about ideas and proposals for action makes a difference to those who are involved and responsible for them.

ANNOTATED BIBLIOGRAPHY

Hollis, Joseph W., and Lucile U. Hollis, *Organizing for Effective Guidance.*
Chicago: Science Research Associates, 1965, 460 pp.
Chapter 12, "In-Service Education," emphasizes how it contributes to the
total educational picture. An overview of techniques and activities for in-
service education is presented.

Ohlsen, Merle M., *Guidance: An Introduction.* New York: Harcourt and Brace and
Company, 1964, 515 pp.
In various parts of the book suggestions are given as to ways pupil behavior
descriptions, the interpretation and use of tests, and counseling techniques may
be improved through in-service education programs.

Shaw, Merville C., *School Guidance Systems.* Boston: Houghton Mifflin Company,
1973, 407 pp.
Chapter 16 (pp. 344–367) deals with promoting changes in existing guidance
programs. How change may be initiated, developing plans for changes and
establishing programs to follow policy are among the topics dealt with in this
chapter. A case study of a school district that changes its program is given.

Improving the Guidance Function through Accountability

Each generation gives new form to the aspirations that shape education in its time. What may be emerging as a mark of our generation is a widespread renewal of concern for the quality and intellectual aims of education —but without abandonment of the ideal that education should serve as a means of training well-balanced citizens for democracy.[1]

From my point of view, counselors should be held accountable not only for helping individuals whether student, staff or parents, but for evidence of the extent to which they have contributed to the whole school function and to change in that function.[2]

Chapter 17

What are some of the current research attempts to bring accountability procedures in guidance and counseling programs?

What difficulties are involved in evaluating the effectiveness of the guidance function?

Why is accountability of guidance so important?

What approaches may be used to evaluate guidance?

What is the role of guidance personnel in organizing guidance evaluation?

Lessinger states that since 1969, "accountability" is the "in" word in education. The current emphasis on accountability started in 1969 through the Elementary and Secondary Education Act of 1965, to the programs for Bilingual Education and Dropout Prevention. All eighty-six funded proposals provided accountability procedures. One of the ten dropout prevention projects had a performance contract with a private agency to achieve stipulated and guaranteed results in reading and mathematics. This caught on, and mushroomed the already embryonic on-rush for accountability. Accountability is a focus on intended and desired results. The correct term would be "outcome accountability." In 1973, twenty-six states had legislation requiring accountability measures in education, and twelve more had pending legislations.[3]

---

[1]Jerome S. Bruner, *The Process of Education.* Cambridge: Harvard University Press, 1961, p. 1.

[2]C. Gilbert Wrenn, *The World of the Contemporary Counselor.* Boston: Houghton Mifflin Company, 1973, p. 260.

[3]Leon M. Lessinger, "Toward a Humanistic Accountability," *Impact,* Vol. 2, No. 3, pp. 4–11.

Evaluation, or accountability of guidance, is the process by which judgments are made as to whether the goals of guidance are being attained. Casual daily evaluation of practices and techniques is made through observation. These everyday observations and reflections are useful in analyzing and synthesizing generalizations made in the program, and in indicating needs of students demanding either further attention or no particular emphasis.

Even though observations are careful, ordered, and reflective, the judgments made from such observations are quite often limited. Error, bias, incompleteness, and lack of uniformity often creep in. For this reason, systematic methods of evaluating guidance functions are necessary.

Evaluation depends upon and involves assessment. Travers distinguishes assessment from evaluation in that no value judgment is involved in the former.[4] Remmers, Gage, and Rummel state that assessment or measurement refers to "observations that can be expressed quantitatively and answer the question 'how much.' Evaluation goes beyond the statement of how much to concern itself with the question 'what value.' "[5] The following researchers are cited to illustrate some of the work being done in guidance evaluation, and accountability from the 1950s to the age of accountability, the 1970s. Accountability of counseling and guidance functions can be gained through a variety of evaluative procedures. Today the various guidance publics demand to know the quantity and quality of guidance functions. Whether by daily log, time spent in the office or in the field, number of self referrals, student feedback, or sophisticated research designs, there is a need for a variety of ways for accounting for guidance functions.

Gephart defines five steps to educational accountability:

1. Know what accountability is and is not.

2. Make educational goals explicit.

3. Negotiate the goals to be achieved and the procedures to be used.

4. Evaluate in selecting goals, in selecting and using educational procedures and in judging products.

5. Recycle.[6]

---

[4]Robert M. W. Travers, *Educational Measurement.* New York: The Macmillan Company, 1955, p. 7.

[5]H. H. Remmers, N. L. Gage, and J. Francis Rummel, *A Practical Introduction to Measurement and Evaluation.* New York: Harper & Row, Publishers, 1960, p. 7.

[6]William J. Gephart, "Five Steps to Educational Accountability," *The Administrator,* Vol. 3, No. 3 (Spring 1973), pp. 12–15. The Buckeye Association of School Administrators, Worthington, Ohio.

SOME CURRENT RESEARCH AND EVALUATIVE EFFORTS

Counseling with Elementary School Children

Kranzler and his associates[7] sought to assess the results of counseling with fourth grade students. The criterion was change in sociometric status and was selected on the basis that sociometric status has been shown to be related to many other personal and social characteristics such as achievement, personality characteristics, social skills, and physical skills. The authors believed that the combination of special attention and close personal relationships provided children assigned to counseling would result in significantly greater gain in sociometric status when compared with a control group.

Procedures. A sociometric instrument was administered by teachers to four fourth grade classes (N not specified) at Indiana University Elementary School during early December, 1963. Each teacher was asked to stress the confidentiality of the instrument, to inform the pupils that they could choose a boy or girl who was absent if they desired, and that groups would be arranged so that members would be able to sit near one or more of the pupils they had chosen. The sociometric instrument asked each pupil to list three individuals with whom he would most like to sit, work on committees, and play. Students were told that those chosen might be the same for all three tasks or they could be different. After tabulation of choices, each teacher was given a seating chart or suggested committee work groupings in which each student was placed with at least one of his choices. The five pupils of lowest sociometric status were placed with their first choices.

Subjects in the investigation were five pupils with the lowest number of choices in each of the four fourth-grade classrooms. The 20 subjects were randomly assigned to one of three conditions: counseling (eight subjects), teacher guidance (four subjects) or control (eight subjects).

The eight subjects assigned to the counseling condition met as a counseling group twice a week for six weeks. After six weeks the counseling group was divided into two groups, each meeting once a week for another 12 weeks. In addition, each subject was counseled individually for 12 weeks. In counseling, subjects were informed that they could discuss any concerns or difficulties that they or their friends might have and that their communications would be held in confidence. The authors state that a client-centered counseling approach was employed. Excerpts of individual counseling pre-

---

[7]Gerald D. Kranzler, G. M. Mayer, C. O. Kyer, and P. F. Munger, "Counseling with Elementary School Children: An Experimental Study," *Personnel and Guidance Journal,* Vol. 44, No. 9 (May 1966) pp. 944–949.

sented by the authors reflect student concern over relationships with teachers and parents.

The authors described the teacher guidance and the control conditions. Essentially, children assigned to teacher guidance were identified and described to the teachers as being of low sociometric status. Teachers were given a list of classroom procedures to use including praise of students' work, assigning them important tasks, and allowing them to work in self-preferred groups. Neither the eight pupils assigned to the control condition nor their teachers were informed that they were subjects and no unusual attention was paid them.

At the end of five months (April, 1964) the sociometric instrument was readministered and in November 1964, seven months after termination of counseling and teacher guidance, the sociometric instrument was administered a third time. At the time of this third administration, all subjects had been promoted to fifth-grade and had been placed in various classrooms.

Results.   Change in sociometric status was assessed by comparing total number of choices received by the subject on a posttest with the number received on the pretest. At the time of the first posttesting (soon after treatment conditions terminated), none of the subjects assigned to the counseling or teacher guidance conditions had decreased in sociometric status while 57 percent of control subjects (four of seven, since one left the school district) had decreased. Indeed, 75 percent of the counseled and 100 percent of the teacher guidance subjects had increased in sociometric status compared to 29 percent of control subjects. Statistical treatment of the pre-post data revealed that the counseled group differed (.05 level) from control but the teacher guidance group did not differ significantly from either the counseled or control group. Results of the second posttesting (seven months after termination of treatment) revealed that the differences between counseled and control groups were still statistically significant and that the relative percentages of subjects in the counseled and control groups who had increased or decreased in sociometric status remained the same. However, sociometric status of pupils assigned to teacher guidance condition decreased between the two posttest administrations.

In their discussion of the findings, Kranzler and his associates recognized the limitations imposed upon their data by the small numbers involved. They believe that their data suggested that certain kinds of behavior modification can be brought about in classroom situations by teachers if they are aware of students' low sociometric status and given suggestions for coping with it. Further, the authors believe that behavioral modifications brought about by teacher guidance do not carry over into a new situation but gains from counseling do.

Group Counseling

In 1965, Marilyn Bates did a study of the effectiveness of group counseling in meeting the goals of guidance in education at Western High School, Anaheim Union High School District in California. Over a period of thirteen weeks, Dr. Bates compared two groups of students, one involved in a traditional situation meeting in a weekly class format, and the other which was involved in an accelerated interaction format concentrated into a two-day continuous session held during school hours. There were thirty-six boys and girls in each group, which was broken down into three subgroups containing an equal number of tenth, eleventh, and twelfth graders. There was a matching of students on the basis of sex, grades, academic potential, socioeconomic level, and academic achievement. There was a control group to parallel each experimental group. Evaluation was done by means of a matched pairs t formula, using the pre-test-post-test gains scores. The Bills' Index of Adjustment and Values (IAV), the Taylor Vocational Choice Cards, The Rotter Incomplete Sentences Blank, academic grades, effort grades, citizenship grades, and attendance patterns made up the instrumentation used before and after the thirteen-week period.

The guidance goals and the group counseling goals were related, and an analysis was made to find if the guidance goals could be implemented through counseling in groups. This analysis is summarized in Table 17–1.

The study concerned itself with finding which counseling format, the traditional or accelerated interaction, might be used more effectively to help the student to be more receptive to the learning process because of a reduction of tensions and hostilities. It was found that if one were interested only in giving students an opportunity to vent their feelings, either format is adequate, but that if additional purposes were involved, cognitive or otherwise, the interchangeability ceased to exist.

On the basis of these findings it was found that the traditionally counseled group demonstrated a statistically significant improvement in terms of positive behavioral change when compared with the accelerated interaction group. This behavioral improvement was seen in terms of the citizenship, effort scores, and the traditionally counseled group's attendance patterns. When group counseling was done on a traditional basis, the occupational horizons of the group counselees were significantly expanded. It was demonstrated by the findings of the study, using the "Self" score of the IAV, that the traditional format of group counseling helped facilitate the individuation process. The traditional group also came to place a great deal more value on others as they listened and responded to the problems of others in the group. The accelerated interaction groups did not experience this same shift in perceiving others.

Table 17-1.   *Summary of Statistical Findings*[8]

Measuring Instrument	Traditional vs. Controls		Accelerated vs. Controls	
	t	Level of Significance	t	Level of Significance
GPA	2.72	0.01	1.41	NS
Attendance	2.10	0.05	0.06	NS
Effort Grades	2.54	0.01	−1.50	NS
Citizenship Grades	2.42	0.05	−1.17	NS
Vocational Choice Cards	2.42	0.05	1.32	NS
Rotter Incomplete Sentences	3.85	0.001	4.27	0.001
Bills IAV − Self Score	1.75	0.05	0.81	NS
Bills IAV − Other Scores	2.86	0.01	1.62	NS

Phoenix High Schools Study

Jenson[9] made an assessment of pupil reaction to the guidance program in the Phoenix Union High Schools during the 1952 school year. His decision to use student opinion as the criterion was based on the belief that it provides an index of what students think of counseling and how they believe their self-understanding and adjustment are affected by it. Jenson and his co-workers used a 20 percent random sample of 8,000 seventh-through twelfth-grade boys and girls in the seven high schools in Phoenix.

Counselor load average was 650 pupils. All counselors had 12-15 semester hours of university credit in guidance training. Pupil reaction to counselor help was obtained by a questionnaire administered by teachers according to prepared instructions.

The district-wide counseling objectives were stated, and students indicated on a five-point scale the help they had received from counselors toward meeting these objectives. Objectives emphasized student self-understanding, decision-making, and personal responsibility for decisions and actions. Jenson also asked students from whom they would seek assistance —parents, counselors, teachers, deans, friends—for certain problems. These problems included knowing more about their abilities, interests, personality, school activities, and work; getting along with others; and the like. A preference score for each individual was obtained by assigning a weight of 3 to first choice, 2 to second choice, and 1 to third choice.

Among his findings were

1.   Over 60 percent believed counselors had helped them "very much" or "some." Eighty-one percent felt they had received positive

---

[8]Marilyn Bates, "A test of group counseling," *Personnel and Guidance Journal,* Vol. 46, (April, 1968), pp. 749–753. Used with permission.
[9]Ralph E. Jenson, "Student Feeling about Counseling Help," *Personnel and Guidance Journal,* Vol. 33 (May, 1955), pp. 498–503.

help in understanding their abilities, interests, ambitions, and personality. Sixty percent indicated they had received help in making progress toward realistically chosen goals.

2. Counselors (28 percent), parents (27 percent), and teachers (19 percent) were the first, second, and third persons, respectively, from whom students would seek help when they wanted to know more about their abilities, ambitions, interests, and personality. In the problem area labeled "desire to know most promising kinds of school activities and work," students indicated they would seek help (in order of preference) from the following people: counselors (38 percent), teachers (22 percent), parents (20 percent), deans (9 percent), friends (8 percent), and others (3 percent). Counselors and teachers ranked highest in terms of persons to whom students would go for help in making progress toward selected goals in school and work. Parents and counselors were rated about the same, followed by friends, for help in getting along better with people at school, at home, or in the community. Parents and counselors were the first ones students would turn to for help in gaining confidence to make sound decisions on their problems, as well as for help in learning to do the things best for the student and society.

3. Overall, counselors were the individuals preferred by students for help with most of their problems. Students preferred counselors and parents to teachers, dean, or friends for help with problems. Teachers received their largest vote in help with school progress, although even here they were second to counselors.

4. Deans received few student choices which Jenson attributed to their authority roles.

Wisconsin Counseling Study

Rothney reported a longitudinal study of the value of all counseling secondary school pupils. He chose as his subjects all sophomore students from four representative high schools in Wisconsin.[10] Eight hundred and seventy students were distributed randomly into control and experimental groups. The experimental group received counseling throughout grades 10, 11, and 12. Followup studies of the 690 who graduated were conducted six months, two and one-half years, five years, and ten years after high school graduation. Evaluative criteria were (1) measures of satisfaction with and adjustment to post-high school status; (2) measures of optimism in outlook;

---

[10]John W. M. Rothney, *Guidance Practices and Results.* New York: Harper & Row, Publishers, 1958, p. 63 ff. Material used with permission.

(3) measures of reflection on post-high school education; and (4) measures of persistency in post-high school endeavors.

During the first year, all control group subjects were interviewed once and experimental subjects were interviewed twice. Guide sheets were used in the initial interviews. Such information as parents' education and occupations, number of siblings and counselee's relationships with them, parents' vocational expectations for counselees, educational and vocational aspirations and plans, school and community activities, health, and the like were discussed. Entries were made in students' cumulative records of such items as name, address, birth date, ninth and tenth grade marks, ability, and other test results.

During the second year, selected parts of the *Differential Aptitude Test* were administered to all subjects of the study. Rapport was maintained with control group subjects. Intensive counseling interviews were carried on with experimental subjects. Again, general guide sheets were used in interviewing, unless the counselees preferred to discuss other topics or subjects. Such things as changes in family situation, present educational and vocational plans, part-time work, school activities, health concerns, and relationships with other pupils, teachers, and parents were topics. In addition, behavioral descriptions, autobiographies, and samples of students' class work were collected.

Interviewing was also the major activity of the third year—the last year the subjects were in school. Again, general interview guides were used. The focus of these interview guides was students' strengths, weaknesses, personal problems, and present and future educational and vocational problems and plans. One month before graduation, all subjects indicated their post-high school plans in terms of one of six categories: education, employment, armed forces, work on parents' farm, uncertain, or married within one year (for girls only). Different forms of a senior report questionnaire were then given to each student according to the post-high school plans category he indicated. Students rated themselves comparatively with other members of the class in such things as reading, mathematics, intelligence, getting along with others, strengths, and weaknesses. Conferences, at the initiative of parents, were conducted. Approximately half of the parents sought interviews.

Rothney stated that follow-up studies over the five years revealed that, compared with noncounseled students, the counseled students

1. Achieved slightly higher academic records in high school and post-high school education;

2. Indicated more realism about their own strengths and weaknesses at the time they were graduated from high school;

3. Were less dissatisfied with their high school experiences;

4. Had differing vocational aspirations;

5. Were more consistent in expression of, entering into, and remaining in their vocational choices, classified by areas;

6. Made more progress in employment during the five-year period following high school graduation;

7. Were more likely to go on to higher education, to remain to graduate, and to plan for continuation of higher education;

8. Were more satisfied with their post-high school education;

9. Expressed greater satisfaction with their status five years after high school and were more satisfied in retrospect with their high school experiences;

10. Participated in more self-improvement activities after completing high school;

11. Looked back more favorably on the counseling they had obtained.[11]

Merenda and Rothney,[12] in a further report on the results of the five-year study, concluded that desirable outcomes may be enhanced by providing intensive counseling services to high school students. They noted that the differences were not large between counseled and uncounseled students on criterion variables obtained five years after high school graduation but speculated that the "more subtle and lasting effects of counseling require a longer period of time in order to become more clearly apparent." This speculation was based upon the likelihood that the early years after high school graduation are given over to exploratory and continued training experiences.

Ten-Year Follow-Up. In 1961, all subjects responded to a four-page questionnaire. This was ten years after high school graduation. While the complete results[13] of this ten-year study have not yet been published in the professional journals, Rothney[14] reported a study of trained and non-trained males ten years after high school graduation. The 179 males who

---

[11] *Ibid.,* pp. 479–480.

[12] Peter F. Merenda and John W. M. Rothney, "Evaluating the Effects of Counseling—Eight Years After," *Journal of Counseling Psychology,* Vol. 5, No. 3 (Fall 1958), pp. 163–168.

[13] John W. M. Rothney, *Educational, Vocational and Social Performances of Counseled and Uncounseled Youth Ten Years After High School.* Report submitted to Cooperative Research Program, Department of Health, Education and Welfare. Washington, D.C., 1963. Project No. SAE 9231.

[14] John W. M. Rothney, "Trained and Non-trained Males Ten Years After High School Graduation," *Vocational Guidance Quarterly,* Vol. 14, No. 4 (Winter 1966), pp. 247–250.

constituted the *training* group continued their education after high school graduation either by enrollment in a school or college or entering a formal apprenticeship. The 142 members of the *no training* group did not enroll in any educational institution or apprenticeship during the ten years after high school graduation. Some members of both groups had attended service schools while serving in the armed forces.

The most significant differences between the counseled and comparison groups in the follow-up studies were in the number of counseled subjects who went to and completed post-high school training. Rothney reports that the training group contained a much higher proportion of counseled students but did not specify the proportion.

Ten years after high school the trained group (and significantly more of them were counseled students) had left their own home towns, married later, earned more money, were more optimistic, looked back more favorably on their high school experience, reported more educational and vocational plans for the future, and belonged to more organizations and held a few more offices in them. No significant difference existed between the trained and nontrained groups in respect to satisfaction with current status, job satisfaction, satisfaction with what they had done during the past 10 years, appraisal of their personal assets, persons to whom they went for advice, confidence in making decisions, numbers of self-improvement activities, and satisfaction with counseling they had received.

In his discussion of the results, Rothney asked "Who can say that the boy who stayed in or near his home town, enjoyed marriage and a family earlier, belonged to fewer organizations (perhaps because fewer were available) and did not burden himself with too many offices was less well off than the boy who went into training?"[15]

Minnesota College Student Counseling Study

Williamson and Bordin[16] sought to determine the effect of counseling provided at the University of Minnesota Student Counseling Bureau. Their subjects were 384 students who, during the years 1933–1936, had come to the Counseling Bureau before November of their freshman year for counseling help with educational, vocational, or other personal problems.

These 384 counseled students were designated as the experimental group and selected solely on the basis of having complete counseling folders. One year later these students were individually paired and matched with other

---

[15] *Ibid.*, p. 249.
[16] E. G. Williamson and E. S. Bordin, "Evaluating Counseling by Means of a Control-Group Experiment," *School and Society,* Vol. 52, No. 1349 (November, 1940), pp. 434–440.

noncounseled students on college entrance test scores, English proficiency test score, high school rank, age, sex, size, and type of high school and college class. This second group was the control group and could have received counseling from other students, administrators, or other staff members. All 768 students were registered in the College of Science, Literature and the Arts (SLA). Half were men; half were women.

Both groups were interviewed roughly one year after counseling (range = 1–4 years, mode = 1 year) and rated on a scale called "Adjustment" which centered mainly around educational-vocational progress. Without benefit of counseling, 68 percent of the control group achieved what was judged by themselves and the evaluating judges to be satisfactory adjustment with respect to their vocational choices and progress in classes. In contrast, 81 percent of the counseled students achieved what was judged to be a correspondingly satisfactory adjustment. Conversely, 27 percent of the noncounseled cases and 15 percent of the counseled students failed to achieve satisfactory adjustment. The two groups were also compared on first-quarter grade point average (GPA). Among the results were that (1) the counseled students rated significantly higher on the Adjustment scale, and (2) the counseled students earned significantly better grades than noncounseled students—2.18 to 1.97, respectively, on a four-point scale.

Since criticism was directed at the Williamson-Bordin study because the two groups were not equated for motivation to seek counseling, Campbell[17] in a 25-year follow-up study of the students, identified a third group (N = 62) of former control students who sought counseling after the original study. For these students, both precounseling and postcounseling measures were available. The results showed that before counseling, this "better" control group resembled the control students; after counseling, the counseled students.

Twenty-Five Year Follow-Up. In 1961–1962, Campbell followed up the individuals in the Williamson-Bordin counseled and noncounseled groups to assess the effects of counseling over a 25 year period. Virtually all "students"—then roughly 45 years old—were located, 761 of the 768. Thirty people had died, about 10 percent would not cooperate, and 62 control students had sought help from the Counseling Bureau during the interval, and therefore could no longer be used as controls. Information was collected in respect to their achievements, job, and life satisfaction.

Campbell reports that counseled students compared to noncounseled students had earned significantly better grades (2.20 versus 2.06 on a 4.00 scale); graduated in roughly one-fourth greater numbers (59 versus 48

---

[17]David P. Campbell, *The Results of Counseling: Twenty-five Years Later.* Philadelphia: W. B. Saunders Company, 1965.

percent); were elected to Phi Beta Kappa (6 versus 2 percent); earned more M. A. degrees (6 versus 2 percent) and more Ph.D. degrees (2 versus 0.3 percent); reported more participation in campus activities and were more often elected to offices in these activities.

Campbell further identified and compared the current achievements of the two groups. While more of the counseled group reported that they had published, won athletic awards, been awarded patents, and given public addresses more so than the noncounseled students, the differences (some statistically significant) were small and discounted by Campbell. The annual family income of counseled males ranged from $1,600 to $150,000 with a median of $14,670 compared to the $4,000 to $70,000 range reported for noncounseled males (their median was $13,500 and the $1,200 difference in median income was not statistically significant). Neither was the difference in annual family income between counseled females and noncounseled females ($13,300 median versus $13,000) statistically significant.

Campbell drew together all achievement data and had each subject rated on a "Contribution to Society" scale by three psychologists working independently (16 raters participated). There was perfect agreement among the raters in 299 of the 724 cases, or 41 percent. In the remaining 59 percent, two of the three raters agreed, and the third deviated by only one point. The differences between the counseled and noncounseled groups were all in favor of the counseled students but were not statistically significant. However, when the counseled male was compared to his matched noncounseled control (123 pairs of males), differences were significant at the .05 level. But this procedure failed to hold for the female matched pairs.

Two conclusions from the follow-up about the effect of counseling on students were drawn by Campbell. First, a very mild difference in achievement existed between counseled and noncounseled students 25 years later, especially among men. Second, counseling did exert a beneficial effect on the students' achievement. While the effect was most visible on immediate criteria such as grades and graduation, and although it withered somewhat, it did not completely disappear over 25 years. Campbell further points out that these conclusions are not too surprising since counselors are more effective in dealing with immediate problems and these frequently concern grades and graduation. It is his judgment that counseling is best justified as immediate help to the student bewildered by an increasingly complex range of educational and occupational opportunities.

Wellman developed one approach suitable to accountability for guidance. He emphasized educational, vocational, and social objectives and evaluative criteria.[18]

---

[18]Frank T. Wellman, Criterion Variables for the Evaluation of Guidance Practices, a Taxonomy of Guidance Objectives. Office of Education Contract, Columbia, Missouri, University of Missouri, 1967.

Humes[19] discusses the four-step accountability procedures of situation, population, outcome, and process. After reading Humes and other articles on accountability, one is struck with the idea of a new name for evaluation, worthwhileness, research, and acceptability. Accountability does seem to emphasize a more direct line of finding out the meaningfulness of objectives, process, and results in terms of better student development—educational, vocational and social-personal.

Pulvino and Sanborn[20] emphasize the need for a feedback system in accountability. This is illustrated in their accountability paradigm (Figure 17–1). Through feedback, counselors decide if goals are appropriate, if clients have made developmental progress, and if there is achievement of goals by the students.

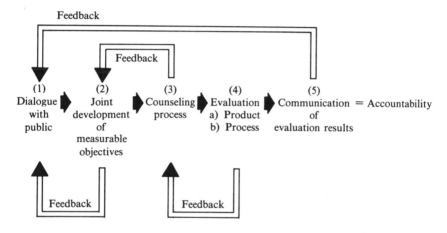

Figure 17–1.   Accountability Paradigm

Wysong[21] reported on the 1968–1972 program evaluations in 175 varied secondary schools in Ohio. Guidance objectives were developed in the cognitive and affective domain. Questionnaires and check lists were developed. Survey and counselor logs are illustrative of the instruments used. Basically the technique was that of consumer feedback. The various "feedbacks" were analyzed and presented to the concerned publics. Above all, this system increased guidance awareness, which is a pristine requirement for accountability of guidance functions.

---

[19]Charles W. Humes II, "Accountability: A Boom to Guidance," *Personnel and Guidance Journal,* Vol. 51, No. 1, (September 1972), pp. 21–26.

[20]Charles J. Pulvino and Marshall P. Sanborn, "Feedback and Accountability," *Personnel and Guidance Journal,* Vol. 51, No. 1 (September, 1972), pp. 15–20. Used with permission.

[21]H. Eugene Wysong, "Accountability: Foibled Fable or Solution?" *Impact,* Vol. 2, No. 3, pp. 34–37.

Warner and Hansen[22] studied the effects of model-reinforcement and verbal-reinforcement group counseling on alienated high school students. Juniors in the three high schools who scored one standard deviation above the mean on a scale of alienation were selected for the research. The students were randomly assigned to one of four treatment groups: control, placebo, model reinforcement, and verbal reinforcement. The reinforcement counseling groups were effective in reducing students' feelings of alienation.

In the accountability analysis, the key weakness is the authors' definition of alienation. The singularity of a behavioristic model does not reflect the web of interactive forces in one's living; that is, the interplay of one behavior on others, subtle or distant as they may seem to be. This study is an effective study in terms of the art and science of the specificity of behavior. The real accountability is in long range behavior.

DIFFICULTIES INVOLVED IN EVALUATION

Evaluation is difficult, expensive, and time consuming. However, evaluation is necessary for a continuing, constantly improving guidance program. During the last twenty years, authors, lecturers, and others have deplored the lack of formalized evaluative guidance studies. Reasons for the paucity of evaluative studies have been advanced by Kitson. In 1948, he thought that (1) research was necessarily limited in scope; hence, its usefulness may be minimal; (2) significant research could only be carried out over a number of years; (3) training and facilities were crucial problems; and (4) some problems were not amenable to research, e.g., contemporary human relations.[23]

In 1957, Coleman listed the following reasons for the lack of evaluative studies in guidance: (1) lack of recognition that efforts and pet beliefs do not guarantee results; (2) lack of competence in evaluative and research skills; (3) preoccupation with service and daily tasks, often enhanced by pressure from higher administrators.[24]

Williamson and Bordin discussed the following difficulties in conducting experimental research in the field of guidance: (1) all evaluational methods have weaknesses; (2) acquiring sufficient data is difficult because records are frequently inadequate or incomplete, and because the purposes of counsel-

---

[22]Richard W. Warner, Jr., and James C. Hansen, "Verbal-reinforcement and model-reinforcement group counseling with alienated students," *Journal of Counseling Psychology,* Vol. 17, No. 2, 1970, pp. 168–172.

[23]Harry D. Kitson, "More and Better Research in Vocational Guidance," *Occupations,* February, 1948, pp. 308–315.

[24]William Coleman, "Role of Evaluation in Improving Guidance and Counseling Services," *Personnel and Guidance Journal,* Vol. 35 (March, 1957), p. 441.

ing often preclude the gathering of certain data; (3) tests on group performance validated by statistical criteria are frequently not applicable because of the uniqueness of the counseling situation; and (4) exact evaluation of guidance is impeded by the inability to control counseling recommendations and to check their effects.[25]

More and more, secondary school personnel are supplanting casual armchair speculation of the effectiveness of their program by more systematic processes. Some of the methodological problems that plague them as they attempt to evaluate guidance procedures are summarized briefly below.

Objectives Not Well Defined

One of the problems in attempting evaluation is that too often the objectives of the guidance program have not been stated in observable behavioral outcomes. In far too many schools where organized programs have existed for some time, there has been little attempt to define guidance objectives in any terms. Where school personnel have identified the objectives of guidance, all too often the stated objectives are so general and broad that they are beyond assessment by either observation or empirical verification.

Objectives must be established for the guidance program before evaluation can be conducted. Since the guidance program is based on the needs of students, the objectives of such a program should be stated in terms of characteristics noticeable in student behavior. This, of course, is not an easy operation, but it is a necessary one. Objectives stated in behavioral terms become the criteria against which guidance programs can be assessed.

Those working on guidance evaluation have the problem of securing appropriate criteria. A criterion may be said to be a behavior, event, or condition which can be described as a goal, aim, or end. In other words, a criterion is a standard of behavior which is established as being desirable. Whether the method used is judged effective or not depends upon the criterion. The method used may be effective when a particular criterion is used, but if another criterion is used, the method may not be effective.

Researchers in guidance and counseling have used many different criteria. Improvement of school marks, improved behavior, reduced discipline problems, reduction of number of student program changes, appropriateness of vocational goal, reduced dropouts, a greater participation in extracurricular activities, and job satisfaction are some of the criteria that have been employed. Each of these criteria, in and of themselves, has severe

[25]E. G. Williamson and E. S. Bordin, "The Evaluation of Vocational and Educational Counseling: A Critique of the Methodology of Experiments," *Educational and Psychological Measurement,* Vol. 1, No. 1 (1941), p. 23.

limitations. Hatch and Stefflre have presented a very thorough discussion of the limitations.[26] All criteria contribute some worthwhile information if the data are used well.

Burck, Cottingham, and Reardon point to the identification, selection, definition, and measurement of the criterion as a major and persistent problem. Their criticism of most counseling evaluation is that "the criteria used are those most available and accessible rather than those most relevant to predetermined counseling objectives." According to Burck et al., criteria (a) generate from the theoretical goals and objectives of counseling, (b) involve the researcher's value orientation, (c) range from the immediate, intermediate, and ultimate, (d) should be stable, definable, relevant, and variable among the general population, and (e) are spread along a continuum ranging from general to specific, objective to subjective, single to multiple, common to individualized, and internal to external.[27]

Cartwright found that these differing criteria may be unrelated. He states, "But suppose that a client changes a great deal on one variable, a little on another, none at all on another, and changes for the worse, or deteriorates, on yet another variable. Suppose, in short, that all or most of the hundreds of variables so far studied were essentially uncorrelated. Which variables would you choose then as your target for prediction purposes?"[28] Patterson believes "Some of them may be negatively related, at some levels of a nonlinear total relationship, to independence. It thus is not wise, nor desirable, to attempt to combine specific criteria into a composite. Multiple criteria should be used."[29]

Travers rejects subjective criteria such as the individual's assessment of happiness, satisfaction with a job, student satisfaction with counseling, and cooperation. He advocates extreme caution in the use of certain objective criteria such as grades, income, change of job, stability of life goals, and completion of educational plans. Although recognizing the problems involved, Travers urges greater use of the control group method.[30]

Finding Suitable Control Groups

A second major problem of those who seek to evaluate guidance functions is that of finding a suitable control group. The control group needs to be

[26]Raymond N. Hatch and Buford Stefflre, *Administration of Guidance Services: Organization, Supervision, Evaluation.* Englewood Cliffs, N.J.: Prentice-Hall, Inc., 1958, pp. 260–265.

[27]Harmon D. Burck, Harold F. Cottingham, and Robert C. Reardon, *Counseling and Accountability.* Elmsford, N.Y.: Pergamon Press, 1973, pp. 31, 39.

[28]D. S. Cartwright, "Methodology in Counseling Evaluation," *Journal of Counseling Psychology,* Vol. 4, No. 4 (Winter 1957), p. 264.

[29]C. H. Patterson, "Methodological Problems in Evaluation," *Personnel and Guidance Journal,* Vol. 39 (December, 1960), p. 271.

[30]Robert W. M. Travers, "A Critical Review of Techniques for Evaluating Guidance," *Educational and Psychological Measurement,* Vol. 9 (1949), pp. 211–225.

similar in all important respects to the experimental group. Many studies have established a control group matched or randomized with the experimental group on measured intelligence, socio-economic background, personality factors, and the like. However, the motivation for counseling is a variable, and a most important one, that typically is not included.

Personnel in the secondary schools are understandably reluctant to withhold services from a segment of their students. Yet, the individual who seeks counseling is probably different in an important aspect of his motivation from another person with whom he might be matched by intelligence, interests, age, or other factors. Attempts to solve this problem have included three procedures: (1) delaying counseling, or the services intended, to one group for a time; (2) using a group as its own control by evaluating it, waiting for a period of time, re-evaluating the group, applying counseling or the service intended, and then evaluating the group for a third time; (3) providing a different type of counseling or service in the contacts with some members of the group.

Sampling

A third problem is that of sampling. Most studies have drawn samples from the population served by the institution in which the study was being conducted. Such a population is usually limited to those persons available to the institution. The results based on such samples are thus generalized only to the population represented by the sample. The usefulness of such studies, therefore, is curtailed because the sample is not representative, but is peculiar to the organization in which the work is carried on.

The sample drawn must be from a known or defined population. Before any generalizations can be made from a study of one high school student body to another, it must be demonstrated that the student populations are similar.

Controlling Numerous Variables

A fourth problem is that of controlling the numerous and complex variables inherent in human beings and human relationships. Many factors correlated with individual differences predispose a person to think and act as only he can. Changes occur in an individual in the absence of any known influence that has been brought to bear on him.

McDaniel has written that

> . . . it is quite impossible, in research involving human relationships, to isolate and control variables and to establish any definite relationship between cause and effect . . . Even in carefully designed research studies

in which matched groups are used and certain variables are controlled, there remain many factors that are beyond the management of the experimenter.[31]

SUMMARY OF CRITICISMS

Dressel summarizes the criticism of evaluative studies under the following seven headings:

1. Lack of clear, acceptable statements of objectives in terms of observable student characteristics and behavior.

2. Failure to relate student personnel objectives to all institutional-educational objectives.

3. The use of immediate and easily available criteria accompanied by failure to validate the immediate criteria against long-term goals.

4. The tendency to regard certain goals as equally desirable for all individuals, thereby ignoring individual differences.

5. Confusion of means with ends or of process with outcomes.

6. Excessive use of subjective reactions.

7. Little or no attention to determining a satisfactory experimental design.[32]

THE IMPORTANCE OF EVALUATION

Guidance is the fastest growing of all services currently conducted by the public schools. Because of this growth, appraisal of its effects is in order, lest size be mistaken for purposeful activity. Claims made in the name of guidance are not necessarily results.

The most essential reason for conducting evaluation is to check whether the guidance function has been adequate to the task. Are guidance methods fitting? Have hypotheses been made appropriately? Are operations conducted properly? Have materials been tailored to the capacities and needs of students? The answers to such questions enable school personnel to

---

[31]H. B. McDaniel and G. A. Shaftel, *Guidance in the Modern School,* p. 40. Copyright © 1956, New York: Holt, Rinehart & Winston, Inc.

[32]Paul L. Dressel, "Personnel Services in High School and College," *Occupations,* Vol. 29, (February, 1951), p. 331.

determine how well they are doing what they are doing. The school exists to serve its pupils, to enable them to move toward certain objectives; evaluation is the means by which school personnel can better judge the extent to which these objectives are being met.

Another important reason for evaluating guidance functions—and inherent in the above reason—is that evaluation serves as a base for developing new services or adapting existing services. Not only does evaluation provide data on how well a school is doing what it is doing, but such data in turn provide a foundation to make decisions as to what might be done. Better planning, coordination, and articulation usually result from well-conceived evaluative studies.

A third value from evaluation of school guidance is that data are secured which aid in interpreting the program to the school's public. As stated in Chapter 15, school personnel have an obligation to report the status of the guidance program to the school community. Parents who are informed can participate better in defining the direction and objectives for the school. Evaluation reveals the strengths and limitations of any program. The accounting to the public enables the school to secure support for needed improvements in the guidance program.

A fourth value resulting from evaluation is that the processes of conducting such a study provide in-service training for staff members. To perform the evaluation service, teachers, counselors, and administrators are involved in many varied activities. The sharing of ideas, the development of plans, the formulation of evaluative devices are learning experiences for all school personnel. Better insight, more understanding of the *why* of guidance services, increased use of services—all result from the interactions of the school staff.

Mahoney cited the values of evaluation, based on ten years of sponsoring systematic and cooperative programs of secondary school evaluation from a state department of education. The following values are paraphrased from his statement.

1. It is an effective means of promoting and extending guidance services.

2. Evaluation is a means for involving lay participation and acquainting the people of the community with the work of the schools in general, and the guidance program in particular.

3. Evaluation is an effective in-service training vehicle. Through evaluation, much can be done to bring unity of thinking relative to the place of guidance. Evaluation sets the stage for followup programs of in-service training.

4. Through evaluation, an opportunity is provided to really see what happens in a school. Determining why is the theme of such activity.

5. Evaluation lends support to the school in its attempt to acquaint the community with the need for guidance services.

6. It is a way to accumulate data which may be used ultimately for research purposes.

7. Evaluation is a means by which school people become more intimately acquainted with other members of the staff.

8. Evaluation builds personal confidence among co-workers.

9. Evaluation is a means of identifying professional talent and potential leaders who may later be used on committees, programs, and similar activities.[33]

In summary, evaluation is valuable as a means: to judge the effectiveness of guidance, to know the program's strengths and weaknesses, and to plan and carry out improvements which benefit students and the community.

APPROACHES TO ACCOUNTABILITY—MODELS AND IDEAS

Stufflebeam[34] gives an overview of three accountability models—transactional accountability, state assessment, and political accountability. These are described here in some detail.

Model 1—Transactional Accountability:

Accountability is the ability of all relevant parties in a given educational setting to supply information about past actions in relation to (1) mutually arrived at agreements and decisions that guided those actions, (2) the logical and empirical bases (rationale) for those agreements and decisions, (3) the extent to which they were efficiently and properly implemented, and (4) the quality of their effects; accountability also leads to the ability to improve future actions on the basis of information about past actions.

---

[33]H. J. Mahoney, "Ten Years of Evaluating Guidance Services," *Occupations,* Vol. 29 (December 1950), pp. 194–197.
[34]Daniel L. Stufflebeam, "An Overview of the State of Accountability Models," *The Administrator.* (The Buckeye Association of School Administrators, Worthington, Ohio) Vol. 3, No. 3 (Spring 1973), pp. 19–23. Used with permission.

Model 2—State Assessment:

Richard Jaeger chaired the team that devised Model 2. Model 2 includes both a short-range and a long-range strategy. The short-range strategy involves applying the methodology of the Program for the National Assessment of Educational Progress to the development of an Ohio Assessment Program.

Initially, this assessment program would focus on four measurement domains, including: (1) basic skills (reading, vocabulary, and arithmetic); (2) students' attitudes toward schooling; (3) citizens' attitudes toward schooling; and (4) professional educators' attitudes toward schooling.

The Jaeger plan for data analysis includes six parts. They are: (1) status of a population on a single variable of interest; (2) status of a population on a category of variable interest; (3) comparison of two or more subpopulations on a variable of interest; (4) comparison of two or more subpopulations on a category of variables of interest; (5) growth over time of a particular subpopulation on a variable of interest; and (6) growth over time of a particular subpopulation on a category of interest.

The long-range strategy implies assessment over a long period of time, with appropriate feedback given to concerned staff.

Model 3—Political Accountability

Model 3 was developed by a team chaired by Raphael Nystrand. The definition of accountability on which Model 3 is based is:

> Accountability is a process in which responsibility is determined and performance is analyzed for the purpose of understanding behavior and allocating resources in relation to specified goals.

The Nystrand team emphasized that while striving to make schools more accountable, the state should also experiment with means to make the schools more effective.

Accountability is, of necessity, closely related to and an integral part of the school guidance program. The ways a school approaches evaluation vary. First a statement of objectives for the program must be developed. As mentioned before, these objectives must be stated in such a way that they can be observed and verified. For example, one objective of a guidance program may be to help students develop an awareness of the educational opportunities available to them.

The second necessary condition to conduct accountability studies is that the specific activities, methods, and practices which are to be used to realize the stated objectives must be identified. For example, if an objective is the one stated above—developing an awareness of educational opportunities—the guidance program will include such procedures, activities, or methods for realizing this objective as (1) interviews with students on educational plans, (2) conferring with parents on students' plans, (3) units within a course or a homeroom on educational opportunities, and (4) organized and supervised use of educational information and opportunities. In other words, practices and services to promote achievement of the objectives must be known.

The third condition is that means must be established to determine whether the activities or methods developed have actually resulted in attaining objectives or moving toward them. In short, the research methodology that is to be used must be decided. What research procedures will disclose to school personnel that the objectives have, or have not, been attained? How can evidence be best marshalled and appraised?

Classifying Evaluative or Accountability Approaches

A number of writers have made suggestions for classifying the evaluative studies made by guidance personnel. Among the early authors, Wrenn formulated three categories from a review of the research: (1) the logical survey method, in which the needs of students are determined and services designed to meet those needs are developed; (2) the experimental cross-section method, in which a counseled group is compared with a noncounseled group; (3) the developmental method, in which evidence of the total achievements of students is collected over a considerable length of time.[35] Kefauver and Hand offered six categories for classifying evaluative studies: (1) analysis or description of practices; (2) relation of practices in a school with a "standard" program; (3) comparison of characteristics of students before and after experience in guidance; (4) study of students after being exposed to a guidance program; (5) comparison of the characteristics of the jobs of workers functioning in different types of guidance programs; (6) projection of a comprehensive program of guidance and the followup of students through this program.[36]

Froehlich, classifying on the basis of methodology used by investigators, suggested the following seven categories: (1) external criteria, the do-you-do-this? method; (2) follow-up, the what-happened-then? method; (3) client opinion, the what-do-you-think? method; (4) expert opinion, the "Informa-

---

[35]C. G. Wrenn, "A Critique of Methods Used in Follow-up Studies of Studies," *Harvard Educational Review,* Vol. 10 (May, 1940), pp. 357–363.

[36]Grayson N. Kefauver and Harold C. Hand, "Evaluation of Guidance Programs," *Occupations,* Vol. 12 (March, 1934), pp. 106–114.

tion Please" method; (5) specific techniques, the little-by-little method; (6) within-group changes, the before-and-after method; (7) between-group changes, the what's-the-difference? method.[37]

Dressel, in a more recent statement of types of evaluation, based his three categories on the significance of the evidence of program effectiveness. To him, the three major types of evaluative studies were (1) appraisal of group development, which studies changes taking place in a group with regard to a universally accepted objective; (2) appraisal of individual development, which determines the extent to which the individual attains goals appropriate to him; (3) appraisal by external opinion, which collects evidence of changes in individuals, based on opinions, external criteria, experts, and the like.[38]

Rushong discusses three classifying methods: (1) survey method, in which existing procedures and techniques are assessed to determine the extent to which they achieve the objectives; (2) scientific method, in which appraisal is attempted by objective instruments of evaluation; (3) comprehensive method, in which clinical judgment is applied to tests, questionnaires, observations, case histories, anecdotal records, and interviews, to estimate the outcomes of the counseling program.[39]

Survey Method

The survey method to evaluation has been most universally used by schools to evaluate guidance services. The survey method (1) uses predetermined criteria or standards for a guidance program, (2) collects evidence of the guidance services being offered, and (3) takes stock of how these existing services compare with the predetermined standards. Knowledge of present services—their extent, strengths, and weaknesses—is the outcome of the survey method. The survey method may involve both subjective judgments and/or objective evidence, depending upon the nature of the method. Generally, little objective evidence is supplied as to whether the goals of the guidance program are being met; with no controls, it is impossible to make more than a guess or an estimate. Many have criticized the survey method because it does not reveal whether changes have taken place because of the services rendered or because of other variables.

A number of checklists, questionnaires, and survey forms containing standards or criteria have been published for use in the survey approach.

---

[37]Clifford P. Froehlich, *Evaluating Guidance Procedures.* Washington: Federal Security Agency, Office of Education, January, 1949, p. 2.

[38]Dressel, *Personnel Services,* pp. 331–340.

[39]H. D. Rushong, "Present Status and Trends in the Evaluation of Counseling," *Educational and Psychological Measurement,* Vol. 9 (1953), pp. 418–430.

Section G, *Guidance Services, Evaluative Criteria* (see also Chapter 10),[40] has been widely employed by state departments of education, county school units, and local systems. Section G contains statements of the conditions, provisions, or characteristics that should be found in a guidance program. These statements are organized into four sections: (1) General Nature and Organization; (2) Guidance Staff, including (a) preparation and qualifications, (b) teacher participation; (c) specialists for consultation and referral; (3) Guidance Services, consisting of (A) individual inventory services, (B) Socioeconomic information services, (C) Counseling, (D) Placement services, (E) Research and Evaluation Services; (4) Special Characteristics of the Guidance Services. Evaluators rate statements in these areas on a seven-point scale: 5—Excellent, 4—Very Good, 3—Good, 2—Fair, 1—Poor, M —Missing, N—Does not apply. A combination of self-evaluation and evaluation from visiting experts is the procedure recommended by *Evaluative Criteria.*

Another checklist that has been rather widely used is *Criteria for Evaluating Guidance Programs in Secondary Schools,* Form B, by the U.S. Office of Education. Developed in 1949, *Criteria* was revised in 1961.[41] Purposes of *Criteria* are to provide a base for evaluating the school guidance program and to stimulate improvement in such programs by identifying the strengths and limitations of its various phases. As in Section G of the *Evaluative Criteria,* statements of the features of a "good" guidance program are organized into sections. The major sections are: (1) Administrative Bases for Guidance Services; (2) Guidance Staff; (3) Guidance Services; (4) Services Complementary to the Guidance Program; (5) Guidance Services as an Influence on Total School Development; (6) Outstanding Characteristics of the Guidance Program; (7) General Evaluation of the Guidance Program. A six-point rating scale similar to that of Section G, *Evaluative Criteria,* is used. Self evaluation and appraisal by a committee of experts are procedures recommended by the *Criteria.*

Hill and Nitzsche reported a study wherein students and parents evaluated a school guidance program by use of questionnaires.[42] (The student and parent questionnaires were also published.) Hill and Nitzsche stated: "Not only do they (students and parents) have opinions but, with reasonable care as to the approach used, they are quite willing to express them on checklists and questionnaires."[43]

---

[40] *Evaluative Criteria,* Section G, Guidance Services, in *National Study of Secondary School Evaluation,* Washington, D.C.: Cooperative Study of Secondary School Standards, 1960, pp. 273–288.

[41] Arthur L. Benson (ed.), *Criteria for Evaluating Guidance Programs in Secondary Schools,* Form B. Washington: U.S. Department of Health, Education and Welfare, Office of Education, 1961.

[42] George E. Hill and Dale F. Nitzsche, *Students and Parents Evaluate the School's Guidance Program.* Athens, Ohio: College of Education, Ohio University, Pupil Services Series, 1960, No. 2, 1960.

[43] *Ibid.,* p. 5.

Scientific Method

The survey method of evaluating guidance programs has involved largely subjective judgments as to the extent of the services rendered and an assumption that the services or activities being offered to students achieve the goals of the program. Therefore, more rigorous attempts to appraise the program's effectiveness have been sought and developed. The scientific method makes use of either *statistical control*—the application of covariance statistical methods to the data, or *experimental control*—the manipulation of dependent variables in a deliberate and predetermined manner.

Experimental control of evaluation has involved designs from any one of several bases: "before-after," "after only," simulated "before-after," or "before-after" with control groups. Hatch and Stefflre summarized these various designs in table form.[44] Briefly, "before-after" means selection of an experimental group; assessment of group; application of experimental variable (e.g., counseling, dissemination of occupational information); reassessment of group; difference between second and first assessment taken as the changes due to application of experimental variable. The "after only" design usually involves selection of experimental variable; assessment of both groups; difference between assessment results from experimental group and control group taken as change induced by application of the experimental variable. Simulated "before-after" designs include selection of experimental and control groups; assessment of control group only; exposure to experimental variable (sometimes even the controls); assessment of experimental group only; difference between measures of control group assessment and experimental group assessment taken as change induced by experimental variable. The "before-after" with control group design usually includes selection of an experimental group and a control group; assessment of both experimental and control groups; differences between second and first assessment of experimental group and second and first assessment of control group attributed to change as a result of experimental variable.

In these experimental approaches, the "before-after" with control group is usually regarded as the best design. It permits a check on the control group to ascertain if changes have occurred through factors other than the application of the experimental variable. Thus value judgments on what should be or can be done are more soundly based.

Comprehensive Method

The comprehensive or case-study method of evaluation is designed to assess the changes that have taken place in an individual in relation to his own goals. The individual formulates objectives appropriate to his desires.

---

[44]Hatch and Stefflre, *Administration of Guidance,* p. 266.

Evaluation is more imperative today in light of the impetus for accountability which has resulted from a perceived confidence gap by the public. Hilderbrand believes that "The public is no longer willing to invest heavily in education without having some assurance that its investments will yield positive results." Today people are disenchanted with the promises that schools have made them. They're looking for concrete results.[45]

With the comprehensive or case-study method of evaluation, the individual formulates objectives appropriate to him (acceptable also to the school or institution); counseling takes place; statements, descriptions, logs of the individual's activities, interactions with others, and the like are systematically collected; experts review and assess the changes that have taken place in the individual. Has he progressed toward the goals or objectives that were established?

This type of evaluation requires expert judgment. It has the advantage of emphasizing the individual and his growth. Such an approach avoids the massing effects of other evaluative methods wherein there is little knowledge as to how or to what extent a particular individual changed. The concern of guidance is with the individual and his maximum development. The comprehensive method or case-study approach to evaluation, though time consuming, seems most appropriate for the work of guidance.

THE ROLE OF GUIDANCE PERSONNEL

Evaluation of guidance programs represents an investment of human intelligence, energy, and resources to determine the extent to which the expectations of such programs are being met. Sound appraisal of accomplishments is of utmost importance. If the assumption is correct that guidance represents an investment by the people of the community to insure the well-being of the total educational enterprise, then it is imperative that the results of guidance be subjected to careful appraisal.

Guidance personnel should not overlook the fact that evaluation is a matter of quality control. Quality control in the social sciences is derived in major part from the personnel conducting the activity, that is, guidance. Every guidance person can improve the quality of his services by extending his personal and professional growth. By constant, critical, objective appraisal of his decisions and recommendations, a sensitivity to quality of improvement will be developed in the counselor, as well as a growing awareness of his social utility.

---

[45]John A. Hilderbrand, "Accountability of the Present," *The Administrator.* Akron, Ohio: University of Akron, Vol. 3, No. 3 (Spring, 1973) p. 8.

Too often, guidance personnel have shied away from attempting evaluation, regarding it as a task for specialists. Such reluctance is not justified. A director of guidance, guidance staff members, administrators, interested teachers, who can and have thought their way through many difficulties to the establishment of an organized program, are also qualified to plan and conduct evaluation. Understandably, some evaluation procedures are more technical than others. If the staff does not have an individual with some training in measurement and statistics, consultant help may be obtained from state departments of education and from universities. But the important responsibilities of evaluation—formulation of objectives, statements of hypotheses, planning of procedures, carrying out of day-to-day activities— can only be carried on by local staff members. Such responsibilities are part of the professional responsibilities of any competent staff.

The director of guidance is the individual responsible for conducting evaluations of the effectiveness of the guidance program. Evaluative processes should be included in the organizational breakdown of duties of guidance personnel. Time should be allocated to carry through work of evaluation. A rule of thumb that has appeared in the literature of guidance is that at least 5 percent of each counselor's time should be spent in evaluation. This may be inadequate, but few existing programs seem to be devoting even that amount of time. Some counselors have more responsibilities for the formal systematic program of evaluation than others. But all counselors and other school personnel should be involved in the development of a master plan of evaluation.

It is a reality that some teachers, counselors, and administrators view evaluation as a threat to their methods, operations, or procedures. An uncooperative faculty may reject any ideas for guidance evaluation. In such situations, it is necessary to introduce evaluative practices gradually. Systematic programs of evaluation can be accomplished only when there is substantial agreement among all staff members that the time has come to ascertain how the guidance program in their school can be improved. The approach to be taken is "Our school *does* conduct guidance activities; how can they be improved?"

In the conduct of a systematic plan of evaluation, a few steps to be taken are suggested. *First,* begin with a clarification of the goals or objectives of the guidance program. Dressel has suggested that guidance personnel start with an all-institutional statement of objectives, and then sort out responsibility for the various objectives to the appropriate parts of the educational program.[46] Some objectives will be the concern of instruction, some of guidance, and some of both. Dressel has also cautioned that a wide range

---

[46]Dressel, *Personnel Services,* pp. 331–340.

of objectives should be kept in mind. This suggestion was made on the premise that guidance personnel have "tended to emphasize intelligence, interests, attitudes, values, and adjustment and ignore or pay slight attention to knowledge and creativity."[47]

A clear statement of objectives of the guidance program, couched in observable behavioral terms, is essential to determining the extent to which such objectives are being realized by the students.

Second, keep careful records of student behavior. There should be a continued effort to obtain longitudinal data on each student. Follow-up on students should be maintained. Careful records should be kept of students who avail themselves of the services of the guidance program. Efforts should be made to improve the efficiency of filing systems. Well kept, complete records of student behavior, maintained over a period of time, are essential to research and evaluation.

Third, involve as many faculty members as possible in some aspects of the program of evaluation. If improvement is to result from evaluation, staff members must understand what is taking place. Those who participate will have a better understanding of results. Greater cooperation can be expected in the data gathering when staff members are a part of the program. Faculty members who participate will more readily accept the results and will more intelligently and willingly follow through on the recommendations.

Fourth, design a master plan that makes use of several types of evaluation. Do not depend solely upon student reactions or faculty opinions. Planning should be carefully conducted. How will data be collected? How will they be analyzed? Can they be interpreted? Hypotheses that form the basis for the study should be stated so as to be testable. Planning eliminates the need for improvising, which often voids and curtails research and evaluation. Design a plan that includes continuous evaluation over an extended period of time.

Fifth, secure competent consultants on experimental designs and statistical treatment of data. Statistical methods for securing and treating data should be decided upon after the development of the statement of hypotheses. If the school staff has no individuals who are competent to do this, consultants must be obtained.

Sixth, act upon and publicize the results. The prime reason for conducting evaluation is to secure indications of what can be done. Evaluation is worthwhile when it leads to improvement. Present the results of evaluation to the community so that it can become better informed and capable of intelligent participation in the school.

---

[47] *Ibid.,* p. 338.

SUMMARY

Current evaluation studies indicate that guidance can be an effective program for aiding in the development of students. Evaluation is a means for determining the effectiveness of the program and serves as a basis for structuring improvements. Problems confronting guidance workers seeking to do evaluation include lack of time, skill, money, adequate criteria, suitable controls, and the like.

The survey method, scientific method, and comprehensive or case study method are approaches commonly utilized to evaluate guidance activities. Guidance processes must be closely observed, and their end products and desirability noted, for evaluations to be sound.

Guidance personnel must exercise their professional responsibilities and provide the time, effort, and leadership to conduct evaluative studies. The ultimate test of the success of a guidance program lies in its developmental effect upon the pupils.

ANNOTATED BIBLIOGRAPHY

Burck, Harman D., Harold F. Cottingham and Robert C. Reardon, *Counseling and Accountability: Methods and Critique.* New York: Pergamon Press, Inc., 1973, 279 pp.

The first part of the book deals with research approaches to studying the guidance functions. Part II contains a variety of summaries of research articles with research-based critiques.

Cramer, Stanley H., Edwin L. Herr, Charles N. Morris and Thomas T. Frantz, *Research and the School Counselor.* Boston: Houghton Mifflin Company, 1970, 202 pp.

The authors present research considerations in the much-needed guidance functions of follow-up, evaluation of the guidance program, and the measurement of attitudes. The counselor and data processing are discussed in Chapter 12.

Phi Delta Kappa National Study, Committee on Evaluation, *Educational Evaluation and Decision Making.* Itasca, Illinois: F. E. Peacock Publishers, Inc., 1971, 368 pp.

This book covers definitions of evaluation, evaluation in educational decision-making and the valuing process. In addition, chapters 6 and 7 present evaluation methodology and types and models. The latter chapters discuss organization and administration of evaluation units together with education of the evaluation specialist.

Guidance Programs in Action

What is the nature of an action-oriented elementary school guidance program?

What forces are involved in the development of guidance programs?

What is the nature of guidance in a community agency?

What are the guidance functions of a state agency?

Chapter 18

This chapter contains descriptions of two local school guidance programs, guidance services provided by a state department of education, and guidance services provided by a community agency. Generally, the descriptions of the two school programs follow the pattern of discussing community and school setting, organization of the school, development of guidance services, organization of guidance services, budget, physical facilities and equipment, and limitations and strengths of the guidance program. Description of the state service seeks to point out its historical development, present organization, and major functions. The descriptions are from the following individuals:

Elementary	Main Street Elementary School Columbus, Ohio	Anne L. Slaughter
Suburban school	Washington Township Schools, Indianapolis, Indiana	Clark Ketterman
State guidance services	Division of Guidance and Testing, Ohio Department of Education	Kenneth Richards
Community Agency		Katherine Cole

Main Street Elementary School Guidance Program

ANNE L. SLAUGHTER
Counselor

COMMUNITY AND SETTING

Columbus, Ohio, is the state's second largest city with a population of approximately 550,000. Columbus is a growing city, the largest city in Ohio in respect to area, and it is strategically located within the state. Columbus has become a many-sided community, with a commercial, cultural, and an industrial balance.

The Columbus Public School System is the seventeenth largest school system in the United States, and the second largest in Ohio. The school district is composed of 126 elementary schools, 27 junior high schools, and 14 high schools. Preferred size for Columbus Schools is 500 to 600 pupils in elementary schools, 700 to 1000 pupils in junior high schools, and 1200 to 1500 pupils in senior high schools.

Main Street Elementary School is located on the east side of Columbus. The school has an enrollment of approximately 550 pupils, a high percentage of which is composed of black students. A majority of the students in the school is from low income families.

551

DEVELOPMENT OF THE SCHOOL'S GUIDANCE PROGRAM

The elementary school guidance program in Columbus primarily serves inner-city and fringe inner-city schools. The district program was begun in September of 1965, with six certified counselors serving twelve schools in the outer-city. The Elementary and Secondary Education Act of 1965 provided funds so that Columbus Public Schools could place counselors in inner-city schools under Title I. The Title I project was begun in January, 1966, with six counselor-teachers (not yet certified counselors) and a project chairman serving twenty-eight "inner-city" schools, including twenty-three public and five diocesan. By 1969, the program had grown rapidly. Some forty-three counselors were serving sixty-eight Columbus Public elementary schools. However, by the 1972–73 school year, the program was reduced to thirty elementary school counselors due to unfortunate local and state financial cutbacks.

The counseling project in 1966 was conducted in Columbus public and private schools which had a significant number of "disadvantaged" children who manifested certain educational problems. The project, federally funded as a pilot project, was an attempt to evaluate whether elementary school guidance could be justified in meeting the needs of these children. It was begun in so-called "inner-city" schools because federal funds were available for those schools. Besides this obvious fact, it was also believed that the project should first be focused upon students experiencing difficulties in meeting individual needs which, although common to all children, are obviously perpetuated in disadvantaged children.

The need to maintain personal dignity and self-respect is less easily satisfied in a disadvantaged child. Needs to understand the school, its structure, its purpose, and its importance may be overlooked or unrecognized by the school. In homes where no model family provider existed, the child's need to understand his or her vocational role in the future sometimes becomes rather confused. Included in the proposed rationale for elementary school guidance and counseling services was the idea that such children are likely to have fewer success experiences in school, to have more reading and other academic difficulties, and to have a higher incidence of dropout rates.

Thus, the primary focus for the original elementary school guidance program in Columbus was to assist so-called "disadvantaged" pupils to achieve a better understanding of themselves, to help them cope more effectively with frustrations within the classrooms and with peers, to assist them in achieving more success experiences in school, and to improve their self-concepts. Elementary school guidance in Columbus has continued to focus upon central city students primarily because of restricted state funding for these priority schools and a lack of local funding for elementary school guidance. However, Columbus counselors believe that guidance must be developmental in nature in order to be effective. They believe that elementary school guidance programs should be operative in all elementary schools, because all children need assistance when they experience critical developmental stages during their elementary years. A preventative approach is more beneficial than a remedial or crisis-oriented one. Therefore, it is strongly believed by Columbus elementary school counselors that an organized guidance program with participation of administrators, teachers, other specialized personnel, paraprofessional staff, and parents, can and should be an integral part of every elementary school, in order to more efficiently meet the developmental needs of all children.

The rationale and philosophical base for elementary school guidance have remained the same since the beginning of guidance programs in Columbus, although the implementation of the guidance programs has varied somewhat from school to school, depending upon the priorities of the particular elementary school counselor as he evaluates the particular needs of his staff, students, and community. The Columbus elementary school counselors, program chairman, supervisor of counselor services, director of child study, and director of pupil personnel have cooperated as a unit in producing the statement, "Counselor Role and Function," (1972), as well as an *Elementary Guidance Handbook* (periodically revised) to provide overall structure and uniformity for the program. These sources establish a "skeletal" picture of possible activities, programs, and responsibilities for elementary counselors, although much flexibility is permitted for the individual counselor in order to implement a program most relevant to his particular school's needs.

Columbus elementary school counselors presently serve thirty-nine schools, twenty-three of which receive a full-time counselor and the remainder of which receive a part-time counselor. Schools which receive a full-time counselor are those schools designated as "high priority" schools and they are given some state funds to support elementary school guidance programs.

ORGANIZATION OF THE ELEMENTARY SCHOOL GUIDANCE PROGRAM

The emphasis of the guidance program at Main Street School has been on the counselor as being a consultant, a coordinator, and a counselor. The program focuses on the following services: the counseling component, classroom guidance, the testing program, parent involvement, referral, placement, information services, and staff development.

The counseling component is directed toward those students referred to the counselor for various reasons by staff members, primarily classroom teachers, but also by administrators, other counselors, by the counselor himself from previous contacts, or by the student himself on a self-referral basis. Students are primarily referred to the counselor because of peer difficulties, aggressive behavior or other unacceptable behavior, academic weaknesses, and for ability testing for special placement. However, students are also referred because of withdrawn behavior or emotional difficulties (incidences of frequent crying, anxieties, nervousness, psychosomatic tendencies). The referral system may either be formal or informal. During orientation meetings with the staff at the beginning of each school year, all staff members are informed of the referral process as well as the possible reasons for counselor referrals. Counselor referral forms, in a check-list format, are made available to all staff members. These forms allow the teacher to check appropriate behaviors which appear to be typical of the student. However, most referrals are made informally to the counselor in person to person contacts with staff members, and most frequently after a positive rapport has been established with a staff member who then feels more secure in receiving assistance from the counselor. Students are also informed as to how and for what reason they might come to see the counselor. Self-referrals are usually informal also; frequently established during recess, on the playground, at lunch time, or in the halls. Some "legitimate" cases for the counseling component are self-referred, but more are either primarily short-term, more crisis-oriented contacts lasting only one or two sessions, or curious onlookers seeking to get out of class for a few minutes.

Counseling

The counseling component consists of both individual and group counseling. Individual counseling is restricted to a few students, possibly four or five during the school day. These may be students who are too withdrawn to relate well enough socially in a group counseling experience, and/or who have more severe emotional difficulties. The bulk of the referred students, approximately fifty to sixty, are seen in counseling groups. The size of the groups vary from two or three members to as many as eight, depending upon the objectives of the group, and the social and emotional needs and abilities of the students. Average size for a group is five or six. Counseling groups may be categorized on a continuum from unstructured to very structured, depending upon the needs of the group members. The most frequent base for group counseling is improvement of peer relationship or interpersonal relationship skills. However, other groups have been structured for improvement of academic progress, self-concept skills, aggressive behavior in the classroom or on the playground, value orientations (lying, stealing), or for more instructionally oriented purposes such as information for vocational education, family living, or drug education.

The establishment of groups for counseling is a very difficult task because of the limiting factors involved: the selection of those students who will be mature enough to cooperate well in a group situation considering physical, social, and academic characteristics, and proximity in the building (same or different room); the selection of as many students as possible from the referred caseload; time established for group sessions, coordinated with each classroom teacher involved, plus any special teachers with whom the students may work; counselor room size (may be limiting to the number who can be accepted and still have the experience be comfortable); objectives and activities planned to best meet the needs of all students in the group; and mobility of students. Even though this process is involved and demands much ambiguity and flexibility, it seems to be more effective and satisfying than individual sessions with a small minority of the school enrollment.

Activities or techniques involved for group counseling are of course dependent upon the orientation of the counselor, but also upon the objectives of the group, and the selected students' abilities, interests, individual and group needs, and personal-social, academic, and physical maturity. Since the most frequent base for groups is to improve interpersonal relationships and to cope with frustrations in a socially acceptable manner, many group activities are focused upon role playing, and sociodramatic play, with or without the use of play media (puppets, props, etc.). Audio-visual aids are used very frequently with all groups. The Department of Child Study has available for counselor use a wide variety of filmstrips, record sets, and films, on topics related to interpersonal relationships, emotional-social growth, self-understanding, vocational education, drug, and family-life education. Audio-visual materials provide an excellent source of stimulating follow-up discussions, and provide opportunities for role-playing activities ("mock situations") to demonstrate alternative choices of behavior and consequences of certain behaviors. Commercially produced guidance-oriented kits for self-understanding are frequently used in group counseling situations, such as *Development and Understanding of Self and Others,* (puppets; cassette-narrated stories relating to feelings and interpersonal relations; Science Research Associates' *Focus on Self*—record, filmstrip-narrated stories, and emotionally stimulating pictures concerning self-understanding and understanding of others).

Bibliotherapy, the use of books, is an excellent way to stimulate group discussions organized for structured purposes, such as for discussing

information concerning vocations or family living. However, this is somewhat limiting in that only those students who can read fluently are able to
benefit by the use of books.

Examples of resources available to Columbus counselors are the *Random
House Series for Elementary Guidance,* books relevant for grades one
through four, relating to emotions and self-understanding; "World of
Work" books applicable for all grades; "Values" series for grades four
through six; and a collection of paperback books for "extracurricular"
reading for the purpose of stimulating interest in reading, although several
may be guidance oriented topics.

Use of Play Media

Play media (games, puzzles, blocks, building sets) are not used as frequently as the previously mentioned activities, although at times such media
may be very effective. For example, in the case of the very withdrawn child
or a child who is evidently experiencing internal feelings of hostility or
rejection, the use of play permits him to express his feelings. That, of course,
provides insight for the counselor and enables him to better understand the
student. This, in turn, enables him to respond to the student better. Play
media is also used as a relaxing technique with students—especially primary
students—before or after testing, and at the start of counseling sessions, as
positive reinforcement for acceptable behaviors in implementing behavior
modification theory in the counseling process.

As was previously mentioned, the group counseling activities will vary
with counselors, depending upon the counselor's training and theory orientation. Approaches or techniques with students depend, once again, upon
the students' needs which the counselor is attempting to meet, the personal
characteristics of the student, and the counselor himself. The counselor
must be familiar with a variety of counseling approaches, and must then be
willing to be flexible enough to experiment with all approaches, constantly
evaluating the effectiveness of these approaches with particular students.
For example, a group of third grade boys who were referred for aggressive
behavior in the classroom responded very well to a structured, behaviorally-
oriented group approach. However, a sixth grade group of girls, referred for
manifesting disobedience to authority, responded in a group situation which
was a very unstructured, awareness-oriented counseling approach. Other
techniques selected from rational-emotive, Adlerian, or transactional analysis approaches have merit with certain counseling groups. Therefore, a
counselor must constantly evaluate whether approaches implemented are
effective, and if they are comfortable for the counselor. No one counseling
approach or technique is a panacea for elementary school students; how-

ever, the overall counseling style, (posture, proximity to client, nonverbal behavior, manner of speaking, tone of voice, manner of rapport) may be relatively constant.

Research on counseling, which is incorporated into the counseling component for the elementary school guidance program, is the State Evaluation Component. This consists of a research experiment involving twenty to thirty students. These students selected for the evaluation program are the "core" of the counseling component, or those in need of a more concentrated counseling experience. The state evaluation group is selected by the fall of the school year, when pre-instruments are administered: a behavior rating scale is completed by each student's teachers, a behavior rating scale is completed by the counselor, and a personality inventory is completed by the student. After four months of counseling experience and after periodic evaluative logs have been kept by the counselor to note progress, post-instruments are administered to each student in the program which are the same as the pre-instruments. The data are then collected from all elementary guidance programs, are analyzed, and are recorded in a report, which is then sent to the State Department of Education to justify future funding of elementary guidance programs.

Classroom Guidance Activities

In the implementation of guidance in the classroom, the counselor serves primarily as a coordinator with the classroom teacher in formulating guidance oriented classroom programs or units. Topics for classroom guidance primarily focus on grooming, family living, career exploration, study skills, drug abuse, interpersonal relationship skills, self-understanding, and orientation to junior high. These units continue simultaneously with counseling groups throughout the school year, and may be scheduled for a period of at least four weeks, one to two sessions weekly, or up to as many as eight weeks. With the exception of study skill units, or those concerning orientation to junior high, all topics may be coordinated at any grade level. A sample of a classroom guidance schedule for the school year is as follows.

Testing

The elementary school testing program is a city-wide, kindergarten-to-sixth grade program. In addition, individual psychological testing is administered where appropriate. The standardized testing program consists of academic aptitude tests for second and fifth grades, reading achievement tests for grades one through six, math achievement tests for grades three through six, and language achievement tests for grades four and six. These

Classroom Guidance Schedule

Topic	Grade	Date	Activities, Materials	Coordinated with
Grooming; Family living	6th (girls) 6th (boys)	Oct.–Nov.	speakers, panels, group discussions, films, filmstrips, books	6th grade teachers, nurse, community resources-agencies, parent groups
Self-Understanding	1st	Jan.	kit — Development and Understanding of Self and Others guidance-oriented films, role-play	1st grade teachers
Self-Understanding	2nd	Feb.	kit — Development and Understanding of Self and Others, or Focus on Self guidance-oriented film, role-play	2nd grade teachers
Career Exploration	6th 3rd	Jan.–April Mar.	filmstrips, films, books, speakers, parent and community involvement	3rd grade–6th grade teachers, community agencies, and parents
Drug Educ.	4th–6th	April–May	speakers, films, agencies, parents, role-playing	4th–6th grade teachers, nurse, agencies, parents
Sixth Grade Orientation	6th	Jan.–May	group activities with junior high, assembly programs, teacher meetings with 6th–7th grade teachers	6th grade teachers, counselors-jr. high teachers

tests are administered the first two weeks in April. A reading readiness test is administered to kindergarten at the end of the school year, and to the first grade at the beginning of the school year.

The counselor's responsibilities, as testing coordinator for the school, include: orienting staff members concerning administering and scoring tests, orienting students concerning the testing program, primarily grades four through six where computer scored answer sheets are used, distributing all testing materials to staff members; planning an in-service meeting concerning the results of the testing; and organizing a testing schedule for tests administered in grades one through six.

The elementary school counselor is also responsible for administering individual psychological tests (such as the Slosson I.Q. test, Goodenough-

Draw-A-Man test, Wide-Range Achievement Test, and the Torrence Test of Creativity), primarily for in-class placement upon request by a teacher, for grade placement upon request by the principal, and as a screening procedure for possible referral to the school psychologist. In addition to this testing throughout the year, the counselor, with the help of kindergarten teachers, is involved in a two-week screening program for kindergarten children. A battery of tests, individual and group, are administered primarily for the purpose of early identification of learning disabilities and for referral to the school psychologist. Also, in May or early June, the counselor is responsible for administering early entrance tests to those children eligible, age-wise, for kindergarten or first grade placements. The instruments used in the early entrance testing include: the Lorge-Thordike Intelligence Test, the Rutgers Drawing Test, and the Star Reading Readiness Test.

All requests—records, data, and schedules for testing—concerning psychological evaluations—are coordinated by the elementary school counselor. Each school psychologist in Columbus presently serves approximately six schools. Consequently, the need is ever present for a screening procedure in order that priority cases can be scheduled for psychological assessment. The counselor is also helpful to the school psychologist in providing immediate feedback to the teacher concerning classroom activities or approaches which might be helpful for the child. The counselor is also instrumental in the referral process in coordinating special services for students who may be recommended for special programs by the school psychologist. These programs may be class or tutoring placements for educable mentally retarded or for children diagnosed as having learning disabilities or emotional difficulties.

Parent Consultation

A very rewarding experience for elementary school counselors is their involvement with parents. This includes planned parent activities designed for any parent to attend regardless of the age of his child, or parent interest groups involving meetings for certain purposes. At Main Street School during the 71–72 school year, a Block Parent Organization was begun by the counselor and parent coordinator. Information letters were sent to all students' parents explaining the purpose for the organization. Attached to the letter was an information slip which parents were to return to the school if they desired to participate in the program. The organization was designed as a preventative service for the school and community, to assist children in time of need when walking to and from school, and as an information source to improve school-community relations, and to include parent input into school policies. This organization thus served as a springboard for formulating a parent interest group. A "core" of parents began meeting monthly first in the school during the 71–72 school year, and then in the homes, during the 72–73 school year. The meetings in the homes proved to be quite successful, as feelings, suggestions for school programs, policies, and educational concerns, could be more comfortably expressed. Meetings varied from being very unstructured to somewhat structured. For example, speakers were asked to speak on school and community-related concerns such as drug abuse or community sanitation; or parents would often informally discuss, using the counselor and parent coordinator as resource people, ways to help their children improve reading skills.

In addition to monthly parent meetings, individual parent conferences were and are conducted during the entire school year. The counselor is continually meeting with parents either on a spontaneous or scheduled basis to discuss particular concerns of a child and ways to improve behaviors. If a parent is unable to come to the school, the counselor will visit the home to discuss these concerns. Along with the parent coordinator, the counselor is responsible for initiating contacts with parents who are new to the district. The counselor and the school nurse are responsible for initiating contacts with those parents whose children have been recommended for a different grade or class placement, or for extra in-school tutoring or class placement in special programs for emotionally or learning disabled children or for the educable mentally retarded.

Referral Procedures

In providing the school with a referral service, the counselor acts as a coordinator with the rest of the staff, involving the administration, nurse, school psychologist, teachers, parents, and the community agencies involved. This service attempts to provide students and parents with assistance for those additional pupil services not offered by the school. Referral services may involve such community agencies as hospitals, mental health clinics, medical clinics, psychiatric clinics and hospitals, family and children counseling centers, welfare departments, and Big Brother associations. The elementary school counselor works very closely with the school nurse in this area of coordinating appointments for children, making parent contacts, and compiling school referral reports for community agencies.

The elementary school counselor again acts as a coordinator with the administration, parents, nurse, school psychologist, and teachers concerning placements of children. This may involve appropriate grade level placements, curriculum placements for instructional purposes, special class or tutoring programs, placements in special schools for special academic assistance, or emotional difficulties.

Resource Agent

The elementary school counselor also acts as a resource staff member in providing information services to staff, parents, and students concerning educational, vocational, and personal-social growth. Various materials (audio-visual guidance materials, books, and pamphlets) are available to staff, students, and parents concerning their particular needs. For example, information available for parents is primarily concerned with child management techniques, child behavior, academic difficulties, and community concerns. Information to staff members primarily focuses on classroom instructional materials which are guidance-oriented to improve classroom management techniques (books, instructional materials, prepared units on various topics, and information concerning learning disabilities and reading programs. Other information provided to the staff includes opportunities for professional growth through university course offerings, adult education programs, or in-service workshops and other staff development programs. Information for student use includes paperback books, pamphlets, audio-visual materials, pictures, and instructional books concerning values, career exploration, self-understanding, and general interest reading.

The elementary school counselor is also instrumental as a liaison person to coordinate school programs or activities such as the student council, and any university-related programs, such as an early experience program involving university students, or a big brother-big sister program involving elementary school students and university students. University-related programs provide an excellent source of staff development activities which the counselor coordinates throughout the school year.

PHYSICAL FACILITIES

The physical facilities available to Columbus elementary school counselors vary, depending upon the particular school to which a counselor is assigned. Most counselors' physical facilities are very adequate. At Main Street School the counselor's room is approximately nine feet by twelve feet. A considerable amount of space is needed for equipment and supplies, including two large file cabinets, a storage cabinet for play media, a bookcase, a table, six to eight chairs, a desk, a desk chair, and a rocking chair. Therefore, the room is limiting in terms of the number of students selected for group counseling sessions. The room is located in the older section of the building; however general maintenance and lighting are very adequate. Audio-visual equipment is made available to Columbus counselors for use in their particular programs by the Department of Child Study of the Columbus Board of Education. Equipment available includes a filmstrip projector, record player, cassette and standard tape recorder, and an adequate supply of tapes.

BUDGET

The Department of Child Study allocates to each counselor a budget of $75 each year with which to purchase guidance materials. In addition to this, each counselor has a school budget of $150. Most of this budget is used to purchase all needed materials (test booklets, answer sheets, manuals, etc.) for the city-wide testing program. Any remaining funds are utilized for purchasing clerical materials the counselor may need during the school year.

STRENGTHS AND WEAKNESSES OF THE PROGRAM

A major strength of the Main Street Elementary School guidance program is the personal and emotional support given to counselors by the supervisory staff of the Child Study Department of the Board of Education. The assistance and support given by the Program Chairman, as well as by other supervisory personnel of the Child Study Department is most appreciated by all Columbus elementary school counselors. Their help has done much to create unity among the total elementary school guidance staff and has contributed to the success of the elementary school guidance program in Columbus.

Along with this emotional support and personal unity is the availability of support concerning guidance materials and professional growth. The Department of Child Study makes available for counselor use a variety of guidance materials, such as recent audio-visual aids, guidance literature, and instructional materials. Many opportunities are available for in-service workshops for professional growth, which are offered periodically throughout the school year.

Another strength of the Columbus elementary school guidance program is the way elementary school counselors are encouraged to formulate a guidance program most relevant to the needs of a particular school and its community. There are a few counselors, however, who have expressed that they would feel more comfortable having more structure given to the program by supervisory staff. They suggest that there is too much ambiguity in the program. This may be seen as a weakness in the program by some counselors; however, most counselors appreciate the flexibility of the program and have learned to cope with the ambiguity—which is often a result of a program which attempts to be flexible to best meet the needs of a school's staff, students, and community.

Because most elementary school counselors believe in providing a program which is flexible to best meet the needs of the school, counselors may have a tendency to attempt to be responsible for more duties than they are capable of handling. One counselor remarked at an elementary school counselor meeting that when she walked into her building, she was handed a slip of paper which read, "Do everything!" Elementary school counselors need to be wary of "spreading themselves too thin." This lessens the effect of their services and also can be detrimental to the counselor's personal mental health. It is very critical that counselors budget their time in scheduling priorities for the program, and then concentrate on accomplishing these priorities. This is not an easy task. Most counselors desire to have flexibility take precedence over schedule. However, in view of the fact that elementary school guidance trends are currently emphasizing more accountability in guidance programs, elementary school counselors will need to aim, for their own personal and emotional satisfaction, for flexibility within a priority-based, systematic program.

Development and Organization of Guidance Services Metropolitan School District of Washington Township Indianapolis, Indiana

Clark S. Ketterman, Ph.D.
Director of Pupil Personnel Services

COMMUNITY AND SCHOOL SETTING

The Metropolitan School District of Washington Township, Marion County, is adjacent to Indianapolis on the immediate north side. It is a horseshoe-shaped area, and since the early 1800s has had its own separate school system. In 1884, there were fifteen public schools in the township, but with condemnation, consolidation, and new construction, the end of World War II found only three large elementary schools. These schools provided an education for students in grades one through eight, with high school students attending the Indianapolis high schools on a tuition basis. There were approximately 1300 pupils in the three elementary schools in the 1945–46 school year. By 1951, the enrollment had grown to 2200, and concerned citizens began to take steps to increase the number of schools when the Township Trustee announced that one-half day sessions would be the order of the day for the 1952 school year. In the Fall of 1953, two additional elementary schools were opened and a third was under construction.

During the early part of 1954, the concerned citizens formed themselves into the School planning Committee to investigate the possibilities of providing a total K–12 school system. Their major efforts during the initial years of operation were to raise money through debenture bonds for the building of junior and senior high schools. In 1955, a sympathetic Trustee candidate was elected and the first Board of School Commissioners was appointed on August 1, of that year. In 1956, a Superintendent of Schools was chosen and the district provided education for youngsters from kindergarten through the twelfth grade in its own schools. The 1972-73 school year found the school district with an enrollment of 15,500 students in grades K–12, which ranked this district as the tenth largest district in the state of Indiana. It is composed of twelve elementary schools, three junior high schools (grades 7 through 9), one senior high school (grades 10 through 12), and a school for trainable retarded children. An Area Vocational School is located on the same campus area as the high school and provides twenty-four different vocational classes for students from this school district as well as those from eight other nearby participating districts. Figure 18–1 depicts the organizational pattern of the Metropolitan School District of Washington Township.

Patrons living in the school community work in a wide variety of vocational settings. The greatest number hold managerial or executive positions in the business world or in the professions. Members of the community embrace the fundamental philosophy of the school: that each individual not only has worth, but also has the potential to be a unique person, capable of making a unique contribution to society; and that in accordance with the democratic idea, each individual is entitled to no less than the opportunity to develop to his fullest potential.

The community is primarily a residential or "bedroom" community with the residents working in the city of Indianapolis or in surrounding areas. There is little industry within the corporation boundaries; primarily, shopping centers and isolated professional office buildings comprise the business community. A relatively recent phenomenon to the township has been the increased number of apartment complexes. At least three of these complexes have been designed for low-income family housing, and they have attracted inner-city families into this suburban district. However, the predominant and most obvious social stratification remains in the middle to upper-middle class range. Racially, the community has approximately 10 percent non-white residents.

The community residents, from the time of the original Planning Committee to the present, continue to demonstrate a high degree of interest and involvement in the schools and their activities. The Planning Committee has continued to function as a liaison advisory committee to the School Board and the school administrators. Various subcommittees of the larger committee have been formulated and these involve themselves with certain aspects of the total school program. One such committee is the Guidance

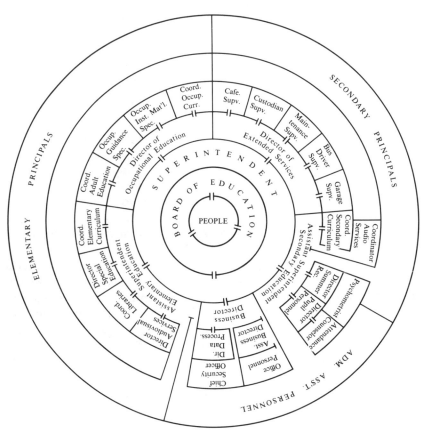

Figure 18-1.   *Organizational Pattern of the Metropolitan School District of Washington Township*

Committee, which has served to keep the community informed of current guidance practices, to offer manpower to appropriate guidance activities, and to serve as a general sounding board for any matters relative to guidance and counseling policies and practices. Likewise, each school parent-teacher organization within the district has a subcommittee directly or indirectly related to guidance and other pupil personnel services. More discussion of parent involvement in guidance functions will be given later in this text.

As would naturally be expected, the school district experiences a very low dropout rate in relation to local, state, and national statistics. A less than 8 percent dropout rate has been demonstrated over the past several years. Approximately 80 percent of the high school graduates move on into post-high school educational settings. Approximately 75 percent enroll in diploma or degree-granting institutions. Prior to the opening of the area vocational school, the greatest curricular deficiency lay in the area of providing appropriate education for the noncollege-bound student. Since the vocational school has been added, the district believes that it is providing for a wide variety of student goals, and coupled with the special education curriculum, it is providing sound educational programs for virtually 100 percent of its school-age children. The high school and junior high schools offer a diverse program of curricular offerings. Although this can complicate the work of the counselors in educational planning, it certainly demonstrates that the school is interested in providing a well-balanced educational program for all its students. The twelve elementary schools within the district might best be described as individually unique and innovative. Three elementary schools have adopted the individually guided education (IGE) approach, four are operating on an open-school concept, and the others, though organized in a self-contained classroom structure, are constantly innovating in the areas of teaching techniques and methodology.

GUIDANCE SERVICES IN PERSPECTIVE

Counselors were employed by the school district when it opened its first secondary school. In 1966 the school district employed a Director of Pupil Personnel Services to coordinate all services which existed at that time and to develop a pupil personnel team approach. Figure 18-2 shows the organization of the district-wide personnel services. The guidance services are one of four pupil personnel services supervised by this individual. Others include: social services (staffed by three social workers); the psychological services (staffed by two psychometrists); and the health services (staffed by school nurses). The school district has utilized the pupil personnel team approach in working with individual students in all aspects of their development. At this time, the most significant deficiency in the overall program is the lack of elementary school counselors. Guidance services at the elementary schools are provided primarily through the building administrators, the principal and/or the assistant principal. The elementary school building administrator is responsible for the pupil appraisal program, for referrals to social workers and psychometrists, and for providing counseling with selected students on an individual or group basis. The Director of Pupil Personnel Services coordinates and supervises a township-wide standardized testing program which provides testing for pupils in kindergarten and in the first, second, fourth, sixth, eighth, and tenth grades, in the area of achievement and ability. The elementary school principal is responsible for coordinating this program within his building and seeing that the results are properly disseminated and utilized.

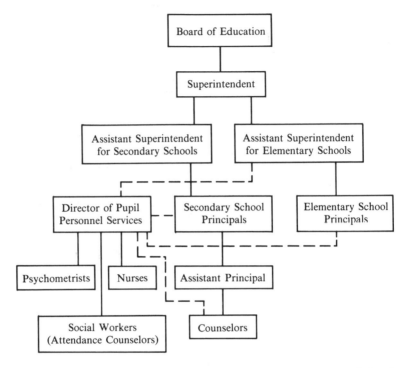

Figure 18-2.   *Organization of Pupil Personnel Services, M.S.D. of Washington Township*

Due to their size, the three junior high schools have a different counseling staff composition. The largest of the three schools, which has an enrollment of approximately 1600 students, has four full-time and two part-time counselors, making an equivalent of approximately five full-time counselors. The next larger junior high school has four full-time counselors with an enrollment of 1,150 students. The smallest junior high school has two full-time counselors and two half-time counselors and an enrollment of 950 students. The senior high school has a staff of eleven full-time counselors. One of these individuals serves as the Chairman of the Guidance Department, but carries a counseling load of approximately 100 students. The Area Vocational School, which falls under the administrative jurisdiction of the township, has two full-time counselors. Since they serve students from several high schools, they depend upon the student's home-school counselor to provide the bulk of the counseling services. The vocational school's counselors do, however, perform a great deal of educational/vocational counseling and work primarily in the planning and placement service area. Close coordination is required between these counselors and the counselors at the feeder high schools.

There are then twenty-seven certified counselors in the school district, including twenty-three full-time and four part-time counselors. During the academic year, a meeting of all counselors is held each month. The primary focus of these meetings is on in-service training with a minimum amount of time devoted to administrative problems. In addition to these monthly meetings, weekly meetings are held at the individual buildings. These weekly meetings are held under the direction of the building administrator or his designated assistant principal. At these building meetings, the social worker and psychometrist serving that building are often invited to attend to discuss concerns regarding individual students they have served during that week. The counselors discuss individual cases and much staff coordination is accomplished.

In 1958, the counselors combined energies and wrote a very comprehensive, detailed description of the functions they performed. In 1967, under the direction of the Director of Pupil Personnel Services, the counselors condensed this paper and developed a statement of Role and Function which was subsequently adopted by the school administration and the Board of Education, and which became part of the administrative handbook used by all building administrators. In 1971, a revision and condensation of this statement was accomplished and again adopted. This time it was not only published in the administrative handbook but also in the teachers handbook. This current Role and Function statement is as follows:

Role

Counselors serve a unique position in the total school program. They are not teachers in the strictest sense, although each counselor has taught prior to being certified. Each is, therefore, aware of classroom activities and problems. They are not administrators, although principals frequently expect counselors to identify student concerns. Rather they are student-advocates, concerned adults with specialized competencies in the behavioral sciences, who will do everything they can to understand and help their students. As a result of this unique status in the school system, counselors serve as communicators with students and all other facets of the school community. To serve effectively, counselors must frequently meet with students, teachers, and parents in a variety of environments—the school halls, the cafeteria, the classroom, the home.

Functions

The primary function of guidance is to assist young people by:

1. Helping them to understand themselves through realistic self-appraisal.

2. Helping them to work through their own problems.

3. Cultivating within them a sense of worth and dignity.

4. Providing them with sources of curricular and occupational information which make possible: (a) the development of saleable skills during public school experience; (b) post high school training in a vocational/technical school setting; (c) post-high school education in a college or university setting; and (d) realistic occupational decisions.

To further serve the student, counselors work closely with a number of people, including:

1. Parents by (a) providing information about their child and the school; and (b) by making themselves available for consultation.

2. Faculty Members, by (a) serving as communicating links among students, parents, and teachers; (b) by providing information to help teachers better understand *all* their students; (c) by consulting with teachers regarding individual students who need special attention; and (d) by being an auxiliary resource for the development of the guidance techniques for classroom use.

3. Administrators, by (a) identifying needs for curriculum revision; (b) by providing information regarding student concerns; (c) by suggesting improvements in scheduling procedures; (d) by interpreting to students established policies and the reasoning behind policy changes; (e) by implementing needed changes in individual schedules; and (f) by serving as their liaison among all schools and employers.

4. Referral agencies within the school corporation, such as social workers, psychometrists, and health service personnel; and outside the school corporation, such as private tutorial services; private physicians, hospitals, legal agencies, and child guidance agencies.

Within each junior high school building, the counselors are immediately supervised by an assistant principal. This individual directs the counseling activities for that building, and is generally considered the Director of Guidance and Pupil Personnel Services. At the high school there is a chairman of the guidance department who serves as guidance director and who is immediately responsible to an assistant principal. The Director of Pupil Personnel Services serves as a coordinator and supervisor of guidance services and reports directly to an assistant superintendent. The Director of Pupil Personnel Services has no direct authority over building principals but works as a central office staff member who consults, advises, and coordinates guidance services throughout the township.

GUIDANCE SERVICES IN ACTION

Organization

All counselors are assigned counselees on the basis of alphabetic distribution. The average counseling load is approximately 330 students per counselor. The junior high counselors will have an equal number of seventh-, eighth-, and ninth-grade students assigned to them, and likewise at the high school, where each counselor will have approximately the same number of students in grades ten, eleven, and twelve. At one junior high school the students are not only assigned on an alphabetic basis but also the girls are assigned to two female counselors and the boys assigned to two male counselors. In the other schools the assignment is made disregarding sex. On a generalist/specialist polarized scale the counselors would be considered closer to the generalist end; however, some flexibility does exist. For example, at the high school there are two black counselors who are assigned counselees on the same basis as all other counselors. If another counselor has a student whom he believes could relate better to one of the black counselors, he can make arrangements for that student to be assigned to that counselor for certain guidance services. This flexibility exists in all buildings, and therefore, arrangements can be made to provide for just about any contingency that may exist which would cause a counselor to request a student being assigned to another colleague.

Counseling

At least two conferences with each student are scheduled by the counselor each year. At these times, the student has the opportunity to discuss educational plans, to explore educational goals, or to discuss any concern for which he feels the counselor could help. Many students seek additional conferences with their counselor throughout the school year in regard to matters of a personal, educational, or vocational nature. Many of the counselors are working with small group counseling activities and several in-service training sessions have been directed toward this activity. Class-room-size guidance activities are also arranged for imparting educational and vocational information of a general nature. A recent in-service training workshop taught the Micro-Lab Technique as developed by Duane Kurpius at Indiana University. This technique enables the counselor to work with a classroom-size group of twenty-five to thirty students, with emphasis upon improving communication skills and indirectly helping students to develop a more positive self-concept. There is a great emphasis on group guidance and counseling activities throughout the school district.

The counseling setting is primarily directed toward helping students gain a better self-understanding and a more complete knowledge of his environment. Therefore, heavy emphasis is placed upon providing information to the student about himself and his world. The results of standardized tests, occupational information, educational materials, and general materials designed to aid students in developing a better self-concept are utilized in the counseling relationship.

Orientation

An orientation program is planned by junior high school counselors and directed towards sixth grade students who will be entering the junior high the following year. It is basically a three-phased program which involves counselors working with students, parents, and sixth-grade teachers. Junior high school counselors, accompanied by administrators and pupils, visit the elementary feeder schools and provide a general orientation program to sixth-grade classes. Later these students are taken on a tour of the junior high during a normal school day. On a subsequent visit to the elementary building, the counselors spend their time in individual conferences with teachers, getting to know individual students better and developing educational plans which will be implemented at the seventh-grade level. Group-parent orientation programs are scheduled during the evenings and parents visit and tour the junior high school buildings. Similar activities are conducted by the high school counselors for the ninth-grade students who will be enrolled at the high school the coming year. The junior high school counselors also meet with the high school counselors to discuss youngsters who need special attention in the area of curriculum and personal-social problems.

Appraisal Services

Counselors maintain the students' cumulative folders in their offices and are responsible for seeing that information gathered through standardized testing, individual psychological testing, teacher anecdotal records, counseling conference records, and teacher personality ratings are collected, analyzed, and used. Counselors record the basic highlights of all counseling interviews. Test results are provided through the school district's data processing center, and come in the form of individual profile sheets. These sheets are shared with the student and his parents and a copy is maintained for the student's cumulative record. Counselors are aware that the appraisal service is a vital aspect of the total guidance program, and work diligently to see that objective and subjective data are collected and utilized for all students.

Planning and Placement Services

In addition to the educational planning referred to previously, conferences are scheduled with all eighth-grade students, and parents are invited to attend. During this conference, the student's ninth-grade program is planned in detail, utilizing all information available to the counselor. Parent interest in this activity is high. The schools have experienced about 95 percent participation from parents, and in most conferences, both parents attend, even though it is scheduled during school hours. During this conference the student is asked to complete a four-year plan record to the best of his ability. Oftentimes only the ninth and tenth grade years are planned in detail, but in some cases a student can project his entire four years of high school work on the plan sheet. The reverse side of the plan sheet contains a personal data questionnaire. The student is asked to list his most-liked subjects, his least-liked subjects, his occupational and educational goals, and other personal data such as hobbies, job experiences, traveling experiences, and reading interests. Again at the ninth grade level, an educational planning conference is scheduled. However, parents are not specifically asked to attend but students are informed that they may invite their parents. Approximately 50 percent of the ninth-grade students are accompanied by their parents when this conference is held. The student and the counselor review the tenth-grade program, and modifications are made in the four-year plan sheet. At the high school, subsequent education planning conferences are held on an individual or small group basis for the students planning eleventh- and twelfth-grade programs. Parents do not attend these conferences, but a subject election form is sent to the home to be returned by the student with a parent's signature. High school counselors also assist junior and senior high school students in planning for education beyond the high school level. As previously mentioned, approximately 80 percent of the students do go on to some form of advanced education, and this requires that counselors provide those services necessary to the student to assist him in making the transition from high school to the post-high school institution. A great deal of energy has been devoted to reducing the amount of paper work involved in all aspects of educational planning. The counselors of Washington Township believe that they have reduced this, with the aid of the computer and special forms, to a minimum. The student himself is responsible for providing much of the data necessary for the completion of college applications. The counselor's involvement in writing recommendations has been streamlined to a high degree. The counselors in the Area Vocational School are heavily involved in placement of graduates in full-time positions. They also maintain a file of part-time jobs available to students within the community. This service has been well advertised throughout the school and the community. Employers and prospective employees constantly seek help from this service.

Physical Facilities

Adequate facilities for guidance in all secondary schools are fundamental for efficient service to the students. The three junior high schools have somewhat different arrangements. In one junior high school, the guidance officers are located in the three grade level wings. These are separated by some distance from the administrative offices and seem to meet the needs of that school's community quite well. Another junior high school has recently undergone a complete remodeling, and the guidance area is based upon an open concept with available private offices for each counselor as well as a large open area where counselors can be visible to the students at all times. The third junior high school, which was formerly a high school building, has the guidance suite near but not adjacent to the administrative suite. All offices are spacious and offer a warm, comfortable environment. Special reception areas are also used for guidance materials. These materials are generally maintained by student assistants. The high school has two full-time secretaries to perform clerical functions for the counselors. Each junior high school has secretarial help available on a part-time basis.

Parent Involvement

As mentioned earlier in this text, the parents of this school district are sincerely interested and actively involved with their schools. Parents are utilized by guidance personnel quite heavily in many activities. Each secondary school has a career day program which is completely organized by parents. Parent-teacher club committees survey student interests, solicit speakers, and coordinate these career day programs in each building. A college night program is similarly operated by parents at the high school once each year. Throughout the year parents are asked to assist in other guidance-related programs sponsored in the individual schools.

Undoubtedly some school districts look upon parent involvement as "parent pressure"; however, the Washington Township schools have accepted this involvement as a sincere and dedicated interest on the part of their patrons and have directed these talents toward a better overall guidance service.

NEW DIRECTIONS

An on-going evaluation of guidance services is built into the overall guidance program. Through the School Planning Committee, parent-teacher organizations, administrators, counselors, teachers and students, input is obtained to identify strengths and areas within the guidance services which need improvement. One of the major shortcomings of the program is the lack of an adequate follow-up service. With the help of parents and administrators, the school district is working towards maintaining an up-to-date mailing list of all graduates and former students. Each year at the end of the first semester a questionnaire is sent to all graduates of the previous year. We recognize that this does not give us the long range evaluation which we vitally need; however, once a good file of former students is begun, it will be possible to conduct follow-up studies on groups four or five years removed from the school. As previously mentioned, we are concerned about the lack of elementary school counselors in our district, but have worked closely with building principals to provide guidance services on a limited basis to the elementary school child.

Washington Township has recently purchased a very sophisticated computer which has been of immeasurable assistance to the guidance counselors. Much more can be done in utilizing this equipment for the information services as well as the education planning and placement services. A committee has been formulated to more thoroughly study the possibility of inaugurating the CIVIS or a similar type education-vocation information program utilizing computers. Another obvious trend in the guidance program in the Washington Township school system is the movement towards heavier utilization of group techniques. This is recognized as an effective and efficient approach to working in many aspects of the guidance services. Finally, we are most proud of our pupil personnel team approach to assisting individual students and their families. We continue to develop this approach each year by increasing staff and by streamlining referral techniques. A heavy emphasis is placed upon the "staffing" approach to an individual student's problem.

Division of Guidance and Testing Ohio State Department of Education

KENNETH W. RICHARDS

The following description portrays that portion of the Department of Education, State of Ohio, which is related to guidance services. The Department is responsible to the State Board of Education which is composed of twenty-three members who are elected by the people of the State on a nonpartisan basis from each of the Congressional districts. Among the responsibilities of the State Board of Education, as the policy-making body for public education in Ohio, are

1. Formulating and administering educational policies relating to instruction, teaching materials, finance, and school district organization.

2. Apportioning and administering the distribution of all State and Federal funds to elementary and secondary schools.

3. Prescribing minimum standards to be applied to all elementary and high schools.

4. Determining who should teach and how they should be prepared.

5. Operating the State Schools for the Blind and Deaf.

6. Serving as the State Board of Vocational Education and the State Board of Vocational Rehabilitation.

7. Hearing important issues as a board of review.

8. Cooperating with other State and Federal agencies concerning the health and welfare of youth.

State Department of Education personnel are responsible to the State's chief school officer, the Superintendent of Public Instruction, who is appointed by the Board. As of November 1, 1973, Ohio Department of Education comprised 573 professional personnel and 450 clerical and maintenance persons. Figure 18–3 is a simplified organizational chart of the Ohio Department of Education.

ORGANIZATION OF STATE DIVISION OF GUIDANCE AND TESTING

It is noted in Figure 18–3 that the Division of Guidance and Testing is a unit within the Department and contains one administrative unit and three service sections. Twenty-three professional staff members are employed by this Division in the capacities indicated in Figure 18–4.

FUNCTION OF STATE DIVISION OF GUIDANCE AND TESTING

The Division provides assistance to Ohio schools in the development of adequate guidance and testing programs. Services provided include: consultation, in-service education, research and evaluation, publications, identification and use of resources, promotion of state and area professional organizations, and cooperation of statewide professional conferences. It cooperates with other Divisions of the State Department of Education and nonschool agencies on projects of mutual concern such as audio-visual workshops, supervisory conferences, vocational surveys, research, development of criteria for counselor certification, high school equivalency testing program, and preservice education of teachers and counselors. The three service sections indicated in Figure 18–4 provide the following services:

1. *Measurement and Evaluation Services Section*
   a. Assists school personnel in the organization and coordination of their total school testing program.

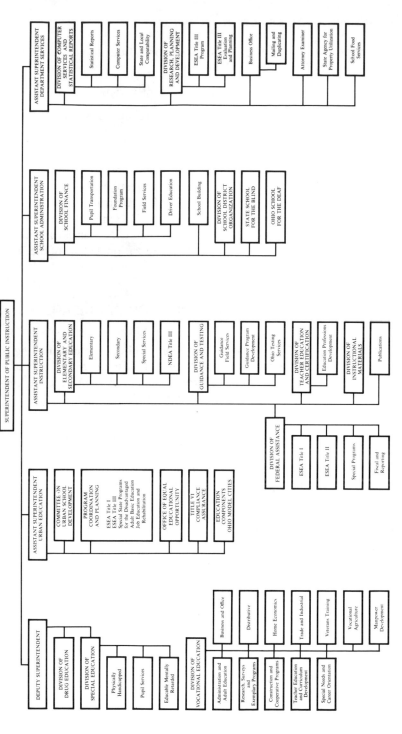

Figure 18-3   The Ohio Department of Education Organization Chart

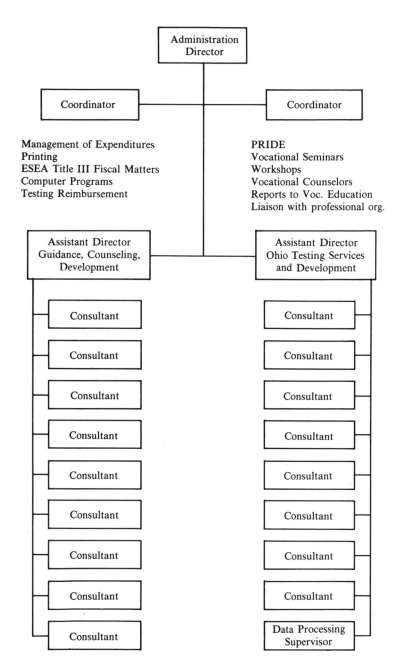

Figure 18–4.   *Organization Division of Guidance and Testing*

    b. Assists school personnel to use test results for instructional, guidance, and administrative purposes.

    c. Administers a program for the release of the General Aptitude Test Battery to secondary schools and conducts related counselor education programs.

    d. Administers funds for reimbursement of school testing programs under NDEA, Title V-A.

2. *Guidance Services Section*

    a. Assists schools to initiate, evaluate, and expand guidance programs at all grade levels.

    b. Administers funds for reimbursement of local guidance programs under NDEA, Title V-A.

    c. Coordinates vocational guidance programs which are funded by the Division of Vocational Education.

3. *Ohio Testing Services Section*

    a. Provides services and materials related to state testing programs which include the Ohio Survey Tests, Ohio Diagnostic Series, Ohio Tests of Scholastic Achievement, Ohio History Test, High School Equivalency Test, and 8th, 9th, and 10th Grade Equivalency Tests.

    b. Coordinates the development of item banks for the Tests of Scholastic Achievement. (2)

CURRENT PRIORITIES

In its statewide guidance system, the Division addresses itself to three priority objectives to assist school systems in developing a written program describing the services which the school community can expect from school counselors. Responsibility for the implementation of school guidance services is placed in the hands of the building principal. He must develop a system to deliver guidance services to the community.

"What does a School Counselor do?" was the question that was answered in fulfilling the first objective in the Division publication *Guidance Service for Ohio Schools*,[1] which clearly defines the functions of a school counselor. This publication lists nine dimensions of guidance services and sets forth the building principal's role in such services. This publication is used as a model for school guidance programs across the state.

---

[1]Martin W. Essex, G. Robert Bowers and Kenneth W. Richards, *Guidance Services for Ohio Schools*. Columbus, Ohio: Ohio Department of Education, 1971.

The second objective consists of a system to deliver the guidance services as defined in *Guidance Services for Ohio Schools.* This system utilizes data obtained from the *Ohio Vocational Interest Survey-General Aptitude Test Battery Combined Report* (OVIS-GATB) to formulate a strategy for career guidance.

The third objective was to provide leadership from the state level to K–12 guidance programs. One thrust of such leadership was in the area of early identification of children for individualized instruction to enhance ongoing elementary school guidance models. The second thrust involved placement and follow-up of graduating students from Ohio high schools. Implemented in 1973, both of these programs continue to be developed and tested in models around the state.

PROFESSIONAL PERSONNEL

To execute guidance services for Ohio schools, the Division of Guidance and Testing employs twenty-three professional staff members and twenty-four support personnel. The professional staff members are funded from three different sources: thirteen from the Elementary and Secondary Education Act (ESEA), Title III; four from Vocational Education; and seven from test sales income. It is not always possible to ascribe specific division activities to specific sources of funding. This report, more or less, highlights the Division activities and services primarily funded by ESEA, Title III, and related state funds.

PROGRAM DEVELOPMENT AND DISSEMINATION

The Division of Guidance and Testing assists local schools in program development by providing consultative services. During the fiscal year (FY) 1973, the Division provided over 900 days of such services, conducted thirty Guidance Services Evaluations, and coordinated twenty *Program Review(s) For Improvement, Development, and Expansion in Vocational Education and Guidance* (PRIDE). These reviews served to assist schools in the implementation of the aforementioned nine dimensions of a guidance program. During FY 1973, a four-phase, five-year Longitudinal Follow-Up System was developed and piloted in ten school systems. (This system had been initiated in 1971.)

The Guidance Program Evaluation materials, developed in 1969, were revised and updated and are being used as a package with *Guidance Services for Ohio Schools* in the development and improvement of guidance services in Ohio schools. Through Ohio Testing Services, a self-supporting unit, the

Division provides the following tests and surveys: (1) *American History Contest;* (2) *Ohio Tests of Scholastic Achievement;* (3) *Ohio Survey Tests;* (4) *General Aptitude Test Battery;* and (5) *Ohio Vocational Interest Survey.* With the exception of the *General Aptitude Test Battery* (not prepared by Ohio Testing Services and of which 50,000 were administered during FY 1973), that section developed and distributed 335,000 tests and surveys to Ohio schools during 1973. In addition, Ohio Testing Services provides consultative services, and develops interpretive materials to assist schools in improving their test program organization, administration, and interpretation. Also, to assist adults who have not completed high school, the Division offers the *Ohio Equivalency Tests for Grades 8, 9, and 10* and the *Tests of General Educational Development.* During FY 1973, 138 persons successfully passed the equivalency tests for grades 8, 9, and 10, and 6, 261 of the adults taking the General Educational Development (GED) tests received a statement of high school equivalency.

Coordination with other Pupil Personnel Services and Resources

The Ohio Division of Guidance and Testing has a very close working relationship with the Ohio Division of Vocational Education, sponsoring jointly a number of projects such as:

1. Seventeen two-week summer seminars, conducted annually for practicing school counselors and covering the vocational aspects of guidance. Participation in at least one of these seminars is required of all counselors who become reimbursed vocational guidance coordinators.

2. Establishment of standards and administration of a program for the reimbursement of vocational guidance coordinators in Ohio schools, including Joint Vocational Schools. Approximately 160 vocational guidance coordinators are currently functioning under this program.

3. Development and piloting of programs of career information (K–6), career orientation (7–8), and career exploration (1–10), in selected Ohio schools, including the development of materials and procedures.

4. Work with vocational education staff members in conducting a PRIDE program for evaluating vocational education programs, including vocational guidance. This program involved the administration of over 25,000 *Ohio Vocational Interests Surveys* (OVIS)

during FY 1973 and the development and administration of more than 40,000 student opinion questionnaires as well as 40,000 parent opinion questionnaires. This is an ongoing activity.

5. Work with new vocational education programs in the development of vocational guidance services and in surveying interests in the careers and vocational education of students in feeder schools.

6. Planning and coordinating an annual three-day conference for all counselor education personnel in the state, to help keep them abreast of new developments in vocational education and vocational guidance and to encourage the strengthening of counselor education programs with reference to the vocational aspects of guidance.

7. Coordination of data collection and publication of informational materials related to vocational education, including the periodic preparation of the *Ohio Vocational Education Notebook* (OVEN) and the distribution of the materials to guidance workers.

Projects administered cooperatively with the Ohio State Department of Education and with professional organizations

In addition to the very close cooperation with the Division of Vocational Education, the Division of Guidance and Testing works in ongoing cooperation with:

1. The Division of Drug Education in developing materials and participating in workshops on drug education and drug abuse.

2. The Division of Elementary and Secondary Education in conducting ten North Central Evaluations and in administering the statewide *Right to Read* project.

3. The Division of Research and Planning in the development and conducting of a statewide needs assessment project, entitled *Search for Consensus.*

4. The Division of Special Education in planning and conducting meetings in connection with Early Identification and Exceptional Children projects.

5. The Division of Teacher Education and Certification in the evaluation of higher learning matters.

6. The Ohio Bureau of Employment Services in the development of programs for local school-employment service cooperation and

for the dissemination of occupational and labor market information.

7. The State Selective Services headquarters in the development and distribution to school counselors of periodic handbooks and bibliographies of resource information concerning selective service and military service.

8. A seven-state consortium project designed to promote professional staff development in state departments of education.

9. The Ohio Association of College Admissions Counselors in data collection and publication of the *Ohio Higher Education Notebook, Volume I,* which is published annually and distributed to all Ohio school counselors and others who work with college-bound youth.

10. The State Board of School and College Registration in data collection and publication of the *Ohio Higher Education Notebook, Volume II* (to be published every five years), which lists all proprietory schools in Ohio and is distributed to all Ohio school counselors, students, and parents.

11. The Bureau of Apprenticeship and Training and the Ohio Apprenticeship Council in data collection and periodic publication of the *Ohio Apprenticeship Notebook,* which lists Ohio's apprenticeship opportunities and requirements.

12. The Ohio Regional Medical Programs office in planning health career information for Ohio school counselors in their work with students on career education. Distribution of health careers materials to school counselor and work with a state planning committee in planning other activities to promote interest in the health career field.

13. Ohio and area governmental, civic, and professional groups serving as committee members, consultants, or program participants for such groups as the Ohio School Counselors Association, the Ohio Personnel and Guidance Association, the Ohio Vocational Association, area guidance groups, the Ohio Civil Rights Commission, the Ohio Youth Commission, the Columbus Urban League, the Columbus Hospital Federation, the Ohio Nurses Association, and the Ohio Education Association.

14. The Ohio School Counselors Association, in planning and conducting three major statewide guidance conferences each year,

one aimed at the total guidance profession, one for elementary guidance workers, and one for junior high school guidance workers.

15. The Ohio Association of College Admissions Counselors in the planning and presenting of five high school-college articulation workshops.

16. The Columbus City Schools, Indiana University, and The Ohio State University in the development and implementation of an EPDA project, *Pupil Personnel Services Program.*

17. The Ohio Association of Pupil Personnel Administrators in developing and conducting a two-day workshop on the use of tests.

Conferences, publications, pilot programs, and studies

The major means of dissemination developed by the Division of Guidance and Testing are state, regional, and local conferences and publications.

Statewide Conferences. In cooperation with the Ohio School Counselors Association, the Division of Guidance and Testing sponsors three major conferences each year: (1) The *All Ohio Guidance Conference,* a two-day program, held the last week in September. It features two national speakers, a series of practical workshops, and a large display area. During FY 1973, approximately 1600 guidance workers attended; (2) The *Elementary School Guidance Conference,* which is held each fall and which focuses on new developments in elementary school guidance. During FY 1973, about 1000 school counselors attended; and (3) The *Junior High School Guidance Conference,* which is held each spring and which highlights new developments in junior high school guidance. During FY 1973, more than 800 attended.

GATB Training Session. The Division conducted seventeen regional three and one-half day workshops on the administration and interpretation of the *General Aptitude Test Battery* (GATB). Approximately 460 counselors, psychologists, and teachers participated in this program during FY 1973 and were trained in the aspects of the administration of this battery and in the counseling techniques involved in its interpretation to students. As a result of 165 workshops conducted since 1961, approximately 2900 individuals have been trained to administer and use the GATB.

In addition to these workshops, about sixteen to twenty retraining sessions are held annually to update counselors on the administration of the GATB, to introduce a new GATB answer sheet, and to report on new

developments, such as the *OVIS-GATB Combined Report* and other *Dictionary of Occupational Titles* (DOT) materials.

College Articulation Conferences. In cooperation with the Ohio Association of College Admissions Counselors, the Division conducted, during FY 1973, five regional high school-college articulation conferences, attended by approximately 1200 school counselors, principals, and other educators. These conferences are an annual event, and focus on trends and current practices in college admissions.

Summer Vocational Guidance Workshops. In cooperation with the Division of Vocational Education, with various counselor education institutions, local school systems, and/or joint vocational school districts, the Division conducted seventeen two-week seminars on vocational guidance and the relationship between vocational education and guidance. Approximately 340 counselors attended these sessions during FY 1973. With few variations, these seminars are an annual affair.

State GED Conference. This is an annual one-day conference on the use of the General Education Development (GED) test, held for the purpose of examining present practices and possibilities of using the GED for adult guidance in Ohio. During FY 1973, about fifty educators who are involved in the administration of the program attended.

Regional Conferences—ESEA Title III. Ten or more regional conferences are held annually for school administrators and school counselors to bring them up-to-date on guidance activities in Ohio, to inform them about application procedures for Guidance ESEA Title III Projects, and to orient them to the services available from the Division of Guidance and Testing. During FY 1973, approximately 1000 administrators and counselors attended these conferences.

Others. Staff members of the Division of Guidance and Testing also participate in local in-service meetings and address graduate classes in counselor education and professional guidance associations stressing new ideas and developments.

Publications

The following publications were developed and distributed by the Division during FY 1973:

1. *News & Views on Guidance Services For Ohio Schools*. This averages four pages. Two issues were sent of the actual guidance newsletter and substituted with two memoranda enclosing publications, either prepared by Division staff members or secured

from other sources at the time of mailing the materials to approximately 5000 guidance workers. The number of enclosures with each issue averaged eight.

2. *Bibliography For Your Guidance Library.* This consists of four pages. It lists low cost career guidance publications and is mailed with the state guidance newsletter.

3. *Directory of Ohio School Counselors.* This is an annual publication, which averages 200 pages, and which indentifies guidance personnel in City, Exempted Village, County and Local school districts, nonpublic schools and Joint Vocational School districts. It also contains an alphabetical listing of all persons mentioned therein.

4. *Ohio Higher Education Notebook, Volume I.* The 1972 edition has 100 pages and lists the Ohio educational opportunities at the college and university, branch and academic center, community, technical and junior college levels, and the United States Service Academies. Included for each college and academy is a profile of data concerning entering freshman classes, section factors, admissions requirements, procedures, and other information to supplement available information.

5. *Ohio Higher Education Notebook, Volume II.* The 1973 edition is the first such publication, prepared in cooperation with the State Board of School and College Registration. It is a 661-page publication listing licensed private post-high school educational institutions in Ohio and in those states which solicit students from Ohio. It is to be updated and revised every five years.

In addition to the above publications, prepared and distributed during FY 1973, there have been more than 800 requests for *Sources of Occupational Information,* a 1970 publication to be revised in the near future, for *Guidance Services for Ohio Schools,* the 1971 State Guidance Plan, for *Referral Resources Directory of Counseling, Rehabilitation, and Treatment Services for Individuals with Drug-Related Concerns,* a 1971 publication, for leaflets, pamphlets and bibliographies on career education. prepared for seminars and conferences by staff members of the Division, as well as numerous requests for the publication, *Guidelines for Planning, Implementing, and Evaluating Career Development Programs, K–12,* a report resulting from a June 1970 seminar on Career Development Programs, K–12, which will be distributed upon completion.

Innovative and Exemplary Programs Studies, and Investigations

During FY 1973, the Division funded and monitored seventeen innovative and exemplary ESEA Title III Projects in guidance, counseling, and
testing. Fifteen projects are designed to develop a meaningful and workable
model for an elementary guidance program which would include a strategy
to implement early identification; one project is to develop a meaningful and
workable model for an adult guidance program; one project is to develop
a meaningful and workable model for Educable Mentally Retarded (EMR)
students; another project is to develop an assessment model for guidance
programs; another project is to develop an assessment model for guidance
programs; and still another project is to develop a model for use of tests.
Guidance and counseling consultants spent 136 days working on the
projects.

The Division of Guidance and Testing is working with the Cuyahoga
Falls City School System in a study designed to develop a curriculum-based
information system to assist ninth-grade students in selecting tenth-grade
educational programs, especially vocational education courses. The study
is designed to determine the relationship between GATB scores and success
in the various educational programs.

SIGNIFICANT GUIDANCE FACTORS IN THE STATE OF OHIO

During FY 1973, the statewide plan for guidance and counseling services
was expanded. The plan included a booklet, *Guidance Services For Ohio
Schools,* and a fourteen-step Guidance Services Evaluation package, which
includes a one-year follow-up.

One-year follow-up data on twelve of the twenty guidance services evaluations conducted in Ohio secondary schools during FY 1973 provided the
following information:

—137 recommendations for guidance program improvement were
made by guidance and counseling consultants in the twelve
schools;

—73 (53%) of the recommendations for improvement have been implemented;

—28 (20%) of the recommendations for improvement were in the
process of being implemented;

—36 (27%) of the recommendations for improvement were not being implemented.

In summary, 101 (73%) of the recommendations made by Division consultants for guidance program improvement in the twelve schools followed up, had either been implemented or were in the process of being implemented.

Guidance Service in Community Agencies

KATHERINE W. COLE
Project Director, National Foundation for
Improvement in Education

Educators increasingly recognize that students need contact with the realities of life; that school experiences are most effective when closely related to the communities they serve; and that students learn best and most quickly when dealing with direct, concrete experiences.[1] Isolation from direct experience in education is a real danger. It is possible for schools to become so removed and remote from parents, community agencies, communication media, and other unifying agencies that they lose touch with the organic life of the community.[2] Educators must prevent the loss of the combined talents of those receiving and disseminating services.

An easily overlooked but nevertheless very fundamental component of any student's educational experience is the availability and utilization of guidance services both within and outside school walls. Such services, in any setting, are expected to provide encouragement for inner-city youth. Many of these youth need encouragement, assistance, and support to contend with the daily exigencies with which they are forced to cope.

Rather than replicate the guidance procedures currently used in schools, guidance services in many community agencies are based upon using a team

---

[1] Miller R. Collings, "How to Utilize Community Resources," *How To Do It Series–Nos. 13–22,* Series No. 13. Washington, D.C.: National Council for Social Studies, 1967, p. 1.
[2] Ibid.

590

approach to remedy or prevent problems encountered by those in the community. Powerful forces within many communities have sought to dramatize the need for expanded and innovative guidance services in community agencies. These forces have compelled many community agencies to initiate and implement feasible programs that better serve young people. Without doubt, the interdependence of home, community, and school cannot be overlooked if the guidance needs of individual girls and boys, as well as young adults, are to be taken into consideration.

Students' needs have changed greatly during the 70s. Therefore, it is even more important for school counselors to make use of the resources available in their community agencies. Too, it should be noted that minority group students have committed themselves to rebuilding rubbled communities that were literally destroyed by riots; other young people are seeking seats on local school boards, or are developing new forums in the community from which their and other voices may be heard. Eighteen-year-olds are voting in state and national elections. Still other groups have found help and solace in communal living, and still others seek ways of expanding their educational programs. Students often turn to the community agencies, such as "walk in" and crisis centers, in attempting to clarify their personal and educational concerns and issues.

The services provided in community agencies are often limited by their staff members' degree of sensitivity to existing problems in the community and by the financial resources which are available. Many community agencies depend upon and use peer counselors. The professionals consult with and supervise those young people who "counsel" their peers. Experience indicates that peer counselors and other support personnel are often able to cut through the bureaucratic structure with fewer annoyances and hassles than their professional counterparts. On the other hand, school counselors contend with a more formalized structure which, in many instances, is needed. However, such structures often slow down, or fail in the delivery of services to its recipients.

One aim of many inner-city community agencies is to identify individuals who need to develop skills in training or educational programs. Counselors or support personnel (paraprofessionals) are used to seek out and encourage high school-age students to return to school, and other individuals to make use of training opportunities. Personal contacts and confidential interviews are conducted with many individuals throughout the community by agency staff members. They encourage community residents, of all age groups, to identify, discuss, and rank their needs in a logical manner so that they can make use of training programs. Also, data obtained by these interviews enable agency personnel to deliver services needed by individuals in order to pursue training opportunities.

A COMMUNITY MODEL

Counselors who work in community agencies and those who work in schools must work closely together if they are to reduce or eliminate many obstacles that prevent personal effectiveness among their clientele. A model that reflects this interface between and among community segments has been developed by Dunn and his associates.[3] His model was formulated to provide work-study experiences and is depicted in Figure 18–5, as "Organizational Model 4.0."

The work-experience program, presented by Dunn, is conducted by a central department (in this instance, the agency and school together); both work and learning experiences are conducted within the firm (agency or school) by its employees. In this model, a wide variety of business organizations, professional firms, and public companies are brought together in a consortium to provide an educational and work experience program. Study (Learning Activity Center) is separated from work. But that which is done at work gives focus to that which is done in the Learning Activity Center, and vice-versa.

Based upon the model supplied by Dunn and his associates, the writer can visualize elements in the community brought together to provide relevant services for their clientele. This has been represented in Figure 18–5 "Suggested Model 4–1." All of the resources identified in 4–1 are urgently needed by those living in inner-cities. The community agency is a focus for all elements upon which many depend.

Many factors impinge on the educational development of students. They are summarized as follows (not necessarily ranked in terms of influence): housing, job opportunities, commodity repositories, medical and mental health services, legal services, religious programs, services for the aged, communication services, recreation services, transportation, and cultural opportunities. Staff members of community agencies are called upon to deliver services in one or more of these areas. Many clients have difficulty in sorting out their specific needs since they are frustrated and blocked in many areas of living. A monumental task for inner-city students is to cope with day to day problems and to function as effective students. Committed counselors and support personnel who work in community agencies have to become very sensitive to the environment in which their clientele function. Only by doing so can they relate in a positive manner to their clientele's needs and expectations and their home influences. Similarly, counselors in inner-city schools need to develop an awareness of the environment of their

---

[3]James A. Dunn, et. al., *Feasibility of Guidance, Counseling, and Pupil Personnel Services in Employer-Based Career Education,* Final Report. Palo Alto, California: American Institutes for Research in the Behavioral Sciences, June 1972.

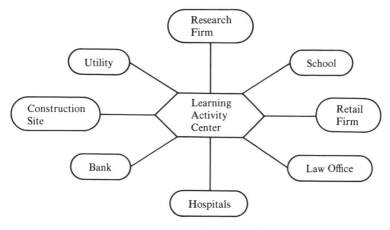

Organization Model 4-0

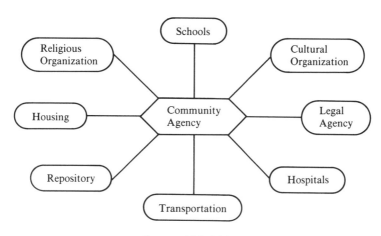

Suggested Model 4-1

Figure 18-5   *Models of Community Support Services*

clients, if for no other reason than to be able to utilize the referral system to connect the student and his family to an appropriate community agency.

POSSIBLE NEEDS OF INNER-CITY YOUTH

The educational development of inner-city youth is influenced by many fundamental but complex forces. The counselor who seeks to help his client cope with these forces knows that solutions are hard to come by. Counselors within school settings frequently feel powerless at the very magnitude of the forces. Some major obstacles confronting students are very complex, even though when they are stated in written terms, they seem trivial or simple. The point is that these matters, so very important to the student's total existence, often require cooperative actions of school and agencies if the problems are to be dealt with. The following statements review some of the needs of students that are served by community agencies.

Housing

The inner-city student and his family often need help in locating low and moderately low income dwellings (fixed by building codes) that provide proper heat, ventilation, plumbing, etc. Community agencies often serve to clarify, for the family, how subsidies are obtained either from the local government, church, or other sources. All too often, families of these students become involved in ill-founded or fraudulent schemes to obtain housing needs. Agencies have sought to develop informational programs about housing arrangements and to design training courses in the upkeep of homes. It may be pointed out that schools could incorporate such courses, at least as "mini" courses, for they would be quite relevant to the student's school curricula experiences, e.g., civic and economic courses. Moreover, an often overlooked outcome of such activities is that students develop leadership capabilities in informing others about housing arrangements and care.

Job Opportunities

Many inner-city youth and members of their families need work. Often these students have few skills, but have great needs for jobs. Many intercity schools and agencies have responded by establishing on-the-job training programs in and outside of the schools. Such work-study programs relate to the student's curricula. Time constraints, attitudinal development, and behavioral skills are topics that are treated in such programs. The meld of education and practical job experience is highly relevant for many students.

A further step is to aid parents in seeking meaningful employment. Career education programs in many schools need to be expanded. Adults need information and need to develop skills that will permit them to enter career areas that are open-ended rather than restrictive. Many intercity schools have sought to implement a career education programs in concert with community agencies to raise students' and parents' levels of job aspiration and skill development. There are basically two types of aspirations: *ideal* and *real*. The ideal aspiration expresses what a person would most like to achieve; the real aspiration expresses what he believes that he will in fact achieve. Henderson points out that the closer the real aspiration approximates the ideal aspiration, the less internal conflict an individual experiences.[4] Without doubt, changing the aspirations of students or adults is a complex, difficult endeavor that requires continuous, sustained effort. The question of values is ever-present in such matters.

A set of guidelines which was designed for social studies teachers is highly relevant for career education programs. These guidelines are reproduced here:

1. All activities should be undertaken with the full knowledge and approval of your supervisor.

2. Whatever transpires in your work should be treated as confidential unless otherwise specified.

3. Punctuality is of prime importance in this work. It is your responsibility to meet the schedule which was agreed upon.

4. If absence is necessary, you are duty-bound to inform the agency (school) and your immediate supervisor of this fact at the earliest possible time. Be sure you know whom you should contact and how to reach them.

5. It is your responsibility to finish the job assigned to you each day.

6. Make sure that you know who your supervisor is each day. Do not hesitate to question your supervisor of guidance.

7. Ask questions but do not express your opinion unless it is requested. It is not your prerogative to criticize.

8. Do not go beyond the duties specifically assigned to you.

9. Volunteer work implies, from the volunteer, the best efforts and the maximum enthusiasm.[5]

Commodity Repositories

Food and clothing repositories that carry quality items within the national price guidelines have been established in many communities. Such repositories give students opportunities for learning buying and selling techniques. In many ways they serve as an OJT program. Students can learn about business operations from them.

---

[4]George Henderson, *Guidance for Urban Disadvantaged Youth,* Edmond C. Hallberg (ed.). Washington, D.C.: American Personnel and Guidance Reprint Series, 1971, p. 213.

[5]M. L. Frankel, "How to Cooperate with Community Agencies," *How To Do It Series, Nos. 13–22,* Series No. 17. Washington, D. C.: National Council for the Social Studies, 1967, p. 4.

Legal Services

Legal Services have been established in many community agencies. These services have been expanded to include information and help about laws that govern due process to protect students from arbitrary and capricious rulings by schools. The Constitution guaranteed rights to all, regardless of knowledge or wealth. Currently, there is less and less reluctance on the part of citizens to seek out legal information and help for events that take place in their communities. In the past, this relatively free service has not been available to the low and moderately low income families. School counselors can contact their local Bar Association to locate legal aid services for their counselees.

Religious Programs

These are fundamental to many students' heritage. Pastoral counseling services are available to all members of families who seek to strengthen their own personal philosophy. Leaders who have been involved in religious programs often serve as character witnesses for the community residents. Students can gain experiences by serving as members of religious education classes, girl and boy scouts, recreation teams, choirs and so forth.

Transportation

Better transportation services at lower cost are badly needed in many communities. People need to be transported from one community to another in less time. The work situation for many people will be improved when the transportation system has been improved.

Cultural Opportunities

All citizens must have exposure to cultural opportunities for their own growth and development. What better place to operate these centers than in the communities? Too, schools can identify cultural opportunities available in the community, and can organize programs that enable students to attend these events. Experience demonstrates that students are motivated to seek new careers by becoming involved in cultural experiences. Many cultural programs provide scholarships, student loans, and part-time jobs.

Medical Service

Many students and their family members need medical attention. Some of our larger communities, by geographical arrangement, have mental health and medical clinic services available for their residents. Too, it may be pointed out that students are able to secure part-time jobs in such programs. Part-time employment gives them an awareness of the total allied health career programs. The credentials needed for health careers range from a high school diploma to a doctor's degree.

SUMMARY

Students must be made aware of all these services, and must be encouraged to utilize them fully. A variety of techniques and practices should be used in helping students transform information into definite goals and objectives.

Counselors from any setting must be cognizant that in a democratic society it is essential that each individual assume as much responsibility for himself as he practically can. It should be borne in mind that some students are starving for real interpersonal relationships. Early years spent "on their own" have left their mark on many. Services other than "9 to 3 o'clock" are needed in many communities. Counselors who serve in agencies can fill this void so that neglected clients are able to bridge gaps in their resources. Otherwise, they will continue to fall behind the more affluent.

Counselors working in community agencies must provide information to their clients about schools, libraries, jobs, clubs, counseling services, and other facilities. They need continuing contact with counselors and personnel in schools and other settings to do so with efficiency.

Community agency counselors who have been characterized as working "where the action is" can outline and explain their services and practices to counselors from other settings through a professional forum, The American Personnel and Guidance Association. Its publications and conventions provide all professionals with the opportunity to share ways to better the delivery of helping services. It is a way by which counselors everywhere can keep informed about the development of new programs in various agencies. In 1954, Frankel[6] pointed out that the community offers an opportunity for student and teacher alike to become aware of a wide scope of problems. In attending to the community, a consciousness is fostered. The local community is a miniature laboratory for, and the motivating force behind, the myriad developments in our complex, interdependent civilization. If the problems of the community are met and understood, the national and international problems will be met and understood.

---

[6]Ibid.

Appendix

Ethical Standards*

PREAMBLE

The American Personnel and Guidance Association is an educational, scientific, and professional organization dedicated to service to society. This service is committed to profound faith in the worth, dignity, and great potentiality of the individual human being.

The marks of a profession, and therefore of a professional organization, can be stated as follows:

1. Posession of a body of specialized knowledge, skills, and attitudes known and practiced by its members.

2. This body of specialized knowledge, skills, and attitudes is derived through scientific inquiry and scholarly learning.

3. This body of specialized knowledge, skills, and attitudes is acquired through professional preparation, preferably on the graduate level, in a college or university as well as through continuous in-service training and personal growth after completion of formal education.

4. This body of specialized knowledge, skills, and attitudes, is constantly tested and extended through research and scholarly inquiry.

5. A profession has a literature of its own, even though it may, and indeed must, draw portions of its contents from other areas of knowledge.

6. A profession exalts service to the individual and society above personal gain. It possesses a philosophy and a code of ethics.

7. A profession through the voluntary association of its members constantly examines and improves the quality of its professional preparation and services to the individual and society.

---

*Ethical Standards. Washington, D.C.: American Personnel and Guidance Association, October 1961.

8. Membership in the professional organization and the practice of the profession must be limited to persons meeting stated standards of preparation and competencies.

9. The profession affords a life career and permanent membership as services meet professional standards.

10. The public recognizes, has confidence in, and is willing to compensate the members of the profession for their services.

The Association recognizes that the vocational roles and settings of its members are identified with a wide variety of academic disciplines and levels of academic preparation. This diversity reflects the pervasiveness of the Association's interest and influence. It also poses challenging complexities in efforts to conceptualize:

    a. the characteristics of members;

    b. desired or requisite preparation or practice; and

    c. supporting social, legal and/or ethical controls.

The specification of ethical standards enables the Association to clarify to members, future members, and to those served by members the nature of ethical responsibilities held in common by its members.

The introduction of such standards will inevitably stimulate greater concern by members for practice and preparation for practice. It will also stimulate a general growth and identification with and appreciation for both the common and diverse characteristics of the definable roles within the world of work of Association members.

There are six major areas of professional activity which encompass the work of members of APGA. For each of these areas certain general principles are listed below to serve as guide lines for ethical practice. These are preceded by a general section which includes certain principles germane to the six areas and common to the entire work of the Association members.

SECTION A, GENERAL

1. The member exerts what influence he can to foster the development and improvement of the profession and continues his professional growth throughout his career.

2. The member has a responsibility to the institution within which he serves. His acceptance of employment by the institution implies that he is in substantial agreement with the general policies and principles of the institution. Therefore, his professional activities are also in accord with the objectives of the institution. Within the member's own work setting, if, despite his efforts, he cannot reach agreement as to acceptable ethical standards of conduct with his superiors, he should end his affiliation with them.

3. The member must expect ethical behavior among his professional associates in APGA at all times. He is obligated, in situations where he possesses information raising serious doubt as to the ethical behavior of other members, to attempt to rectify such conditions.

4. The member is obligated to concern himself with the degree to which the personnel functions of non-members with whose work he is acquainted represent competent and ethical performance. Where his information raises serious doubt as to the ethical behavior of such persons, it is his responsibility to attempt to rectify such conditions.

5. The member must not seek self-enhancement through expressing evaluations or comparisons damaging to other ethical professional workers.

6. The member should not claim or imply professional qualifications exceeding those possessed and is responsible for correcting any misrepresentations of his qualifications by others.

7. The member providing services for personal remuneration shall, in establishing fees for such services, take careful account of the charges made for comparable services by other professional persons.

8. The member who provides information to the public or to his subordinates, peers, or superiors has a clear responsibility to see that both the content and the manner of presentation are accurate and appropriate to the situation.

9. The member has an obligation to ensure that evaluative information about such persons as clients, students, and applicants shall be shared only with those persons who will use such information for professional purposes.

10. The member shall offer professional services only, through the context of a professional relationship. Thus testing, counseling, and other services are not to be provided through the mail by means of newspaper or magazine articles, radio or television programs, or public performances.

SECTION B, COUNSELING

This section refers to practices involving a counseling relationship with a counselee or client and is not intended to be applicable to practices involving administrative relationships with the persons being helped. A counseling relationship denotes that the person seeking help retain full freedom of choice and decision and that the helping person has no authority or responsibility to approve or disapprove of the choices or decisions of the counselee or client. "Counselee" or "client" is used here to indicate the person (or persons) for whom the member has assumed a professional responsibility. Typically the counselee or client is the individual with whom the member has direct and primary contact. However, at times, "client" may include another person(s) when the other person(s) exercise significant control and direction over the individual being helped in connection with the decisions and plans being considered in counseling.

1. The member's *primary* obligation is to respect the integrity and promote the welfare of the counselee or client with whom he is working.

2. The counseling relationship and information resulting therefrom must be kept confidential consistent with the obligations of the member as a professional person.

3. Records of the counseling relationship including interview notes, test data, correspondence, tape recordings, and other documents are to be considered professional information for use in counseling, research, and teaching of counselors but always with full protection of the identity of the client and with precaution so that no harm will come to him.

4. The counselee or client should be informed of the conditions under which he may receive counseling assistance at or before the time he enters the counseling relationship. This is particularly true in the event that there exist conditions of which the counselee or client would not likely be aware.

5. The member reserves the right to consult with any other professionally competent person about his counselee client. In choosing his professional consultant the member must avoid placing the consultant in a conflict of interest situation, *i.e.,* the consultant must be free of any other obligatory relation to the member's client that would preclude the consultant being a proper party to the member's efforts to help the counselee or client.

6. The member shall decline to initiate or shall terminate a counseling relationship when he cannot be of professional assistance to the counselee or client either because of lack of competence or personal limitation. In such instances the member shall refer his counselee or client to an appropriate specialist. In the event the counselee or client declines the suggested referral, the member is not obligated to continue the counseling relationship.

7. When the member learns from counseling relationships of conditions which are likely to harm others over whom his institution or agency has responsibility, he is expected to report *the condition* to the appropriate responsible authority, but in such a manner as not to reveal the identity of his counselee or clients.

8. In the event that the counselee or client's condition is such as to require others to assume responsibility for him, or when there is clear and imminent danger to the counselee or client or to others, the member is expected to report this fact to an appropriate responsible authority, and/or take such other emergency measures as the situation demands.

9. Should the member be engaged in a work setting which calls for any variation from the above statements, the member is obligated to ascertain that such variations are justifiable under the conditions and that such

variations are clearly specified and made known to all concerned with such counseling services.

SECTION C, TESTING

1.   The primary purpose of psychological testing is to provide objective and comparative measures for use in self-evaluation or evaluation by others of general or specific attributes.

2.   Generally, test results constitute only one of a variety of pertinent data for personnel and guidance decisions. It is the member's responsibility to provide adequate orientation or information to the examinee(s) so that the results of testing may be placed in proper perspective with other relevant factors.

3.   When making any statements to the public about tests and testing care must be taken to give accurate information and to avoid any false claims or misconceptions.

4.   Different tests demand different levels of competence for administration, scoring, and interpretation. It is therefore the responsibility of the member to recognize the limits of his competence and to perform only those functions which fall within his preparation and competence.

5.   In selecting tests for use in a given situation or with a particular client the member must consider not only general but also specific validity, reliability, and appropriateness of the test(s).

6.   Tests should be administered under the same conditions which were established in their standardization. Except for research purposes explicitly stated, any departures from these conditions, as well as unusual behavior or irregularities during the testing session which may affect the interpretation of the test results, must be fully noted and reported. In this connection, unsupervised test-taking or the use of tests through the mails are of questionable value.

7.   The value of psychological tests depends in part on the novelty to persons taking them. Any prior information, coaching, or reproduction of test materials tends to invalidate test results. Therefore, test security is one of the professional obligations of the member.

8.   The member has the responsibility to inform the examinee(s) as to the purpose of testing. The criteria of examinee's welfare and/or explicit prior understanding with him should determine who the recipients of the test results may be.

9.   The member should guard against the appropriation, reproduction, or modifications of published tests or parts thereof without express permission and adequate recognition of the original author or publisher.

Regarding the preparation, publication, and distribution of tests reference should be made to:

"Tests and Diagnostic Techniques"—Report of the Joint Committee of the American Psychological Association, American Educational Research Association, and National Council of Measurements used in Education. Supplement to *Psychological Bulletin,* 1954, 2, 1–38.

SECTION D, RESEARCH AND PUBLICATION

1. In the performance of any research on human subjects, the member must avoid causing any injuries effects or after-effects of the experiment upon his subjects.

2. The member may withhold information or provide misinformation to subjects only when it is essential to the investigation and where he assumes responsibility for corrective action following the investigation.

3. In reporting research results, explicit mention must be made of all variables and conditions known to the investigator which might affect interpretation of the data.

4. The member is responsible for conducting and reporting his investigations so as to minimize the possibility that his findings will be misleading.

5. The member has an obligation to make available original research data to qualified others who may wish to replicate or verify the study.

6. In reporting research results or in making original data available, due care must be taken to disguise the identity of the subjects, in the absence of specific permission from such subjects to do otherwise.

7. In conducting and reporting research, the member should be familiar with, and give recognition to, previous work on the topic.

8. The member has the obligation to give due credit to those who have contributed significantly to his research, in accordance with their contributions.

9. The member has the obligation to honor commitments made to subjects of research in return for their cooperation.

10. The member is expected to communicate to other members the results of any research he judges to be of professional or scientific value.

SECTION E, CONSULTING AND PRIVATE PRACTICE

Consulting refers to a voluntary relationship between a professional helper and help-needing social unit (industry, business, school, college, etc.)

in which the consultant is attempting to give help to the client in the solving of some current or potential problem.*

1. The member acting as a consultant must have a high degree of self-awareness of his own values and needs in entering a helping relationship which involves change in a social unit.

2. There should be understanding and agreement between consultant and client as to directions or goals of the attempted change.

3. The consultant must be reasonably certain that he or his organization have the necessary skills and resources for giving the kind of help which is needed now or that may develop later.

4. The consulting relationship must be one in which client adaptability and growth toward self-direction are encouraged and cultivated. The consultant must consistently maintain his role as a consultant and not become a decision maker for the client.

5. The consultant in announcing his availability for service as a consultant follows professional rather than commercial standards in describing his services with accuracy, dignity, and caution.

6. For private practice in testing, counseling, or consulting the ethical principles stated in all previous sections of this document are pertinent. In addition, any individual, agency, or institution offering educational and vocational counseling to the public should meet the standards of the American Board on Professional Standards in Vocational Counseling, Inc.

SECTION F, PERSONNEL ADMINISTRATION

1. The member is responsible for establishing working agreements with supervisors and with subordinates especially regarding counseling or clinical relationships, confidentiality, distinction between public and private material, and a mutual respect for the positions of parties involved in such issues.

2. Such working agreements may vary from one institutional setting to another. What should be the case in each instance, however, is that agreements have been specified, made known to those concerned, and whenever possible the agreements reflect institutional policy rather than personal judgment.

3. The member's responsibility to his superiors requires that he keep them aware of conditions affecting the institution, particularly those which may be potentially disrupting or damaging to the institution.

---

*This definition is adapted from "Dimensions of the Consultant's Job" by Ronald Lippitt, *The Journal of Social Issues,* Vol. 15, No. 2, 1959.

4. The member has a responsibility to select competent persons for assigned responsibilities and to see that his personnel are used maximally for the skills and experience they possess.

5. The member has responsibility for constantly stimulating his staff for their and his own continued growth and improvement. He must see that staff members are adequately supervised as to the quality of their functioning and for purposes of professional development.

6. The member is responsible for seeing that his staff is informed of policies, goals, and programs toward which the department's operations are oriented.

SECTION G, PREPARATION FOR PERSONNEL WORK

1. The member in charge of training sets up a strong program of academic study and supervised practice in order to prepare the trainees for their future responsibilities.

2. The training program should aim to develop in the trainee not only skills and knowledge, but also self-understanding.

3. The member should be aware of any manifestations of personal limitations in a student trainee which may influence the latter's provision of competent services and has an obligation to offer assistance to the trainee in securing professional remedial help.

4. The training program should include preparation in research and stimulation for the future personnel worker to do research and add to the knowledge in his field.

5. The training program should make the trainee aware of the ethical responsibilities and standards of the profession he is entering.

6. The program of preparation should aim at inculcating among the trainees, who will later become the practitioners of our profession, the ideal of service to individual and society above personal gain.

Index